Looking in Classrooms

Sixth Edition

Thomas L. Good
University of Arizona

Jere E. Brophy
Michigan State University

 HarperCollins*CollegePublishers*

Executive Editor: Christopher Jennison
Design Supervisor: Molly Heron
Cover Design: Mary McDonnell
Production Manager: Willie Lane
Compositor: BookMasters, Inc.
Printer/Binder and Cover Printer: Malloy Lithographing, Inc.

Looking in Classrooms, Sixth Edition

Library of Congress Cataloging-in-Publication Data
Good, Thomas L., 1943–
    Looking in classrooms / Thomas Good, Jere E. Brophy. — 6th ed.
        p.   cm.
    Includes bibliographical references and indexes.
    ISBN 0-06-501918-0
    1. Teaching.   2. Classroom management.   3. Observation
(Educational method)   I. Brophy, Jere L.   II. Title.
LB1025.3.G66   1994   93-31886
371.1′02—dc20   CIP
 94 95 96 9 8 7 6 5 4 3 2

Contents in Brief

Contents in Detail

Preface

As with previous editions, we have designed the sixth edition of *Looking in Classrooms* to help teachers, principals, and supervisors observe and describe classroom behavior. We also provide strategies teachers can use to enhance the interest, learning, and social development of their students.

One difficulty of teaching is being aware of all of the complex behavior that occurs in classrooms. Teaching in modern classrooms involves information processing, decision making, and the application of knowledge of students and pedagogy in classrooms. Hence, we describe a variety of techniques teachers can use to increase their ability to think and to make decisions in the classroom. We believe that when teachers become cognizant of what happens in the classroom and can monitor their own thinking and decision making, they can more easily achieve their instructional and personal goals.

We also present important knowledge, concepts, and research findings that teachers can use to improve instruction. In particular, recent research provides compelling evidence that teachers' decisions about curriculum and instruction significantly affect students' attitudes and achievement. This text focuses on both quantitative and qualitative methods (ways students can observe and reflect on classrooms). We review both types of classroom research, thus providing a useful integration of multiple approaches to the study of classroom learning.

We have updated and edited all of the text in order to provide the most comprehensive and current knowledge about teaching. For example, the revised edition describes findings of policy commissions that have urged greater recognition of the student role in learning; emphasizes maintaining the best of traditional classrooms; and at the same time discusses exciting and workable new directions in classroom instruction that can be implemented in modern schools.

In this edition we present up-to-date reviews of research on teacher expectations, classroom organization and management, student motivation, classroom instruction, and several other topics related to successful teaching in today's classroom.

We provide detailed advice about teaching in heterogeneous classrooms, including strategies for dealing with student diversity. For example, cooperative learning is considered in detail. Several models are presented and critiqued so that common potential problems with this strategy and means of overcoming them are detailed.

The book contains a new chapter integrating social constructivist instructional issues. This chapter stresses that teaching is more than just transmission of knowledge, that it often involves construction of new understandings, and accordingly, the chapter emphasizes the role of socially situated knowledge (i.e., how knowledge is constructed in a social setting) and discusses strategies for transferring responsibility for management of learning from the teacher to students. Also included are an authoritative analysis of traditional instructional methods and helpful strategies for organizing models of effective teaching as traditionally defined (lectures, classroom discussion and recitation, certain forms of inquiry).

We stress the teacher's role in evaluating teaching and argue that staff development programs should recognize the growing authority and competence of classroom teachers in planning their own programs of self-development. The book includes detailed discussions of professional collaboration and ways that schools can support teachers' professional growth.

In Chapters 1 and 2 we emphasize that it is difficult for teachers, observers, or supervisors to monitor accurately and understand what takes place in classrooms because life there is so complex and proceeds at such a rapid pace. To make valid suggestions about how to improve classroom behavior, however, strategies that allow effective classroom observation are necessary. Chapters 1 and 2 discuss general principles of observation and describe quantitative and qualitative procedures that teachers and supervisors can use to record classroom observations that provide a basis for reflective thinking and classroom decision making.

In Chapters 3 through 10 we suggest important dimensions and concepts to consider in analyzing classroom instruction. Chapter 3 provides extensive coverage of the relationship between teacher expectations and student performance. Chapter 4 describes methods of preventing classroom problems, and Chapter 5 discusses strategies for dealing effectively with misbehavior. Chapter 6 deals with motivation; it suggests how teachers can make assignments more attractive to students. This chapter also introduces project-based learning and discusses school supports necessary for enhancing classroom motivational strategies.

In Chapter 7 we discuss ways in which students can actively engage in dialogue and learning with other students. Here we discuss issues such as peer tutoring, small group learning, and project-based learning. In Chapter 8 we discuss ways in which teachers can deal effectively with issues of teaching in heterogeneous classrooms, and the chapter discusses various organizational strategies that are more effective than tracking and other strategies which have been used historically for dealing with diversity. The chapter provides a philosophical argument for an educational system of inclusion rather than exclusion.

Chapter 9 provides an authoritative analysis of traditional instructional methods, and Chapter 10 presents a new chapter detailing teaching for understanding, designing authentic classroom learning activities, and considering the role of socially situated knowledge.

We argue in Chapter 11 that good teachers need continuing opportunities to learn and grow. Teachers can further their professional development through personal reflection and cooperation with their peers to obtain needed feedback. There is growing evidence that school effectiveness can be enhanced when teachers are willing to share knowledge and help one another.

We believe that much of teaching is an art. Successful teachers must be able to observe, comprehend, and respond to the rapid pace of complex classroom behavior. Ultimately, teachers must also develop and continue to refine their own teaching styles. We offer a method for observing, describing, reflecting, and understanding classroom behavior—an important first step in developing a teaching style that is both effective and personally satisfying.

We wish to thank the following reviewers for helpful suggestions: Kay Alderman, University of Akron; Ronald D. Anderson, University of Colorado; Michael Andrew, University of New Hampshire; Manon P. Charbonneau, College of Santa Fe; Walter Doyle, University of Arizona; Carol Goodenow, Tufts University; Laurie Hart, University of Georgia; Leslie McClellan, University of South Florida; DeWayne Mason, University of California–Riverside; Donna Merkley, Iowa State University; Ludgwig Mossberg, University of Delaware; Barbara Redier, College of Santa Fe; and Allen Warner, University of Houston.

Thomas L. Good
Jere E. Brophy

To the instuctor: For the first time, Looking in Classrooms *is accompanied by a comprehensive and innovative Instructor's Guide. Organized according to the text's chapter order, each chapter of the guide includes a text chapter overview, Intended Outcomes, key terms and concepts, Tips for Teaching, in-class applications, follow-up activities, observational forms, case studies, transparency masters, objective test items, short essay questions, and application items. The guide is available on request to instructors considering the text for adoption, as well as adopting instructors.*

Chapter
1

Classroom Life

*T*his book has four major purposes. The first is to help teachers and prospective teachers develop ways of describing what goes on in classrooms. The second is to make teachers aware of the influences of their own previous teaching and life experiences and of how historical and contemporary factors in their lives influence their classroom decisions (Carter, 1992; Goodson, 1992). The third is to suggest ways in which teachers can have a positive influence on the interests, learning, and social development of their students. Our fourth goal is to help teachers understand extant research knowledge (e.g., Alkin, 1992; Jackson, 1992; Wittrock, 1986), to use related theories and concepts appropriately, and to combine knowledge of research with knowledge of their own classrooms in ways that lead to new understanding and improved teaching. We want teachers to become reflective about classroom practice and capable of providing instructional leadership (Smylie, 1992).

Teachers are sometimes unaware of what they do or why they engage in a practice, and this lack of perception can result in unproductive behavior. Our intent is to show that teachers need to learn how to observe and describe classroom behavior in order to improve their teaching. If teachers can become aware of what happens in the classroom and can monitor accurately both their own intentions and behaviors and those of their students, they can function as *decision makers*. To the extent that teachers cannot do this, they are controlled by classroom events.

Classroom decision making is not easy, in part because classrooms are complex environments in which teachers often must make quick decisions while using incomplete information. For example, Doyle (1986) cites the following aspects of classrooms that teachers must necessarily accommodate:

1. *Multidimensionality.* Many different tasks and events occur. Records and schedules must be kept, and work must be monitored, collected, and evaluated. A single event can have multiple consequences. Waiting a few seconds for one student to answer a question may increase that student's

motivation but negatively influence the interest of another student who would like to respond, and slow the pace of the lesson for the rest of the class.

2. *Simultaneity.* Many things happen at the same time in classrooms. During a discussion, a teacher not only listens and helps improve students' answers but also monitors unresponsive students for signs of comprehension and tries to keep the lesson moving at a good pace.

3. *Immediacy.* The pace of classroom events is rapid. Sieber (1979) found that teachers evaluated pupil conduct in public an average of 15.89 times per hour, or 87 times a day, or an estimated 16,000 times a year.

4. *Unpredictable and public classroom climate.* Things often happen in ways that are unanticipated. Furthermore, much of what happens to a student is seen by many other students as well. For example, students can infer how the teacher feels about certain students by the way the teacher interacts with them in class.

5. *History.* After a class has met for several weeks or months, common norms and understandings develop. Events that happen early in the year sometimes influence how classrooms function for the rest of the year.

ACTION-SYSTEM KNOWLEDGE

Leinhardt and Smith (1985) distinguish between subject-matter knowledge and action-system knowledge. *Subject-matter knowledge* includes the specific information needed to present content. *Action-system knowledge* refers to skills for planning lessons, making pacing decisions, explaining material clearly, and responding to individual differences.

In this book we deal with action-system knowledge. Systematic study of such knowledge will help you learn how to manage classrooms and to present information, concepts, and assignments effectively. We hope also to provide knowledge that will help you design engaging learning environments that allow students to be active learners and to develop the capacity for self-regulated learning. This information will complement the subject-matter knowledge you gain in other courses.

Even with both kinds of knowledge, however, some teachers may fail because they do not apply the knowledge they possess. They may have inappropriately low expectations for students' ability to learn or for their own ability to teach. Or they may not be active decision makers. Lacking an integrated set of theories and belief systems to provide a framework for informed decision making, they may not have effective strategies for organizing information gleaned from monitoring and interpreting the rapid succession of events in their classrooms.

We provide useful information to help you consider various issues related to classroom teaching and begin to develop an integrated approach that reflects your teaching style. In addition to knowledge, however, much teaching involves hypothesis testing. For example, a teacher might assume that a student who has been out of his or her seat creating behavior problems needs more structure (e.g., more explicit directions, self-checking devices) to work alone productively. However, other factors may be producing the misbehavior. If the problem is not improved by the correction strategies suggested by the first hypothesis, other strategies will have to be used. Teachers who have a rich fund of action-system knowledge are able to develop better hypotheses and adapt their behavior more appropriately to the needs of their students. Indeed, teachers who learn how to reflect on classroom instruction may even develop insights that challenge traditional views of practice (see, for example, Gitlin & Smyth, 1989).

Teaching presents enduring problems. For example, teachers must teach a class or group much of the time but still try to respond to the needs of individuals. Individual students not only differ in how much knowledge they have about a subject but also may vary widely in terms of how they view adults and how they cope with ambiguity. Students' previous experiences and home cultures have important consequences for their beliefs about schooling (Heath, 1982; Hiebert, 1991; McCaslin & Murdock, 1991; Moll, 1992).

Unless we carefully consider a particular manifestation of teaching practice, we may interpret it in terms of our own history as children and students (for better or worse). For example, many of us have been socialized not to appreciate loud, spontaneous behavior. This socialization pattern may make us more likely to interpret such behavior as aggressive than someone who was socialized differently. Similarly, many of us have learned to expect that genuine interest in something (like a school subject) is accompanied by verbal animation ("Isn't this exciting?" "Look how important this is!"), and we may not realize that others may express interest differently (carefully selecting and organizing materials, etc.). The point we are making here is quite simple: that we are shaped by our history and socialization and, hence, our view of appropriate behavior in a third-grade class is likely to depend heavily on our own experiences in intermediate elementary grades unless we attempt to benefit from research, scholarship, and the experience of others.

Another difficulty for teachers is that they are constantly faced with the task of covering a broad range of topics, yet doing so in sufficient depth to allow meaningful learning. To provide you with increased awareness of the complexities associated with teaching, and to help you learn to describe and understand classroom behavior, we have included many examples and practice exercises. To illustrate classroom life, we begin with simulated dialogue from a classroom.

CLASSROOM NARRATIVE: AN ELEMENTARY SCHOOL EXAMPLE

As you read the following example, try to identify teaching behaviors that you believe are effective or ineffective—and consider why you feel that way. Think about what you would have done differently if you had been the teacher. Jot down your ideas as you read.

Sally Turner is a fifth-grade teacher at Maplewood Elementary School, which is located in a moderate-sized midwestern community. She has 30 students, who come primarily from lower-middle-class and working-class homes. The majority are white (20 students), 8 are black, and there is 1 Hispanic and 1 Asian student. Sally has taught at Maplewood since graduating from college three years ago.

The following classroom scene takes place in October. The students have been reading about Columbus. The scene begins as Sally passes out copies of a map showing the sea routes that Columbus followed on each trip.

BILLY: (*Almost shouting*) I didn't get no map.

TEACHER: (*Calmly and deliberately*) Billy, share Rosie's map. Tim, you can look with either Margaret or Larry.

TIM: Can I look with Jill?

TEACHER: (*Slightly agitated*) Okay, but don't play around. You and Jill always get into trouble. (*Most of the students turn to look at Jill and Tim.*) I don't want you two fooling around today! (*smiling but stated with some irritation*). Okay, class. Now, does everybody have a map? I wanted to pass out these maps before we start. You can see that the route of each voyage is traced on the map. It might help you to understand that there were different trips and different routes. Pay special attention during the discussion because you'll need to know the information for tomorrow's quiz. If the discussion goes well, I have a special treat for you—two filmstrips.

CLASS: (*In a spontaneous, exuberant roar*) Yea!

TEACHER: Who can tell me something about Columbus's background?

KAY: (*Calling out*) He was born in 1451 in Italy.

TEACHER: Good answer, Kay. I can tell you've been reading. Class, can anyone tell me who influenced Columbus's urge to explore unknown seas? (*She looks around and calls on Jerry, one of several students who have raised their hands.*)

JERRY: He'd read about Marco Polo's voyage to Cathay and about the fantastic riches he found there.

TEACHER: Okay. Jan, when did Columbus first land in America?

JAN: 1492.

TEACHER: Terrific! I know you've been reading. Good girl! Where did Columbus stop for supplies?

JIM: (*Laughingly*) But Mrs. Turner, the date was on the map you passed out.

TEACHER: (*With irritation*) Jim, don't call out without raising your hand!

BILLY: (*Calling out*) The Canary Islands.

TEACHER: Okay, Billy. Now, what were the names of the three ships? (*She looks around the room and calls on Biff, who has his hand up.*) Biff, you tell us. (*Biff's face turns red and he stares at the floor.*) Biff Taylor! Don't raise your hand unless you know the answer. Okay, class, who can tell me the names of the three ships? (*She calls on Andrew, who has his hand up.*)

ANDREW: (*Hesitantly*) The *Santa Maria*, the *Nina*, and the . . .

TEACHER: (*Supplying the answer*) *Pinta*. Nancy, how long did this first voyage to the New World take?

NANCY: (*Shrugging her shoulders*) I don't know.

TEACHER: Think about it. It took a long time, Nancy. Was it less or more than 100 days? (*Silence*) The answer was on the first page of the reading material. Class, can anyone tell me how long the voyage took? (*No hands are raised.*) Class, you better learn that because it will be on the exam! Now, who can tell me why Columbus came to the New World? (*Mary and two other students raise their hands.*) Mary?

MARY: (*Firmly and loudly*) Because they wanted to discover new riches, like explorers in the East.

TEACHER: (*She pauses and looks at Max and Helen, who are talking, and at Jim, who is headed for the pencil sharpener. Max and Helen immediately cease their conversation.*) Jim, sit down this minute. (*Jim heads for his seat.*) What were you doing, anyway?

JIM: (*Smiling sheepishly*) Jan wanted me to sharpen her pencil.

JAN: (*Red-faced and alarmed*) Mrs. Turner, that's not true! (*Class laughs.*)

TEACHER: Quiet, both of you. You don't need a sharp pencil. Sit down. (*Resuming discussion*) Good answer, Mary. You were really alert. Why else, Mary? Can you think of any other reason?

NANCY: (*Calling out*) Because they wanted to find a shortcut to the Eastern treasures. The only other way was over land, and it was thousands of miles over deserts and mountains.

TEACHER: (*Proudly*) Good, Nancy! Now, who were "they"? Who wanted the riches?

BILLY: (*Calling out*) Queen Isabella and King Ferdinand. She paid for the trip because she thought Columbus would make her rich.

TEACHER: Okay, Billy, but remember to raise your hand before speaking. Why do you think Columbus was interested in making the trip? Just to find money?

CLASS: (*Calling out*) No!

TEACHER: Well, what problems did the sailors have? (*She looks around and calls on Jim, who has his hand up.*)

JIM: Well, they were away from home and couldn't write. Sort of like when I go to summer camp. I don't write. I was lonely the first few days, but . . .

TEACHER: (*Somewhat confused and irritated*) Well, that's not exactly what I had in mind. Did they get sick a lot? Class, does anyone know? (*She looks around the room and sees Claire with a raised hand.*)

CLAIRE: Well, I don't remember reading about sailors getting sick with Columbus, but I know that sailors then got sick with scurvy and they had to be careful. (*Hank approaches the teacher with great embarrassment and asks in hushed tones if he can go to the bathroom. Permission is granted.*)

TEACHER: Yes. Good answer, Claire. Claire, did they try to prevent scurvy?

CLAIRE: They carried lots of fruit. . . . You know, like lemons.

TEACHER: Okay, Claire, but what special kind of fruit was important to eat? (*Claire blushes and Mrs. Turner silently forms the soft "c" sound with her mouth.*)

CLAIRE: Citrus.

TEACHER: Very good! What other problems did the sailors have? (*She calls on Matt, who has his hand up.*)

MATT: Well, they didn't have any maps and they didn't know much about the wind or anything, so they were afraid of the unknown and scared of sailing off the earth. (*Laughter*)

TEACHER: (*Noticing that many students are gazing at the floor or looking out the window, she begins to speak louder and more quickly.*) No, educated people knew that the earth was round. Don't you read very carefully?

ALICE: (*Calling out*) But even though educated people knew the earth was round, Columbus's sailors didn't believe it. They called the Atlantic Ocean the "Sea of Darkness," and Columbus had to keep two diaries. He showed the sailors the log with the fewest miles so they wouldn't get scared. But the men threatened mutiny anyway.

TEACHER: (*With elation*) Excellent answer, Alice. Yes, the men were afraid of the unknown; however, I think most of them knew that the earth was round. Okay, Matt, you made me drift away from my question: Why did Columbus want to go? What were the reasons for his trip other than money? James, what do you think? (*James shrugs his shoulders.*) Well, when you read your lesson, class, look for that answer. It's important and I might test you on it. (*With exasperation*) Tim! Jill! Stop pushing each other this instant! I told you two not to play around. Why didn't you listen to me?

TIM: (*With anger*) Jill threw the map in her desk. I wanted to use it so I could trace my own map.

JILL: But it's my map and . . .

TEACHER: (*Firmly*) That's enough! I don't want to hear any more. Give me the map and the three of us will discuss it during recess.

PRINCIPAL: (*Talking over the PA system*) Teachers, I'm sorry to break in on your classes, but I have an important announcement to make. The high school band will not be with us this afternoon. So 2:00 to 2:30 classes will not be canceled. Since I have interrupted your class, I would also like to remind you that tonight is PTA. Teachers, be sure that the students remind . . . (*During the announcement many pupils begin private conversations with their neighbors.*)

TEACHER: (*Without much emotion or enthusiasm*) It's not recess time yet. Listen, we still have work to do. Tell you what we're going to do now. I've got two videotapes: one describes the United States astronauts' first trip to the moon; the other describes Columbus's first trip to the New World. Watch closely when we show these films because after we see them, I'm going to ask you to tell me the similarities between the two trips. Ralph, turn off the lights.

HANK: (*Returning from his trip to the restroom*) Hey, Mrs. Turner, why are the lights out? It's spooky in here!

ALICE: (*Impishly*) It's the Sea of Darkness! (*Class breaks out in a spontaneous roar.*)

TEACHER: Quiet down, class! It's time to see the videotape—a long, dangerous, and exciting trip is about to begin.

JUAN: (*Speaking audibly but not loudly*) If I had been there, I'd have said "Buena suerte y buen viaje, Señor Columbus." (*Classmates clap and acknowledge their interest.*)

Teacher and class watch 20-minute videotape of voyage.

HANK: (*Calling out as soon as the program finishes*) My sister told me that Columbus was a mean man!

TEACHER: Hank, what do you mean when you say "mean"?

HANK: My sister told me she had read that Columbus lied to his men to get here, that he brought slaves, and that he brutally killed the Indians.

TEACHER: During the next two days we'll spend time discussing the voyage and its importance. We'll talk about what happened on the trip and what happened once they reached North America. Hank is right, some cruel things happened, and we will talk about "means and ends" issues as we did last week when we discussed the environment and jobs.

We need to discuss various aspects of history—history from everybody's point of view, what we want, and how we get there.

Our example illustrates many points, such as that teachers are busy, teaching is complex, and the pace of classroom life is hurried. Sally had a constant stream of student behavior to react to, and she had to make a number of decisions instantaneously. We offer this example to illustrate that teaching problems are by no means simple to conceptualize.

What were the teacher's *weaknesses* and *strengths*? If you were to discuss this classroom dialogue with the teacher, what would you tell her? You may want to repeat this exercise when you finish reading the book in order to assess the information you have gained or any changes in your perspective that may occur between now and then. Complete the exercise now; then read some of our reactions to this teaching incident in the following section.

ANALYSIS OF THE CLASS DISCUSSION

Like most teachers, Sally Turner has some strengths and some weaknesses. We have organized our comments around four topics that are basic to most teaching/learning situations: motivation, management, instruction, and expectations. These topics are discussed at length in separate chapters; the discussion here provides an introduction.

Motivation

Sally's attempt to breathe life into history by linking Columbus's explorations to a significant event in the students' lives is notable. In her efforts to help students identify more personally with the content, she has gone to the trouble to order videotapes both of Columbus's voyage (a simulation description) and of the astronauts' trip to the moon. However, even the latter trip occurred before these students were born. It might have been more effective if Sally had attempted to stimulate students' thoughts about the unknown with events that were more personal (e.g., first trip to a camp) or more immediate (soldiers in Desert Storm). Or, if several of the students had seen one of the movies or television shows made in connection with the 1992 quincentenary of Columbus's voyages, the discussion of these movies or shows might have stimulated all of the students' interest.

Feedback Sally does a fair job of giving feedback to students about the correctness of their responses. Although this point may seem unimportant, teachers frequently fail to provide students with this information when they should do so (i.e., whenever they are not *deliberately* withholding comments in order to encourage brainstorming or to allow students to discover and correct misconceptions on their own). They do not respond to students' answers, or they respond in a way that makes it difficult for some students to know whether their responses are correct. An example of such ambiguous teacher feedback is, "So, you think it's 1492?" Many students, especially low achievers, will not know whether a response is right or wrong unless the teacher specifically tells them. If students are to learn basic facts and concepts, they must know whether their statements are adequate.

Introducing the Lesson Some of what Sally communicates to students is likely to harm their motivation. Perhaps most striking is her tendency to emphasize that the discussion is important only because it will prepare students to take a test. Her behavior does not suggest that learning is enjoyable or important for its own sake and does not focus on positive learning goals (see Chapter 6). Note especially Sally's poor introduction to the lesson. She stresses that students will be tested but provides little additional rationale for the discussion of Columbus's voyage. Her introduction should have focused more on positive learning goals and less on tomorrow's quiz.

Although it is probably useful to tell students once that material is important and will be on a quiz, Sally comments several times that listening is important because of future testing. Such behavior may convince students that learning is arbitrary, an irrelevant exercise done only to please adults or to receive high grades (see Chapters 3 and 6).

Sally's attempt to make the history associated with Columbus's discovery of America more personal and meaningful to students is good. Nevertheless, the lesson itself is dry, and students' role in the discussion is relatively passive (see Chapters 9 and 10).

Classroom Management

In the area of classroom management (e.g., creating a learning environment, maintaining student involvement), Sally appears to be an average teacher. Her students are generally attentive, and there are few interruptions to the discussion. Although students do not seem enthusiastically engaged, she has established at least minimal conditions of classroom rapport and management structure.

Sally could improve in several areas. First, she did not have enough maps for all students. Equipment and material shortages inevitably lead to trouble, especially when students are to keep the material. A more careful count of the maps might have prevented both the minor delay at the beginning of the discussion and the major disruption (students fighting over a map) that occurred later. Upon discovering the shortage and after hearing Tim's request to sit with Jill, Sally might have responded, "Okay, that's fine. Sit with Jill, because I know that you and Jill can share cooperatively. Billy and Tim, I'm sorry you didn't get maps. I didn't make enough copies, but I'll draw each of you a *special* map this afternoon." This way of handling the situation would have accomplished two important things: (1) It would have assured Billy and Tim that they would get maps and made it less likely that they would "take the law into their own hands." (As we point out in Chapter 4, what a teacher does to prevent misbehavior is more important than what is done after misbehavior occurs.) (2) It would have encouraged more appropriate expectations, and perhaps better cooperation, from Jill and Tim. The teacher's original remark ("You and Jill always get into trouble") placed Jill and Tim in the spotlight by implying that misbehavior was expected from them. By subtly condoning misbehavior in this way, the teacher actually made it more likely (see Chapter 3).

Credibility   Sally has developed the bad habit of not following up on what she says. During the discussion, she says on several occasions, "Don't call out answers, raise your hand." However, she repeatedly accepts answers that are called out. Recall this instance:

> TEACHER: (*With irritation*) Jim, don't call out without raising your hand!
> BILLY: (*Calling out*) The Canary Islands.
> TEACHER: Okay, Billy . . .

Such discrepant teacher behaviors may lead to countless discipline problems if they convince students that teachers do not mean what they say or are not aware of much that happens in the classroom.

Rhetorical Questions   In two situations involving off-task behavior, Sally uses rhetorical questions that cause needless difficulty. For example, Jim has already started back to his seat when she needlessly asks, "What were you doing, anyway?" This question evokes a more serious disruption. Similarly, in her exchange with Jill and Tim, Sally pointlessly queries, "Why don't you listen to me?" Again, this situation deteriorates and the whole class is distracted. Such rhetorical questions that communicate negative expectations typically lead to clowning or other disruptive student behavior. Consider how you feel when someone says to you, "Why don't you listen?" "Can't you do anything right?" or "Why are you always the difficult one?" These questions irritate most people.

Classroom Instruction

The instructional aspects of the illustrated lesson are limited and in that sense unsatisfactory. It is difficult to understand what Sally wants students to learn and how this lesson fits into the overall unit (how students will use the information later). Effective teaching requires that teachers plan sequences of lessons, not just isolated lessons.

Teacher Questions   The instructional component of the lesson resides in the teacher's questions. For the most part, these appear to be rather mechanical—time-filling rather than thought-provoking. Table 1.1 presents the first ten questions Sally asks. Two things seem apparent from an examination of these questions. First, most of them are factual (students can answer them by reading the material). Second, the questions seem more like an oral quiz than an attempt to initiate a meaningful discussion.

Assessment of students' factual knowledge is important, but if it is overemphasized in discussion, students may believe that the teacher is interested only in finding out who knows the answers. Thus, discussion becomes a fragmented ritual rather than a meaningful, enjoyable process.

A teacher can influence students' answers both through the types of questions asked originally and through follow-up questions posed to students after they respond. Sally Turner's initial questions are primarily factual. Her students might have been more interested in the class discussion if they had been involved more directly in it through questions of value and opinion, such as, "How would you feel if isolated from your parents and friends for several days? How would you feel being in a 5-by-7-foot room and unable to leave it? Would you like to be a sailor working on a ship week after week, not knowing where you were going or what you would see? Would you volunteer for such a voyage? Why? Is mutiny ever justified? Would you have felt like mutinying if you had been on Columbus's crew?

Table 1.1   PARTIAL LIST OF CONTENT QUESTIONS SALLY ASKED

1. Who can tell me something about Columbus's background?
2. When did Columbus first land in America?
3. Where did Columbus stop for supplies?
4. What were the names of the three ships?
5. How long did this first voyage to the New World take?
6. Was it less or more than 100 days?
7. Why did Columbus come to the New World?
8. Can you think of any other reason?
9. Who wanted the riches?
10. Why do you think Columbus was interested in making the trip? Just to find money?

Was the discovery of the New World important? Why? Would it be important to explore a new planet like Venus? Why?"

Some of these questions (e.g., "Why was the discovery of the New World important?") could be considered factual if the book gives answers to them. How students react to such questions depends on the teacher. Too often teachers' questions implicitly say, "Tell me what the book said." Students should be encouraged to process and respond to what they read, not just memorize it. For example, Sally might ask, "The book states two reasons why the Spaniards sponsored voyages of discovery. What were these reasons, and what beliefs and values underlay them?" Or instead of asking, "When did Columbus discover the New World?" she might ask why the trip was not made before 1492.

Similarly, Sally could ask students to evaluate the social consequences of the events discussed. Was it worth the time and money to send astronauts to the moon? What did we learn (e.g., technological or medical information) as a result of the space program? Alternatively, she could initiate discussion of the risks of explorations, perhaps by noting the numerous ships that have been lost at sea or tragedies in space exploration (e.g., the explosion of the space shuttle *Challenger*). Or, she could comment on the expanding role of women astronauts. In the example, however, Sally asks too many factual questions and too few questions of value and opinion that might have stimulated greater interest in the discussion.

Teacher Questions After Student Responses   Sally seldom encourages students to evaluate their own thinking (e.g., "Well, that's one way; what are some other ways that Columbus could have boosted his crew's morale?" "That's an accurate statement of how the crew members felt, but what about Columbus? Do you think he was fearful?"). Nor does she ask questions to help students evaluate their classmates' answers (e.g., "Sam gave his opinion about sailing with Columbus. Bill, do you agree with him? How do you feel?" "What are some other reasons in addition to the good ones that Tim gave?"). Such opportunities to explore a question in depth make a discussion more enjoyable to students, place less emphasis on just reciting facts, and help teacher and students alike to determine whether they *really* understand the material.

To reiterate, Sally does a good job of giving students feedback about the correctness of answers, and on occasion she does probe for additional information. That is, she seeks an additional response from a student after the first response, for clarification (e.g., "What do you mean?") or elaboration (e.g., "Why do you think that is so?" "How does this relate to . . . ?").

Unfortunately, the word *probe* conjures up a negative image to many teachers. They react to it as though it means "to pick the student's answer apart." No such usage is intended here. Appropriate probing helps students to consider thoughtfully the implications of what they do and say—to think about the material. Probing techniques should be gentle ways to focus students' attention and to help them think. For example, an automatic response to "When did Columbus discover America?" is an unthinking "1492." However, the question "Why not 1400?" forces consideration of what the world was like in 1400 and, more generally, extends understanding and appreciation of Columbus's voyage.

Factual questions should be used with other types of questions so that students also consider the implications of facts or the circumstances that produce them. Probing questions help students think more fully about material. Teachers need to provide conditions that encourage students to engage classroom content thoughtfully. These conditions include questions that press students to reflect and integrate material (Blumenfeld, 1992).

Controlling Classroom Interaction   Sally calls on only one student who does not volunteer. Otherwise, either students call out the answer or Sally calls on a student who has a hand up. However, it is often useful for teachers to call on students who seldom raise their hands, such as shy students or low achievers. Students who avoid public-response situations need to be given opportunities to learn that they can participate successfully. Another consideration is that if students learn that their teacher calls only on those who raise their hands, they may become inattentive. Calling on students who do not have their hands up may increase student attention.

We do not know why Sally fails to call on students who do not raise their hands during this particular lesson, but if this behavior is typical, a clue is provided by one incident. Recall that she scolds Biff for having the audacity to raise his hand without knowing the answer. This reaction suggests that Sally wants "correct" answers, that she is more interested in establishing a point and moving on with the lesson than in promoting the learning of individual students. If a teacher typically responds this way, students learn not to raise their hands unless they are absolutely sure of their answers.

Some teachers unconsciously call only on students who are likely to know the answer as a strategy to provide self-reinforcement. Teachers need to recognize that no matter how well they plan, students often fail to understand ideas and require reteaching using different procedures and examples. If teachers are to make good decisions about whether students understand material, they need to get feedback from a representative sample of students, including timid students and low achievers (Rohrkemper & Corno, 1988).

Student Questions   Sally does not encourage students to ask questions or to evaluate responses of classmates. She could have encouraged students in this way: "Today I have several questions that I want to find answers for, and you probably have some questions that weren't answered in the reading material. Maybe the class and I can help you answer these questions. Any questions that we can't answer we'll look up in the encyclopedia or in the school library. I wonder why Queen Isabella picked Columbus to head the voyage? Why not some other sailor? I think that's an interesting question! Now let's have *your* questions. We'll list them on the board and see if we have answered them at the end of the discussion."

Although it is not necessary to solicit questions for every discussion period, it is wise to do so frequently, because this technique tells students that the purpose of discussion is to satisfy their needs and interests as well as the teacher's. Furthermore, in asking for questions the teacher communicates the following messages to students:

1. I have important questions, and I want your viewpoint.
2. You certainly must have important questions too.
3. We'll have an interesting discussion as we address one another's questions.
4. If you need more information, we'll get it.

If used consistently, such an approach will, in time, teach students that discussion is not a quiz but a profitable and enjoyable process of sharing information (see Chapter 9).

Teachers should communicate enthusiasm and respect for students who ask questions. Some teachers call for student questions but then react to them in ways that discourage students from asking about issues that interest them. Comments such as "Well, that is not directly related to our discussion" or "That was answered in the book" may convince a student that the teacher doesn't really want questions or that the student is the only one in class who does not know the answer.

Teacher Expectations

As we see in Chapter 3, teachers hold expectations about individual students, about groups, and about whole classes. Furthermore, teachers sometimes communicate these expectations in their classroom behavior and assignments. The communication of expectations has both positive and negative consequences.

Much research has focused on teachers' interactions with high and low achievers. Since we do not identify students' achievement in the example, it is not possible for us to determine whether Sally acts differently toward students she believes to be high and low performers (e.g., calls on one group more frequently than the other, asks them different types of questions). However, we can assess her behavior toward boys and girls and comment on her gender expectations.

Teacher Behavior Toward Male and Female Students   Sally does not praise boys but frequently praises girls. It is not possible to say unequivocally that she always favors girls, but during this class discussion, she is more responsive and supportive to female students. Also, though Sally makes few attempts to improve poor responses by any of the students, she more often does so with girls than with boys. When a boy gives a poor response, she accepts it and either provides the answer herself or calls on another student. However, on two occasions she prompts a girl who is having difficultly responding. When Nancy fails to answer the question "How long did the voyage take?", Sally first provides a clue ("It took a long time") and then reduces the complexity of the question ("Was it less or more than a hundred days?"). Similarly, when Claire cannot remember the word *citrus*, Sally provides a nonverbal clue.

Sally questions boys and girls with similar frequency (there are no differences in *quantity* of questions), but the *quality* of her feedback to students' responses differs. She is more likely to praise the performance of girls and to work with them when they do not answer correctly, at least during this lesson.

Teacher Sensitivity to Cultural Diversity   When the teacher announces the start of the videotape, Juan, with evident interest, wishes Columbus "Good luck and a pleasant trip" in Spanish, and the class appears to appreciate his good humor. It's not possible to determine Sally's sensitivity to students from different cultural and socioeconomic backgrounds, but she did not take advantage of Juan's heritage and possible personal interest by discussing Spanish culture or even Spain's role in the world at that time. (See Chapter 8 for more discussion of multicultural issues.) After the videotape, however, it is clear that Sally is willing (and perhaps had always planned) to discuss the controversial issues that surround the voyage. When teachers discuss history, it's appropriate to discuss everybody's history (i.e., from the standpoint of the Indians as well as the Spaniards). In this sense, Sally's awareness of cultural issues is evident in her willingness to engage in this type of analysis in the classroom.

Reaction to Students' Spontaneous Comments   Sally also fails to discuss even directly relevant topics that students introduce spontaneously. Part of her plan is to get students to appreciate the sense of adventure and apprehension that explorers face. When two students mention their sense of fear, however, Sally fails to respond. Jim talks about his loneliness during the first few days of summer camp. Sally could have asked, "Why did you feel this way during the first few days of camp?" "How did you feel on your first day at school?" "Why are we uncomfortable when we do something for the first time?" After such a discussion, the students would likely better appreciate the newness of the situation the explorers faced as well as the related stress and excitement.

A similar opportunity arises when Hank alludes to the spookiness of the room and Alice cleverly labels it the Sea of Darkness. Sally could have profitably paused to point out that Alice's remark was a good one, and perhaps to add in a quiet voice, "Okay, now listen. For one minute, no one will make a noise. Let's pretend that we are on the *Pinta*. We have been at sea for two months. It is now completely dark, and the only noise is the roar of the sea and the creaking of the boat. We are all scared because no one has ever sailed this sea! What will we run into in the darkness? What will our destination be like? Will the people there be hostile?" Teachers often stimulate good discussions when they capitalize on spontaneous student comments or questions. If teachers do not react positively to students' self-initiated questions and concerns, however, the students will stop asking.

LEARNING TO ANALYZE CLASSROOMS

Our brief analysis of Sally's teaching yields some inferences about her classroom behavior and beliefs. Admittedly, one example is enough information on which to base only the most speculative conclusions; however, it should encourage an observer to look for more information to confirm or negate tentative hypotheses (e.g., that Sally does not want students to respond unless they know the answer). Some teachers, especially beginners, unwittingly fall into the trap of discouraging students from responding unless they know the answer perfectly. They find that silence or incorrect answers are difficult to respond to and are often embarrassing or threatening.

The incident with Biff illustrates two important points: (1) Teachers may encourage students not to listen by falling into ineffective but consistent questioning styles. (2) Often we can get enough evidence from what we observe in classrooms to make decisions and give firm suggestions to teachers, but at other times (e.g., the exchange with Biff), we may only note clues about a teacher's general behavior patterns or assumptions about students. These speculations need to be checked by talking with the teacher and/or with students or by making additional observations (see Chapters 2 and 11).

CLASSROOM NARRATIVE: TWO SECONDARY SCHOOL EXAMPLES

As you read the following classroom dialogues (Mrs. Wilson and Ms. Chavez) make notes about effective and ineffective teaching techniques and why you identify them that way. We do not analyze these dialogues, because we want you to form your own impressions and complete your own analyses. After you have read Chapters 3 through 10, return to these narratives to see how your reactions to them have changed.

Example 1: Mrs. Wilson*

Begin
1:20

1. The students are filing in. The teacher is outside by the
2. door in the hallway. The teacher pokes her head in and says
3. to the class, "You'd better be in your seats when the bell
4. rings or it's going to be demerits for you. Hurry." One
5. student runs to sharpen her pencil and says, "I can make it."

1:26
6. Another student sharpens his pencil. One student is passing
7. out folders. The teacher comes in and closes the door. The
8. bell has not rung. The teacher is at the front of the
9. room looking at the lost and found section. She says,
10. "Here are somebody's clothes," and she opens a sack. Students
11. say, "What does it have in it?" The teacher says,
12. "White corduroy slacks and a shirt." No one claims it.
13. The teacher says, "Okay," folds the clothes, puts them
14. back in the sack, and puts the sack back on the shelf.
15. The teacher says, "Now open your books. I want the
16. number of your textbook when I call your name. If you
17. don't have your textbook, you'll get a demerit." Students
18. make noises like, "Oohs, aahs, nos, Miss," from the
19. class. "No, Miss, that's not fair." The teacher says,

---

*This narrative was taken from an actual observation in the classroom management project at the Research and Development Center for Teacher Education, University of Texas, Austin, Texas. Carolyn Evertson, Ed Emmer, and Walt Doyle provided leadership for this project.

20. "You will just have to remember from now on." She calls
21. the first two names. They have their books, and they
22. give their numbers. The teacher calls on Bruce. Bruce
23. says, "I do not have my book." The teacher says, "Then
24. you'll get a demerit." Bruce says, "Why?" The teacher
25. says, "Because you are supposed to remember to bring your
26. book to class." Bruce says, "I don't have a book." The
27. teacher says, "You need to remember to bring it." Bruce
28. says, "I don't have a book." The teacher says, "Then you
29. had better pay for the lost book and get a new one."
30. The teacher continues calling out other names. Bruce
31. says, "I don't think it's fair that I get a demerit."
32. The teacher says, "Bruce, if you can't afford to pay for
33. the book, then talk with me later and we will see what

1:28   34. can be done." Bruce says, "I can afford it." The teacher
35. says, "Bruce, then you had better get one soon so you
36. won't get any more demerits." Bruce blurts out, "Can you
37. take that demerit off?" The teacher says, "No, Bruce."

1:30   38. Bruce goes, "Gah." The bell rings. The teacher
39. continues calling out names. Four more students get
40. demerits for not having their books. When the students
41. do not have their own books, they get demerits, but they
42. can borrow a book from the shelf to use in the class.

1:31   43. The teacher says, "All right, let's open our books to
44. page 44 and spend two minutes looking over the book to be
45. sure to see if there are any questions that I might ask
46. you." The teacher goes outside the door and can be heard

1:32   47. talking to a man outside the door. The observer does not
48. know who the man is or why the two are talking. While
49. the teacher is gone, five students are talking, four
50. students are looking at the book, and others are just

1:33   51. looking about the room. Now eight students are talking, one
52. student is marking on her desk, six students are reading,
53. three students are looking around the room, but are

1:35   54. quiet. The teacher returns and says, "All right, you
55. should have had enough time to look over page 44." Bruce
56. goes back to the pencil sharpener and grinds away at his
57. pencil. The teacher ignores him and wipes off the transparency
58. that she had used in the previous class. The
59. teacher asks, "What does it tell us on the top of
60. page 44?" Three hands go up. The teacher says, "Don?"
61. Don says, "To divide." The teacher says, "So okay, we
62. are starting off with division. What does it say up
63. there in bold black type?" A student reads, "Basic
64. division facts." The teacher says, "What does 'basic'
65. mean?" Several students blurt out several different
66. answers. One student says, "Simple." The teacher says,
67. "Right, simple. The foundation of something. Okay, we
68. start off looking at the basic facts of division." The
69. teacher writes, "Division—page 44," on the overhead

1:38

70. transparency. The teacher has Bruce read the instructions
71. on the first part. The teacher writes on the overhead
72. as she is explaining. Bruce reads the directions.
73. The teacher says, "Okay, let's look up here." She writes
74. the example shown to the side.
75. The teacher explains that they
76. should substitute six for
77. the N, and they have their problem. "What would it be
78. if I put 15 on the left-hand side of this line? What
79. will it look like on the right-hand side?" Several students
80. raise their hands. The teacher calls on Janet.
81. She answers. The teacher says, "Yes, you're on the right
82. track, Janet, but you said it wrong." Janet repeats it.
83. The teacher says, "You said it wrong, Janet. You said
84. three divided by fifteen. There is a big difference." Janet
85. says, "What?" the teacher says, "There just is. You
86. can't—if you divide three by fifteen, you would come
87. out with a fraction. So what should it be, Janet?"
88. Janet says, "Fifteen divided by three equals five." The
89. teacher says, "Right. Let's do one more." She writes,
90. "12" "So what would we put on the right side? A student
91. answers, "Twelve divided by three equals four."
92. The teacher writes this on the transparency. She says,
93. "How about a nine?" The same hands go up. The teacher
94. says, "Let's get someone who hasn't answered yet." The
95. teacher calls on Larry. Larry answers. The teacher
96. says, "Right." The teacher continues asking for problems
97. with 30, 27, and 18. She tries to call on different
98. students each time. (It seems like the same group
99. of hands go up every time. Students answer well. They
100. seem to understand this.) The teacher says, "That's the
101. way you are going to answer all the rest of the problems.

1:40

102. Look at the problems one through nine and see if
103. you have any questions." There was no response from the
104. class; no one seemed to have any questions. The teacher
105. says, "Okay, who would like to read the instructions for
106. problems ten through twenty?" Three hands go up. The teacher
107. says, "Okay, Sarah." Sarah reads. The teacher says,
108. "Okay," and she writes "3, 21, 7" on the transparency.
109. She asks. "Can someone give me a multiplication problem
110. using these three numbers? Jeff?" Jeff answers, "Three
111. times seven equals twenty-one." The teacher says, "Very good.
112. Can anyone give me a division problem using those three
113. numbers?" Four hands go up. "Terry?" Terry says,
114. "Twenty-one divided by seven equals three." The teacher
115. says, "Very good. Let's look at one more. How about
116. the numbers seven, fifty-six, and eight? What's a good multiplication
117. problem using those numbers? Bruce?" Bruce
118. says, "What?" Apparently Bruce was not paying attention.
119. The teacher says, "Greg, can you help Bruce out?"

EXAMPLE
N   N÷3
6   $6 \div 3 = 2$
15 $15 \div 3 = 5$
12 $12 \div 3 = 4$

120. Greg says, "Eight times seven equals fifty-six." The teacher
121. says, "Very good." She writes this on the overhead
122. transparency. Greg turns to smirk at Bruce. The teacher
123. says, "Very good." Now, who can give me a division
124. problem?" A student answers, "Fifty-six divided by
125. eight equals seven." The teacher says, "Right." There
126. is one more, which is fifty-six divided by seven equals eight."
127. The teacher writes these on the overhead transparency.
128. The teacher says, "All right, any questions on ten
129. through twenty?" There are no questions. The teacher says,
130. "You must put two multiplication and two division problems

1:45 131. on each one of these." "Are there any questions?"
132. There are no questions. The teacher says, "All right,
133. homework for tonight is page forty-four, one through twenty. Do not
134. talk. You may begin." Students look at her with forlorn
135. looks. The teacher says, "It's only homework if
136. you do not finish in class." The students say, "Oh,
137. yea." Students go to sharpen pencils, and they talk at
138. the pencil sharpener. The teacher says, "Let's take
139. care of those lost books as soon as possible." Students
140. settle down to work now. One student is at the teacher's

1:48 141. desk, Bruce and Greg are talking quietly, the girl in front
142. of Bruce is listening and picking her nose, all other students
143. seem to be working. The teacher leaves the light
144. of the overhead projector on so that a student can see an
145. example of what they just worked as a class. The teacher is
146. at her desk working on demerit slips. There is lots of noise

1:49 147. from the hallway and/or other classes outside this classroom.
148. The teacher flips off the overhead light. Students are working
149. quietly. The teacher looks up from her desk to survey the
150. class from time to time. David is talking to the girl next
151. to him. He is having a hard time settling down to work.

1:50 152. Students work very quietly. The teacher is at her desk. She
153. does not move around to help at this time. Students go up to
154. her desk from time to time and ask for help. Bruce is copying
155. off his neighbors' papers. He tries to crane his neck around
156. to see the girl's paper who sits behind him. She has already
157. moved her desk away from his desk, and when he turns around

1:55 158. she covers her paper automatically with her hand. Bruce gets
159. the message. He turns back around. Students go to the teacher's
160. desk for help. All students are very quiet in the classroom.
161. All seem to be working on something. (Observer thinks
162. that the teacher is working on her demerit file. She is
163. filing cards into a cardboard box.) A student at
164. the teacher's desk asks a question. The teacher shakes her
165. head. Observer could not hear the question. The teacher
166. says, "Maybe, but we won't get to leave any earlier. We will

2:00 167. leave at 20 minutes after." The student goes back to work.
168. All is quiet again. Bruce goes to the teacher's desk to ask
169. her a question. The class is so quiet that the teacher

170. lecturing across the hall comes in loud and clear. Every now
171. and then a student in this class will look at another student
172. and laugh at something the across-the-hall teacher has said
173. to her class. She is really giving it to her students. The

2:03   174. teacher hears a lot of rustling now, and she is up and moving
175. about. Two students are up out of their desks. There is
176. no real reason for them to be out of their desks. The teacher
177. says, "Sit down," to the two students. The teacher helps one
178. student with a question; other students are working. The
179. teacher is moving about, looking over shoulders, and helping
180. where needed. A student goes to the teacher to tell her that
181. she figured a problem out. The teacher follows the student

2:09   182. back to her desk and looks at the student's paper. She says,
183. "Great," and she smiles. The student smiles and is pleased

2:10   184. with herself. The teacher returns to her desk to work.
185 Another student follows the teacher there with a question,
186. then another student goes to her with a question. (Observer
187. feels that maybe the teacher sat down too soon.) A third
188. student goes to her desk to ask the teacher a question. The
189. second student now returns to the teacher's desk with book and
190. folder in hand. The teacher and student are going to grade
191. one of the student's past papers that had been turned in for
192. makeup work. Bruce is playing with a ruler. Greg blurts
193. out, "Miss, may I go home?" The teacher does not say anything
194. because she is helping two students. (Observer thinks that
195. maybe she did not even hear the comment. Observer feels that

2:12   196. Greg might as well go home because he has only written three words
197. on his paper.) Don asks the teacher what do they do when they
198. are finished. The teacher says, "Then you don't have any
199. homework." He says, "Then we just sit here?" The teacher
200. says, "No, go to the extra-credit box and get something to
201. work on." A girl goes to the box, and when she returns to her
202. desk, she blurts out, "Miss, can we write on these papers?"
203. The teacher says, "What paper?" The student points to the

2:13   204. extra-credit box. The teacher says, "Yes, they are yours."
2:14   205. The teacher is very busy helping two students at a time.
206. Several students finish. There is a murmur in the class.
207. It's quiet, but there are still murmurs. There is loud pencil
208. sharpening. A student stops at the observer and asks, "Do you
209. write Spanish?" The observer answers, "Just fast and sloppy."
210. The student smiles and goes on. The teacher is now helping
211. a boy and girl at her desk. Students are quiet, but there are

2:18   212. lots of restless body movements. Two students are talking and
213. laughing; one student is talking to the teacher about the
214. bottle that is on the teacher's desk. Greg is sitting and
215. staring; others are sitting quietly and still working. Greg

2:18   216. says, "Miss, it's time to clean up." The teacher says, "Let's
217. pass folders up to the front. Bruce, let me have my ruler
218. back." The teacher repeats, "Let's pass our folders up to the
219. front. No talking," but there is still talking. It is quiet

2:19   220. talking, but there is talking in the classroom. The teacher
            221. is busy helping students put up folders. The teacher says,
            222. "Everybody in their chairs now so we can go when the bell
            223. rings." One girl goes over to look at the metric poster.
            224. (Observer feels maybe she just does this out of spite to the
            225. teacher.) Two girls are taking up the folders. Others are
            226. sitting in their desks. The bell rings. The teacher says,
            227. "First and second row may go." A student blurts out, "First
            228. and second from what side?" The teacher points to the first
            229. and second row by the door. She says, "Okay, the third row
            230. may go." The teacher pauses to let the fourth and fifth rows
            231. get quiet. The teacher says, "Okay, fourth and fifth rows may
            232. go. Bye-bye, you all have a nice evening." The students say
            233. bye-bye to the teacher as they leave class.

Example 2: Ms. Chavez*

Ms. Chavez has rolled the math department computer into her class for the morning and has connected it to her LCD viewer. Her 28 first-year algebra students, seated at round tables in groups of threes and fours, are working on a warm-up problem. The day before they had had a test on functions. For the warm-up to today's class, Ms. Chavez has asked students to set up a table of values and graph the function $y = |x|$.

She has chosen this problem as a way to introduce some ideas for a new unit on linear, absolute value, and quadratic functions. During the warm-up, students can be heard talking quietly to one another about the problem: "Does your graph look like a V-shape?" "Did you get two intersecting lines?" Walking around the room, Ms. Chavez listens to these conversations while she takes attendance. After about five minutes, she signals that it is time to begin the whole-group discussion.

A girl volunteers and carefully draws her graph on a large wipe-off grid board at the front of the room. As she does this, most students are watching closely, glancing down at their own graphs, checking for correspondence. A few students are seen helping others who had some difficulties producing the graph.

Another student suggests that they enter the function into the computer and watch it produce the graph. Several other students chime in, "Yeah!" The first girl does this, and the class watches as the graph appears on the overhead screen. It matches the graph she sketched, and the class cheers, "Way to go, Elena!"

Ms. Chavez then asks the class to sketch the graphs of $y = |x| + 1$, $y = |x| + 2$, and $y = |x| - 3$ on the same set of axes and write a paragraph that compares and contrasts the results with the graph of $y = |x|$. "Feel free to work alone or with the others in your group," she tells them.

After a few minutes, two students exclaim, "All the graphs have the same shape!"

---

*This narrative is taken from National Council of Teachers of Mathematics (1991). *Professional Standards for Teaching Mathematics* (pp. 47–49). Reston, VA: Author. Reprinted by permission.

A few other students look up. Another student observes, "They're like angles with different vertex points." "Then they're really congruent angles," adds his partner.

Ms. Chavez circulates through the class, listening to the students' discussions, asking questions, and offering suggestions. She notices one group has produced only one branch of the graphs. "Why don't you choose a few negative values for x and see what happens?" Another group asks, "What would happen if we tried $|x - 3|$?" "Try it!" urges Ms. Chavez.

The students continue working, and the conversation is lowered to murmurs once again. Then the members of one group call out, "Hey, we've got something! All these graphs are just translations of $y = |x|$, just like we learned in the unit on geometry."

"That's an interesting conjecture you have," remarks Ms. Chavez. She looks expectantly at the other students. "Do the rest of you agree?" They are still, many looking hard at their graphs. One student says, slowly, "I'm not sure I get it."

A boy in the group that made the conjecture about translations explains, "Like $y = |x| + 2$ is like $y = |x|$ moved up two spaces and $y = |x| - 3$ is moved down three spaces. It's like what Louella said about them being like angles with different vertex points."

Ms. Chavez decides to provoke the class to pursue this. She asks if anyone thinks they can graph $y = |x| + 4$ without first setting up a table of values. Hands shoot up. "Ooooh!!" Scanning the class, Ms. Chavez notices Lionel, who does not volunteer often, has his hand up. He looks pleased when she invites him to give it a try.

Lionel sketches his graph on the dry-erase board. Elena again enters the equation of the graph into the computer and the class watches as the graph is produced. The computer-generated graph verifies Lionel's attempt. Again there are cheers. Lionel gives a sweeping bow and sits down.

Ms. Chavez asks the students to write in their journals, focusing on what they think they understand and what they feel unsure about from today's lesson. They lean over their notebooks, writing. A few stare into space before beginning. She gives them about ten minutes before she begins to return the tests. She will read the journals before tomorrow's class.

At the end of the period, she distributes the homework that she has prepared. The worksheet includes additional practice on the concept of $y = |x| \pm c$ as well as something new, to provoke the next day's discussion: $y = |x \pm c|$.

Over the next couple of weeks, students explore linear, quadratic, and absolute value functions. Nearing the end of this unit, Ms. Chavez decides to engage students in reflecting on and assessing how far they have come.

As she assigns homework for that evening, she announces, "I'd like each of you to write two questions that you think are fair and would demonstrate that you understand the major concepts of this unit. I'll use several of your ideas to create the test. And here's a challenge for the last part of your assignment: you just drew the graph of $f(x) = x^2 - 2x$ as a part of the review. Think about everything we've done so far this semester, and see if you can remember any ideas that will help you draw the graph of $|f(x)|$."

Different Types of Observational Procedures

There are many different ways to collect data in classrooms, but they are usually divided into two broad classifications called quantitative and qualitative. In *quanti-*

tative approaches, observers use checklists or coding schemes to record each occurrence of particular categories of events, and then analyze the resulting frequency profiles. Quantitative approaches provide information on how often certain
things occurred in the classroom, considered either in their own right or in comparison with other things that might have occurred instead. Thus, quantitative
scales allow measurement of particular behaviors or sequences of behavior, and
their focus is relatively narrow. The observer may decide what scale to use, or the
decision may be based on the teacher's goal or request (e.g., the teacher asks a
peer to look for differences in questions posed to male and female students). Further, the decision about what to look for in a classroom is relatively closed—once
the form(s) is (are) selected, that decision guides the focus of the observation (at
the end of Chapters 3 to 10 we will include examples of quantitative scales). Two
popular types of quantitative coding are time sampling and event sampling. Examples of these types of coding can be found in Appendix A at the end of Chapter 2.

In *qualitative approaches*, observers do not concentrate on assigning classroom
events to categories but instead attempt to collect detailed descriptive information
about them. These rich descriptive data are preserved and then analyzed with emphasis on qualitative aspects of the events recorded (i.e., on the specifics of how
they unfolded and how they were likely to have been experienced by the teacher
and students).

Although there have always been qualitative studies in educational research,
the use of qualitative inquiry has become especially popular in the past decade
(Erickson, 1986; Goetz & LeCompte, 1984). Qualitative studies generally describe
classrooms as richly as possible. These descriptions not only include observation of
behavior (as in quantitative studies) but also may include interviews with teachers
and students. These studies attempt to understand how individual classroom participants see and interpret behavior. An example of a qualitative study appears at
the end of Chapter 2, and in Chapter 2 we provide a brief introduction to case
study methods. Further, at the ends of Chapters 3 through 10 we include suggestions about possible qualitative explorations that could be conducted.

We realize that access to classrooms varies widely. Some readers are classroom
teachers, whereas others are still preparing to teach. In the questions and activities
at the end of the chapters we offer you some opportunity to engage in qualitative,
interpretative work. For example, the first question typically asks you to gather
data about how you, other teachers or peers, or students react to events. Although
you will have to adjust these activities to the circumstances you are in, the purpose
of the activities is to emphasize that behavior is only one factor to be considered in
analyzing classrooms (one has to understand participants' intentions and interpretations as well). Still, many of the questions focus on examination of behavior per se
because the first step in understanding classrooms is to clarify what has occurred.
We hope that these questions illustrate the difficulty but also importance of analyzing classrooms.

In Appendix A at the end of Chapter 2, we provide descriptions of two popular
types of qualitative methods, the anecdotal record and the running record. The
Mrs. Wilson narrative that appeared earlier is an example of a *running record*
wherein the observer listed the major events that occurred during the observation.

SUMMARY

In this chapter we suggested that teachers need to be aware of their own formative learning experiences (e.g., how discussions were handled in their family, instructional and management strategies used by their cooperating teacher, preferences of their initial principal, etc.) because these formative experiences may affect their classroom decision making and instruction in subtle but important ways. We argued that, to become active decision makers and to develop their own personal styles, teachers need to understand the knowledge base that supports teaching, including information not only about instructional strategies but also about student development, learning, and motivation. We also noted that teachers need to be reflective (e.g., analyze classroom processes, discuss curriculum and instruction with peers, etc.) and to be sensitive to both the context in which they teach and the instructional goals that are most important to them. Thus, teachers who are aware of their own development, who are knowledgeable about research on classroom instruction and student learning, and who frequently reflect on their teaching will be the most active decision makers.

We also noted that there are many methods for observing and analyzing instructional behavior. We introduced two broad types of classroom observational methods—quantitative and qualitative. Other important distinctions will be made in Chapter 2. We emphasize, however, that there is no one correct way to observe and to study classrooms, and that there is critical comment available on both quantitative and qualitative approaches (e.g., Hammersley, 1992; Stodolsky, 1990). The desirability of a particular observational method or research plan depends on the purposes for which one is observing. Different observational methods have different strengths and weaknesses. The desirability of a method resides not in its form but rather in the extent to which it generates useful information and insights.

SUGGESTED ACTIVITIES AND QUESTIONS

1. What were the primary reasons you decided to become a teacher? How will (or how do) these reasons influence how you see your role? Why did your classmates or peers decide to become teachers? What does it mean to become a more effective teacher? How can you tell if you are improving as a teacher? How do your criteria differ from those of others?

2. Consider the grade you teach (or plan to teach) and identify the ten most important skills, attitudes, or behaviors a teacher must possess in order to instruct effectively at this level. Keep this list so you can compare it with a list you make after you have read the entire book.

3. If you could talk with Sally Turner about her lesson, what questions would you ask? Why? How might additional information change your opinion of her teaching?

4. Reread the example of Sally Turner's class and identify four instances in which she could have probed for improved student responses. Write the questions you would have used.

5. We evaluated Sally's teaching. What teaching strengths or weaknesses did you identify that we did not mention? Explain why these behaviors are strengths or weaknesses.

6. We criticized Sally's introduction to the lesson. Improve the introduction by writing your own. In general, what steps should a good introduction include? Why?

7. Reread the questions that Sally asks her class. How could you improve them? Write ten questions of your own. Why are your questions better than hers?

8. If Sally' classroom were composed entirely of inner-city students, how would you assess her instruction? Does teaching have to be adjusted to the characteristics of students? Explain.

9. After reading the secondary classroom narratives, how would you describe each teacher's relative strengths and weaknesses?

10. If you were going to talk to Mrs. Wilson, what would you want most to discuss? Why? What questions would you have for Ms. Chavez? Why?

11. How might home influences affect how students try to learn in the classroom? For example, how did your parent(s) or guardian react when you asked them a question or they asked you one? How often did your guardian or parent ask about school or particular assignments? How do your experiences vary from those of classmates?

12. Why do teachers have a difficult time being aware of everything that occurs in classrooms?

13. We suggested that before conducting a class discussion, it is often a good idea to solicit questions from students. Why? Under what circumstances might this be a poor approach?

REFERENCES

Alkin, M. (Ed.). (1992). *Encyclopedia of educational research* (6th ed.). New York: Macmillan.

Blumenfeld, P. (1992). The task and the teacher: Enhancing student thoughtfulness in science. In J. Brophy (Ed.), *Advances in research on teaching* (Vol. 3, pp. 81–114). Greenwich, CT: JAI Press.

Carter, K. (1992). *The place of story in research on teaching.* Division K vice presidential address presented at the annual meeting of the American Educational Research Association, San Francisco.

Doyle, W. (1986). Classroom organization and management. In M. Wittrock (Ed.), *Handbook of research on teaching* (3rd ed., pp. 392–431). New York: Macmillan.

Erickson, F. (1986). Qualitative methods in research on teaching. In M. Wittrock (Ed.), *Handbook of research on teaching* (3rd ed., pp. 119–161). New York: Macmillan.

Gitlin A., & Smyth, J. (1989). *Teacher evaluation: Educative alternatives.* New York: Falmer Press.

Goetz, J., & LeCompte, M. (1984). *Ethnography and qualitative design in educational research.* New York: Academic Press.

Goodson, I. (1992). Studying teachers' lives: Problems and possibilities. In I. Goodson (Ed.), *Studying teachers' lives* (pp. 234–249). New York: Teachers College Press.

Hammersley, M. (1992). *What's wrong with ethnography?* London: Routledge.

Heath, S. B. (1982). Questioning at home and school: A comparative study. In G. Spindler (Ed.), *Doing the ethnography of schooling* (pp. 102–131). New York: Holt, Rinehart, and Winston.

Hiebert, F. (Ed.). (1991). *Literacy for a diverse society.* New York: Teachers College Press.

Jackson, P. (Ed.). (1992). *Handbook of research on curriculum.* New York: Macmillan.

Leinhardt, G., & Smith, D. (1985). Expertise in mathematics instruction: Subject matter knowledge. *Journal of Educational Psychology, 77,* 247–271.

McCaslin, M., & Murdock, T. (1991). The emergent interaction of home and school in the development of students' adaptive learning. In M. Maehr & P. Pintrich (Eds.), *Advances in motivation and achievement* (Vol. 7, pp. 213–260). Greenwich, CT: JAI Press.

Moll, L. (1992). Bilingual classroom studies and community analysis. *Educational Research, 21,* 20–24.

Rohrkemper, M., & Corno, L. (1988). Success and failure on classroom tasks: Adaptive learning and classroom teaching. *Elementary School Journal, 88,* 299–312.

Sieber, R. (1979). Classmates as workmates: Informal peer activity in the elementary school. *Anthropology and Education Quarterly, 10,* 207–235.

Smylie, M. (1992). Teachers' reports of their interactions with teacher leaders concerning classroom instruction. *Elementary School Journal, 93,* 85–98.

Stodolsky, S. (1990). Classroom observation. In J. Millman & L. Darling-Hammond (Eds.), *The new handbook of teacher evaluation.* New York: Sage.

Wittrock, M. (Ed.). (1986). *Handbook of research on teaching* (3rd ed.). New York: Macmillan.

Chapter
2

Increasing Teacher Awareness Through Classroom Observation

Our brief glimpse into Sally Turner's classroom in Chapter 1 revealed that it is very busy and that she is probably unaware of much of her behavior and its effects on students. In this chapter, we discuss research indicating that classrooms are complex, that the fast pace in Sally Turner's class is common, and that teachers are unaware of much of their behavior. We argue that teachers do not perceive many classroom events because (1) classroom interaction involves fast and complex communications, (2) different life experiences lead teachers to be more sensitive to some issues than others, (3) teachers are not trained extensively to monitor and study their instructional behavior, and (4) they rarely receive systematic or useful feedback about their behavior. Finally, we emphasize that neither teachers nor observers are likely to understand classroom behavior unless they know what behaviors to look for, know how to collect information accurately, and have a conceptual framework to use in analyzing their observations. The final section of the chapter provides detailed information about strategies that can be used to collect reliable and useful information in classrooms.

CLASSROOMS ARE COMPLEX

In a single day, an elementary teacher may engage in more than a thousand interpersonal exchanges with students (Jackson, 1968). Teachers in secondary schools may have interactions with 150 different students a day. Yet teachers must *interpret* and respond to student behavior on the spot. It is not surprising that most teachers are hard pressed to keep track of the number and substance of the contacts they have with each student. It may not be important for teachers to remember all such contacts; however, they must recall certain information (the ten students who did not get a chance to present their class reports; the student who had trouble with vowel sounds during reading, etc.).

Because teachers constantly respond to immediate needs while they teach, they have little time during teaching to consider what they are doing or planning to do. Unless they look for signs of student boredom or difficulty, they may not see them. Teachers are so absorbed in their work that it is difficult for them to get a perspective on what happens in their classrooms. Gloria Channon (1970), an elementary teacher in New York City, compared the role of the teacher to that of a doctor in the middle of an epidemic "so busy with daily doings that she finds it hard to get some distance between herself and her functions, to see what is happening."

Those who study teachers often comment on how busy teachers are. For example, according to Maeroff (1988, p. 36):

> Being a schoolteacher is having so much to do and so little time to do it that keeping up with the growth in knowledge is a luxury. Even the most dedicated teacher finds that trying to stay abreast of subject matter is like paddling upstream on a fast-moving river. For the typical high school teacher, meeting with 125 to 175 students a day, marking many of the papers at night, and preparing for the next day's classes—not to mention maintaining a family life and possibly a part-time job—it is a task without beginning or ending.

Teachers not only are busy but they also work alone. Freedman, Jackson, and Boles (1983, p. 270) quote one teacher who described the problem: "We never had any administrative encouragement to work together. There was never any time, there was never any made, there were very few group decisions. It's a very individual thing. If you found someone you wanted to share materials with you did it on your own. No, nobody has ever encouraged that route."

If teachers are to grow as professionals, they have to overcome these problems by learning to monitor their teaching as it occurs, to reflect on it afterward, and to engage in professional development activities with colleagues. Obviously, administrators must allow teachers time to reflect on teaching and to work collaboratively.

TEACHERS' PERCEPTIONS OF THEIR CLASSROOM BEHAVIOR

A study conducted by Good and Brophy (1974) provided clear evidence that teachers are unaware of some of their behavior. These researchers found that teachers differed widely in the extent to which they stayed with students in failure situations (repeated or rephrased a question, asked a new question) or gave up on them (gave the answer or called on someone else). Interviews with teachers showed that they were largely unaware of the extent to which they generally gave up on or stayed with students, let alone of their behavior toward specific students. Teachers were so preoccupied with running the classroom that awareness of this dimension of classroom life eluded them.

Other researchers have reached similar conclusions. Indeed, even a seemingly simple aspect of teacher-student interaction can be a complex perceptual problem in a fast-moving, complicated social setting such as a classroom. Many teachers cannot accurately recall the extent to which they call on boys versus girls, the frequency with which students approach them, the number of private contacts they initiate with students, or the amount of class time they spend on procedural matters. This lack of awareness is one reason why, in too many classrooms, student gender, race, ethnicity, or culture predict the quality of students' learning opportunity (AAUW Report, 1992; Hiebert, 1991).

CLASSROOM PROBLEMS
CAUSED BY LACK OF TEACHER AWARENESS

In the following sections, we describe classroom problems that occur in part because of lack of teacher awareness and information. Most of the problems presented here are discussed again later in the book. The material in this chapter is designed to help you begin thinking about factors that affect teacher behavior and student achievement.

Teacher Domination of Classroom Communication

Teachers dominate classroom discussion, even though they sometimes do not want to and are not aware of their behavior. Adams and Biddle (1970) concluded that teachers are the principal actors in 84 percent of classroom communication episodes. Cuban (1984) found that the basic structure of classrooms (heavy reliance on teacher-student recitation) has remained unaltered for decades. School critics often decry the fact that students are not active enough in school settings (Boyer, 1983; Goodlad, 1984).

We believe that teachers can talk either too much or too little and that both types of teachers may be unaware of their behavior. In any case, the quality of teacher talk is just as important as its quantity. The same is true, of course, for student talk. For example, there is growing agreement among researchers that teachers spend too much time asking (and students answering) isolated factual questions (Goodlad, Soder, & Sirotnik, 1990).

Lack of Emphasis on Meaning

What teachers talk about is important. Durkin (1978–1979) found after 300 hours of observing in reading and social studies classrooms that less than 1 percent of the time was devoted to comprehension instruction. Students were expected to learn by reading, but were not being taught how to do so. Another study indicated that mathematics teachers who actively instructed and emphasized the meaning of concepts obtained higher achievement from students than teachers who used instructional time for other purposes (Good, Grouws, & Ebmeier, 1983).

Few Attempts to Motivate Students

After over 100 hours of observation in six intermediate-grade classrooms, Brophy and Kher (1986) found that only a third of the teachers' task introduction statements included comments judged likely to enhance student motivation. These few comments mostly consisted of predictions that students would enjoy a task or do well on it. There were only nine attempts to explain to students why it was important to learn material, and none to explain how students could derive personal satisfaction from learning relevant skills or knowledge.

Not Cognizant of Effects of Seat Location

Teachers often group students by ability in order to reduce the range of individual differences within each group. Some teachers segregate low- and high-ability students by seating them apart. The top readers sit at the same table, the next best group sits together, and so on. Such seating patterns may create status differences among students and engender an attitude of inferiority in low achievers that removes them from the mainstream of classroom life. Many teachers are probably unaware of how seat assignments and group practices influence student behavior and peer relations.

Overreliance on Repetitive Seatwork

Many students spend considerable time doing seatwork while the teacher instructs other students. During such times some students may engage in off-task behavior that escapes teacher attention. Anderson et al. (1985) conducted one of the few studies that examined in depth what students do during seatwork times and how they attempt to understand and complete their assignments. Results showed that the 32 students studied in first-grade classes spent from 30 to 60 percent of the time allocated to reading instruction doing some type of seatwork. Furthermore, an average of 50 percent of seatwork assignments involved commercial products such as workbooks, dittos, and reading material, often of questionable value (copying sentences with blanks and choosing the correct word from several options). Anderson et al. found that teacher instruction related to seatwork assignments seldom included statements about what would be learned or how the assignment related to other things the students had learned. When teachers observed students who were doing seatwork, they typically monitored students' task engagement but not their understanding of what they were doing. Other researchers have made similar comments about the poor quality of seatwork assignments, especially for low-ability students (Allington, 1991).

DIFFERENTIAL TEACHER-STUDENT INTERACTION

There is evidence that some students receive more opportunity than others to participate in classroom events (Allington, 1991). These differences are associated with differences in student achievement levels, gender, and race.

Student Achievement

Perhaps the most consistent finding concerning teacher-student interaction is that teachers tend to call more frequently on students they believe to be the most capable. However, qualitative differences in teacher-student interaction patterns also have been observed, even where there were no quantitative differences.

Brophy and Good (1970) studied the classroom behavior of four first-grade teachers toward high- and low-achieving students. They reported only minor differences in the *frequency* of teacher contact with students of different achievement levels but found important variations in the *quality*. Teachers were more likely to praise high-achieving students, even when differences in the correctness of students' answers were taken into account.

When high achievers gave a right answer, they were praised 12 percent of the time. Low achievers, however, were praised only 6 percent of the time. Even though they gave fewer correct answers, low achievers received proportionately less praise. Yet low achievers were more likely to be criticized for wrong answers (18 percent of the time compared to only 6 percent for high achievers). Furthermore, teachers were twice as likely to stay with high achievers (repeat the question, provide a clue, ask a new question) when they made no response (or said "I don't know," or answered incorrectly).

Teachers vary widely in the extent to which they are influenced by their expectations and treat low achievers inappropriately. Some teachers show this tendency more than others; many teachers call on high- and low-achieving students equitably, and some even call on low achievers more often than highs (see Chapter 3). Many teachers develop appropriate expectations for low achievers and treat them fairly (Brophy & Good, 1974; Cooper & Good, 1983). Many others, however, especially teachers who are unaware of their behavior, favor high achievers (Allington, 1991; Eder, 1981). Moreover, differences in contact between teachers and certain students may be controlled by students rather than teachers. For example Jones and Gerig (in press) found that some sixth graders, particularly shy students, avoided classroom participation.

Student Gender

Gender affects the quantity and quality of students' communication with teachers. Studies consistently show that boys have more interactions with teachers than girls (Brophy & Good, 1974), with the difference being greatest for disciplinary exchanges and smallest for instructional ones. Some of these differences in interaction patterns are partly due to student behavior. Morse and Handley (1985) studied seventh- and eighth-grade students during science instruction over two consecutive years and found that in the seventh grade, 41 percent of the student-to-teacher academic interactions were initiated by girls; in the eighth grade, these same girls initiated only 30 percent of the interactions. Thus, as they matured, girls initiated fewer interactions in science classes. In contrast, boys' initiation of interactions increased correspondingly over the two years.

A considerable body of literature has examined gender issues in both elementary and secondary schools (e.g., AAUW Report, 1992; Sadker, Sadker, & Klein, 1991). Unfortunately, although there has been concern with differential interaction in classrooms on the basis of gender for over two decades, there is still evidence that students sometimes receive notably different opportunities in classrooms as a function of their gender.

Subject Matter and Gender

Subject matter can affect teachers' treatment of boys and girls. Leinhardt, Seewald, and Engel (1979) studied teacher-student interactions in 33 second-grade classrooms and found that in reading, girls had a higher percentage of academic contacts with teachers and received somewhat more instructional time than boys. The opposite was true in mathematics, however. In all classrooms, boys had more management contacts with teachers than girls. The authors suggested that differential instructional behavior was linked to student achievement in reading. Although there were no differences in initial abilities, significant gender differences were found in end-of-year reading achievement, presumably because the teachers spent relatively more time with girls in reading.

In related research Jones and Wheatley (1990) examined teacher-student dyadic interactions in 30 physical science classes and 30 chemistry classes. They report that males received more teacher contact than females on all types of classroom interaction (both positive and negative).

Race

Teacher-student interactions are affected not only by gender but also by other student characteristics such as race (see Grant, 1985). Leacock (1969) found that teachers generally rated black students less favorably than they rated white students, and showed particular hostility and rejection toward the *brightest* black students. The latter result is a reversal of the usual finding in studies involving white students.

However, in some classes black students may be treated differentially on the basis of gender. Ross and Jackson (1991) studied elementary teachers' reactions to questionnaires containing case histories of hypothetical black fourth- and fifth-grade students. Even though the performance abilities of male and female students were constructed in equivalent ways, teachers consistently reported lower expectations for black males and preferred to have black females in their classes.

Teachers need to be aware of differences in students that they may overreact to if they are not careful (see Allington, 1991; Brophy & Evertson, 1981; Eisenhart &

Cutts-Dougherty, 1991; Grant, 1985; Ogbu, 1992; Wilkinson & Marrett, 1985 for reviews of this literature). The most successful teachers are not merely sensitive to the cultural diversity of the students they teach: They use this diversity to enrich the learning experiences they provide to the class as a whole (Hiebert, 1991; Natriello, McDill, & Pallas, 1990).

COOPERATIVE GROUP LEARNING

The research data described above were usually collected when teachers were teaching the class as a whole. There is growing interest in the potential of cooperative small groups for helping students to learn more actively and for ameliorating differences among students in classroom interaction and participation. The effects of grouping, however, are mixed. For example, some students can monopolize small groups just as they dominate whole-class discussions (King, 1993; Mulryan, 1989). Blumenfeld (1992) reported that students found small-group work more motivating and enjoyable but noted that active learning declined during small-group work.

When small-group tasks are poorly designed, students often spend more time carrying out superficial procedures than thinking about the meaning of the task (Good, Mulryan, & McCaslin; 1992; McCaslin & Good, 1992). Moreover, classroom environments become much more complex when the teacher tries to monitor the academic and social progress of seven or eight groups. Hence, unless teachers monitor students carefully as they work in groups, teachers may unintentionally create caste systems in which some groups, or some students within groups, have much more status and power than others. Clearly, shifting the unit of instruction from whole class to small group does not necessarily reduce the complexity of teachers' observing in classrooms.

FACTORS THAT INFLUENCE ACHIEVEMENT

Use of Time in Classrooms

Allocated Time Teachers vary widely in *how much* instructional time they allocate to school subjects. For example, Berliner (1979) found that average daily time allocated for second-grade math ranged from a low of 24 minutes to a high of 61 minutes. The range for second-grade reading was from 32 to 131 minutes. Some students received as much as four times more instructional time in a given subject than other students in the same grade. Teachers also vary significantly in how they *use* time. Freeman and Porter (1989) reported that teachers in some math classes focused on conceptual ideas, whereas other teachers emphasized drill and practice of computation skills.

Variations in time use are found in secondary classrooms as well. Some teachers use 40 minutes of a 45-minute period to develop concepts; others use only 20 to 25 minutes for developing subject-matter content. Stallings (1980) studied 87 secondary classrooms and reported that teachers who obtained relatively poor achievement from students used more class time for noninteractive instruction. Most teachers are probably not aware of how their time allocations differ from those of other teachers.

Teachers' Attitudes Some research suggests that teachers devote time to subjects partly on the basis of their attitudes toward these subjects. Schmidt and Buchmann (1983) found that teachers who enjoyed teaching reading more than writing tended to stress reading over language arts instruction and that teachers who enjoyed mathematics more than social studies allocated more time to mathematics. Indeed, the teachers who enjoyed teaching mathematics spent over 50 *percent* more time teaching math than teachers who did not. Variation among teachers in time allocated to particular subjects was tremendous (e.g., one teacher averaged 2 minutes on science, while another averaged 43.2 minutes). Thus, in addition to becoming aware of how they spend time, teachers may need to alter their knowledge of or attitudes toward certain subjects so that they feel comfortable teaching them.

Opportunity to Learn

Student opportunity to learn also affects achievement. Teachers who are teaching ostensibly the same curriculum present varied information, assignments, and activities to their students, so that even if time allocation is equal, students receive different content and learning opportunities. Much of this scheduling occurs as a result of conscious decision making, but some of it also happens without teacher awareness. Brophy (1982) argued that teachers play a key role in determining the curriculum that students actually receive, even if clear curriculum guidelines and adopted materials are in place. The enacted curriculum is further modified by the students themselves when their efforts to make sense of what they are learning cause them to interpret information differently from the way the teacher intended (Doyle, 1992).

Curriculum-Test Match

Many school districts use standardized achievement tests that are poorly matched to textbooks or to the instructional approach of particular teachers (Freeman et al., 1983). Clearly, unless the curriculum and the test are aligned, incorrect conclusions are likely to be drawn about the effects of schooling. In our opinion, curriculum goals should determine the test used and not vice versa.

Related problems occur when curriculum materials are inappropriate for students. Jorgenson (1977) reported that in some classes 85 percent of the students used learning materials that were too difficult for them. Teachers probably were unaware of this mismatch or else did not know what to do about it.

Selection of Classroom Tasks

Doyle (1983) has contended that tasks are a critical aspect of academic work, arguing further that tasks vary widely in the cognitive complexity required (memorize versus analyze) and in the degree of risk taking they require of students. If teachers routinely assign memory work, students will spend their time memorizing isolated facts. In contrast, if tasks require students to integrate and organize information in order to understand concepts, then notably different performance expectations will be communicated. Thus, task structure affects how students think about assigned work in powerful ways.

Following the seminal work of Doyle (1983), many researchers have examined how task structure influences student learning and curriculum enactment (for comprehensive reviews see Blumenfeld and Meece, 1988; Fisher and Hiebert, 1990; and Mergendoller, 1988). Researchers have not only conducted task research but have moved this conceptualization into particular subject-matter domains including social studies (e.g., Alleman & Brophy, 1992), literacy (e.g., Fisher & Hiebert, 1990), math (e.g., Good, McCaslin, & Reys, 1992), art (e.g., May, 1992), and science (e.g., Blumenfeld, 1992).

Empirical studies suggest that typical tasks assigned to students (laboratory exercises, workbooks, etc.) place only minimal demands for thinking (see for example, Mergendoller et al., 1988). Further, some teachers do not design and implement tasks in classrooms that "press" for students' cognitive engagement and understanding of material (Blumenfeld, 1992). It seems clear that some classroom teachers do not attend to the distribution of types of classroom tasks and to the impact of such assignments on students' thinking and performance.

HOW STUDENTS AFFECT TEACHERS

Impression Management

The ways that students present themselves to teachers may make teaching decisions more difficult. Spencer-Hall (1981) described how some students were much better at impression management than others because they had learned to misbehave in ways that escaped the teachers' attention. One such student even was selected by teachers for a good citizenship award, despite the fact that the student had often engaged in disruptive behavior when teachers were nearby. Students who were skilled at misbehaving when the teacher had his or her back turned also were adept at looking appropriately involved when the teacher was monitoring classroom behavior.

There are many examples of the influence of individual students or classes of students on teachers and on classroom procedures. Most students and teachers are aware of students who have successfully manipulated instructors into giving them extra time and help. One of our favorite examples, provided by Professor Myron Dembo (personal communication), concerns successful manipulation by a college student to get extra time to prepare for exams by requesting permission to take exams *early* (due to a supposed conflict). Instructors typically preferred (for purposes of test security) that she take the exam late, however, and often gave her the same exam that was given in class. Hence, she often received extra time and knew the test content. Furthermore, instructors often viewed the student favorably because of her "willingness" to take the exam early.

Students who appear interested in class discussions may be more likely to get a clue or a second chance than students who seem less attentive. More generally, students' self-presentations can lead teachers to make erroneous assumptions about students' knowledge and motivation, especially when teachers have to make rapid decisions in a complex classroom setting. Teachers, for example, may misinterpret the behavior of some students because of cultural reasons (Allington, 1991; Hiebert, 1991). Some students prefer not to participate in class discussions and attempt to keep a "low profile" (Jones, 1990; Jones & Gerig, in press).

Students' Reactions to Classroom Tasks

Carter and Doyle (1982) provided an excellent example of how a teacher and students influenced one another during a writing assignment in a junior high language arts class. When the lesson was familiar in format and response demand (e.g., a grammar lesson), the class moved in a smooth and predictable fashion. However, when the class focused on writing, work periods were slow to begin and were frequently interrupted by student-initiated questions about requirements and procedures. Much of the students' behavior during these more complex and ambiguous writing tasks was directed at trying to get more information from the teacher about an acceptable product. Some of the most sophisticated attempts to get the teacher to give more exact information about good work included

1. "Trying out" answers for assignments, to get the teacher's reactions
2. "Guessing" to elicit prompts from the teacher
3. Responding incorrectly, to secure answers from the teacher
4. Bringing work in progress to the teacher for suggestions and corrections
5. Bargaining as a group for information about accomplishing a task
6. "Contracting" with one student (with a history of success) to get answers from the teacher

This research suggests that when some students are asked to make new and somewhat unpredictable responses, they attempt to make the assignment more routine and predictable.

Doyle (1983) argued that various academic activities or tasks are associated with different levels of ambiguity and risk. Memory tasks (e.g., What happened in 1588? What is the product of 9 × 8?) are low in *ambiguity* because students know in advance what kinds of answers are required. In contrast, students must construct rather than simply reproduce answers for tasks that involve understanding, and they may not have a clear idea about what to do.

Risk refers to the likelihood that students will be unable to produce an acceptable answer or product. Although memory tasks are typically low in ambiguity, they can be high or low in risk, depending on what must be recalled. Academic tasks that require understanding are at least moderately high in ambiguity and tend to be high in risk because the precise answer cannot be predicted in advance, so the constructive process is problematic. An accountability system has to be operating for risk to be an important variable: That is, if a teacher accepts any answer, there is no risk.

Carter and Doyle's (1982) study also demonstrated the powerful influence of the teacher's grading system on classroom behavior and, reciprocally, of students on teachers. They write:

> Many of the teacher's comments on graded writing assignments were directed to grammar and mechanics, and grades for those aspects of written work were typically lower than those for content. In other words, grammar actually carried more weight in writing assignments (although this policy was not explicitly stated by the teacher), and students directed their efforts to this facet of the task.

We suspect that teachers often make decisions and behave in ways that they do not intend because of students' responses to classroom events. Moreover, teachers do not perceive some student influences on their behavior.

Individual Differences in Students

Differences in response opportunities often arise in classrooms because of important differences in students. Some students are more active, have more curiosity, and ask more questions than other students. Because of previous experiences, some students are better able than others to use adults as resources. Many differences in classroom participation among students are not attributable to teachers but rather to early socialization or influences outside the classroom (e.g., piano or gymnastics teachers, etc.).

Yet, at least some teachers socialize young girls mostly to be responsible and dependable in following conduct rules rather than to use initiative in learning (Grant, 1985). Differential teacher behavior toward male and female students (or high and low achievers) is an individual difference variable. Although some teachers differentiate content and interaction on the basis of student gender, other teachers show little of such behavior (e.g., Eccles & Blumenfeld, 1985). Furthermore, as we have noted, student behavior influences teacher behavior. Brophy and Evertson (1981, p. 118) concluded that most gender differences in teacher-student interactive patterns "are attributable to differences in the behavior of the students themselves and not to significant teacher favoritism of girls or rejection of boys."

Bossert (1981) notes that when students work in mixed-gender groups on projects or experiments, boys are likely to manipulate objects and set up equipment, whereas girls are likely to watch and listen or to perform note-taking duties. Bossert found that boys and girls have varied interests and behave differently, so that even if teachers do not assign girls to act as recorders, most girls may assume these duties on their own. He contended that teachers need to be aware of the different interests that students bring to the classroom and be prepared to encourage all students to participate in a variety of classroom work.

Although the above discussion has focused mainly on gender issues, the argument applies largely to any discussion of individual differences. Many differences in student performance are due to home, cultural, and/or societal influences. Although we discuss individual student characteristics such as achievement level or race, we must recognize that students have multiple characteristics and that teachers must respect the complex interconnections of student gender, ethnicity, cultural background, ability, personality, and so on (Peshkin, 1991).

MULTIPLE VIEWS OF CLASSROOM LIFE

There are multiple perspectives from which to view classroom life, and some of these viewpoints are strikingly different. Discrepancy between the viewpoints of a classroom observer and the teacher does not necessarily indicate a weakness on the part of the teacher. Observers can draw inappropriate conclusions about what occurs in classrooms. Similarly, teachers who work together often see or interpret classroom behavior in different ways (Gitlin & Smyth, 1989), and such differences can lead to useful dialogue, insight, and reflection.

Also, students often see things differently from their teacher or observers. Peterson and Swing (1982) studied relationships among students' thought processes, time on-task, and achievement. They reported that students' descriptions of their attending (active listening) to teacher presentations were better predictors of achievement than were observers' ratings of students' time on-task during teacher presentations. In fact, observers' reports of students' attending behaviors were not good predictors of students' self-reports of attention. Rohrkemper (1985), Weinstein (1982), and Weinstein and Middlestadt (1979) also have demonstrated the value of obtaining students' views of classrooms. As Rohrkemper (1985) argued, information describing how students perceive their classroom experiences is a prerequisite to adequate interpretation of observed classroom interactions.

WHY TEACHERS ARE UNAWARE

We have discussed behaviors that teachers engage in without full awareness and noted that even when teachers are aware of their behavior they may not realize its effects. We believe that teachers' lack of awareness about their behavior or its effects lessens their classroom effectiveness. In this section, we discuss some of the reasons why teachers are unaware.

The most fundamental factor making it difficult for teachers to assess classroom behavior is that so much happens so rapidly. This problem can be solved in part through training. Awareness of everything that occurs is impossible, but with practice teachers can become more aware of their classroom behavior.

A second factor limiting awareness is that, historically, many teacher education programs have failed to equip teachers with specific teaching techniques or with skills for labeling and analyzing classroom behavior. Too often they gave teachers global advice (e.g., teach the whole child, individualize instruction) without linking it to specific behaviors. Recently, teacher education programs have made important strides in helping teachers to enhance their capacity for self-awareness.

Conceptual labels are powerful tools in helping teachers to become aware of what they do. Brophy and Good (1970) found that teachers gave up on low-achieving students who had difficulty responding to questions. However, the teachers did not view their behavior as giving up. Rather, they said that they were embarrassed by the silence, afraid that the students were embarrassed by the silence, or eager to keep the discussion moving. Similarly, teachers in the Rowe (1969) study probably did not realize that they were giving low achievers less time to respond and thereby making a response more difficult, and teachers in the Leinhardt, Seewald, and Engel (1979) study were probably not aware of their differential behavior toward male and female students.

These findings suggest that teacher education programs have not given teachers ways of labeling and monitoring their behavior. We are not saying that teachers should never give up on students in recitation sequences, for there are times when it is appropriate to move on. Teachers should be aware, however, that they are giving up when they do so and should known how often they do it with low achievers. Otherwise, they will teach low achievers that the easiest way to react to a question is to make no response.

Similarly, teachers should know the alternative responses they can make when students make no response or respond incorrectly: providing clues, probing, asking a simpler question, repeating the question, and so forth. Teachers can learn to make such alternative responses if they learn concepts with which to identify and label specific teaching situations and the skills to use in responding to them.

A third obstacle to awareness is that there is no system in place for providing teachers with information about what to do. McNeil (1971) and Pambookian (1976) pointed out that teachers are most likely to change when provided with information that shows a discrepancy between what they want to do and what they are doing. In-service teachers are unlikely to obtain such information, however, unless they meet with a supervisor several times during the year or have the chance to observe in other classrooms and exchange information with fellow teachers. Yet teachers rarely see supervisors. A survey by the National Education Association revealed that only 34 percent of secondary teachers were observed even once during the year for five minutes or longer. The median number of observational visits in secondary schools was one, the median in elementary schools was two, and only half of these visits were followed by a conference (McNeil, 1971). Unless they have unusual principals or supervisors, teachers seldom receive direct, useful feedback about their teaching (Rosenholtz, 1989.

IMPROVING TEACHING THROUGH OBSERVATIONAL FEEDBACK

Principals are beginning to visit classrooms more frequently in some school districts; however, visits are typically for purposes of evaluating teaching (Gitlin & Smyth, 1989) rather than for helping teachers to become more aware of their behavior or to improve instruction. Evaluation must occur, but teachers need information about what they are doing and suggestions for improvement as well (see Chapter 11).

Under the supervisory structure used in many schools, teachers may view feedback from supervisors with suspicion or hostility. Teachers know that supervisors' ratings are sometimes unreliable. Also, teachers frequently disagree with supervisors over goals (Gitlin & Smyth, 1989). When teachers believe that supervisors do not spend enough time in the classroom to assess their behaviors adequately, employ vague or irrelevant criteria, or lack the necessary subject-matter knowledge, teachers may reject supervisors' advice (Rosenholtz, 1989; Tuckman & Oliver, 1968).

There is reason to believe, however, that teachers want more frequent feedback about their classroom performance, particularly when they help to determine the criteria for evaluation (Rosenholtz, 1989). Indeed, one source of teacher dissatisfaction is infrequency of evaluation (Natriello & Dornbusch, 1980–1981; Wise et al., 1985).

Considering the recent interest in making teaching more of a profession by creating more opportunities for professional growth (Griffin, 1985; Rosenholtz & Smylie, 1984; Smylie, 1992), we hope that in the next few years there will be a significant increase in opportunities for in-service teachers to obtain useful feedback about their classroom performance (see Chapter 11).

Griffin (1983) found that during supervisory interactions little attention was paid to developing a knowledge base that would help student teachers subsequently when they had their own classrooms. These interactions focused mostly on reacting to immediate, specific problems and a "let's see if this works" style of offering suggestions. Unfortunately, rationales for these suggestions typically were not provided, and there were few references to learning theory, child development, instructional models, and so on. The supervisory interactions were dominated by the cooperating teacher, who selected the topics for conversation and controlled how they were discussed. Conversations usually focused on a particular classroom at a certain time; they seldom involved alternative ways to understand and respond to classroom events.

The ability to describe behavior heightens awareness of it as it unfolds in the classroom. A conceptual system allows teachers to classify what they are doing as they do it, making it possible for them to be aware of what they do and to remember it later. Many school districts now have video equipment so that teachers can see themselves in action. At first glance, videotaping seems like a useful learning aid—what better way for teachers to improve than to see themselves as others do? Unfortunately, studies report that after teachers have viewed tapes, the changes in their teaching behavior are not impressive.

Seeing a film of oneself teaching is like sitting in a classroom watching another teacher. The behavior on the film is still rapid and complex. If teachers do not know what to look for, they do not see much. However, when teachers view tapes with a consultant who can provide specific feedback or with materials describing what to look for, positive change occurs. Thus, video- and audiotapes are likely to help teachers improve their classroom behavior only if specific teaching behaviors are highlighted and discussed (Fuller & Manning, 1973). Further, there is some evidence that when teachers are given suggestions about ways to think about teaching (as opposed to directives), teacher conferences are more likely to be productive.

The terms *conceptual and observational tools* refer to a descriptive vocabulary. Every social organization, game, or system has a language of its own. For example, bridge has a unique descriptive vocabulary, as does football. Persons who do not understand such terms as *three no-trump* or *first down* cannot understand the games. Language for describing classrooms is necessarily much more complex, but learnable. We want to make teachers more familiar with this language to enable them to describe and understand what they do in the classroom.

BENEFITS OF CLASSROOM OBSERVATION

We believe that providing you with concepts that describe classroom processes will help you to monitor more of your behavior. For example, knowledge of variables such as *wait time* can help you increase the time you wait for students to respond when it is appropriate to do so. Similarly, awareness of a tendency to *give up* on low achievers can enable you to ask new questions, provide clues, rephrase questions, or otherwise seek to improve the performance of these students more frequently.

Teachers who are trying to understand their behavior can apply observational techniques such as those presented here. Consider the "Sea of Darkness" example in Chapter 1. If the teacher had tape-recorded the lesson, most of the dimensions discussed in our analysis might have become evident to her (high rates of factual questions, lack of a clear pattern to the questions, different reactions toward boys and girls, and so forth). Teachers who tape-record their lessons occasionally (e.g., once every two weeks) could derive many of the same benefits as having an observer in the classroom. However, neither teachers nor observers are likely to understand classroom behavior unless they know how to collect information, know what behaviors to look for, and have a conceptual or theoretical framework to guide their analyses. Thus, in addition to a willingness to understand, teachers must also have concepts and methods for analyzing instruction. Given increased emphasis on teacher leadership in reforming American schools, it seems plausible that increasing numbers of teachers will have the opportunity to observe one anothers' classrooms (Smylie, 1992).

Thus, we stress observation skills in order to allow you (1) to observe skillfully in other teachers' classrooms, (2) to interpret the comments of supervisors and other teachers who observe in your classroom, and (3) to analyze videotapes of your own teaching more effectively. As you examine and modify your teaching style, observational feedback from others will usually be of immense assistance; still, you need to be aware that all observations have some error.

PROBLEMS WITH OBSERVATION

Teachers' perceptions of classroom behavior differ in some respects from those of students and observers (Cooper & Good, 1983; Weinstein, 1983). Part of the reason is that teachers and observers may miss some classroom occurrences because so many things happen so quickly. Further, teachers are intimately involved in running the classroom. Also, teachers and observers can and do *misinterpret* classroom behavior. That is, the problem of observing in classrooms is a bit more complex than we have described so far. Not only is our ability to perceive behavior in the classroom reduced by a fast classroom pace and not knowing what to look for, but on occasion, what we think we see is not congruent with reality. Our beliefs, past experiences, and prejudices can lead us to interpret what we see incorrectly rather than to see, describe, and analyze objectively what really happened.

Personal Biases

Supporters of various theories of teaching may interpret what they see in classrooms differently (Posner, 1985). Those who hold a didactic view believe that teaching is primarily aimed at transmitting knowledge and providing clear explanations or demonstrations that show how the knowledge operates. A discovery view focuses on student experimentation and opportunity to learn inductively from inquiry activities, with a minimum of teacher structure and explanation. An observer who prefers a didactic approach might find it difficult to assess fairly a teacher who uses a discovery approach, and vice versa. Thus, in addition to the problems discussed earlier (speed, complexity, lack of conceptual vocabulary for describing classroom behavior), personal biases (values, preferences) may distort what we see in the classroom.

Those who wish to observe accurately must identify and examine their biases. A classroom observer who is irritated by assertive, highly verbal teachers may see such teachers as punitive and rigid, whereas another observer may view them as well organized and articulate. Similarly, a teacher may see two students exhibit the same behavior yet interpret the students' behavior differently. Imagine the following situation. Mr. Fulton, who teaches tenth-grade American history, is talking when Bill Rink calls out, "Why are we talking about this?" Knowing Bill to be a troublemaker and class clown, Mr. Fulton assumes Bill wants to waste time or provoke an argument, so he responds aggressively, "If you would pay attention, you'd know what we're doing. Pay attention!" Compare this response with Mr. Fulton's reply to Jim, who calls out in the same tone, "Why are we talking about this?" Because Mr. Fulton knows that Jim is a good, dependable student, he views Jim's words not as a threat but as a serious question. He reasons that if Jim does not understand the purpose of the discussion, nobody does. He responds, "Jim, I probably haven't made this clear. Last Friday we discussed . . ."

Teachers react according to their *interpretations* of what students say, and their past experiences with a student often influence their response. We do not suggest that teachers should not interpret students' comments, but we argue that teachers should be *aware* of doing so. Some teachers fall into the trap of expecting a student to behave in a certain way and then systematically coloring their interpretations of the student's behavior, so that the behavior appears to fulfill the teacher's expectation. Often the distinction between observed behavior and the teacher's interpretation of that behavior is lost.

Anyone who tries to observe behavior must guard against this tendency to let personal biases color what is seen. We provide an exercise at the end of the chapter to help you identify your classroom biases. After you become more aware of various teacher and student behaviors and your attitudes toward them, you will be able to interpret classroom behavior more objectively. Suggestions are also presented to help you gather classroom data without unduly influencing the behavior of teachers and students.

Teacher Anxiety

Teachers who are insecure and possess a poor teaching self-concept are especially unlikely to seek information about themselves and apt to distort so-called threatening information when they receive it. Insecure teachers often see instructional difficulties as reflecting factors other than their own lack of competency ("TV has spoiled students. You can't motivate them anymore.").

How teacher anxiety influences teacher behavior, as well as the anxiety and classroom behavior of students, is complex, but a teacher who is excessively concerned about self is likely to have difficulty monitoring classroom interaction and seeing how others are affected by classroom events. Hence, some teachers may need more peer association than others.

DANGERS OF INTERPRETATION

It is hard to overstate the value of interpreting behavior only after data are collected. Quantitative and qualitative theorists agree on this important point (Evertson & Green, 1986). Quantitative researchers often ask questions before they observe (Is instruction meaningful or rote? Do girls and boys have equally challenging assignments? etc.) and develop coding systems that are specifically designed to answer these questions. In contrast, qualitative researchers tend to ask questions only after collecting considerable observational data. As Erickson (1986) notes, however, the stereotype of a classroom observer (field worker) arriving with a tabula rasa mind (carrying only a toothbrush and hunting knife), first to find and then to study a question, is romantic and extreme.

Erickson suggests that the observer's task is to become aware of possible frames of interpretation of those who are observed (i.e., How did teachers and students view the behavior?) and to subject observed behaviors to multiple interpretations. According to Erickson, the classroom observer, or field worker, should perform as a progressive problem solver. That is, observers' decisions about whom to talk to and what to observe next are determined as data are collected and analyzed. Thus, whether coders are using categories or field notes, they must be nonjudgmental during data collection. Knowing the question in advance is not likely to prejudice the outcome of research if the question calls for collection of descriptive facts rather than ratings or value judgments and the observer concentrates on collecting these facts before exploring their implications for classroom participants. Indeed, in many ways, formulating questions in advance guarantees that the information collected is relevant to the teacher and classroom being observed.

The teaching incident involving Mr. Fulton also illustrates that inferences should be made after observers have collected and examined descriptive information. As we have noted, observers' backgrounds, particularly their experiences as students and their views of good teaching, can lead them to draw erroneous conclusions (e.g., Goodson, 1992). If the teacher does something an observer especially likes (e.g., asks questions before calling on students), the observer may rate the teacher high in all areas. Similarly, if the teacher does something an observer particularly dislikes (e.g., humiliates a student who provides a wrong answer), the observer may evaluate the teacher as low on all dimensions of classroom behavior, even if the teacher performs well on some. Thus, observers need to guard against generalizing about behavior. Also, they must not evaluate behavior as positive or negative independent of its effects on students. For example, a teacher whom an observer sees as overly critical may be perceived by students as a person who sets high standards and cares about them (Kleinfeld, 1975; Mitman, 1985).

It is difficult for an observer to record behavior without interpreting it. Observers should concentrate on observing and coding or recording. Looking for specific behaviors is one way to minimize the effects of observers' attitudes and biases on their perceptions. For example, if an observer believes a teacher to be caustic and ineffectual, it is less likely that such an attitude will interfere with the description of classroom life if the observer pays attention to behavior (e.g., how often the teacher calls on low-achieving male students) than it will if the observer tries to describe the teacher in global, inferential terms (warm, friendly, fair, etc.). Behavior can be seen accurately if an observer wants to do so and is willing to practice and to compare his or her observations with those of others.

Common sources of error that can occur during observation appear in Table 2.1. As Everston and Green (1986) note, these issues need attention if we are to observe accurately in classrooms.

CASE STUDY TECHNIQUES

One useful way to improve observational skills is by conducting case studies that focus on one or a few students. Case studies that involve reporting of observed behaviors are particularly helpful. Such assignments facilitate our ability to observe and describe behavior accurately, and these skills are necessary to the generation of effective, concrete plans for dealing with students. Traditional case studies are excellent analytical tools for expanding our ability to see and to interpret student behavior.

Those of you seeking more detailed advice about ways to conduct scientific inquiries using case studies and field notes can profitably consult other sources (e.g., Erickson, 1986). Our focus here is on practical techniques for studying students in one's classroom.

Discovering Bias

We have noted that observers and teachers often misinterpret behavior because of their backgrounds and biases or because they try to interpret their findings prematurely. The first step in overcoming these problems is to become aware of them.

Table 2.1 SOURCES OF ERROR IN OBSERVATIONAL RESEARCH

Type of Error	Definition
1. Central tendency	When using rating scales, the observer tends toward the subjective midpoint when judging a series of stimuli.
2. Leniency or generosity	When using rating scales for which a "yes," "sometimes," "rarely," or "no" is required, the observer tends to be lenient or generous.
3. Primacy or recency effects	Observers' initial impressions have a distorting effect on later judgments (primacy). Observers' ratings may be unduly influenced by their most recent observations (recency).
4. Logical errors	Observer makes judgment errors based on theoretical, experiential, or commitment-based assumptions (e.g., the assumption that because a teacher shows warmth to a class, she or he is also instructionally effective).
5. Failure to acknowledge self	The influence of the observer on the setting is overlooked. The investigator's role may lead to the establishment of particular expectations. Judgments can be made in accordance with these expectations.
6. Classification of observations	Construction of macro categories loses fine distinctions. Such categories permit quantification but lose information about the process and fine-grained differences.
7. Generalization of unique behavior	Judgments may be based on evidence from an unrepresentative sample. Can lead to false conclusion or incorrect classifications of people or events.
8. Vested interests and values of observer	Findings become value-laden or otherwise distorted because of unchecked personal bias.
9. Failure to consider perspective of the observed	For investigators interested in a clear picture of everyday life, failure to obtain participants' perspectives may lead to identification of unvalidated factors, processes, or variables.
10. Unrepresentative sampling	Errors may occur based on samples that do not represent the general group of behaviors, that do not occur frequently enough to be observed reliably, or that are inconsistent with the theory guiding the observations.
11. Reactions of the observed	Reactions of participants being observed can distort the process or phenomena being observed (e.g., teachers who are anxious about being observed may behave differently than they would at a calmer time).
12. Failure to account for situation or context	Leads to incorrect conclusions from assumptions of functional equivalents (e.g., reading time 1 = reading time 2). Can lead to overlooking what is being taught, changes in activities, variations in rights and obligations for participation, hence can distort conclusions.
13. Poorly designed observation systems	Lead to problems with reliability and validity.
14. Lack of consideration for the rapid speed of relevant action	Errors may occur based on the omission of crucial features because of the rapidity of actions in the classroom.
15. Lack of consideration for the simultaneity of relevant action	Errors may occur based on failure to account for more than one activity occurring at a time; more than one message being sent at a time (e.g., use of different channels—verbal and nonverbal); and more than one function of a message at a time.
16. Lack of consideration of goal-directed or purposive nature of human activity	False conclusion that a behavior lacks stability because of failure to consider the purposes of human behavior.

Table 2.1   SOURCES OF ERROR IN OBSERVATIONAL RESEARCH, continued

Type of Error	Definition
17. Failure to ensure against observer drift	Errors caused by changes in the way the observer uses a system as time goes on. Can lead to obtaining descriptions that do not match the original categories or that vary from each other.

Source: Adapted from Evertson, C., & Green, J. (1986).Observation as inquiry and method. In M. Wittrock (Ed.), *Handbook of research on teaching* (3rd ed.). New York: Macmillan.

When we become aware of our attitudes, we can often control our behavior better. For example, the teacher who unhesitatingly says, "I am a fair grader, I am never influenced by the student as a person, and I grade only the paper," may be an unfair grader. The fact is that knowing who wrote a paper does influence most graders. With certain students, especially high achievers, teachers tend to read more into an answer than is there. They may demand more proof from other students (e.g., although a student's first paragraph in an essay is excellent, the teacher suspects that this student does not really know the material).

Once teachers realize that they do have biases that interfere with grading fairly, they can take steps to reduce the effects of those biases. For example, teachers can mask the identity of the student who wrote the paper before grading it, grade all papers on the first question before going to the next question, and score only content and not handwriting. In the same way, we can improve other weak spots if we become aware of them.

Difficulties of Self-Study

It is difficult to admit to feelings and reactions that we are afraid are unprofessional or inappropriate. For example, we tend not to accept the fact that we react differently to various students. Greenberg (1969) described some of the myths that frequently produce teacher problems, such as the illusion of liking all students equally. Such magnanimous behavior is impossible. Teachers treat students in equally fair and facilitating ways if and when they are aware of their feelings about the students. This does not mean identical behavior toward all students, however, because some students need more teacher contact, others need more opportunity to work on their own, and so forth. As human beings, teachers experience the full range of human emotions: They distrust some students, are proud of others, find some delightful, and want to avoid others. Similarly, observers have different reactions toward different teachers. If we are not careful, these feelings interfere with our ability to perceive classroom events accurately. Once we identify our feelings, it is possible to monitor classroom behavior more objectively.

Using Case Study for Self-Study

The case study assignment described in this section provides you with an opportunity to study your values, preferences, and attitudes. It forces you to consider the types of students (or teachers) whom you find fun and exciting to work with and to identify the types who annoy or bore you.

From the following list, select two contrast groups for study—any two except pairs 1 and 4. If you are not in an observation course, select peers who are in your class or select two college instructors and analyze their behavior. Better yet, arrange to observe in a class similar to the one you teach or will be teaching.

1. Select the two students with whom you would most enjoy working; that is, as a teacher, which two students would you choose first to be in your own room? (Positive feelings)
2. Select the two students whom you dislike the most. (Negative feelings)
3. Select two students for whom you have no strong feeling whatsoever. Use the class roster here so that you do not forget about anyone. (Apathy, indifference, not noticing when they are absent)
4. Select two students (one boy, one girl) who best represent the child you would want your son or daughter to be like at this age. (Identification)
5. Select two students who come from a cultural background that differs from your own. (Need for new knowledge or understanding.)

After selecting the four students, observe them more closely. If you choose to take notes during class, be sure to obtain the teacher's permission and let him or her know that the notes are about students and not the teacher. Some of you will be busy teaching during the day, so your notes will have to be made after class. The notes are for your own use, so their form is completely open. Bear in mind that any information you record in classrooms is confidential; students should never be identified by name. Even notes that you take in class should include no *actual* student names (notes are often lost). For this case study, it is not necessary to collect data from the school files, which might influence the observation anyway. Normal classroom behavior is sufficient.

Analyze the similarities and differences among the four students to get clues regarding the types of student behavior that are likely to elicit positive or negative responses in you. This activity will help you to understand why you behave as you do and to learn to interact more positively with students who irritate or confuse you. Consider the following questions when you compare and contrast the students:

1. What are they like physically? How do they look? Do they have nice clothes? Are they attractive? Clean? Large or small for their age? Male or female?
2. What are their favorite subjects? What lessons bore them? What are their strong and weak points as students? As persons?
3. What are their most prominent behavioral characteristics? Do they smile a lot? Thank you for your attention? Seek you out in the classroom more or less than the average student? Do they raise their hands to answer often? Can they be depended on to do their own work? How mature are they? Are they awkward or clumsy?
4. What are their social characteristics? What socioeconomic level do they come from? What is their ethnic background?

5. What aspects of classroom life seem most satisfying to them? What is least enjoyable or threatening?

The goal of this exercise is to start you thinking about possible linkages between your feelings about students and the way students treat you and you treat them in the classroom. A valuable parallel exercise would be to list the teacher behaviors that provoke your interest or boredom.

Conducting Case Studies

If you are puzzled about particular students, or merely interested in learning more about them, concentrated and sustained observation usually will reveal new insights and suggest interpretations and explanations. Case studies help teachers overcome the tendency to see students only within the student role. Attention is focused on students as unique individuals, and an attempt is made to empathize with them. This study involves trying to see the classroom environment as students see it and to understand what students are trying to accomplish when they respond to it.

First, who are the students? What are their background characteristics (age, gender, family background)? What are their orientations toward school? Toward the teachers? Toward classmates? What are their hobbies and interests? Their strengths and weaknesses as individuals? As students? Thinking about such questions and jotting down tentative answers can help in developing an open mind toward students and learning to look at them in new ways. These steps may improve your knowledge of a certain student before you spend any time observing that student. For example, if you cannot name several strengths *and* weaknesses, your view of the student is probably biased. In our desire for simplicity and consistency in our perceptions, we tend to emphasize characteristics that fit together and reinforce our biases, and to slight those that do not.

No special preparation or equipment is required to observe a student systematically. An ordinary notebook and pen or pencil will do. You should be near enough to see and hear the student, but not so close as to be inhibiting. Ideally, the student should not know you are observing him or her. If possible, observe the student outside class as well (during recess, at lunch, and between classes), when the student's behavior is likely to be more characteristic than when constricted by the student role.

If the student presents a problem, try to formulate it as specifically as you can, using terms that translate into observable behavior. Include any relevant information about the contexts in which behavior occurs (subject matter, size of group, time of day, type of situation). Patterns in the student's behavior may increase your understanding of it. You also might notice important differences between situations in which the student is and is not a problem (interest in the topic, structure in the activity, active versus quiet activity, type of antecedent experience, presence of peers or other distractors, etc.). Whatever the activity, focus on the student, including times when he or she is a passive spectator. There is a tendency to observe the teacher or whoever else is the center of attention at times like these, but when you are doing a case study, it is important to concentrate on the student.

Keep a running log of the student's behavior during periods of observation. Observations should be dated and clearly separated from one another in the continuous log, and they should be subdivided into natural units according to what was going on at the time (class periods and breaks between periods, different activities and settings within classes, etc.). The log should contain narrative descriptions of behavior along with interpretations about its possible meanings. It is important to keep objective descriptions of behavior separate from subjective interpretations concerning meaning, because interpretations may change as more information is collected. Probably the easiest way to do this is to use only the left half of the page for keeping the log of behavior. Interpretations can be written on the right half of the page later, when you review your notes and think about what you have observed.

If you interviewed students, you may find that their beliefs about school subjects and other topics differ from what you had concluded on the basis of your observation. Students can be excellent sources of information about how classrooms work. Interview techniques are beyond the scope of this book, but excellent suggestions about the use of student interviews as well as how to conduct them can be found elsewhere (Cazden, 1986; Meichenbaum et al., 1985; Rohrkemper, 1981, 1985; Spradley, 1979; Weinstein, 1983). The Meichenbaum et al. (1985) chapter provides valuable ideas for planning and conducting various types of interviews (observation of spontaneous private speech, think-aloud method, and how to infer metacognition from task performance).

Cazden (1986) argues that much research on teaching is designed to develop knowledge of teacher behavior and is often used to provide teachers with feedback in order to enhance their self-knowledge. However, she suggests that information about students' beliefs and behavior is more valuable to teachers than information about the teachers themselves. Cazden offers valuable tips for researchers or observers who are attempting to track individual children's learning, students' peer-peer interaction, students' elaboration in group projects, and peer tutoring. This information would be useful for teachers or researchers who are interested in studying students' perceptions and behavior in the classroom.

Fact Versus Interpretation

When recording information for a case study, the goal is to include as much pertinent and interpretable information as possible but to stick with the facts and avoid unsupported and perhaps incorrect interpretations. This objective is not difficult to achieve, but it may take some practice to learn to separate vague information from interpretable facts, and interpretable facts from interpretations themselves.

An Example   Suppose an observer were watching Ron, a white student, at a time when he became involved in an incident with Ralph, a black student, and recorded the following information: "Ralph taps Ron, points, and speaks. Ron replies, shaking head. Ralph gestures, speaks. Ron strikes Ralph, and a fight starts." This information is factual, but it is too vague to be much good. Even if the words of the boys are not heard, their gestures and the general nature of their interaction can be described much more clearly. Let's look at another example.

> Ron is working quietly until bothered by Ralph. He listens, then refuses. Ralph becomes angry and abusive. Ron becomes aggressive, triggering a major racial incident.

Assuming that the observer could not hear what was said, this example is not so much an observation as an interpretation. Ron may or may not have "refused" whatever Ralph wanted, Ralph may or may not have "provoked" Ron, and the incident may or may not be "racial." These are interpretations. They fit the facts and may be true, but this also can be said of many other possible interpretations. A competent observer would have recorded the facts as follows:

> Ralph taps Ron on shoulder, shows his assignment, points to something, speaks. Ron looks, shakes head no, says something. Ralph replies with disgusted look, downward gesture of arm. Turns away when finished speaking. Ron says something to Ralph from behind, then slaps Ralph's head. Ralph responds as if attacked, fight begins.

This description contains about as much useful information as could be recorded without becoming interpretive. About all that is missing is a description of Ron's facial expression and general manner when slapping Ralph. This information would be helpful in judging whether the head slap really was meant as an attack (if so, it would be an unusual behavior).

The interpretation of this information would raise questions about its meaning. Who actually started the trouble, and what started it? Is it accurate to call this a racial incident, or is the fact that one boy is black and the other white irrelevant? What really happened?

Ordinarily, the observer would get answers to these and related questions, because interactions as intense as fights usually involve loud talk, which is easy to hear. However, without more information, the interpretation of these facts would have to be confined to speculation. The first fact is that Ralph interrupted Ron by tapping his shoulder, pointing to the assignment, and saying something. The shoulder tap apparently did not bother Ron because he did not show any reaction to it. In fact, he did not appear angry until later. The fact that Ralph showed the assignment and pointed to something suggests that he was seeking help or information about it or was expressing an opinion. However, it is possible that Ralph did these things just to give the appearance of discussing the assignment and that what he had to say to Ron had nothing to do with the assignment. If so, he could have made a provocative statement, but not necessarily.

Ron responded by shaking his head no and saying something. This response could have been a refusal to listen, a refusal of a request, or an answer to Ralph's question, among other things. If Ralph had expressed an opinion, this could have been a disagreement by Ron. In any case, it is clear that Ron responded negatively to whatever Ralph asked or said.

Ralph's gesture and facial expression in his reply suggest disgust and/or anger, although it is not at all clear whether he provoked Ron in some way. He might have, but he might also have been expressing his own frustration with whatever

Ron had said. He might even have been giving an opinion. For example, he might have originally pointed out what he considered to be a stupid question and asked Ron if he understood it. Ron might have said that he didn't understand it either, and Ralph might have responded with a gesture and look of disgust while saying something like, "Why do they ask us stuff like this?"

Just as Ralph's behavior may or may not have involved provocation, Ron's behavior may or may not have involved aggression. It could have been an attack on Ralph, perhaps in retaliation for something Ralph said, but it also could have been horseplay. Boys frequently poke or slap one another as a way of teasing (but not attacking), and that could be what happened.

With a little imagination, we can think of several other interpretations of what occurred between Ron and Ralph, but the ones just given are sufficient to indicate the difference between facts and interpretations. Such ambiguous situations are common when classroom observations are collected in case studies, which is why it is important physically to separate facts about observations from interpretations of these observations. The factual record will remain constant even when interpretations change in the light of new evidence. Even when you are not entering observations in a case study record, the distinction between fact and interpretation should be kept in mind. The ability to maintain and be aware of this distinction is an important part of learning to be accurate when observing in classrooms.

Avoiding Bias Recording and interpreting behavior are two distinct issues. You must determine what behavior to record and how to record it, and then you interpret the behavior. You may have to experiment in order to find the appropriate degree of generality to use in describing behavior. You should not try to record literally everything that you see. Even if this were possible, you would be recording a great deal of information about trivial behaviors and expressions that have no interpretive importance. In contrast, in the interest of objectivity, it is important that you record observable behaviors. Thus, it would be appropriate to note that the student smiled or even smiled at the teacher, but it would be an interpretation to say that the student showed friendly warmth (as opposed to self-satisfaction, for example). Similarly, it would be appropriate to state that the student spent time apparently absorbed in thinking and problem solving, but it would be an interpretation to say that the student *was* thinking and problem solving. Perhaps the student has learned to give this appearance while daydreaming (Peterson & Swing, 1982; Spencer-Hall, 1981).

You want to highlight information relevant to your concerns about the student, but your record should keep everything in proper perspective. For example, if you are watching a student who gets into trouble with peers, you should have detailed descriptions of what happened on two occasions when the student became involved in arguments. It should be clear from the record, however, that these two occasions involved only a few minutes, and the record should provide a running account of what the student was doing during the rest of the period. In fact, when you observe a problem student, it can be helpful to keep in mind the question "What does the student do when not misbehaving?" This question will cue your attention to positive behavior that a teacher should learn about and build on in future interactions with the student. To obtain this information, it is important to fight the tendency to let halo effects structure your perceptions. Just as outstanding students have weaknesses, problem students have strengths.

Behavioral records should be reviewed and checked for completeness and accuracy at the first opportunity. At this time, you can also make initial interpretations, add clarification, and edit your notes. You may or may not be able to interpret everything you see, but your notes should be complete and unambiguous concerning what actually happened. In addition to a description of what transpired, there should be information about the qualitative aspects of the student's behavior (Was it random or purposeful? Was there anything unusual or noteworthy about it?) and explanations for the behavior (What stimulated it? What was its purpose?).

In reviewing behavioral comments, look for correlations and contradictions. Try to identify repeated patterns. Are they well known, or do they suggest new insights? Look for places where a particular pattern might have been expected but did not occur. These could be keys to explaining patterns or to developing ideas about how to get the student to change. If your notes suggest certain hypotheses but do not contain enough information to allow you to evaluate them, try to identify what information you need. Perhaps you can identify specific situations you could observe soon. For example, suppose the student challenged the teacher on two occasions when asked to read aloud. This response could be a defense mechanism used in an attempt to avoid reading, perhaps because the student cannot read. You cannot tell from only two instances, but you could watch for this behavior in the future whenever the class is involved in oral reading, and you could check the student's reading achievement. Such supplementary information then can be added to the log at appropriate places to assist you in interpreting the student's behavior.

SIMPLIFYING THE OBSERVATIONAL TASK

We have emphasized the need to study observer and teacher biases to prevent them from interfering with assessment of classroom events. Another major obstacle to accurate perception of classrooms is their sheer physical complexity. While the teacher instructs a reading group, four students may be at the science table, three listening to tapes at the listening post, four reading at their desks, and three writing at the blackboard. No observer can monitor everything that takes place. Even relatively simple tasks may be impossible to code simultaneously. For instance, if an observer wants to code the number of hands raised when a teacher asks a question and note whether the student called on by the teacher has a hand up, the observer may still be counting hands when the teacher calls on the student and will thus be unable to determine whether the student had a hand up.

One excellent way to overcome this complexity, especially when you begin observing in classrooms, is to study the behavior of a few students. You can study these students intensively, and their behavior will probably mirror what is taking place in the entire classroom. An observer can focus on a few students (perhaps two high, two middle, and two low achievers—one female and one male at each level) or on a particular group of students (low achievers). Then a record can be made of certain things these students do. One might record the following information about high, middle, and low achievers:

1. How often do they raise their hands?
2. Do all students approach the teacher to receive help, or do some seldom approach the teacher?
3. How long does each reading group last?
4. Are the students involved in their work? How long do they work independently at their desks?
5. How often are students in different groups praised?
6. What do students do when they finish their experiment, while other students are still completing their lab assignment?

Another useful strategy is to limit the number of behaviors you observe at one time, perhaps restricting attention initially to five to ten behaviors. When we attempt to monitor too many things, we become confused and cannot record objectively. It is better to concentrate on a few behaviors for a while and then to code a new set.

RELIABILITY OF OBSERVATIONS

You should assess your ability to code classroom behavior accurately by comparing your observations with those of others. This method is perhaps the easiest way to determine whether you are observing what happens and not allowing your personal biases to interfere with your observing.

In general, the observation forms presented following Chapters 3 through 10 can be used reliably with little practice. After discussing an observation scale for a short time (5 to 20 minutes, depending on the scale), observers should be able to achieve general agreement (60 to 90 percent) and thus be able to use the scale reliably to code classroom behavior. If observers are watching a videotape and coding the number of academic questions a teacher asks, one observer may have tallied 16 academic questions, whereas another tallied only 10. Agreement between the two observers can be estimated by using this simple formula suggested by Emmer and Millet (1970):

$$\text{agreement} = 1 - \frac{A - B}{A + B}$$

The formula tells us to subtract the difference between the two observers' counts and to divide by the sum of their counts. The *A* term is always the larger number. Thus, agreement in this example would be:

$$1 - \frac{16 - 10}{16 + 10} = 1 - \frac{6}{26} = 1 - 0.23 = 77\%$$

GENERAL PLAN FOR OBSERVING IN CLASSROOMS

What you observe in a classroom will vary from situation to situation and from individual to individual. Some observers will be able to focus on six behaviors; others may be able to code ten. Some may be in the classroom eight hours a week, some only four. Some may see two or three different teachers; others will remain in the same room. Despite such situational differences, some general principles will apply when observing in classrooms.

First, observers often try to reduce the complexity of classroom coding by focusing their attention exclusively on the teacher. This is particularly true for teachers in training, who are still trying to determine what teachers do, but it is misplaced emphasis. *The key to thorough classroom observation is student response.* If students are actively engaged in worthwhile learning activities, it makes little difference whether the teacher is lecturing, using discovery techniques, or using small-group activities for independent study.

Earlier we noted that some observers may see a teacher as punitive and rigid, whereas others see the same teacher as well organized and articulate. A good way to reduce your own bias in viewing teacher behavior is to supplement your observations by examining both teacher and student behaviors. Students influence teachers as much as teachers influence students.

Teachers who want to receive relevant feedback about their behavior and that of their students, and observers who want to see what life in a classroom is like must be careful not to disturb the natural behavior in the classroom. By *natural* we mean the behavior that would take place in the classroom if the observer were not present. Students, especially young ones, adjust quickly to the presence of an observer if teachers prepare them properly and if the observer behaves appropriately. The teacher should explain the observer's presence briefly, so that the students do not have to wonder about the observer or try to question him or her to find out for themselves. For example, a second-grade class might be told, "Mr. Ramon will be with us today and the rest of the week. He is learning about being a teacher. Mr. Ramon will not disturb us because we have many things we want to finish, and he knows how busy we are. Please do not disturb him because he, too, is busy and has his own work to do."

The observer can help the teacher by avoiding eye contact with the students and by refusing to be drawn into long conversations with them or to aid them in their seatwork—unless, of course, the observer is also a participant in classroom life. (Some university courses call for students to serve as teacher aides before they do their student teaching.)

Observers should not initiate contact with students or do anything to draw special attention to themselves (e.g., loudly ripping pages out of a notebook). It is especially important when two observers are in the same room that they not talk with each other, exchange notes, and so forth. Such behavior bothers both the teacher and the students and causes attention to be focused on the observers, so that natural behavior is disturbed.

Before coming into a classroom, observers should talk with the teacher about where they will sit in the room, how they should be introduced to the students, and how they should respond when a student approaches them. Without such preparation, both teachers and observers frequently are paralyzed when students approach the observer. Teachers are embarrassed because students are out of their seats, and they are indecisive about what to do because they do not know whether the observer wants to inspect the students' work or would prefer not to be bothered. Observers are often unskilled at dealing with students. They are not sure how to act when approached, except that they don't want to be a rude guest. The teacher and observers should agree on how to deal with students who are intent on making themselves known to the observer. At such meetings, observers can obtain curriculum materials and information about the students (seating chart, achievement ranking). Such information is necessary if the observer plans to conduct an intensive study of only a few students at different achievement levels. The information needed to use the rating systems at the end of subsequent chapters is presented in this chapter. If you wish detailed information about more advanced coding systems, consult Appendix A at the end of this chapter.

In the first two chapters, we have identified many factors that can interfere with your perception of classroom behavior, and we have discussed ways to reduce problems of bias and complexity (students who will conduct research in classrooms can find more detailed discussions about conducting observational research elsewhere). In the following chapters, we develop the theme of looking in classrooms by providing detailed comments about *what* to look for. In these chapters we discuss what could and should be occurring in classrooms. At the end of most chapters are rating scales that can be used to record the presence or absence of the teaching behaviors discussed in this chapter.

USING RESEARCH AND OBSERVATIONAL FEEDBACK

Research findings and concepts provide a way of thinking about classroom instruction, but they must be used as tools, not rules. Consider Adams and Biddle's (1970) discussion of the action zone, describing their finding that students who sat in the front row and in seats extending directly up the middle aisle received more opportunities to talk than other students. The action zone is a useful concept for identifying *possible* problems in the classroom; it suggests that students in some areas of a classroom may receive more response opportunities than students in other areas. If interpreted too literally, however, the work of Adams and Biddle could be interpreted to mean that action zones are always located in the front row and the middle of the class.

A study by Alhajri (1981) showed that only 1 of 32 classrooms had an action zone like the one described by Adams and Biddle, although some kind of action zone was present in many classrooms. This research reaffirmed the value of the action zone concept as a tool for analyzing classroom instruction, even though it showed that action zones can take many forms. If observers or teachers were monitoring classes for only one type of action zone, they would not notice zones that took a different form.

We discuss research findings in terms of concepts that enable teachers to examine classrooms. Research results do not provide answers because they must be applied to particular teachers and students. Research-based concepts can, however, enable educators to observe more behaviors more rapidly. They also can stimulate additional analysis.

Considering the complexity of and variation among instruction-learning settings, research findings—no matter how clear the relevant theory or how robust the findings—must be interpreted in relation to individual teachers and individual schools. Effective use of any concept taken from research on teaching can take many forms, and a teaching behavior may be appropriate in some contexts but not in others. Even behaviors that have wide applicability are not useful in some schools or classrooms. Teachers must analyze and discuss findings and concepts from research on teaching in terms of their own teaching situations. Teachers must learn to reflect carefully, define their classroom problems, and explore research findings and concepts within the dictates of their classroom contexts.

TEACHERS AS DECISION MAKERS

We noted in Chapter 1 that teachers need to be decision makers and to understand that knowledge has to be applied to a particular social and academic setting. Here we want to elaborate on the importance of viewing teaching as decision making. Teachers must *continuously* reflect on their classroom experiences and adapt their teaching to the students in their classes. Teachers also need to obtain new information from research about concepts and ideas they can use to analyze their teaching or improve curriculum and instruction for students.

In a comprehensive review of research on teachers' thought processes, Clark and Peterson (1986) concluded that teaching involves reflective, thoughtful adaptation. They contend that research substantiates the view that teaching is a complex and cognitively demanding process. Adding to this complexity is the fact that teachers hold countless beliefs about students and the learning process, as well as beliefs about the content of various types of subject matter and the ways to teach the content.

A skillful, adaptive teacher may realize that students have not grasped the essential point of a lesson (because the teacher knows to check for understanding and to call on a diverse range of students); still, this knowledge does not predict what action the teacher should take. On a given day, for example, late in the afternoon and with a difficult concept, the teacher may move to a new lesson and not reteach the concept until the next day. Alternatively, the teacher might give the students a reading assignment or ask them to engage in some experimental assignment in order to prepare them for the instruction that will come later. The teacher might make a different decision in other circumstances—to reteach the concept immediately. In this case, the key issue is that the teacher *knows* that the students do not understand the material; hence, the teacher is in a position to take corrective action. Teachers who lack such awareness cannot be decision makers.

Fenstermacher (1983) distinguished the structural elaboration from the personal elaboration of research. Structural elaboration involves using research findings as answers or prescriptions. If, for example, researchers found that ten minutes of homework were effective in a particular program, structural elaboration would advocate that all teachers use ten minutes of homework. In contrast, when research is used for personal elaboration, the decision about how to apply research and about its value resides with the individual teacher, who thinks about the needs of his or her students. It is vital that teachers have access to recent research-based knowledge—knowledge derived from observation of classrooms—but it is important that teachers reflect and form their own ideas about the value of the knowledge and its relevance to their contexts.

Kindsvetter, Wilen, and Ishler (1989) pointed out that many teachers' classroom practice is heavily influenced by their past experience and involves no innovations based on reflection. Some teachers simply teach the way they were taught when they were in school or model more immediate experiences (e.g., teach the way their cooperating teachers did). Some teachers develop a thoughtful approach when they begin teaching but subsequently fail to update curriculum materials or to monitor changes in students' interests that are related to variation in societal expectations, experiences, and so on. Examples that worked fine five years ago may be less compelling to today's students. Instruction in a subject or at a grade level cannot be planned in any final way. Teachers must revise plans and expectations on the basis of new knowledge and new students.

Kindsvetter et al. (1989, pp. 8–9) characterize the limitations of decisions based largely on personal experiences:

> To the extent that teachers operate primarily on the basis of experience, they perform analogously to the tribal medicine man. Through his use of both mystique and proficiency with primitive medicines, he may actually perform a valuable service for his fellow tribespeople. His practice, however, lacks a rationally developed base. Little change occurs in his practice from generation to generation because there is essentially no understanding of the causes, and instead simply a recognition and treatment of the symptoms.

Kindsvetter et al. note that their statement is intended only as an informal, casual analogy; they recognize that changes have obviously occurred in education. Nevertheless, they stress that some teachers fail to avail themselves of new knowledge and hence teach without important information that could improve classroom learning.

One important change is that the field of teaching now has a substantial knowledge base from research (Jackson, 1992; Wittrock, 1986) that teachers can use to think about their classrooms and to make decisions. We emphasize the value of personal experience in making teaching decisions. In many respects, teaching involves values (fairness, sensitivity) and is an art at times (spontaneous deviation from intended plans, etc.). However, although intuitive sources of knowledge can be valuable, they are also affected by biases and self-perceptions.

SUMMARY

Teachers are not aware of everything that goes on in the classroom, and this lack of awareness may interfere with their effectiveness. This problem exists for at least two basic reasons. First, classrooms are busy places, and teachers (and students as well) are so busy responding that they have little time to think about what they are doing. Many factors contribute to classroom complexity. The second problem is that teachers are seldom observed systematically, so they rarely receive valuable information about ways to increase their effectiveness. When they are observed, it is typically for purposes of evaluation. Fortunately, this situation is changing in some schools.

Objective recording of behavior provides a way to guard against our biases and gain the most benefit from classroom observations. Personal bias in observing can be reduced by (1) becoming aware of our biases; (2) observing specific behaviors, to alleviate the complexity of the classroom; and (3) checking our observational data against the observations of others. Exercises were suggested to help you observe your own or another's behavior objectively. We also discussed procedures for minimizing the observer's effect on the classroom, along with techniques for observing unobtrusively. These considerations should be borne in mind when you use the observation schedules following Chapters 3 through 10.

Finally, we have suggested that although research and, particularly, observational data about classrooms are important, they should not dictate successful practice. Teachers must integrate rich data with their own beliefs, values, and purposes regarding instruction. Effective classroom teachers function as active decision makers.

SUGGESTED ACTIVITIES AND QUESTIONS

1. Sometimes problems and/or potential are in the eye of the beholder. What one person views as appropriate curiosity or initiative another may believe is unwarranted intrusion or aggression. To explore more fully the ambiguity of behavior (and the need to interpret it), consider what selected behaviors (e.g., cooperation, initiative, leadership, etc.) mean to you in a particular instructional context. What student behaviors would imply appropriate initiative in a first-grade versus a seventh-grade classroom? How would you define appropriate cooperative behaviors at these two grades? How do your classmates define these terms at different grade levels? How do first- and seventh-grade students define cooperation? How do teachers at the two grade levels define these terms?

2. After reading the chapter, do you have any questions about the facts or concepts presented? Are there topics that you would like more information about? If so, write two or three questions of your own and turn them in to your instructor for feedback, or trade questions with fellow teachers or students.

3. Most of us find it difficult to monitor our teaching behavior initially, but improvement comes with practice. When you teach (whether micro, simulated, or real), try to monitor your behavior (e.g., the ratio of fact to thought questions) and see how your mental record compares with a record taken by a coder or with what you hear when you play back your tape-recorded lesson. Practice monitoring your behavior, listening to what you say as you teach, and comparing your perceptions with objective records.

4. How can teachers improve their ability to see behavior in classrooms?

5. Why is it important that an observer have a conceptual system for describing classroom behavior and for noticing significant occurrences?

6. Teachers obviously want low achievers to do well, but some low achievers receive less teacher contact and help than high achievers. How can teachers improve their interaction patterns with low achievers without reducing their effectiveness with other students?

7. Why is the use of video equipment (allowing teachers to see themselves teach) relatively ineffective unless it is combined with specific directions concerning what to look for or descriptions of what took place?

8. Visit a classroom or watch a videotape of a discussion and tally the number of times that the teacher: (a) asks a question, (b) responds to a student's answer, and (c) praises a student. Compare your tallies with another observer's by calculating the percentage of agreement between your observations.

9. Think about all your previous teachers and list the major characteristics of your favorite teacher. What was he or she like as a person? What were the chief elements of the teacher's teaching style?

10. Similarly, list the distinguishing factors of your least liked or least effective teacher. Why were you more comfortable or more stimulated in one class than the other? Was it because of the teacher, the subject matter, the students in the class, or a combination of factors?

REFERENCES

Adams, R., & Biddle, B. (1970). *Realities of teaching: Explorations with video tape.* New York: Holt.

Alhajri, A. (1981). *Effect of seat position on school performance of Kuwaiti students.* Unpublished doctoral dissertation, University of Missouri-Columbia.

Alleman, J., & Brophy, J. (1992). Analysis of the activities in a social studies curriculum. In J. Brophy (Ed.), *Advances in research on teaching* (Vol. 3, pp. 47–80). Greenwich, CT: JAI Press.

Allington, R. (1991). Children who find learning to read difficult: School responses to diversity. In E. Hiebert (Ed.), *Literacy for a diverse society* (pp. 237–252). New York: Teachers College Press.

American Association of University Women. (1992). *How schools shortchange girls.* Washington, DC: American Association of University Women Educational Foundation.

Anderson, L., Brubaker, N., Alleman-Brooks, J., & Duffy, G. (1985). A qualitative study of seatwork in first-grade classrooms. *Elementary School Journal, 86,* 123–140.

Berliner, D. (1979). Tempus educare. In P. Peterson & H. Walberg (Eds.), *Research on teaching: Concepts, findings, and implications.* Berkeley, CA: McCutchan.

Blumenfeld, P. (1992). The task and the teacher: Enhancing student thoughtfulness in science. In J. Brophy (Ed.), *Advances in research on teaching* (Vol. 3, pp. 81–114). Greenwich, CT: JAI Press.

Blumenfeld, P., & Meece, J. (1988). Task factors, teacher behavior, and students' involvement and use of learning strategies in science. *Elementary School Journal, 88,* 236–250.

Bossert, S. (1981). Understanding sex differences in children's classroom experiences. *Elementary School Journal, 81,* 255–268.

Boyer, E. (1983). *High school*. New York: Harper & Row.

Brophy, J. (1982). How teachers influence what is taught and learned in classrooms. *Elementary School Journal, 83*, 1–14.

Brophy, J., & Evertson, C. (1981). *Student characteristics and teaching*. New York: Longman.

Brophy, J., & Good, T. (1970). Teachers' communication of differential expectations for children's classroom performance: Some behavioral data. *Journal of Educational Psychology, 61*, 365–374.

Brophy, J., & Good, T. (1974). *Teacher-student relationships: Causes and consequences*. New York: Holt, Rinehart and Winston.

Brophy, J., & Kher, N. (1986). Teacher socialization as a mechanism for developing student motivation to learn. In R. Feldman (Ed.), *Social psychology applied to education*. Cambridge: Cambridge University Press.

Carter, K., & Doyle, W. (1982). *Variations in academic tasks in high and average ability classes*. Paper presented at the annual meeting of the American Educational Research Association, New York.

Cazden, C. (1986). Classroom discourse. In M. C. Wittrock (Ed.), *Handbook of research on teaching*, 3rd ed. (pp. 432–463). New York: Macmillan.

Channon, G. (1970). *Homework*. New York: Outerbridge and Dienstfrey.

Clark, C., & Peterson, P. (1986). Teachers' thought processes. In M. C. Wittrock (Ed.), *Handbook of research on teaching* (3rd ed., pp. 255–298). New York: Macmillan.

Cooper, H., & Good, T. (1983). *Pygmalion grows up: Studies in the expectation communication process*. New York: Longman.

Cuban, L. (1984). *How teachers taught: Constancy and change in American classrooms 1890–1980*. New York: Longman.

Doyle, W. (1983). Academic work. *Review of Educational Research, 53*, 159–199.

Doyle, W. (1992). Curriculum and pedagogy. In P. Jackson (Ed.), *Handbook of research on curriculum* (pp. 486–516). New York: Macmillan.

Durkin, D. (1978–1979). What classroom observations reveal about reading comprehension instruction. *Reading Research Quarterly, 14*, 481–533.

Eccles, J., & Blumenfeld, P. (1985). Classroom experiences and student gender: Are there differences and do they matter? In L. Wilkinson & C. Marrett (Eds.), *Gender influences in classroom interaction*. New York: Academic Press.

Eder, D. (1981). Ability grouping as a self-fulfilling prophecy: A microanalysis of teacher-student interaction. *Sociology of Education, 54*, 151–161.

Eisenhart, M., & Cutts-Dougherty, K. (1991). Social and cultural constraints on students' access to school knowledge. In E. Hiebert (Ed.), *Literacy for a diverse society* (pp. 28–43). New York: Teachers College Press.

Emmer, E., & Millet, G. (1970). *Improving teaching through experimentation: A laboratory approach*. Englewood Cliffs, NJ: Prentice-Hall.

Erickson, F. (1986). Qualitative methods in research on teaching. In M. C. Wittrock (Ed.), *Handbook of research on teaching* (3rd ed., pp. 119–161). New York: Macmillan.

Evertson, C., & Green, J. (1986). Observation as inquiry and method. In M. C. Wittrock (Ed.), *Handbook of research on teaching* (3rd ed., pp. 162–213). New York: Macmillan.

Fenstermacher, G. (1983). How should implications of research on teaching be used? *Elementary School Journal, 83,* 496–499.

Fisher, C., & Hiebert, E. (1990). Characteristics of tasks in two approaches to literacy instruction. *Elementary School Journal, 91,* 3–18.

Freedman, S., Jackson, J., & Boles, K. (1983). Teaching: An imperiled "profession." In L. Shulman & G. Sykes (Eds.), *Handbook of teaching and policy.* New York: Longman.

Freeman, D., Kuhs, T., Porter, A., Floden, R., Schmidt, W., & Schwille, J. (1983). Do textbooks and tests define a national curriculum in elementary school mathematics? *Elementary School Journal, 83,* 501–513.

Freeman, D., & Porter, A. (1989). Do textbooks dictate the content of mathematics instruction in elementary schools? *American Educational Research Journal, 26,* 403–421.

Fuller, F., & Manning, B. (1973). Self-confrontation review: A conceptualization for video playback in teacher education. *Review of Educational Research, 43,* 469–528.

Gitlin A., & Smyth, J. (1989). *Teacher evaluation: Educative alternatives.* New York: Falmer Press.

Good, T., & Brophy, J. (1974). Changing teacher and student behavior: An empirical investigation. *Journal of Educational Psychology, 66,* 390–405.

Good, T., Grouws, D., & Ebmeier, H. (1983). *Active mathematics teaching: Empirical research in elementary and secondary classrooms.* New York: Longman.

Good, T., McCaslin, M., & Reys, B. (1992). Investigating work groups to promote problem solving in mathematics. In J. Brophy (Ed.), *Advances in research on teaching* (Vol. 3, pp. 115–160). Greenwich, CT: JAI Press.

Good, T., Mulryan, C., & McCaslin, M. (1992). Grouping for instruction in mathematics: A call for programmatic research on small-group processes. In D. Grouws (Ed.), *Handbook of research on mathematics teaching and learning* (pp. 165–196). New York: Macmillan.

Goodlad, J. (1984). *A place called school.* New York: McGraw-Hill.

Goodlad, J., Soder, R., & Sirotnik, K. (Eds.). (1990). *Places where teachers are taught.* San Francisco: Jossey Bass.

Goodson, I. (Ed.). (1992). *Studying teachers' lives.* New York: Teachers College Press.

Grant, L. (1985). Race-gender status, classroom interaction, and children's socialization in elementary school. In L. Wilkinson & C. Marrett (Eds.), *Gender influences in classroom interaction.* New York: Academic Press.

Greenberg, H. (1969). *Teaching with feeling.* New York: Macmillan.

Griffin, G. (1983). *Student teaching and the common places of school* (Report No. 9038). Austin: University of Texas, Research and Development Center for Teacher Education.

Griffin, G. (1985). The school as a workplace and the master teacher concept. *Elementary School Journal, 86,* 1–16.

Hiebert, E. (Ed.). (1991). *Literacy for a diverse society.* New York: Teachers College Press.

Jackson, P. (1968). *Life in classrooms.* New York: Holt.

Jackson, P. (Ed.). (1992). *Handbook of research on curriculum.* New York: Macmillan.

Jones, M. (1990). Action zone theory and target students in science classrooms. *Journal of Research in Science Teaching, 27,* 651–660.

Jones, M., & Gerig, T. (in press). Silent students: Characteristics, achievement, and teacher expectations. *Elementary School Journal*.

Jones, M., & Wheatley, J. (1990). Gender differences in student-teacher interactions. *Journal of Research in Science Teaching, 27*, 861–874.

Jorgenson, G., (1977). Relationship of classroom behavior to the accuracy of match between material difficulty and student ability. *Journal of Educational Psychology, 69*, 204–232.

Kindsvetter, R., Wilen, W., & Ishler, M. (1989). *Dynamics of effective teaching*. New York: Longman.

King, L. (1993). High and low achievers' perceptions and cooperative learning in two small groups. *Elementary School Journal, 93*, 399–416.

Kleinfeld, J. (1975). Effective teachers of Eskimo and Indian students. *School Review, 83*, 301–344.

Leacock, E. (1969). *Teaching and learning in city schools*. New York: Basic Books.

Leinhardt, G., Seewald, A., & Engel, M. (1979). Learning what's taught: Sex differences in instruction. *Journal of Educational Psychology, 71*, 432–439.

Maeroff, G. (1988). *The empowerment of teachers*. New York: Teachers College Press.

May, W. (1992). Designing worthwhile activities in elementary art. In J. Brophy (Ed.), *Advances in research on teaching* (Vol. 3, pp. 225–275). Greenwich, CT: JAI Press.

McCaslin, M., & Good, T. (1992). Compliant cognition: The misalliance of management and instruction goals in current school reform. *Educational Researcher, 21*, 4–17.

McNeil, J. (1971). *Toward accountable teachers: Their appraisal and improvement*. New York: Holt.

Meichenbaum, D., Burland, S., Gruson, L., & Cameron, L. (1985). Metacognitive assessment. In S. Yussen (Ed.), *The growth of reflection in children*. New York: Academic Press.

Mergendoller, J. (Ed.). (1988, January). Schoolwork and academic tasks. *Elementary School Journal, 88*, special issue.

Mergendoller, J., Marchman, B., Mitman, A., & Packer, M. (1988). Task demands and accountability in middle-grade science classes. *Elementary School Journal, 88*, 251–265.

Mitman, A. (1985). Teachers' differential behavior toward higher- and lower-achieving students and its relationship with selected teacher characteristics. *Journal of Educational Psychology, 35*, 149–161.

Morse, L., & Handley, H. (1985). Listening to adolescents: Gender differences in science classroom interaction. In L. Wilkinson & C. Marrett (Eds.), *Gender influences in classroom interaction*. New York: Academic Press.

Mulryan, C. (1989). *A study of intermediate-grade students' involvement and participation in cooperative small groups in mathematics*. Unpublished doctoral dissertation, University of Missouri-Columbia.

Natriello, G., & Dornbusch, S. (1980–1981). Pitfalls in the evaluation of teachers by principals. *Administrator's Notebook, 29*(6), 1–4.

Natriello, G., McDill, E., & Pallas, A. (1990). *Schooling disadvantaged children: Racing against catastrophe*. New York: Teachers College Press.

Ogbu, J. (1992). Understanding cultural diversity and learning. *Educational Researcher, 21*, 5–14.

Pambookian, H. (1976). Discrepancy between instruction and student evaluation of instruction: Effect on instruction. *Instructional Science, 5*, 63–75.

Peshkin, A. (1991). *The color of strangers, the color of friends: The play of ethnicity in school and community.* Chicago: University of Chicago Press.

Peterson, P., & Swing, S. (1982). Beyond time on task: Students' reports of their thought processes during classroom instruction. *Elementary School Journal, 82*, 481–491.

Posner, G. (1985). *Field experience: A guide to reflective teaching.* New York: Longman.

Rohrkemper, M. (1981). *Classroom perspectives study: An investigation of differential perceptions of classroom events.* Unpublished doctoral dissertation, Michigan State University.

Rohrkemper, M. (1985). The influence of teacher socialization style on students' social cognitions and reported interpersonal classroom behavior. *Elementary School Journal, 85*, 245–275.

Rosenholtz, S. (1989). *Teachers' work place: The social organization of schools.* New York: Longman.

Rosenholtz, S., & Smylie, M. (1984). Teacher compensation and career ladders. *Elementary School Journal, 85*, 149–166.

Ross, S., & Jackson, J. (1991). Teachers' expectations for black males' and black females' academic achievement. *Personality and Social Psychology Bulletin, 17*, 78–82.

Rowe, M. (1969). Science, silence, and sanctions. *Science and Children, 6*, 11–13.

Sadker, M., Sadker, D., & Klein S. (1991). The issues of gender in elementary and secondary education. In G. Grant (Ed.), *Review of research in education* (Vol. 17, pp. 269–334). Washington, DC: American Educational Research Association.

Schmidt, W., & Buchmann, M. (1983). Six teachers' beliefs and attitudes and their curricular time allocations. *Elementary School Journal, 84*, 162–172.

Smylie, M. (1992). Teachers' reports of their interactions with teacher leaders concerning classroom instruction. *Elementary School Journal, 93*, 85–98.

Spencer-Hall, D. (1981). Looking behind the teacher's back. *Elementary School Journal, 81*, 281–290.

Spradley, J. (1979). *The ethnographic interview.* New York: Holt.

Stallings, J. (1980). Allocated academic learning time revisited, or beyond time on task. *Educational Researcher, 9*, 11–16.

Tuckman, B., & Oliver, W. (1968). Effectiveness of feedback to teachers as a function of source. *Journal of Educational Psychology, 59*, 297–301.

Weinstein, R. (1982, May). Students in classrooms. *Elementary School Journal, 83*, special issue.

Weinstein, R. (1983). Student perceptions of schooling. *Elementary School Journal, 83*, 287–312.

Weinstein, R., & Middlestadt, S. (1979). Student perceptions of teacher interactions with male high and low achievers. *Journal of Educational Psychology, 71*, 421–431.

Wilkinson, L., & Marrett, C. (Eds.). (1985). *Gender influences in classroom interaction.* New York: Academic Press.

Wise, A., Darling-Hammond, L., McLaughlin, M., & Bernstein, H. (1985). Teacher evaluation: A study of effective practices. *Elementary School Journal, 86*, 61–121.

Wittrock, M. (Ed.). (1986). *Handbook of research on teaching* (3rd ed.). New York: Macmillan.

APPENDIX A

Coding Vocabulary: Blumenfeld and Miller

There has been rapid growth in the use of observation systems in training and research, and the types of systems used to code classroom behavior have become more varied (Evertson & Green, 1986). The following material was prepared by Phyllis Blumenfeld and Samuel Miller for their students at the University of Michigan. It is an effective device for describing different means of collecting narrative and frequency-count information.

NARRATIVE STRATEGIES

Anecdotal Record

Characteristics:
a. Provides a brief sketch or illustration about a student's behavioral pattern or learning style (e.g., several brief anecdotes might be used to illustrate how a student reacts to a particular situation).
b. Indicates that students have mastered or applied concepts (e.g., brief anecdotes might be used to illustrate that students used knowledge from a subtraction lesson to solve a problem in another subject or outside of class).

Procedure:
a. Write down the incident as soon after it occurs as possible.
b. Identify the basic action of the key person and what was said.
c. Include a statement that identifies the setting, time of day, and basic activity.
d. In describing the central character's actions or verbalizations, include the responses or reactions of other people in the situation.
e. Whenever possible note exact words used, to preserve the precise nature of the conversation.
f. Preserve the sequence of the episode.
g. Be objective, accurate, and complete (i.e., do not interpret).

Running Record

Characteristics:
a. Running records are used to record the situation in a manner that lets someone else read the description later and visualize the scene or event as it occurred.
b. As opposed to anecdotal records, which provide a brief illustrative episode on a student, running records provide a detailed, continuous, or sequential descriptive

account of the behavior and its immediate environmental context (eyewitness account par excellence).

c. Running records can be used to help locate the source of the problem or pattern of behavior. (If you wanted to know whether the teacher used effective questioning strategies, you could collect running records of lessons and later go to the records to pinpoint instances of the teacher using effective and ineffective questions.)

Procedure:

a. Describe the scene as it is when the observer begins the description.

b. Focus on the subject's behavior and whatever in the situation affects this behavior.

c. Be as accurate and complete as you can about what the subject says, does, and responds to within the situation.

d. Put brackets around all interpretive material generated by the observer so that the description stands out clearly and completely.

e. Include the "how" for whatever the subject does (e.g., teacher said to be quiet in a high voice while pointing her right hand at the students vs. the teacher said to be quiet).

f. Give the "how" for everything done by anyone interacting with the subject (i.e., emphasis on the details, not on inferences).

g. For every action report all the main steps in their proper order.

h. Describe behavior positively, rather than in terms of what was NOT done.

i. Use observational tools whenever possible (tape recorders, cameras, or videotape).

Comparison of Anecdotal and Running Records

Comparison is related to the following points:

a. *Length of Observation.* Anecdotal records require shorter periods of time and are normally completed after the event has occurred, whereas running records are recorded as events occur and usually continue for extended periods of time.

b. *Amount of Detail.* Running records demand a greater number of details than anecdotal records. Additionally, compared to anecdotal records, running records place little emphasis on impressions or interpretations (whenever they occur they are set off by brackets).

c. *Breadth of Focus.* While both records are targeted on a particular student(s) or event(s), the running record includes much more information on the environmental context than does the anecdotal record. Anecdotal records are less sophisticated than running records—they are similar to a diary, whereas the running record is similar to a verbatim report.

d. *Systematicness.* Anecdotal records do not provide generally systematic evidence. They are brief illustrative sketches of incidents rather than evidence collected across situations and at different times.

FREQUENCY COUNTS

We present two frequency count approaches—time sampling and event sampling. Read the characteristics and procedures for conducting each in order to understand the similarities and differences between the two approaches.

Time Sampling

Characteristics:

a. In time sampling behaviors are observed over repeated intervals for different periods of time (e.g., 3 recordings of a behavior per ten minutes for 4 one-hour periods).

b. Time sampling is appropriate only for behaviors that occur fairly frequently, at least once every 15 minutes on average.

c. This behavior is then looked upon as a "sample" of the person's usual behavior(s).

Procedure:

a. Identify behaviors that occur regularly and define the behaviors so that others will agree with what the focus of the observation will be (e.g., on-task behavior that may be defined as (1) on-task, engrossed, (2) on-task, at work but not engrossed, (3) off-task, quietly disengaged, or (4) off-task, disruptive).

b. Decide how long the observation period will be and how many observations are needed within this period (e.g., 3 one-hour observation periods during math where the observer codes on-task behavior of 5 children for 3 minutes, waits 7 minutes, records behavior during another 3-minute period, waits 7 minutes, etc.). If the behavior occurs during an observer wait period, it is not recorded.

Event Sampling

Characteristics:

a. In event sampling, the observer waits for the selected behavior to occur and records it (i.e., all selected behaviors that occur are recorded).

Procedure:

a. Clearly identify the kind of behavior you want to study (e.g., how students get the teacher's attention during seatwork).

b. Determine what kind of information you want to record (e.g., call the teacher's name, hold an object in front of his or her face, stand in front of teacher, ask teacher for assistance, cause a disruption, etc.).

c. Decide how many times you will observe and how long you will observe during each time (e.g., ten 40-minute seatwork classes).

Comparison of Time Sampling and Event Sampling

a. Both event and time sampling are useful for determining the frequency of behaviors or events, and both allow the collection of a large number of observations in a relatively short time.

b. Time sampling is limited to frequently or regularly occurring behaviors and counts only those behaviors that occur during a recording interval. Event sampling counts all instances of the behavior's occurrence, and the behavior does not have to occur frequently.

c. With both approaches the observer must determine what behaviors are to be observed, when they are to be observed, and for how long they are to be observed to obtain a sample set of behaviors typical of the student(s) in question.

Method	Focus	Advantages/Disadvantages
Case study narratives	Single student	+ Provides a rich, detailed account of an individual's actions + Allows an in-depth examination of a single problem – Descriptions may be affected by the observer's biases – Conclusions may not apply to the same student in other classes or to other students
Frequency counts	Single student Small groups	+ Gives actual number of behaviors per unit of time, which allows comparisons among students or across classes + Allows teacher to receive immediate information on a problem without having to receive extensive training – Actual behaviors recorded may not explain all facets of the problem – Apart from the behavior in question, the teacher will not know what students are doing during the observation time
Classroom observation scale (COS)	Single student Small groups Whole class	+ Gives actual number of behaviors per unit of time, which allows comparisons among students or across classes – Usually involves more observer training than do other methods – Apart from the behavior in question, the teacher will not know what students are doing during the observation time
Questionnaire	Single student Small groups Whole class	+ Allows the collection of information on a variety of topics in a relatively short time + Since students respond to the same set of questions, questionnaires allow comparisons among individuals or across classes – Question construction is more difficult than it may appear (e.g., responses may be affected by how questions are worded) – Responses may not truly represent what students will do in actual situation (validity) – Responses may differ if questionnaire was given at another time (reliability)
Interview	Single student Small groups	+ Yields more student information than do other methods + Allows greater flexibility to probe a student's response more deeply – Since students give more information, comparisons among students may be difficult

Method	Focus	Advantages/Disadvantages
		− Responses given may be affected by student biases
		− Usually will take longer to conduct than other methods
Ethnography	Whole class	+ Relative to other methods it provides more information on the social context of the classroom
		− Since the purpose is to interpret behaviors, the analysis may be affected by observer bias
		− Since the focus is not on a particular set of behaviors for all students, comparisons among students or across classes are difficult
		− The purpose is not to answer specific questions but to describe the norms governing interactions in social settings—therefore, the information collected may not be appropriate for answering specific questions

APPENDIX B

Brophy-Good Dyadic Interaction System

There are many observational systems we can use to code classroom behavior. All systems are selective and code certain behaviors while ignoring other aspects of the classroom. Hence, the usefulness of a particular observation system depends on your goal. We present one observation system, the Brophy-Good Dyadic Interaction System, briefly.

In this particular system, the goal is to determine whether individual students receive more or less of certain behaviors than other students (e.g., Are high-achieving female students treated differently than low-achieving male students?). After you read the definitions and examine the coding sheets that follow, go back to Chapter 1 and examine the long classroom scenes. Do the teachers provide equal opportunity for all students? Coding systems like the Brophy-Good system help us to be more systematic in our observations.

BRIEF DEFINITIONS OF VARIABLES CODED IN BROPHY-GOOD DYADIC INTERACTION SYSTEM

The coding sheet (see Figure 2.1) uses the following definitions (presented in the order that they appear on the coding sheet). For an extended discussion of these definitions and coding examples see Brophy and Good (1970).

Student-initiated question. A student asks the teacher a question in a public setting.

Reading or recitation. Student is called upon to read aloud, go through an arithmetic table, and so on.

Discipline question. The discipline question is a unique type of direct question in which the teacher uses the question as a control technique, calling on the student to force him or her to pay better attention rather than merely providing a response opportunity in the usual sense.

Direct question. Teacher calls on a student who is not seeking a response opportunity.

Open question. The teacher creates the response opportunity by asking a public question and also indicates who is to respond by calling on an individual student, but the teacher chooses one of the students who has indicated a desire to respond by raising a hand.

Call-outs. Response opportunities created by students who call out answers to teachers' questions without waiting for permission to respond.

Process question. Requires students to explain something in a way that requires them to integrate facts or to show knowledge of their interrelationships. It most frequently is a "why?" or "how?" question.

Product question. Product questions seek to elicit a single correct answer that can be expressed in one word or a short phrase. Product questions usually begin with "who," "what," "when," "where," "how much," and "how many."

Choice question. In the choice question, the student does not have to produce a substantive response but may instead simply choose one of two or more implied or expressed alternatives.

Self-reference question. Asks the student to make some nonacademic contribution to classroom discussion ("show-and-tell"; questions about personal experiences, preferences, or feelings; requests for opinions or predictions, etc.).

Opinion question. Much like a self-reference question (i.e., there is no single correct answer) except that it elicits a student opinion on an academic topic ("Is it worth putting a person on the moon?").

Correct answer. If the student answers the teacher's question in a way that satisfies the teacher, the answer is coded as correct.

Part-correct answer. A part-correct answer is one that is correct but incomplete as far as it goes, or correct from one point of view but not what the teacher is looking for.

Incorrect answer. A response that is treated as simply wrong by the teacher.

Don't know. Student verbally says "I don't know" (or its equivalent) or nonverbally indicates that he or she doesn't know (shakes head).

No response. Student makes no response (verbally or nonverbally) to teacher question.

Praise. Praise refers to the teacher's evaluative reactions that go beyond the level of simple affirmation or positive feedback by verbally complimenting the student.

Affirmation of correct answers. Affirmation is coded when the teacher indicates that the student's response is correct or acceptable.

Summary. Teacher summarizes the student's answer (generally as part of the affirmation process).

No feedback reaction. If the teacher makes no verbal or nonverbal response whatever following the student's answer to the question, the teacher is coded for no feedback reaction.

Negation of incorrect answer. Simple provision of impersonal feedback regarding the incorrectness of the response, without going farther than this by communicating a negative personal reaction to the student. As with affirmation, negation can be communicated both verbally ("No," "That's not right," "Hmm-mm") and nonverbally (shaking the head horizontally).

Figure 2.1 The Brophy-Good dyadic coding sheet.

Criticism. Evaluative reactions that go beyond the level of simple negation by expressing anger or personal criticism of the student in addition to indicating the incorrectness of the response.

Process feedback. Coded when the teacher goes beyond merely providing the right answer and discusses the cognitive or behavioral processes that are to be gone through in arriving at the answer.

Gives answer. This category is used when the teacher gives the student the answer to the question but does not elaborate sufficiently to be coded for process feedback.

Asks other. Whenever the student does not answer a teacher question and the teacher moves to another student in order to get the answer to that same question, the teacher's feedback reaction is coded for *asks other.*

Call out. The call-out category is used when another student calls out the answer to the question before the teacher has a chance to call on someone.

Repeats question. Teacher asks a question, waits some time without getting the correct answer, and then repeats the question to the same student.

Rephrase or clue. In this feedback reaction, the teacher sustains the response opportunity by rephrasing the question or giving the student a clue as to how to respond to it.

New question. When the first question is not answered or is answered incorrectly, the teacher asks a new question that is different from the original, although it may be closely related. A question requiring a new answer is coded as a new question.

Expansion. Teacher responses to vague or incomplete statements that ask the student to provide more information ("I think I understand, but tell me . . .").

DYADIC TEACHER-STUDENT CONTACTS

The preceding material has dealt primarily with the coding of response opportunities and reading and recitation turns.

Dyadic teacher-student contacts differ from response opportunities and reading and recitation turns in that the teacher is dealing privately with one student about matters idiosyncratic to him or her rather than publicly about material meant for the group or class as a whole.

Dyadic teacher-student contacts are divided into work-related contacts, procedural contacts, and behavioral or disciplinary contacts. They are also separately coded according to whether they are initiated by the teacher (teacher-afforded) or by the student (student-created). The coding also reflects certain aspects of the teacher's behavior in such contacts.

Work-Related Contacts

Work-related contacts include those teacher-student contacts that have to do with the student's completion of seatwork or homework assignments. They include clarification of the directions, soliciting or giving help concerning how to do the work, or soliciting or giving feedback about work already done. Work-related interactions are considered *student-created* if the student brings his or her work up to the teacher to talk about it, raises a hand, or otherwise indicates a desire to discuss it with the teacher. Work-related interactions are coded as *teacher-afforded* if the teacher gives feedback about work when the student has not solicited it (the teacher either calls the student to come up to his or her desk or goes around the room making individual comments to the students). *Created* contacts are not planned by the teacher and occur solely because the student has sought out the teacher; *afforded* contacts are not planned by the student and occur solely because the teacher initiates them.

Separate space is provided for coding *created* and *afforded* work-related interactions on the coding sheets, and the coder indicates the nature of an individual dyadic contact by where the interaction is coded.

In addition to noting the interaction as a work interaction and as an interaction that is student-created or teacher-afforded, the coder also indicates the nature of the teacher's feedback to the student during the interactions. He or she indicates this by using one or more of the five columns provided for coding teachers' feedback in work-related interaction: praise (+ +), process feedback (pcss), product feedback (fb), criticism (−), or "don't know" (?). The first four of these categories have the same meaning as they have in other coding of teacher feedback. The additional "don't know" category is added for this coding because frequently the individual teacher-student interaction that occurs in the dyadic contacts is carried on in hushed tones or across the room from the coder, where it is not possible to hear the content of the interaction. In such cases, the coder notes the occurrence of the work-related interaction and the fact that it was either teacher-afforded or student-created but enters the student's identification number in the "don't know" column (identified by the question mark on top).

Procedural Contacts

The category of *procedural contacts* includes all dyadic teacher-student interactions that are not coded as work-related contacts or as behavioral contacts. Thus it includes a wide range of types of contacts, most of which are initiated on the basis of the immediate needs of the teacher or student involved. Procedural contacts are *created* by the student for such purposes as seeking permission to do something, requesting needed supplies or equipment, reporting some information to the teacher (tattling on other students, calling attention to a broken desk or pencil, etc.), seeking help in putting on or taking off clothing, getting permission or information about how to take care of idiosyncratic needs (turning in lunch money, delivering a note from the parent to the principal, etc.), as well as a variety of other contacts. In general, any dyadic interaction initiated by the student that does not fit the definition of *work-related contacts* is coded as a *procedural contact*.

Behavioral Contacts

Behavioral contacts are coded whenever the teacher makes some comment on the student's classroom behavior. They are subdivided into *praise, warnings,* and *criticism*. The coder notes the information by entering the student's identification number under the appropriate column. Behavioral evaluation contacts are considered to be *teacher-afforded*, although they usually occur as reactions to the student's immediately preceding behavior. Nevertheless, they are teacher-afforded in the sense that the student usually does not want and does not expect the interaction and that the teacher chooses to single the student out for comment.

APPENDIX C

Emmer Observation System

In Appendix B, we examined parts of the Brophy-Good Dyadic Interaction System, and we have seen that it allows us to code and/or think more systematically about the two classroom scenes presented in Chapter 1. However, teachers do more than interact with individual students, and we need ways to classify and think about these aspects of classroom interaction as well.

One interesting and useful observational manual has been prepared by Ed Emmer at the University of Texas. We can present only a small part of this system here; if you are interested in more of the observational scales included in the manual and in details of training and reliability, consult Emmer (1971).

Emmer recommends that the scales be used approximately every 15 minutes, because longer periods may reduce reliability by placing too much reliance on the observer's memory, and shorter intervals may fail to provide sufficient information to use the scale. He also suggests that the observer should sit where he or she can observe the teacher and students and be in a position to see the faces of as many students as possible.

What follows are examples of 5 of the 12 scales that appear in the Emmer system.

LEVEL OF ATTENTION

Attention as defined for this scale refers to pupil orientation toward the teacher, the task at hand, or whatever classroom activities are appropriate. If pupils are attending to inappropriate activities or are engaged in self-directed behavior when they are supposed to be engaged in a class activity, this behavior is not considered attentive. Therefore, you should look for behavior that is focused on or engaged in whatever activity is appropriate, be it individual seatwork, group discussion, or listening to the presentation of information. Useful cues in recognizing attentive behavior include eye contact, body orientation, response to questions or other eliciting cues, and participation in class activity. Useful cues in recognizing inattentiveness include inappropriate social interaction, repetitive body movement, visual wandering, and engagement in behavior other than the sanctioned class activity. At times, it will be difficult to determine whether a student is attentive, such as when the teacher presents information and the student sits facing the teacher, with no observable behaviors indicating inattention. In such instances, the pupils are considered attentive until they behave otherwise.

To code behavior on this scale, scan the class on several occasions during each 15-minute observation period. Note how many pupils appear attentive or inattentive at a given time. After some practice you will find it easier to keep in mind your estimate of the number of inattentive students. Average your estimates of attention and record this average using the following scale.

1. Fewer than half of the students are attentive most of the time.
2. One-half to three-fourths of the students appear attentive most of the time; the remainder are attentive only some of the time.
3. Most of the students are attentive, but several (four to six) are attentive only some of the time.
4. Nearly all students are attentive, but a few (one, two, or three) are attentive only some of the time.
5. All of the students are attentive most of the time.

Note—the phrase "most of the time" means at least 75 percent of the time the observer checks the pupils for attentiveness.

Some examples from which inattention or attention may be inferred.

Inattention: Moving around the room at an inappropriate time
Reading a book during class discussion

Two students whispering
Sitting with elbows on desk, fingers holding eyelids open
Doodling with a pencil
Laying head on desk
Asking a question unrelated to the activity of the class
Staring fixedly at an object not related to class activity

Attention: Raising hand to volunteer a response
Maintaining eye contact, following teacher's movements
Turning to watch another student who is contributing to the class
activity
Working on assigned activity
If a free-activity period, pupils engaged in some task

TEACHER PRESENTATION

The teacher presentation scale measures only one type of behavior. The observer's task is to estimate the relative amount of class time occupied by teacher presentation of substantive information. *Teacher presentation* means substantive (content-oriented) verbal or nonverbal behavior that provides information and does not imply or require pupil response or evaluate pupil behavior. Thus teacher questions, procedural directions, praise, and criticism are not instances of teacher presentation. Lecturing, reading to the class, answering pupil questions, and any other activity in which the teacher gives information are all instances of teacher presentation.

To use this scale, observe the teacher's behavior and note the amount of teacher presentation as compared to the total of all teacher behavior, pupil behavior, and periods of seatwork or other activities in which there is no verbal interaction.

1. Teacher presentation occurs 0–20 percent of the period.
2. Teacher presentation occurs 21–40 percent of the period.
3. Teacher presentation occurs 41–60 percent of the period.
4. Teacher presentation occurs 61–80 percent of the period.
5. Teacher presentation occurs 81–100 percent of the period.

Note that in order for a 5 to be scored, the observation period must be taken up almost entirely by teacher information-giving. Even a small amount of discussion or other activity is likely to cause the rating to be a 4 or less. On the other hand, a score of 1 occurs only when there is a very small amount of teacher information-giving (less than 20 percent of the time).

Teacher presentation should not be confused with *teacher talk,* since the former may be only a small part of the latter. Although a question-and-answer session might contain 70 percent teacher talk, much of it may be teacher questions and evaluation rather than presentation. Be sure to distinguish teacher presentation from other teacher behaviors.

REFERENCE

Emmer, E. (1971). *Classroom observation scales.* Austin: Research and Development Center for Teacher Education, University of Texas.

APPENDIX D

An Ethnographic Research Study Conducted by Susan Florio

Some qualitative researchers study a single classroom for a long time in order to describe and understand its unique characteristics and functioning. The following article provides one example of how qualitative researchers conduct classroom inquiry. Notice that this research attempts to describe and understand both the social and cognitive tasks of classrooms.

The Problem of Dead Letters:
Social Perspectives on the Teaching of Writing*

SUSAN FLORIO
Institute for Research on Teaching, Michigan State University,
East Lansing, Michigan

Dead letters! does it not sound like dead men? Conceive a man by nature and misfortune prone to a pallid hopelessness, can any business seem more fitted to heighten it than that of continually handling these dead letters . . . ?

HERMAN MELVILLE
Bartleby the Scrivener [1]

Why is it so hard to get students writing in school? Of the language arts, writing is the most troublesome. While the value of literacy is unquestioned by educators and researchers alike, writing, as part of literacy, is typically slighted in the course of a day in school and in research on the basic skills (2).

In attempting to account for this neglect, some have noted that writing—and its pedagogy—require hard work. Thus it could be argued that teachers and students assiduously avoid difficult tasks, and so they avoid writing. Yet, all of us can think of difficulty endured in the pursuit of a valued goal. What is more, from the ranks of the few who have taken a look at the teaching of writing comes a recommendation that is disturbing in its simplicity. We are advised, in a variety of voices, that the best way to teach writing is simply to let students do it! (2, 3, 4).

Why, then, is it so hard to get students writing in school?

When researchers at the Institute for Research on Teaching set out to address this question, they were confronted with much the same finding as the lawyer who set out to discover the roots of Bartleby the Scrivener's "derangement." The problem, in each case, was the lack of meaningfulness. At the heart of a student's successful engagement in the complex and difficult task of writing, experienced teachers told us, was the requirement that the writing task have meaning. Writing requires having something to express, an intended audience, and a chance for some kind of response (4). Apparently the teachers with whom we spoke had shared just about enough of Bartleby's experience to abhor it.

---

*From Susan Florio, "The problem of dead letters . . . ," *Elementary School Journal,* *80* (1979), 1–7. Reprinted with permission.

Bartleby's first job involved reading and sorting letters that were undeliverable—dead letters. From that job he went to work as a scribe, or copier of the manuscripts of others, for a lawyer. Is it any wonder that, after years of such meaningless inter-action with truncated human communication, his only response when asked by the lawyer to perform written tasks was, "I prefer not to"? Teachers told us that they preferred not to read "dead letters" from their students—exposition going nowhere and written only to fulfill academic requirements. Similarly, the teachers preferred not to ask their students merely to put their own words to someone else's ideas. The teachers knew that the perseverance and the practice needed to master a craft as complex as writing were likely to be present only when school writing tasks had mean-ingful communicative functions in the lives of their students.

The teachers' insight suggests that writing may be avoided in school not simply because of its inherent difficulty, but also because writing, as one of many tasks in a busy school day, typically is not connected to anything or anyone else in the lives of students or teachers. If this is true, then "letting children write" may amount to far more than pedagogical laissez faire. The teaching of writing may require vigilant at-tention to the learning environments in which writing occurs to insure that written expression is motivated and that it goes somewhere.

Perhaps teachers can best serve the acquisition of writing by structuring both for and with students social occasions in which writing functions meaningfully as commu-nication. The possibility parallels what we know about the acquisition of speaking, another complex communicative skill. Both research and experience tell us that spo-ken language is acquired literally "in the doing." Children are welcomed as commu-nicators even before their first words are uttered. Early in life, children find that their moves and sounds elicit action from other people. Children, in effect, practice the use of language not as preparation or training for social life, but as social life itself (5).

Research on language acquisition has shown us that requisite grammatical skills are seldom taught directly to children by the adults with whom they communicate. For teachers of writing, an essential lesson from research on language acquisition is that even the most flawed and rudimentary communicative attempts of novices are functional in that they have social meaning. Critical to acquiring language is the social fact that a child's emergent and stumbling efforts are heeded by others. Early talk is meaningful by virtue of the child's membership in the family, the first community.

Classrooms contain the stuff of community, too, and therein lies potential that writing done in them will be meaningful. Classrooms are located in organized social worlds where meanings are shared and values held, and at the same time classrooms individually constitute small communities with cumulative histories, shared beliefs, and rights and responsibilities of membership.

To learn more about the acquisition of writing skills and the ways in which writ-ing in school can be meaningful to students, researchers at the Institute for Research on Teaching have been looking closely at one second-grade classroom in central Michi-gan. The classroom is notable because children do a great deal of writing there and because a strong sense of community can be found there as well.

To get to Mrs. Frank's second grade you must travel to the small community of Haslett, Michigan. The town of nearly seven thousand is located in the shadow of the state capitol and a large public university. Although some of the residents are farmers, the parents of most of the children in Mrs. Frank's room are employed in one of the area's major activities—state government, education, and manufacturing.

Mrs. Frank's students attend the Ralya School, one of three elementary schools in Haslett. The contemporary school building houses about 170 students and contains

Figure 2.2 Map drawn by students on 6/2/78. Instructions were to fill in "important things and places—as many as you can remember."

one room for each grade from Kindergarten through Grade 5. Approaching Mrs. Frank's room, you already have a sense of why she is well known in and around Haslett and why children look forward to being in her class. The classroom literally spills out into the corridor with bright colors and activity. Upon entering the classroom, you encounter yet another small community, one that the children have dubbed, "Betterburg."

As the map in Figure 2.2 drawn by one of Mrs. Frank's students illustrates, the child-sized, cardboard buildings of Betterburg dominate the physical space of the classroom. We have found that Betterburg dominates as well the social life and the attendant writing that is done in that physical space.

The members of Mrs. Frank's class populate Betterburg, filling its civil offices and making its laws. Betterburg has all the accoutrements of a community—law enforcement, cultural activities, commerce, welfare and, most important for our purposes, a postal system. Of course, the room also has all the other features of standard classrooms—blackboards, desks, bookshelves, and the like; but the dominance of the town is clear. One day upon leaving the class the children were asked to draw maps of the important things and places in the room. The children's maps included, often in considerable detail, each aspect of the town. The content of their drawings is summarized in Table 2.2.

During the year that the children in Mrs. Frank's class were observed, they wrote often and produced a wide variety of documents. Table 2.3 displays the written products and the occasions when writing occurred on March 15, 1978, a typical day in the classroom. Activities recorded in Table 2.3 include everything from the practice of motor skills, spelling, and the rules of punctuation to the use of metaphor, simile, and the complex rhetoric of persuasion. Table 2.3 also illustrates the fact that the variety of writing activities done in this classroom involves the practice of a wide range of skills. Sometimes spelling and punctuation are in the foreground for teacher as well as students. At other times, self-expression is most highly valued, and correct spelling is incidental. Such changes in emphasis are accompanied by changes in the behaviors of

Table 2.2 CLASSROOM AREAS AND OBJECTS AND PERCENTAGE OF
STUDENTS NAMING THEM IN CLASSROOM MAPS

Area or object	Percentage of children including area on classroom map
→ Capitol building	83
→ police station/jail	78
student desks	78
→ post office*	74
→ Department of Health, Education & Welfare	70
library	70
teacher's desk	70
→ bank	65
→ mailboxes*	55
reading table	35
other tables	35
chairs	22
blackboard	13
plants	13
coatrack	13
toys	13
bulletin board, art work, books, shelves, cabinets, wastebasket, school bell, wall	10

→town-related area

* area related to letter writing

teacher and students. The teacher's role may vary from that of helper or resource to that of editor or critic. Similarly, what children need to do to complete adequately the various kinds of writing activities changes depending on the particular activity in which they are engaged.

On the day that information for Table 2.3 was compiled, one of the most daring and most sustained writing activities was the writing of letters to manufacturers of the children's favorite games and candies. Betterburg was establishing a store, and the children needed to acquire goods to sell in the store. To turn a profit, it was necessary to buy the goods at the wholesale price. Despite inexperience with the nuances and the intricacies of spelling, punctuation, and sentence structure, the children undertook the sophisticated task of writing persuasively. They needed to interest their readers in the doings of Betterburg. To this end, the children needed to take the perspective of someone who had never heard of the classroom town. Writing from this point of view, the students had to weave into their letters sufficient information to make subsequent requests for goods sensible. It might be said that the children were out of their depth in such a task but, like young children acquiring speech, they were learning in the doing.

In Betterburg the performance of such complex social and linguistic operations through the medium of the letter was typical. Letter-writing was observed almost

Table 2.3 PRODUCTS AND OCCASIONS FOR WRITING

Field notes, March 15, 1978

I. Writing Headlines: Teacher as Scribe

It is a typically busy morning in the second-grade classroom. First, the children who have brought in articles from the previous evening's newspaper share them with the class. The teacher acts as scribe, making a headline out of each article.

N. M. builder recycles tin cans into households. Until recently U.S.'s spendthrifts didn't conserve nation's resources.

We're expecting a blackout because miners haven't obeyed President Carter's demands.

Bicycles and motorcycles aren't safest, insurance company reports. They're larger than children and teen-agers can handle, and we've got record highway injuries.

At the end of the presentation of news, children volunteer to come to the board and circle in the headlines instances of abbreviations, compound words, prefixes, suffixes, contractions, and the like. The noise level rises as children wave their hands in the air, jump up and down, and call "Me! I know it!"

II. Expository Writing and Editorial Work

Later in the morning some of the children work on the manuscript of a book the class is writing. The book is intended for very young children and their parents. It is going to be about becoming a good and happy person. Children have written entries and have drawn pictures to illustrate them. Now the task of layout—the spacing and matching of pictures and words—remains. Some of the entries with which children are working include the following:

Don't be crool to people because they mite be crool to you because you're teaching them to be crool.

It's like planning how to make a building. You have to think how you want it before you start if you want it to be a beautiful building.

The teacher comments about the manuscript that is taking shape, "It came out real well considering how much they agonized over it."

III. Writing Answers on Worksheets

While the teacher spends the better part of an hour working with reading groups children work quietly at their desks. Some of them catch up on their reading—from primers or from library books. Others work busily on dittoed worksheets, circling, marking with x's and writing an occasional word in answer to a fill in the blank question.

IV. Writing Letters

During seatwork, some of the children are polishing up letters that they have written to companies manufacturing their favorite toys and candies. Because the entire class is planning to have a store this spring, the children have decided to solicit help from the companies. Children have written to makers of Flair pens, Cracker Jacks, Mounds, DC Comics. Here is an example:

Dear Parker Brothers:
Hi! My name is Marnie at Ralya School in second grade and we have a town in our classroom. Our town's name is Betterburg because we want to make things better. We'll have a store in our town. We have a police station, Bank, capitol, Library, H.E.W. and a Post Office. My teacher

Table 2.3 PRODUCTS AND OCCASIONS FOR WRITING, continued

said I could sell anything in the world I wanted to and I chose you because we have some of your games and we play with them all the time and we like them alot. I always want to buy the games but we don't get enough money. When I'm over to somebody's house I look at the games. If I find a Parker Brothers game I want to play it but if they don't have a Parker Brothers game I don't want to play a game. I have to buy your good games at a good wholesale price or we won't make any money. Please, please give us it at a good wholesale price. We really need it bad. Just send the games and bill. We'll be sure to pay the bill if you send the games with the letter. Thank you for reading my letter.

Your friend,
Marnie

V. "Meta Writing" Spelling Words, Making Concrete Sentences

After the children return from recess, the teacher, standing at the front blackboard, asks them to clear their desks and take out pencils and spelling books. She draws lines on the blackboard. Then she says, "We've been *neglecting* your spelling words." She asks them to pick out the two hardest words from this week's spelling list and write a sentence using each word. "In order to be a sentence, it has to *tell* something. I'm not going to spell any words for you: just sound them out. It isn't a spelling test. The only word I care about your spelling correct is the spelling word."

The children write quietly at their desks. As they finish, a few of them bring their sentences up to the teacher. She tells them, "Sit down." Finally, as the whispering and shifting in seats increases, the teacher says, "Stand up if you are ready." The teacher calls on children standing at their desks to read their sentences. Here is a bit of what follows:

Teacher calls on Christy.
CHRISTY: Do you want to clean your room now?
TEACHER: I should have . . . OK you can either *tell* something or *ask* something. She asked. What did she put at the end of her sentence?
CHILDREN: A question mark!
Another child is called on.
KRISTINA: I clean my room every day.
TEACHER: Oh, you do really? Is she telling or asking?
CHILDREN: Telling.
TEACHER: I'm going to ask your mother about that, Kristina!
JACK: I clean the living room every day.
TEACHER: He *told* you right. Jack, would you like to come over to my house tonight?
CHILDREN: Laughter.
SAM: He is sleeping.
TEACHER: What did Sam do to the word? He put the *ing* on a suffix. Don't do that on the spelling test tomorrow, but it's all right.

VI. Cursive Writing Practice

After many children have shared their sentences, the teacher turns to the lines she has drawn on the blackboard. She says as she does this in brisk, clipped speech, "Up, up! Sit up! Feet on floor. When I say 'ready,' what do you do?" The students reply, "Do we have to write in *cursive?*" The teacher, smiling says, "Yup." What follows is a lesson in cursive writing in which students use the spelling words from their sentences. The teacher coaches in colorful language—each motion of the pen corresponds to a phrase that the children know. Some of them talk along with her: "Rainbow up, straight back. Rocker, come around, straight, rocker." As children finish their words, they are asked to bring them up to show the teacher.

Table 2.3   PRODUCTS AND OCCASIONS FOR WRITING, continued

VII. Imaginative Writing

After the children finish their cursive writing, the teacher asks them to sit in a circle at her feet at the front of the room. It is nearing St. Patrick's Day, and the teacher has brought in a story about leprechauns. The children listen quietly. Sometimes the teacher stops to ask questions about the story. The children answer in chorus. After the story there is just time enough before lunch for the children to do one more thing. The teacher, in a soft voice, says, "I want you to think. Shut your eyes. You're a leprechaun now, hiding under your mushroom and you're thinking. 'If I were a leprechaun, what magic would I play?' What magic would you play if you were a leprechaun?"

As the children open their eyes and are sent back to seats, the teacher passes out bright green paper shamrocks. She asks them to write down on lined paper the trick they thought of to play. She says that after writing them, the children will paste them onto the shamrocks and put them in the hall "for everyone to see." She also says they can copy them over into St. Patrick's Day cards to bring home to their mothers.

After the assignment is made, the room is alive with whispering and children leaning over one another's papers. The teacher stands at the board, and as children call out words she spells them for them on the board. As children finish, they bring their tricks up to the teacher. One student reads his aloud to the teacher. "If I were a leprechaun, I'd use my magic finger to turn trash into flowers because I'd like to make the world into a better place." The teacher replies, "He accomplished something with his trick. It wasn't wasted."

---

daily over months of field work in the classroom, and when the children were interviewed at the end of the year about their activities, the only writing activity on which they commented in detail was letter-writing. Here are excerpts from the interviews.

INTERVIEWER: I want to know about all the things you wrote this year.
STUDENT 1:   Yeah, we wrote people to come to our store.
STUDENT 2:   Letters.
STUDENT 3:   Oh, yeah. We wrote to our moms and dads and wrote to kids in our class.
STUDENT 4:   Our post office would get mail.

Additional evidence of the importance of letter-writing in this classroom community can be found in Table 2.3. The post office is among the places most frequently included in the classroom maps. The mailboxes—the one outside the post office as well as those fastened to the children's desks—are included in the maps of more than half the students. Finally, when Mrs. Frank and the students recorded the history of Betterburg in a yearbook, the text was made up almost entirely of the letters that had been written during the existence of the town.

The celebration of community in the classroom in the form of Betterburg appears to be related powerfully to the use of letter-writing as an expressive activity. Dewey suggests that education fundamentally involves the child, whose "understandings are primarily personal and concrete," and the transmission of "values incarnate in the mature experience of the adult" (6:4). From this perspective, teaching of writing can be thought of as occurring at the place where the personal world and the wider community meet. Writing is the private struggle of an individual with pen and paper, and writing is the social activity of communication with another. Furthermore, writing occurs within communities. A pedagogy of writing that slights any of these features risks engaging students in the generation of dead letters rather than in communication.

Betterburg enables immediate and explicit sharing of classroom membership, and the town is a powerful organizer of the students' personal experiences. The classroom town also provides the occasion for students to venture outside its borders into the wider adult community. This movement is fundamental to writing. It constitutes, in the words of Elsasser and John-Steiner, a "critical shift in the consciousness of the learner, a shift of attention from an immediate audience that shares the learner's experience and frame of reference to a larger, abstract, and unfamiliar audience" (7:358).

In the classroom community of Betterburg, there is need for discourse across the boundaries. Because Betterburg operates, in microcosm, very much like Haslett, students write to government officials in the town and in the nearby state capital for guidance in the establishment and the enforcement of laws. Similarly, Betterburg, as we have already seen, has a commerce. Haslett and other nearby towns are potential markets for the goods that children sell in their store. Haslett citizens are reached by means of letters to individuals and to the local newspaper.

Because letters are a meaningful medium for Mrs. Frank's class, the postal system of Betterburg is important. In a sense, the postal system epitomizes Betterburg's integrity and links the class to the wider world. The system insures that letters can leave the confines of the classroom, that responses can be distributed, and that letters can be noted officially. Mailboxes serve as a tangible reminder that it is possible to communicate with someone who is not physically present. Perhaps even more dramatically, however, the post office of Betterburg stands for the potential efficacy of the students in the world of communication. An address is not only a place from which to express oneself, it is also a place where one can be reached when someone wants to respond.

Some educators say that one writes if one can realistically expect a response, if one does not feel isolated and powerless. But one does not feel isolated and powerless because one writes and is responded to (7, 8). Bartleby the Scrivener was immobilized by a social order that stymied both the chance for expression and the opportunity for response. Although Mrs. Frank's classroom is perhaps novel in its design, it paints in bold strokes a community spirit that is potentially available in all classrooms. That community spirit stems from recognition both of shared classroom meanings and of access of the class to a world beyond itself by means of the written word. Understanding and using the classroom as a community can rescue children from academic writing activities that are mere copying or expressions falling on deaf ears. As one child in Mrs. Frank's class put it, reflecting on the writing he had done in Betterburg, "I made my own words, and I didn't copy people. The more I learned to write good letters, the better they got."

NOTES

The work reported here is sponsored by the Institute for Research on Teaching, College of Education, Michigan State University. The Institute for Research on Teaching is funded primarily by the Teaching Division of the National Institute of Education, United States Department of Health, Education, and Welfare. The opinions expressed in this article do not necessarily reflect the position, policy, or endorsement of the National Institute of Education. (Contract No. 400-76-0073)

1. HERMAN MELVILLE. "Bartleby the Scrivener," in *Eight Great American Short Novels*, p. 52. Edited by Philip Rahv. New York, New York: Berkeley Publishing Company, 1963.

2. DONALD H. GRAVES. *Balance the Basics: Let Them Write*. New York, New York: The Ford Foundation, 1978.

3. KENNETH KOCH. *Wishes, Lies, and Dreams*. New York, New York: Chelsea House, 1970.

4. JAMES MOFFETT. *Teaching the Universe of Discourse*. New York, New York: Houghton Mifflin, 1968.

5. COURTNEY B. CAZDEN. *Child Language and Education*. New York, New York: Holt, Rinehart and Winston, 1972.

6. JOHN DEWEY. *The Child and the Curriculum* and *The School and Society*. Chicago, Illinois: The University of Chicago Press, 1956.

7. NAN ELSASSER and VERA P. JOHN-STEINER. "An Interactionist Approach to Advancing Literacy," *Harvard Educational Review*, 47 (August, 1977), 355–69.

8. PAULO FREIRE, *Cultural Action for Freedom*. *Harvard Educational Review* and Center for the Study of Development and Social Change, Monograph Series No. 1. Cambridge, Massachusetts: *Harvard Educational Review* and Center for the Study of Development and Social Change, 1970.

Chapter 3

Teacher Expectations

Teachers' behavior is goal directed and thus shaped by their beliefs and expectations about how to accomplish their goals. In planning for and interacting with students, teachers are guided by their beliefs about what students need and by their expectations about how students will respond if treated in particular ways. Also, teachers' beliefs about the academic ability of the class or of individual students may influence their curricular or instructional decisions.

A great deal of research has been done on the effects of teachers' expectations on teacher-student interaction and student performance. *Teachers' expectations* are inferences that teachers make about the future behavior or academic achievement of their students, based on what they know about these students now. *Teacher expectation effects* are effects on student outcomes that occur because of the actions that teachers take in response to their expectations.

In this chapter we will discuss different types of expectation effects and present models suggesting how sequences of teacher behavior may communicate differential expectations in ways that hinder or enhance student performance. The chapter will also present models of how students may internalize teacher expectations and reciprocally how students' beliefs and behavior may influence teachers. Although much of the chapter will deal with how expectations influence classroom interaction, the chapter will also explore other areas where expectation effects may be generated (e.g., teachers' knowledge of subject matter; Carlsen, 1991). Finally, the chapter will explore ways that teachers can express realistic and supportive expectations.

AN EXAMPLE

Before we discuss types of expectation effects, read the following example and think about the expectations for performance that the teacher communicates to students. How effective is the communication?

Bill Peeler is a third-year teacher at the Boonville Community High School. The school serves students from a full range of socioeconomic backgrounds. Its student population is 55 percent Anglo, 35 percent African-American, and 10 percent Asian. Bill teaches two sections of trigonometry, one of calculus, and one of consumer math. As a third-year teacher, he also advises the student yearbook committee and coaches the tennis team. During the first class period he approaches his class this way. "Since fifth grade, your math has been pretty much the same year after year. We're going to do some of the things you've done in the past, but when we do these things, we're going to use them in practical problem-solving situations. The modern world requires all types of mathematics skills, and you need to be able to estimate and to think mathematically as well as to do calculations. But only about one-fourth of the material we study in this course will be review. I want to introduce some new ideas including geometry and algebra principles. These topics are sometimes seen as complex, but they are really only a way of thinking, and I think you'll enjoy these topics and learn a lot. As I hand out the course syllabus, I want you to start thinking about why mathematics is important to today's world. I want each of you to think of five ways you use math now and will use math in the future."

TYPES OF EXPECTATION EFFECTS

Researchers have examined two types of teacher expectation effects (Cooper & Good, 1983). The first is the *self-fulfilling prophecy effect*, in which an originally erroneous expectation leads to behavior that causes the expectation to become true. Merton (1948), who coined the term, gave bank failures as an example. He noted that a false rumor that a bank was about to fail could cause depositors to panic and flock to clear out their accounts. If enough depositors acted on this unfounded rumor and demanded their money, the bank's financial position would deteriorate rapidly and failure would occur, even though it would not have occurred if the false rumor had not circulated in the first place. As a classroom example, consider a first-grade teacher who decides that Juana will be one of her best readers, because last year Juana's older sister Rosa was an excellent first-grade reader. Let us assume that Juana is actually a student with average potential, but that the teacher warms up to her right away, expresses confidence that she will be a good reader, calls on her often in class, and arranges for her to practice at home with Rosa. Chances are that this treatment will make Juana a top reader before long, even though this probably would not have happened if the teacher had not treated her specially. Juana's rapid progress in reading can be seen as a self-fulfilling prophecy effect of her teacher's expectations and related instructional decisions.

The second type of expectation effect is the *sustaining expectation effect*. Here, teachers expect students to sustain previously developed patterns, to the point that teachers take these patterns for granted and fail to see and capitalize on change in students' potential. The findings described in Chapter 2 on teachers' differential treatment of high versus low achievers are examples of sustaining expectation effects. To the extent that teachers wait longer for high achievers to respond to questions, provide them with more second chances following initial failures, and react to their answers with more praise and less criticism, teachers are likely to sustain (and probably increase somewhat) achievement differences between the two groups.

Self-fulfilling prophecy effects are more powerful than sustaining expectation effects because the former introduce significant change in student behavior instead of merely minimizing such change by sustaining established patterns. Self-fulfilling prophecy effects can be powerful when they occur, but the more subtle sustaining expectation effects occur more often. This chapter is organized around the concept of self-fulfilling prophecies, but both types of expectation effects are important and provide useful concepts for examining classroom events.

TEACHERS' EXPECTATIONS AS SELF-FULFILLING PROPHECIES

Robert Rosenthal and Lenore Jacobson's *Pygmalion in the Classroom* (1968) created wide interest in and controversy about self-fulfilling prophecies. In their book they described research in which they manipulated teachers' expectations for student achievement to see whether these expectations would be fulfilled. The study involved several classes in each of the first six grades at Oak School. Expectations were created by claiming that a test (actually a general achievement test) had been developed to identify students who were about to bloom intellectually and therefore could be expected to show unusually large achievement gains during the coming school year. A few students in each class were identified to the teachers as such "bloomers." Actually, the students had been selected randomly rather than on the basis of test scores, so there was no real reason to expect unusual gains from them.

Yet, the "bloomers" did show greater gains than other students on achievement tests given at the end of the year (although primarily in the first two grades). Rosenthal and Jacobson interpreted these results in terms of the self-fulfilling prophecy effects of teachers' expectations. They reasoned that the expectations they created had caused the teachers to treat the "bloomers" differently, so that these students did make unusually high achievement gains that year.

At first, this conclusion was accepted enthusiastically, and secondary sources sometimes even made exaggerated claims that went far beyond those Rosenthal and Jacobson made. For example, an ad in the *Reader's Digest* read: "Actual experiments prove this mysterious force can heighten your intelligence, your competitive ability, and your will to succeed. The secret: Just make a prediction! Read how it works." Soon, however, critics began to attack the study, and a replication attempt failed to produce the same results, leading to debates over the Oak School experiment that continued for 20 years (Wineburg, 1987). Meanwhile, other investigators did related studies using a variety of approaches, and attention shifted from debates over the original study to attempts to make sense of a growing literature on teacher expectation effects and related topics (Brophy & Good, 1974). This process continues, although it has produced a consensus that teachers' expectations can and sometimes do affect teacher-student interaction and student outcomes, along with a recognition that the processes involved are much more complex than originally believed (Brophy, 1983; Good, 1993; Jones, 1986; Jussim, 1986).

To make sense of the research, one must distinguish between two types of studies. The first, which includes the Rosenthal and Jacobson study, involves experimental attempts to induce teacher expectations by identifying "late bloomers," by using phony IQ scores, or by providing some other fictitious information about students. The second type of study uses the expectations that teachers form naturally on the basis of whatever information they have available (test scores and cumulative folders, information from other teachers, previous experience with the family, etc.).

EFFECTS OF INDUCED EXPECTATIONS

Studies conducted in quite different settings have shown that student achievement can be affected by expectations induced in instructors. Beez (1968), studying adult tutors teaching Headstart children; Eden and Shani (1982), studying Israeli army instructors teaching military skills; and Schrank (1968), working with Air Force mathematics instructors all obtained similar results. In each study, teachers' expectations were manipulated by causing the teachers to believe that certain students or classes they would work with had unusually high learning potential. In fact, the students had been matched or selected randomly. Nevertheless, in each study, the students of instructors who had been led to hold high expectations achieved more than other students.

Some experimental studies failed to produce positive results, apparently because the teachers did not acquire the expectations that the experimenters were trying to induce. In the most obvious case, teachers knew that the expectations were not true, as in Schrank's (1970) adaptation of his earlier study of Air Force mathematics courses. For this second study, Schrank merely simulated the manipulation of teachers' expectations; the teachers knew that their students had been grouped randomly rather than by ability, but were asked to pretend that they were teaching a higher ability group. Negative results also were reported by Fleming and Anttonen (1971), who tried to induce expectations using falsely inflated IQ scores but found that teachers did not accept the phony IQs or allow the scores to affect their treatment of students. Jones (1990) provides a thorough analysis of related research that has been conducted in social psychology laboratory experiments.

Induced expectation experiments have produced clear-cut positive results often enough to demonstrate that teachers' expectations can have self-fulfilling prophecy effects on student achievement (see Jones, 1990). Such demonstrations are necessary because studies of teachers' naturally formed expectations cannot prove cause-and-effect relationships. This is because naturally formed expectations typically are based on real differences in student potential and thus are merely accurate predictions rather than indirect causes of differences in student progress. Studies linking teachers' naturally formed expectations to their classroom interactions with students are also needed, however, because they provide information about *how* teachers' expectations can become self-fulfilling.

STUDIES OF NATURALLY FORMED EXPECTATIONS

In this type of study, teachers' expectations are assessed either prior to their interactions with students (ideally) or early in the term before the teachers have had a chance to obtain much firsthand information about students. Usually, teachers are asked to rank or rate their students on either current achievement or expected improvement over the term. Student outcome data are then examined for differences between groups of students rated low versus high by their teachers.

Palardy (1969) studied the reading achievement produced by two groups of first-grade teachers. Using a questionnaire, he identified 10 teachers who believed that boys in their classes would make just as much progress in reading as girls, and another 14 teachers who expected the girls to do better. Five teachers from each group were selected for further study. All taught in middle-class schools, used the same basal reading series, and worked with three reading groups in heterogeneously grouped, self-contained classrooms.

The two groups did not differ on reading readiness tests given in September. However, on reading achievement tests given in March, boys whose teachers believed that they could achieve as well as girls averaged 96.5, but boys whose teachers did not believe that they could perform as well as girls averaged only 89.2. The girls in these classes averaged 96.2 and 96.7, respectively. Thus, boys did achieve less when taught by teachers who did not think that boys could progress as rapidly as girls.

Most studies of teachers' naturally formed expectations have related such expectations to teacher-student interaction measures rather than to student outcomes. Such studies typically demonstrate that teachers interact differently with high-expectation students than with low-expectation students, and they suggest the mechanisms that mediate sustaining expectation effects.

HOW EXPECTATIONS BECOME SELF-FULFILLING

Teacher expectation effects in classrooms are just special cases of the more general principle that any expectation can become self-fulfilling (Jones, 1986; Miller & Turnbull, 1986). Although it is not true that "wishing can make it so," our expectations affect the way we behave, and the way we behave affects how other people respond. Sometimes, our expectations about people cause us to treat them in ways that make them respond just as we expected they would.

An Example

For example, look ahead (or back) to your first teaching assignment. Unless they already know the situation, most new teachers want to find out about the school and the principal with whom they will be working. Suppose you spoke to a teacher at the school who said, "Ms. Jackson is wonderful. You'll love working for her. She's warm and pleasant, and she really takes an interest in you. Feel free to come to her with your problems; she's always glad to help." If you heard this about Ms. Jackson, how would you respond to her when you met her? Think about this for a few moments, and then consider a different situation. Suppose the teacher had said, "Ms. Jackson? well, she's hard to describe. I guess she's all right, but I don't feel comfortable around her; she makes me nervous. I get the feeling that she doesn't want to talk to me, that I'm irritating her or wasting her time." How would you act when meeting Ms. Jackson after you heard this?

If you are like most people, your behavior would differ depending on which description you heard. If you had received the positive information, you probably would look forward to meeting Ms. Jackson and approach her with confidence and a friendly smile. You would likely tell her that you had heard good things about her and were looking forward to working with her. Having heard the other description, however, you probably would not look forward to the meeting, and you might be nervous, inhibited, or overly concerned about making a good impression. You might approach with hesitation, wearing a serious expression or a forced smile, and speak in reserved or formal tones. Even if you said the same words, chances are that they would sound more like a prepared speech than a genuine personal reaction.

Now, put yourself in Ms. Jackson's place. Assume she knows nothing about you. Take time to think about how she might respond to these two disparate approaches. Chances are, Ms. Jackson would respond positively to the first approach. Faced with your warmth, friendliness, and genuine-sounding compliments, she likely would respond in kind. Your behavior would put her at ease and cause her to see you as a likeable, attractive person. When she smiled and said she would be looking forward to working with you, too, she would really mean it.

But what if you took the more nervous, formal approach? Again, Ms. Jackson probably would respond in kind. Your self-presentation would likely make her feel nervous and formal, if she were not already. She would respond in an equally bland and formal manner, and this probably would be followed by an awkward silence that would make you both increasingly nervous.

Brophy and Good's Model

The example shows that it is not just the existence of an expectation that causes self-fulfillment; it is the behavior that the expectation produces. This behavior then affects other people, making them more likely to act in the expected ways. In our early research on teacher expectation effects on individual students (Brophy & Good, 1970), we suggested the following model for how the process might work:

1. Early in the year, the teacher forms differential expectations for student behavior and achievement.
2. Consistent with these differential expectations, the teacher behaves differently toward different students.
3. This treatment tells students something about how they are expected to behave in the classroom and perform on academic tasks.

4. If the teacher's treatment is consistent over time, and if students do not actively resist or change it, it will likely affect their self-concepts, achievement motivation, levels of aspiration, classroom conduct, and interactions with the teacher.

5. These effects generally will complement and reinforce the teacher's expectations, so that students will come to conform to these expectations more than they might have otherwise.

6. Ultimately, this will affect student achievement and other outcome measures. High-expectation students will be led to achieve at or near their potential, but low-expectation students will not gain as much as they could have gained if taught differently.

Self-fulfilling prophecy effects of teachers' expectations can occur only when all elements in the model are present. Often, however, one or more elements is missing. A teacher may not have clear-cut expectations about every student, or those expectations may change continually. Even when expectations are consistent, the teacher may not necessarily communicate them through consistent behavior. In this case, the expectations would not be self-fulfilling even if they turned out to be correct. Finally, students might prevent expectations from becoming self-fulfilling by counteracting their effects or resisting them in a way that makes the teacher change them.

PRACTICE EXAMPLES

In this section we provide some practice examples you can use to improve your understanding of the self-fulfilling prophecy concept. Read each example and determine whether you think a self-fulfilling prophecy is involved. If so, you should be able to identify: (1) the original expectation; (2) behaviors that consistently communicate this expectation in ways that make it more likely to be fulfilled, and (3) evidence that the original expectation has been confirmed. If the example does not contain all three elements, it does not illustrate a self-fulfilling prophecy.

1. Coach Winn knows that Sarah Brown is the daughter of a former professional tennis player. Although he has never seen Sarah play, she predicts, "Sarah will help our team in her sophomore year." In practice sessions, Sarah is treated like all the other team members. She plays the same number of matches and does the same drills, and the coach praises her only when her performance merits its. Sarah is the top-ranked player on the team in her sophomore year and is named to the league's all-star team.

2. Rick Wilson, a tenth-grade social studies teacher, believes that Antonio Navarro and Julia Suárez can be better students. Although they have earned only average grades, he has seen flashes of insight in them that suggest higher potential. Furthermore, their aptitude test scores are higher than their achievement profiles. However, both students have poor work habits. Neither spends much time working on seatwork assignments, and it is not uncommon for Antonio and Julia to fail to hand in homework

two or three times a week. Mr. Wilson believes that both students can do better if he can motivate them to work harder, so he begins to call on them more often and to provide more detailed feedback on their seatwork and homework papers. By December, he has seen no progress. Nevertheless, he continues his efforts, and by May, Antonio is performing at a much higher level, but Julia's classroom behavior and test scores have not improved.

3. Jean Rogers is giving directions to John Greene, a second grader who is frequently in trouble. She has no confidence in John's sense of responsibility, so she gives him detailed instructions: "John, take this note to Ms. Turner's room. Remember: Don't make noise in the hall, don't stop to look in other classrooms, and above all, don't go outside." John responds with an obviously pained look, "Ms. Rogers, don't you trust me?"

4. As the school year begins, Tom Bloom is assigned to Dean Smith for academic counseling. The dean knows that Tom will probably flunk out at the end of the term. He has low entrance scores and poor writing skills. He is also shy, making it unlikely that he will get to know his instructors well or receive much help from them. The dean tells Tom that he is at risk for academic difficulty and urges him to enroll in the study skills clinic and to devote extra time on weekends to his studies. In addition, he has Tom report to his office once a week. Tom realizes that the dean expects him to have trouble unless he works hard, so he works as hard as he can, ultimately earning two Bs and three Cs.

5. Bob Graney knows that Beth Blanton will be a problem. He had her older sister the year before and she was uncontrollable. Trying to keep Beth out of trouble, Bob seats her at a table away from the other third graders in the room. Before long, though, Beth begins to throw things at her peers to attract their attention.

6. Tom Burton teaches a consumer business course at Mill Tour High School. He believes that students need and want to perform enjoyable drill activities in class but are not interested in tasks that require higher-order thinking. Therefore, in his taxation unit he emphasizes how to fill out tax forms and quick ways to check for computation errors. His other units also emphasize practical exercises involving much drill and practice but comparatively little analysis (Why are taxes collected? How legitimate is the present system? What alternative taxation plans would yield the same revenue but distribute the burden differently?).

7. Judy Jones, a seventh-grade mathematics teacher, uses tests emphasizing speed rather than ability to group students for instruction. At the beginning of the year she teaches new material to her high group (students who did well on the speed test) but requires her low group to review sixth-grade material in order to build up their speed. However, the slower students work only a few of the review problems because they know how to do them and because they want to listen to the teacher work with the high group so that they will be ready to do the work. Their failure to complete the review work during class strengthens the teacher's belief that these

students need still more drill. In time the low-group students become bored with the easy, repetitive drill work, do even fewer problems, and even lose interest in listening to the teacher work with the high group (in part because they do not get to work on similar problems). By the end of the year, many slow-group students are engaging in disruptive behavior.

8. Jennifer Ball is concerned about the peer-group adjustment of Dick Stewart, one of her second-graders. Dick had participated all year long in the races and games conducted during recess, but he began to withdraw from the group in the spring, when she introduced baseball. Although Dick is coordinated well enough, he had not played much baseball and had difficulty hitting and catching the ball. As a result, he was usually one of the last children chosen when teams were selected. After this happened a few times, Dick began to withdraw, claiming that he did not want to play because he had a headache or sore foot. Jennifer recognized that embarrassment was the real reason.

To help Dick compensate for his deficiencies and maintain peer status, Jennifer began allowing him to serve as umpire for ball games. This gave him an important, active role that she reinforced by praising Dick and calling other children's attention to his umpiring. In private contacts, she reassured Dick that he should not feel bad because he was not playing, because there could not be a ball game without an umpire.

In the last few days of school, Jennifer decided to let Dick play again, now that his confidence was built up. She was gratified to see that he was picked earlier than usual by the team captain. However, his batting and catching were just as bad as before. The next day, he was the last one chosen and he begged off, complaining of a headache.

ANALYSIS OF EXAMPLES

Let us see how well you were able to identify self-fulfilling prophecies. If we have been successful in describing the process, you should have identified each example correctly.

In Case 1, Coach Winn's original expectation about Sarah is fulfilled. However, there is no evidence that the coach caused this through special behavior toward Sarah. Thus, the coach's prediction did not act as a self-fulfilling prophecy, even though it was accurate.

Case 2 is a self-fulfilling prophecy for Antonio but not for Julia, even though the teacher believed that both students could do better. Rick Wilson's determined teaching apparently was successful in changing Antonio's perceptions and beliefs ("I can do math," "I should do it," "I want to"), thus improving his effort and achievement. However, Mr. Wilson's behavior did not improve Julia's performance (perhaps she viewed his increased questioning as nagging or as a lack of confidence in her ability).

In Case 3, the teacher gives John explicit instructions because she fears that he will misbehave. She subconsciously communicates this expectation through her behavior, and he picks it up. However, there is no evidence that his behavior changes accordingly, so this is not an example of self-fulfilling prophecy. If Jean Rogers were to continue to treat John this way, though, he might begin to behave as she expects. At this point, her expectation would have become self-fulfilling.

Case 4 is especially interesting and instructive. The dean fears that Tom will flunk, and he communicates this expectation. Tom gets the message, but he reacts by working hard to prove himself. He ends up doing well, despite the dean's original expectation. This occurs because the dean communicates serious concern but follows up with attempts to deal with the problem (referring Tom to the study skills clinic, calling for extra study time, scheduling regular counseling appointments). In effect, the dean works against his own expectation by engaging in what might be called "counter-prophetic compensation" behaviors (Brophy, 1985) designed to prevent the feared outcome. If, instead, the dean had communicated hopelessness and had done nothing to change the situation, his expectation probably would have been fulfilled.

Goldenberg (1992) presented two case studies that related to the story of our fictional Tom Bloom. One was remarkably parallel, describing a student whose teacher feared low achievement from her but alleviated it by working hard with her and enlisting special help at home. The other case was the obverse of the first. Here, the teacher had confidence that the student was bright and well-motivated, so she didn't get concerned when the student began to skip assignments and perform less capably. As a result, this student's achievement level kept slipping as the year progressed. By the time the teacher realized what was happening, it was too late to do much about it.

Goldenberg's case studies of actual students illustrate that students sometimes can benefit from initially low teacher expectations if those expectations cause the teacher to take action intended to counteract the feared consequences. Conversely, students can suffer negative consequences from initially high teacher expectations if those expectations cause the teacher to fail to notice changes that call for corrective action.

Case 5 is a classic illustration of a self-fulfilling teacher expectation. Bob Graney expects Beth to be a problem and begins to treat her as one. His treatment involves separating her from her peers, which leads her to misbehave to get attention and causes his expectation to become fulfilled.

In Case 6, we do not know whether Tom's expectation is correct or not. Many of his students probably do prefer drill and practice tasks over tasks that require higher-order thinking, but other students may want to know why things exist and how they operate. If these students' attitudes change over the year so that they develop a preference for repetitive practice tasks, then a self-fulfilling prophecy will have occurred. From the information given in the example, it is not possible to tell. In any case, Tom's behavior can be seen as communicating low and inappropriate expectations likely at least to *sustain* undesirable behavior and attitudes among students who prefer drill and practice activities. The teacher's approach denies these students the chance to develop a broader understanding of the topic through higher-order thinking activities.

Case 7 is not a self-fulfilling prophecy, although it exhibits some of the same characteristics. First, it involves an inappropriate teacher belief (that students' slowness is due largely to low ability rather than to motivational factors). Second, the teacher does engage in differential group treatment. However, she does so in an attempt to provide each group with the curriculum and instruction that she thinks they need; she does not "write off" the slow group as hopeless. Nevertheless, the result is much like a self-fulfilling prophecy effect (the gap between the slow and the fast students is widened), because the teacher's beliefs about students' needs are incorrect and lead to counterproductive slow-group teaching.

Case 8 illustrates how a teacher's expectation can be self-fulfilling even though it is unformulated and unrecognized by the teacher. Jennifer Ball intends to build Dick's confidence so that he will participate in ball games. However, her approach takes into account only his attitude and not his need for practice in hitting and catching the ball. Although she does not think about it this way, her approach reflects the expectation that Dick cannot hit or catch and, therefore, needs some alternative role. This is very different from the idea that Dick cannot hit or catch and, therefore, needs to be taught to do so. The teacher's attempt to solve the problem involves many good things for Dick but not the things he needs most: instruction and practice in hitting and catching the ball. As a result, by the end of the year he is even farther behind in these skills than he was earlier.

The last two examples show that teachers may adopt inappropriate strategies if they define a problem incorrectly. Teachers who worry about their students' self-concepts often do this because they think that they have to improve students' self-concept before their ability will improve. Usually, the opposite is true (Eccles & Wigfield, 1985). Low self-concept results from poor performance, and improvement in performance will produce improvement in self-concept. When students show handicaps, inhibitions, or lack of skill, the appropriate strategy is to provide remedial instruction and extra practice or opportunities to learn. Although well-meant, attempts to make students feel better by providing compensation in other areas will not solve the root problem.

HOW TEACHERS FORM EXPECTATIONS

We now consider some of the research on teacher expectation effects, along with its implications for teachers. Most of this research has focused on teachers' expectations for students' achievement rather than for other student outcomes (motivation, conduct, social adjustment), and most has focused on expectations about individual students rather than groups or whole classes. Therefore, we emphasize research on teachers' expectations for individual students' achievement, considering the research in terms of the steps in the Brophy and Good model.

The model begins with the statement that teachers form differential achievement expectations for different students at the beginning of the school year. Investigators have studied the nature of the information that teachers use to form these expectations and the degree to which the expectations are accurate.

One body of literature consists of experimental studies of expectation formation in which subjects (not necessarily teachers) are given only carefully controlled information about, and little or no opportunity to interact with, the "students" (usually fictional) about whom they are asked to make predictions. For example, all of the subjects might be given cumulative record forms containing identical test scores, grades, and comments presumably written by previous teachers, but half of the forms would be accompanied by a picture of a white child and the other half by a picture of a black child (to see if knowledge about the fictional student's race would affect predictions about his or her achievement). Such experiments have shown that expectations can be affected significantly by information about performance on tests or assignments, track or group placement, classroom conduct, physical appearance, race, socioeconomic status, ethnicity, gender, speech characteristics, and various diagnostic or special education labels (see Jones, 1990).

These findings are not surprising, given the limited information that experimental subjects had to work with. Unfortunately, however, such results are often cited in discussions about teachers' formation of expectations concerning their actual students, so that teachers sometimes are made to appear to be both gullible (willing to accept whatever phony information someone gives them) and prejudiced (tending to jump to conclusions based on students' race, gender, etc.). However, studies focusing on real teachers' expectations concerning their actual students, conducted under more natural conditions, suggest a much more positive picture. First, teachers will not passively accept phony information if it is contradicted by other information that they have from more credible sources or from their own tests, assignments, or interactions with their students (Bognar, 1982; Raudenbush, 1984). Furthermore, although evidence of teacher bias based on student gender (Jussim, 1989) or ethnicity (Clifton et al., 1986; Trujillo, 1986) has been reported occasionally, studies of in-service teachers' achievement expectations for their actual students do not reveal much evidence of grossly biased judgments. For example, most impressions that teachers form from interacting with their students are based primarily on students' participation in academic activities and performance on tests and assignments rather than on physical or other status characteristics. More generally, most teachers' perceptions of students are largely accurate and based on the best available information, and most of the inaccuracies that may exist are corrected when more dependable information becomes available (Brophy & Good, 1974; Short, 1985). Consequently, teachers' predictions about student achievement are usually quite accurate, sometimes even more accurate than predictions based on test data (Coladarci, 1986; Helmke & Schrader, 1987).

In summary, in-service teachers usually develop accurate expectations about their students, and they correct inaccurate expectations as more or better information becomes available. This limits the possibilities for self-fulfilling prophecy effects (which are based on false or unjustified expectations), although it still leaves a great deal of room for sustaining expectation effects.

HOW TEACHERS COMMUNICATE EXPECTATIONS TO STUDENTS

Given that teachers have formed differential expectations for different students, the next step of the Brophy and Good model postulates that teachers communicate these differential expectations by treating students differently. Researchers have addressed this issue by documenting differences in the ways teachers interact with students who differ in current or expected achievement.

Rosenthal (1974) reviewed the research on mediators of teacher expectation effects and identified four general factors. Focusing on positive self-fulfilling prophecy effects, he suggested that teachers will maximize student achievement if they

1. Create warm social-emotional relationships with their students (climate)
2. Give them more feedback about their performance (feedback)
3. Teach them more (and more difficult) material (input)
4. Give them more opportunities to respond and to ask questions (output)

This four-factor model is a useful summary, but we prefer a longer list of potential mediating mechanisms, for three reasons. First, teachers and teacher educators can use each of the items in a more detailed list as a basis for observing in classrooms. Second, we want to complement Rosenthal's emphasis on enhancing student achievement through positive expectation effects with an emphasis on ways that teachers might minimize the learning progress of low-expectation students through negative or undesirable expectation effects. Unfortunately, research suggests that teachers are more likely to be affected by information leading to negative expectations than by information leading to positive expectations (Mason, 1973; Persell, 1977). Third, we want to emphasize that teachers can communicate their expectations in a variety of ways, including some that are much more subtle than the direct ways summarized in Rosenthal's model. Reviews of the literature (Brophy, 1983; Brophy & Good, 1974) suggest that the following behaviors sometimes indicate differential teacher treatment of high and low achievers:

1. Waiting less time for lows to answer a question (before giving the answer or calling on someone else)
2. Giving lows answers or calling on someone else rather than trying to improve their responses by giving clues or repeating or rephrasing questions
3. Inappropriate reinforcement: rewarding inappropriate behavior or incorrect answers by lows
4. Criticizing lows more often for failure
5. Praising lows less often for success
6. Failing to give feedback to the public responses of lows
7. Generally paying less attention to lows or interacting with them less frequently
8. Calling on lows less often to respond to questions, or asking them only easier, nonanalytic questions
9. Seating lows farther away from the teacher
10. Demanding less from lows. This differential treatment is evidenced by a variety of behaviors. Beez (1968) found that tutors who did not have high expectations not only taught fewer words but also taught them less rapidly and with more extended explanation and repetition of definitions and examples. The inappropriate reinforcement findings mentioned above indicate that teachers may accept low-quality or even incorrect responses from lows. Graham (1984) suggested that excessive teacher sympathy or

offers of gratuitous, unsolicited help may communicate low expectations, especially if these behaviors occur instead of behaviors designed to help low achievers meet success criteria.

11. Interacting with lows more privately than publicly, and monitoring and structuring their activities more closely

12. Differential administration or grading of tests or assignments, in which highs but not lows are given the benefit of the doubt in borderline cases

13. Less friendly interactions with lows, including less smiling and fewer other nonverbal indicators of support

14. Briefer and less informative feedback to questions of lows

15. Less eye contact and other nonverbal communication of attention and responsiveness (forward lean, positive head nodding) in interaction with lows

16. Less use of effective but time-consuming instructional methods with lows when time is limited

17. Less acceptance and use of lows' ideas

18. Exposing lows to an impoverished curriculum (overly limited and repetitive content, emphasis on factual recitation rather than on lesson-extending discussion, emphasis on drill and practice tasks rather than application and higher-level thinking tasks)

Several points should be made about these forms of differential treatment that have been documented in research. First, they do not occur in all classrooms. Teachers differ considerably in how much they differentiate in their treatment of students toward whom they hold different expectations (more on this later). Second, sometimes these differences in treatment are due mostly or even entirely to the students rather than to the teacher. For example, if lows seldom raise their hands, it is difficult for the teacher to ensure that they get as many response opportunities as highs, and if their contributions to the lesson are of lower quality, the teacher cannot accept and use their ideas as frequently.

Third, some forms of differential treatment are appropriate at times and may even represent appropriate individualizing of instruction rather than inappropriate projection of negative expectations. Lows appear to require more structuring of their activities and closer monitoring of their work, for example, and one could argue that it makes sense to interact with them more privately than publicly or to ask them easier questions. It is difficult to distinguish seatwork monitoring that includes just the right degree of extra structuring and assistance from seatwork monitoring that amounts to giving students answers without requiring them to think and learn. Similarly, it may be difficult to determine whether a teacher is challenging a student below, at, or above the optimal level. Thus, one should not assume that the forms of differential treatment described above are necessarily inappropriate whenever they are observed.

These teacher behaviors are danger signals, however, especially if the differentiation is large and occurs on many dimensions rather than one or two. Such a pattern suggests that the teacher is merely going through the motions of instructing low-expectation students, without genuinely trying to encourage their academic progress.

Note also that some of these forms of differential treatment could directly affect students' opportunity to learn. To the extent that lows get less content and feedback, they are almost certain to make less progress than highs, regardless of whether or not lows are aware of this differential treatment and its implications about their teacher's expectations for them. (For more technical information on teacher expectation effects see Brophy, 1983; Jussim, 1990; and Rosenthal & Rubin, 1978.)

In addition to these expectation effects that occur directly through differences in exposure to content, indirect effects may occur through teacher behavior that affects students' self-concepts, motivation, performance expectations, or attributions for success or failure. This brings us to Step 3 of the Brophy and Good model, which postulates that students perceive differential treatment and its implications about what is expected of them.

STUDENTS' PERCEPTIONS OF DIFFERENTIAL TEACHER TREATMENT

Students are aware of differences in teachers' patterns of interaction with different students in the class. Interviews with elementary school students indicate that they see their teachers as projecting higher achievement expectations and offering more opportunity and choice to high achievers, while structuring the activities of low achievers more closely and providing them both with more help and with more negative feedback about their academic work and classroom conduct. Furthermore, students are more aware of such differentiation in classes where more of it occurs (Weinstein et al., 1987).

Cooper and Good (1983) reported similar findings. Compared to low-expectation peers, elementary students for whom their teachers held high expectations reported themselves as engaging more often in teacher-initiated public interactions but less often in teacher-initiated private interactions, supplying correct answers more frequently, and receiving more praise and less criticism from teachers. Observed differences were in the same directions but less extreme, suggesting that students not only perceive differential treatment but exaggerate the differentiation that exists.

Combining their student interview findings with classroom observation of teachers' patterns of interaction with students who differ in expectation or achievement, Good and Weinstein (1986) produced the summary shown in Table 3.1. To the extent that such differentiation exists in a teacher's classroom, expectation effects on student achievement are likely to occur both directly through opportunity to learn (differences in the amount and nature of exposure to content and opportunities to engage in various types of academic activities) and indirectly through differential treatment that is likely to affect students' self-concepts, attributional inferences, or motivation.

Individual differences among students also affect the size of teacher expectation effects. Some students may be more sensitive than others to voice tones or other subtle communication cues, so that they may interpret teachers' communica-

Table 3.1   GENERAL DIMENSIONS OF TEACHERS' COMMUNICATION OF DIFFERENTIAL EXPECTATIONS AND SELECTED EXAMPLES

	Students believed to be MORE capable have:	Students believed to be LESS capable have:
Task Environment Curriculum, procedures, task definition, pacing, qualities of environment	More opportunity to perform publicly on meaningful tasks.	Less opportunity to perform publicly, especially on meaningful tasks (supplying alternate endings to a story vs. learning to pronounce a word correctly).
	More opportunity to think.	Less opportunity to think, analyze (since much work is aimed at practice).
Grouping Practices	More assignments that deal with comprehension, understanding (in higher-ability groups).	Less choice on curriculum assignments—more work on drill-like assignments.
Locus of Responsibility for Learning	More autonomy (more choice in assignments, fewer interruptions).	Less autonomy (frequent teacher monitoring of work, frequent interruptions).
Feedback and Evaluation Practices	More opportunity for self-evaluation.	Less opportunity for self-evaluation.
Motivational Strategies	More honest/contingent feedback.	Less honest/more gratuitous/less contingent feedback.
Quality of Teacher Relationships	More respect for the learner as an individual with unique interests and needs.	Less respect for the learner as an individual with unique interests and needs.

tions of expectations more often and accurately. Younger and more teacher-dependent students may also be more susceptible to teacher expectation effects (Persell, 1977).

STUDENTS' RESPONSES TO DIFFERENTIAL LEARNING OPPORTUNITIES

Students not only develop inferences about what teachers think of and expect from them; over time they develop beliefs about their potential and roles as students. Some come to believe that they can learn with relative ease, but others come to believe that they can learn only with great difficulty or perhaps cannot learn at all. Some are willing to try hard to learn, but others conclude that the costs (embarrassment, long hours of effort) are simply not worth the benefits. Some students learn to ask questions when they are confused, but others view such question asking as a form of public humiliation. The latter students learn to hide rather than confront their learning difficulties, and if necessary to turn in incomplete work, affect an air of apathy or disdain, or in other ways project the notion that they are unwilling rather than unable to do the work. This is because they would rather have the teacher or peers question their motivation than their ability.

Students who need the most help often are the least likely to seek assistance, especially once they have been in school long enough to learn that asking questions sometimes yields teacher criticism (for asking at the wrong time, for not having listened carefully, etc.) or causes the teacher or peers to infer that one is not very bright. Good et al. (1987) found that low achievers were just as likely to ask questions as other students in kindergarten classes but that low achievers asked significantly fewer questions than their classmates did in upper-elementary and secondary classes. Similarly, in a study involving grades 2, 4, and 6, Newman and Goldin (1990), found that among sixth graders the lowest achievers had both the greatest perceived need for help and the greatest resistance to asking for it.

Students' ambivalence about asking questions or getting help from teachers becomes especially acute at adolescence, when they have become both more concerned about how they are perceived by peers and more sensitive to the costs as well as the benefits of help seeking. Newman (1990) found that students' attitudes about help seeking were explained by various factors (including intrinsic striving for challenge and dependence on the teacher) at grades 3 and 5, but that by grade 7 students' help-seeking behavior was predicted completely by their beliefs about its probable benefits and costs (e.g., the likelihood that their help seeking would actually yield help that would enable them to learn, balanced against the expected embarrassment that it would entail).

Teachers must recognize and learn to cope effectively with forms of student passivity or resistance that stem from students' attempts to protect themselves from embarrassment. At minimum, teachers should avoid being conditioned by such students to lower expectations for them and thus abandon serious attempts to get them to achieve to their potential. Better yet, teachers should counter these students' fears and pessimistic expectations by convincing them that they can learn if they put forth reasonable effort, and then follow up by teaching students strategies for managing their learning effectively (more on this in subsequent chapters).

Given that a teacher forms differential expectations and acts on them by treating students differently, and that students perceive this differential treatment and draw inferences about what is expected of them, the stage is set for teacher expectation effects on student achievement that are mediated through effects on students' self-concepts, motivation, expectations, and attributions. The remaining steps in the Brophy and Good model suggest that such effects occur but do not say much about how the process might work. Others have developed models to offer such explanation. We will review one such model here (for information on other models see Cooper, 1985; Darley & Fazio, 1980; and Eccles & Wigfield, 1985).

Good's Model of Student Passivity

Good (1981, 1993) suggested that certain forms of teacher treatment induce passivity in low achievers through two mechanisms. First, many teachers call on low achievers less often and wait a shorter time for them to respond than they do for highs. They also give them answers rather than try to improve their poor responses and are less likely to praise their successes but more likely to criticize their failures. Given that low achievers are less likely to be able to answer correctly in the first place and that their mistakes occur in public, they must bear considerably more than the usual levels of ambiguity and risk when they participate actively in lessons. Under the circumstances, a good strategy for them is to remain passive—not to volunteer and not to respond when called on.

A second possible path toward passivity is that low achievers often must adjust to more varied teacher treatment than other students. Their teachers are likely to treat them inconsistently over the course of the school year, trying one approach after another in an attempt to find a strategy that works. Also, they may have more teachers (if they are involved in compensatory or special education), which means exposure to more contrasting strategies. Some teachers call on them frequently in an attempt to get them to participate, but others mostly avoid them. Some rarely praise their successes, but others praise almost everything they do, even responses that are not correct. Student passivity is a likely outcome of such diversity of treatment. Not knowing what to do, low achievers may learn to avoid initiating and wait for the teacher to structure their behavior.

Student Internalization

We have argued that students may receive different types of expectations from different teachers. However, student self-views are affected by many factors. Another type of inconsistency that some students experience is between home and school environments. For example, Heath (1983) has noted that lower-class parents generally do not ask their children a question when they, the adults, already know the answer. However, middle-class parents and teachers often engage in this practice. McCaslin and Murdock (1991) have provided detailed case analysis to illustrate how students' home learning may support or conflict with students' understanding and valuing of classroom activities and achievement (e.g., the role of effort may mean notably different things in some homes than what it means to teachers). Much remains to be learned about how students are socialized to accept or to reject the norms that teachers, parents, and other significant adults hold. Sometimes students will react to the same type of teacher behavior in dissimilar ways (some students will hear challenge and appropriate concern; others will hear criticism). If students are consistently exposed to low expectations, however, they will tend to internalize those expectations in time.

FACTORS THAT AFFECT EXPECTATION COMMUNICATION

Context

School contexts vary in the opportunities that they provide for differential teacher-student interaction, and thus for expectation effects to occur. *Grade level* is one such factor. Other things being equal, expectation effects should be greater in the early grades, before students' records of academic achievement and their academic self-concepts and attribution patterns become firmly established. This is what Raudenbush (1984) found in his review of 18 experiments on induced teacher expectations. Effects were stronger in grades 1 and 2 than in grades 3 through 6. Then effects became strong again at grade 7, the first year of junior high school for most students. This suggests that strong effects might also be seen in the first year of high school, college, or graduate school, or whenever students are new to an institution and their instructors.

Differences between the elementary and secondary grades create variation in the types of differential treatment that occur. Elementary students have the same teacher all day and often interact with that teacher individually. Secondary students see most of their teachers for only an hour or less per day and do not spend much time interacting with them individually. Consequently, in the early grades expectations are likely to be communicated through qualitative aspects of individualized teacher-student interaction (the teacher interacts frequently with all students but may treat highs and lows in quite different ways), but in the secondary grades differentiation is more likely to occur through the number of individualized teacher-student interactions (the teacher interacts with highs much more often than with lows, because highs contribute to lessons more often).

Time of year is another relevant context factor. Greater expectation effects would be expected early in the year (Brophy & Good, 1974). As the year progresses, teachers may pay relatively less attention to within-class differences between individuals or subgroups and begin to pay more attention to the progress of the class as a whole, adjusting the pace of instruction to suit the potential of the class as they have come to perceive it (Cooper & Good, 1983).

Subject matter is another significant context variable. Smith (1980) reported larger expectation effects on reading achievement than on math achievement. This may be because a greater variety of grouping and instructional practices tends to be used in teaching reading than in teaching math, so that there is more room for teachers to translate differential expectations into differential treatment of students.

The most important context factor is probably *the nature of the learning environment* that the teacher establishes. The potential for expectation effects (especially for undesirable effects of low expectations) is greatest in classrooms that feature uniform rather than multiple goals, a narrow rather than a broad range of activity structures, norm-referenced achievement standards, a competitive atmosphere, public performance evaluation, emphasis on achievement rather than effort, and frequent publicly perceived differential treatment of high and low achievers (Rosenholtz & Simpson, 1984).

Teachers' Personal Characteristics

More important than context and setting factors in determining teacher expectation effects are individual differences among teachers, especially in their personal characteristics and their beliefs about teaching and learning. Some teachers are likely to show sizable self-fulfilling prophecy effects, especially negative effects that reduce student achievement gains.

For example, Brattesani, Weinstein, and Marshall (1984) compared classrooms where the students described the teachers as differentiating considerably in their treatment of high versus low achievers with classrooms where the students reported little such differentiated treatment. They found that including teacher expectation measures added 9–18 percent to the variance in year-end achievement beyond what could be predicted from prior achievement in the high-differentiation classes, but added only 1–5 percent in the low-differentiation classes. Thus, "high-differentiating" teachers produced sizable expectation effects, but "low-differentiating" teachers did not.

Brophy and Good (1974) suggested that teachers can be ranked on a dimension of expectation formation from proactive through reactive to overreactive. *Proactive* teachers are guided by their own beliefs about what is appropriate in setting goals for the class as a whole and for individual students. If they set realistic goals and have the needed skills, they are likely to move their students systematically toward fulfilling the expectations associated with these goals. Proactive teachers are the most likely to have positive expectation effects on their students.

At the other extreme are *overreactive* teachers who develop rigid, stereotyped perceptions of students based on students' prior records and on first impressions of their behavior. Overreactive teachers tend to treat students as stereotypes rather than as individuals, and they are the most likely teachers to have negative expectation effects.

In between these extremes are *reactive* teachers who hold expectations lightly and adjust them as a result of new feedback. Reactive teachers have minimal expectation effects on their students, tending to maintain existing differences between high and low achievers (although these differences will increase slightly because of different behavior by students themselves that the teachers do not compensate for).

Research has supported these distinctions, but with an important qualification: Unfortunately, most sizable teacher expectation effects on student achievement appear to be negative ones in which low expectations lead to lower achievement than students might have attained otherwise (Brophy, 1983; Simon & Willcocks, 1981). There is little evidence that even proactive teachers significantly augment the achievement of individual students by projecting positive expectations, but much evidence that overreactive teachers minimize student progress by acting on low expectations.

One cluster of traits likely to be found in overreactive or "high-bias" teachers is a tendency toward conventionalism, authoritarianism, or dogmatism (Babad, 1985). Other such personal traits that are less well documented but seem likely are (1) a tendency to maintain expectations rigidly once they are formed; (2) a teacher role definition that minimizes the teacher's personal responsibility for ensuring that students master the curriculum; (3) a tendency to view student ability as unitary and fixed rather than as multiple and open to improvement through instruction and practice; (4) a tendency to notice, think about, and comment on the differences rather than similarities between students, and to take these into account when planning instruction; (5) a tendency to repress or rationalize teaching failures rather than recognize and try to overcome them; and (6) poorly developed classroom management and instructional skills (which give the teacher more to be defensive about and thus more to repress or rationalize).

These personal characteristics of teachers interact with their beliefs about appropriate curriculum and instruction to determine the nature and strength of expectation effects on the achievement of individual students in their classes. Teachers with all of the above-listed characteristics, for example, would tend to have powerful (and mostly negative) expectation effects, including self-fulfilling prophecy effects, on substantial numbers of their students if they were teaching in the primary grades using approaches that maximized the time that they spent with individuals and small groups but minimized the time spent with the class as a whole. In contrast, these same teachers might have relatively minor sustaining expectation effects if they were teaching mathematics to high school students and relying exclusively on a whole-class approach that provided the same instruction, tasks, and requirements to all students and minimized the time spent with individuals.

GROUP, CLASS, AND SCHOOL EXPECTATION EFFECTS

So far we have been discussing expectation effects on individual students in the same class. However, expectation effects can operate on groups, classes, or entire schools. Less research is available on such expectation effects, but they appear to be at least as important as effect on individuals. After all, low expectations for an entire class can affect all students in the class.

Group Effects

Expectation effects at the group level are possible whenever teachers group students according to ability or achievement, as is commonly done for elementary reading instruction. Weinstein (1976) showed that reading group membership information added 25 percent to the variance in mid-year reading achievement that could be predicted beyond what was predictable from readiness scores taken at the beginning of the year. Placement into high groups accelerated achievement rates, but placement into low groups slowed them down (relative to the rates expected based on initial readiness levels).

Research comparing instruction in different reading groups (reviewed by Allington, 1991) suggests some of the reasons for this. Teachers tend to give longer reading assignments, to provide more time for discussion of the story, to ask more higher-level comprehension questions, and to be generally more demanding with high groups than with low groups. Teachers are quicker to interrupt low-group students when they make reading mistakes, and more likely to just give them the word or prompt them with graphemic (phonetic) cues rather than to offer semantic or syntactic cues that might help them intuit the word from its context.

The nature and extent of such differential treatment vary across teachers, and at least some of it can be seen as appropriate differential instruction. Even so, widespread and powerful patterns of differential treatment of groups should be cause for concern. Too often, low groups continually get less interesting instruction, less emphasis on meaning and conceptualization, and more rote drill and practice activities (Good & Marshall, 1984).

Eder (1981) compared instruction in the high and the low reading groups in a first-grade class in a school serving a relatively homogeneous middle-class population. None of the students could read prior to entering first grade, and given their relative homogeneity of background, it is not clear that ability grouping was needed.

The teacher did use "ability grouping" however, based on kindergarten teachers' recommendations that, in turn, were based on students' maturity in addition to their perceived ability. Consequently, a major reason that the low group progressed slowly was that it contained several immature, inattentive students who frequently disrupted lesson continuity. Compared with those in the high group, low-group students spent almost twice as much time off task and were more likely to call out words or answers that were supposed to be supplied by other students. Thus, low-group student progress can be slowed not only by low teacher expectations but also by the undesirable social contexts that develop when groups are short on academic peer leaders and long on attention and conduct problems.

A "low-group psychology" often develops when ability grouping is practiced, even in schools whose low-group students would be high-group students somewhere else. Often, low groups are taught at a slower pace and exposed to less interesting and varied activities than they are capable of handling.

Class Effects

Brophy and Evertson (1976) found that the most successful teachers believed that their students were capable of mastering curriculum objectives, and that they (the teachers) were capable of meeting students' instructional needs. These expectations were associated with behaviors such as augmenting or even replacing curriculum materials or tests if these did not appear to be suited to students' needs.

Ashton and Webb (1986) reported similar findings for teachers who differed in *sense of efficacy*. Teachers who were high in sense of efficacy believed that they were capable of motivating and instructing students successfully. Teachers who were low in sense of efficacy believed either that no teachers could have important effects (because students' motivation and performance depends mostly on their home environments) or that some teachers could have such effects but they personally could not (presumably because they lacked needed knowledge or skills).

Research done in 48 basic-level (i.e., low-achieving) mathematics and communication classes in four high schools revealed relationships between teachers' sense of efficacy, patterns of teacher-student interaction, and student achievement gains. Teachers high in sense of efficacy were more confident and at ease in their classrooms, more positive (praising, smiling) and less negative (criticizing, punishing) in interactions with their students, more successful in managing their classrooms as efficient learning environments, less defensive, more accepting of student disagreement and challenges, and more effective in stimulating achievement gains.

Midgley, Feldlaufer, and Eccles (1989) found that students' motivational profiles also can be affected by their teachers' efficacy beliefs. In particular, students who were taught mathematics by high-efficacy teachers one year showed notable drops in their self-concepts as mathematics learners if they were taught by low-efficacy teachers the next year.

Teacher expectation effects at the class level are especially likely to appear in schools using tracking systems. Evertson (1982) identified several ways in which students in low-track classes slowed pacing and shifted teachers' attention from academic to procedural or behavioral matters. However, she also noted differences in how the teachers taught their high- and low-track classes, suggesting that teacher expectation effects were operating in addition to student effects on teachers. Compared with their behavior in high-track classes, many teachers of low-track classes were observed to be less clear about objectives, to introduce content less clearly or completely, to make fewer attempts to relate content to students' interests or backgrounds, to be less reasonable in their work standards, to be less consistent in their discipline, and to be less receptive to student input (see also Oakes, 1985; Oakes et al., 1993).

Teachers also tend to assign more independent projects and to introduce more high-level and integrative concepts in high-track classes (Oakes, 1985), but to stress more structured assignments dealing with basic facts and skills in low-track classes (Borko, Shavelson, & Stern, 1981). Finally, teachers tend to plan more thoroughly in order to be prepared for the academic challenges that high-track classes present but to be less well prepared for low-track classes and to spend more time allowing students to do activities of their own choosing rather than teaching academic content (Brookover et al., 1979; Gamoran & Berends, 1987; Rosenbaum, 1976).

Good and Weinstein (1986) offered the following suggestions for improving classrooms that feature low expectations and boring, unchallenging routines.

1. Broaden goals of lessons and activities. Students need to practice and master basic content and skills, but they also need application opportunities. Something is wrong if students are usually working on phonics exercises but rarely reading, often practicing penmanship or copying spelling words but rarely writing, or regularly working on arithmetic computations but rarely trying to formulate or solve problems.
2. Pay more attention to students' ideas and interests, and encourage them to play a larger role in assessing their own performance. Students are often much more passive and teacher-dependent in their learning efforts than they need to be.
3. Increase opportunities for students to participate actively and use materials in meaningful ways. Teacher-led lessons should require more than just quiet listening, and follow-up assignments should require more than just working through highly structured practice exercises.
4. Besides asking factual questions, ask questions that require students to think, analyze, synthesize, or evaluate ideas. Include questions that can be answered at a variety of levels from a variety of points of view, so that a greater range of students can participate and experience success.

5. Focus on the positive aspects of learning. Encourage, reinforce, and note group progress toward learning goals. Minimize public comparisons of students with one another, criticisms of the class as a whole, or suggestions that material to be learned is overly difficult or unrewarding.

School Effects

High expectations and commitment to bringing about student achievement are part of a pattern of attitudes, beliefs, and behaviors that characterize schools that are successful in maximizing their students' learning gains. Brookover et al. (1979), for example, found that teachers in effective schools not only held higher expectations but acted on them by setting goals expressed as minimally acceptable levels of achievement (rather than using prior achievement data to establish ceiling levels beyond which students were not expected to progress). These teachers viewed student failure as a challenge and required students to redo failed work (with individualized help as needed) rather than writing them off or referring them to remedial classes. They responded to mistakes and response failures during class with appropriate feedback and reinstruction rather than with lower standards or inappropriate praise.

Rosenholtz (1989) found quite different beliefs about the kinds of professional behavior expected among teachers in more and less effective schools. The teachers in more effective schools looked for ways to share ideas and educational materials and tried to work together to facilitate students' achievement. In contrast, the teachers in less effective schools avoided such professional collaboration with peers and, in particular, avoided discussion of problems. Consequently, they had fewer resources to draw on in trying to solve those problems.

Stevenson and Stigler (1992) compared schooling in China, Japan, and the United States. They noted that in Asian classrooms more emphasis is placed on effort and hard work, but that an emphasis on innate ability in American schools lowers expectations about what can be accomplished through persistent effort. Thus, in terms of international norms, it may be that students perceived to be less talented in American schools receive too little academic demand.

EFFECTS OF EXPECTATIONS ON STUDENTS' PERSONAL AND SOCIAL DEVELOPMENT

In this chapter we have concentrated on teacher expectation effects on student achievement. However, there is reason to believe that teacher expectation effects also play a significant role in shaping students' personal and social development, at least within the school setting.

Experiments on the direct labeling of children by adults (Toner, Moore, & Emmons, 1980) have shown that children labeled as possessing prosocial traits such as patience or charity were more likely to demonstrate these traits in follow-up test situations than control children who were not so labeled. Unfortunately, less desirable outcomes such as learned helplessness can also result from direct labeling effects (Langer & Benevento, 1978).

Self-perceptions and behavior also can be affected by expectations communicated indirectly. Hauserman, Miller, and Bond (1983) found that children's self-concepts could be improved by stimulating them to make positive statements about themselves each day. Riggs et al. (1983) showed that even self-perceptions can be induced indirectly (people who were asked questions implying that the experimenter believed them to be introverted later described themselves as more introverted than people who had been asked questions suggesting that they were considered extroverted). Brophy et al. (1983) showed that students were less engaged in activities that teachers introduced in ways suggesting negative expectations (i.e., suggesting that the activities would be very difficult or unenjoyable) than they were in other activities.

Beliefs, attitudes, expectations, and behavior can be socialized, both through deliberate actions and through other behaviors that communicate one's beliefs, attitudes, or expectations. Thus, the success of a teacher's classroom management efforts probably is determined in part by expectations communicated about student conduct; the classroom atmosphere likely depends in part on expectations communicated about student cooperation and interpersonal relationships; and student responsiveness to lessons and assignments is probably affected by expectations communicated about the meaningfulness, interest, or utility of school activities. Thus, besides affecting student achievement, teacher expectations can be expected to affect students' attitudes, beliefs, attributions, expectations, motivational patterns, and classroom conduct. We discuss these topics in more detail in Chapters 4–6.

NEW DIRECTIONS FOR EXPECTATION RESEARCH

Expectation research can be expanded in many ways to enhance our understanding of classroom teaching and learning (Good, 1993). In this section we briefly discuss three of many research topics that would yield information about how expectations influence students' performance: teachers' decisions about content, teachers' knowledge of subject matter, and the effects of different teachers' expectations across consecutive years.

Selection of Curriculum Content

Many educators have contended that textbooks define the curriculum. However, recent research challenges this simplistic view and suggests that teachers act as decision makers, modifying the curriculum in relation to factors such as teachers' beliefs about students' aptitude, their instructional intentions, and their subject-matter knowledge. If teachers influence the curriculum, then their decisions about curriculum help to determine performance expectations for students, just as teacher behaviors and activity structures do.

According to Freeman and Porter (1989), teachers make many decisions that influence how much content students receive. For example, teachers decide how much time to spend on mathematics on a certain day, what topics should be taught, how much time should be allocated for each topic, whether all students are taught the same topics, and in what order topics should be presented.

Freeman and Porter (1989) conducted detailed case studies of how four fourth-grade teachers used textbooks to make decisions about what mathematics content to teach. One particularly interesting comparison of two teachers who used the same textbook showed that they presented substantially different content to students. Teacher A allocated her mathematics time in the following ways: conceptions, 23 percent; skills, 59 percent; and applications, 18 percent. In contrast, Teacher B allocated 17 percent to conceptions, 70 percent to skills, and 13 percent to applications. Students in Class A received 13 additional lessons on concepts and 10 additional lessons on applications.

Freeman and Porter (1989) also contrasted time allocation in Class A (7764 minutes) with that in Class C, which was divided into two instructional groups. Teacher C provided only 5830 minutes of instruction for the low group. Using 50 minutes as a class unit, the low group in Class C received 7½ fewer weeks of instruction than did students in Class A. The time spent on instruction and the focus of instruction are two important ways in which expectations might be communicated. Subsequent research could profitably attempt to integrate study of teachers' decisions about how much and what type of content to present with study of teachers' expectations for students (how much students are likely to learn, etc.).

Subject-Matter Knowledge

Teachers' subject-matter knowledge is likely an important factor affecting the performance expectations they communicate to students. Teachers know more about some subjects or concepts than others, and their beliefs about subject matter and how to present it to students can affect their expectations concerning what students should learn and in what way.

Carlsen (1991) documented the effects of four beginning biology teachers' subject-matter knowledge on discourse and activity focus in their classrooms. Teachers taught an equal number of lessons on topics about which they had either high or low knowledge. These teachers were more likely to use lectures and relatively open-ended laboratory activities to teach high-knowledge topics but to use seatwork assignments and non-laboratory projects for topics about which they had low knowledge.

The findings imply that choice of instructional activity affects students' participation in classroom discussion. Teachers used lectures and laboratory activities, which are characterized by high rates of student questioning, with topics they were knowledgeable about. They tended to use classroom activities that involved few student questions when they were unfamiliar with the subject matter.

As Good (1993) has argued, research that examines teachers' performance expectations for individual students along with teachers' subject-matter knowledge would be profitable. When teachers instruct students in topics about which teachers have little knowledge, they may exaggerate differential treatment (i.e., avoid unpredictable questions by low achievers; over-depend on students believed to be more capable). They also may depend heavily on the textbook for their curriculum content, on fill-in-the-blanks worksheets for their activities, and on multiple-choice tests for assessing student learning.

Expectations Across Consecutive Years

As we noted earlier, Midgley et al. (1989) reported that students who moved from high- to low-efficacy math teachers during the transition from elementary to junior high school ended the first junior high year with low performance expectancies (even lower than students who had low-efficacy teachers both years) and high perceptions of task difficulty. The transaction had more of an effect on low-achieving than on high-achieving students. In the spring of both years, students with more efficacious teachers had higher expectancies for and perceptions of their performance in math than did students with less efficacious teachers. Moreover, in the spring of their seventh-grade year, students with more efficacious teachers rated math as less difficult than did students with less efficacious teachers.

There is growing evidence that students' views of their potential to understand subject matter and perform in classrooms are not simply a product of the current classroom environment but are also influenced by previous school experiences. Fetterman (1990) found that fifth-grade teachers were unable to implement a process approach to mathematics (teaching students to understand content, explain solution paths) because fourth-grade teachers had encouraged a product approach (quick right answers) and also because of students' expectations about what would happen in the sixth grade. Hence, another important way to think about how expectations affect student performance is through an examination of the match or mismatch of expectations across consecutive school years.

INCREASING EXPECTATIONS

There is growing evidence that the performance of low achievers improves when they are allowed to enroll in more challenging courses or when course content is altered to include more challenging material that traditionally is not available to them. The decision to allow students to engage in more challenging academic work (e.g., move to a higher reading group) can be a powerful strategy for increasing teacher and student performance expectations (see Weinstein, 1976).

A Junior High/Middle School Example

Mason et al. (1992) described a study in which 34 average-achieving eighth-grade math students were assigned to prealgebra classes rather than traditional general mathematics classes. Results showed that students placed in prealgebra classes benefited from advanced placement in comparison to average-achieving eighth graders from the previous year who took general math. Prealgebra students outperformed the comparison cohort group on a concepts subtest while maintaining equivalent performance on the problem-solving and computation subtests. Subsequently, the average-achieving prealgebra students enrolled in more advanced mathematics classes during high school and obtained higher grades in these classes. Moreover, the presence of average achievers in prealgebra classes did not lower the performance of higher-achieving students in these classes.

Comprehensive Intervention in a High School

Efforts to change low expectations for student performance can go beyond altering the practices of one teacher (e.g., how students are assigned to reading groups) or a few teachers (e.g., the criteria math teachers set for entry into prealgebra classes) to include an entire school. For example, Weinstein et al. (1991) reported positive findings from a comprehensive intervention program designed to raise expectations for student achievement. This quasi-experimental field study involved collaboration between university researchers and teachers and administrators at an urban high school. The cooperating teachers attended university classes that focused on ways in which teachers can inadvertently maintain low expectations, and on the special motivational problems of low-achieving students. Teachers and researchers collaborated to develop a program for preventing and remediating low expectations.

This program has had some notable positive effects. For example, teachers were able to implement program procedures designed to increase communication of positive expectations to low achievers. Project teachers' expectations for students, as well as their attitudes toward colleague teachers, became more positive. Project teachers also expanded their roles and worked to change school tracking practices. Positive changes were also evident for the 158 project students. In contrast to 154 comparison students, project students had improved grades, fewer disciplinary referrals postintervention, and increased retention in school a year later.

AVOIDING NEGATIVE EXPECTATION EFFECTS

How can teachers avoid having negative expectation effects, and perhaps have positive expectation effects, on their students? Some authors have suggested that teachers should avoid forming any expectations at all: Refuse to discuss students with their previous teachers and ignore cumulative records and test information. We reject this suggestion, for two reasons.

First, expectations cannot be suppressed or avoided. We remember experiences that make an impression on us. When events occur repeatedly, they become seen as expected and normal. Thus, teachers will form expectations simply from interacting with students, even if they try to avoid other sources of information (Jones, 1990). Second, whether other sources of information are examined is not as important as *how information is used*. Information about students will create expectations, but if the information is accurate it can be useful in planning individualized instruction to meet students' specific needs.

Other authors have suggested that teachers should have only highly positive expectations. This idea is superficially appealing, because confidence and determination are important teacher qualities, and a "can do" attitude helps cut problems down to a workable size. However, positive expectations should not be carried to the point of distorting reality. Students show large individual differences in learning abilities and interests, and these cannot be eliminated through wishful thinking. Teachers will only frustrate both themselves and their students if they set unrealistically high standards that students cannot reach.

Expectations should be *appropriate* given students' current capabilities, and they should be followed by appropriate instructional behavior; that is, planned learning experiences that move students through the curriculum at a pace that fosters continued success and improvement. The pace will necessarily vary for different students. As long as students are working up to their potential and progressing steadily, a teacher has reason to be satisfied.

Regular patterns of student behavior will build up strong expectations in all teachers, including those who try to deny or suppress them. Inevitably, some of these expectations will be pessimistic. However, teachers can avoid undesirable self-fulfilling prophecy effects if they remain alert to the formation of, and changes in, their expectations, and if they monitor their behavior to see that negative expectations are not communicated. To the extent that such expectations do exist, they should take the "Dean Helpful" form in which the teacher combines expressions of concern with behavior designed to remediate difficulties. Thinking that a student needs help is bad only if the teacher does not provide that help in a positive, supportive way.

In Developing Expectations, Consider Students' Full Range of Abilities

Students' scores on intelligence and achievement tests provide useful, but only partial, information about students' abilities. Along with the abilities emphasized in these tests, students possess other forms of intellectual aptitude that they can bring to bear as learning resources if the forms of curriculum and instruction in use in the classroom allow them to do so. For example, Howard Gardner (1983, 1991) argued that people possess at least seven types of intellectual abilities in varying degrees:

Linguistic: Sensitivity to the meaning and order of words and ability to make varied use of language; exhibited by translators and poets.

Logical-mathematical: Ability to handle chains of reasoning and recognize patterns; exhibited by mathematicians and scientists.

Spatial: Ability to perceive the visual world accurately and re-create or transform its aspects based on those perceptions; exhibited by sculptors and architects.

Musical: Sensitivity to pitch, melody, rhythm, and tone; exhibited by composers and singers.

Bodily-kinesthetic: Ability to use the body and handle objects skillfully; exhibited by athletes, dancers, and surgeons.

Interpersonal: Ability to notice and make distinctions among other people; exhibited by politicians, salespeople, and religious leaders.

Intrapersonal: Ability to understand one's own feelings and emotional life; exhibited by therapists and social workers.

Gardner noted that the curriculum content and especially the tests traditionally emphasized in schooling have focused on linguistic and logical-mathematical abilities to the relative neglect of the others. He advocated better rounded curricula and more use of project learning methods that would allow students to develop their complete range of abilities and bring them to bear as learning resources.

We mention his ideas here because they also serve as a reminder that the traditional emphasis on linguistic and logical-mathematical abilities can condition teachers to restrict themselves to these areas when developing expectations about the performance of their students. A narrow focus on these abilities, especially when they are expressed in a single score such as an IQ score or an achievement-level stanine score, can lead to rigid stereotyping of students. Thus, in getting to know one's students and beginning to develop expectations about them, it is important to pay attention to their full ranges of abilities and to view these abilities not as limiting factors but as resources that students will both develop and use as they participate in classroom activities.

Keeping Expectations Flexible and Current

Expectations based on recurring classroom events can be very compelling. If Susan frequently fails to do homework assignments, her teacher may gradually stop trying to change Susan's work habits and begin to accept her poor performance as "what is to be expected." To avoid falling into this rut, teachers need to keep their expectations flexible and bear in mind their role as instructors. If expectations are allowed to become too strong or too fixed, they can distort perception and behavior. Teachers may notice only those behaviors that fit their expectations and as a result may deviate from good teaching practice.

Once formed, expectations tend to be self-perpetuating because they guide both perceptions and behavior. When we expect to find something, we are much more likely to see it than when we are not looking for it. For example, most people do not notice counterfeit money or slight irregularities in clothing patterns. However, treasury department officials and inspectors for clothing manufacturers will notice them. Hidden abilities and aptitudes also may not be noticed except by those who are on the lookout for them. This is part of the reason why teachers often fail to notice the strengths of students who are frequent discipline problems. When expecting misbehavior, teachers may miss many of these students' academic accomplishments that someone else might have noticed and reinforced.

Expectations not only cause us to notice some things and fail to notice others, they also affect the way we *interpret* what we do notice. The optimist, for example, perceives a glass as half full, whereas the pessimist sees it as half empty. Mistaken beliefs about other people can be difficult to correct because of their tendency to influence how we interpret what we see. Consider a teacher who asks a difficult question and then calls on Johnny, an intelligent and well-motivated student. Johnny remains silent, pursing his lips and knitting his brow. The teacher knows that Johnny is working out the problem, so he patiently gives him more time. Finally, Johnny responds with a question, "Would you repeat that last part again?" The teacher is happy to do so, because this indicates that Johnny has partially solved the problem and may be able to do it by himself with a little more time. The teacher repeats and then waits eagerly, but patiently, for Johnny to respond again. If someone interrupted the teacher at this point to ask what he was doing, he might respond that he was "challenging the class to use creativity and logical thinking to solve problems."

Suppose, however, that the teacher had called on Sammy instead. Sammy is a low achiever, and the teacher does not think Sammy is very motivated, either. When called on, Sammy remains silent, although the teacher notes his pursed lips and furrowed brow. This probably means that Sammy is hopelessly lost, although it may mean that he is merely acting, trying to give the impression that he is thinking about the problem. After a few seconds, the teachers says, "Well, Sammy?" Now Sammy responds, but with a question instead of an answer: "Would you repeat that last part again?" This confirms the teacher's suspicions, making it clear that any more time spent with Sammy on this question would be wasted. After admonishing Sammy to listen more carefully, the teacher calls on someone else. If interrupted at this point and asked what he was doing, the teacher might say that he was "making it clear that the class is expected to pay close attention to the discussion, so that they can respond intelligently when questioned."

In this example, the teacher's expectations for the two students caused him to draw inferences from their behavior different from those a more neutral observer would have drawn. Although the behavior of the two boys was the same and they made the same response to the initial question, the teacher interpreted the behavior quite differently by reading initial meaning into it. His interpretations about the two boys may have been correct, but we (and he) cannot tell for certain because he did not verify them. Instead, he acted as if his interpretations were observable facts, so that his treatment of Sammy may have been unjustified.

The fact that a student could not do something yesterday does not mean that he or she cannot do it today, but the teacher will not find out unless the student is given a chance. Expectations stress the stable, unchanging aspects of the world. Teachers, however, are change agents trying to make students different from what they are today. Therefore, teachers must keep their expectations in perspective. To the extent that expectations are negative, they represent problems to be solved, not definitions of reality to which a teacher must adapt.

Emphasizing the Positive

The implication of all this seems to be that teachers should form and project expectations that are as positive as they can be while still remaining realistic. Such expectations should represent genuine beliefs about what can be achieved and therefore should be taken seriously as goals toward which to work in instructing students. Brophy (1983) suggested that teachers might accomplish this through several steps, including the following:

1. Keep expectations for individual students current by monitoring their progress closely; stress present performance over past history.
2. Set goals for the class and for individuals in terms of floors (minimally acceptable standards), not ceilings. Let group progress rates, rather than limits adopted arbitrarily in advance, determine how far the class can go within the time available.
3. When individualizing instruction and giving students feedback, stress their continuous progress relative to previous levels of mastery rather than how they compare with other students or with standardized test norms.
4. In responding to student performance, do not evaluate only success or failure. In addition, provide students with feedback or additional instruction they will need to meet the objectives.
5. When students have not understood an explanation or demonstration, diagnose their learning difficulty and follow through by reteaching in a different way rather than merely repeating the same instruction or giving up in frustration.
6. In general, think in terms of stretching the students' minds by stimulating them and encouraging them to achieve as much as they can, not in terms of "protecting" them from failure or embarrassment.

SUMMARY

In this chapter, we have shown how teachers' attitudes and expectations about different students can lead them to treat the students differently, sometimes to the extent of producing self-fulfilling prophecy effects. A particular danger is that low expectations combined with an attitude of futility will be communicated to certain students, leading to erosion of their confidence and motivation for school learning. This will confirm or deepen their sense of hopelessness and cause them to fail when they could have succeeded under different circumstances.

Expectations tend to be self-sustaining. They affect both *perception*, by causing teachers to be alert for what they expect and less likely to notice what they do not expect, and *interpretation*, by causing teachers to interpret (and perhaps distort) what they see so that it is consistent with their expectations. In this way, some expectations can persist even though they are not justified.

Research on teacher expectancies in the classroom was a rich and exciting area in the 1970s and 1980s, and many useful constructs have been derived from this work. Although the importance of teacher expectation effects has sometimes been overstated, it is clear that these effects are important, especially when considered with other teaching abilities (Anderson & Burns, 1989; McCaslin & Good, 1992) and other general variables (e.g., home-school correspondence; see McCaslin & Murdock, 1991).

Sometimes teachers give up on certain students and accept failure rather than trying to do anything further with them, and the students are blamed for their failure. This attitude psychologically frees the teacher from continuing to worry about the students' progress and from seeking more successful ways to teach them.

It is natural for teachers to form differential attitudes and expectations, because each student is an individual. To the extent that these expectations are accurate and up to date, they are helpful in planning ways to meet each student's needs. However, expectations must be monitored and evaluated to ensure that they change appropriately in response to changes in students.

Remember, teaching attitudes and expectations can be your allies and tools if properly maintained and used. However, if accepted unquestioningly and allowed to solidify, they can become defense mechanisms that lead you to ignore or explain away problems rather than solve them. Therefore, learn to control your attitudes and expectations—don't let them control you!

SUGGESTED ACTIVITIES AND QUESTIONS

1. How do teachers determine at what pace to teach content and for what level of understanding to hold students accountable? How do teachers make such decisions if they work in a high school that is very different from the high school they attended? How do elementary school teachers develop appropriate expectations for student performance when they do their observational work in a first-grade class, perhaps student teach in a third-grade class, and eventually accept their first job teaching in a sixth-grade class? Try to interview two teachers from the level at which you intend to teach, and determine how they developed expectations for class performance. If teachers are not available, arrange interviews with three or four classmates and discuss for a given academic subject (e.g., third-grade math or American history) and a particular topic how you would decide about what concepts to emphasize and the type of understanding students should demonstrate. What are the major differences in the way individuals approach these important decisions?

2. Which students in your preservice teacher education courses (or teachers at your school) are the brightest? What behavioral evidence and information have you used to form your opinions? How accurate do you think your estimates are?

3. Reread the example that appears at the beginning of the chapter. How appropriate were Mr. Peeler's expectations? Why? Can teachers' expectations be too high as well as too low?

4. Do you think that teachers tend to underestimate or overestimate the learning potential of the following: loud, aggressive males; quiet passive males; loud, aggressive females; quiet, passive females; students who are neat and follow directions carefully; students with speech impediments; and students who complain that schoolwork is uninteresting? Why might teachers over- or underestimate the ability of these student types?

5. Analyze your own attitudes about classroom learning. As a student, did you find school assignments enjoyable? If so, why? Was it just because you did well, or for other reasons? What reasons? When learning was unrewarding, was it due to particular teachers or subjects?

6. What are ways in which teachers might inadvertently support the stereotyping of students by projecting classroom messages like "Asian students always do well in math"?

7. Write an original example of a self-fulfilling prophecy, based on something that happened to you, a relative, or a classmate. Include each of these three steps: an original expectation, behaviors that consistently communicated this expectation, and evidence that the expectation was confirmed.

8. Role-play the beginnings and endings of lessons. (You be the teacher and let classmates play students at a specific grade level.) Try to communicate appropriate expectations.

9. How can a teacher's overemphasis on praise of right answers interfere with student learning?

10. How might you as a beginning teacher guard against accepting indiscriminately the expectations of other teachers in your school?

11. How might teachers communicate high or low performance expectations to new teachers in their school?

12. How might the school principal communicate high and low expectations to teachers in a school?

13. Why do the authors stress that expectations should be appropriate rather than necessarily positive and that they must be followed up with appropriate behavior?

14. How do teachers form their expectations about students?

15. Explain in your own words why expectations, once formed, tend to be self-perpetuating.

16. How might a teacher's use of homework and seatwork assignments communicate low expectations to students?

17. Select some of the forms in the following Appendix designed to measure behaviors that communicate teacher expectations, and use them to rate actual or videotaped teaching segments.

REFERENCES

Allington, R. (1991). Children who find learning to read difficult: School responses to diversity. In E. Hiebert (Ed.), *Literacy for a diverse society* (pp. 237–252). New York: Teachers College Press.

Anderson, L., & Burns, R. (1989). *Research in classrooms: The study of teachers, teaching, and instruction.* Oxford: Pergamon Press.

Ashton, P., & Webb, R. (1986). *Making a difference: Teachers' sense of efficacy and student achievement.* New York: Longman.

Babad, E. (1985). Some correlates of teachers' expectancy bias. *American Educational Research Journal, 22,* 175–183.

Beez, W. (1968). Influence of biased psychological reports on teacher behavior and pupil performance. *Proceedings of the 76th Annual Convention of the American Psychological Association, 3,* 605–606.

Bognar, C. (1982). Dissonant feedback about achievement and teachers' expectations. *Alberta Journal of Educational Research, 28,* 277–287.

Borko, H., Shavelson, R., & Stern, P. (1981). Teachers' decisions in the planning of reading instruction. *Reading Research Quarterly, 16,* 449–466.

Brattesani, K., Weinstein, R., & Marshall, H. (1984). Student perceptions of differential teacher treatment as moderators of teacher expectation effects. *Journal of Educational Psychology, 76,* 236–247.

Brookover, W., Beady, C., Flood, P., Schweitzer, J., & Wisenbaker, J. (1979). *School social systems and student achievement: Schools can make a difference.* New York: Bergin.

Brophy, J. (1983). Research on the self-fulfilling prophecy and teacher expectations. *Journal of Educational Psychology, 75,* 631–661.

Brophy, J. (1985). Teachers' expectations, motives, and goals for working with problem students. In C. Ames & R. Ames (Eds.), *Research on motivation in education, Vol. II: The classroom milieu.* Orlando, FL: Academic Press.

Brophy, J., & Evertson, C. (1976). *Learning from teaching: A developmental perspective.* Boston: Allyn and Bacon.

Brophy, J., & Good, T. (1970). Teachers' communication of differential expectations for childrens' classroom performance: Some behavioral data. *Journal of Educational Psychology, 61,* 365–374.

Brophy, J., & Good, T. (1974). *Teacher-student relationships: Causes and consequences.* New York: Holt, Rinehart and Winston.

Brophy, J., Rohrkemper, M., Rashid, H., & Goldberger, M. (1983). Relationships between teachers' presentations of classroom tasks and students' engagement in those tasks. *Journal of Educational Psychology, 75,* 544–552.

Carlsen, W. (1991). Subject-matter knowledge and science teaching: A pragmatic perspective. In J. Brophy (Ed.), *Advances in research on teaching* (Vol. 2, pp. 115–144). Greenwich, CT: JAI Press.

Clifton, R., Perry, R., Parsonson, K., & Hryniuk, S. (1986). Effects of ethnicity and sex on teachers' expectations of junior high school students. *Sociology of Education, 59,* 58–67.

Coladarci, T. (1986). Accuracy of teacher judgments of student responses to standardized test items. *Journal of Educational Psychology, 78,* 141–146.

Cooper, H. (1985). Models of teacher expectation communication. In J. Dusek (Ed.), *Teacher expectancies.* Hillsdale, NJ: Erlbaum.

Cooper, H., & Good, T. (1983). *Pygmalion grows up: Studies in the expectation communication process.* New York: Longman.

Darley, J., & Fazio, R. (1980). Expectancy confirmation processes arising in the social interaction sequence. *American Psychologist, 35,* 867–881.

Eccles, J., & Wigfield, A. (1985). Teacher expectations and student motivation. In J. Dusek (Ed.), *Teacher expectancies.* Hillsdale, NJ: Erlbaum.

Eden, D., & Shani, A. (1982). Pygmalion goes to bootcamp: Expectancy, leadership, and trainee performance. *Journal of Applied Psychology, 67,* 194–199.

Eder, D. (1981). Ability grouping as a self-fulfilling prophecy: A micro-analysis of teacher-student interaction. *Sociology of Education, 54,* 151–161.

Evertson, C. (1982). Differences in instructional activities in higher- and lower-achieving junior high English and math classes. *Elementary School Journal, 82,* 329–350.

Fetterman, N. (1990). *The meaning of success and failure: A look at the social instructional environments of four elementary school classrooms.* Unpublished doctoral dissertation, Bryn Mawr College, Bryn Mawr, PA.

Fleming, E., & Anttonen, R. (1971). Teacher expectancy or My Fair Lady. *American Educational Research Journal, 8,* 214–252.

Freeman, D., & Porter, A. (1989). Do textbooks dictate the content of mathematics instruction in elementary schools? *American Educational Research Journal, 26,* 403–421.

Gamoran, A., & Berends, M. (1987). The effects of stratification in secondary schools: Synthesis of survey and ethnographic research. *Review of Educational Research, 57,* 415–435.

Gardner, H. (1983). *Frames of mind: The theory of multiple intelligences.* New York: Basic Books.

Gardner, H. (1991). *The unschooled mind: How children think and how schools should teach.* New York: Basic Books.

Goldenberg, C. (1992). The limits of expectations: A case for case knowledge about teacher expectancy effects. *American Educational Research Journal, 29,* 517–544.

Good, T. (1981). Teacher expectations and student perceptions: A decade of research. *Educational Leadership, 38,* 415–423.

Good, T. (1993). Teacher expectations. In L. Anderson (Ed.), *International encyclopedia of education* (2nd ed.). Oxford: Pergamon.

Good, T., & Marshall, S. (1984). Do students learn more in heterogeneous or homogeneous achievement groups? In P. Peterson, L. Cherry-Wilkinson, & M. Hallinan (Eds.), *The social context of instruction: Group organization and group processes.* Orlando, FL: Academic Press.

Good, T., Slavings, R., Harel, K., & Emerson, H. (1987). Student passivity: A study of student question-asking in K–12 classrooms. *Sociology of Education, 60,* 181–199.

Good, T., & Weinstein, R. (1986). Teacher expectations: A framework for exploring classrooms. In K. K. Zumwalt (Ed.), *Improving teaching.* (The 1986 ASCD Yearbook.) Alexandria, VA: Association for Supervision and Curriculum Development.

Graham, S. (1984). Teacher feelings and student thoughts: An attributional approach to affect in the classroom. *Elementary School Journal, 85,* 91–104.

Hauserman, N., Miller, J., & Bond, R. (1983). A behavioral approach to changing self-concept in elementary school children. *Psychological Record, 26,* 111–116.

Heath, S. (1983). *Ways with words.* New York: Cambridge University Press.

Helmke, A., & Schrader, F. (1987). Interactional effects of instructional quality and teacher judgement accuracy on achievement. *Teaching and Teacher Education, 3,* 91–98.

Jones, E. (1986). Interpreting interpersonal behavior: The effects of expectancies. *Science, 234,* 41–46.

Jones, E. (1990). *Interpersonal perception.* New York: W. H. Freeman.

Jussim, L. (1986). Self-fulfilling prophecies: A theoretical and integrative review. *Psychological Review, 93,* 429–445.

Jussim, L. (1989). Teacher expectations: Self-fulfilling prophecies, perceptual biases, and accuracy. *Journal of Personality and Social Psychology, 57,* 469–480.

Jussim, L. (1990). Social reality and social problems: The role of expectancies. *Journal of Social Issues, 46*(2), 9–34.

Langer, E., & Benevento, A. (1978). Self-induced dependence. *Journal of Personality and Social Psychology, 36,* 886–893.

Mason, E. (1973). Teachers' observations and expectations of boys and girls as influenced by biased psychological reports and knowledge of the effects of bias. *Journal of Educational Psychology, 65,* 238–243.

Mason, D., Schroeter, D., Combs, R., & Washington, K. (1992). Assigning average-achieving eighth graders to advanced mathematics classes in an urban junior high. *Elementary School Journal, 92,* 587–599.

McCaslin, M., & Good, T. (1992). Compliant cognition: The misalliance of management and instructional goals in current school reform. *Educational Research, 21,* 4–17.

McCaslin, M., & Murdock, T. (1991). The emergent interaction of home and school in the development of students' adaptive learning. In M. Maehr & P. Pintrich (Eds.), *Advances in motivation and achievement* (Vol. 7, pp. 213–260). Greenwich, CT: JAI Press.

Merton, R. (1948). The self-fulfilling prophecy. *Antioch Review, 8,* 193–210.

Midgley, C., Feldlaufer, H., & Eccles, J. (1989). Change in teacher efficacy and student self- and task-related beliefs in mathematics during the transition to junior high school. *Journal of Educational Psychology, 81,* 247–258.

Miller, D., & Turnbull, W. (1986). Expectancies and interpersonal processes. In M. Rosenzweig & L. Porter (Eds.), *Annual Review of Psychology* (Vol. 37, pp. 233–256). Palo Alto, CA: Annual Reviews, Inc.

Newman, R. (1990). Children's help seeking in the classroom: The role of motivational factors and attitudes. *Journal of Educational Psychology, 82,* 71–80.

Newman, R., & Goldin, L. (1990). Children's reluctance to seek help with school work. *Journal of Educational Psychology, 82,* 92–100.

Oakes, J. (1985). *Keeping track: How schools structure inequality.* New Haven: Yale University Press.

Oakes, J., Quartz, K., Gong, J., Guiton, G., & Lipton, M. (1993). Creating middle schools: Technical, normative, and political considerations. *Elementary School Journal, 93,* 461–480.

Palardy, J. (1969). What teachers believe—what children achieve. *Elementary School Journal, 69,* 370–374.

Persell, C. (1977). *Education and inequality: The roots and results of stratification in American schools.* New York: Free Press.

Raudenbush, S. (1984). Magnitude of teacher expectancy effects on pupil IQ as a function of the credibility of expectancy induction: A synthesis of findings from 18 experiments. *Journal of Educational Psychology, 76,* 85–97.

Riggs, J., Monach, E., Ogburn, T., & Pahides, S. (1983). Inducing self-perceptions: The role of social interaction. *Personality and Social Psychology Bulletin, 9,* 253–260.

Rosenbaum, J. (1976). *Making inequality.* New York: Wiley-Interscience.

Rosenholtz, S. (1989). *Teachers' work place: The social organization of schools.* New York: Longman.

Rosenholtz, S., & Simpson, C. (1984). Classroom organization and student stratification. *Elementary School Journal, 85,* 21–37.

Rosenthal, R. (1974). *On the social psychology of the self-fulfilling prophecy: Further evidence for Pygmalion effects and their mediating mechanisms.* New York: MSS Modular Publications.

Rosenthal, R., & Jacobson, L. (1968). *Pygmalion in the classroom: Teacher expectation and pupils' intellectual development.* New York: Holt, Rinehart and Winston.

Rosenthal, R., & Rubin, D. (1978). Interpersonal expectancy effects: The first 345 studies. *The Behavioral and Brain Sciences, 3,* 377–386.

Schrank, W. (1968). The labeling effect of ability grouping. *Journal of Educational Research, 62,* 51–52.

Schrank, W. (1970). A further study of the labeling effect of ability grouping. *Journal of Educational Research, 63,* 358–360.

Short, G. (1985). Teacher expectation and West Indian underachievement. *Educational Research, 27,* 95–101.

Simon, B., & Willcocks, J. (Eds.). (1981). *Research and practice in the primary classroom.* London: Routledge and Kegan Paul.

Smith, M. (1980). Meta-analysis of research on teacher expectation. *Evaluation in Education, 4,* 53–55.

Stevenson, H., & Stigler, J. (1992). *The learning gap.* New York: Summit Books.

Toner, I., Moore, L., Emmons, B. (1980). The effect of being labeled on subsequent self-control in children. *Child Development, 51,* 618–621.

Trujillo, C. (1986). A comparative examination of classroom interactions between professors and minority and non-minority college students. *American Educational Research Journal, 23,* 629–642.

Weinstein, R. (1976). Reading group membership in first grade: Teacher behaviors and pupil experience over time. *Journal of Educational Psychology, 68,* 103–116.

Weinstein, R., Marshall, H., Sharp, L., & Botkin, M. (1987). Pygmalion and the student: Age and classroom differences in children's awareness of teacher expectations. *Child Development, 58,* 1079–1093.

Weinstein, R., Soulé, C., Collins, F., Cone, J., Mehorn, M., & Simontacchi, K. (1991). Expectations and high school change: Teacher-researcher collaboration to prevent school failure. *American Journal of Community Psychology, 19,* 333–364.

Wineburg, S. (1987). The self-fulfillment of the self-fulfilling prophecy. *Educational Researcher, 16*(9), 28–44.

APPENDIX

Observation forms are presented here for measuring teacher behavior related to the basic teacher attitudes and expectations discussed in the chapter. Each form has a numbered title, a definition of the classroom situations in which it should be used, and a description of its purpose. Although all the forms possess these common properties, they differ from one another in several ways. Some are confined to strictly behavioral categories and require simple counting of observed events; others require the coder to make inferences or judgments and score the teacher on more global rating scales. Also, some call for only a single coding for a single event; others involve coding several items of information about series of events that occur in sequences.

Skilled coders can use many of the observation forms during a single observation, so long as they do not attempt to code two things at the same time. At the beginning, however, it is best to start with one or two forms while you acquire basic observation and coding skills.

The observation forms define the applicable classroom situation and then list several alternative ways in which the teacher could respond in the situation. The different teacher behaviors listed are most often mutually exclusive, but sometimes more than one could occur in a given situation. To use the observation forms correctly, you must be able to (1) recognize when relevant situations are occurring that call for use of the form, (2) accurately observe the teacher's handling of the situation, and (3) accurately record this information on the form. If the teacher shows more than one codable behavior in the situation, simply number the different behaviors consecutively. This method will preserve not only the information about different techniques that were used but also the sequence in which they were used.

USING CODING SHEETS

An example (Figure 3.1) of how the coding sheet would be used and how the information recorded on it can be recovered later is presented on page 122. This example includes the form used for teacher behavior when introducing lessons or activities or making assignments (Form 3.1). This form is used to measure the teacher's motivation attempt (if any) as opposed to specificity or completeness in presenting the assignment (the latter is covered on a different form).

On this form, the observer would note carefully what attempt the teacher made to build up interest or *motivate* the students to work carefully on the lesson or assignment; this information is numbered by categories, and these numbers are used to record the behavior in the coding columns.

In the example, the coding sheet shows that three such instances were observed by the coder (the coding sheet has room for 50 instances). Note that the first code entered is a 4, which indicates that the teacher began a lesson or gave an assignment with no attempt at all to motivate or build up interest. Some directions may have been given to get the group started, but no attempt was made to promote the activity ("Yesterday we finished page 53. Open your books to page 54. Mark, begin reading with the first paragraph."). The teacher also did not promise rewards or threaten punishment for good or bad performance in the activity.

The teacher's behavior the second time he or she introduced a lesson or activity is coded in the next row. Here the coder has entered both a 1 and a 3, indicating that the teacher began with a gushy buildup but later also mentioned the information or skills that would be learned in the activity.

The third row also shows a 1 followed by a 3 indicating again that the teacher introduced a lesson or activity with an excessive buildup followed by mention of the information or skills to be learned.

Although not enough instances are recorded to make interpretations with great confidence, a pattern is noticeable in the three instances coded. The teacher appears to be basi-

MOTIVATION, ATTEMPT, INTRODUCING ACTIVITIES	EVALUATIONS AFTER ACTIVITIES	INDIVIDUAL PRAISE	INDIVIDUAL CRITICISM
1. Gushy buildup	1. Praises specific progress	1. Perseverance, effort	1. Poor persistence, effort
2. Enjoyment	2. Criticizes specifically	2. Progress	2. Poor progress
3. New information, skills	3. Praises general progress	3. Success	3. Failure
4. No motivation attempt	4. Criticizes general performance	4. Good thinking	4. Faulty thinking, guessing
5. Apologizes	5. Ambiguous praise	5. Imagination, originality	5. Triteness
6. Promises reward	6. Ambiguous criticism	6. Neatness, care	6. Sloppiness, carelessness
7. Warns of test	7. Praises good behavior	7. Obedience, attention	7. Breaks rules, inattentive
8. Threatens to punish	8. Criticizes misbehavior	8. Prosocial behavior	8. Antisocial behavior
9. Gives as punishment	9. No group evaluation	9. Other (specify)	9. Other (specify)
10. Other (specify)	10. Other (specify)		

CODES		CODES		STUDENT NUMBERS AND CODES		STUDENT NUMBERS AND CODES	
_4_ 1.	— 26.	_5_ 1.	— 26.	_14_ 1. 3	— 26.	_16_ 1. 3	— 26.
_4,3_ 2.	— 27.	_5_ 2.	— 27.	_23_ 2. 3,4	— 27.	_21_ 2. 3	— 27.
_4,3_ 3.	— 28.	— 3.	— 28.	_6_ 3. 3	— 28.	_5_ 3. 3,4	— 28.
— 4.	— 29.	_9_ 4.	— 29.	_18_ 4. 3	— 29.	_12_ 4. 3	— 29.
— 5.	— 30.	— 5.	— 30.	— 5.	— 30.	— 5.	— 30.
— 6.	— 31.	— 6.	— 31.	— 6.	— 31.	— 6.	— 31.
— 7.	— 32.	— 7.	— 32.	— 7.	— 32.	— 7.	— 32.
— 8.	— 33.	— 8.	— 33.	— 8.	— 33.	— 8.	— 33.
— 9.	— 34.	— 9.	— 34.	— 9.	— 34.	— 9.	— 34.
— 10.	— 35.	— 10.	— 35.	— 10.	— 35.	— 10.	— 35.
— 11.	— 36.	— 11.	— 36.	— 11.	— 36.	— 11.	— 36.
— 12.	— 37.	— 12.	— 37.	— 12.	— 37.	— 12.	— 37.
— 13.	— 38.	— 13.	— 38.	— 13.	— 38.	— 13.	— 38.
— 14.	— 39.	— 14.	— 39.	— 14.	— 39.	— 14.	— 39.
— 15.	— 40.	— 15.	— 40.	— 15.	— 40.	— 15.	— 40.
— 16.	— 41.	— 16.	— 41.	— 16.	— 41.	— 16.	— 41.
— 17.	— 42.	— 17.	— 42.	— 17.	— 42.	— 17.	— 42.
— 18.	— 43.	— 18.	— 43.	— 18.	— 43.	— 18.	— 43.
— 19.	— 44.	— 19.	— 44.	— 19.	— 44.	— 19.	— 44.
— 20.	— 45.	— 20.	— 45.	— 20.	— 45.	— 20.	— 45.
— 21.	— 46.	— 21.	— 46.	— 21.	— 46.	— 21.	— 46.
— 22.	— 47.	— 22.	— 47.	— 22.	— 47.	— 22.	— 47.
— 23.	— 48.	— 23.	— 48.	— 23.	— 48.	— 23.	— 48.
— 24.	— 49.	— 24.	— 49.	— 24.	— 49.	— 24.	— 49.
— 25.	— 50.	— 25.	— 50.	— 25.	— 50.	— 25.	— 50.

Figure 3.1 Sample coding sheet combining four observation forms.

cally positive in the presentation of lessons and activities. No negative motivation attempts (apology, threat of test, or punishment) appear. However, in attempting to provide positive motivation, the teacher may be overdoing it, in that the observer coded two instances of overdramatic buildup.

If this sequence did indeed develop as the teacher's stable pattern, some guidelines for additional questions and observations would emerge. What would be the effects of this over-dramatizing on the class? Would it tend to amuse them or cause them to lose respect for

---

FORM 3.1. Introducing Lessons, Activities, and Assignments

USE: When the teacher is introducing new activities or making assignments
PURPOSE: To see whether or not the teacher pictures school work as
worthwhile or enjoyable
Observe teacher behavior when introducing activities and making
assignments. For each codable instance observed, record the numbers
(consecutively) of each category applicable to the teacher's behavior.

BEHAVIOR CATEGORIES	CODES	
1. Gushes, gives overdramatic buildup	1. _4_	26. ___
2. Predicts that group will enjoy the activity	2. _1,3_	27. ___
3. Mentions information or skills the group will learn	3. _1,3_	28. ___
	4. ___	29. ___
4. Makes no attempt to motivate; starts right into activity	5. ___	30. ___
5. Apologizes or expresses sympathy to group ("Sorry, but you have to . . .")	6. ___	31. ___
	7. ___	32. ___
6. Bribes, promises external reward for good attention or work	8. ___	33. ___
	9. ___	34. ___
7. Warns group, or reminds them, about test to be given later	10. ___	35. ___
8. Threatens punishment for poor attention or work	11. ___	36. ___
9. Presents the activity itself as a penalty or punishment	12. ___	37. ___
	13. ___	38. ___
10. Other (specify)	14. ___	39. ___
	15. ___	40. ___
	16. ___	41. ___
NOTES:	17. ___	42. ___
	18. ___	43. ___
	19. ___	44. ___
	20. ___	45. ___
	21. ___	46. ___
	22. ___	47. ___
	23. ___	48. ___
	24. ___	49. ___
	25. ___	50. ___

---

the teacher? Would it train them to begin to complain or suspect unenjoyable activities if the teacher failed to give the coming activity a big buildup? If there was evidence that the teacher's overacting was having these kinds of effects on the class, he or she might be advised to tone down the motivation attempts. If there appeared to be no adverse effects on the class, it might be advisable for the teacher to continue the present style of motivating the class and instead work on changing problem behaviors that appear to have negative consequences.

The observation forms here, as well as all of the forms following subsequent chapters, will be partially filled in to show how they look after being used in the classroom. However, we will no longer add our interpretations of the data shown on these sample coding sheets. Studying the partially filled-in coding sheets will help you quickly grasp what is involved in using each observation form. In addition, it will provide a basis for practicing interpretation

FORM 3.2. Evaluations After Lessons and Activities

USE: *When teacher ends a lesson or group activity*
PURPOSE: *To see whether the teacher stresses learning or compliance in making evaluations*
        When the teacher ends a lesson or group activity, code any summary evaluations he or she makes about the group's performance during the activity.

BEHAVIOR CATEGORIES
1. Praises progress in specific terms; labels knowledge or skills learned
2. Criticizes performance or indicates weaknesses in specific terms
3. Praises generally good performance, for doing well or knowing answers
4. Criticizes generally poor performance (doesn't detail the specifics)
5. Ambiguous general praise ("You were very good today.")
6. Ambiguous general criticism ("You weren't very good today.")
7. Praises good attention or good behavior
8. Criticizes poor attention or misbehavior
9. No general evaluations of performance were made
10. Other (specify)

CODES

1.	5	26.	
2.	5	27.	
3.	9	28.	
4.		29.	
5.		30.	
6.		31.	
7.		32.	
8.		33.	
9.		34.	
10.		35.	
11.		36.	
12.		37.	
13.		38.	
14.		39.	
15.		40.	
16.		41.	
17.		42.	
18.		43.	
19.		44.	
20.		45.	
21.		46.	
22.		47.	
23.		48.	
24.		49.	
25.		50.	

NOTES:

Teacher uses stock phrase ("You were really good today; I'm very pleased").

#13 cut off by bell; might have praised otherwise.

1 = Homework Review

2 = Division Facts Drill

3 = Board Work

of coded data. If possible, compare your interpretations of these data with those of a friend or colleague. Discuss any disagreements in detail to discover the reasons for them and to determine what additional information (if any) would be needed to resolve the matter with confidence. Your instructor or in-service leader can help you to resolve coding difficulties.

The observation forms are divided so that each measures just one or a small number of related teacher behaviors. Thus each form is a self-contained observation instrument that can be used independently of the others. Once you have acquired some skill as a coder, however, you will want to observe several aspects of teacher behavior, using several different forms. You may find it convenient to combine several forms onto a single coding sheet. There are many ways to do this, and personal preferences and convenience are the primary criteria for deciding whether a given method is desirable. We have provided a sample coding sheet in Figure 3.1 that combines Forms 3.1, 3.2, 3.3, and 3.4.

FORM 3.3 Individual Praise

USE: *Whenever the teacher praises an individual student*
PURPOSE: *To see what behaviors the teacher reinforces through praise, and to see how the teacher's praise is distributed among the students*
Whenever the teacher praises an individual student, code the student's number and each category of teacher behavior that applies (consecutively).

BEHAVIOR CATEGORIES	STUDENT NUMBER	CODES
1. Perseverance or effort, worked long or hard	14	1. _3_
	23	2. _3,4_
2. Progress (relative to the past) toward achievement	6	3. _3_
	18	4. _3_
3. Success (right answer, high score), achievement	8	5. _1_
4. Good thinking, good suggestion, good guess or nice try	8	6. _1_
	8	7. _1_
5. Imagination, creativity, originality		8. __
6. Neatness, careful work		9. __
7. Good or compliant behavior, follows rules, pays attention		10. __
		11. __
8. Thoughtfulness, courtesy, offering to share; prosocial behavior		12. __
		13. __
9. Other (specify)		14. __
		15. __

NOTES:

All answers occurred during social studies discussion.

Was particularly concerned about #8, a low-achieving male

16. __
17. __
18. __
19. __
20. __
21. __
22. __
23. __
24. __
25. __

The four forms were compressed onto a single coding sheet by using key terms rather than the full behavior category descriptions that appear on the originals. Use and purpose descriptions are omitted entirely, since it is assumed that the coder is already familiar with the four original forms. The result is a sheet with spaces to code up to 50 instances of each of the four teacher behaviors. A coder would use this sheet until all 50 spaces were used for one of the four behaviors and then switch to a new sheet.

Figure 3.1 shows only one of many ways that these four forms could be combined onto a single coding sheet. Feel free to create coding sheets that meet your own preferences and needs. There is no single ideal coding sheet; the one that you like and that does the job is the one you should use.

Generally, all the information you need to code is on the sheet. For example, in Figure 3.1, column 1, you can see that most of the ways a teacher can motivate students when

FORM 3.4. Individual Criticism

USE: *Whenever the teacher criticizes an individual student*
PURPOSE: *To see what behaviors the teacher singles out for criticism, and to see how the teacher's criticism is distributed among the students*
    Whenever the teacher criticizes an individual student, note the student's name or number and code the behavior that is criticized.

BEHAVIOR CATEGORIES	STUDENT NUMBER	CODES
1. Lack of effort or persistence, doesn't try, gives up easily	16	1. 3
	21	2. 3
2. Poor progress (relative to expectations), could do better, falling behind	5	3. 3,4
	12	4. 3
3. Failure (can't answer, low score), lack of achievement	5	5. 1
4. Faulty thinking, wild guess, failure to think before responding		6. ___
		7. ___
5. Trite, stereotyped responses, lack of originality or imagination		8. ___
		9. ___
6. Sloppiness or carelessness		10. ___
7. Misbehaves, breaks rules, inattentive		
8. Selfish, discourteous, won't share; antisocial behavior		11. ___
		12. ___
9. Other (specify)		13. ___
		14. ___
		15. ___

NOTES:
    All answers during social studies discussion.
    Teacher sharply critical of student #5; seems irritated with her generally.

16. ___
17. ___
18. ___
19. ___
20. ___
21. ___
22. ___
23. ___
24. ___
25. ___

introducing a lesson have been summarized into nine categories; if the teacher's behavior cannot be described in one of these nine categories, use the tenth category. Occasionally, users will have to supply some information of their own. Notice scales representing Forms 3.3 and 3.4 (individual praise and individual criticism) in Figure 3.1. When individual students must be identified, as in these examples, users will have to supply their own identification codes. In the first instance, under *individual praise*, we see that student 14 received teacher praise for successful accomplishment (category 3).

Thus, depending on their coding goals, users will have to supply appropriate code numbers. For example, if you are interested in how teachers praise male and female students, respectively, then you need only use a 1 when girls are praised and a 2 when boys are praised. Obviously, in Figure 3.1 the coder is coding the entire class, because in the second instance of a teacher praising an individual student, the student's number is 23. If you are interested in coding the behavior of an entire class, simply assign each student a unique number and use this number whenever interactions involving that student are coded.

FORM 3.5. Positive Expectations Communicated to the Class

USE: At any time
PURPOSE: To document the frequency and nature of the teacher's
communication of positive expectations for the class as a whole
*   If the teacher's remarks made to the class as a whole include positive*
expectations or statements about the class, check the type of statement
made and record the statement in the space below the checklist.

_____ 1. General goodness of class (they are a fine group of students, the teacher enjoys working with them, etc.)
_____ 2. Intelligence/ability (the students are bright, alert, sharp, etc.)
_____ 3. Careful work (they work carefully on their assignments)
_____ 4. Good ideas/thoughtful (they ask good questions and make good comments about the content; write interesting essays, etc.)
_____ 5. Eager to learn (they are curious, interested in the content, eager to master skills, etc.)
_____ 6. Steady progress (they are making steady progress in mastering material and approaching long term goals)
_____ 7. Improvement (their work shows notable improvement over earlier levels).
_____ 8. Mature/responsible (they know how to act, use good judgment, can assume responsibility, live up to the teacher's confidence in them, etc.)
_____ 9. Achievement oriented (they work hard because they want to do their best)
_____ 10. Cooperative with teacher (they want to cooperate by following the teacher's and the school's rules, and in general, conducting themselves appropriately)
_____ 11. Prosocial attitudes and behavior (they are, or are striving to be, kind, considerate, and helpful in their dealings with peers and with people generally)
_____ 12. Other (indicate)

NOTES:

Chapter 4

Management I: Preventing Problems

INTRODUCTION

Classroom management is important to everyone connected with education. New teachers often fear that students will not respect them. Experienced teachers usually cite establishing management as a major goal in the first few weeks of the year. Principals give low ratings to teachers who lack control of their classes.

Classroom Vignettes

Teachers constantly have to ask questions and make decisions about management (Brophy & McCaslin, 1992; Kauffman et al., 1993). Consider the following three vignettes that illustrate these decisions. As you read each vignette, think about how you would respond as a teacher.

Jan Thorton, who teaches physics at Riverside High School, has become concerned that students are not reading basic assignments before laboratory work. Hence, students are doing the experiments but not really understanding the work they do. She decides to start giving pop quizzes over assigned readings. Is this a good idea? What does this action convey to students?

Bill Reid, a sixth-grade teacher at Truman Middle School, gives students at least 30 minutes of uninterrupted seatwork each day. He expects students to work alone, and he is largely unavailable for assistance because he grades papers during this time. He believes that after a 15- to 20-minute lecture-discussion, students should be able to work independently and that this practice builds self-reliance. What are possible advantages and disadvantages of this "management" of instruction?

José Cruz is a ninth-grade English teacher at St. John High School. He likes to write the names of students on the board when they misbehave. He believes this is a good strategy because as soon as he writes a name on the board, the "named" student settles down and other students in the class seem less disturbed than when he speaks aloud to a misbehaving student. After all, students know the consequences if their name goes on the board twice; thus, Mr. Cruz finds this a very efficient management system. How would you describe the possible advantages and disadvantages of this management technique?

Management Research

Until recently, advice to teachers about classroom management was based mostly on untested theory or unsystematic individual testimonials about "what works best for me." Much of it was contradictory and very little was based on solid evidence. During the past 20 years, however, research on classroom management has yielded a knowledge base that offers a coherent set of principles to guide teachers in making decisions about how to manage their classrooms (Brophy, 1983, 1988; Doyle, 1986; Emmer & Aussiker, 1990; Evertson & Harris, 1992; Gettinger, 1988; McCaslin & Good, 1992). The findings converge on the conclusion that teachers who approach classroom management as a process of establishing and maintaining effective learning environments tend to be more successful than teachers who place more emphasis on their roles as authority figures or disciplinarians. Teachers *are* authority figures and will need to require their students to conform to certain rules and procedures. However, these rules and procedures are not ends in themselves but means for organizing the classroom as an environment that supports teaching and learning. Thus, classroom management should be designed to support instruction.

It is important to recognize that most classroom management research has been conducted in elementary and junior high school settings (Doyle, 1992; Evertson & Harris, 1992). Thus, care must be exercised in applying the findings to high school situations. Also, little classroom management work has been done in classrooms that are characterized by high levels of gang activity, drug use, or violence; thus, it is not clear to what extent research that has been conducted in "regular" classrooms can be applied to classrooms where the problems of order are the most serious. However, with these important qualifications in mind, the research on classroom management is a rich and valuable literature providing general principles and guidelines that teachers can adapt to local conditions.

Student Role

Teachers' expectations about appropriate student activities and behavior can be called the *student role*. Unfortunately, popular notions of the student role usually include elements such as regimentation of activity, restriction of movement, and subordination of individual desires to the personal authority of the teacher and the less personal but often restrictive school and classroom rules (Doyle, 1986). This is a reminder that although rules help provide for orderly and reasonably satisfactory group functioning within the school setting, they do so at a price. Much behavior that is considered natural and appropriate elsewhere, such as boisterous talk or play, is forbidden in the classroom, and certain forms of peer cooperation or helping are considered cheating.

These considerations suggest the value of a cost/benefit approach to classroom management, in which proposed techniques are assessed with an eye toward what side effects they may have. This approach suggests that practices such as requiring students to remain absolutely silent at all times unless addressed by the teacher are inappropriate because they are not essential to any worthwhile goal. Other practices, such as persistently authoritarian and punitive techniques, are inappropriate because their positive effects are outweighed by their negative ones. Our recommendations on classroom management will emphasize an approach that has been shown to be effective for establishing good learning environments in classrooms, while at the same time being the least costly to the classroom atmosphere or to teacher-student relationships.

CLASSROOM EXAMPLES

To help you begin thinking about some of the key issues involved, we invite you to consider four common types of classrooms:

1. This class features chaos and uproar. The teacher continually struggles to establish control but never fully succeeds. Directions and even threats are often ignored, and punishment does not seem to be effective for long.

2. This class is also noisy, but the atmosphere is more positive. The teacher tries to make school fun by introducing lots of stories, films, games, and enrichment activities. Still, even though the teacher holds academic activities to a minimum and tries to make them as pleasant as possible, attention to lessons is spotty and seatwork often is not completed or not done carefully.

3. This class is quiet and well disciplined because the teacher has established many rules and makes sure that they are followed. Infractions are noted quickly and cut short with stern warnings or if necessary with punishment. The teacher appears to be a successful disciplinarian because the students usually obey him, although the classroom atmosphere is uneasy. Trouble is always brewing under the surface, and whenever the teacher leaves the room, the class "erupts."

4. This class seems to run by itself. The teacher spends most of her time teaching, not handling discipline problems. When working independently,

students follow instructions and complete assignments without close supervision. They often interact with one another as they do so, but the noises they produce are the harmonious sounds of productive involvement in activities, not the disruptive noises of boisterous play or disputes. When noise does become disruptive, a simple reminder from the teacher usually suffices. Observers sense warmth in the atmosphere of this class and go away positively impressed.

These contrasting types of classrooms are found in all kinds of schools, so their differences cannot be attributed entirely to the types of students involved. Furthermore, within any given school, some teachers have chronic control problems, while others regularly gain good cooperation even from students who were problems the year before. We have described four teacher prototypes. The first "can't cope," the second "bribes the students," the third "runs a tight ship," and the fourth "has cooperative students." Before reading on, take time to think about these four teachers. Assume that they each began the year with roughly equivalent groups of students. List three attitudes or behaviors for each teacher that might help explain why the classrooms have evolved along the lines described. What might be their expectations about students and assumptions about the learning process? What might their students learn from observing them as models?

MANAGEMENT AS MOTIVATION AND PROBLEM PREVENTION

The purpose of the previous exercise was to help you focus on the teacher's role in shaping the learning environment. The classroom learning environment develops gradually, in response to the teacher's communication of expectations, modeling of behavior, and approach to classroom management. The same class that is interested and attentive with one teacher can be bored or rebellious with another.

The most important determinant is the teacher's method of classroom management, especially his or her techniques for keeping the class actively engaged in lessons and productively involved in independent or small-group activities. This is why the chapter title refers to management rather than to discipline or control. The latter terms have a connotation that we wish to avoid: the idea that managing students is mostly a matter of handling their misbehavior successfully. Until recently, classroom management was equated with classroom discipline and considerable emphasis was placed on what to do *after* students misbehaved. However, we now know that the key to good management is use of techniques that elicit student cooperation and involvement in activities and thus *prevent* problems from emerging in the first place.

Kounin's (1970) Study

This phenomenon was shown originally by Kounin (1970), who studied teachers using interviews, on-the-spot note taking, and the coding of videotapes. Kounin observed in classrooms to develop information about relationships between teacher behavior and student behavior. Surprisingly, he found that the teachers' methods of responding to discipline problems were unrelated to the frequency and seriousness of such problems in their classes. That is, the teachers who minimized discipline problems did not differ from those who had frequent and serious discipline problems, *on measures of teacher response to student misbehavior.*

The teachers did differ in other ways, however. In particular, the effective managers minimized the frequency with which students became disruptive in the first place by maximizing the time that students spent profitably involved in academic activities and by resolving incidents of minor inattention before they developed into major disruptions. The following were keys to their success:

"Withitness"   Effective managers monitored their classrooms regularly. They positioned themselves so that they could see all students and they continuously scanned the room to keep track of what was going on, no matter what else they were doing at the time. They also let their students know that they were "with it"—aware of what was happening and likely to detect inappropriate behavior early and accurately. This enabled them to nip problems in the bud before they could escalate into serious disruptions.

Overlapping   Effective managers could do more than one thing at a time when necessary. When teaching reading groups, for example, they responded to students from outside the group who came to ask questions, but at times and in ways that did not disrupt ongoing group activities. When circulating to check on seatwork progress, they conferred with individuals but still kept an eye on the rest of the class. In general, they handled routine housekeeping tasks and met individual students' needs without disrupting the ongoing activities of the class as a whole.

Signal Continuity and Momentum in Lessons   Effective managers were well prepared and thus able to teach smooth lessons that provided students with a continuous "signal" to attend to. They seldom had to interrupt the flow in order to consult the manual to see what to do next or to obtain a prop that should have been prepared earlier, and they seldom confused the students with false starts or backtracking to present information that should have been presented earlier. They ignored minor, fleeting inattention but dealt with sustained inattention before it escalated into disruption, using methods that were not themselves disruptive (moved near inattentive students, used eye contact when possible, etc). They realized that when teachers deliver extended reprimands or otherwise overreact to minor inattention, they lose the "momentum" of the lesson and break the "signal continuity" that provides focus for student attention.

Variety and Challenge in Seatwork   Students often worked independently rather than under the direct supervision of the teacher. To help ensure that their students remained continuously engaged in productive activities during these times, the effective managers provided the students with tasks that were both (1) familiar and easy enough for them to do successfully and yet (2) challenging and varied enough to sustain motivation.

Other Studies

Subsequent work by other investigators confirms that these teacher behaviors are keys to successful classroom management (Doyle, 1986) and also shows that they are associated with student learning gains (Brophy & Good, 1986). Furthermore, other researchers have elaborated on Kounin's findings by showing how successful managers establish an effective learning environment at the beginning of the year and then maintain it thereafter.

In summary, research has established that the key to successful classroom management is a proactive approach that features clarity in communicating expectations. Three characteristics of this proactive approach are (1) it is preventive rather than just reactive; (2) it integrates management methods that encourage appropriate student conduct with instructional methods that encourage student achievement of curricular objectives; and (3) it focuses on managing the class as a group, not just on the behavior of individual students (Gettinger, 1988).

ESSENTIAL TEACHER ATTITUDES

Certain key teacher attitudes must be present if these general principles of classroom management are to succeed. *The attitudes and principles to be described complement one another to form a systematic approach. Attempts to use parts of this system as isolated techniques will not succeed.*

Certain attitudes and personal qualities are basic to successful management because they make the teacher someone whom students will respect and want to please, not merely obey. First, teachers must like their students and respect them as individuals. They need not be demonstratively affectionate; enjoyment of students and concern for their individual welfare will come through in tone of voice, facial expressions, and other everyday behavior.

Teachers should make an effort to get to know students individually. Students who like and respect their teachers will want to please them and will be more likely to imitate their behavior and adopt their attitudes. They also will be more likely to sympathize when the teachers are challenged or defied, instead of allying with the defiant students.

Teachers must also establish credibility early in the school year and then maintain it thereafter. Because many students have experienced discrepancies between what adults preach and what they practice, such students will doubt or even discount what a new teacher tells them. Credibility is established largely by making sure that words and actions coincide and by pointing this out to the class when necessary. With some students, this may mean discussing the subject directly and pointing to the record: "George, you've got to understand that I mean what I say. I'm not playing games or talking just to hear myself talk. Think—have I misled you or made a promise that I didn't keep? . . . Well, try to remember that. It's frustrating for me to know that you always think I'm trying to put something over on you. Maybe other people have let you down in the past, but I'm not them, and you've got to remember that. I try to give you and everyone else in the class a fair deal, and in return I expect all of you to respect me and trust me. If I ever do anything to let you down, let me know about it right away so that we can straighten it out."

Credibility provides structure that students want and need. If they can depend on what teachers say, they will be less likely to test teachers constantly and more able to accept responsibility for their own behavior. When teachers establish fair rules and enforce them consistently, rule breakers can get angry only at themselves. However, if teachers make empty threats or enforce rules inconsistently, rule breakers who are punished will likely feel picked on.

Appropriate expectations are also involved in establishing credibility. Students tend to conform not so much to what teachers say as to what they actually expect. If students learn that "No talking over there" really means "Keep the noise down to a tolerable level," they will respond to the second message, not the first. This would be all right, except that sometimes the teacher really means "No talking." At these times, the students will react in the usual way, and misunderstanding and resentment may result.

To avoid this, teachers must think through what they really expect from their students and then ensure that their own behavior is consistent with those expectations. Such self-monitoring will help eliminate empty, overgeneralized, or inconsistent statements. Observers can be helpful here, since teachers are often unaware of inappropriate expectations. Teachers who bribe students to learn provide one example. They think of school-related tasks as unrewarding drudgery and do not expect students to enjoy them. Their students soon learn to wince, sigh, or protest at the mention of assignments, which further reinforces the teacher's expectations and bribery behaviors. In general, to establish groundwork for successful classroom management, teachers must (1) earn the respect and affection of the students; (2) be consistent and, therefore, credible and dependable; (3) assume responsibility for seeing that their students learn; and (4) value and enjoy learning and expect the students to do so, too.

GENERAL MANAGEMENT PRINCIPLES

If teachers have these personal qualities, what specific steps can they take to establish good classroom management? We begin with several general principles of classroom organization, all of which are based on the following assumptions.

1. Students are likely to follow rules that they understand and accept.
2. Discipline problems are minimized when students are regularly engaged in meaningful activities geared to their interests and aptitudes.
3. Therefore, management should be approached with an eye toward establishing a productive learning environment, rather than from a negative viewpoint stressing control of misbehavior.
4. The teacher's goal is to develop inner self-control in students, not merely to exert control over them.

Plan Rules and Procedures in Advance

Effective classroom management begins with advanced planning, in which the teacher thinks through the intended curriculum and its implications about the kind of learning environment that will be needed to support it. Advanced planning should attend to both rules and procedures. *Rules* define general expectations or standards for classroom conduct. Useful general rules include "be in your seat and ready to work when the bell rings" and "listen carefully when others speak." Usually, four or five general rules, suited to the grade level and the instructional goals, are sufficient.

Procedures are methods for accomplishing daily routines and other specific activities that recur frequently in classrooms (Emmer, 1987). Teachers need to think about the different *activities* that they plan to use and the procedures that would be appropriate for implementing them: (1) whole-class presentations, recitations, and discussions; (2) teacher-led small groups; (3) independent small-group or project work; (4) individual seatwork; (5) transitions between activities and into and out of the room; and (6) room and equipment use. In addition, procedures need to be planned for *the handling of academic work:* (1) communication of assignments and related work requirements; (2) handling of makeup work and other procedures related to student absences; (3) monitoring of student progress on and completion of assignments, and assisting students who encounter difficulty with these assignments; (4) feedback to students about their progress and procedures for dealing with students who fail to complete work; and (5) grading procedures and related record keeping.

Similarly, Evertson (1987) suggested that procedures are needed for the following *activities:* (1) room use (teacher's desk and storage areas, students' desks and storage areas, wastebasket, lavatories, learning centers or stations); (2) transitions in and out of the room; (3) group work (student movement to the group setting, expected behavior in and out of the group); and (4) teacher-led instruction and seatwork (obtaining help, out-of-seat procedures, talk among students, and what to do after seatwork is completed). Evertson also identified the need for procedures concerning the following aspects of *managing student work:* (1) communicating assignments and work requirements (posting of assignments, accepting incomplete or late work, arranging for makeup work and assistance to absentees, grading procedures); (2) monitoring progress and completion of assignments (what forms of monitoring and checking to use, what records to keep, how to monitor special projects or lengthy assignments); (3) feedback to students (grading procedures that are consistent with the school's policies; what you will do if a student stops doing assignments; how you will communicate with parents; where you might display student work; what work records, if any, students will be expected to keep); and (4) the grading system (what components it will have, the weight or percentage for each component, how to organize the grade book, policies concerning extra credit assignments). The more carefully that teachers have thought out their preferred rules and procedures, the more prepared they will be to explain them clearly to students and to be consistent in ensuring their implementation.

Establish Clear Rules and Procedures Where Needed

Certain aspects of classroom management are part of the daily routine (e.g., use of the toilets and drinking fountains, access to paper and other supplies, use of special equipment, behavior during periods of independent work).

In these or other situations where procedural rules are required, they should be explicit, and the rationales for them should be explained. Explanation is especially important at the beginning of the year and with students in kindergarten or first grade, who are new to school. Some will never have used or even seen pencil sharpeners or certain audiovisual or arts and crafts equipment, so that verbal explanation alone may not be enough. A *demonstration* followed by the *opportunity to practice* the use and care of such equipment may be needed. Demonstrations and practice are less necessary with older students, but still are important for introducing new responsibilities (such as the use and care of laboratory equipment). Older students will need thorough discussion of rules and procedures, however. Each new grade adds experiences that they have not been through before. More importantly, last year's teacher may have demanded behavior that differs from what this year's teacher wants, especially on the matter of what things the students must seek permission to do and what may be done without permission.

Behavioral rules should be kept to a minimum and stated clearly with convincing rationales. They should be presented to the class as means, not ends in themselves. For example, the rationale underlying rules about behavior during seatwork times might stress that students should not disrupt concurrent group lessons or work by other students on assignments. The range of activities that students who finish seatwork can engage in without disturbing others needs to be explained. An overgeneralized rule such as "When you finish your seatwork you will remain quiet and not talk to anyone or leave your seats for any reason," would not be justifiable. This is much more restrictive than it should be and will cause more problems than it solves. Instead, the teacher should stress the basic goal of avoiding disturbances to students involved in lessons or seatwork and then list examples of acceptable and unacceptable behavior.

When rules or procedures are no longer needed or no longer do the job they were meant to do, they should be modified or dropped. Teachers should explain the reasons for any such changes, not just announce them. Sometimes, it may be worthwhile to explain the problem and invite students to suggest solutions. In summary, good management involves establishing clear rules and procedures where these are needed, reviewing them periodically and changing or dropping them when appropriate, and involving students actively in this process.

Let Students Assume Responsibility

There is no reason for teachers to do what students can do for themselves. With proper planning and instruction, even the youngest students can assume many responsibilities (e.g., pass out supplies, carry chairs, and form orderly lines). Older students can also work independently or in small groups, check their own work, and edit one another's paragraphs and short essays. Teachers who unnecessarily do these things themselves or control them by calling on students one by one only create delays, lose time that could have been spent teaching, and retard students' development of independent responsibility.

Teachers will sometimes say, "I tried to get them to do it themselves, but they couldn't." Often students only need a demonstration lesson or an opportunity to practice the behavior. Time spent giving such explanations and patience in responding to slowness and mistakes early in the year pay great dividends later.

Some teachers adopt overly rigid rules on the grounds that they are needed ("If I put out supplementary books, they'll steal them," "If I allow them to work in groups, they'll just copy from one another or waste time"). This attitude avoids the problem rather than solving it, and it communicates negative expectations by treating students as if they were infants or criminals.

Teacher/Student Cooperation

The application of classroom management research does not imply blind obedience or rigid exercise of teacher authority. Certain types of activities may require a noiseless classroom (when students are reading silently for comprehension or writing essays). However, at other times an orderly classroom may be filled with movement, conversation, and noise that facilitates a productive exchange of information. Doyle (1992) put it this way: "Cooperation in the complex action systems of classrooms is elicited and jointly constructed by teachers and students rather than imposed or coerced by the teacher. Teachers play their part in achieving and sustaining order by introducing, monitoring, and guiding classroom action systems that organize students for accomplishing curriculum tasks" (p. 3). Students in return do their part by applying their talents to school tasks when students feel that teachers are fair and that tasks are appropriate. Teachers can help to develop cooperative relations with students by deleting unneeded rules, encouraging students to take more responsibility, and allowing students to voice concerns.

Minimize Disruptions and Delays

Management problems start and spread more easily when students are idle or distracted by disruptions than when everyone is involved in productive activity. Teachers can do many things to minimize delays, disruptions, and distractions.

One is avoid creating situations in which students must idly wait for something, with no clear focus for their attention. Delays frequently result when there is high demand for something that is in short supply, as when the entire class must use paste from a single jar or get laboratory supplies from a single container or shelf. Much time can be saved by storing items in several containers and by breaking the class into subgroups or appointing assistants to help instead of lining up the entire class to do something at one time.

The time needed for distributing supplies can be reduced by having one student from each row pass things out. Items should be stored low enough for students to reach them and arranged neatly for easy identification and replacement. They also should be stored as close as possible to where they will be used. Store frequently used items where they can be taken out and returned most conveniently. Items that are used rarely or at a different time of the year can be stored in the harder-to-reach areas.

The room should be arranged to promote smooth traffic flow. Heavily used traffic lanes should not be obstructed. Traffic lanes should be wide enough for students to move freely without bumping into furniture or one another.

In junior high and high school, complicated diagrams, maps, or mathematical computations should be prepared on the chalkboard or overhead before class begins or distributed on mimeographed sheets rather than constructed during class. Similarly, many science experiments and other demonstrations can be partially prepared ahead of time when the preparations themselves do not need to be demonstrated (unless it is important for the teacher to model the motions involved).

Bear in mind that when students must wait with nothing to do, four things can happen, and three of them are bad: (1) students may remain interested and attentive; (2) they may become bored or fatigued, losing the ability to concentrate; (3) they may become distracted or start daydreaming; or (4) they may actively misbehave. Therefore, plan room arrangement, equipment storage, preparation of lessons, and transitions between activities to avoid needless delays and confusion.

Plan Independent Activities as Well as Organized Lessons

Disruptions often originate with students who are not working on their assignments or who have finished and have nothing else to do. Teachers who fail to provide worthwhile assignments or to have backup plans prepared for times when seatwork is completed more quickly than anticipated have more management problems than their better-prepared colleagues (Kounin, 1970).

Seatwork is (or should be) a basic part of the curriculum, not merely a time filler. It should provide students with opportunities to practice what they are learning or to apply it in solving problems. Therefore, teachers should plan seatwork as carefully as they plan their lessons, make its importance clear to students when assigning it, and then follow up by monitoring progress and providing additional instruction to students who do not understand. Students must be held accountable for careful work on the assignment if it is to have its desired effects.

In addition to being specific about expected work on assignments, teachers should provide clear expectations about what students should do when they finish. This may involve additional specific assignments, or there may be a range of optional activities to select from. In any case, students should know what options are available if they finish seatwork early. Nor should students have to interrupt their seatwork frequently to get help. Teachers often give students tasks that are too difficult for them (Fisher et al., 1980). This not only impedes their learning progress but also invites management problems, especially when the teacher is trying to teach a small group while the rest of the students work independently. To work independently, students must understand what to do and be able to do it with little or no help. Teachers can accomplish this by assigning seatwork that is appropriate in the first place and by making sure that the students understand the directions before "turning them loose" to work independently.

Similarly, teachers must not assign students work that is too easy. Work that is too easy not only may lead to boredom or misbehavior by the more talented students, it also fails to provide less talented students with opportunities to overcome initial failure and to develop skills of adaptive problem solving (Rohrkemper & Corno, 1988).

Assignments should be written on the board or available in some other place so that students who are not sure about what to do can check for themselves rather than interrupt the teacher. There should also be clear procedures for students to follow when they know what to do but not how to do it. Different teachers will prefer different procedures, but whatever procedure is adopted should be made clear to the students.

Even when the teacher circulates around the room during seatwork times, disruptions are likely if students must wait for long periods before the teacher gets to them. Sometimes (when everyone seems to need help) the problem is overly difficult work or poor directions. At other times, problems occur because the teacher becomes absorbed with individual students to the point of neglecting the rest of the class. In addition to monitoring continuously and showing "withitness" at these times, teachers need to perfect the art of keeping themselves in circulation and available to give immediate help to students who need it. Interactions with individuals normally should be brief. The teacher should provide them with enough guidance to sustain their work on the assignment but should not necessarily cover everything they eventually will need to know (the teacher can return again after the student does the next set of problems). When many students seem to have the same question or misconception, it is probably worthwhile to briefly clarify the problem to the class as a whole. Otherwise, it is usually best to provide private help to those who need it while allowing the rest of the students to work on the assignment without interruption.

In summary, students must be provided with appropriate independent activities during times when the teacher is busy with small-group instruction. Students should know what their assignments are, what to do if they need help, and what they can or should do when they finish. These activities will provide a basis for responsible self-guidance and will minimize problems resulting from boredom, idleness, or confusion about what to do.

MANAGEMENT OF SMALL-GROUP LEARNING

Although we will say more about the management of small-group instructional settings when we discuss small group instruction and learning later in the text, we want to point out that we believe the general principles of managing small groups are similar to those already described. However, we should acknowledge that managing small groups (e.g., seven groups of 4) is typically more difficult than managing one class of 28 or two groups of 14. A critical difference is that the teacher can interact with only a small portion of the class at a given moment. Thus, the design of curriculum tasks and their appropriateness for given groups of students become critical factors. Tasks must engage group members in ways that are appropriate both for learning (task is meaningful and challenging to all students) and for student self-management (students can handle minor disagreements, students know how to get help when needed).

Obviously teachers can help to make group work more meaningful by explaining the task and allowing students to actively discuss its purpose and related procedures before moving into small groups. Students also may need to role-play or receive direct instruction in various aspects (what cooperation means, how to handle conflict, helping versus giving answers without explaining, etc.).

Monitoring groups is difficult because the teacher can observe only one group at a time. Thus, it is possible that in some groups one or two students will do all the work or that some students will engage in undesirable social behavior. Accordingly, teachers will have to devise monitoring procedures that are appropriate for their context (i.e., the age and ability of their students, their instructional goals, etc.). Individual students need to be held accountable for their work in small groups (e.g., through class discussion following group work, performance exams, etc.).

When all students are working in small, cooperative groups, groups should know what to do when they finish the task first. Some researchers have found that one of the frequent management problems associated with small groups is finding teacher time for involvement with all groups (Good et al., 1989–1990).

Some groups will finish before others, so teachers need clear procedures for how students can productively turn to other tasks while they wait for their classmates to finish. Teachers will also need to socialize students against the norm of quick work (as students see other groups finish, they may hurry their work) (Good et al., 1989–1990). Thus, although the basic management tasks are similar in large-group and small-group settings, there are special issues that teachers will need to address in small groups (Dunne & Bennett, 1990; Weinstein & Mignano, 1993). This issue will vary with the type of small-group format being used, the instructional goal, and the age of students. However, one unique need of the small-group setting is to learn to respect diverse responses and perspectives and use them constructively.

GETTING THE SCHOOL YEAR OFF TO A GOOD START

In a series of studies conducted at both elementary and secondary schools, Evertson, Emmer, and their colleagues developed detailed information about how teachers who varied in classroom management effectiveness handled the first day and the first few weeks of the school year. They took detailed notes about what rules and procedures the teachers introduced, how they did so, and how they followed up when it became necessary to use the procedures or enforce the rules. They also scanned the room every 15 minutes to record the percentage of students who were attentive to lessons or engaged in other teacher-approved activities. They then analyzed the data for relationships between teacher management behaviors and student engagement rates that would provide clues to how the more effective managers accomplished their goals.

Third-Grade Study

The first study (Emmer, Evertson, & Anderson, 1980) was conducted in 28 third-grade classrooms. The study showed that the seemingly automatic, smooth functioning of the classrooms of successful managers resulted from thorough preparation and organization at the beginning of the year. Room arrangement, materials storage, and other physical factors were prepared in advance, and teachers spent much time introducing rules and procedures in the early weeks. On the first day and throughout the first week, they gave special attention to matters of greatest concern to the students (information about the teacher and their classmates, review of the daily schedule, procedures for lunch and recess, where to put personal materials, when and where to get a drink). Procedures and routines were introduced gradually as needed so as not to overload the students with too much information at one time.

Effective managers not only described what they expected, but also modeled correct procedures, took time to answer questions, and, if necessary, arranged for the students to practice the procedures and get feedback. In short, key procedures were formally taught to students, just as academic content is taught.

Although they focused more on instruction than on "control," effective managers were thorough in following up on their expectations. They reminded students about procedures shortly before they were to carry them out, and they scheduled additional instruction and practice when students did not carry out procedures properly. Consequences of appropriate and inappropriate behavior were clear in their classrooms and sanctions were applied consistently. Inappropriate behavior was stopped quickly. In general, the effective managers showed three major clusters of behavior.

Conveying Purposefulness   Students were held accountable for completing work on time (after being taught to pace themselves by using the clock, if necessary). Regular times were scheduled each day to review independent work. Completed papers were returned to students promptly, with feedback. In general, effective managers tried to maximize use of the available time for instruction and to see that their students learned the curriculum (not just that they remained quiet).

Teaching Students Appropriate Conduct   Effective managers were clear about what they expected and what they would not tolerate. They focused on what students should be doing and taught them how to do it when necessary. This included not only conduct and housekeeping guidelines, but also learning-related behaviors such as how to read and follow directions for assignments. When students failed to follow procedures properly, the teachers stressed specific corrective feedback rather than criticism or threat of punishment.

Maintaining Students' Attention   Effective managers continuously monitored students for signs of confusion or inattention and were sensitive to their concerns. Seating was arranged so students could easily face the point in the room where they most often needed to focus attention. Variations in voice, movement, or pacing were used to refocus attention during lessons. Activities had clear beginnings and endings, with efficient transitions in between. The active attention of all students was required when important information was given.

Effective managers followed up this intensive activity in the early weeks by consistently maintaining their expectations. They no longer needed to devote much time to procedural instruction and practice, but they continued to give reminders and occasional remedial instruction, and they remained consistent in enforcing their rules.

Junior High Study

A related study of junior high school teachers (Evertson & Emmer, 1982a) revealed similar findings, as well as a few differences. Junior high teachers did not need to spend as much time teaching their students how to follow rules and procedures, but they did have to communicate expectations concerning student responsibility for engaging in and completing work assignments. Evertson and Emmer (1982b) listed the following as characteristic of effective managers at the junior high school level.

Instructing Students in Rules and Procedures   All teachers had rules and procedures, but the effective managers described their rules more completely and installed their procedures more systematically. They were notably more explicit about desirable behavior (the dos, not just the don'ts).

Monitoring Student Compliance with Rules   The better managers monitored compliance more consistently, intervened to correct inappropriate behavior more consistently, and were more likely to mention the rules or describe desirable behavior when giving feedback at these times.

Communicating Information   The better managers were clearer in presenting information, giving directions, and stating objectives. They broke down complex tasks into step-by-step procedures.

Organizing Instruction   Effective managers wasted little time getting organized or accomplishing transitions between activities, and they maximized student attention and task engagement during activities by maintaining signal continuity and momentum in lessons, overlapping their own activities, and using the other techniques identified by Kounin (1970).

Subsequent Studies

Subsequent work by Evertson, Emmer, and their colleagues involved training teachers in effective classroom management techniques. This work showed that teachers could learn these techniques and thereby decrease classroom disruptions and increase student engagement in academic activities, without undermining classroom climate. Teacher training was accomplished using manuals that summarized research findings about effective classroom management and provided examples, checklists, and step-by-step instructions about how to implement recommended procedures. For reports of the research findings, see Evertson (1985) and Evertson et al. (1983). For classroom management guidelines based on this research, see Emmer et al. (1993) and Evertson et al. (1993).

Research sources are a good place for information about useful guidelines. However, as we have stressed earlier, research has to be adjusted to your context. Also, research guidelines provide only a starting point, since the goal is not to control students but help students over time to develop self-control.

Others who have studied the factors involved in getting off to a good start on the first day and in the early weeks of the school year have reached conclusions very similar to those of Evertson, Emmer, and their colleagues. The consensus is that although teachers should be friendly and personable rather than austere, they also should be businesslike in visibly taking charge and establishing the desired classroom atmosphere and learning environment (Brooks, 1985; Doyle, 1986; Evertson, 1987; Moskowitz & Hayman, 1976; Smith, 1985). It helps to install basic everyday lesson and work routines quickly, but to do so using relatively simple formats and tasks that students are likely to be able to accomplish successfully. Once students become accustomed to everyday routines and begin to follow them habitually without much special direction, the teacher can begin to phase in more challenging work and more complex formats (supplementing whole-class lesson and seatwork activities with small-group activities, special projects, learning centers).

MAINTAINING AN EFFECTIVE LEARNING ENVIRONMENT

In previous sections, we have identified basic attitudes that are essential to success in managing classrooms and have emphasized the need for proactive behavior (planning rules and procedures in advance) and presented research-based principles for getting the year off to a good start. In the next sections, we describe how teachers can build on this good start by cueing and reinforcing desirable behavior and providing any on-the-spot instructions that may be needed.

Use Positive Language to Cue Desirable Behavior

Learning is easier and more pleasant when we are shown what *to* do rather than told what *not to* do. This is why so many lessons begin with explanation or demonstration. Teachers would not think of teaching addition by naming all the sums that 2 + 2 do not equal, but they (and adults generally) often do not realize that a direct, positive approach is just as important in socializing behavior as it is in teaching school subjects. A string of "don'ts," emphasizing what students should *not* be doing, fails to develop students' understanding and may create anxiety or resentment against the teacher. Teachers should specify desirable behavior in positive terms, as in the following examples.

Positive Language

Close the door quietly.

Try to work these out on your own without help.

Quiet down—you're getting too loud.

Always dispose of used chemicals like this (demonstration).

Sit up straight.

Raise your hand if you think you know the answer.

When you finish, put the scissors in the box and bits of paper in the wastebasket.

These crayons are for you to share—use one color at a time and then put it back so others can use it too.

Use your own ideas. When you do borrow ideas from the author, be sure to acknowledge them. Even here, try to put them in your own words.

When you make your class presentation speak naturally, as you would when talking to a friend.

Note the caution statements in the instructions. Be sure to check the things mentioned there before proceeding to the next step.

Be ready to explain your answer—why you think it is correct.

Negative Language

Don't slam the door.

Don't cheat by copying from your neighbor.

Don't make so much noise.

That's not how you dispose of chemicals.

Don't yell out the answer.

Don't leave a mess.

Stop fighting over those crayons.

Don't plagiarize.

Don't just read your report to us.

Take your time when doing this experiment or you'll mess it up.

Don't just guess.

Sometimes negative statements are appropriate, as when a student is doing something that must be stopped immediately (fighting, causing a major disruption). Even here, however, negative remarks should be followed with positive statements about what to do instead. Teachers should phrase instructions in positive, specific language that indicates the desired behavior clearly.

Recognize and Reinforce Desired Behavior

Most sources of advice to teachers urge them to recognize and reinforce students' good conduct, contributions to lessons, or academic work. The idea is that students' accomplishments should be rewarded not only with high grades, but also with verbal praise, public recognition (hanging examples of good work for public display, describing accomplishments in the school newspaper), symbolic rewards (stars, happy faces, stickers), extra privileges or activity choices, or material rewards (snacks, prizes). Social learning theorists and behavior modifiers see reinforcement as essential in providing both motivation and guidance to learners: Behavior that is reinforced is likely to be repeated, but behavior that is not reinforced is likely to be extinguished. Other writers see reinforcement as desirable, if not essential, on the grounds that it helps students to appreciate their successes, develops positive self-concepts, boosts motivation, or develops a sense of accomplishment. Whatever their rationale, most writers state or at least imply that reinforcement is highly desirable and should occur regularly in classrooms.

We accept the validity of the general principle of reinforcement (behaviors that are reinforced will be retained, but those that are not reinforced will be extinguished). However, we question some of the suggestions that have been made for implementing this principle in the classroom. We believe that too much emphasis has been placed on quantity or frequency of reinforcement and not enough on quality issues and questions such as whom to reinforce, under what conditions, and with what kinds of reinforcement. We believe that teachers' attempts to reinforce are valuable under certain circumstances, but ineffectual or even counterproductive under other circumstances.

Let us begin by noting that a great deal of reinforcement of student behavior occurs simply as a natural consequence of performing that behavior. Attention to the teacher and effort on assignments typically lead to successful performance, which in turn leads to high grades and feelings of satisfaction. Succeeding in school and gaining the respect of teachers and peers are important goals to most students, so that any behaviors that students recognize as supporting progress toward those goals will be reinforced automatically. Thus the issue is not whether reinforcement should occur in the classroom, but whether (and if so, how much) the teacher should inject additional reinforcement beyond what occurs as a natural consequence of student behavior. Our position is that such additional reinforcement is not necessary, although it may be appropriate.

It is not necessary because humans possess thinking and speaking abilities that enable us to learn by observing models and by being instructed, so that, unlike lower animals, we are not dependent on shaping through reinforcement as our primary learning mechanism. Also, we respond to a great many motives (self-actualization, cognitive consistency, curiosity) in addition to, and sometimes instead of, the desire for extrinsic reinforcement. Even when reinforcement is a primary motivator, reinforcement from sources other than the teacher (winning a competition, for example, or gaining peer acceptance) may be more important than anything the teacher does. Thus, reinforcement from the teacher is only one of many factors influencing students' behavior.

Even when reinforcement from the teacher is relevant, there are limits on how much reinforcement is productive. Overly frequent reinforcement is unnecessary to sustain behavior and may become intrusive.

Another complicating factor is individual differences in students' motivational systems (Heckhausen, 1991). Eden (1975) has shown that for a given person and situation, certain motives will be relevant and others will not, so that the success of a motivational effort will depend on how well it fits with the person's present motives. In the classroom, teachers are likely to increase students' motivation to perform a desired behavior only if they deliver some *relevant* motivational consequence following performance of the behavior. If they should deliver a consequence that is irrelevant to the students' currently operating motives, there is likely to be a small *decrease* in overall motivation to continue the behavior. Thus, teachers' motivational efforts may have (slightly) negative effects when they are based on incorrect assumptions about students' motives. Teachers need to monitor their students' responses to consequences intended to be reinforcing, not just assume that all students actually experience these consequences as reinforcing.

Some educational theorists have opposed reinforcement even in principle. These writers urged teachers to capitalize and build on students' intrinsic motivation to learn, without trying to supplement it through extrinsic reinforcement (including praise). Several studies by attribution theorists supported this view to some extent (attribution theorists are concerned about what happens when we try to explain our successes or failures to ourselves—when we *attribute* our performance to causes). It has been shown that if you begin to reward people for doing what they already were doing for their own reasons, you decrease their intrinsic motivation to continue the behavior in the future (Deci & Ryan, 1985; Heckhausen, 1991; Lepper & Greene, 1978). Furthermore, to the extent that their attention becomes focused on the reward rather than the task itself, their performance tends to deteriorate (Condry & Chambers, 1978). They develop a piecework mentality, doing whatever will garner them the most rewards with the least effort, rather than trying to do the job as well as they can to create a high-quality product.

For a time, it was thought that these undesirable effects were inherent in the use of extrinsic reinforcement, including praise. More recently, it has become clear that the effects of reinforcement depend on the nature of the reinforcement used and especially on how it is presented. Decreases in performance quality and in intrinsic motivation for subsequent repetition of the behavior are most likely when reinforcement has the following characteristics:

High salience (large or highly attractive rewards, or rewards presented in ways that call attention to them)

Noncontingency (rewards are given for mere participation in activities, rather than being contingent on achieving specific performance objectives)

Unnatural/unusual (rewards are artificially tied to behaviors as control devices, rather than being natural outcomes of the behaviors)

In short, reinforcement is likely to undermine students' intrinsic motivation when it implies that their behavior is controlled externally—that they are engaging in an activity only because they must do so in order to earn a reward. Actually, this effect will occur not only with reinforcement, but also with any factor that leads students to attribute their behavior to external pressures rather than their own intrinsic motivation. Other examples include teacher reminders to students that they are under surveillance and student awareness of pressure to meet a time deadline (Lepper, 1982).

In summary, reinforcement of student behavior is likely to be effective only to the extent that the consequences intended to function as reinforcers are actually experienced as reinforcing by the student, are contingent on the achievement of specific performance objectives, and are awarded in ways that complement rather than undermine intrinsic motivation and other natural outcomes of the behavior.

PRAISING EFFECTIVELY

Praise is usually described as a form of reinforcement, although it does not always have this effect (Brophy, 1981). Sometimes teachers do not even intend their praise to be reinforcing, as when they use praise in an attempt to build a social relationship with an alienated student ("I like your new shirt, John"). Even when teachers do intend their praise to be reinforcing, some students will not perceive it that way. In particular, public praise may be more embarrassing than reinforcing to certain students, especially if it calls attention to conformity behavior rather than to some more noteworthy accomplishment. This is especially likely when teachers try to shape the behavior of onlookers by praising peers ("I like the way that Susie is sitting up straight and ready to listen"). Praise has been oversold to teachers as a form of reinforcement, partly because reinforcement in general has been oversold, but also because praise does not always function as reinforcement.

Correlations between teachers' rates of praise and their students' learning gains are not always positive and in any case are usually too low to be of practical importance (Brophy, 1981). Neither teachers nor students see teacher praise as an important or powerful reinforcer (Ware, 1978). In general, teachers' strategies for eliciting desirable student behavior in the first place are much more important than their praising such behavior after it appears. To the extent that praise is important, the key to its effectiveness lies in its quality rather than its frequency.

Effective praise calls attention to students' developing learning progress or skill mastery. It expresses appreciation for students' efforts or admiration for their accomplishments in ways that call attention to the efforts or accomplishments themselves rather than to their role in pleasing the teacher. This helps students to learn to attribute their *efforts* to their own intrinsic motivation rather than to external manipulation by the teacher, and to attribute their *successes* to their own abilities and efforts rather than to dependency on the teacher, lack of challenge in the task, or sheer luck.

Unfortunately, much teacher praise is directed more toward controlling students than toward expressing admiration for their efforts or accomplishments. Also, much teacher praise functions less as reinforcement than as an indication of teachers' expectations or attitudes. Brophy and Evertson (1981) found that teachers were credible and spontaneous when praising students whom they liked, often smiling as they spoke and praising genuine accomplishments. They praised students whom they disliked just as often, but usually without accompanying spontaneity and warmth and often with reference to appearance or behavior rather than to academic accomplishments. Dweck et al. (1978) found that teachers tended to praise boys only for objectively successful performance but sometimes praised girls for neatness, for following instructions to the letter, or for answering in proper form. Teachers sometimes even praise poor responses, especially when interacting with low achievers (Nafpaktitis, Mayer, & Butterworth, 1985; Natriello & Dornbusch, 1985).

Such praise is part of a well-intentioned attempt to encourage low achievers, but it often backfires because it undermines credibility and confuses or depresses the students, especially if they realize that they are being treated differently from their classmates. Research by Blumenfeld et al. (1982) suggests there is little point in teachers' trying to shield students from classroom realities. Younger students (in the early elementary grades) tend to think of themselves as successful as long as they complete their work successfully (regardless of what other students are doing), and older students are aware of how their performance compares to that of others, even when their teachers try to hide this. Students (especially those who are struggling) need encouragement, but they also need accurate feedback about their performance.

Praise is most likely to be effective when delivered as spontaneous, genuine reaction to student accomplishment rather than as part of a calculated attempt to manipulate the student. Other guidelines for effective praise are given below and in Table 4.1.

1. Praise simply and directly, in a natural voice, without gushing or dramatizing.
2. Praise in straightforward, declarative sentences ("I never thought of that before") instead of gushy explanations ("Wow!") or rhetorical questions. The latter are condescending and more likely to embarrass than reward.
3. Specify the particular accomplishment being praised and recognize any noteworthy effort, care, or perseverance ("Good! You figured it out all by yourself. I like the way you stuck with it without giving up" instead of "Good"). Call attention to new skills or evidence of progress ("I notice you've learned to use different kinds of metaphors in your compositions. They're more interesting to read now. Keep up the good work").
4. Use a variety of phrases for praising students. Overused stock phrases soon begin to sound insincere and give the impression that the teacher has not really paid much attention to the accomplishments.
5. Back verbal praise with nonverbal communication of approval. "That's good" is rewarding only when delivered with a smile and a tone that communicates appreciation or warmth.
6. Avoid ambiguous statements (e.g., "You were really good today") that students may take as praise for compliance rather than for learning. Instead,

Table 4.1 GUIDELINES FOR EFFECTIVE PRAISE

Effective praise	Ineffective praise
1. Is delivered contingently	1. Is delivered randomly or unsystematically
2. Specifies the particulars of the accomplishment	2. Is restricted to global positive reactions
3. Shows spontaneity, variety, and other signs of credibility; suggests clear attention to the student's accomplishment	3. Shows a bland uniformity that suggests a conditioned response made with minimal attention
4. Rewards attainment of specified performance criteria (which can include effort criteria, however)	4. Rewards mere participation, without consideration of performance processes or outcomes
5. Provides information to students about their competence or the value of their accomplishments	5. Provides no information at all or gives students information about their status
6. Orients students toward better appreciation of their own task-related behavior and thinking about problem solving	6. Orients students toward comparing themselves with others and thinking about competing
7. Uses student's own prior accomplishments as the context for describing present accomplishments	7. Uses the accomplishments of peers as the context for describing student's present accomplishments
8. Is given in recognition of noteworthy effort or success at difficult (for this student) tasks	8. Is given without regard to the effort expended or the meaning of the accomplishment
9. Attributes success to effort and ability, implying that similar success can be expected in the future	9. Attributes success to ability alone or to external factors such as luck or (easy) task difficulty
10. Fosters endogenous attributions (students believe that they expend effort on the task because they enjoy the task and/or want to develop task-relevant skills)	10. Fosters exogenous attributions (students believe that they expend effort on the task for external reasons—to please the teacher, win a competition or reward, etc.)
11. Focuses students' attention on their own task-relevant behavior	11. Focuses students' attention on the teacher as an external authority figure who is manipulating them
12. Fosters appreciation of, and desirable attributions about, task-relevant behavior after the process is completed	12. Intrudes into the ongoing process, distracting attention from task-relevant behavior

Source: Brophy, J. (1981). Teacher praise: A functional analysis. *Review of Educational Research, 51,* 5–32.

be specific in praising learning efforts: "I'm very pleased with your reading this morning, especially the way you read with so much expression. You made the conversation between Billy and Mr. Taylor sound very real. Keep up the good work."

7. Ordinarily, individual students should be praised privately. Public praise will embarrass some students and even may cause them problems with peers. Delivering praise during private interactions helps show the student that the praise is genuine and avoids the problem of sounding as though you are holding the student up as an example to the rest of the class.

When used appropriately, teacher attention and praise can reinforce desired behavior by helping students to know that their efforts are seen and appreciated. This is especially likely if praise is delivered in natural, genuine language that includes a description of the specific behavior being commended.

GETTING AND HOLDING ATTENTION

In this section we suggest techniques for dealing with everyday problems of minor inattention and disruption caused by boredom, fatigue, or situational distractions. We have already noted that the most successful way to minimize situational distraction is to create engaging lessons and activities that prevent it from happening. When it does occur, however, it may need to be checked before it becomes more serious. This is accomplished mostly with "low profile" techniques that minimize disruptions to ongoing activities.

Focus Attention When Beginning Lessons

Teachers should establish that they expect each student's full attention to lessons. First, they should have everyone's attention before beginning lessons. Some teachers fail to do this, or even deliberately start the lesson in a loud voice in an attempt to get students to pay attention. This involves talking *at* rather than *to* students, and it causes many of them to miss the beginnings of lessons. Teachers should use a standard signal that tells the class "We are now ready to begin a lesson." Routines for introducing lessons tell the students that the transition between activities is over and a new activity is about to begin.

After giving the signal, teachers should pause briefly to allow it to take effect. Then, when they have attention, they should begin briskly, ideally by describing what will be done in an overview that will provide motivation and an attention set for learning. The pause between giving the signal and beginning the lesson should be brief, just long enough for students to focus their attention. If the pause is too long, some students will lose this sharp focus. Therefore, the teacher should act quickly if a few students do not respond. If they are looking at the teacher, expressions and gestures can be used to indicate that they should pay attention. If not, the teacher should call their names. Usually this will be enough by itself; if not, a brief focusing statement can be added ("Look here").

Keep Lessons Moving at a Good Pace

Teachers often begin with good attention but lose it by spending too much time on minor points or by causing everyone to wait while students respond repetitively, while equipment is passed out, and so forth. Attention will wander when students are waiting or when something they clearly understand is being rehashed needlessly. Review lessons are often abused in this way. If only a few students need further review, work with them individually or form them into a special group.

Monitor Attention During Lessons

Teachers should regularly scan the class or group throughout the lesson. Students are much more likely to maintain attention if they know that the teacher regularly watches everyone (both to see whether they are paying attention and to note signs of confusion or difficulty). Teachers who bury their nose in the manual, rivet their eyes on the board, or look only at the student who is speaking are asking for trouble.

Stimulate Attention Periodically

When things become too predictable and repetitive, the mind tends to wander. There are several things teachers can do to help ensure continual attention as a lesson or activity progresses. One is to provide variation. There is no need for theatrics, but lectures delivered in a dull monotone with few facial expressions or gestures soon produce yawns. Teachers should speak loudly enough for everyone to hear and should modulate their tone and volume to break monotony. It also helps to use a variety of techniques. Lectures should be mixed with questions or activities; group responses with individual responses; and reading or factual questions with thought-provoking discussion questions.

Extended presentations usually can be broken into several parts. By changing voice inflections or using transitional signals ("In summary," "The second reason . . . "), teachers can stimulate attention by cueing students that they are moving into a new phase.

Attention also can be stimulated more directly. For example, the teacher can challenge the class. "Here's a tricky question—let's see if you can figure it out," or create suspense, "So, what do you think happened next?" When the type of question changes, this can be noted in a statement that not only calls attention to the change, but also stimulates interest: "All right, you seem to know the theory, let's see if you can apply it to a practical problem."

Maintain Accountability

All students should be accountable for attending to lessons continuously, not just when they respond to questions or demonstrate. Several techniques are useful with students whose attention tends to wander. One is to develop variety and unpredictability in asking questions (Kounin, 1970), so that students learn that they may be called on at any time, regardless of what has gone on before. Teachers should occasionally question students again after they have answered an earlier question or ask them to comment about an answer just given by another student ("Paul, do you agree with Ted's answer?"). Note that these techniques are intended to challenge the class, stimulate interest, and avoid predictability, not to catch inattentive students in order to embarrass or punish them. If misused this way, they will cause resentment and probably not have the desired positive effects. Thus, teachers ordinarily should not say, "Remember, I might call on you at any time to tell me what's happening, so pay attention." It is better just to use this technique without calling attention to it, meanwhile stimulating interest in the topic and communicating expectations for attention in more positive ways as well.

Also, note the emphasis on *occasional* use of these accountability devices; they may be counterproductive if used too often or in the wrong situations. Teachers who use accountability devices moderately are more successful than those who used them either too often or not often enough. Accountability devices are essentially methods of recapturing lost attention, so that frequent use implies that the teacher is not doing enough of the fundamental things that establish and maintain good attention in the first place.

In the early grades, such accountability devices are not as important as careful monitoring, because the main problem facing teachers in these grades is helping students to be *able* to follow lessons, not making sure that they *choose* to follow them. This is accomplished through such techniques as teaching the children in small groups, having them follow with their finger or a marker, or monitoring them regularly to see that they have their place. Here, predictability is probably helpful. Brophy and Evertson (1976) and Anderson, Evertson, and Brophy (1979) found that teachers who had students read in a predictable order during reading groups got better results than those who called on students to read "randomly." This may have been because the predictable pattern provided structure that helped students follow the lesson. When students become able to keep track without help, and especially when they learn to anticipate what they will be held accountable for and practice it ahead of time, teachers will have to call on them in less predictable patterns.

Because brighter and more assertive students tend to seek response opportunities and get called on more often than reticent students, teachers should keep track of who has responded and who has not. Teachers can monitor this by tallying response opportunities in a log book (in fact, using a simple coding system, they also can keep track of students' rates of success in handling questions of varying difficulty levels).

Continuing accountability for attention also can be fostered by putting questions to the class as a whole and allowing time for thinking before calling on a student to respond. Students who know they may be called on to answer are likely to think about the question and try to form an answer if given time to do so. If the teacher names a student to answer a question before asking it, however, the rest of the class will know they are not going to be called on. This may cause some of them to turn their attention elsewhere.

Terminate Lessons That Have Gone on Too Long

When the group is having difficulty maintaining attention, it is better to end the lesson early than to continue doggedly. When lessons continue beyond the point where they should have been terminated, more of the teacher's time is spent compelling attention and less of the students' time is spent thinking about the material. Teachers usually know this but sometimes pursue lessons anyway because they do not want to get off schedule. This attitude is self-defeating, because students do not learn efficiently under these conditions and the material will probably have to be retaught. The wise teacher tailors the schedule to the needs of the students.

Teachers sometimes prolong an activity needlessly because they want to give each student a chance to participate individually. This intention is usually laudable, but when recitation becomes boringly repetitive it is time to move on to something else.

Some teachers deliberately prolong repetitive activities in order to use them as time fillers or to create opportunities for them to do paperwork. Students know that if activities are really important, teachers will participate actively and pay careful attention to what is happening. They also know an uninterested babysitter when they see one.

INDEPENDENT WORK

Typical elementary school teachers instruct small reading groups for about 20 minutes each. To create time for sustained interaction with these small groups, they must organize the class so that students not in the group being taught at the time can work productively on their own. Students in most secondary classes also spend much time working independently (e.g., writing essays, solving proofs, etc.). In this section we discuss some of the special management problems that are associated with seatwork supervision. We will focus on elementary reading, although the problems are similar (conceptually) in other grades and subjects.

Anderson, Brubaker, Alleman-Brooks and Duffy (1985) found that in most classrooms the assigned seatwork was low-level and repetitive, the directions seldom included statements about what would be learned or how the assignment related to other learning, and teachers' monitoring of progress focused on students' behavior rather than their levels of understanding or performance. When providing feedback, teachers' explanations were usually procedural (e.g., "Read the sentence and then pick the word that completes it"), with little attention to the cognitive demands of the task (i.e., strategies for selecting the appropriate word). Likewise, much teacher feedback focused on correctness of answers or neatness of work.

Low Achievers' Assignments

Anderson et al. noted that low achievers often received inappropriate assignments, did poorly on them, and derived answers by using strategies that allowed them to complete the assignments without understanding what they were supposed to be learning. One student commented as he finished his seatwork, "There! I didn't understand that, but I got it done."

In these classrooms, the teachers generally emphasized keeping busy and finishing work rather than understanding what was being taught. Anderson et al. suggested that low achievers who often work on assignments they do not understand may come to believe that schoolwork does not have to make sense, and that consequently, they do not need to obtain assistance when they do not understand it (see also the discussions of Good's Passivity Model in Chapter 3).

Criteria for Worthwhile Assignments

Osborn (1984) noted that much of what appears in workbooks is confusing or trivial. Teachers who are effective instructional managers can prevent much wasted time by carefully reviewing seatwork assignments and identifying tasks that should be skipped or substituted because they lack instructional value. We believe that successful seatwork activities have the following characteristics: (1) they allow students to work successfully and independently, (2) they are interesting and reflect variety in type of assignment and in how it is to be completed, (3) they frequently allow students to read for comprehension and pleasure, and (4) they relate the content to students' personal lives. (See Chapter 9 for more extensive guidelines for evaluating activities and assignments.)

From time to time it is necessary for teachers to work in a concentrated, sustained manner with small groups. During these times, the rest of the students will need seatwork that they can complete successfully without needing to interrupt the teacher to get help. Such seatwork does not have to be dull or mechanical, but too often it is. Many of the activities included in workbooks require only a limited level of reading and do not ask students to draw conclusions or reason about the material they read. Few workbook activities foster fluency or strategic reading (Anderson, Hiebert, Scott, & Wilkinson, 1985). Almost none require extended writing. Rather, responses usually involve filling a blank, circling or underlining a word, or selecting one of several choices. The exercises often have difficult-to-understand directions, yet drill students on skills that have little value in learning to read. Furthermore, workbook activities are often unrelated to the current reading lesson.

Classroom research consistently shows that the amount of time devoted to worksheets is unrelated to students' year-to-year gains in reading proficiency. This is not surprising, given the typically low level of these assignments. For these reasons, teachers need to either improve their worksheets and supplement them with more meaningful activities or use such materials less frequently.

Instead of always filling in worksheets, students could be assigned to read and answer questions, write an alternative ending to a story, write a story, write an ending for a story that another student started, or engage in any of a great many different language arts tasks. Similarly, instead of always working alone, students could work together on some assignments (two or more students may debate issues in a story or compare and contrast endings that they have written independently).

Assignments that students are interested in may also encourage sustained effort over a long period of time. For example, one of the authors observed a small group of fifth-grade students write and rewrite with great enthusiasm and intensity their descriptions of a baseball card during several free time periods over two weeks. Students displayed considerable imagination in their writing (e.g., detailing records of players' accomplishments with various baseball clubs) and had a chance to practice several skills (organizing and editing information) during an enjoyable activity.

At least occasionally, assignments should allow students to influence other persons or future classroom events. Third- and fourth-graders could prepare and share stories with kindergarten and first-graders in order to provide the older students with a real audience for their writing. Similarly, third- and fourth-graders will benefit from seeing or reading plays written by sixth-graders and from the chance to write letters in response (expressing thanks, seeking more information, or providing critiques). Even kindergarten students can learn from communicating with others (e.g., preparing valentines for parents or senior citizens) and gain satisfaction from doing so. Students also enjoy and become involved in activities that allow them to influence classroom events (e.g., respond to themes like, "If I could be the teacher for the day, . .").

We have discussed elementary reading and language arts as a special instance, but it is clear that seatwork management is important at all levels of schooling and in all subjects. For example, in an intensive analysis of junior high English classes, Doyle (1984) found that successful managers established an activity system early in the year and then supervised it closely, ushering it along and protecting it from intrusion or disruption. For the first three weeks, contacts with individual students during seatwork were brief as the teachers circulated the room and maintained a whole-group perspective. In response to disruptions, they tended to push the curriculum and talk about completing the assignment successfully rather than about misbehavior. Less successful managers focused attention on misbehavior by their frequent public reprimands, so that eventually all work ceased. Observations indicated that if a work system was established effectively by November, the teacher then could spend less time supervising the class and more time with individual students. By this point, the work system itself seemed to keep students productively engaged in work on assignments and the teacher was free to attend to other classroom events.

Doyle's findings illustrate that establishing a functional work system is important to overall success in managing classrooms. Bear in mind, however, that assignments are means to instructional ends, not ends in themselves. Thus, assignments are not necessarily appropriate just because they are easy for the teacher to manage. If they are to be productive, they will need to be meaningful for the students as well as functional in moving them toward instructional goals.

SELF-REGULATED MANAGEMENT

Students should assume as much responsibility for self-management as they can handle. Opportunities for self-evaluation should be provided for both academic areas (e.g., students should be encouraged to compare a composition written in September with one written in May and to make their own assessment of growth) and social areas (e.g., the chance to work collaboratively with peers in increasingly complex ways). Rules that are no longer needed should be deleted or revised in ways that recognize and value students' increasing capacity for self-evaluation (no more than one student out of the room at a time; no more than six students at the library at the same time). In many school situations, the modern curriculum emphasizing adaptive problem solving and meaningful learning is "sabotaged" by a management system that encourages student passivity and obedience (McCaslin & Good, 1992).

Students must come to take responsibility for the management system as they progress through school. They cannot learn self-regulation and self-control if the teacher does all of the alerting, accountability, and so on (McCaslin & Good, 1992). Students need to be taught to manage time (we have 15 minutes to finish a task) and to define their own work and procedures (what is the critical problem—how else might the problem be approached?). Thus, appropriate management necessitates that rules and structures—the scaffolding—be progressively altered to encourage more responsibility for self-control.

What constitutes student self-regulation, of course, varies markedly in terms of students' age, background experiences, and teachers' instructional intentions and expectations. We believe that students should be able to regulate both their instruction and their behavior to the maximum extent possible. Although younger students need much more structuring, support, and teacher guidance than do older students, the goal of classroom socialization should be to help all students become as autonomous and as adaptive as possible (McCaslin & Good, 1992).

Students should be able to maintain both a focus on learning and the intention to understand and to master material (Corno, 1992, 1993) without constant teacher monitoring or encouragement. In time, students need to learn to transform information and to make it their own rather than simply accepting someone else's words or definitions. Students must develop the capacity for integrating current instruction with previous instruction and their own life experiences (Lave & Wenger, 1992).

In the areas of classroom management and personal behavior, students should be encouraged to develop numerous dispositions and skills over time. For example, they should learn how to set goals and to delay gratification (e.g., "I'll do two drafts of the paper before seeking feedback"). Students should know how to seek resources appropriately in the classroom (when to get information and how to get it) from teachers, peers, library, and computers.

Students need to develop rudimentary self-control of learning situations (judge the amount of time it will take to complete an assignment, decide whether it is useful to do something at home or to wait for a study period the next day, etc.) and to set guidelines that help them to organize their time ("I will do at least three problems before class ends so that I can get help if I need it"). Students must also develop the capacity for self-assessment (knowing when they understand an assignment and the topic they are dealing with and when they are confused) and should be able to engage in self-reward as appropriate (recognizing when something is finished or relatively complete).

Over time, students need to learn more sophisticated strategies for intervening in their environment. Rohrkemper and Corno (1988) argued persuasively that students should be able to change themselves, change the task, or change the environment when it is appropriate to do so. For example, students should recognize inappropriate self-affect that renders them to passivity (undue thoughts about how hard the task is, how long it will take, what will happen if they do not complete the task). These researchers indicated that students should be able to change tasks to make them more interesting ("I'll see if I can do the first two in five minutes"; "I'll see if I can come up with a general rule that explains the relationship across these problem sets") or change the environment (move away from a noisy friend who is interfering with task completion).

As students become more sophisticated they should become adept at allocating their personal resources adaptively (realizing how much time to spend on a biology homework assignment and how much time to spend studying for a Spanish quiz). Students must recognize that an adaptive aspect of self-regulation is changing goals as well as maintaining them. That is, sometimes students have to decide to cut their losses and recognize when they have reached the point of diminishing returns. For example, after reviewing material three times, a fourth review is unlikely to help. Instead, getting new information or a new perspective or simply moving to a different area might be more productive.

Johnson and Johnson (1989–1990) suggest that teachers construct a T-chart on which the skill being developed is listed and then add two columns of information solicited from students indicating what the skill (e.g., participation; active listening) should look and sound like. If the teacher were developing the concept of encouraging participation, descriptors in the "looks like" column might include eye contact and smiles. The "sounds like" column would include comments such as "good idea, I never thought of that before."

SUMMARY

The key to successful classroom management is prevention—teachers do not have to deal with misbehavior that never occurs. Many problems originate when students are crowded together or forced to wait.

Classroom management and equipment storage can be planned so that traffic is minimized and needed items are accessible. Problems that occur when everyone needs the same item can be reduced by stocking several items rather than just one. Waiting can be minimized by allowing students to handle most management tasks on their own, by eliminating needless rituals and formalities, and by assigning various jobs to be done simultaneously by different subgroups. Confusion and idleness can be minimized by preparing appropriate independent work assignments in sufficient quantity and variety and by seeing that students know what to do if they finish or if they need help.

Teachers need to specify desired behavior in positive terms, provide instruction and opportunities to practice routines, offer cues or reminders when particular procedures are to be followed, and monitor students for compliance with expectations. Teaching strategies should maximize student involvement in productive activities. Teachers should establish clear signals to gain students' attention and alert them when an activity is beginning, provide a brief overview or advance organizer to help them prepare for it, and then keep the activity moving at a brisk pace, avoiding unnecessary delays. If an activity has gone on too long, it should be terminated. When it is necessary to hold students accountable for material and to stimulate their continuing attention, teachers should vary their questioning patterns and avoid falling into predictable patterns that tempt certain students to try to "beat the system." The more directive aspects of classroom management can be faded to minimal levels as students acquire the ability to manage their own learning with increasing degrees of autonomy and responsibility.

Teachers who consistently apply the strategies presented in this chapter will maximize productive student activity and minimize the time students spend "in neutral" or misbehaving. To be most effective, however, all aspects of good management must occur in combination as a system. Attempts to use certain techniques in isolation are unlikely to succeed for long.

SUGGESTED ACTIVITIES AND QUESTIONS

1. Students constantly mediate teachers' instructional statements. That is, students interpret the meaning behind the teacher's message, just as people interpret the meaning of even ordinary, everyday events (for example, is the honking of a car horn a friendly hello or a threat?). Think about some of the instructional behaviors mentioned in this chapter (e.g., accountability, alerting, etc.), Is it possible that some students might interpret teachers' alerting behaviors as nagging while other students see them as helpful hints? If you have access to a classroom, try to interview three or four different types of students and determine what they think about a particular teacher behavior (do they like reminders—why, what type?). If you do not have access to students, arrange to interview or form a discussion group with three or four classmates to see how you may view the Kounin variables discussed in the chapter differently. The interview or discussion might focus on the appropriateness of these variables in a college setting (e.g., is a predetermined set of dates for quizzes appropriate organization and good alerting or needless control?).

2. Reread the three vignettes that appear at the start of the chapter. Which of the strategies do you agree with? Why?

3. What routines and procedures might you want to establish early in the school year?

4. In one section of this chapter, we advise that requests be phrased in positive language. The examples given on page 144 are primarily elementary school examples. Write five examples of positive language that would be appropriate at the high school level.

5. Teachers sometimes conduct meaningful and worthwhile learning activities only to undermine students' intrinsic motivation by telling them such things as "You've done so well today that I am going to give you a free hour after lunch so you can do the things you really want to do." What guidelines should teachers follow when they summarize learning activities? Apply your ideas to the case study of Mrs. Turner in Chapter 1. What would be an effective way to end the lesson she presented? Write out your ending in a few sentences and compare it with the endings written by others.

6. Describe in your own words how teachers can praise appropriately. What type of student will be most difficult for *you* to praise? Why?

7. Why is it suggested that teachers show variety and unpredictability in asking questions?

8. Specify the minimum set of rules that will be observed in your room. Be sure to state them in positive terms. Are your rules essential for establishing a good learning climate? Why?

9. Why is it important to prevent classroom disruptions before they occur? What preventive steps can teachers take to reduce the number of disruptions they will face?

10. Using the criteria given in this chapter for praising effectively, describe how you should respond to these situations:
    a. The class as a whole, except for two students, does very well on a test.
    b. One of your slowest students struggles but eventually succeeds in doing a relatively easy math problem at the board, in front of the class.

c. One of your alienated underachievers does very well on a test, but you suspect cheating or lucky guessing.

d. Mary and Joe turn in perfect papers again this week, as they have all term long.

e. Randy asks a question that is relevant to the topic and indicates interest and good thinking on his part, although he would have known the answer to his question if he had read the assignment.

f. Your lowest reading group finally finishes a reader that the other groups finished weeks ago.

g. Dull, methodical Bernie turns in a composition that is trite but neat and error free. Creative but erratic Linda turns in one that contains exciting content written sloppily with many spelling errors.

11. Think about the seatwork assignments you will make. What kinds are appropriate for the subject/grade you will teach? Why?

12. In what ways can you as a teacher establish credibility with your students? Be explicit.

REFERENCES

Anderson, L., Brubaker, N., Alleman-Brooks, J., & Duffy, G. (1985). A qualitative study of seatwork in first-grade classrooms. *Elementary School Journal, 86,* 123–140.

Anderson, L., Evertson, C., & Brophy, J. (1979). An experimental study of effective teaching in first-grade reading groups. *Elementary School Journal, 79,* 193–223.

Anderson, R., Hiebert, E., Scott, J., & Wilkinson, I. (1985). *Becoming a nation of readers: The report of the Commission on Reading.* Washington, DC: National Institute of Education.

Blumenfeld, P., Pintrich, P., Meece, J., & Wessels, K. (1982). The formation and role of self-perceptions of ability in elementary classrooms. *Elementary School Journal, 82,* 401–420.

Brooks, D. (1985). The teacher's communicative competence: The first day of school. *Theory Into Practice, 24,* 63–70.

Brophy, J. (1981). Teacher praise: A functional analysis. *Review of Educational Research, 51,* 5–32.

Brophy, J. (1983). Classroom organization and management. *Elementary School Journal, 83,* 265–285.

Brophy, J. (1988). Educating teachers about managing classrooms and students. *Teaching and Teacher Education, 4,* 1–18.

Brophy, J., & Evertson, C. (1976). *Learning from teaching: A developmental perspective.* Boston: Allyn & Bacon.

Brophy, J., & Evertson, C. (1981). *Student characteristics and teaching.* New York: Longman.

Brophy, J., & Good, T. (1986). Teacher behavior and student achievement. In M. Wittrock (Ed.), *Handbook of research on teaching* (3rd ed.). New York: Macmillan.

Brophy, J., & McCaslin, M. (1992). Teachers' reports of how they perceive and cope with problem students. *Elementary School Journal, 93,* 3–68.

Condry, J., & Chambers, J. (1978). Intrinsic motivation and the process of learning. In M. Lepper & D. Greene (Eds.), *The hidden costs of reward: New perspectives on the psychology of human motivation.* Hillsdale, NJ: Erlbaum.

Corno, L. (1992). Encouraging students to take responsibility for learning and performance. *Elementary School Journal, 93*(1), 69–84.

Corno, L. (1993). The best-laid plans: Modern conceptions of volition and educational research. *Educational Researcher, 22,* 14–22.

Deci, E., & Ryan, R. (1985). *Intrinsic motivation and self-determination in human behavior.* New York: Plenum.

Doyle, W. (1984). How order is achieved in classrooms: An interim report. *Journal of Curriculum Studies, 16,* 259–277.

Doyle, W. (1986). Classroom organization and management. In M. Wittrock (Ed.), *Handbook of research on teaching* (3rd ed.). New York: Macmillan.

Doyle, W. (1992). *Research on classroom organization and management.* An invited paper prepared for OERI.

Dunne, E., & Bennett, N. (1990). *Talking and learning in groups.* London: Macmillan Education.

Dweck, C., Davidson, W., Nelson, S., & Enna, B. (1978). Sex differences in learned helplessness: II. The contingencies of evaluative feedback in the classroom, and III. An experimental analysis. *Developmental Psychology, 14,* 268–276.

Eden, D. (1975). Intrinsic and extrinsic rewards and motives: Replication and extension with Kibbutz workers. *Journal of Applied Social Psychology, 5,* 348–361.

Emmer, E. (1987). Classroom management and discipline. In V. Richardson-Koehler (Ed.), *Educators' handbook* (pp. 233–256). New York: Longman.

Emmer, E., & Aussiker, A. (1990). School and classroom discipline programs: How well do they work? In O. C. Moles (Ed.), *Student discipline strategies: Research and practice.* Albany: State University of New York Press.

Emmer, E., Evertson, C., & Anderson, L. (1980). Effective classroom management at the beginning of the school year. *Elementary School Journal, 80,* 219–231.

Emmer, E., Evertson, C., Sanford, J., Clements, B., & Worsham, M. (1993). *Classroom management for secondary teachers* (3rd ed.). Englewood Cliffs, NJ: Prentice-Hall.

Evertson, C. (1985). Training teachers in classroom management: An experimental study in secondary school classrooms. *Journal of Educational Research, 79,* 51–58.

Evertson, C. (1987). Managing classrooms: A framework for teachers. In D. Berliner & B. Rosenshine (Eds.), *Talks to teachers* (pp. 54–74). New York: Random House.

Evertson, C., & Emmer, E. (1982a). Effective management at the beginning of the school year in junior high classes. *Journal of Educational Psychology, 74,* 485–498.

Evertson, C., & Emmer, E., (1982b). Preventive classroom management. In D. Duke (Ed.), *Helping teachers manage classrooms.* Alexandria, VA: Association for Supervision and Curriculum Development.

Evertson, C., Emmer, E., Clements, B., Sanford, J., & Worsham, M. (1993). *Classroom management for elementary teachers* (3rd ed.). Englewood Cliffs, NJ: Prentice-Hall.

Evertson, C., Emmer, E., Sanford, J., & Clements, B. (1983). Improving classroom management: An experiment in elementary classrooms. *Elementary School Journal, 84*, 173–188.

Evertson, C., & Harris, A. (1992). What we know about managing classrooms. *Educational Leadership, 49*, 74–78.

Fisher, C., Berliner, D., Filby, N., Marliave, R., Cahen, L., & Dishaw, M. (1980). Teaching behaviors, academic learning time, and student achievement: An overview. In C. Denham & A. Lieberman (Eds.), *Time to learn.* Washington, DC: National Institute of Education, U.S. Department of Education.

Gettinger, M. (1988). Methods of proactive classroom management. *School Psychology Review, 17*, 227–242.

Good, T., Reys, B., Grouws, D., & Mulryan, C. (1989–1990). Using work groups in mathematics instruction. *Educational Leadership, 47*, 56–62.

Heckhausen, H. (1991). *Motivation and action.* (P. Leppman, Trans.). Berlin, Heidelberg, Germany: Springer-Verlag.

Johnson, D., & Johnson, R., (1989–1990). Social skills for successful group work. *Educational Leadership, 47*, 30–32.

Kauffman, J., Hallahan D., Mostert, M., Trent, S., & Nuttycombe, D. (1993). *Managing classroom behavior: A reflective case-based approach.* Boston: Allyn & Bacon.

Kounin, J. (1970). *Discipline and group management in classrooms.* New York: Holt, Rinehart and Winston.

Lave, J., & Wenger, E., (1992). Situated learning: Legitimate peripheral participation. New York: Cambridge University Press.

Lepper, M. (1982). Extrinsic reward and intrinsic motivation: Implications for the classroom. In J. Levine & M. Wang (Eds.), *Teacher and student perceptions: Implications for learning.* Hillsdale, NJ: Erlbaum.

Lepper, M., & Greene, D. (1978). *The hidden costs of reward: New perspectives on the psychology of human motivation.* Hillsdale, NJ: Erlbaum.

McCaslin, M., & Good, T. (1992). Compliant cognition: The misalliance of management and instructional goals in current school reform. *Educational Researcher, 21*, 4–17.

Moskowitz, G., & Hayman, J. (1976). Success strategies of inner-city teachers: A year-long study. *Journal of Educational Research, 69*, 283–289.

Nafpaktitis, M., Mayer, G., & Butterworth, T. (1985). Natural rates of teacher approval and disapproval and their relation to student behavior in intermediate school classrooms. *Journal of Educational Psychology, 77*, 362–367.

Natriello, G., & Dornbusch, S. (1985). *Teacher evaluative standards and student effort.* New York: Longman.

Osborn, J. (1984). Workbooks that accompany basal reading programs. In G. Duffy, L. Roehler, & J. Mason (Eds.), *Comprehensive instruction: Perspectives and suggestions.* New York: Longman.

Rohrkemper, M., & Corno, L. (1988). Success and failure on classroom tasks: Adaptive learning and classroom teaching. *Elementary School Journal, 88*, 299–312.

Smith, H. (1985). The marking of transitions by more and less effective teachers. *Theory Into Practice, 24,* 57–62.

Ware, B. (1978). What rewards do students want? *Phi Delta Kappan, 59,* 355–356.

Weinstein, C., & Mignano, A., Jr. (1993). *Elementary classroom management: Lessons from research and practice.* New York: McGraw-Hill.

FORM 4.1. Transitions and Group Management

USE: During organizational and transition periods before, between, and after lessons and organized activities
PURPOSE: To see if teacher manages these periods efficiently and avoids needless delays and regimentation
        How does the teacher handle early morning routines, transitions between activities, and clean-up and preparation time?

Record any information relevant to the following questions:

1. Does the teacher do things that students could do for themselves?

2. Are there delays caused because everyone must line up or wait his turn? Can these be reduced with a more efficient procedure?

3. Does the teacher give clear instructions about what to do next before breaking a group and entering a transition? *Students often aren't clear about assignment so they question her during transitions and while she is starting to teach next group.*

4. Does the teacher circulate during transitions, to handle individual needs? Does he take care of these before attempting to begin a new activity? *Mostly, problem is poor directions before transition, rather than failure to circulate here.*

5. Does the teacher signal the end of a transition and the beginning of a structured activity properly, and quickly gain everyone's attention? *Good signal but sometimes loses attention by failing to start briskly. Sometimes has 2 or 3 false starts.*

Check if applicable:

_____ 1. Transitions come too abruptly for students because teacher fails to give advance warning or finish up reminders when needed

_____ 2. The teacher insists on unnecessary rituals or formalisms that cause delays or disruptions (describe)

____✓_____ 3. Teacher is often interrupted by individuals with the same problem or request; this could be handled by establishing a general rule or procedure (describe) *See # 3 above.*

____✓_____ 4. Delays occur because frequently used materials are stored in hard to reach places *Pencil sharpener too close to reading group area, causing frequent distractions.*

_____ 5. Poor traffic patterns result in pushing, bumping, or needless noise

_____ 6. Poor seating patterns screen some students from teacher's view or cause students needless distraction

_____ 7. Delays occur while teacher prepares equipment or illustrations that should have been prepared earlier

FORM 4.2. Classroom Rules and Routine

USE: Whenever sufficient information is available
PURPOSE: *To assess the adequacy of the teacher's system of classroom*
rules and routines
Students should be clear about each of the following issues. Check
each issue that is handled adequately through classroom rules or routines,
and explain the problem when the issue is not handled adequately.

_____ 1. What books and supplies are to be brought to class routinely
_____ 2. Where to sit and store personal belongings
_____ 3. Precisely when class begins and what is expected at that
   time (in terms of attention to the teacher and advance
   preparation of materials)
_____ 4. When and for what purposes students may leave their seats
_____ 5. When and for what purposes students may converse with
   one another
_____ 6. Rules for participation in whole-class or small group lessons
   (when, if at all, it is allowable to call out responses without
   first raising one's hand and being recognized)
_____ 7. When it is permissible to approach the teacher with personal
   concerns and when the teacher should not be interrupted
   except for emergencies
_____ 8. What to do if you enter the class late or leave it early
_____ 9. Rules regarding use of equipment and learning centers
_____ 10. Procedures for distributing and collecting work or supplies
_____ 11. What forms of student cooperation in working on
   assignments are allowed or encouraged
_____ 12. Due dates for assignments and penalties for unexcused late,
   incomplete, or missing work
_____ 13. What will be taken into account in assigning grades
_____ 14. Other (sources of student confusion or managerial difficulty
   that could be eliminated by clarifying rules or procedures)

NOTES:

Chapter
5

Management II: Coping with Problems Effectively

Consistent application of the principles discussed in the previous chapter will minimize problems of inattention and misbehavior. Some such problems will occur, however, and teachers must be prepared to cope with them. The present chapter contains suggestions on how to interpret such problems, identify their causes accurately, and respond effectively. As a way to begin to think about management issues, read the vignettes that follow and consider how you would respond to each of the issues.

CLASSROOM VIGNETTES

Elementary School Example

Mr. Brandon is a fifth-grade teacher at Willow Heights Elementary School, which is located in a rich suburban school district about 10 miles from a major urban city. Students at the school are all from upper-class families, and the enrollment is 90 percent white, 8 percent Asian, and 2 percent black. Mr. Brandon has been using small cooperative groups to teach social studies twice a week for 30 minutes after lunch. He divides his 28 students into seven groups of four, and students are assigned to groups primarily on the basis of achievement.

During the small-group work period when students are discussing social studies issues, Mr. Brandon typically prepares for the science class that follows. He occasionally walks around the room to assure himself that students are still on task, and after the students have worked for about 25 minutes, he takes 5 minutes for a whole-class discussion of the issues students have been talking about in small groups.

Today, while working with a group that has a procedural problem, he inadvertently overhears the discussion taking place at a nearby table. Janis (apparently holding back tears) says, "Alice, that's a cruel thing to say! I am too mature! I've grown up a lot this year!" Alice shrugs her shoulders, and Tim says, "That's right, you have grown up a lot this year." Then Bill, Alice, and Tim exchange glances, laugh and say together, "Not!" Now Janis begins to sniffle.

If you were the teacher, what would you say or do now, if anything? What would you do or say later? How can teachers monitor discussions that take place during academic group work?

Middle School Example

Nick Rawlings is an eighth grader at Pattonville Middle School. Pattonville is a small town of about 8000 located in an agricultural area in a midwestern state. Nick is sitting in the principal's office awaiting the principal's decision about an out-of-school suspension.

The problem started three weeks ago when Nick and five other students created a disturbance during study hall. All of the students received a three-day after-school detention for their misbehavior. A week after that, a student who disliked Nick shoved him in the locker room after football practice. Nick shoved the player back, and when the coach entered the locker room, Nick and Jason Benedict were fighting. The football coach reported the players to the principal (as required by school rules), and the principal gave Nick a three-day in-school suspension (Nick comes to school but has to stay in the study hall).

After this episode, Nick became "fair game." Nick is not popular, in part because he comes from a poor family. Further, he has limited academic ability; he was retained twice—in the first and third grades. Many of his peers like to poke fun at him because of his poor academic record and his family. One area in which Nick excels is sports. He won the local Punt, Pass, and Kick Contest and represented his city in the state competition. Nick has been looking forward to playing basketball after the football season ends, but the school has a rule that a student who receives an out-of-school suspension is automatically banned from sports for the rest of the year.

For several consecutive days Nick has been needled relentlessly by three football team members who dislike him. To his credit, Nick has refrained from reacting to their comments. Finally, they go too far, and he shoves one of them, knocking him over a bench. The coach reports the episode to the principal, who, according to school rules, should give Nick an out-of-school suspension because this is Nick's fourth infraction.

Nick tries to tell his side of the story, but the principal does not want to listen. He says, "Nick, there are always reasons why one loses self-control, but there is no acceptable reason. You'll have to live with the consequences of your behavior. I don't like doing this, it probably hurts me more than it hurts you, but rules have to be enforced. I have no alternative but to give you an out-of-school suspension."

Do you agree with the principal's decision? Can school rules create unintended consequences? Can teachers and administrators enforce rules without understanding why students misbehaved? Why or why not?

Junior High School Example

Carolyn Reid is a first-year teacher at Southern Junior High, which is one of three junior highs in a city of about 50,000 located in the Southeast. The school enrolls a wide mixture of students from various socioeconomic levels, races, and ethnic backgrounds. Carolyn teaches ninth-grade science and physics. Her third-period physical science class is one of those "fated" classes in which everything that can go wrong does.

Today, there are too few lab sheets available for students, and while the teacher is rummaging through her desk to find extra lab sheets, a pair of students (students are working with lab partners) begin the experiment and inadvertently mix the wrong chemicals, causing a small fire that Ms. Reid hurriedly puts out. In the haste of putting out the fire, the bunsen burner is knocked off the table and damaged so that the two students cannot use it and must be reassigned to work with other pairs.

Five minutes later, the class is finally working productively on their assigned experiments, when Chris Vaughn throws a spitball at Kate Wood, who is sitting at an adjoining table. Kate watches the object land in front of her and smiles to herself. Chris, not satisfied with her response, says in subdued voice, "Hey, Kate, look here and give me a smile." Kate beams, and as she turns, gesturing in Chris's direction, she knocks the test tube from her lab table.

How might the teacher have prevented this situation? What should she do at this point, if anything? What should she do later?

High School Example

Judy Burden teaches an honors English course for seniors at Owensboro High School, the only high school in a town of about 20,000 located in a western state. Judy is worried about one of her students, Allen Thorton, who has been late about half the time for her first-period class and has missed six classes during the first month of school. When Allen is in class, he is cooperative but lethargic and appears haggard. His late arrivals are becoming a joke (and very disruptive). However, Allen has turned in two acceptable papers. Ms. Burden is meeting with him after class to discuss his excessive tardiness and absences. She confronts him directly: "Allen, I'm concerned about your excessive tardiness and absences. In fact, I examined school records and found that last year you were almost always in class and on time. What's going on?"

Allen (looking embarrassed and staring at the floor) says, "Everything's falling apart this semester! But your class is the only one that I've been tardy for. The only other class I've missed a lot is second period. Some mornings I just can't get out of bed and get going, but I always get here by mid-morning so I don't miss my third-period class."

Ms. Burden: "But what's the problem? Why can't you get up in the morning?" Allen: "I took a job last May at a fast-food chain, and the manager really liked me. In August I was promoted to manager. Now I'm in charge of the 9 to midnight shift. After midnight, I have to clean up, so I don't get home until 1 A.M. Also, if anything goes wrong, like some equipment is dirty or inventories aren't complete, the manager calls me at 6 A.M. complaining or asking questions. I'm trying to get it under control so it won't interfere with my schoolwork, but I really need the job. My family . . . ".

If you were Judy Burden, what would you say or do? Should the teacher talk to Allen's parents? Should schools work with businesses that employ students to develop policies that minimize conflicts between students' work and school? Should consequences be imposed for Allen's excessive absences and tardiness?

DEALING WITH MINOR INATTENTION AND MISBEHAVIOR

Techniques for dealing with minor inattention or misbehavior are designed to achieve a single goal: *eliminate the problem quickly and with minimal distraction of other students*. These techniques should be used whenever students are engaged in minor mischief and the teacher wants to refocus their attention on the lesson or activity.

Monitor the Entire Classroom Regularly

Successful classroom managers display "withitness"—their students know that they always "know what is going on" in the room (Evertson et al., 1993; Kounin, 1970). Teachers who regularly scan the room can respond to problems effectively and nip most of them in the bud. Those who fail to notice what is going on are prone to such errors as failing to intervene until a problem becomes disruptive or spreads to other students, attending to a minor problem while failing to notice a more serious one, or rebuking a student who was drawn into a dispute instead of the one who started it. Teachers who regularly make such errors convince students that the teachers do not know what is happening. This will make the students more likely to misbehave and also to test teachers by talking back or trying to confuse them.

Most disruptions begin when one student "starts something" while the teacher's back is turned. Once one student becomes inattentive, it is likely that at least some of the others will too (Felmlee, Eder, & Tsui, 1985). Thus, it is important for teachers to monitor their classrooms regularly, even while conducting small-group lessons, writing on the board, or talking with individual students.

Ignore Minor, Fleeting Misbehavior

Teachers should not intervene every time they notice a problem, because such intervention may be more disruptive than the problem itself. For minor misbehavior, it is better to delay action or simply ignore the problem. For example, suppose a student has dropped a pencil or neglected to put away some equipment. Such incidents rarely require immediate action, so teachers should wait until they can deal with them without disrupting the continuity of ongoing activities.

Much minor misbehavior can be ignored, especially when it is fleeting. If the group is distracted momentarily because someone snaps a pencil, or if two students briefly whisper and then return attention to the lesson, it is usually best to take no action at all since students' attention is already back on the lesson.

Stop Sustained Minor Misbehavior

When minor misbehavior is repeated or intensified, or when it threatens to spread or become disruptive, teachers cannot simply ignore it; they must take action to stop it. Unless the misbehavior is serious enough to call for investigation (and it seldom is), teachers should try to eliminate it as quickly and inconspicuously as possible, without disrupting the flow of classroom activity. The following techniques are preferable to more disruptive ones when the goal is simply to redirect inattentive students to ongoing activities.

1. *Eye contact.* When it can be established, teachers can compel attention with simple eye contact, perhaps adding head nods or gestures such as looking at the book the student is supposed to be reading. Eye contact is doubly effective for "with-it" teachers who monitor regularly. When students know that a teacher continuously scans the room, they tend to look at the teacher when they misbehave (to see if the teacher is watching). This makes it easier for the teacher to intervene through eye contact.
2. *Touch and gesture.* When the students are close by, as in small groups, teachers can use touch to gain attention. A light tap, perhaps followed by a gesture toward the book, delivers the message without need for verbalization. Such touching is most useful in the early grades, when much teaching is done in small groups and distraction is a frequent problem. Also, some adolescents resent any touching by teachers. Gestures are helpful for dealing with events going on elsewhere in the room. Teachers may be able to communicate by shaking their heads, and so forth.
3. *Physical proximity.* When checking seatwork or moving about the room, teachers often can eliminate minor misbehavior simply by moving close to the offending students. If students know what they are supposed to do, the teacher's presence will motivate them to get busy.
4. *Asking for responses.* During lessons, the simplest method of capturing students' attention may be to ask them questions or otherwise call for responses. Such requests compel attention automatically, without requiring mention of the misbehavior.

   This technique should be used with care, however, because it can backfire. If teachers use it too often, students may perceive this method as an attempt to "catch" them. Also, the questions must be ones that students can answer, so that they will not feel embarrassed and end up disrupting the lesson by admitting that they were not paying attention or, if they dare, by responding with an aggressive remark. Thus, it would be appropriate to ask a clearly inattentive student a question that she or he can respond to even if the student did not hear the previous question (e.g., "Mary, Tom says that the villain was motivated by jealousy. What do you think?").

5. *Name dropping.* When giving information or instructions rather than asking questions, a teacher can call for the attention of a particular student by inserting his or her name into the middle of an instructional statement ("The next step, Mary, is to . . . ").

These "low-profile" techniques enable teachers to eliminate minor problems without disrupting ongoing activity by calling attention to the misbehavior (McDaniel, 1986).

DEALING WITH PROLONGED OR DISRUPTIVE MISBEHAVIOR

When misbehavior is prolonged, dangerous, or seriously disruptive, teachers will have to stop it directly by calling out the students' names and correcting them. *Because such direct correction is itself disruptive, it should be used only when necessary.*

Also, like the techniques described in the previous section, *direct correction should be used only when no information is needed*—when the disruptive students know what they are supposed to be doing and the nature of the misbehavior is obvious and does not require investigation. Faced with loud socializing, shooting of rubber bands, or horseplay, for example, teachers do not need additional information to be able to act. They only need to stop the misbehavior and get the students back on task. In more ambiguous situations where students may not know what they are supposed to be doing or where the teacher is not sure what is going on (e.g., two students are talking but may or may not be discussing the assignment), the teacher may need to get more information and make some decisions before issuing directives.

Appropriate Direct Correction

There are two ways for teachers to intervene directly. First, they can *demand appropriate behavior.* Such demands should be short and direct, naming the students and indicating what they should be doing. The teacher should speak firmly but not shout or nag. Commands such as "Jerry! Get back to your seat and get to work" and "Gail, Laura! Stop talking and pay attention to me" unnecessarily call attention to the misbehavior. Instead, a brief direction telling the students what to do is sufficient: "Jerry, finish your work" and "Gail and Laura, look here."

A second direct correction technique is to *remind students of rules and expectations.* If clear rules have been established, with thorough discussion of the reasons for them, teachers can use brief reminders of these rules to correct misbehavior without sermonizing or embarrassing students unnecessarily. During independent work periods, rule reminders are often the best responses when the class becomes noisy. Rather than naming offenders, the teacher can say, "Class, you're getting too loud. Remember, talk only about the physics assignment, and speak softly."

As with other forms of direct intervention, rule reminders should be brief and firm. Usually they are preferable to demanding appropriate behavior because they help students internalize behavioral control. When students are clear about rules and the reasons for them, rule reminders help them to accept responsibility for their own misbehavior and help keep down conflict.

Inappropriate Direct Correction

There are several things that teachers should *not* do in response to easily interpretable misbehavior. First, *teachers should not ask questions about obvious misbehavior*. If the situation is clear and the goal is simply to return students to productive work, there is no need to conduct an investigation. Also, the questions asked in such situations tend to be counterproductive and rhetorical. The meaninglessness of these questions and the tone in which they are asked show that they are not really questions at all but attacks on the student: "What's the matter with you?" "How many times do I have to tell you to get busy?" Such questions do no good and may cause embarrassment, fear, or resentment.

Teachers should also *avoid unnecessary threats and displays of authority*. By simply stating how they want the student to behave, teachers communicate the expectation that they will be obeyed. However, if they add a threat ("Do it or else. . ."), they not only invite power struggles with students but also suggest indirectly that they are not sure students will obey.

If students ask why they are being told to do something, teachers should give reasons. Teachers who become defensive and appeal to authority ("You do it because I say so!") will produce resentment. Also, because such authoritarian comments directly challenge students and can cause them to lose face before their peers, they may even produce an outburst against the teacher. Furthermore, if onlookers believe teacher is acting unfairly, the teacher's relationship with them will suffer too.

Finally, teachers must *avoid dwelling on misbehavior (nagging)*. In a direct correction situation, there is no reason to describe the present problem in detail or to catalog the student's past misbehavior. Attacks on students place the teacher in conflict with the students and endanger credibility and respect. If a teacher attacks students regularly, students may come to see it as funny. Some may even begin to provoke the teacher deliberately.

Teachers sometimes forget to stress desired behavior and instead just *describe* misbehavior instead of *changing* it. In effect, they tell students that they have given up hope of change ("Phyllis, every day I have to speak to you for fooling around instead of doing your work. It's the same again today. How many times do I have to tell you? You never learn."). Chances are that it will be the same story tomorrow and the day after too unless the teacher attempts to effect change. Instead of merely nagging Phyllis, the teacher should try to identify the cause of her misbehavior and develop a solution. Perhaps the seatwork is too easy, too difficult, or otherwise inappropriate for her. Perhaps Phyllis is "fooling around" with a classmate, so that a conference, and possibly a new seating arrangement, is required. In any case, rather than let the situation continue, the teacher should discuss it with Phyllis and come to an agreement with her about the future.

In summary, teachers should avoid the following behaviors when intervening to correct misbehavior: (1) rhetorical or meaningless questions, (2) unnecessary threats or displays of authority, and (3) dwelling on misbehavior (nagging). These reactions do no good and may cause needless anxiety or resentment.

Conducting Investigations

When situations are not clear enough to allow teachers to act without additional information, they will need to question one or more students. Such questions should be genuine attempts to get information, not rhetorical questions. They should be direct and addressed primarily to matters of *fact*. Some questions about students' *intentions* may also be needed to establish what the student was doing and why ("Why did you leave the room?" "Why haven't you turned in your homework?"). However, any questions about intentions should not berate students, impugn their motives ("Did you think you could get away with it?"), or confuse them by raising issues that they cannot answer ("Why didn't you remember to be more careful?").

When questioning to establish the facts in a dispute, it usually is best to talk in private. This avoids putting individuals on the spot in front of the group, where they may be tempted to try to save face with lies or confrontations. When questioning two or more students together, teachers should insist that each individual be allowed to respond without interruption (otherwise students are likely to argue over who did what to whom first).

When responses conflict, teachers must guard against making premature judgments or accusations of lying. They should point out the discrepancies and perhaps indicate that they find certain statements hard to believe. This avoids rejecting anyone's statement out of hand and leaves the door open for someone to change his or her story.

Teachers should make it clear that they expect the truth and should back their words with credible actions that cast them as helpers who want the best for all concerned and not as authority figures interested only in assessing guilt. There must be no reward for lying and no punishment for telling the truth.

The facts need not always be established in detail. If the goal is to promote long-term development of integrity and self-control, not merely to settle a single incident, it may be desirable to leave contradictions unresolved or even to accept a lie or exaggeration without labeling it as such. This is especially true when teachers suspect that students are not telling the truth but are unable to prove it. Even when such students are guilty, they will respond poorly to a teacher who insists that they are lying (conclude that the teacher is picking on them, etc.). Thus, teachers confronted with unresolvable discrepancies should remind the students that they try to treat them fairly and honestly and expect them to reciprocate; state that they "just don't know what to think," in view of the discrepancies and contradictions; state that there is no point in further discussion without new information; and restate expectations. Compared with the alternatives (punishing everyone or affixing blame without proof), this procedure promotes progress toward long-run goals by increasing the probability that the students who lied will admit this to themselves and feel remorseful about it.

CONFLICT RESOLUTION

Most misbehavior can be either prevented or handled on the spot with techniques described so far. However, students with chronic personality or behavioral problems will require more intensive treatment. Two approaches to such treatment are Gordon's "Teacher Effectiveness Training" and Glasser's "Ten Steps to Good Discipline."

Gordon

Gordon (1974) advocates what he calls the "no lose" approach to resolving conflicts. He begins by analyzing the degree to which each party "owns" the problem. The teacher owns the problem when the teacher's needs are being frustrated (as when a student persistently disrupts class by clowning). Students own the problem when their needs are frustrated (as when a student is rejected by the peer group). Finally, teachers and students share problem ownership whenever each is frustrating the needs of the other (other researchers have provided empirical support for these classifications, e.g., Brophy & McCaslin, 1992).

Gordon believes that student-owned problems call for the teacher to provide sympathy and help, especially in the form of *active listening*. Active listening involves not only listening to students describe their side of a conflict and trying to understand it from their point of view but also reflecting students' statements back to them to show that they have been understood accurately. It also involves listening for the personal feelings and reactions that students express to the events being described and reflecting these well.

When the teacher owns the problem, Gordon believes the teacher should explain it using *"I" messages* that explicitly describe the student's behavior, show how it frustrates the teacher's needs, and specify the effects of this on the teacher's feelings (discouragement, frustration). The idea is to get the student to recognize both the problem behavior and its effects on the teacher (but without blaming or rejecting the student).

Gordon believes that active listening and "I" messages will help teachers and students to achieve shared rational views of problems and to assume a cooperative, problem-solving attitude. Research by Peterson et al. (1979) showed that "I" messages reduced disruptive behavior in most students, and other studies (reviewed by Emmer & Aussiker, 1987) have shown mixed but mostly positive results.

When conflicts are involved (i.e., when problem ownership is shared), Gordon advocates the following six-step "no lose" method for finding the solution that best satisfies all concerned:

1. Define the problem.
2. Generate possible solutions.
3. Evaluate those solutions.
4. Decide which is best.
5. Determine how to implement the best solution.
6. Assess the effectiveness of this solution after it is implemented. If it is not working satisfactorily to all concerned, begin again and negotiate a new agreement.

Glasser

Glasser's (1977) ten-step approach is intended for use with students who persistently violate rules that are reasonable and are administered fairly by teachers who maintain a positive, problem-solving stance in dealing with those students. It emphasizes showing students that they will be held responsible for their in-school behavior. The ten steps are as follows. Starting with Step 4, each new step escalates reaction to the problem, so new steps are not taken unless previous steps have not solved the problem.

1. List your typical reactions to the student's disruptive behavior.
2. Analyze the list to see what techniques do or do not work and resolve not to repeat the ones that do not work.
3. Improve your relationship with the student by providing extra encouragement, asking the student to perform special errands, showing concern, or implying that things will improve.
4. Focus the student's attention on the disruptive behavior by requiring the student to describe what he or she has been doing. Continue until the student describes the behavior accurately and then request that it be stopped.
5. Call a short conference and again have the student describe the behavior. Then have the student state whether or not the behavior is against the rules or recognized expectations and ask the student what he or she should be doing instead.
6. Repeat Step 5, but this time add that the student will have to formulate a plan to solve the problem. The plan must be more than a simple agreement to stop misbehaving. The plan must include commitment to positive actions designed to eliminate the problem.
7. Isolate the student from the class until he or she has devised a plan for ensuring that the rules will be followed in the future, gotten the plan approved, and made a commitment to follow it.

8. If this does not work, the next step is in-school suspension. Now the student must deal with the principal or someone other than the teacher, but this person will repeat earlier steps in the sequence and press the student to devise a plan that is acceptable. The student will either follow the reasonable rules in effect in the classroom or continue to be isolated outside of class.

9. If students remain out of control or do not comply with in-school suspension rules, their parents are called to take them home for the day, and they resume in-school suspension the next day.

10. Students who do not respond to the previous steps are removed from school and referred to another agency.

There is little systematic research available on the approaches advocated by Gordon and Glasser. The general principles underlying their approaches were supported by Brophy and McCaslin's (1992) research, which examined teachers' strategies for coping with students who present chronic personality or behavior problems. Two factors were associated with principals' and observers' ratings of teacher effectiveness in dealing with such students. The first was a willingness to assume responsibility for solving the problem. Higher-rated teachers tried to deal with such problems personally, whereas lower-rated teachers often disclaimed responsibility or competence to deal with the problem and tried to refer it to the principal or counselor. Second, higher-rated teachers used long-term, solution-oriented approaches to problem solving, whereas lower-rated teachers concentrated on controlling misbehavior in the immediate situation, often by relying on threat or punishment. *Higher-rated teachers concentrated on helping their students understand and cope with the conflicts or problems that caused their misbehavior. These teachers usually did not find it necessary to punish problem students*, although they sometimes included punishment as part of the larger solution strategy. The following section offers suggestions about how to punish effectively when punishment becomes necessary.

PUNISHMENT

Teachers' use of punishment signifies that they have not been able to cope with the problem. It also communicates lack of confidence in students, indicating that the teacher thinks that their misbehavior is deliberate and that they are not trying to improve. Even if these perceptions are accurate, communicating them can damage students' self-concepts and further reduce their willingness to cooperate.

Teachers who rely heavily on punishment can achieve only limited and temporary success. They may achieve grudging compliance, but at the cost of chronic group tension and conflict. Their students may obey them out of fear when they are present but then go out of control when teachers are not in the room. Thus, teachers are well advised not to use punishment if other methods will suffice. Punishment sometimes is necessary, however, and teachers should use it appropriately when circumstances call for it.

Effective Punishment

Generally, punishment is used only in response to *repeated* misbehavior. It is a treatment of last resort for students who persist in misbehaving despite continued teacher expressions of concern and assistance. It is a way to exert control over students who will not control themselves. Thus, punishment is not appropriate for dealing with isolated incidents, even severe ones, if there is no reason to believe that the student will repeat the action. Even with repeated misbehavior, punishment should be minimized when students are trying to improve. Teachers should give students the benefit of the doubt by assuming their good will, and punishment should be used only when students repeatedly fail to respond to more positive treatment.

A great body of evidence (reviewed in Bandura, 1986, 1989) shows that *punishment can control misbehavior, but by itself it will not teach desirable behavior or even reduce the desire to misbehave*. Thus, punishment is never a solution by itself; it can only be part of a solution.

When used, punishment should be employed deliberately as part of a planned response to repeated misbehavior. It should not be applied unthinkingly or vengefully. When teachers punish in response to their own anger, the punishment is usually accompanied by statements or thoughts like "We'll fix your wagon" or "We'll see who's boss." Such statements do not indicate use of punishment as a deliberate control technique; they are emotional outbursts indicating poor self-control and emotional immaturity.

The effectiveness of a punishment will depend in part on the way the teacher presents it to students. Punishment should be threatened before actually being used, so that students have fair warning (recall our discussion of alerting). They also should know that punishment is used as a last resort and not because the teacher wants to get even or enjoys punishing. They should see that their own behavior has made punishment necessary because they have left the teacher no other choice.

Tone and manner are important. The teacher should avoid dramatizing ("All right, that's the last straw!" "Now you've done it!") or implying a power struggle ("I'll show you who's boss"). The need for punishment should be stated in a quiet, almost sorrowful voice, in a manner that communicates a combination of deep concern, puzzlement, and regret over the student's behavior. Whether or not it is stated overtly, the implied message should be, "You have misbehaved continually. I have tried to help with reminders and explanations, but your misbehavior has persisted. I cannot allow this to continue. If it does, I will have to punish you. I don't want to, but I must if you leave me no choice."

If punishment becomes necessary, it should be related to the offense. If a student misuses materials, for example, it may be most appropriate to restrict or suspend his or her use of them for a while. If students continually get into fights during recess, they can lose recess privileges or be required to stay by themselves. If they are continually disruptive, they can be excluded from the group.

The teacher should explain why students are being punished and what they must do to restore normal status. Students should know that they are being punished solely because of their unacceptable behavior and that they can regain normal status by changing the behavior.

This is in contrast to the "prison sentence" approach ("You have to stay here for ten minutes." "No recess for three days") and the "I am the boss" approach ("You stay here until I come and get you"). These statements include no explicit improvement demands, and they make it easy for the student to get angry or feel picked on. Even worse are overreactive inflexible statements ("You'll stay after school for a week, . . get an 'F' in conduct, . . have to get special permission to leave your seat from now on") that leave teachers stuck with either enforcing them or taking them back. Either way they lose. If they follow through and "execute the sentence," they will deepen the student's discouragement or resentment. If they back off, they will appear wishy-washy.

Exclusion from the Group If not handled properly, exclusion from the group may actually function as a reward rather than a punishment. Excluded students should be placed where they cannot easily attract peer attention, perhaps behind the other students and facing a corner or wall. The idea is to make them *feel* excluded, psychologically as well as physically.

Withdrawal of privileges and exclusion from the group should be tied closely to remedial behavior whenever possible. This means telling students not only why they are being punished, but also what they may do to regain their privileges or rejoin the group. ("When you share with the others without fighting." "When you pay attention to the lesson."). Students should have only themselves to blame for their punishment, but they should also be given a way to redeem themselves, to focus their attention on positive behavior and provide an incentive for changing.

Exclusion should be terminated when excluded students indicate that they are ready to behave properly. Stated intentions to behave should be accepted without "grilling" the students to extract specific promises ("You'll stop calling out answers without raising your hand?" "You'll stop making fun of other students during small-group lessons?").

Also, when students request readmittance, the teacher should respond in ways that clearly accept them back into the group. Avoiding vague phrases like "Well, we'll see," teachers should show excluded students that they have accepted their intention to reform and then should instruct them to rejoin the class ("Well, John, I'm glad to hear that. I hate to have to exclude you from the class. Go back to your seat and get ready for math.").

Sometimes, excluded students may offer only halfhearted pledges to reform, and the teacher may wish to hold out for a more credible commitment, especially if there has been a previous history of failure to take exclusion seriously. This should be done with caution, since it is usually better to give students the benefit of the doubt than to risk undermining reform efforts. When a pledge is rejected, the reasons must be made clear. The students must see that the teacher is acting on the basis of observed behavior ("I'm sorry, John, but I can't accept that. Several times recently you promised to behave and then broke that promise as soon as you rejoined the group. I don't think you realize how serious this problem has become.

Go back to the corner and stay there until I get a chance to come and talk to you about this some more").

Inappropriate Punishment

Abusive Verbal Attacks   These are never appropriate. Severe personal criticism cannot be justified on the grounds that the student needs it. It has no corrective function and will only cause resentment, both in the victim and in the rest of the class.

Physical Punishment   We do not recommend physical punishment, even where it is legal, for several reasons. First, by its very nature, it places the teacher in the position of attacking students, physically if not personally. This can cause injury, and in any case, it will undermine the teacher's chances of dealing with the students effectively in the future.

Although physical punishment still exists in many schools and often is defended by principals and teachers, research reveals that it typically is used ineffectively and counterproductively, mostly by inexperienced or poorly trained personnel who have not learned effective alternatives; most often against younger students from lower-class and minority groups, who are unlikely to defend themselves physically or legally; and for such offenses as tardiness, unfinished homework, or forgotten gym clothing rather than for physical aggression or insubordination (Hyman & Wise, 1979). In short, it is used by the ineffective to take out their frustrations on the weak and vulnerable.

Also, physical punishment is intense and focuses attention on itself rather than on the misbehavior that led to it. Yet, it is over quickly and has an air of finality about it, so that it usually fails to induce guilt or acceptance of personal responsibility for misbehavior. The offenders are more likely to be sorry for having gotten caught than for having misbehaved. Finally, physical punishment's long-term costs outweigh its short-term benefits. The least-controlled, most hostile students usually come from homes where their parents beat them regularly. Criminals convicted of assault and other violent crimes almost always have home backgrounds in which physical punishment was common. In general, physical punishment teaches people to attack others when angry. It does not teach them appropriate behavior, which is the purpose of discipline.

Extra Work   We do not recommend assigning extra schoolwork as punishment because this may cause students to view schoolwork as drudgery. Both teachers and students should see work assignments as useful learning devices, not as punishments.

Requiring students to copy rules or write compositions about them may or may not be effective punishment, depending on how it is handled. Writing "I must not disrupt the class" five or ten times might help students remember the rule. However, requiring them to write it 50 or 100 times calls attention more to the punishment than the rule.

Ordinarily, it is more effective to ask older students to write a composition about how they should behave. This will force them to think about the rationales underlying the rules rather than just copy rules by rote. The teacher should follow up by discussing the composition with the student. The punishment itself is only part of the treatment.

Lowering Academic Grades   Punishment that is closely related to the offense is more easily seen as fair. Students can blame only themselves if they lose a privilege because they have abused it, but they can easily feel picked on if the teacher punishes by imposing restrictions in an entirely unrelated area. An especially bad practice of this type is to lower the students' academic grades as punishment for misbehavior or to deny students the chance to play sports or be in the band because of school tardiness, and so forth. Students who misbehave frequently are often low achievers as well, and lowering their grades as punishment for misbehavior is likely to further alienate or discourage them from academic efforts. Except where the punishment is *directly related* and *proportional* to the offense, as when a student who cheats on a test is given a failing grade for that test (and only that test), students should *not* be punished by having their grades lowered.

Punishment as a Last Resort

We cannot stress too strongly that punishment is a measure of last resort, appropriate only as a way to curb misbehavior in students who know what to do but refuse to do it. It should not be used when misbehavior is not disruptive or when problems exist because students do not know what to do or how to do it.

This does not mean that all nondisruptive problems should be ignored. Withdrawal, daydreaming, or sleepiness can be serious problems if they are characteristic and continuing (especially if they are related to drug use). However, punishment is not an appropriate response to such behavior, nor is it helpful for problems such as failure to answer questions or to do assigned work. Students who fail to turn in work should not be punished beyond imposition of standard penalties for late or missing work. More importantly, they should be made to complete the work during free periods or after school (this is not punishment, but simply insistence that students meet their responsibilities). Finally, when students do not know what to do or how to do it, they need instruction, not punishment.

Bear in mind that punishment focuses attention on undesirable behavior, and it tends to reduce work involvement and increase the tension in the room (Kounin, 1970). Using it in response to one problem may cause several others. This is one reason why teachers who rely on punishment have more, not fewer, control problems.

CHOOSING YOUR ROLE

Different grade levels offer different opportunities and challenges to teachers in their roles as managers of classrooms and socializers of students. As students progress through school, their personal and social development affects the role of the teacher and the goals and techniques of classroom management. Brophy and Evertson (1978) identified four developmental stages:

1. *Kindergarten and the early elementary grades.* Here students are social- ized into the student role and instructed in basic skills. The emphasis is on teaching students what to do rather than on getting them to comply with familiar rules. Most still are predisposed to do what they are told and are likely to feel gratified when they please teachers and upset when they do not. They turn to teachers for directions, encouragement, solace, and per- sonal attention. Teachers spend considerable time teaching students how to carry out basic routines and procedures.

2. *The middle elementary grades.* This stage starts when basic socialization to the student role is completed and continues as long as most students re- main adult-oriented and relatively compliant. Students are familiar with most school routines and the serious disturbances seen frequently in later years are not yet common. Creating and maintaining an appropriate learn- ing environment remain central to teaching success, but these tasks con- sume less time and teachers are able to concentrate on instructing students in the formal curriculum.

3. *The upper elementary or junior high school grades.* As more and more students change their orientation from pleasing teachers to pleasing peers, they begin to resent teachers who act as authority figures. Certain stu- dents become more disturbed and harder to control than they used to be. As a result, classroom management again becomes a prominent part of the teacher role. Now, however, the teacher's primary problem is motivating students to behave as they know they are supposed to, not instructing them in how to behave, as in the first stage.

4. *The upper high school grades.* As many of the most alienated students drop out of school and the rest become more mature, classrooms once again assume an academic focus. Classroom management requires even less time than it did during the second stage, because students handle most student role responsibilities on their own. Teaching at this level is mostly a matter of instructing students in the formal curriculum, although socialization occurs during informal, out-of-class contacts with individ- ual students.

These developmental aspects of classroom management should be considered when thinking about the grade level one is preparing to teach. Teachers who like to provide nurturant socialization as well as instruction, who enjoy working with young children, and who have the patience and skills needed to socialize them into the student role would be especially effective in the primary grades. Elementary teachers who want to concentrate mostly on instruction would be best placed in the middle grades. Grades 7 to 10 would be best for teachers who enjoy or at least are not bothered by "adolescent" behavior and who see themselves as socialization agents and models at least as much as instructors. The upper high school grades are best for teachers who want to function mostly as subject-matter specialists.

There has been much debate, but little research and certainly no conclusive evidence, about how to handle the most serious behavioral problems: racial and other group tensions; severe withdrawal and refusal to communicate; hostile, antisocial acting out; truancy; drug abuse; refusal to work or obey; vandalism; and severe behavior disorders or criminality. Psychotherapists have not achieved much success in dealing with behavior disorders, and neither they nor correctional institutions have dealt effectively with severe delinquency and criminality. Yet, teachers must cope with such problems while at the same time instructing all their students in the curriculum.

Some teachers respond to this challenge by addressing the full spectrum of responsibilities with determination to solve whatever problems come along, but others conclude that it is better to concentrate on a few tasks and perform them well than to try to do too much. The latter position is quite understandable. A teacher with little interest in pupil socialization, who recognizes this predisposition and chooses to teach at grades where socialization is a minimal problem and to concentrate on becoming highly skilled at teaching subject matter, probably is making a wise decision. Teachers who recognize their own limitations and work within them probably will have more positive effects in the long run than they would have if they had tried to do everything and ended up doing nothing very well.

However, there are limits to how much teachers can minimize their roles as authority figures and socializers of students. Jones (1988) outlined a schoolwide systematic approach to responsible management of disruptive behavior of at-risk students and cited research showing that administrators and teachers work together in schools that respond effectively to problem students (Anderson, 1985; Gottfredson & Gottfredson, 1986; Metz, 1978). In contrast, there tend to be more problems with student misbehavior in schools where teachers place most discipline issues immediately into the hands of administrators and emphasize control and punishment over attempts to assist students in developing more productive behavior (Hawkins, Doueck, & Lishner, 1988; Wu et al., 1982). Jones argued that teachers should assume responsibility at least for initial efforts at corrective intervention. We also encourage teachers to take a proactive role in guiding and socializing at least some of their troubled students, especially the ones who appear to have no other positive influences in their lives.

THE TEACHER AS A SOCIALIZATION AGENT

Teachers who do want to socialize students can accomplish this goal by making a commitment to deal with student problems in addition to providing academic instruction. However, teachers who do so must be prepared to

1. Cultivate close personal relationships with students that go far beyond those necessary for purely instructional purposes.
2. Spend considerable time outside of school hours dealing with students and their families, and perhaps even to be "on call" as a counselor to students who have no one else to turn to.

3. Receive no extra financial compensation for such efforts, and perhaps even some opposition from school officials.
4. Deal with the wrath of a student's parents or others who may be involved in the situation.
5. Deal with complex problems that have developed over a period of years.

Difficulties of Socialization

Teachers typically do not have special training in methods of dealing with serious personality or behavior disorders, nor do they have the luxury of interacting with students in a friendly, nonauthoritarian therapist's role. Indeed, they must find ways to reach disturbed students while still playing the role of authority figure and dealing with them every day in class. As a result, even the most energetic, determined, and skilled teachers will have only limited success. This is not bad in itself, because the success rates even of professionally trained therapists are not impressive. However, teachers who want to help students with serious problems must be able simultaneously to expect the best and yet be prepared for the worst. Teachers who expect consistent successes or expressions of love and gratitude will be disappointed. Rewarding experiences occur, but so do frustrations. Many students will not respond despite continued and appropriate attempts to reach them. Others will make initial progress only to regress and end up worse than when they started. Furthermore, not all "success cases" will respond with overt gratitude or other direct reinforcement of the teacher.

Finally, teachers can work intensively with only so many students at one time. Overcommitment will cause diminishing returns. Therefore, teachers will have to be selective about their "caseloads," holding them within a manageable limit.

If you think that you can try to reach students persistently despite a steady diet of frustrations, you probably have a good chance to be a successful socialization agent. In fact, if you find the prospect challenging rather than daunting, you might consider teaching in grades 6 to 10, where student socialization needs are most frequent and intense.

Coping with Serious Adjustment Problems

Most classrooms have students whose serious and continuing problems require individualized treatment beyond that suggested so far. This section presents suggestions for dealing with them. Although different problems require different treatment, certain general considerations apply to all of them.

Do Not Isolate Students or Label Them as Unique Cases   Because expectations and labels can act as self-fulfilling prophecies, it is important that problem students not be labeled or treated as qualitatively different from their peers. This is doubly important for students with continuing behavior problems, because problems are harder to eliminate once they become labeled as characteristic of a student. Labels call undue attention to the misbehavior and suggest that more of the same is expected.

Stress Desired Behavior   Teachers should stress desired behavior, not the misbehavior the student is showing. Teachers must not only talk, but also think and act in a manner consistent with the intention of moving the student toward desired behavior. This even applies to such behaviors as stealing or destroying property. If destruction is due to impulsiveness or carelessness, the teacher can instruct the student about how to handle property carefully. If stealing results from real need (poverty), teachers can plan with students ways they can borrow the stolen items or earn the right to keep them. Meanwhile, students can be praised for progress in acting responsibly or respecting the property rights of others. If students have been stealing or destroying property to seek attention or express anger, teachers can help them recognize this and develop better ways to meet their needs. Here again, the teacher should label and praise any positive progress students show.

By defining problems positively, teachers give students a goal and suggestions about how to work toward it. This helps both teachers and students feel that they are making progress. When the problem is defined negatively ("You've got to stop . . . "), both teachers and students are left where they started, and the cycle is likely to repeat itself over and over again.

Focus on Students' School-related Behavior   Seriously disturbed behavior in school is usually part of a larger pattern of disturbance caused by many factors, including some that the teacher can do little or nothing about (parental conflict, inadequate or sadistic parent, poor living conditions). Even so, all students can learn to play the student role by behaving in ways that teachers expect. Factors in the home or out-of-school environments may need to be taken into account, but teachers should not use them as excuses for failing to deal with school-related misbehavior.

Generally, teachers are advised to confine their treatment efforts to school behavior and to aspects of the home environment that are closely related to school behavior (such as asking parents to see that students get to bed early enough on nights before school or that they do their homework). Going beyond such appropriate and expected teacher concerns is risky unless the teacher has both therapeutic expertise and a good relationship with the student and the family.

Build a Close Relationship with the Student   It is important for the teacher to build close relationships with problem students as individuals, both to develop better understanding of their behavior and to earn the respect and affection that will make the students want to respond to change efforts. To do this, teachers need to take time to talk with such students individually, either after school or at conferences during school hours, making clear their concern about the students' welfare (not merely about their misbehavior) and willingness to help them improve. They should encourage students to talk about their problems in their own words, listening carefully and asking questions when they do not understand.

Ideally, the student will say something that suggests treatment procedures. If teacher behavior has been part of the problem, the teacher should admit this and promise to change. Reasonable student suggestions should be accepted. For example, a seventh grader may request that he not be asked to read aloud from the history book, since he reads at the second-grade level. This request could be granted, provided that a plan is devised to see that the student learns to read better. When students' suggestions cannot be accepted, the reasons should be explained. The teacher may also wish to offer suggestions and elicit the students' opinions about whether the suggestions would help. Serious, deep-rooted problems will not be solved in one day with one conference. It is sufficient as a first step if both parties communicate honestly during the conference and come away from it feeling that progress has been made. Discussions should continue until mutual understanding is reached and both parties agree to try a particular suggested solution.

With serious problems, then, the teacher should arrange a conference and question the students to discover how they see the situation, then attempt to work out agreements about suggested solutions. More specific suggestions about treatment of several common behavior problems are given in the following sections.

Showing Off Some students continually seek attention by trying to impress or entertain teachers or peers. They can be enjoyable if they have the talent for the role and confine their showing off to appropriate times. Often, though, they are exasperating or disruptive. The way to deal with show-offs is to give them the attention and approval they seek, but only for appropriate behavior. Ignore inappropriate behavior, or when it is too disruptive to be ignored, do not call attention to it or make the student feel rejected. Thus, a comment like "We're having our lesson now" is better than "Stop acting silly." Students who seek attention at an awkward time should be delayed (i.e., told that the teacher will see them later at a specified time) rather than refused.

Show-offs need constant reassurance that they are liked, and teachers should try to fill this need. However, praise and rewards should be reserved for appropriate behavior. Inappropriate behavior should go unrewarded and, as much as possible, unacknowledged.

Defiance Most teachers find defiance threatening, even frightening. What is the teacher to do with students who vehemently talk back or refuse to do what they are asked to do? To begin with, the teacher must remain calm so as not to get drawn into a power struggle. The natural tendency of most adults is to get angry and strike back with a show of force designed to show such students that they "can't get away with it." This may suppress the immediate defiance, but it will probably be harmful in the long run, especially if it involves loss of temper by the teacher or public humiliation of the student.

Teachers who overcome the tendency to react with immediate anger will gain two advantages by pausing a moment before responding to defiance: (1) they gain time to control their tempers and think about what to do before acting, and (2) the mood of the defiant student is likely to change from anger and bravado to fear and contrition during this time. Therefore, it helps to ponder the situation for a few moments before responding, letting the class wait in silent anticipation.

When teachers do act, they must do so decisively, although in a calm and quiet manner. If possible, they should give an assignment to the class and then remove the defiant student for a private conference. If this is not possible or if the defiant student refuses to leave for a conference, he or she should be told that the matter will be discussed after school. The teacher's tone and manner should communicate serious concern, but no threats should be made. The defiant student and the rest of the class should know that action will be taken but should not be told exactly what it will be. The following response would be appropriate: "John, I can see that something is very wrong here and that we'd better do something about it before it gets worse. Please step into the hall and wait for me—I'll join you in a minute." Stating that the matter will be dealt with in a private conference tells the class that the teacher will handle the situation yet does not humiliate the defiant student or incite further defiance. The teacher can even afford to let the student "get in the last word," because the matter will be taken up again later.

Defiant acts usually culminate a buildup of student anger and frustration. Difficulties at home or in relationships with peers may be part of the problem, but the teacher is almost always part of the problem too. Students are unlikely to defy their teachers unless they resent the teachers for some reason. Therefore, teachers must be prepared to hear defiant students out. There must be a discussion, not a lecture or argument. When students claim unfair treatment, teachers must entertain the possibility that this is true. When mistakes have been made, teachers should admit them and promise to change.

It is usually best to encourage angry students to say everything they have on their minds *before* responding to the points they raise. This helps teachers to get the full picture and allows them some time to think about what they are hearing. If they try to respond separately to each point as it is raised, the discussion may turn into a series of accusations and rebuttals. Such exchanges usually leave students feeling that their objections have been "answered" but that they still are right in accusing the teacher of general unfairness.

With some defiant students, it may be important to review the teacher's role. Students should understand that teachers are interested primarily in teaching them, not in ordering them around or playing police officer, but this requires the students' cooperation. Regardless of the points students raise, teachers should express concern for these students and a desire to treat them fairly. This reassurance (backed, of course, by appropriate behavior) will be more important to the students than responses to specific accusations.

Even serious defiance can usually be handled with one or two sessions like these, if teachers are honest in dealing with students and if they follow up the discussion with appropriate behavior. Although unpleasant, incidents of defiance can be blessings in disguise. They bring out into the open problems that have been smoldering for a long time. Defiant acts usually have cathartic effects on students, releasing built-up tensions and leaving students more receptive to developing a constructive relationship with the teacher.

Aggression Against Peers Aggressive students must not be allowed to hurt classmates or damage property. When such harmful or destructive behavior appears, teachers should demand an end to it immediately. If the student fails to respond, the teacher should send another student for help and, if necessary and feasible, should physically restrain the student who is out of control. Most teachers rarely will be required to intervene in this way, but all should be prepared to do so. Such preparation should include training in techniques of restraining students and breaking up fights effectively, as well as development of clear procedures for emergency situations with the principal, other teachers, and support staff who may be available. A good rule of thumb is that teachers' responsibilities in these situations are first to the safety of themselves and the other students, then to the aggressive student, and then to property.

While being restrained, students may respond by straining to get away, making threats, or staging temper tantrums. If so, they should be held until they regain self-control. The teacher should speak firmly but quietly, telling them to calm down and get control of themselves. The students should be reassured that the problem will be dealt with, but not until they calm down. If they insist that the teacher let go, they should be told firmly that this will happen as soon as they stop yelling and squirming. Such verbal assurance can be reinforced nonverbally by relaxing the grip as the student gradually tones down resistance.

Restraint may be required if two students are fighting and do not respond to demands that they stop. Do not try to stop a fight by getting between the participants and trying to deal with both at the same time. This will result in delay, confusion, or even the teacher getting hit. Instead, restrain one of the participants, preferably the more belligerent, or the one with whom you have less rapport, by pulling him back and away from his opponent so that he is not hit while being held (pull at the belt or waistband, leaving the arms free for self-defense). This will stop the fight, although it may be necessary to order the other participant to stay away. It is helpful if the teacher does a lot of talking at this point, calming the students down and explaining that the matter will be dealt with when they comply. If the teacher does not take over here, the students are likely to exchange threats and other face-saving actions.

Humor is helpful if the teacher has the presence of mind to use it. Threats or face-saving actions are effective only when taken seriously. If teachers respond to them with smiles or little remarks to show that they are considered funny or ridiculous ("All right, let's stop blowing off steam"), they are likely to stop quickly.

Once aggressive students calm down, teachers should talk with them individually. (If two students were fighting, it may be necessary to talk to both together.) As usual, the teacher should begin by hearing the students out. It is important to help aggressive students see the distinction between feelings and behavior. Feelings should be accepted as legitimate or at least understandable. Students who state that they hate someone or that they are angry because of unfair treatment should be asked to state their reasons for feeling this way. The feeling itself should not be denied or attacked. If the student has been treated unfairly, the teacher should express understanding and sympathy.

If angry feelings are not justified, the teacher should explain in a way that recognizes the reality of the feelings but does not legitimate them ("I know you want to be first, but others do too. They have the same rights as you. So there's no point in getting angry because they went first. You'll have to wait your turn. If you try to be first all the time, everyone will think you are selfish."). Although teachers should accept and sometimes expressly encourage legitimate *feelings*, they should not accept *misbehavior*. They should state clearly that students will not be allowed to hit others, destroy property, or otherwise act out angry feelings in destructive ways.

Habitually aggressive students must learn that frustration and anger do not justify aggressive behavior. They should be given suggestions about how to express feelings verbally rather than physically. For example, students who "hit first and ask questions later" need instruction about how to resolve conflict through discussion and negotiation. In response to classmates who cause them problems, they should ask what the classmates are doing and why (instead of assuming that the classmates are provoking them deliberately) and should express their feelings verbally when others cause them to become angry (because peers may not even realize that they have made them angry or why).

Teachers should also appeal to the Golden Rule to try to help aggressive students see the consequences of their behavior. Students usually can see that if they dislike and avoid others who bully, cheat, or destroy property, others will dislike and avoid them for the same reasons. It is helpful to show by examples the value of verbalizing feelings and seeking solutions to problems instead of striking out at others. Aggressive students must learn that others will know why they are angry only if they tell them and that hitting will only make the others angry too.

If aggression results mostly from students' poor handling of certain situations (failure to share, failure to wait one's turn, tendency to overreact to teasing or to accidental physical contact), teachers should work with students on the situational problem, stressing that part of the problem is not only the students' behavior, but also their overreactive emotions. This does not mean instructing students to deny their feelings; their anger and resentment are real. However, it does mean that students need to learn to control their feelings in frustrating situations. They must see that certain frustrations are unavoidable and that overreacting to them only makes one unhappy and unpopular.

Cases in which a student attacks others for no apparent reason are more serious. Students who do this regularly may require professional treatment. Sometimes a child acquires a self-image as a "tough guy" and may actually want others to fear and dislike him. Even so, a teacher can provide assistance in many ways. As with any serious problem, the teacher should deal with aggressive acting out as it occurs and talk with the student to develop understanding and to explain behavioral expectations. In addition, the teacher can cope with the problem indirectly, to help both the student and others in the class to see him in a more positive light.

First, the teacher should avoid labeling the student or reinforcing any negative label he may apply to himself. Labels imply that there is something permanently wrong with the student or that he cannot exert self-control. They should be avoided in favor of statements that imply confidence. The teacher can help the student practice a more positive role by arranging for him to play such a role toward his classmates. It might be helpful for this student to be used as a tutor to teach academic content or other skills that he may know (tying shoes, operating equipment, arts and crafts, music, or other talents). In reading and role-playing situations, he should be assigned parts that feature kindness, friendship, and help-fulness toward others. Such a student would be ideal for the part of an ogre who everyone feared and disliked until they found out how good he was underneath.

Cooperative and helpful behavior can be acknowledged and praised whenever it occurs. Also, potentially serious conflicts can be nipped in the bud if teachers spot them early enough and turn them into cooperative situations by suggesting how students can resolve the problem. For good measure, teachers can add that they are pleased to see the students cooperating. Such behaviors help change a negative self-concept and make students see themselves as persons whom others will like as friends.

So far, we have noted what teachers *should* do with aggressive students. Before leaving this topic, it is worth discussing one frequently advocated technique that we do *not* recommend. This is the practice of providing substitute methods for expressing aggression, such as telling the student to hit a punching bag instead of another student. By encouraging students to act out hostility against substitute ob-jects, teachers merely prolong and reinforce immature emotional control. If kept up long enough, this will produce adults who are prone to temper tantrums at the slightest frustration and who spend much of their time building up and then re-leasing hostile feelings. This sort of person is neither happy nor likeable.

Instead of trying to get students to act out all emotions, teachers should help students to distinguish between emotions and behavior and between appropriate and inappropriate emotions. Inappropriate emotions (unjustified anger or other emotional overreactions) should be labeled as such, and the reasons why they are inappropriate should be explained. Teachers must not tolerate behavior that is sim-ply unacceptable, no matter how strong the student's emotions or impulses to act out. Acceptable (and more effective) alternatives should be explained and insisted upon. All aspects of the teacher's behavior should communicate the expectation that students can and will achieve mature self-control.

These guidelines are reflected in the findings of Brophy and McCaslin (1992), who interviewed elementary teachers concerning their perceptions of and strate-gies for coping with persistently hostile and aggressive students who were depicted in vignettes. These researchers found that teachers who were rated by their prin-cipals as highest in ability to deal with problem students reported responding to aggression as a serious behavioral problem calling for resocialization of aggressive students' responses to situations in which they tended to act out, not as a neurotic symptom or a relatively minor problem that could be handled through brief man-agement responses. These teachers placed firm limits on aggressive students, de-manded that they curb their aggressive behavior, and were prepared to back their demands with punishment if necessary. However, high-rated teachers also reported that they would try to encourage change by providing aggressive students with counseling or instruction in more effective ways of handling frustration, controlling their tempers, solving conflicts through communication and negotiation rather than aggression, and expressing anger verbally rather than physically.

Unresponsiveness Some students lack the self-confidence to participate nor-mally in classroom activities. They do not raise their hands to answer questions and they copy, guess, or leave an item blank rather than ask the teacher about their seatwork. When they are called on and do not know an answer, they stare at the floor silently or perhaps mumble incoherently. Sometimes this "strategy" is successful, because many teachers become uneasy and give the answer or call on someone else rather than keep such students "on the spot."

The key to success in working with shy or inhibited students appears to be application of steady but indirect and patient pressure for change. Brophy and McCaslin (1992) found that teachers rated high in effectiveness in coping with problem students reported that they would take problems of shyness or inhibition seriously and work to change students' behavior but would do so in indirect and supportive ways (private talks and special activities or assignments to draw students out, minimizing stress or embarrassment, praising accomplishments and encouraging efforts, and where necessary, building up students' academic self-concepts). Effective teachers said they would use these methods routinely to apply consistent pressure for change but would avoid direct confrontations, demands, or threats; would back off temporarily if they met resistance; and would be prepared to spend several months patiently working to achieve substantial improvement with unresponsive students.

Teachers should generally treat inhibitions about classroom participation indirectly. Attacking the problem directly by labeling it and urging the students to overcome it can backfire by making students more self-conscious and inhibited (much research on stuttering, for example, shows this). The teacher should stress what the students should be doing rather than what they are not doing. Questions should be asked directly rather than prefaced with stems such as, "Do you think you could . . . ", which suggest uncertainty and make it easy for students to remain silent. Also, the teacher should pose questions in a conversational tone. More formally stated questions may sound like test items and thus produce anxiety.

Questions should be accompanied by appropriate gestures and expressions to communicate that the teacher is talking to the student and expects an answer. The teacher should look at the student expectantly after asking the question. If the student answers, the teacher can respond with praise or relevant feedback. If the answer is too soft, the teacher might say, "Good! Say it louder so everyone can hear." When students appear to be about to answer, but hesitant, teachers can help by nodding their heads or encouraging verbally, "Say it!" When students do not respond at all, teachers can give the answer and then repeat the question or ask students to repeat the answer. If students mumble or partially repeat, they should be asked to repeat again and then praised when they do so. All this is designed to make clear to students that they are expected to speak up, to give them practice in doing so, and to reassure and reward them when they do.

Interactions with reticent students should be deliberately extended at times, both to give them practice at extended discussions and to combat the idea that students can keep interactions short by offering brief responses. When such students answer initial questions correctly, teachers should sometimes ask them another question or have them elaborate on the response. When they fail the initial question, the follow-up question should be a simpler one that they can handle. Students who do not respond to any level of questioning can be asked to repeat things or to imitate actions. Once they begin to respond correctly, the teacher can move to more demanding questions as confidence grows (Blank, 1973).

Inhibited students need careful treatment when they do not respond. As long as they appear to be trying to answer the question, teachers should wait them out. If they begin to look anxious, as if they are worrying about being in the spotlight instead of thinking about the question, teachers should intervene by repeating the question or giving a clue. They should not call on another student or allow others to call out the answer.

Teachers should not allow students to "practice" resistance or nonresponsiveness (Blank, 1973). Anxiety or resistance should be cut off before it builds. Students who do not respond to questions requiring a verbal answer can be asked to make nonverbal responses such as shaking their heads or pointing. It is important to get some form of positive response before leaving the student.

Students at all levels should be instructed to say "I don't know" rather than remain silent when they cannot respond. Many students hesitate to say "I don't know," because previous teachers reinforced the idea that such responses are shameful through such comments as "What do you mean you don't know?" By legitimating "I don't know," the teacher makes it possible for students to respond verbally even when they do not know the answer.

These methods are difficult to apply in large-group situations with extremely unresponsive students who often do not say anything at all. Such students may have to be brought along slowly in individual and small-group situations first. Getting rid of strong inhibitions or fears takes time, and much progress can be undone by trying to push too far too fast. With continued progress and regular success, confidence will grow and students' tolerance for being "on the spot" will increase. The teacher should continue to obtain a response of some kind from unresponsive students every time they have an interaction and should see that the students do not become regarded as students who do not answer and therefore are no longer asked to respond. If this type of inhibition is widespread among students, the teacher may be causing or contributing to it (e.g., overvaluing correct answers, showing impatience or disgust at failure, or criticizing instead of helping students who come with questions). Although some educators recommend placing shy students in small groups (to make it easier for them to get a turn, etc.), a smaller setting does not necessarily make communication easier. The teacher will need to be careful to monitor the behavior of shy students when using small-group cooperative methods because research suggests that these students are encouraged by other students to remain passive (Mulryan, 1989).

Failure to Complete Assignments Certain students fail to complete seatwork or homework assignments. Methods for dealing with this depend on why assignments are not turned in. Some students do not turn in work because they have not been able to figure out how to do it. This is not a motivational problem; it is a teaching problem calling for remedial work to help the students learn what they do not understand. This may seem obvious, but students report that teachers often not only fail to provide this help to slow learners but also routinely collect seatwork assignments before students have had a chance to finish (Weinstein & Middlestadt, 1979).

Patience and determination are needed in working with slow students because they need support and encouragement just to keep trying. If the teacher criticizes them, embarrasses them before the group, or shows impatience, they will likely begin to copy from neighbors rather than continue to try to do the work themselves. Teachers can encourage these students by pointing out the progress they are making, regardless of where they stand in relation to others in the class. Teachers will need to make time for remedial teaching with them or to plan some other remediation arrangement.

A different problem is presented by students who can do the work but do not finish it or turn it in. The best way to deal with this problem is to stop it early, before it becomes entrenched. From the beginning of the year, teachers should be clear about expectations for seatwork and homework. Their purpose and importance should be explained, and the assignments should be collected, checked, and followed up with feedback and, when necessary, remedial work.

Although the teacher may wish to make open-ended assignments (such as identifying problems to do for extra credit or "to see if you can figure them out"), all students should have a clear-cut minimum amount of work for which they are accountable. There should be a clear understanding about what to turn in, when it is due, and the consequences for missing the deadline.

Teachers should also make clear that students are expected to finish assignments before doing anything else during seatwork time. Students involved in seatwork should be monitored to see that they are working productively. The established policy must be enforced consistently so that everyone forms the habit of doing the seatwork.

Failure to turn in homework is a more difficult problem, because teachers cannot monitor and intervene if students are not working properly. They can keep track of whether homework is being turned in, however, and can assign students who did not complete it to do so during free periods. Students who do not complete the job during free periods should be kept after school. Here again, the policy that assignments are to be completed and turned in on time must be established from the beginning of the year. If homework is not turned in, completion of the assignment will be first priority whenever the student is not involved in a lesson or other instructional activity. Of course, this advice assumes that homework assignments are relevant in content and appropriate in difficulty level. If failure to turn in homework is common, teachers should review and adjust the homework assigned and the way it is monitored and corrected.

ANALYZING PROBLEM BEHAVIOR

Many forms of problem behavior have not been discussed in this chapter: student habits that irritate or disgust the teacher, students who bait the teacher with provocative remarks, and various signs of mental or emotional disorder. When faced with such symptomatic behaviors, teachers need to try to find out why the students are behaving as they are, and in the process, develop clues to successful treatment.

Finding Out What Problem Behavior Means

To the extent that behavior problems occur in the classroom, teachers should question students and systematically observe them. What is the meaning of the behavior? Why does the student act this way? *Remember, surface misbehavior may be just a symptom of an underlying problem, and the symptomatic behavior may not be as important as the reasons that are producing it.*

If the behavior is just a habit, not part of a larger complex of problems, the teacher should insist that the student drop it. This demand should be supported by an appropriate rationale. Where objectionable habits are not fundamentally immoral but merely violate school rules, social convention, tact, good taste, or the teacher's personal preferences, this distinction should be noted. Students should not be made to feel guilty or to believe that their habits indicate something seriously wrong with them. Teachers are justified in forbidding habits that are disruptive or irritating but should not describe such habits as worse than they really are.

If the problem behavior is more serious or complex than a simple habit and the student has not given an adequate explanation for it, careful observation is needed. Observations should begin by describing the behavior more precisely. Is it a ritual that is repeated pretty much the same way over and over (masturbating, spitting, nose picking), or is it a more general tendency (aggression, suspiciousness, sadistic sense of humor) that is manifested in many different ways? Perhaps the description can be narrowed. Is there a recognizable pattern? For example, do students' suspicions center around a belief that others are talking about them behind their backs, or do they think they are being picked on or cheated? If they think others are talking about them, what do they think is being said? If students laugh inappropriately, what makes them laugh? Such information provides clues to what the behavior means.

Besides enabling the teacher to describe the behavior more specifically, observations should establish the conditions under which it occurs. Is it a chronic problem or something that started recently? Does it happen at a particular time of the day or week? Does it occur when tests are given, for example, or when a student has lost a competition? Such common elements might point to events that trigger the reaction. In addition, discussing these observations with the student may produce insights that increase both the teacher's and the student's understanding of the behavior and lead to useful suggestions for problem solving (see Rohrkemper, 1982).

Teachers should also note what they themselves were doing immediately before the students acted out. Perhaps they triggered the behavior by treating students in ways that the students think are unfair. Analyses of this sort help teachers place students' behavior in context and allow the teacher to see the behavior as symptoms that may help identify underlying causes. This will move teachers away from essentially negative, describe-the-problem-but-don't-do-anything-about-it approaches ("How can I get Lynn to stop sulking?") and toward diagnosis and treatment ("How can I help Lynn see that I am not rejecting her personally when I refuse her requests?").

Arranging a Conference

The simplest and often best way to understand students' behavior is to talk to them about it in a conference during a free period or after school. Teachers should note what they have observed, express concern about the behavior, and ask for an explanation. Students usually lack the insight to explain fully why they act as they do, and teachers should not expect them to. Instead, the hope is that helpful information will emerge from the discussion. If it does produce a breakthrough, fine. If not, something is still accomplished if students learn that the teacher is concerned about them and wishes to help.

Conferences should be concluded in ways that give students a feeling of closure. If the problem behavior has been disruptive, teachers should clarify expectations and limits as well as reach agreements with students about any special actions to be taken. If the problem requires no special action or if it is not yet clear what action to take, teachers can conclude by telling students that they are glad to have had a chance to discuss the problem and that they will help in any way they can if students will let them know how.

Bringing in Parents and Other Adults

Teachers should think twice before involving parents, principals, counselors, or other adults, because this escalates the problem in the minds of all concerned and labels the student as a "problem student." The expected benefits of involving adults must be weighed against the damage that could result from such labeling.

Help may be available from a counselor, social worker, or school psychologist. By discussing the situation with a resource person, preferably one who has observed in the classroom several times, teachers may gain new insights or get specific suggestions. A knowledgeable principal or fellow teacher might also play this role. The resource persons' titles are less important than the quality of their observations and advice.

Some resource people deal with students directly rather than through teachers. Again, this may or may not be helpful. There is usually little point in having students tested, for example, unless a physical problem is suspected. Knowledge of the students' scores on intelligence or personality tests usually contributes nothing to the solution of their problems. In fact, testing may lead to undesirable labeling or self-fulfilling prophecy effects. Also, merely sending students to outside "disciplinarians" will not do much good over the long run. If a student's behavior problem is in the classroom, it must be dealt with there.

Many educators are encouraging closer working relationships between teachers and families. For example, Kauffman et al. (1993) argue that if teachers are to be effective, they must develop skills for working with parents. Theoretically, there are many advantages to having close collaborative relationships between school and family. Collaboration enables the teacher to have more information to use in understanding students' classroom behavior. Reciprocally, families who are better informed about teachers' and schools' intentions can provide more support. Further, there is some research to suggest that family involvement in children's education is often associated with better attendance, more positive attitudes toward school, and higher academic achievement. It is beyond the scope of this chapter to provide detailed information about strategies for creating, maintaining, and improving home-school relationships. Fortunately, several excellent sources are available (e.g., Hoffman, 1991; Kauffman et al., 1993; Weinstein & Mignano, 1993). In this chapter we simply suggest that working with parents is one possible way to get information to use in understanding students' misbehavior in schools and perhaps in developing programs and expectations that are mutually supportive both in the family and at school.

Although, in general, we think that enhancing communication between home and school is desirable, some special caveats need to be observed when contacting parents in problem situations. Teachers need to recognize that many parents are reluctant to become involved in school for various reasons including the fact that they are busy, feel that schooling should be left to teachers and principals (the experts), or that parents support teachers best by not bothering them. Other parents remember school as a place where they were uncomfortable and hence do not want to come into contact with the institution again (Weinstein & Mignano, 1993). Finally, some parents are embarrassed because they believe that their children's difficulties for their academic (or behavioral) problems are their fault. Further, it is important to recognize that in some cases parents are responsible for a student's misbehavior. For example, Parkway and Stanford (1992) estimate that about 2 million school-age children are victims of child abuse and neglect each year. Moreover, such parents are likely to react to their children's school misbehavior or other problems with physical punishment. Thus, unless you are prepared to spend considerable time attempting to understand and clarify parents' behavior and motivation, you may only deepen a problem by contacting parents about students' problems at school.

Thus, contacting parents about problems is risky. After all, to the extent that students have serious emotional or behavioral problems, their parents are probably the biggest single cause. Merely informing the parents will do no good. If they get the impression that they are expected to "do something," the parents might just threaten or punish the student and let it go at that.

Sometimes teachers can suggest how parents can help, as when teachers enlist parents' help in seeing that the students get enough sleep, do their homework, or eat breakfast. When making suggestions, teachers may need to tell parents many of the things discussed in this chapter. The need to think of punishment as a last resort and the need for confidence and positive expectations are two principles that many parents violate when their children have problems.

If teachers call parents mostly to get information, teachers should make this clear and then state their observations and concern about the student and ask if the parents can add anything that might increase teachers' understanding. They should see how much the parents know about the problem and what their explanation for it is. If some plan of action emerges, it should be discussed and agreed on with the parents.

If no parental action seems appropriate, the conference should be brought to some form of closure ("We'll, I'm glad we've had a chance to talk about George today. You've given me a better understanding of him. I'll keep working with him in the classroom and let you know about his progress. Meanwhile, if anything comes up that I ought to know, give me a call"). The parents should emerge from the conference knowing what to tell their child about it and what, if anything, the teacher is requesting them to do.

OTHER APPROACHES TO CLASSROOM MANAGEMENT

Our approach to classroom management is eclectic, stressing principles gathered from many theories. A few systematic approaches stress principles developed within one theory or point of view. Four of the most prominent are assertive discipline, contingency contracting, cognitive behavior modification, and classroom-meeting applications of reality therapy.

Assertive Discipline

Assertive discipline is an approach developed by Canter (1976, 1981) and promoted through in-service training workshops sponsored by his corporation. Described as a "take-charge approach for today's educator," assertive discipline stresses the rights of teachers to define and enforce standards for student behavior that allow the teachers to carry out instruction in a manner that is consonant with their capabilities and needs. Teachers who do this are described as assertive teachers and are contrasted both with submissive teachers who fail to enforce standards and hostile teachers who do so but in ways that violate the best interests of students. Recommended methods focus on developing clearly specified expectations for student behavior, translating these into a set of rules that specify acceptable and unacceptable behavior, and linking these to a system of rewards and punishments. The teacher then articulates the rules and consequences to students and follows through by consistently delivering promised rewards for compliance and imposing threatened punishments for noncompliance. The most widely used punishment is a penalty system in which the names of misbehaving students are written on the board and check marks are added following their names for repeated offenses. Students whose names are written on the board are subject to detention, and those whose names are followed by one or more check marks are also subject to progressively more serious punishments including notes sent home to parents, time out from the classroom, or referral to the principal.

There has been considerable controversy over assertive discipline. Canter (1988) claims that the approach is supported by research, and both he and his supporters (e.g., McCormack, 1989) cite testimonials and survey data to suggest that the method is popular among practitioners because they are convinced that it works. However, independent reviewers have concluded that Canter and his associates have failed to conduct systematic research on the effectiveness of the approach they have been promoting for 18 years, and that the limited research available on the approach simply does not support Canter's claims for its effectiveness (Emmer & Aussiker, 1987; Render, Padilla, & Krank, 1989).

Several authors have also voiced philosophical objections to the assertive discipline model. Curwin and Mendler (1988) characterized it as an example of an *obedience model*, in which power-based methods are used to compel students to conform to rules. They consider such obedience models less desirable than *responsibility models*, in which the goal is to develop responsibility for inner self-guidance in students, using methods that emphasize rationale explanations and natural consequences of behavior rather than threats and punishment. Similarly, McDaniel (1989, p. 82) criticized assertive discipline as being "not much more than applied behavior modification and take-charge teacher firmness with rules and consequences."

We see value in several aspects of the assertive discipline approach (especially its emphasis on developing and communicating clear expectations for student behavior), but we share the concerns voiced by its critics. We believe that the approach places too much emphasis on threat and punishment, so that it is a much less desirable alternative than the approach outlined here, which is based on replicated findings obtained by several research teams working independently in different parts of the country. Further, we believe that any management system is incomplete if it relies on teachers to regulate student behavior but lacks a concomitant emphasis on student self-control. As McCaslin and Good (1992) noted, it is foolish to try to teach a problem-solving curriculum while undermining it by using rigid behavior control management systems.

Contingency Contracting

Skinner (1953) described behavior as controlled by contingent reinforcement. Behavior that brings on or maintains reinforcement will be repeated, and behavior that is not reinforced will be extinguished. This idea is simple in theory, but it becomes complex in practice because people respond differently to the same stimuli. Some are not motivated by stimuli that most others experience as rewards, and some respond positively to stimuli that most others view as punishments. Thus, the same stimulus can be rewarding, punishing, or irrelevant for different people or even for the same people in different situations.

To deal with this complexity, behavior modifiers use the Premack principle (Premack, 1965) to define reinforcers. This principle states that preferred behaviors that appear frequently under free-response conditions can be used as reinforcers to elicit and maintain behaviors that would not appear otherwise. That is, high-frequency behaviors experienced as rewarding can be used as reinforcers by making the opportunity to engage in these preferred behaviors contingent on performance of less-preferred behaviors. Applying the Premack principle, teachers can provide reinforcement when students pay attention, do their work, or keep the rules and can withhold it when they do not.

Students can be given a more active role through *contingency contracting*, in which students receive reinforcement contingent on meeting work or behavioral requirements that are negotiated and then formalized into contractual agreements. For example, teachers can determine the levels of performance (assignments done according to specified criteria, possibly along with earning an acceptable test score) that will be required for particular grades. A level of performance that will require sustained effort (for a particular student) can be required for a grade of "A," with lesser requirements for lower grades.

Contracts for behavioral improvement can be developed using the same principles. Conduct that represents the best that can be expected from *this* student at *this* time can be required for maximum reinforcement, with less acceptable levels producing less reinforcement. As students become able to control themselves more successfully, new contracts requiring better behavior can be introduced.

Contingency contracting usually works best when students are presented with a variety of attractive reinforcements. These "reinforcement menus" might include opportunities to spend time in learning centers or other enrichment activities, to go to the library, to play games, or even just to converse with friends. Specified good behavior or acceptable completion of assignments is rewarded with so many points, and these points can be "spent" on reinforcements. The "prices" of reinforcements may vary according to their attractiveness and the demand for them. The most popular ones are the most expensive. Occasional changes in reinforcement menus or prices provide variety and help avoid satiation with the reinforcers.

It is harder than it might seem to arrange contingencies so that desired behaviors are reinforced. Sometimes proper contingencies are not established; at other times, the problem is in the presumed reward that is supposed to function as a reinforcer. Analyze the behavior modification attempts presented in the examples below. Are they likely to be successful? Why or why not?

1. Ms. Bussey has set up a contingency-contracting system. Students who complete assignments get tokens they can spend on reinforcers. However, the work must be correct. If students come with incomplete or incorrect work, they must return to their desks and finish it correctly.

2. Mr. Cornucopia gives out goodies every Friday afternoon as a way to motivate students to apply themselves. He sees that everyone gets something but makes sure to give the more desirable items to students who appear to have worked hard during the week. He refers to this as "payday," and says "Good work" to each student when passing out the goodies.

3. Ms. Calvin announces that from now on, the student who finishes the afternoon math assignment first will be allowed to dust the erasers.

4. Mr. Caries is frustrated because his students do not keep orderly desks. To encourage better habits, he occasionally (and unpredictably) announces that today students who do a good job of cleaning their desks will get candy. After allowing enough time, he goes around to check and gives candy to those who have neat desks.

Superficially, all four examples are similar: the teacher offers rewards to improve some performance. However, subtle differences make it likely that only Ms. Bussey will succeed. She has attractive reinforcers available, and students can get them only by turning in complete and correct work. Assuming that all students can do the work assigned to them, the contingencies are such that rewards will function as reinforcement for sustained and careful work on assignments.

Mr. Cornucopia will not succeed because there is no clear contingency between performance of the behaviors he is trying to reinforce and delivery of the reinforcements. All students get some kind of reward whether they apply themselves or not, and differences in the attractiveness of the rewards given to individuals depend on his unsystematic perceptions and fallible memory rather than on objective evidence of effort. Some students get more than they deserve, and others get less than they deserve because Mr. Cornucopia does not realize how deserving they are. His students will learn that there is no clear contingency between reward and performance, so that few of them will be motivated to work harder by this gimmick, even though they will enjoy the goodies.

Ms. Calvin's scheme is almost certain to fail, for three reasons. First, she should reward effort and accomplishment, not speed. Second, the possibility for reinforcement exists for only those few students who can work fast enough to finish first. Finally, it is unlikely that many students will be motivated by the opportunity to dust erasers. Ms. Calvin is offering a weak reinforcer, susceptible to early satiation.

Mr. Caries will also fail. His reinforcements are contingent on performance of the desired behavior, but they are offered only occasionally and always announced beforehand. Thus, the contingency here is not "Students who have neat desks every day will get rewarded," but "Students who clean their desks whenever Mr. Caries promises rewards will get rewarded." By always announcing the availability of rewards ahead of time, Mr. Caries eliminates their power to reinforce clean-up efforts even when they are not available.

These examples illustrate some of the problems involved in using contingency contracting in schools. The proper contingencies are hard to establish, and satiation with the available rewards is a continuing problem. Although the method has been used successfully as a system for managing entire classrooms (Robinson, Newby, & Ganzell, 1981), most teachers will find it valuable primarily as a supplement for students who need extra incentives (Macmillan & Kolvin, 1977).

Cognitive Behavior Modification

Experience with goal setting, self-monitoring, and other cognitive elements of contingency contracting led to the realization that they have important positive effects of their own, independent of the effects of reinforcement. For example, inducing students to set work output goals for themselves can improve performance, especially if the goals are specific and difficult rather than vague or too easy (Rosswork, 1977). Even more powerful than inducing students to set goals is inducing them to monitor and maintain daily records of their own study behavior (Sagotsky, Patterson, & Lepper, 1978). If taught properly, students can learn to monitor their behavior more closely and control it more effectively (Hughes, 1988; Kendall & Hollon, 1979; O'Leary & Dubey, 1979; Rosenbaum & Drabman, 1979).

The simplest forms of self-monitoring require students only to judge whether or not they are on task when a "beep" signal is given or a five-minute period has elapsed on the clock. Thus, students might place a card with plus signs (on task) or minus signs (off task) in boxes provided for self-recording of task engagement. Or, they might record and graph the number of math problems completed in each day's seatwork period and the percentage of these problems completed correctly. With proper training, even 8-year-olds can learn to record qualitative aspects of performance, such as the number of action words and describing words that they include in daily compositions (Ballard & Glynn, 1975).

Self-control skills are taught using procedures that Meichenbaum (1977) has called cognitive behavior modification. One particularly powerful technique combines modeling with verbalized self-instructions. Rather than just tell students what to do, the teacher demonstrates the process, not only by going through the physical motions involved but also by verbalizing the thoughts and other self-talk (self-instructions, self-monitoring, self-reinforcement) that direct the activity.

Meichenbaum and Goodman (1971) originally used the technique with cognitively impulsive students who made frequent errors on matching tasks because they responded too quickly, settling on the first response alternative that looked correct rather than taking time to examine all of the alternatives before selecting the best one. As the models "thought out loud" while demonstrating the task, they made a point of carefully observing each alternative, resisting the temptation to settle on the first one that looked correct, reminding themselves that one can be fooled by small differences in detail that are not noticed at first, and so on. Variations of this approach have been used not only to teach cognitively impulsive students to approach tasks more reflectively, but also to teach all students to be more creative in problem solving, to help social isolates learn to initiate activities with peers, to help aggressive students to control their anger and respond more effectively to frustration, and to help defeated students learn to cope with failure and respond to mistakes with problem-solving efforts rather than resignation. Various approaches have in common the attempt to teach students that they can exert control over their own behavior and handle frustrating situations effectively through rational planning and decision making.

A simple example is the "turtle" technique of Robin, Schneider, and Dolnick (1976), in which teachers teach aggressive students to assume a turtle position when upset. The students learn to place their heads on their desks, close their eyes, and clench their fists. This gives them an immediate response to use in anger-provoking situations and enables them to delay inappropriate behavior and to think about constructive solutions. Actually, the turtle position itself is mostly a gimmick; the key is training students to postpone impulsive responding while they gradually relax and consider constructive alternatives.

Douglas et al. (1976) trained hyperactive students to approach seatwork tasks carefully. They used modeling and verbalized self-instruction designed to enable the students to think before acting ("What plans can I try?" How would it work if I did that?"), to monitor their performances during the task ("What shall I try next?" "Have I got it right so far?"), to check and correct mistakes ("See, I made a mistake there—I'll correct it." "Let's see, have I tried everything I can think of?"), and finally, to reinforce themselves ("I've done a pretty good job").

The "Think Aloud" program of Camp and Bash (1981) is a structured curriculum designed to teach students to use their cognitive skills to cope with social problems. It teaches the students to pose and develop answers to four basic questions: "What is my problem?" "How can I do it?" "Am I using my plan?" and "How did I do?" Think Aloud activities can be used with the class as a whole, although they are probably of most value with impulsive and aggressive students taught in small groups.

Classroom Meetings

Glasser (1969) developed an approach to classroom management that emphasizes self-control based on insight and group control based on social pressure. His ideas involve application of *reality therapy,* in which people are taught to see themselves as they really are by learning how others see them. When they find out that others react negatively to things they say and do, people usually are motivated to change.

There is continuing stress on the notion that every student has responsibilities to cooperate and help maintain a good learning environment. Students who fail to fulfill these responsibilities are warned that they will not be allowed to continue this way but also led to see that they have power to solve their own problems. Problems are discussed during classroom meetings in which the teacher presides but functions as a group leader rather than an instructor or authority figure. The problems are presented as belonging to the class, not just the teacher.

In addition to problems brought up by the teacher, the class discusses problems that students bring up in relation to themselves, other students, or the teacher. Students are encouraged to speak freely. The teacher may occasionally clarify or try to keep the discussion on the topic until a solution is achieved but does not criticize students or their contributions to the discussion. The continuing focus is on searching for agreeable solutions, not fixing blame.

These meetings can produce insight and change behavior (Marandola & Imber, 1979), but skill and judgment are involved in leading them successfully. Teachers must be able to shed the authority figure role and shift decision-making power from themselves to the group as well as be prepared to deal with accusations, arguments, and emotional outbursts. Such strong emotional reactions provide excellent opportunities to build insight and foster psychological development, but the group leader must deal with them constructively. Even for teachers who do not want to use the technique regularly, occasional class meetings of this kind can be useful (e.g., in developing and revising classroom rules).

Research on classroom meetings and other aspects of Glasser's reality therapy approach has produced mixed but generally positive results (Emmer & Aussiker, 1987). Glasser (1986) later updated and expanded his ideas, mostly by calling for use of learning teams or cooperative learning groups for teaching content addition to classroom meetings for socialization.

BEARING THE UNBEARABLE

Teachers often must cope with problems that cannot be solved. If enough seriously disturbed students are in the room, the teacher cannot deal with all of them successfully and teach the curriculum too. When things get unbearable, something has to give; either the problem has to be reduced or the teacher needs help from professionals outside the school. Unfortunately, outside resources adequate to do the job usually are not available, and available resources often are not successful. Genuinely therapeutic treatment is available, but unless the family is able and willing to pay high professional fees, students will likely have to go on waiting lists. They may get treated some months later, but not immediately.

Removing the student from the school is rarely an effective strategy. Suspension from school merely deepens students' alienation and makes it harder for them to cope when they come back (*if* they come back). Placement in a class for the retarded, disturbed, or delinquent, although well meant and often considered "treatment," generally is another step toward total failure.

Thus, the only effective treatment that most disturbed students get must come from their classroom teachers, with the assistance of counselors, social workers, psychologists, and administrators. For students who are almost old enough to drop out of school or are in danger of being thrown out, this may be the last real chance to head off a lifelong pattern of failure and misery. Thus, teachers in some instances can play crucial roles.

SUMMARY

Consistent use of the preventive techniques described in the previous chapter will prevent most problems, and the rest can be handled with techniques described in the present chapter. Many major disruptions start as minor misbehavior, so teachers should monitor the classroom continuously and know how to stop minor problems quickly and nondisruptively.

Much misbehavior can be ignored. When it is fleeting and not disruptive, there is no point in interrupting activities to call attention to it. If misbehavior is prolonged or begins to become disruptive, direct intervention is needed. When students know what they are supposed to be doing and when the nature of their misbehavior is obvious, there is no need to question them. Return them to productive activity as quickly and nondisruptively as possible. When it is not possible to use nondisruptive techniques, call the students' names and correct their behavior by telling them what they are supposed to be doing or reminding them of the rules. Such interventions should be brief, direct, and focused on desirable behavior. Questions, threats, and nagging should be avoided.

It is necessary to question students when misbehavior has been serious or disruptive and the teacher is unclear about the facts. Such investigations should be conducted privately so that students will have less reason to engage in face-saving behavior. Teachers should not make decisions until they have heard everyone out. After gathering the facts, teachers should take action aimed at both resolving the present problem and preventing its return. This will mean clarification of expected behavior and perhaps a new rule or agreement. Ordinarily, there will be no need for punishment.

Because punishment is a stopgap measure rather than a solution and because it involves many undesirable side effects, it should be used only as a last resort. When it is used, everyone should understand that punished students brought on the punishment through repeated misbehavior, leaving the teacher no other choice. Appropriate forms of punishment include restriction of privileges, exclusion from the group, and assignments that force students to reflect on the rules and their rationales. Punishment should be related to the offense, as brief and mild as possible, and flexible enough to allow students to redeem themselves by correcting their behavior.

A few students with long-standing and severe disturbances will require extraordinary corrective measures. Suggestions for dealing with several common types are given in this chapter. Such serious problems require careful observation and diagnosis, followed by individualized treatment.

Although it is almost always useful to gather information and solicit advice, teachers should think carefully before involving anyone else in their dealings with problem students. This step may escalate the problem in the minds of everyone and lead to undesirable self-fulfilling prophecy effects. Most relevant information can be gotten by observing and questioning the students themselves, and most beneficial changes will come as a result of time spent establishing and using a good relationship. Classroom problems must be solved in the classroom, regardless of problems a student may have outside.

This chapter and the last have been eclectic, drawing ideas about classroom management from many sources. Readers wanting more information can consult sources that describe methods based on particular points of view, such as contingency contracting, cognitive behavior modification, or the classroom meetings approach of Glasser.

SUGGESTED ACTIVITIES AND QUESTIONS

1. Part of dealing with problems effectively is the ability to recognize and conceptualize problems and potential solution strategies. However, behavior one teacher views as a problem and reacts to quickly and strongly may not seem noteworthy to another teacher. Think about the teaching situation you envision yourself in and identify behaviors that, although relatively minor, you would want to eliminate—behaviors that you would deal with overtly and publicly. How do your perceptions of minor problems correspond with those of your classmates? If you have not student-taught, try to find two or three friends who have done so to see if their lists are different from yours. Would students and teachers with more experience be more or less likely to react to minor problems? To what extent do you think students would agree with your examples of minor problems that you would not tolerate? Would students be more or less lenient than you would be? Why?

2. Reread the three cases presented in Chapter 1, pinpoint any management errors the teacher made, and describe which of the three teachers in Chapter 1 is the best manager. Why? How could the teacher have behaved more profitably?

3. Reread the four cases that appear at the beginning of this chapter. Analyze each case and indicate ways in which the situation could be improved on.

4. Summarize in five brief paragraphs the guidelines for dealing with showing off, defiance, aggression, unresponsiveness, and failure to complete assignments. Practice your ability to deal with these problems in role-playing situations. Specify a hypothetical problem,

assign some participants to the student and teacher roles, and allow the rest to observe and provide feedback.

5. Review or construct a list of student behaviors or characteristics that are most likely to embarrass you or to make you anxious. Practice how you will deal with these. For example, if you dislike threats to your authority, list student behaviors likely to anger you and practice how you would respond. Then role-play your response with other participants. For example, how would you respond (or would you respond) in this situation?

    TEACHER: You're right, Frank. What I told you yesterday was incorrect.
       HERB: (Gleefully bellowing from the back of the room) You're always wrong! We never know when to believe you!

6. Why do the authors not recommend the use of physical punishment?

7. What steps can teachers follow to make exclusion from the group effective punishment? In particular, how should teachers behave when excluding or readmitting students to group activities?

8. A ninth-grade teacher sees Bill Thomas (without apparent provocation) grab Tim Grant's comb and throw it on the floor. Bill and Tim begin to push each other. What should the teacher do? Be specific. Write out or role-play the actual words you would use. Would you behave differently if you had not seen what preceded the pushing?

9. Compare how you responded to the vignettes about contingency contracting on page 197 with the responses of a few classmates.

REFERENCES

Anderson, C. (1985). The investigation of school climate. In G. Austin & H. Garber (Eds.), *Research on exemplary schools*. New York: Academic Press.

Ballard, K., & Glynn, T. (1975). Behavioral self-management in story writing with elementary school children. *Journal of Applied Behavioral Analysis, 8*, 387–398.

Bandura, A. (1986). *Social foundations of thought and action: A social cognitive theory*. Englewood Cliffs, NJ: Prentice-Hall.

Bandura, A. (1989). Human agency in social cognitive theory. *American Psychologist, 44*, 1175–1184.

Blank, M. (1973). *Teaching learning in the preschool: A dialogue approach*. Columbus, OH: Merrill.

Brophy, J., & Evertson, C. (1978). Context variables in teaching. *Educational Psychologist, 12*, 310–316.

Brophy, J., & McCaslin, M. (1992). Teachers' reports of how they perceive and cope with problem students. *Elementary School Journal, 93*, 3–68.

Camp, B., & Bash, M. (1981). *Think aloud: Increasing social and cognitive skills—a problem-solving program for children, primary level*. Champaign, IL: Research Press.

Canter, L. (1976). *Assertive discipline: A take-charge approach for today's educator*. Santa Monica, CA: Canter & Associates, Inc.

Canter, L. (1981). *Assertive discipline follow-up guidebook*. Santa Monica, CA: Canter & Associates, Inc.

Canter, L. (1988). Let the educator beware: A response to Curwin and Mendler. *Educational Leadership, 46*(2), 71–73.

Curwin, R., & Mendler, A. (1988). Packaged discipline programs: Let the buyer beware. *Educational Leadership, 46*(2), 68–71.

Douglas, V., Perry, P., Marton, P., & Garson, C. (1976). Assessment of a cognitive training program for hyperactive children. *Journal of Abnormal Child Psychology, 4,* 389–410.

Emmer, E., & Aussiker, A. (1990). *School and classroom discipline programs: How well do they work?* In O. C. Moles (Ed.), *Student discipline strategies: Research and practice.* Albany: State University of New York Press.

Evertson, C., Emmer, E., Clements, B., Sanford, J., & Worsham, M. (1993). *Classroom management for elementary teachers* (3rd ed.). Englewood Cliffs, NJ: Prentice-Hall.

Felmlee, D., Eder, D., & Tsui, W. (1985). Peer influence on classroom attention. *Social Psychology Quarterly, 48,* 215–226.

Glasser, W. (1969). *Schools without failure.* New York: Harper & Row.

Glasser, W. (1977). Ten steps to good discipline. *Today's Education, 66,* 61–63.

Glasser, W. (1986). *Control theory in the classroom.* New York: Harper & Row.

Gordon, T. (1974). *T.E.T. Teacher effectiveness training.* New York: McKay.

Gottfredson, G., & Gottfredson, D. (1986). *Victimization in six hundred schools: An analysis of the roots of disorder.* New York: Plenum.

Hawkins, D., Doueck, H., & Lishner, D. (1988). Changing teaching practices in mainstream classrooms to improve bonding and behavior of low achievers. *American Educational Research Journal, 25,* 31–50.

Hoffman, S. (Ed.). (1991). Educational partnerships: Home and school community. *Elementary School Journal, 91*(3). Special Issue.

Hughes, J. (1988). *Cognitive behavior therapy with children in schools.* Elmsford, NY: Pergamon.

Hyman, I., & Wise, J. (Eds.). (1979). *Corporal punishment in American education: Readings in history, practice and alternatives.* Philadelphia: Temple University Press.

Jones, V. (1988). *A systematic approach for responsibly managing the disruptive and irresponsible behavior of at-risk students.* Paper presented at the annual meeting of the American Educational Research Association, New Orleans.

Kauffman, J., Hallahan, D., Mostert, M., Trent, S., & Nuttycombe, D. (1993). *Managing classroom behavior: A reflective case approach.* Boston: Allyn & Bacon.

Kendall, P., & Hollon, S. (1979). *Cognitive-behavioral interventions: Theory, research, and procedures.* New York: Academic Press.

Kounin, J. (1970). *Discipline and group management in classrooms.* New York: Holt, Rinehart and Winston.

Macmillan, A., & Kolvin, I. (1977). Behavior modification in teaching strategy: Some emergent problems and suggested solutions. *Educational Researcher, 20,* 10–21.

Marandola, P., & Imber, S. (1979). Glasser's classroom meeting: A humanistic approach to behavior change with preadolescent inner-city learning disabled children. *Journal of Learning Disabilities, 12,* 383–387.

McCaslin, M., & Good, T. (1992). Compliant cognition: The misalliance of management and instructional goals in current school reform. *Educational Researcher, 21,* 4–17.

McCormack, S. (1989). Response to Render, Padilla, and Krank: But practitioners say it works! *Educational Leadership, 47*(7), 77–79.

McDaniel, T. (1986). A primer on classroom discipline: Principles old and new. *Phi Delta Kappan, 68*, 63–67.

McDaniel, T. (1989). The discipline debate: A road through the thicket. *Educational Leadership, 47*(7), 81–82.

Meichenbaum, D. (1977). *Cognitive-behavior modification: An integrated approach.* New York: Plenum.

Meichenbaum, D., & Goodman, J. (1971). Training impulsive children to talk to themselves. *Journal of Abnormal Psychology, 77*, 115–126.

Metz, M. (1978). *Classrooms and corridors.* Berkeley: University of California Press.

Mulryan, C. (1989). *A study of intermediate-grade students' involvement and participation in cooperative small groups in mathematics.* Unpublished doctoral dissertation, University of Missouri-Columbia.

O'Leary, S., & Dubey, D. (1979). Applications of self-control procedures by children: A review. *Journal of Applied Behavior Analysis, 12*, 449–465.

Parkway, F., & Stanford, B. (1992). *Becoming a teacher* (2nd ed.). Boston: Allyn & Bacon.

Peterson, R., Loveless, S., Knapp, T., Loveless, B., Basta, S., & Anderson, S. (1979). The effects of teacher use of I-messages on student disruptive and study behavior. *Psychological Record, 29*, 187–199.

Premack, D. (1965). Reinforcement theory. In D. Levine (Ed.), *Nebraska symposium on motivation* (Vol. 13). Lincoln: University of Nebraska Press.

Render, G., Padilla, J., & Krank, H. (1989). What research really shows about assertive discipline. *Educational Leadership, 47*(7), 72–75.

Robin, A., Schneider, M., & Dolnick, M. (1976). The turtle technique: An extended case study of self-control in the classroom. *Psychology in the Schools, 13*, 449–453.

Robinson, P., Newby, T., & Ganzell, S. (1981). A token system for a class of underachieving hyperactive children. *Journal of Applied Behavior Analysis, 14*, 307–315.

Rohrkemper, M. (1982). Teacher self-assessment. In D. Duke (Ed.), *Helping teachers manage classrooms.* Alexandria, VA: Association for Supervision and Curriculum Development.

Rosenbaum, M., & Drabman, R. (1979). Self-control training in the classroom: A review and critique. *Journal of Applied Behavior Analysis, 12*, 467–485.

Rosswork, S. (1977). Goal-setting: The effects of an academic task with varying magnitudes of incentive. *Journal of Educational Psychology, 69*, 710–715.

Sagotsky, G., Patterson, C., & Lepper, M. (1978). Training children's self-control: A field experiment in self-monitoring and goal-setting in the classroom. *Journal of Experimental Child Psychology, 25*, 242–253.

Skinner, B. (1953). *Science and human behavior.* New York: Macmillan.

Weinstein, C., & Mignano, A., Jr. (1993). *Elementary classroom management: Lessons from research and practice.* New York: McGraw-Hill.

Weinstein, R., & Middlestadt, S. (1979). Student perceptions of teacher interactions with male high and low achievers. *Journal of Educational Psychology, 71*, 421–431.

Wu, S., Pink, W., Crain, R., & Moles, O. (1982). Student suspension: A critical reappraisal. *Urban Review, 14*, 245–303.

FORM 5.1. Teacher's Reaction to Inattention and Misbehavior

USE: *When the teacher is faced with problems of inattention or misbehavior*
PURPOSE: *To see if teacher handles these situations appropriately*
    *Code the following information concerning teacher's response to mis-
behavior or to inattentiveness. Code only when teacher seems to be aware of
the problem; do not code minor problems that teacher doesn't even notice.*

BEHAVIOR CATEGORIES   CODES

A. *TYPE OF SITUATION*   A B C
    1. Total class, lesson or discussion   1. 3 3 4
    2. Small group activity—problem in group   2. 3 3 4,6
    3. Small group activity—problem out of group   3. 1 2 2
    4. Seatwork checking or study period   4. 1 3 4
    5. Other (specify)   5. 4 3 2

B. *TYPE OF MISBEHAVIOR*   6. __ __ __
    1. Brief, nondisruptive, should be ignored   7. __ __ __
    2. Minor, but extended or repeated. Should   8. __ __ __
       be stopped nondisruptively   9. __ __ __
    3. Disruptive, should be stopped quickly. No   10. __ __ __
       questions needed   11. __ __ __
    4. Disruptive, questions needed or advisable   12. __ __ __
    5. Other (specify)   13. __ __ __
                                                   14. __ __ __
C. *TEACHER'S RESPONSE(S)*   15. __ __ __
    1. Ignores (deliberately)
    2. Nonverbal; uses eye contact, gestures or   16. __ __ __
       touch, or moves near offender   17. __ __ __
    3. Praises someone else's good behavior   18. __ __ __
    4. Calls offender's name; calls for attention or 19. __ __ __
       work; gives rule reminder. No overdwelling 20. __ __ __
    5. Overdwells on misbehavior, nags
    6. Asks rhetorical or meaningless questions   21. __ __ __
    7. Asks appropriate questions—investigates publicly 22. __ __ __
    8. Investigates privately, now or later   23. __ __ __
    9. Threatens punishment if behavior is repeated 24. __ __ __
    10. Punishes (note type)   25. __ __ __
    11. Other (specify)

CHECK IF APPLICABLE
_____ 1. Teacher delays too long before acting, so problems escalate
_____ 2. Teacher identifies wrong student or fails to include all involved
_____ 3. Teacher fails to specify appropriate behavior (when this is not
            clear)
_____ 4. Teacher fails to specify rationale behind demands (when this is
            not clear)
_____ 5. Teacher attributes misbehavior to ill will, evil motives
_____ 6. Teacher describes misbehavior as a typical or unchangeable trait;
            labels student

NOTES:
    *#1, 2, and 4 were all for student #12 (he seems
to be the only consistent problem as far as
management goes).*

FORM 5.2. Teacher's Response to Problem Students

USE: When the class contains one or more students who present chronic,
severe problems in personal adjustment or classroom behavior
PURPOSE: To inventory the teacher's coping strategies
Pick a particular problem student and check the strategies that the
teacher uses for coping with this student.

A. GENERAL STRATEGIES

_____ 1. Control undesirable behavior through demands or threats of
punishment

_____ 2. Offer incentives or rewards for improved behavior

_____ 3. Provide modeling, training, or other instruction designed to
teach the student more effective ways of coping (either in
general or in particular situations in which problem behavior is
frequent for this student)

_____ 4. Identify and treat underlying causes believed to be
responsible for the student's symptomatic behavior (home
pressures, self-concept problems, etc.)

_____ 5. Provide counseling designed to increase the student's insight
into the problem behavior and its causes or meanings

_____ 6. Attempt to change the student's troublesome attitudes or
beliefs through logical appeal or persuasion

_____ 7. Attempt to provide encouragement, reassurance, or support
to the student's self-concept through creating a supportive
environment

_____ 8. Attempt to develop a close personal relationship with the
student

_____ 9. Other (describe)

B. SPECIFIC STRATEGIES

_____ 1. Minimize conflict by intervening as seldom and as indirectly
as possible

_____ 2. Use humor or other face-saving or tension reduction
techniques when direct intervention is necessary

_____ 3. Maintain close physical proximity or monitor the student's behavior closely

_____ 4. Use time-out procedures to extinguish disruptive behavior by removing the opportunity for the student to misbehave and be reinforced for it

_____ 5. Use time-out procedures to allow the student an opportunity to calm down and reflect after an outburst

_____ 6. Use behavior contracts to formalize offers of reward for improved behavior

_____ 7. Use modeling or role play procedures to help student learn the self talk that controls adaptive responses to frustrating or threatening situations

_____ 8. Adjust work expectations or assignments if these seem inappropriate and appear to be contributing to the problem

_____ 9. Adjust seat assignment, group assignment, or other social environment/peer relationship factors

_____ 10. Attempt to develop peer support for the problem student

_____ 11. Attempt to develop peer pressure on the problem student (to stop behaving inappropriately)

_____ 12. Active listening, "I" statements, or attempts to negotiate "no-lose" solutions (Gordon's techniques)

_____ 13. Attempt to get the student to recognize problem behavior, accept responsibility, and commit to a plan for improvement (Glasser's techniques)

_____ 14. Contact with family members

_____ 15. Involvement of mental health professionals

_____ 16. Other (describe)

C. ASSESSMENT

Which of these strategies appear to be helpful, and which do not? Which might be more helpful if they were implemented more often, more systematically, or in a different way? Are there strategies that the teacher doesn't use that might be helpful?

FORM 5.2. (Continued)

Chapter
6

Motivation

INTRODUCTION

"You can lead a horse to water, but you can't make him drink." Teachers face the problem summed up in this familiar saying. Appropriate curricula and good teaching are necessary but not sufficient for ensuring that students accomplish instructional goals. If students minimize their investment of attention and effort, not much will be learned. The degree to which students invest attention and effort in classroom activities depends on their *motivation*—their willingness to engage in the activities and their reasons for doing so.

The concept of motivation refers to subjective experience and thus cannot be observed directly. Instead, it must be inferred from students' self-reports and classroom behavior. For example, a student may be staring in the direction of the clock at the time when the class is working on an assignment. Without more information, it is difficult to know the meaning of this behavior or the motivation that lies behind it. Is the student thinking about the assignment or about something else? If he is thinking about the assignment, is he focused on the task and thinking productively, or might he be upset and worried because he is "lost"? If he is not thinking about the task, is this because he has completed it successfully, or might he be bored or preoccupied with some personal matter? The teacher may need to address these questions, especially if the behavior continues. If investigation reveals that the student has not completed the task yet has not been working on it, the teacher will need to intervene in a way that refocuses the student on accomplishing the intended goals. To the extent that the problem is motivational, this intervention will need to address these motivational aspects in addition to or instead of helping the student understand what needs to be done.

Seemingly similar behavior patterns can result from quite different underlying motivational patterns, although the dynamics involved might remain hidden from teachers unless they get to know their students as individuals and spend time talking to them personally. For example, McCaslin (1990) interviewed sixth graders about how they handle the "hard stuff" in mathematics. The following excerpts are from interviews with two girls who were best friends and were viewed by their teacher as sharing a tendency to be persistent and effortful in working on assignments. Despite this teacher-perceived similarity, the girls were quite different in their approach to difficult math problems. Both girls persistently tried to solve the problems, but the first one did so mostly in order to get the assignment finished so that she could interact with her friends. She made strategic use of fantasies connected with this goal as a way to help her get through the rough spots:

> A lot of times I get sick of things so I just want to stop. And I do . . . I always, whenever I'm working and I just get sick of working, I just stop because I can't stand it anymore. I think of things that I like to do. Like in school, I'm going to play with my friends, I think of all the things that are fun that we do, and stuff. But I have to get this done and *right* before I can go to do that.

In contrast, her friend was more focused on learning with understanding (not just getting correct answers). She was also less successful in avoiding the frustration and worry that accompanied failure to solve difficult problems easily. Not having developed her friend's ability to use fantasy strategically, she had to distract herself by engaging in alternative activities:

> Well, I think I'm going to get them all wrong. And I kind of feel like I have to get up and walk around and think about it. I feel like I have to stop and work on something else for a little bit. I might get up and work on spelling for a minute 'cause that's pretty easy and I don't have to think about it, 'cause spelling I just know the answers and they're right there. I can't think about the math and what I'm going to do. . . . (It's time for a break) when I get pretty frustrated, I think to myself "You can't do this," and I start tearing, I start biting my pencil. Then I know I have to get up and do something else. I just get so frustrated with it I can't think. . . . I start to fiddle with my hands, go like that. I know I have to do something else. 'Cause I really get mad. I don't take a real long (break) time, maybe just 10 minutes. Then I come back to work again. Just to get it out of my mind for a minute.

McCaslin's analyses and other recent studies indicate that students differ dramatically in the motivational patterns that they bring to the classroom and in the related strategies that they employ for setting goals, addressing task demands, and seeking to make "repairs" when their initial efforts do not succeed. Their motives and coping strategies are affected by what they learn at home, by interaction with peers, and by the norms and expectations that prevail in the room and the larger school environment, in addition to what their teacher says and does. Whatever backgrounds and motivational patterns students bring into the classroom with them, however, teachers need to do what they can to encourage students to engage in activities with the intention of developing the intended knowledge and skills. Consequently, in this chapter we address student motivation from the point of view of the teacher. That is, we focus on conditions that teachers can create and strategies that teachers can use to increase the likelihood that their students will be motivated to learn with understanding.

We begin with two brief vignettes depicting teachers starting instruction on the *Declaration of Independence* and the *U.S. Constitution*. Read each vignette and then record your answers to the questions.

Frank Thomas's Class

Teacher Frank Thomas begins the week with the following statement:

> Read Chapter 17 carefully because it is a key chapter; in fact, questions on it will represent about 50 percent of the next unit test. I'm going to ask a lot of questions about the facts in Chapter 17 because it covers an important part of American history. In particular, the *Declaration of Independence* is a key document that you should know "cold." You should also understand the Preamble to the *Constitution* and be able to discuss it at length. Let's begin by considering the important facts. First, who was the most important person involved in drafting the *Declaration?*

Jane Strong's Class

Jane Strong is teaching the same material to similar students. She begins in the following way:

> Before beginning our discussion of important ideas associated with the *Declaration of Independence* and the *Constitution* and their roles in American history, I want to raise four questions to provide some structure. Write down these four questions now. Later, I'll give you time to talk about them in small-group discussions: (1) What is protest? (2) Under what circumstances is it appropriate? (3) Think about the rights and privileges that you have in this school and the constraints that apply here. If you were going to write a constitution for this school, what are three important points you would include? (4) To what extent do you think that your view of a good government for this school is shared by other students?
>
> We need to consider these questions before we begin formal discussion so that you can see the problems of consensus that the framers of our *Constitution* faced. To what extent do different individuals see government in the same way? Do they have common expectations for services that facilitate their needs and regulations that inhibit their freedom? Tomorrow we are going to draft a constitution for the class.
>
> Toward the end of the week we will consider the *Declaration of Independence* more formally as we attempt to organize our understanding of the document in the following ways: (1) the historical background of its development; (2) the philosophical ideas that influenced its framers; (3) its continuing effects on life in American society.

Questions

Given these brief glimpses into the two classrooms, how would you answer the following questions: Would you rather have Frank Thomas or Jane Strong as your history teacher? Why? Which teacher's students are likely to be more motivated to learn about the *Declaration of Independence* and the *U.S. Constitution*? To be more concerned about passing the test and getting a good grade? How might the two classes differ in (1) how they would describe the nature and purposes of history classes, (2) how they would approach the content when studying, and (3) what they would learn from the unit?

Skill in Motivating Students

Skill in motivating students to learn is basic to teachers' effectiveness. Like classroom management, however, motivation did not receive much scholarly attention until recently, so that teachers were forced to rely on unsystematic "bag-of-tricks" approaches or on advice stemming from questionable theorizing. Much of the latter advice was based on one of two contradictory yet frequently expressed views that are both incorrect (at least in their extreme form). The first view is that learning should be fun and that motivation problems appear because the teacher somehow has converted an inherently enjoyable activity into drudgery. We believe that students should find academic activities meaningful and worthwhile, but not fun in the same sense that recreational games and pastimes are fun. The other extreme view is that school activities are necessarily boring, unrewarding, and even aversive, so that we must rely on extrinsic rewards and punishments in order to force students to engage in these unpleasant tasks.

Recent theory and research on motivation have led to rejection of both of these extreme views in favor of a more balanced and sophisticated approach and have suggested a rich range of motivational strategies. We summarize this theory and research here. For more information see Ames (1987, 1990); Ames and Ames (1984, 1985, 1989); Corno and Rohrkemper (1985); Deci and Ryan (1985); Dweck (1991); Good and Brophy (1990); Heckhausen (1991); Keller (1983); Lepper and Greene (1978); Maehr and Kleiber (1987); McCombs (1984); Renninger, Hidi, and Krapp (1992); Stipek (1988); Weiner (1992); and Zimmerman and Schunk (1989).

BASIC MOTIVATIONAL CONCEPTS

We begin with definitions of basic motivational concepts and discussion of some key points about motivation in the classroom. Psychologists traditionally use motivational concepts to account for the initiation, direction, intensity, and persistence of behavior. *Motives* are hypothetical constructs explaining why people are doing what they are doing. Motives are distinguished from related constructs such as *goals* (the immediate objectives of particular sequences of behavior) and *strategies* (the methods used to achieve goals and thus to satisfy or at least respond to motives). For example, a person responds to hunger (motive) by going to a restaurant (strategy) to get food (goal). Motives, goals, and strategies are less easily distinguished in analyses of classroom situations that call for intentional learning of cognitive content, because optimal forms of motivation to learn and cognitive strategies for accomplishing that learning tend to occur together (Meece, Blumenfeld, & Hoyle, 1988; Nolen & Haladyna, 1990; Pintrich & DeGroot, 1990; Schiefele, 1991; Wentzel, 1989; Zimmerman and Schunk, 1989). We can make conceptual distinctions for purposes of analysis, but it can be difficult to separate motives, goals, and strategies as well as to separate motivation from cognition.

Consider the vignettes presented earlier in this chapter. If the two classes responded solely to what their respective teachers emphasized in introducing the *Declaration* and *Constitution*, they would develop contrasting motives, goals, and strategies. Frank Thomas's students would be motivated primarily by a desire to do well on the unit test. Furthermore, given what Frank said about the test, their primary study goal would be to memorize the *Declaration*, the *Preamble*, and various facts (names, dates, etc.). Consequently, their study efforts would emphasize rote memorizing strategies (repeating the material until they could regurgitate it "by heart").

In contrast, Jane Strong's students are more likely to *want* to learn about the *Declaration* and *Constitution* because they find the information interesting and important, not just because they need it to pass a test. Given Jane's introduction, they are likely to adopt goals and strategies that involve concentrating on the meanings and implications of the material, placing it in historical context, relating it to personal ideas and experiences, and thinking about its applications to the modern world. This is a much more broad-ranging, personalized, and meaningful way of processing the information than merely committing facts to memory. It involves a broader range of goals and more diverse strategies for accomplishing those goals (posing and answering questions about the material, discussing it with peers, putting oneself in the place of the framers and considering the documents as vehicles constructed to communicate ideas and accomplish political purposes rather than merely as text to be learned).

The motives, goals, and strategies that students develop in response to classroom activities depend on the nature of the activities themselves (Blumenfeld, Mergendoller, & Swarthout, 1987) as well as on how the teacher presents them to the students. If students are motivated solely by grades or other extrinsic rewards, they are likely to adopt goals and strategies that concentrate on meeting minimum requirements that entitle them to acceptable reward levels. They will do what they must to prepare for tests, then forget most of what they learned. It is better when students find academic activities intrinsically rewarding. However, they may not learn what their teacher would like them to learn if the basis for their intrinsic motivation is primarily affective or emotional (they enjoy the activity) rather than cognitive or intellectual (they find it interesting, meaningful, or worthwhile to learn what the activity is designed to teach). Consequently, it is important that teachers use strategies designed to *motivate their students to learn* from academic activities—to seek to gain the intended knowledge and skill benefits from these activities and to set goals and use cognitive strategies that are appropriate for doing so.

Motivation as Expectancy × Value

Most approaches to motivation, including the present one, fit within *expectancy ×
value theory* (Feather, 1982). This theory holds that the effort people are willing to
expend on a task is a product of (1) the degree to which they *expect* to be able to
perform the task successfully if they apply themselves (and thus the degree to
which they expect to get whatever rewards that successful task performance will
bring), and (2) the degree to which they *value* those rewards. Effort investment is
viewed as the product rather than the sum of the expectancy and value factors
because it is assumed that no effort at all will be invested in a task if one factor is
missing entirely. People do not invest effort in tasks that do not lead to valued
outcomes even if they know that they can perform the tasks successfully, nor do
they invest in even highly valued tasks if they believe that they cannot succeed on
these tasks no matter how hard they try. Thus, *expectancy × value theories of motivation imply that teachers need to both help their students appreciate the value of
school activities and make sure that the students can achieve success in these activities if they apply reasonable effort.*

Until recently, motivation research had concentrated on expectancy issues
(Berndt & Miller, 1990). This work produced suggestions about how to develop the
success expectations that are so crucial to students' willingness to commit themselves to challenging achievement goals. Recently, researchers have begun to focus
on task value issues (e.g., why students should want to succeed on the tasks in the
first place). Eccles and Wigfield (1985) suggest that subjective task value has three
major components; (1) *attainment value* (the importance of attaining success on the
task in order to affirm our self-concept or fulfill needs for achievement, power, or
prestige); (2) *intrinsic or interest value* (the enjoyment that we get from engaging in
the task); and (3) *utility value* (the role that engaging in the task may play in advancing our career or helping us to reach other larger goals). We believe that this is
a useful classification scheme, although we place more emphasis on the cognitive
aspects of student motivation to learn academic content. Thus we include *the pleasure of achieving understanding or skill mastery* under attainment value; *aesthetic
appreciation of the content or skill* under intrinsic value; and *awareness of the role
of learning in improving the quality of one's life or making one a better person*
under utility value.

The rest of the chapter is organized according to these expectancy × value theory ideas. After discussing basic preconditions that must be in place if teachers are
to be successful in motivating their students, we discuss approaches to motivation
that involve establishing and maintaining success *expectations* in students. Then we
describe three sets of motivational strategies designed to enhance the subjective
value that students place on school tasks: extrinsic motivational strategies, intrinsic
motivational strategies, and strategies for stimulating motivation to learn.

ESSENTIAL PRECONDITIONS FOR SUCCESSFUL USE OF
MOTIVATIONAL STRATEGIES

The following four preconditions should be established to set the stage for use of
the motivational strategies to be discussed.

Supportive Environment

To be motivated to learn, students need both ample opportunities to learn and steady encouragement and support of their learning efforts. Because such motivation is unlikely to develop in a chaotic classroom, it is important that the teacher organize and manage the classroom as an effective learning environment (see Chapters 4 and 5).

Furthermore, because anxious or alienated students are unlikely to develop motivation to learn, it is important that learning occurs within a relaxed and supportive atmosphere. *The teacher should be a patient, encouraging person who supports students' learning efforts.* Students should feel comfortable taking intellectual risks because they know that they will not be embarrassed or criticized if they make a mistake. The instructional emphasis should be on helping students to achieve mastery rather than on displaying their current abilities to perform, and the evaluation emphasis should be on assessing their progress toward instructional goals rather than on comparing them with one another (Ames, 1987; Ames & Archer, 1988; Marshall, 1990; McGowen, Sutton, & Smith, 1990; Mitman & Lash, 1988; Stipek & Daniels, 1988).

Appropriate Level of Challenge or Difficulty

Activities should be at an appropriate level of difficulty. If tasks are so familiar or easy that they constitute nothing but busywork, and especially if they are so unfamiliar or difficult that even persistent students cannot succeed on them, no strategies for inducing motivation are likely to succeed. *Tasks are of appropriate difficulty when students are clear enough about what to do and how to do it so that they can achieve high levels of success if they persistently employ appropriate strategies.* When students encounter such tasks routinely, they are able to concentrate on learning without worrying about failure.

Meaningful Learning Objectives

Activities should teach things that are worth learning. Students are not motivated to learn when engaged in pointless or meaningless activities such as the following: continued practice on skills that have already been mastered thoroughly; memorizing lists for no good reason; looking up and copying definitions of terms that are never used meaningfully in readings or assignments; reading material that is written in such sketchy, technical, or abstract language as to make it essentially meaningless; and working on tasks assigned merely to fill time rather than to fulfill worthwhile instructional objectives. Where skills must be practiced until they become smooth and automatic, much such practice should occur within whole-task application activities rather than be confined to isolated practice of part skills. Elementary students should be given opportunities to read for information or pleasure in addition to practicing word attack skills, to solve problems and apply mathematics in addition to practicing number facts and computations, and to write prose or poetry compositions or actual correspondence in addition to practicing spelling and penmanship. Secondary students should learn how and why knowledge was developed in addition to acquiring the knowledge itself and should have opportunities to apply what they are learning to their own lives or to current social, political, or scientific issues.

Moderation and Variation in Strategy Use

Motivational strategies can be overused in two respects. First, the need for such strategies varies with the situation. When content is unfamiliar and its value is not obvious to students, significant motivational effort involving several strategies may be needed. In contrast, little or no special motivational effort may be needed when the activity involves things that students are already eager to learn. Thus, motivational strategies can be counterproductive if they are used when they are not needed, go on too long, or are carried to extremes. Second, any particular strategy may lose its effectiveness if used too often or too routinely. Thus, teachers should master and use a variety of motivational strategies.

With these four preconditions in mind, let us consider the motivational strategies that various writers have suggested.

MOTIVATING BY MAINTAINING SUCCESS EXPECTATIONS

Much of the best-known research on motivation has focused on students' success expectations. Research on *achievement motivation* (Dweck & Elliott, 1983) has established that effort and persistence are greater in individuals who set goals of moderate difficulty (neither too hard nor too easy), seriously commit themselves to pursuing these goals rather than treat them as mere "pie-in-the-sky" hopes, and concentrate on trying to achieve success rather than on trying to avoid failure. Research on *efficacy perceptions* (Bandura, 1989; Bandura & Schunk, 1981) has shown that effort and persistence are greater in individuals who believe that they are capable of performing a task successfully and thus earning the rewards that such success will bring. These individuals view themselves as competent or efficacious. Research on *causal attributions* for performance suggests that effort and persistence are greater in individuals who attribute their performance to internal and controllable causes rather than to external or uncontrollable causes (Weiner, 1984, 1992).

These and related approaches suggest that teachers need to encourage their students to develop the following perceptions and attributional inferences concerning their performance at school:

Effort-outcome covariation. Recognition that there is a predictable relationship between the level of effort invested in a task and the level of success or mastery that can be expected (Cooper, 1979).

Internal locus of control. Recognition that the potential to control outcomes (the degree of success achieved) lies within themselves rather than in external factors that they cannot control (Stipek & Weisz, 1981; Thomas, 1980).

Concept of self as origin rather than pawn. Recognition that they can bring about desired outcomes through their own actions (act as origins) rather than feeling that they are pawns whose fate is determined by factors beyond their control (deCharms, 1976).

Sense of efficacy/competence. Confidence that they have the ability (including the specific strategies needed) to succeed on a task if they choose to invest the necessary effort (Bandura, 1989; Bandura & Schunk, 1981; Schunk, 1991; Schunk & Hanson, 1985; Weisz & Cameron, 1985).

Attribution to internal, controllable causes. Tendency to attribute successes to a combination of sufficient ability and reasonable effort and to attribute failures either to insufficient effort (if this has been the case) or to confusion about what to do or reliance on inappropriate strategies for trying to do it (but not to lack of ability or to uncontrollable factors such as bad luck) (Butkowsky & Willows, 1980; Frieze, Francis, & Hanusa, 1983; Weiner, 1992; Whitley & Frieze, 1985).

Incremental concept of ability. Perception of academic ability as potential that is developed continually through learning activities rather than as a fixed capacity that determines and limits what can be accomplished (Dweck & Elliott, 1983).

Several strategies have been suggested for helping students to maintain success expectations and these associated perceptions and attributions. All assume that students are given tasks of appropriate difficulty and receive timely and informative feedback about the correctness of their responses and about the progress they are making toward ultimate goals. Thus, these strategies involve helping students to make and recognize genuine progress rather than misleading them or offering them only empty reassurances.

Programming for Success

The simplest way to ensure that students expect success is to make sure that they achieve it consistently so that they can adjust to each new step without much confusion or frustration. However, two points need to be made about this strategy so that it is not understood as suggesting that teachers should mostly assign under-challenging busywork.

First, we speak here of *success that leads to gradual mastery of appropriately challenging objectives,* not to quick, easy success achieved through "automatic" application of overlearned skills to overly familiar tasks. Students should be paced through the curriculum as briskly as they can progress without undue frustration. Thus, programming for success is a means toward the end of maximizing ultimate achievement, not an end in itself.

Second, keep in mind *the role of the teacher.* Potential levels of success depend not only on the difficulty of the task itself, but also on the degree to which the teacher prepares the students for the task through advance instruction and assists their learning efforts through guidance and feedback. A task that would be too difficult for students left to their own devices might be just right when learned with assistance. In fact, contemporary theorists believe that instruction should focus on the *zone of proximal development,* which refers to the range of knowledge and skills that students are not yet ready to learn on their own but could learn with help from teachers (see Chapter 10).

Programming for success means continually challenging students within their zones of proximal development, yet making it possible for them to meet these challenges by providing sufficient instruction, guidance, and feedback. It may be necessary to provide extra instruction to slower students, to monitor their progress more closely, and to give them briefer or easier assignments if they cannot handle the regular ones even with extra help and support. Nevertheless, teachers should continue to demand that they put forth reasonable effort and progress as fast as their abilities allow. Effective teachers do not give up on low achievers or allow them to give up on themselves.

Teaching Goal Setting, Performance Appraisal, and Self-Reinforcement

Students' reactions to their own performance depend not just on their absolute levels of success but also on their perceptions of what they have achieved. Some students may not fully appreciate their own accomplishments unless helped to identify appropriate standards to use in judging their progress.

This process begins with *goal setting.* Research indicates that setting goals and making a commitment to trying to reach these goals increase performance (Bandura & Schunk, 1981; Locke & Latham, 1990; Tollefson et al., 1984). Goal setting is especially effective when the goals are (1) *proximal* rather than distal (they refer to performance on a task to be attempted here and now rather than to attainment of some ultimate goal in the distant future), (2) *specific* (complete a page of math problems with no more than one error) rather than global (do a good job), and (3) *challenging* (difficult but reachable) rather than too easy or too hard. For example, a struggling mathematics student faced with an assignment involving 20 problems of varying difficulty levels might be asked to adopt the goals of making a serious attempt to solve each problem and persisting until confident that at least 15 of the problems have been solved correctly. Such a suggestion is likely to lead to more persistent and higher quality problem-solving efforts, and ultimately to better performance, than suggestions such as "Do the best you can," or "Do as many as you can." These suggestions are too vague to function as specific challenges toward which students can work as goals.

For a brief assignment, meeting the instructional objective is the appropriate goal. However, perfect performance on more comprehensive assignments or tests is not a realistic goal for many students, and these students may need help in formulating challenging but reachable goals. In the case of a long series of activities that ultimately leads to some distal goal, it is important to establish specific goals for each activity and make students aware of the linkages between these activities and achievement of the ultimate goal (Bandura & Schunk, 1981; Morgan, 1985).

Goal setting is not enough by itself; there must also be *goal commitment*. Students must take the goals seriously and commit themselves to trying to reach them. It may be necessary to negotiate goal setting with some students, or at least to provide them with guidance and stimulate them to think about their performance potential. One way is to provide a list of potential goals and ask students to commit themselves to particular goals (and associated levels of effort). Another is performance contracting, in which students formally contract for a certain level of effort or performance in exchange for specified grades or rewards (Tollefson et al., 1984). This method is time consuming and may call more attention to rewards than is desirable, but it does ensure active teacher-student negotiation about goal setting and it formalizes student commitment to goals.

Finally, students may need help in using *appropriate standards for judging levels of success*. In particular, they may need to learn to compare their work with absolute standards or with their own previous performance rather than with the performance of others. Feedback about specific responses must be accurate (errors must be labeled as such if they are to be recognized and corrected), but more general evaluative comments should provide encouragement. The teacher might note levels of success achieved in meeting established goals or describe accomplishments with reference to what is reasonable to expect rather than to absolute perfection. Some students need *specific, detailed feedback* concerning both the strengths and weaknesses of their performance (Butler, 1987; Elawar & Corno, 1985; Krampen, 1987). They may have only a vague appreciation of when and why they have done well or poorly, so that they need not only general evaluative feedback but concepts and language that they can use to describe their performance with precision. This is especially true for compositions, research projects, laboratory experiments, and other complex activities that are evaluated qualitatively. Concerning compositions, for example, teachers can comment on the relevance, accuracy, and completeness of the content; the organization of the content into a coherent beginning, middle, and end; the sequencing and subdivision of the content into appropriate paragraphs; the structuring of paragraphs to feature main ideas; the appropriateness of the style and vocabulary; and the mechanics of grammar, spelling, and punctuation.

Recent research conducted in Russia indicates that even first graders can learn to apply individual reference norms and self-evaluation processes when assessing their learning (Zuckerman, in press). In this study, students were taught to pay attention to the match between teacher- and self-evaluation. If these two evaluations of student performance coincided (regardless of the level of success achieved), a child was praised for accurate self-evaluation. Clear over- or underestimations were confronted. Evaluative responses that were not related to objective criteria were treated as opinions (individual points of view that cannot be characterized as either correct or incorrect). Over time, the students became more accurate and evidence-based in assessing their work against objective criteria.

Students who have been working toward specific proximal goals and who have the concepts and language needed to evaluate their performance accurately are in a position to *reinforce themselves* for their successes. Many do this habitually, but others need encouragement to check their work and take credit for their successes (that is, to attribute such successes to the fact that they had the ability and were willing to make the required effort). If necessary, teachers can focus students' attention on their progress more directly by comparing their current accomplishments with performance samples from earlier times or by having them keep portfolios, graphs, or other records to document their progress.

Helping Students Recognize Effort-Outcome Linkages

The following strategies are useful for developing an internal locus of control and a sense of efficacy in students and for helping them to recognize that they can achieve success if they put forth reasonable effort.

Modeling   Teachers can model beliefs about effort-outcome linkages when talking to students about the teachers' own learning and when demonstrating tasks by thinking out loud as they work through them. It is especially useful if, when teachers encounter frustration or temporary failure, they model confidence that they will succeed if they persist and search for a better strategy or for some error in their application of the strategies already tried (Zimmerman & Blotner, 1979).

Socialization and Feedback   Teachers can also stress effort-outcome linkages when socializing students or giving them feedback. They can explain that curriculum goals and instructional practices have been established to make it possible for students to succeed if they apply themselves. When necessary, teachers can reassure students that persistence (perhaps augmented by extra help) eventually pays off. Some students may need repeated statements of the teacher's confidence in their abilities to do the work or the teacher's willingness to accept slow progress so long as they consistently put forth reasonable effort.

Extra socialization is needed with low achievers when grades must be assigned according to fixed common standards or comparisons with peers or norms rather than by degree of effort expended or degree of success achieved in meeting individually prescribed goals. Low achievers may need to be socialized to take satisfaction in receiving Bs or Cs when such grades represent, for them, significant accomplishment. When this is the case, teachers should express to these students (*and* their parents) recognition of the accomplishment and appreciation of the effort it represents.

Portray Effort as Investment Rather than Risk   Students need to be made aware that learning may take time and involve confusion or mistakes, but that persistence and careful work eventually should yield knowledge or skill mastery. Furthermore, they need to realize that such mastery not only represents success on the task involved but also provides them with knowledge or skills that will make them more capable of handling higher-level tasks in the future. If they give up on a task because of frustration or fear of failure, they cheat themselves out of this growth potential.

Portray Skill Development as Incremental and Domain-specific Students need to know that their intellectual abilities are open to improvement rather than fixed and that they possess a great many such abilities rather than just a few. Difficulties in learning usually occur not because students lack ability or do not make an effort but because they lack *experience* with the type of task involved. With patience, persistence, and help from the teacher, students can acquire knowledge and skills specific to the domain that the task represents, and such *domain-specific knowledge and skills* will enable them to succeed on this task and others like it. Difficulty in learning mathematics need not imply difficulty in learning other subjects, and within mathematics, difficulty in learning to graph coordinates need not mean difficulty in learning to solve differential equations or to understand geometric relationships. Even within a particular problem area, students can expect to build up knowledge and skills gradually if they persistently apply themselves, accept teacher help, and do not lose patience or give up whenever success is not achieved easily.

Focus on Mastery In monitoring performance and giving feedback, teachers should stress the quality of students' task engagement and the degree to which they are making continuous progress toward mastery rather than comparisons with how other students are doing (Ames, 1987; Krampen, 1987; McColskey & Leary, 1985). Errors should be treated as learning opportunities, not test failures, and should lead to additional instruction and practice opportunities. Makeup exams or extra-credit assignments should be used to provide struggling students with opportunities to overcome initial failures through persistent efforts.

Encouraging Effort: An Example

If students appear convinced that they cannot do the work, teachers must pursue a fine line between two extremes. First, they must repeatedly encourage the students and express the belief that they will be able to succeed with continued effort. The students' expressions of inability should not be accepted or even legitimatized indirectly through such comments as "Well, at least try." Students should know that they learn the most by doing as much as they can for as long as they can, and therefore that they should not seek help at the first sign of difficulty. On the other hand, teachers should make it clear that they are available and willing to help if help is really needed. Here is how the situation might be handled appropriately:

STUDENT: I can't do number 4.
TEACHER: What part don't you understand?
STUDENT: I just can't do it, it's too hard!
TEACHER: I know you can do part of it because you've done the first three problems correctly. The fourth one is similar, but just a little harder. You start out the same way, but there's one extra step. Review the first three; then see if you can figure out number 4. I'll come back in a few minutes to see how you're doing.

Compare this with the following inappropriate scenario.

STUDENT: I can't do number 4.

TEACHER: You can't! Why not?

STUDENT: I just can't do it, it's too hard!

TEACHER: Don't say you can't do it—we never say we can't do it. Did you try hard?

STUDENT: Yes, but I can't do it.

TEACHER: You did the first three. Maybe if you work a little longer you could do the fourth. Why don't you do that and see what happens?

In the first example, the teacher communicated positive expectations and provided a specific suggestion about how to proceed, yet did not give the answer or do the work. Also, in providing feedback about performance on the first three problems, this teacher was more specific in noting that the answers were correct and in attributing this success to the student's knowledge and abilities, thus supporting the student's self-efficacy beliefs. In the second example, the teacher communicated halfhearted and somewhat contradictory expectations, leaving the student with no reason to believe that further effort would succeed. Students need to be socialized to recognize and rely on their own capabilities and to respond to frustration with coping strategies rather than withdrawal or dependency.

Remedial Work with Discouraged Students

Some students become discouraged to the point of "failure syndrome" or "learned helplessness." They tend to give up at the first sign of difficulty or frustration and need more intensive and individualized encouragement.

A few of these are bright students who have become accustomed to consistent, easy success that they attribute to high ability (rather than to the combination of ability and effort). When they finally encounter challenges that they cannot meet with ease, they may overreact to their difficulties and conclude that they lack ability for that content or task. Such students need to be helped to see that abilities can be developed, but the process requires active learning efforts rather than mere activation of already available knowledge and skills. Also, the process may take some time and involve some confusion or frustration. These students need to view academic activities as opportunities to learn, not just to display already developed skills.

Teachers may also encounter a few "committed underachievers" who set low goals and resist "accepting responsibility for their successes" because they do not want to be expected to maintain a high level of performance. These students need reassurance that they can attain consistent success with reasonable effort (that is, that it will not take superhuman effort). They also may benefit from counseling designed to show them that their deliberately underachieving behavior is contrary to their own long-run best interests.

Most students who need remedial work on their expectations are low achievers of limited ability who have become all too accustomed to failure. These students may benefit from the strategies used in *mastery learning* approaches: Make success likely by giving them tasks that they should be able to handle, provide them with individualized tutoring as needed, and allow them to contract for a particular level of performance and to continue to study, practice, and take tests until that level is achieved (see Chapter 7 for more on mastery learning). By virtually guaranteeing success, this approach builds confidence and increases discouraged students' willingness to take the risks involved in seriously committing themselves to challenging goals (Grabe, 1985).

Discouraged students may also benefit from "attribution retraining" approaches (Craske, 1988; Dweck & Elliott, 1983; Fowler & Peterson, 1981; Medway & Venino, 1982) in which they are given modeling, socialization, practice, and feedback designed to teach them to (1) concentrate on the task rather than worry about failure; (2) cope with failure by retracing their steps to find their mistake or by trying another approach rather than giving up; and (3) attribute their failures to insufficient effort, lack of information, or reliance on ineffective strategies rather than to lack of ability. Discouraged students are especially likely to benefit from exposure to programs that combine attribution retraining with training in strategies for accomplishing tasks (Ames, 1987; VanOverwalle, Segebarth, & Goldschstein, 1989), and from exposure to "coping models" who maintain their composure and focus on developing solutions when confronted with failure (as opposed to "success models" who sail through problems without making mistakes) (Borkowski, Weyhing, & Carr, 1988). Thus with discouraged students it is important to model not only initial problem-solving strategies but also *repair strategies*—how to diagnose and make corrections when they discover that they made an error in executing an appropriate strategy, or worse, that they were using the wrong strategy in the first place.

Finally, some students may need extra help because they suffer from severe *test anxiety*. They may learn effectively in informal, pressure-free situations but become highly anxious and perform considerably below their potential on tests or during any testlike situation in which they are aware of being monitored and evaluated. Teachers can minimize such problems by

Avoiding time pressures unless they are truly central to the skill being taught

Stressing the feedback functions rather than the evaluation or grading functions of tests when discussing tests with the students

Portraying tests as opportunities to assess progress rather than as measures of ability

Where appropriate, telling students that some problems are beyond their present achievement level so that they should not be concerned about missing them

Giving pretests to accustom the students to "failure" and to provide base rates for comparison when posttests are administered later

Teaching stress management skills and effective test-taking skills and attitudes

(See Hembree, 1988; Hill & Wigfield, 1984; Naveh-Benjamin, 1991; Wigfield & Eccles, 1989; Zeidner, Klingman, & Papko, 1988).

Concluding Comments About Success Expectations

The expectancy aspects of student motivation depend less on the degree of objective success that students achieve than on how they view their performance: what they see as possible for them to achieve with reasonable effort, whether they define this achievement as success or not, and whether they attribute their performance to controllable factors (effort, choice of strategies) or to uncontrollable factors (fixed general abilities, luck). Therefore, the motivation of all students, even the most extreme cases of learned helplessness, is open to reshaping. Empty reassurances or a few words of encouragement will not do the job, but a combination of appropriately challenging demands, socialization designed to make the students see that success can be achieved with reasonable effort, and coaching in needed cognitive strategies should be effective.

Teachers and students need to learn to view academic frustrations and failures realistically and to respond to them adaptively. As Rohrkemper and Corno (1988) pointed out, not only is some student failure inevitable, but a manageable degree of student failure is desirable. When students are challenged at optimal levels of difficulty, they make mistakes. The important thing about these mistakes is not that they occur but that learning conditions be arranged so that the students get useful feedback concerning their mistakes and use it to respond to them with renewed motivation rather than discouragement.

INDUCING STUDENTS TO VALUE ACADEMIC ACTIVITIES

The expectancy × value approach to motivation stresses that student motivation is affected not only by expectations and attributions concerning performance (Can I succeed on this task? Why did I achieve the level of success that I did?) but also by attributions concerning the reasons for their engaging in the tasks in the first place and by expectations concerning goals and objectives (What am I trying to accomplish here? What benefits can I expect to obtain from my efforts?). Traditionally, teachers have been advised to supply answers to the latter questions either by offering incentives for good performance (extrinsic motivation approach) or by teaching content and designing activities that students find enjoyable (intrinsic motivation approach). We discuss each of these approaches and then turn to a third approach that we believe is deserving of more attention than it has received to date: stimulating students' motivation to learn what is being taught.

STRATEGIES FOR SUPPLYING EXTRINSIC MOTIVATION

Extrinsic motivation strategies are in some ways the simplest, most direct, and most adaptable of the methods for dealing with the value aspects of classroom motivation. Extrinsic strategies do not attempt to increase the value that students place on the task itself, but instead link task performance to delivery of consequences that students do value. Three common forms of extrinsic motivation are rewards, emphasis on the instrumental value of tasks, and competition.

Offer Rewards as Incentives for Good Performance

Rewards are one proven way to motivate students to put forth effort, especially when the rewards are offered in advance as incentives for striving to reach specified levels of performance. Commonly used types include (1) material rewards (money, prizes, trinkets, consumables); (2) activity rewards and special privileges (opportunity to play games, use special equipment, or engage in self-selected activities); (3) grades, awards, and recognition (honor rolls, displaying good papers); (4) praise and social rewards; and (5) teacher rewards (special attention, personalized interaction, opportunities to go places or do things with the teacher).

Rewards are more effective for increasing effort than for improving quality of performance. They guide behavior more effectively when there is a clear goal and a clear strategy to follow than when goals are more ambiguous or when students must discover or invent new strategies rather than merely activate familiar ones. Thus, rewards are better used with boring or unpleasant tasks than with attractive or interesting ones, better with routine tasks than with novel ones, better with specific intentional learning tasks than with incidental learning or discovery tasks, and better with tasks where speed of performance or quantity of output is of more concern than creativity, artistry, or craftsmanship. It is better to offer rewards as incentives for meeting performance standards (or performance *improvement* standards) on skills that require a great deal of drill and practice (arithmetic computation, typing, spelling) than it is for work on a major research or demonstration project.

Rewards are effective as motivators only for those students who believe that they have a chance to get the rewards if they put forth reasonable effort. Therefore, if rewards are to be incentives for everyone and not just the high-ability students, it is necessary to ensure that everyone has equal (or at least reasonable) access to the rewards. This may require performance contracting or some less formal method of individualizing criteria for success.

The comments in Chapter 4 about using rewards and praise to motivate students to conform to classroom expectations also apply to the use of these incentives to motivate students' learning efforts. In particular, it is important that incentives be offered and delivered in ways that encourage students to appreciate their developing knowledge and skills rather than just to think about the rewards. Teachers can do this by following the guidelines in Table 4.1.

Call Attention to the Instrumental Value of Academic Activities

Some knowledge and skills taught in school can be applied immediately in the students' lives or will be needed as "life skills" later. If students are made aware of them, these natural consequences of task mastery are likely to be more effective for motivating learning efforts than would more arbitrary extrinsic rewards. When possible, teachers should note that the knowledge or skills developed by a task are useful in enabling students to meet their own current needs, in providing them with a "ticket" to social advancement, or in preparing them for occupational or other success in life. Better yet, teachers can cite examples by relating personal experiences or telling anecdotes about individuals with whom the students can identify (famous people they look up to or former students from the same school).

This strategy probably is not employed as often as it could be, and when it is, it is often used in self-defeating ways. Rather than stress the present or future application value of what is being learned, many teachers stress personal embarrassment ("You don't want people to think you are ignorant") or future educational or occupational disasters ("You'll never get through the sixth grade"; "How are you going to get a job if you can't do basic math?"). Other teachers use variations that cast the student in a more positive light but portray society as a hostile environment (urging the students to learn to count so that merchants don't cheat them or to learn to read so that they don't get taken when signing contacts).

We suggest that teachers be more positive in their efforts to help students appreciate specific applications of what they are learning. Basic language arts and mathematics skills are used daily when shopping, banking, driving, reading instructions for using some product, paying bills, carrying on business correspondence, and planning home maintenance projects or family vacations. Scientific knowledge is useful for everything from coping effectively with minor everyday challenges to making good decisions in emergency situations. Knowledge of history and related social studies topics is useful for everything from voting on local issues to determining national policy. In general, a good working knowledge of the information, principles, and skills taught in school prepares people to make well-informed decisions that can save time, trouble, expense, or even lives, and it empowers people by preparing them to recognize and take advantage of the opportunities that society offers. Teachers should help their students to appreciate this and to see academic activities as enabling opportunities to be valued rather than as unwelcome impositions.

Structure Appropriate Competition

The opportunity to compete can add excitement to classroom activities, whether the competition is for prizes or merely for the satisfaction of winning. Competition may be either individual (students compete against everyone else) or group (students are divided into teams that compete with one another). Traditionally, competitions have been structured around test scores or other performance measures, but it also is possible to build competitive elements into ordinary instruction by including activities such as argumentative essays, debates, or simulation games that involve competition (Keller, 1983).

Several important qualifications concerning competition should be noted, however. First, bear in mind that participating in classroom activities involves risking public failure and that a great deal of competition is already built into the grading system. Therefore, it may be counterproductive to introduce additional competitive elements.

Second, competition is even more salient and distracting than rewards for most students, so it is important to depersonalize the competition and to emphasize the content being learned rather than who won or who lost. For example, a teacher might divide the class into six teams and require each team to develop a campaign speech based on specified criteria. Next, the teams would use the criteria to rate the speeches produced by the other teams. Then, each team would take the best features from all six of the initial versions and produce an improved speech that represents the class's best thinking. Such a task involves competitive elements, but it focuses on the content rather than on the competition.

Third, the qualifications that apply to use of rewards as incentives also apply to competition. In particular, competition is more appropriate for use with routine practice tasks than with tasks calling for discovery or creativity, and it can be effective only if everyone has a good (or at least an equal) chance of winning. To ensure the latter, it is necessary to use team competition in which the teams are balanced by ability profiles or to use individual competition in which a handicapping system enables each student to compete with his or her own previous performance rather than the other students. Combined approaches that feature both a handicapping system to supply individual criteria for scoring each student's work and an incentive system involving group rewards for winners of competitions between teams provide the most desirable forms of competition—they can be structured so that students cooperate in addition to competing (Slavin, 1983). These student team learning approaches are discussed in Chapter 7.

Finally, a root problem with competition is that it creates losers as well as winners (usually many more losers than winners). Even when there is no rational reason for it, a loser's psychology tends to develop whenever individuals or teams lose competitions. Individuals may suffer at least temporary embarrassment, and those who lose consistently may suffer more permanent losses in confidence, self-concept, and enjoyment of school. Losing team members may devalue one another and scapegoat individuals they hold responsible for the team's loss (Ames, 1984; Johnson & Johnson, 1985). Thus teachers who are thinking about introducing competition should minimize its risks by making sure that everyone has an equal chance to win, that winning is determined primarily by degree of effort (and perhaps a degree of luck) rather than by ability, that attention is focused on the task rather than on who wins and who loses, and that the emphasis is on the positive (winners are congratulated but losers are not criticized or ridiculed; the accomplishments of the class as a whole, and not just of the winners, are acknowledged).

Concluding Comments About Extrinsic Motivational Strategies

Extrinsic strategies can be effective in certain circumstances, but teachers should not rely on them too heavily. If students are preoccupied with rewards or competition, they may not pay much attention to what they are supposed to be learning or appreciate its value. The quality of task engagement and of ultimate achievement is higher when students perceive themselves to be engaged in a task for their own reasons rather than in order to please an authority figure, obtain a reward, or escape punishment (Deci & Ryan, 1985; Lepper, 1983). If students perceive themselves as performing a task solely to obtain a reward, they tend to concentrate on meeting minimum standards for performance rather than on doing a high-quality job (Condry & Chambers, 1978; Kruglanski, 1978). As a result, they may write

300-word essays containing exactly 300 words or read only those parts of the text that they need to read in order to answer the questions on an assignment. In view of these dangers, teachers should use extrinsic approaches sparingly, keeping in mind the qualifications just described and the guidelines in Table 4.1.

STRATEGIES FOR CAPITALIZING ON STUDENTS' INTRINSIC MOTIVATION

The intrinsic motivation approach is based on the idea that teachers should emphasize academic tasks that students find inherently interesting and enjoyable so that they engage in these tasks willingly without need for extrinsic incentives. This is an appealing idea, although research on characteristics of tasks that people tend to find intrinsically rewarding (Deci & Ryan, 1985; Lepper & Greene, 1978; Malone & Lepper, 1987) suggests that this is difficult for teachers to accomplish in typical classroom settings.

For one thing, the simplest way to ensure that people value what they are doing is to maximize their free choice and autonomy—let them decide what to do and when and how to do it. However, schools are not recreational settings designed primarily to provide entertainment; they are educational settings that students are required to come to for instruction in a prescribed curriculum. Some opportunities exist for teachers to take advantage of existing intrinsic motivation by allowing students to select activities according to their own interests, but most of the time teachers must require students to engage in activities that they would not have selected on their own.

A second factor is that intrinsically rewarding activities are usually free of pressures or risks (beyond those that people assume voluntarily when they choose to engage in the activities). However, teachers' motivational attempts in the school setting are complicated by the grading system and the public nature of most teacher-student interaction. Anxiety about public embarrassment or low grades is a significant impediment to the learning efforts of many students (Covington, 1992). Even when this is not a problem, students usually want to predict, and if possible control, the relationship between their academic performance and their grades. They may try to avoid tasks that involve ambiguity (about what will be needed to earn high grades) or risk (due to high difficulty or strict grading standards) and to avoid asking questions or seeking to probe deeper into the content because they want to stick with safe, familiar routines (Doyle, 1983; Hughes, Sullivan, & Mosley, 1985). Thus, even if students enjoy particular school activities, this potential for intrinsic motivation may be negated by concerns about embarrassment or failure.

Finally, teachers act as authority figures and not just as instructors. They evaluate and grade student performance, and they enforce classroom rules. In the process, they sometimes engender resentment that may interfere with their attempts to motivate.

Even so, teachers can take advantage of students' existing intrinsic motivation by selecting or designing classroom activities that contain elements that students are likely to find enjoyable or intrinsically rewarding. No single element will be rewarding to *all* students, but there do appear to be elements that *most* students find rewarding. We describe some of these in the following sections.

Opportunities for Active Response

Students prefer activities that allow them to respond actively—to interact with the teacher or one another, manipulate materials, or do something other than just listen or read. This is one function of drill, recitation, board work, and seatwork activities. However, students also should get opportunities to go beyond the simple question-answer formats seen in typical recitation and seatwork activities in order to do projects, experiments, discussions, role play, simulations, computerized learning activities, educational games, or creative applications. Language arts instruction should include dramatic readings and prose and poetry composition; mathematics instruction should include problem-solving exercises and realistic application opportunities; science instruction should include experiments and other laboratory work; and social studies instruction should include debates, research projects, and simulation exercises. Such activities allow students to feel that school learning involves *doing* something.

Inclusion of Higher-Level Objectives and Divergent Questions

Even within traditional lesson formats, teachers can create more active student involvement by going beyond factual questions to stimulate their students to discuss or debate issues, offer opinions about cause-and-effect relationships, speculate about hypothetical situations, or think creatively about problems. Students need to learn basic facts, concepts, and definitions, but a steady diet of lower-level content soon becomes boring. Therefore, there should be frequent activities or parts of activities devoted to higher-level objectives (application, analysis, synthesis, or evaluation of what has been learned at the knowledge and comprehension level).

Students often complain about problems in this area ("We never get to *do* anything"). So do curriculum experts ("Schools were established to promote higher-level objectives—to get students to think about and use what they learn— but you wouldn't know this from visiting classrooms. Most 'discussions' are really just recitations or oral quizzes on basic facts, and seatwork usually means workbooks, dittos, or pages of computation problems"). Yet curriculum developers usually do not provide much help to teachers in this regard. Curriculum packages (including software for computerized learning) seldom include many higher-level questions or activities, let alone systematic plans for structuring thorough discussion and engaging application of the content. Part of the problem is that higher-level activities can be time consuming to implement and difficult to evaluate. Yet it is important to include such activities, not only for motivational reasons but to ensure that school learning is meaningful and applicable.

There also should be questions designed to elicit opinions, predictions, suggested courses of action, solutions to problems, or other divergent thinking. Such questions and related activities encourage students to respond more actively and creatively to content than do activities built around questions about facts, definitions, or concepts.

The same principles apply to skills instruction. Students need to learn basic skills and often must practice them until mastery, to the point of smooth, rapid, and "automatic" correct performance. However, most of this practice should be embedded within application opportunities. Students should not be spending most of their time practicing penmanship without getting opportunities to compose essays or other meaningful communications, and they should not continually practice mathematical computations without solving problems or applying what they are learning.

Feedback Features

Students enjoy tasks that allow them not only to respond actively but to get immediate feedback that they can use to guide subsequent responses. Such feedback features are among the reasons for the popularity of computer games and other pastimes featured in arcades (Malone & Lepper, 1987). Automatic feedback features are also built into many educational toys and Montessori materials used in preschools and kindergartens, and into programmed materials and computerized learning systems used in elementary and secondary classrooms.

Teachers can build feedback into more typical classroom activities by providing such feedback themselves when leading the class or a small group through an activity or by circulating to supervise progress during independent seatwork times. When teachers are less available for immediate response (such as when they are teaching a small group), they still can arrange for students to get feedback by consulting answer keys, following instructions about how to check their work, consulting with an adult volunteer or appointed student helper, or reviewing and discussing the work in pairs or small groups.

Feedback provides immediacy and impact to an activity. Psychologically, most students find it much more difficult and less rewarding to go back and try to relearn something that "we did already" than to respond to immediate feedback when learning something for the first time. Therefore, teachers should avoid putting students in the position of having to respond for lengthy periods of time without knowing whether their responses are correct. There are three basic ways to accomplish this: (1) Where possible, design or select activities that include built-in opportunities to make responses and get immediate feedback; (2) for other activities, give sufficiently thorough instructions and work through enough practice examples to enable the students to evaluate the correctness of their responses on their own; (3) circulate to supervise progress and provide immediate feedback and help to those who need it.

Incorporation of Gamelike Features into Activities

Practice and application activities can be structured to include features typically associated with games or recreational pastimes (Keller, 1983; Malone & Lepper, 1987). With a bit of imagination, ordinary seatwork assignments can be transformed into "test-yourself" challenges, puzzles, or brain teasers. Some such activities involve clear goals but require the student to solve problems, avoid traps, or overcome obstacles in order to reach the goals (such as exercises calling for students to suggest possible solutions to science or engineering problems or to find a shortcut that will substitute for a tedious mathematical procedure). Other activities challenge students to "find the problem" by identifying the goal itself in addition to developing a method for reaching the goal (many "explore and discover" activities follow this model). Some gamelike activities involve elements of suspense or hidden information that emerges as the activity is completed (puzzles that convey some message or provide the answer to some question once they are filled in). Other such activities involve a degree of randomness or uncertainty about what the outcome of one's performance is likely to be on any given trial (knowledge games that cover a variety of topics at several difficulty levels and are assigned according to card draws or dice rolls—Trivial Pursuit is an example).

Note that most of these gamelike features involve presenting intellectual challenges appropriate for use with either individuals or cooperative groups. We mention this to call attention to the fact that the term *gamelike features* is intended to have a much broader meaning than *games,* a term that most teachers associate specifically with team *competitions* (Which team will win by getting the most answers?). The gamelike features described above are likely to be both less distracting from curriculum objectives and more effective in promoting student motivation to learn than are competitive games, especially competitive games that emphasize speed in supplying memorized facts rather than integration or application of knowledge.

Opportunity for Students to Create Finished Products

Industrial psychologists have shown that workers enjoy jobs that allow them to create a product that they can point to and identify with more than jobs that do not yield such tangible evidence of the fruits of their labor. Students probably will respond similarly to academic tasks. That is, they are likely to prefer tasks that have meaning or integrity in their own right over tasks that are mere subparts of some larger entity, and are likely to experience a satisfying sense of accomplishment when they finish such tasks. Ideally, task completion will yield a finished product that the students can use or display (a map, diagram, or other illustration; an essay or report; a scale model; or something other than just another ditto or workbook page).

Inclusion of Fantasy or Simulation Elements

If more direct applications are not feasible, teachers can introduce fantasy or imagination elements that will engage students' emotions or allow them to experience events vicariously. In studying poems or stories, teachers can encourage their students to debate the authors' motives in writing the work or to learn about formative experiences in the authors' lives. In studying scientific or mathematical principles and methods, teachers can help students to appreciate the practical problems that needed to be solved or the personal motives of the discoverers that led to development of the knowledge or skills being taught. Alternatively, teachers can set up role-play or simulation activities that allow students to identify with real or fictional characters or to deal with academic content in direct, personalized ways. Rather than just assign their students to read history, for example, elementary teachers can make it come alive by arranging for students to role-play Columbus and his crew debating what to do after 30 days at sea, and secondary teachers can do so by arranging for students to take the roles of the American, British, and Russian leaders meeting at Yalta.

Simulation activities include, but are not confined to, full-scale drama, role-play, simulation games, and other "major productions." Other, more modest simulation exercises can be incorporated into everyday instruction. In teaching a mathematical procedure, for example, teachers might ask students to name problems in everyday living that the procedure might be useful in solving (and then list these on the board). Secondary social studies teachers might "bring home" material on totalitarian societies by asking students to imagine and talk about what it would be like to seek housing in a country where the government owned all of the property or to get accurate information about world events in a country where the government controlled all the media. Such brief fantasy or simulation exercises do not take much time or require special preparations, but they can stimulate students to relate to the content more personally and to take greater interest in it.

Opportunities for Students to Interact with Peers

Many students especially enjoy activities that allow them to interact with peers. Teachers can build peer interaction into whole-class activities such as discussion, debate, role-play, or simulation. In addition, they can plan follow-up activities that allow students to work together in pairs or small groups to tutor one another, discuss issues, develop solutions to problems, or work as a team preparing for a competition, participating in a simulation game, or producing some group product (a report, display, etc.).

Peer-interactive activities are likely to be most effective if (1) they are worthwhile learning experiences and not merely occasions for socializing, and (2) every student has a substantive role to play in carrying out the group's mission (see Chapter 7 for more information about peer-interactive activities).

An Example: Project-Based Learning

Blumenfeld et al. (1991) have described *project-based learning*, a comprehensive approach to classroom teaching and learning that incorporates most of these principles for capitalizing on students' intrinsic motivation. Harking back to ideas originally suggested by John Dewey and other early educational theorists, this approach calls for involving students in *projects*: relatively long-term, problem-focused, and meaningful units of instruction that integrate concepts from a number of disciplines or fields of study. Within this framework, students pursue solutions to authentic problems by asking and refining questions, debating ideas, making predictions, designing plans or experiments, collecting and analyzing data, drawing conclusions, communicating their ideas and findings to others, asking new questions, and creating products.

There are two essential components to projects: they require a question or problem that organizes and drives activities, and the activities result in a series of products that culminate in a final product that addresses the driving question. The final products are representations of the students' problem solutions, organized and presented in a form (e.g., a model, report, videotape, or computer program) that can be shared with others and critiqued. Feedback from others permits the learners to reflect on and extend their emergent knowledge and to revise their products if necessary. Motivational elements of project work include tasks are varied and include novel elements, problems are authentic and challenging, the work leads to closure in the form of production of the final product, students exercise choice in deciding what to do and how to do it, and they collaborate with peers in carrying out the work.

Blumenfeld et al. (1991) cautioned that these motivational elements of project work do not automatically ensure that students engage in the work by investing the effort necessary to acquire information, generate and test solutions, and evaluate their findings carefully. Projects need to be planned and implemented with attention to the complex nature of student motivation and knowledge needed to engage in cognitively difficult work. The novel, dramatic, or unique elements of projects should support learning goals and not be distracting "bells and whistles." The projects should be interesting and authentic to the students, not just to subject-matter experts. Students should view the products they create as worthwhile, not just as artificial school exercises, and creating the products should require the students to integrate information and use complex thought. In addition, students will need to have certain prior knowledge in place if they are to engage in project work successfully. In particular, they will need sufficient knowledge of the content and specific skills to explore information pertinent to the problem (skills for using cognitive tools like computers and accompanying software programs, and proficiency in using cognitive and metacognitive skills to generate plans, systematically make and test predictions, interpret evidence in the light of these predictions, and determine solutions). They also need to view errors as natural consequences of attempts to solve difficult and demanding problems, so that they can sustain their learning efforts and avoid becoming overly frustrated.

Projects can be developed for any subject, although they are especially well suited to science and social studies. Blumenfeld et al. (1991) suggest ways in which projects can be designed to maximize their motivational impact. They also describe some of the ways in which emerging technology is making project-based learning more interesting and challenging (by enabling students to work with computerized data bases in conducting their research and to use computerized design, video technology, and other innovations in developing their products). Gardner (1991) proposes a radical restructuring of K-12 schooling in which students would spend most of their time engaged in project-based learning, in and out of classroom settings.

Concluding Comments About Intrinsic Motivational Strategies

Schooling should be as enjoyable as it can be for both teachers and students. Therefore, whenever curriculum objectives can be met through a variety of activities, wise teachers will emphasize activities that students find rewarding and avoid ones that they find boring or aversive. However, there are two important limitations on what can be accomplished through intrinsic motivational strategies.

First, opportunities to use intrinsic motivational strategies in the classroom are limited. Teachers must teach the whole curriculum, not just the parts that appeal to students. Also, content coverage pressures and time constraints built into the daily schedule further limit opportunities to provide choice, autonomy, gamelike features, and the other intrinsic motivation strategies. Thus, even in classrooms where teachers make optimal use of these strategies, the students will still be in school rather than in a recreational setting. Learning will often be enjoyable, but it will still require concentration and effort.

Second, although intrinsic motivational strategies should increase students' enjoyment of classroom activities, they do not directly stimulate an intention to accomplish the activities' learning goals. Therefore, even when intrinsic strategies are used, they will need to be supplemented with strategies for stimulating student motivation to learn (described in the next section). Otherwise, students may enjoy classroom activities but fail to derive the intended knowledge or skills from them.

In this connection, it is worth noting that our colloquial language for discussing intrinsic motivation is misleading. We commonly describe certain topics or tasks as "intrinsically interesting" and speak of engaging in activities "for their own sake." Such language implies that motivation resides in activities rather than in people. In reality, *people generate intrinsic motivation*; it is not somehow built into topics or tasks. We study or do something not for *its* sake but for *our* sake—because it brings us pleasure, meets our needs, or in some other way provides enjoyable stimulation or satisfaction. Each of us has his or her own amount and patterning of intrinsic motivation, developed in response to experiences and to socialization from significant persons in our lives. In the case of motivation to learn academic knowledge and skills, teachers are important "significant persons." Therefore, rather than just confining themselves to accommodating classroom activities to students' existing motivational patterns, teachers can think in terms of *shaping* those motivational patterns through socialization designed to stimulate student motivation to learn the curriculum.

STRATEGIES FOR STIMULATING STUDENT MOTIVATION TO LEARN

By *motivation to learn*, we mean a student's tendency to find academic activities meaningful and worthwhile and to try to get the intended learning benefits from them. In contrast to intrinsic motivation, which is primarily an affective response to an activity, motivation to learn is primarily a cognitive response involving attempts to make sense of the activity, understand information and relate it to prior knowledge, and master the skills that it promotes (Brophy, 1983; Brophy & Kher, 1986).

This definition of motivation to learn implies a distinction between learning and performance: *Learning* refers to the information processing, sense making, and advances in comprehension or mastery that occur while one is acquiring knowledge or skill; *performance* refers to the demonstration of such knowledge or skill after it has been acquired. Strategies for stimulating student motivation to learn apply not only to performance (work on tests or assignments) but also to the information-processing activities (attending to lessons, reading for understanding, comprehending instructions, putting things into one's own words) that are involved in learning content or skills in the first place. Thus, these strategies emphasize encouraging students to use thoughtful information-processing and skill-building strategies when they are learning. This is quite different from merely offering them incentives for good performance later.

Student motivation to learn can be thought of both as a *general trait* and as a *situation-specific state* (Brophy, 1983; Gottfried, 1985). As a general *trait*, it is an enduring disposition to value learning—to approach the process of learning with effort and thought and to take pride in acquiring knowledge and skill. In specific situations, a *state* of motivation to learn exists when students engage purposefully in an activity by adopting its goal and trying to learn the concepts or master the skills involved. Even students who do not have much motivation to learn as a general trait may display such motivation in specific situations because the teacher has sparked their interest or made them see the importance of the content (Deci et al., 1991).

The learning taught in schools is mostly cognitive learning—abstract concepts and verbally coded information. In order to make efficient progress in such academic learning, students need to develop and use *generative learning strategies* (Weinstein & Mayer, 1986). That is, they need to process information actively, relate it to their existing knowledge, put it into their own words, make sure that they understand it, and so on. Therefore, motivating students to learn means not only stimulating them to take an interest in and see the value of what they are learning, but also providing them with guidance about how to go about learning it. We recommend the following strategies for teachers who want to stimulate students' motivation to learn the content or skills that instructional activities were designed to develop.

The first three strategies are general ones that describe pervasive features of the learning environment that should be established in every classroom. These strategies help develop student motivation to learn as a general trait. They involve socializing students to understand that the classroom is primarily a place for learning and that acquiring and applying knowledge and skills are important contributors to quality of life (not just to report card grades).

Teacher Modeling of Motivation to Learn

Teachers should routinely model interest in learning throughout all of their interactions with their students. This modeling should encourage the students to value learning as a rewarding, self-actualizing activity that produces personal satisfaction and enriches one's life. Therefore, in addition to teaching what is in the textbooks, teachers should share their interests in current events and items of general knowledge (especially as they relate to aspects of the subject matter being taught). Teachers can call attention to current books, articles, television programs, or movies on the subject and to examples or applications in everyday living, in the local environment, or in current events.

By "modeling," we mean more than just calling students' attention to examples or applications of concepts taught in school. We mean that *teachers should act as models by sharing their thinking about such examples or applications so that the students can see how educated people use information and concepts learned in school* to understand and respond to everyday experiences in their lives and to news about current events occurring elsewhere. Without being preachy about it, teachers can relate personal experiences illustrating how language arts knowledge enables them to communicate or express themselves effectively in important life situations, how mathematical or scientific knowledge enables them to solve everyday household-engineering or repair problems, or how social studies knowledge helps them to appreciate things they see in their travels or to understand the significance of events in the news. Through teacher modeling, students should come to see how it is both stimulating and satisfying to understand (or even just to think, wonder, or make predictions about) what is happening in the world around us.

Teachers' modeling of ways of thinking about subjects can affect their students' interest in subjects (Woolfolk, Rosoff, & Hoy, 1990) or their self-concepts of ability to learn the subjects (Midgley, Feldlaufer, & Eccles, 1989). Often teachers are unaware of the attitudes they communicate to students. Consider the following dialogue:

TEACHER: We started out with 18 links and divided them into groups of 3, so how many groups are we going to get?

JONATHAN: Six.

TEACHER: Six groups. You're right. We could say 6 groups of 3 make 18, right? Okay, this time, let's say I'm going to take away 1. How many would I have then? Seventeen. I want someone to come up and put these 17 into groups of 2. How many do you end up with?

JONATHAN: Eight groups plus 1 left over.

TEACHER: Can't you put it in with one of the others? Well, okay, we counted 8 groups of 2, but what else have we got?

STUDENT: One left over.

TEACHER: One left over. Okay, in math what do we call a leftover?

STUDENT: A remainder.

TEACHER: Right. So this problem is a little more interesting—we have a remainder.

While instructing third graders in division with remainders, this teacher is teaching attitudes about mathematics as well. She presents the concept of remainders in a positive and problem-solving fashion that encourages students to view mathematics with interest and a "can do" attitude. Another teacher might have made the mistake of introducing the new level of complexity with a sense of futility or irritation ("You don't know what to do now, do you?" "This problem has a remainder, so it's more difficult"). If made consistently, such comments might teach students to view division as complicated and frustrating.

One important place for teachers to model curiosity and interest in learning is when responding to students' questions, especially questions that are not covered in the textbook. Questions from the class indicate that students are interested in the topic and thinking actively about it rather than just listening passively. Consequently, teachers should respond in ways that show that such questions are valued. First, acknowledge or praise the question itself: "That's a good question, Jean. It does seem strange that the people of Boston would throw the tea into the water, doesn't it?" Then, answer the question or refer it to the class: "How about it, class? Why would they throw the tea in the water instead of taking it home with them?"

If the question is one that no one is prepared to answer, some strategy should be adopted to address it. The teacher might promise to get the answer, or better yet, assign the student who asked the question to go to the library (or another resource) to find the answer and then report back to the class. Teachers also can model curiosity in responding to questions for which they do not have ready answers: "I never thought about that before. Why didn't they take the tea home with them? It was valuable, and they must have considered stealing it. So they must have decided not to steal it but throw it into the water instead. How come?" The teacher could continue in this vein or invite suggestions at this point.

Curiosity and interest in learning can be modeled in information that teachers give about their lives outside of school. When teachers read a book, magazine article, or newspaper item of interest, they should mention it so that students can read it for themselves if they wish (ideally, have the item available for loan). Teachers should also announce television programs, museum exhibits, or other special events of educational or cultural value.

Teachers can also reinforce curiosity and interest in learning through comments made in passing during class. Without belaboring the point, they can communicate that they regularly read the newspaper ("I read in the paper that . . . "), watch the news ("Last night on the news they showed . . . "), and participate in various educational and cultural pursuits. Students should be aware that their teacher thinks carefully about and participates in elections, keeps abreast of current events, and otherwise shows evidence of an active, inquiring mind.

We observed one teacher use modeling effectively in connection with an assignment involving reading about current events in the newspaper. He began by noting that he reads the editorial page regularly, sometimes agreeing and sometimes disagreeing, but always finding the material thought provoking. He went on to discuss the newspaper's position and his own position on a forthcoming summit meeting, noting that he was initially relatively uninformed about, uninterested in, and pessimistic about the likely outcome of this meeting but that he had become more interested and optimistic about it as he became better informed by reading the paper and watching news programs on television. This led to a stimulating discussion that clarified for the students, and provoked many questions about, the position of the United States and the Soviet Union on major issues to be discussed at the meeting. The teacher went on to provoke further interest and curiosity by noting that, although he was sharing his own position on the issues discussed that day, he often deliberately withheld his positions on issues discussed in class to encourage students to think for themselves and to avoid inhibiting those who might disagree with him. This teacher probably increased his students' interest in newspaper articles and television programs about current events, as well as giving them a model to follow in responding to those news sources in active, thoughtful ways.

Communicating Desirable Expectations and Attributions

Teachers should routinely project attitudes, beliefs, expectations, and attributions (statements about the reasons for students' behavior) implying that students share the teachers' enthusiasm for learning. To the extent that teachers *treat students as if they already are eager learners,* the students are more likely to become eager learners. Teachers should let their students know that they are expected to be curious, to want to learn with understanding, and to see what they are learning as applicable to their everyday lives (Marshall, 1987).

Minimally, this means avoiding suggestions that students will dislike academic activities or work on them only to get good grades. Preferably, it means treating students as active, motivated learners who care about their learning and are trying to learn with understanding (Blumenfeld & Meece, 1988). One teacher we observed communicated positive expectations by announcing at the beginning of the year that she intended to make her students into "social scientists." She referred to this idea frequently throughout the year in comments such as, "Since you are social scientists, you will recognize that the description of this area as a tropical rain forest has implications about what kinds of crops will grow there," or "Thinking as social scientists, what conclusions might we draw from this information?"

Minimize Performance Anxiety

Motivation to learn is likely to develop most fully when students are goal oriented but relaxed enough to be able to concentrate on the task at hand without worrying about whether they can meet performance expectations. Teachers can accomplish this by making clear distinctions between instruction or practice activities designed to promote learning and tests designed to evaluate performance. *Most classroom activities should be structured as learning experiences rather than as tests.*

If instruction or practice activities include testlike events (recitation questions, practice exercises), these should be treated as opportunities for the students to work with and apply the material rather than as opportunities for the teacher to test students' mastery. If teachers expect students to engage in academic activities with motivation to learn (which implies a willingness to take intellectual risks and make mistakes), they will need to protect the students from anxiety or premature concern about performance adequacy.

Eventually, of course, teachers will have to evaluate student performance and assign grades using tests or other assessment devices. Until that point, however, the emphasis should be on teaching and learning rather than on performance evaluation, and students should be encouraged to respond to performance demands in terms of "Let's assess our progress and learn from our mistakes," rather than "Let's see who knows it and who doesn't." If necessary, teachers may also want to make statements such as "We're here to learn, and you can't do that without making mistakes," or to caution students against laughing at the mistakes made by peers.

The three *general strategies* just described should be pervasive aspects of the learning environments that teachers establish in their classrooms. If used consistently, they should subtly encourage students to develop motivation to learn as a general personal trait. In particular learning situations, teachers can supplement these general strategies with one or more of the following *specific strategies* for motivating students to learn what an activity is designed to teach.

Project Intensity

Teachers can use timing, nonverbal expressions and gestures, and cueing and other verbal techniques to project a level of intensity that tells students that the material is important and deserves close attention. Often, an intense presentation will begin with a direct statement of the importance of the message ("I am going to show you how to invert fractions—now pay close attention and make sure that you understand these procedures"). Then, the message itself is presented using verbal and nonverbal public speaking techniques that convey intensity and cue attention: a slow-paced, step-by-step presentation during which key words are emphasized, unusual voice modulations or exaggerated gestures that focus attention on key terms or procedural steps, and intense scanning of the group following each step to look for signs of understanding or confusion (and to allow anyone with a question to ask it immediately). In addition to the words being spoken, *everything about the teacher's tone and manner communicates to the students that what is being said is important* and that they should give it full attention and ask questions about anything that they do not understand.

Teachers will have to "pick their spots" for deliberately using an intensive communication style. They cannot be intense all the time, and even if they could, students would adjust to it so it would lose much of its effectiveness. Therefore, teachers should reserve intensity for the times when they want to communicate "This is important; pay especially close attention." Likely occasions include introduction of important new terms or definitions, especially those that may be confusing to students; demonstration of procedures and problem-solving techniques, including instructions for assignments; and instruction that is intended to eliminate misconceptions (and thus requires making students aware that even though they think they already understand the point at issue, their "knowledge" is incorrect). Exaggerated intensity is less appropriate for more routine instructional situations, although teachers are well advised to slow the pace and be alert for signs of confusion or student desire to ask a question whenever they are covering new or complex material.

Project Enthusiasm

Students take cues from their teachers about how to respond to school activities. If teachers present a topic or assignment with enthusiasm, suggesting that it is interesting, important, or worthwhile, students are likely to adopt this same attitude (Bettencourt et al., 1983).

In suggesting that teachers project enthusiasm we do not mean pep talks or unnecessary theatrics. Instead, we mean that *teachers identify their own reasons for being interested in the topic or for finding it meaningful or important and project these reasons to the students* when teaching about the topic. Teachers can use dramatics or forceful salesmanship if they are comfortable with these techniques, but if not, low-key but sincere statements of the value that they place on a topic or activity will be just as effective. Thus, a brief comment showing that the topic is food for thought or illustrating how it is interesting, unique, or different from previously studied topics may be sufficient. The primary objective of projecting enthusiasm as a strategy for motivating students to learn is to induce the students to value the topic or activity, not to amuse, entertain, or excite them.

We observed a history teacher generate a great deal of interest (and also pull together a great many concepts) by enthusiastically explaining to his students that during the Middle Ages, the Mediterranean was the center of the world. Mediterranean seaports were major trade centers and places like England were outposts of civilization, but this changed drastically with the discovery of the New World and the emergence of new centers of trade and culture. His presentation included references to maps, reminders about the primary modes of transportation at the time, and characterizations of the attitudes of the people and their knowledge about other countries and trade possibilities. Another teacher brought ancient Israel alive by enthusiastically telling his students about David as the slayer of Goliath and ancestor of Jesus, Abraham leading his people to the Promised Land, Solomon as a wise man and builder of the temple, and Moses as the man who presented the Ten Commandments and led the people out of the wilderness. This included locating Jerusalem, Israel, and the Sinai Peninsula on a map and speculating about whether the temple might be rebuilt in modern Jerusalem (noting that a major Moslem temple is located next to the spot occupied by Solomon's temple). In each of these cases, the teacher was able to parlay personal interest and detailed knowledge about the topic into an effective presentation that sparked interest and elicited many questions and comments.

Induce Task Interest or Appreciation

Teachers can induce appreciation for a topic or activity by verbalizing reasons that the students should value it (Newby, 1991). If it has connections with something that students already recognize as interesting or important, these connections should be noted. When the knowledge or skills to be taught have applications to everyday living, these applications should be mentioned, especially those that will allow students to solve problems or accomplish goals that are important to them. Teachers can also mention new or challenging aspects of activities that the students can anticipate.

We observed a history teacher motivate students to read about the ancient Greek legal system by noting that it was similar to our own system in many ways but that it called for 501 jurors. A geography teacher motivated his students to study the map of Greece with interest and appreciation by explaining that no place in Greece was more than 40 miles from the sea and that the country's jagged contours gave it far more coastline than most larger countries.

Induce Curiosity or Suspense

Teachers can stimulate curiosity or suspense by posing questions or doing "setups" that make students feel the need to resolve some ambiguity or obtain more information about a topic. To prepare their students to read material on the former Soviet Union, for example, teachers could ask the students if they knew that Russia was just part of the USSR, what the term *Iron Curtain* means, how many time zones there were in the USSR, or how the United States acquired Alaska. Such questions help transform "just another reading assignment" into an interesting learning experience by encouraging students to make connections between the new information and what they already know (or think they know). Furthermore, by inducing curiosity or suspense, such questions make new information food for thought rather than merely more material to be memorized. Most students will think that the Soviet Union was just another name for Russia and will be curious to find out about the difference once they have been alerted to it. Most will have heard the term *Iron Curtain* but will not have thought about it and will become curious to read about it when stimulated to think about it in interesting ways (Was there an actual curtain? Was it made of iron? If not, why was the term used?). Similarly, it is mind-boggling for most students to discover that one country encompassed eleven time zones or that the United States purchased Alaska from Russia. These are just four basic facts found in most treatments of the history or geography of the USSR. Whether students will find them (or a great many others that could have been mentioned) interesting and will think about them rather than merely attempt to memorize them will depend largely on the degree to which their teachers stimulate curiosity about them and provide a context for thinking about their associations with existing knowledge or beliefs. This is another illustration of points made earlier: Interest resides in people rather than in topics or activities, and motivation that develops in particular situations does so as a result of interactions among persons, tasks, and the larger environmental context.

Teachers can encourage their students to generate such interest by (1) asking them to speculate or make predictions about what they will be learning; (2) raising questions that successful completion of the activity will enable them to answer; and (3) where relevant, showing them that their existing knowledge is not sufficient to enable them to accomplish some valued objective, that their knowledge is internally inconsistent or inconsistent with the new information, or that the knowledge they currently possess in scattered form can be organized around certain general principles or powerful ideas (Malone & Lepper, 1987). More generally, teachers can put their students into an active information-processing or problem-solving mode by posing interesting questions or problems that the activity will address (Keller, 1983).

Make Abstract Content More Personal, Concrete, or Familiar

Definitions, principles, and other abstract information may have little meaning for students unless made more concrete. One way to accomplish this is to promote personal identification with the content by relating experiences or telling anecdotes illustrating how the content applies to the lives of individuals whom the students are interested in and likely to identify with.

We observed a history teacher read aloud a brief selection about Spartacus in order to personalize a selection that students were to read about slavery in ancient times. When covering the crusades, this teacher gave particular emphasis to the Children's Crusade, noting that the children involved were "your age and younger" and that most of them died before the crusade ultimately ended in failure. He also made poignant connections to contemporary Iran, where religion-based zeal recently caused preadolescents to volunteer to go to war. Another teacher brought the medieval guilds alive for her students by describing them in detail and soliciting the students' reactions to the fact that if they had lived during the Middle Ages, to become a journeyman they would have had to leave their homes as children and spend seven years apprenticed to a master craftsman.

Teachers can make abstractions concrete by showing objects or pictures or by conducting demonstrations. They also can help students to relate new or strange content to their existing knowledge by using examples or analogies that refer to familiar concepts, objects, or events. We have observed teachers make the following connections: (1) the Nile River flooding and its effects on Egyptian customs compared to the spring flooding in Michigan rivers and its effects on local customs; (2) the Washington Monument as a modern example of an obelisk; (3) three times the size of the Pontiac Silverdome as an example of the size of the largest Roman circus colosseums; (4) identification of students in the class (or failing that, famous personalities) descended from the ancient peoples or the geographical areas being studied; (5) linking of students' family names to the guilds (Smith, Tanner, Miller, Baker); (6) similarities in climate and potential for flower raising and dairy farming as reasons why the Dutch were drawn to the Holland, Michigan, area; (7) similarities in the customs associated with the Roman Saturn Festival compared to those associated with modern Christmas festivities; and (8) explanation of how the medieval social and political systems worked by describing the local (rural central Michigan) area as part of the outlying lands surrounding a manor based in Lansing, which in turn would be under the protection of and would pay taxes to "the King of Detroit."

Sometimes the problem is not that the content would be too abstract or unfamiliar for the students to understand if it were explained sufficiently, but that the text simply does not provide enough explanation. A good teacher looks on a text as an outline to be elaborated on, not as the entire curriculum. For example, it is not enough to say that Russia exited World War I because "the revolution came and a new government was established." This brief statement does not supply enough details to enable students to understand and visualize the events surrounding the Russian Revolution. To make these events more understandable, teachers would have to elaborate on the text by explaining why and (especially) how the communists and others organized political and eventually military resistance to the Czar's regime, how they killed or expelled the Czar's family and key officials, and how they established a new government. Such elaboration on the text transforms the relatively meaningless statement that "the revolution came and a new government was established" into a meaningful story that students can explain in their own words because they can relate it to their prior knowledge and visualize the events to which it refers. Thus, they can actively process the content instead of just trying to memorize it.

Finally, teachers may need to adapt their curriculum content to make sure that it features gender equity and suitable adaptation to the ethnic and cultural backgrounds of their students. Even when content is selected and taught effectively in other respects, certain students may feel excluded and lose interest if they come to believe that a school subject is about "them" rather than "us" (Alton-Lee, Nuthall, & Patrick, 1993). Consequently, treatment of history should include sufficient attention to social history, women's roles, and the lives of everyday people along with political and military events, and should include multiple perspectives on their meanings and implications. Similarly, study of literature, biography, and contributions to society and culture should include sufficient attention to contributions by women and members of minority groups, especially groups represented in the class. Research assignments connected with this content should include opportunities for students to choose biographical subjects, literature selections, or historical events on which to focus. In this way, students who wish to do so can pursue their interests in content with which they identify in part because of its relevance to gender or cultural identity issues that are important to them.

Induce Dissonance or Cognitive Conflict

If the topic of a text is already familiar, students may think that they already know all about it and thus may read the material with little attention or thought. Teachers can counter this tendency by pointing out unexpected, incongruous, or paradoxical aspects of the content; by calling attention to unusual or exotic elements; by noting exceptions to general rules; or by challenging students to solve the "mystery" that underlies a paradox.

We have observed several teachers use this strategy effectively. One introduced a unit on the Middle Ages by telling students that they would learn about "our ancestors" who chose to remain illiterate and ignorant and who persecuted people who did not share their religion. Later he contrasted the Moslem advances in mathematics, medicine, and the construction of libraries with the illiteracy of most Christian kings and lords during the Middle Ages. Another teacher stimulated curiosity about the Persian Empire by noting that Darius was popular with the people he conquered and asking students to anticipate reasons why this might be so. Another introduced a selection on the Trojan War by telling the students that they would read about "how just one horse enabled the Greeks to win a major battle against the Trojans." Another introduced a movie on the fall of the Roman Empire by saying, "Some say that the factors that led to the decay of the Roman Empire are currently at work in the United States—as you watch the film, see if you notice parallels."

The school curriculum includes a great many "strange but true" phenomena, especially in mathematics and science. Teachers should call attention to such phenomena and get their students to begin asking themselves "How can that be?" Otherwise, students may treat new material as just more information to be absorbed without giving it much thought or even noticing the fact that it seems to contradict previously learned information.

Induce Students to Generate Their Own Motivation to Learn

Teachers can induce students to generate their own motivation to learn by asking them to think about topics or activities in relation to their own interests and pre-conceptions. For example, they can ask the students to identify questions about the topic that they would like to get answered or to note things that they find to be surprising as they read. Such exercises help students to understand that motivation to learn must come from within themselves—that it is a property of the learner rather than the task to be learned (Ortiz, 1983).

One increasingly popular way to accomplish this is through the K-W-L technique (Ogle, 1986). Developed originally as a way to facilitate reading comprehension, K-W-L promotes learning by helping students to retrieve relevant background knowledge and learn with awareness of purpose and accomplishment. Students complete the K-W-L exercise in two steps. As they are about to begin study of a topic, they write down what they already *Know* (or think they know) about the topic and what they *Want* to learn about it (alternatively, this can be done as a teacher-led group activity, in which students tell what they know about the topic and the teacher lists their contributions on the board or the overhead). During study of the topic, the teacher follows up by addressing any misconceptions that emerged and by providing answers (or arranging for the students themselves to get answers) to the questions they raised. As a culmination to the study of the topic, the students describe what they *Learned* about it. They may wish to change some of the statements they made earlier, if they have discovered that some of what they thought they knew was incorrect. The K-W-L technique is useful not just for its originally intended purpose of helping students to read content selections with greater interest and understanding, but also for developing productive learning sets when introducing new topics in science, social studies, and other content areas.

State Learning Objectives and Provide Advance Organizers

Instructional theorists have shown that learners retain more information when their learning is goal directed and structured around key concepts. Such theorists commonly advise teachers to introduce activities by stating learning objectives and by providing advance organizers characterizing what will be learned in general terms that enable the learners to know what to expect and help them prepare to learn efficiently (Alexander, Frankiewicz, & Williams, 1979; Ausubel, Novak, & Hanesian, 1978; Mayer, 1979). This is good advice for motivational reasons as well (Lane, Newman, & Bull, 1988; Marshall, 1987). Learning objectives and advance organizers call students' attention to the benefits that they should receive from engaging in a task, and this helps them establish a learning set to use in guiding their responses (see Chapter 9 for more discussion of these teaching techniques).

Provide Informative Feedback

Feedback is another factor that is important from a motivational as well as a purely instructional point of view. If students are to function as self-regulated learners, they will need opportunities to assess their progress in understanding content or mastering skills. As soon as possible after being exposed to information through reading or teacher presentation, students should be given questions or assignments that will require them to restate the information in their own words, to show that they can apply it successfully, or to summarize, integrate, or evaluate what they have learned. Note the guidelines presented in Chapter 4 and earlier in the present chapter concerning when and how to provide informative feedback to students.

Model Task-Related Thinking and Problem Solving

The information-processing and problem-solving strategies needed for thinking about particular content or responding to particular tasks will be unknown to many students unless teachers make them overt and observable by modeling them. Therefore, teachers should model the processes involved by showing students what to do and thinking out loud as they demonstrate. Such modeling should include the thinking that goes into selecting the general approach to use, deciding on what options to take at choice points that arise during the process, checking on progress as one goes along, and making certain that one is on the right track. It also should include recovery from false starts and from use of inappropriate strategies, so that students can see how one develops a successful strategy even when one was not sure about what to do at first (Diener & Dweck, 1978; Schunk & Hanson, 1985).

This kind of cognitive modeling is powerful not just as an instructional device but as a way to socialize student motivation to learn. It allows the teacher to *show students what it means to approach a task with motivation to learn*. That is, it allows the teacher to model the beliefs and attitudes that are associated with such motivation (patience, confidence, persistence in seeking solutions through information processing and rational decision making, benefiting from the information supplied by mistakes rather than giving up in frustration, concentrating on the task and how to respond to it rather than focusing on the self and worrying about one's limitations).

Induce Metacognitive Awareness of Learning Strategies

When motivated to learn, students do not merely let information "wash over them" and hope that some of it will stick. Instead, they process the information actively by concentrating their attention, making sure that they understand, integrating new information with existing knowledge, and encoding and storing this information in a form that will allow them to remember it and use it later. The mere intention to learn in this fashion is not sufficient to ensure that such learning will occur. In addition, students must possess and use cognitive and metacognitive skills for learning and studying effectively. Therefore, when opportunities arise, teachers should train their students to be aware of their goals during task engagement, to monitor the strategies they use in pursuing these goals, to note the effects of these strategies as they are employed, and to monitor subjective responses to these unfolding events (Pressley, in press; Pressley et al., 1989).

Actively Preparing to Learn   Teachers can train their students to prepare to learn actively by mobilizing their resources and approaching tasks in thoughtful ways: getting ready to concentrate, previewing tasks by noting their nature and objectives, and developing plans before trying to respond to complex tasks.

Committing Material to Memory   If material must be memorized, teachers can help by teaching their students techniques for memorizing efficiently. Such techniques include active rehearsal; repeating, copying, or underlining key words; making notes; or using imagery or other mnemonic strategies.

Encoding or Elaborating on the Information Presented   Usually it is not appropriate (or even possible) to expect students to rely on rote memory to retain information verbatim. More typically, students must retain the gist of the information and be able to apply it later. It helps if they learn strategies for identifying and retaining the gist: paraphrasing and summarizing the information to put it into their own words, relating it to what they already know, and assessing their understanding by asking themselves questions.

Organizing and Structuring the Content   Students also need to learn to identify or impose organizational schemes that will allow them to structure extensive content by dividing it into sequences or clusters. Teachers can train their students to note the main ideas of paragraphs, outline the material, and notice and use the structuring devices that have been built into it. Students will also benefit from instruction in effective note-taking (Carrier & Titus, 1979; Kierwa, 1985; Ladas, 1980).

Monitoring Comprehension   In giving instructions for assignments, teachers can remind their students to remain aware of the instructional objectives, the strategies that they use to pursue these objectives, the relative success of these strategies, and the corrective efforts they undertake if the strategies have not been effective. They also can teach strategies for coping with confusion or mistakes: backing up and rereading, looking up definitions, identifying previous places in the text where the confusing point is discussed, searching the recent progression of topics for information that has been missed or misunderstood, retracing steps to see whether the strategy has been applied correctly, and generating possible alternative strategies.

Maintaining Appropriate Affect   Finally, teachers can model and instruct their students in ways of approaching academic activities with desirable affect (relaxed but alert and prepared to concentrate, ready to enjoy or at least take satisfaction in engaging in the task) and ways of avoiding undesirable affect (anger, anxiety, etc.).

Such instruction should include modeling of self-reinforcement for success and of coping skills for responding to frustration or failure (reassuring self-talk, refocusing of attention on the task at hand, using strategies listed at the end of the previous paragraph).

Educators interested in teaching school subjects for understanding have developed information about additional, more specific strategies that students can use for guiding their learning in each subject area. Information about these strategies, especially strategies for reading with comprehension, can be found in Chapter 10.

BUILDING MOTIVATION INTO THE SCHOOL ENVIRONMENT

Over the years, researchers studying motivation in education have assembled a formidable list of strategies for potential use by teachers, as this chapter illustrates. Recently, they have begun to consolidate these findings and develop programs that integrate various motivational strategies and connect them with strategies for accomplishing related goals such as establishing productive classroom and schoolwide learning environments and helping students to assume more responsibility for managing their own learning.

An example is the TARGET program for managing classrooms in ways that promote student motivation to learn (Ames, 1990). The TARGET acronym stands for the program's six major facets: task, authority, recognition, grouping, evaluation, and time. The program encourages teachers to manage these facets in ways that encourage students to engage in activities with a focus on task mastery rather than on their public performance and how it reflects on their abilities. *Tasks* are selected so as to provide an optimal level of challenge and to emphasize activities that students find interesting and intrinsically engaging. *Authority* is shared with students and exercised with consideration of their needs and feelings. *Recognition* is provided to all students who make noteworthy progress, not just the highest achievers. *Grouping* is managed in ways that promote cooperative learning and minimize interpersonal competition and social comparison. *Evaluation* is accomplished using multiple criteria and methods, focusing on individualized assessment of progress rather than comparisons of individuals or groups. Finally, *time* is used in creative ways that ease the constraints of rigid scheduling and allow for more use of activities that are widely recognized as valuable but seldom used in classrooms because they are hard to fit into 45-minute periods (or whatever time constraints apply at a given school).

Maehr and Midgley (1991) have extended Ames's TARGET model from the classroom level to the school level, reasoning that the motivational efforts of individual teachers in a school will have much more powerful cumulative effects on students if they reinforce one another and if the environment in the school as a whole supports students' motivation to learn. Maehr and Midgley have been working with school leaders to help them think through how their school-level policies might be adjusted to create a schoolwide psychological environment that reflects the principles behind the TARGET model. Key principles of their approach are summarized in Table 6.1. The table is included here as an illustration of ways in which motivational principles can be integrated with classroom management principles and applied at the level of the school as a whole, in addition to being applied within each classroom.

BUILDING MOTIVATIONAL STRATEGIES INTO INSTRUCTIONAL PLANS

Teachers who are planning courses from scratch can apply these strategies for motivating students to learn by building them directly into their plans. Teachers who are already working with given curricula and materials can use the strategies by adjusting their instructional plans as needed.

For All Activities

The following questions should be considered in planning for any academic activity. First, what are its *goals*? Why will the students be learning this information or skill? When and how might they use it after they learn it? Answers to these questions suggest information that should be conveyed when introducing the activity to the students.

Before getting into the activity itself, is there a way to characterize it using familiar, general terms that indicate its nature and provide students with organizing concepts? If so, such advance organizers should be communicated to the students.

What elements of the activity could be focused on to create interest, identify practical applications, or create curiosity, suspense, or dissonance? Does the activity include information that the students are likely to find interesting, or build skills that they are eager to develop? Does it contain unusual or surprising information? Can the content be related to current events or events in the students' lives? Is there information that the students are likely to find surprising or difficult to believe? Are there ways to stimulate curiosity or create suspense by posing interesting questions?

For Listening and Reading Activities

Teachers might consider the following questions when planning activities that require students to attend to an oral presentation, watch a visual presentation, or learn by reading. First, what aspects of the content are interesting, noteworthy, or important, and why? Answers to these questions will help teachers identify reasons for enthusiasm about the topic, and these reasons should be communicated to the students.

Can personal experiences be related or artifacts be displayed in relation to the content? Are there content-related anecdotes about the experiences of others or about how the knowledge was discovered that could add spice to the presentation?

Will the lesson contain sufficient variety in the cognitive levels of information communicated and the types of responses demanded? If it appears that there will

Table 6.1 GENERAL FRAMEWORK EMPLOYED IN DEVELOPMENT OF A SCHOOLWIDE STRESS ON TASK GOALS IN LEARNING

TARGET Area	Focus	Goals	Strategies
Task	Intrinsic value of learning	Reduce the reliance on extrinsic incentives Design programs that challenge all students Stress goals and purposes in learning Stress the fun of learning	Encourage programs that take advantage of students' backgrounds and experience Avoid payment (monetary or other) for attendance, grades, or achievement Foster programs that stress goal setting and self-regulation/management Foster programs that make use of school learning in a variety of nonschool settings (e.g., internships, field experiences, and cocurricular activities)
Authority	Student participation in learning/school decisions	Provide opportunities to develop responsibility, independence, and leadership skills Develop skills in self-regulation	Give optimal choice in instructional settings Foster participation in cocurricular and extracurricular settings Foster opportunities to learn metacognitive strategies for self-regulation
Recognition	The nature and use of recognition and reward in the school setting	Provide oportunities for all students to be recognized Recognize progress in goal attainment Recognize efforts in a broad array of learning activities	Foster "personal best" awards Foster policy in which all students and their achievements can be recognized Recognize and publicize a wide range of school-related activities of students
Grouping	Student interaction, social skills, and values	Build an environment of acceptance and appreciation of all students Broaden range of social interaction, particularly of at-risk students Enhance social skill development Encourage humane values Build an environment in which all can see themselves as capable of making significant contributions	Provide opportunities for group learning, problem solving, and decision making Allow time and opportunity for peer interaction to occur Foster the development of subgroups (teams, schools within schools, etc.) within which significant interaction can occur Encourage multiple group membership to increase range of peer interaction

Table 6.1, *continued*

TARGET Area	Focus	Goals	Strategies
Evaluation	The nature and use of evaluation and assessment procedures	Increase students' sense of competence and self-efficacy Increase students' awareness of progress in developing skills and understanding Increase students' appreciation of their unique set of talents Increase students' acceptance of failure as a natural part of learning and life	Reduce emphasis on social comparisons of achievement by minimizing public reference to normative evaluation standards (e.g., grades and test scores) Establish policies and procedures which give students opportunities to improve their performance (e.g., study skills and classes) Create opportunities for students to assess progress toward goals they have set
Time	The management of time to carry out plans and reach goals	Improve rate of work completion Improve skills in planning and organization Improve self-management ability Allow the learning task and student needs to dictate scheduling	Provide experience in personal goal setting and in monitoring progress in carrying out plans for goal achievement Foster opportunities to develop time-management skills Allow students to progress at their own rate whenever possible Encourage flexibility in the scheduling of learning experiences

Source: Maehr, M., & Midgley, C. (1991). Enhancing student motivation: A schoolwide approach. *Educational Psychologist, 26,* 399–427.

be too much uninterrupted lecture or reading, the teacher can plan to ask questions, initiate a discussion, or allow time for students to take notes or do a brief assignment.

How should the students respond to the presentation or text? Should they take notes or underline key ideas? Keep particular issues or questions in mind as they listen or read? Outline the material or respond to a study guide? Identify organizational structures embedded in the material? If students are to do something more specific than just pay attention, teachers should tell them what to do, and if necessary, help by supplying questions, outlines, study guides, or information about how the material is organized.

Is there some key point that the students might easily miss if not forewarned? Are there abstractions that will not be meaningful without additional explanation or concrete examples? Are there concepts that may be troublesome because they are subtle or difficult, because they are not well explained in the text, or because they conflict with the students' experiences? If so, teachers may want to call attention to these trouble spots to prepare students for viewing or reading.

For Activities Requiring Active Response

Teachers might consider the following questions when planning activities that require students to do something more than just listen or read (answer questions, prepare a report, work on a project, etc.). Is the activity presented as an opportunity to apply knowledge or develop skills rather than as a test (unless it *is* a test)? When and how might the students be encouraged to ask questions or seek help?

Does the activity demand new or complex responses that should be modeled? If so, what steps should be modeled at what level of detail? Are there important hypothesis-testing strategies (considering alternatives at a choice point and then selecting the correct one after reasoning or brief experimentation) or troubleshooting or repair strategies (responding to confusion or errors with diagnosis of the problem or generation of alternative strategies) that should be modeled?

When, how, and from whom will the students get feedback on their performance? What should they do if they do not understand a question or are not sure about how to begin a response? What should they do when they think they are finished? How might they be encouraged to check their work, to generate and respond to their own questions about it, or to engage in follow-up discourse with peers?

SUMMARY

The effort that students are likely to invest in an academic task will be determined by how much they value the rewards associated with completing it successfully and the degree to which they expect to be able to succeed on the task and thus reap the rewards. A complete motivational program will attend to both the expectancy aspects and the value aspects of student motivation.

The following four essential preconditions set the stage for use of recommended motivational strategies: (1) The teacher organizes and manages the classroom as an efficient learning environment and creates an atmosphere that supports students' learning efforts, (2) students are given tasks of appropriate difficulty, (3) activities have been selected with worthwhile academic objectives in mind, and (4) the teacher shows moderation and variation in using motivational strategies.

Four sets of motivational strategies were reviewed in the chapter. *The first set is designed to motivate by maintaining students' success expectations and related perceptions and beliefs* (perception of covariation between effort and outcome, internal locus of control, concept of self as origin rather than pawn, sense of efficacy or competence, attribution of outcomes to internal and controllable causes, incremental concept of ability). The most basic strategy is programming for success by assigning tasks on which students can succeed if they apply reasonable effort and by instructing them thoroughly so that they know what to do and how to do it. Other strategies include helping students to set appropriate (proximal, specific, challenging) goals, to commit themselves to these goals, to use appropriate standards for appraising their levels of success, and to reinforce themselves for the success that they do achieve; helping students to recognize the linkages between effort and outcome through modeling, socialization, and feedback; portraying effort as an investment rather than a risk; portraying skill development as incremental and domain specific; focusing on mastery; and doing remedial work with discouraged students.

The other three sets of strategies address the *value aspects* of student motivation. *Extrinsic motivation strategies* do not attempt to increase the value that students place on academic activities themselves but instead link task performance to delivery of consequences that the students do value. They include offering rewards as incentives for good performance, calling attention to the instrumental value of academic activities (their potential for developing "life skills" or providing "tickets" to social advancement), and using individual or team competition to enhance interest in an activity. Teachers who use rewards or competition should keep in mind the undesirable side effects that these approaches can have (undermining intrinsic motivation to engage in academic activities, distracting attention from the academic goals that the activities were intended to accomplish). In this regard, the comments made about use of rewards in Chapter 4 and the guidelines summarized in Table 4.1 should be kept in mind.

The next set of motivational strategies calls for *taking advantage of students' existing intrinsic motivation* by designing or selecting activities containing elements that students enjoy: opportunities to respond more actively than by merely listening or reading; opportunities to pursue higher-level objectives and respond to divergent questions that call for creative or challenging application of the content (rather than just memorizing facts or practicing basic skills); tasks that provide immediate feedback to students' responses and thus allow them to experiment and improve with practice; activities that include gamelike features such as "test-yourself" challenges, puzzles, or brain teasers; activities that allow students to create a finished product; activities that include fantasy or simulation elements; and activities that provide opportunities to interact with peers. Opportunities to use intrinsic motivational strategies are limited by the teacher's responsibility to teach the established curriculum within time constraints. Even when such strategies can be used, they merely increase the likelihood that students will enjoy an activity; they do not directly stimulate the students' motivation to learn what the activity was designed to teach.

To accomplish the latter goal, *strategies for stimulating student motivation to learn* are needed. Viewed either as a general personal trait or as a situation-specific state, motivation to learn is a tendency to find learning activities meaningful and worthwhile and to try to get the intended academic benefits from them. The concept emphasizes learning (acquiring information or skills in the first place) and not merely performing (activating the knowledge or skills later in an attempt to meet performance standards), and it carries cognitive implications (goal-oriented information processing, sense-making, and use of generative learning strategies) in addition to more purely motivational implications. Three general strategies describe pervasive features of the classroom learning environment that support development of student motivation to learn as a general trait: modeling the thinking and actions associated with motivation to learn, communicating expectations and attributions implying motivation to learn in the students, and creating a supportive environment for learning.

Other strategies for inducing student motivation to learn are more situation-specific and would be included in the planning for particular academic activities: projecting intensity that communicates the importance of an activity; projecting enthusiasm for the topic; inducing task interest or appreciation by pointing out aspects that the students should find interesting or important; inducing curiosity or suspense by raising interesting questions that the students will get a chance to answer in the process of carrying out the activity; elaborating on vague or abstract content to make it more personal, concrete, or familiar; inducing dissonance or cognitive conflict by mentioning strange but true aspects of the content; inducing students to generate their own motivation to learn by identifying their own interests and the questions that they would like to get answers to; stating learning objectives and providing advance organizers; providing informative feedback to students' responses; modeling the information-processing and problem-solving strategies that would be used when approaching the activity with motivation to learn; and inducing students' metacognitive awareness of their own learning efforts by teaching them strategies for actively preparing to learn, committing material to memory, encoding or elaborating on the information presented, organizing and structuring the content, monitoring their comprehension or mastery, and maintaining appropriate affect.

The chapter concludes with suggestions on ways that teachers can build these motivational strategies into their instructional plans by asking themselves questions about the content or skills involved in an academic activity and then using the answers to these questions as guidelines for planning motivational elements.

SUGGESTED ACTIVITIES AND QUESTIONS

1. What does it mean to say that a student "is motivated" or "has no motivation?" What evidence would lead you to make such judgments? How does your answer to these questions compare with those of your peers?

2. Think back to when you were a student similar (in grade level, subject matter, etc.) to the students you plan to teach. What were your *favorite* learning activities? What were your *most valuable* learning experiences? Compare your answers with those of peers who plan to teach similar students. What do your answers imply about effective motivation strategies?

3. How does motivation to learn differ from intrinsic motivation to engage in classroom activities?

4. To what extent do you think it necessary or advisable to use extrinsic motivation approaches (rewards, competition) in the classroom? If you intend to use extrinsic approaches, how do you plan to minimize their undesirable side effects?

5. As a person who chose to go into teaching, you probably were a well-adjusted student who felt comfortable in classrooms and enjoyed academic activities. Yet, teachers have to cope with students who have histories of failure and find schooling to be boring or aversive. How will you cope with such students? With a friend or colleague, role-play your interaction with a student who is alienated to the point of persistent inattention to lessons and failure to complete assignments.

6. Sometimes the toughest part of motivating students is meeting the essential preconditions for developing student motivation to learn, especially those calling for worthwhile learning objectives and appropriate difficulty levels. What should you do if you find that several activities in the workbooks that come with your adopted curriculum appear to be pointless? Discuss this issue with friends or colleagues.

7. What should you do if certain students cannot handle the same material and move at the same pace as the rest of the class? What might you begin to do differently with these students and how might you explain it to them in ways that would support rather than erode their motivation to learn?

8. Why do the authors make a point of distinguishing between learning and performance when talking about motivating students to *learn*?

9. The authors note that intrinsic motivation resides in persons rather than in topics or activities, but they talk about capitalizing on students' existing intrinsic motivation by emphasizing topics or activities that students find interesting or enjoyable. Explain this seeming contradiction.

10. Similarly, the authors speak of motivation to learn as generated by learners themselves, but suggest that teachers can stimulate their students to develop such motivation to learn through general modeling and socialization and various more specific strategies. Again, explain this seeming contradiction. How can teachers stimulate the development of something that students must develop themselves?

11. Explain the implications of the following statement for motivating students in the classroom: We don't do something for *its* sake, we do it for *our* sake.

12. How would you respond to unmotivated students who genuinely want to know why they are asked to study Shakespeare's sonnets or the history of ancient Greece?

13. Take any three topics in English, science, or mathematics and write a one-page introduction to each topic. In planning your introduction, consider the following questions. What are some elements that could be focused on as a means to create interest, identify application potential, or create curiosity? Is there information that the students are likely to find surprising or difficult to believe? Can the content be related to current events or events in the students' lives?

14. Obtain students' textbooks in English, science, or mathematics and examine the exercises presented there. Given the considerations discussed in this chapter, how satisfactory are the questions and exercises? Find three or four examples that need to be improved, and write out your strategy for improving them or write different questions that have more motivational (and presumably instructional) value.

15 How can teachers model curiosity and interest in learning?

REFERENCES

Alexander, L., Frankiewicz, R., & Williams, R. (1979). Facilitation of learning and retention of oral instruction using advance and post organizers. *Journal of Educational Psychology, 71,* 701–707.

Alton-Lee, A., Nuthall, G., & Patrick, J. (1993). Reframing classroom research: A lesson from the private world of children. *Harvard Educational Review, 63,* 50–84.

Ames, C. (1984). Competitive, cooperative, and individualistic goal structures: A cognitive-motivational analysis. In R. Ames & C. Ames (Eds.), *Research on motivation in education. Vol. 1: Student motivation.* New York: Academic Press.

Ames, C. (1987). The enhancement of student motivation. In M. Maehr & D. Kleiber (Eds.), *Advances in motivation and achievement*. Vol. 5. *Enhancing motivation* (pp. 123–148). Greenwich, CT: JAI Press.

Ames, C. (1990). Motivation: What teachers need to know. *Teachers College Record, 91,* 409–421.

Ames, C., & Ames, R. (Eds.). (1985). *Research on motivation in education*. Vol. 2. *The classroom milieu*. Orlando, FL: Academic Press.

Ames, C., & Ames, R. (Eds.). (1989). *Research on motivation in education*. Vol. 3. *Goals and cognitions*. San Diego: Academic Press.

Ames, C., & Archer, J. (1988). Achievement goals in the classroom: Students' learning strategies and motivation processes. *Journal of Educational Psychology, 80,* 260–267.

Ames, R., & Ames, C. (Eds.). (1984). *Research on motivation in education*. Vol. 1. *Student motivation*. New York: Academic Press.

Ausubel, D., Novak, J., & Hanesian, H. (1978). *Educational psychology: A cognitive view*. New York: Holt, Rinehart and Winston.

Bandura, A. (1989). Human agency in social cognitive theory. *American Psychologist, 44,* 1175–1184.

Bandura, A., & Schunk, D. (1981). Cultivating competence, self-efficacy, and intrinsic interest through proximal self-motivation. *Journal of Personality and Social Psychology, 41,* 586–598.

Berndt, T., & Miller, K. (1990). Expectancies, values, and achievement in junior high school. *Journal of Educational Psychology, 82,* 319–326.

Bettencourt, E., Gillett, M., Gall, M., & Hull, R. (1983). Effects of teacher enthusiasm training on student on-task behavior and achievement. *American Educational Research Journal, 20,* 435–450.

Blumenfeld, P., & Meece, J. (1988). Task factors, teacher behavior, and students' involvement and use of learning strategies in science. *Elementary School Journal, 88,* 235–250.

Blumenfeld, P. C., Mergendoller, J. R., & Swarthout, D. W. (1987). Task as a heuristic for understanding student learning and motivation. *Journal of Curriculum Studies, 19,* 135–148.

Blumenfeld, P., Soloway E., Marx, R., Krajcik, J., Guzdial, M., & Palcinsar, A. (1991). Motivating project-based learning: Sustaining the doing, supporting the learning. *Educational Psychologist, 26,* 369–398.

Borkowski, J., Weyhing, R., & Carr, M. (1988). Effects of attributional retraining on strategy-based reading comprehension in learning-disabled students. *Journal of Educational Psychology, 80,* 46–53.

Brophy, J. (1983). Conceptualizing student motivation. *Educational Psychologist, 18,* 200–215.

Brophy, J., & Kher, N. (1986). Teacher socialization as a mechanism for developing student motivation to learn. In R. Feldman (Ed.), *Social psychology applied to education*. New York: Cambridge University Press.

Butkowsky, I., & Willows, D. (1980). Cognitive-motivational characteristics of children varying in reading ability: Evidence for learned helplessness in poor readers. *Journal of Educational Psychology, 72,* 408–422.

Butler, R. (1987). Task-involving and ego-involving properties of evaluation: Effects of different feedback conditions on motivational perceptions, interest, and performance. *Journal of Educational Psychology, 79,* 474–482.

Carrier, C., & Titus, A. (1979). The effects of notetaking: A review of studies. *Contemporary Educational Psychology, 4,* 299–314.

Condry, J., & Chambers, J. (1978). Intrinsic motivation and the process of learning. In M. Lepper & D. Greene (Eds.), *The hidden costs of reward: New perspectives on the psychology of human motivation.* Hillsdale, NJ: Erlbaum.

Cooper, H. (1979). Pygmalion grows up: A model for teacher expectation communication and performance influence. *Review of Educational Research, 49,* 389–410.

Corno, L., & Rohrkemper, M. (1985). The intrinsic motivation to learn in classrooms. In C. Ames & R. Ames (Eds.), *Research on motivation in education.* Vol. 2: *The classroom milieu.* Orlando, FL: Academic Press.

Covington, M. (1992). *Making the grade: A self-worth perspective on motivation and school reform.* Cambridge: Cambridge University Press.

Craske, M. (1988). Learned helplessness, self-worth motivation and attribution retraining for primary school children. *British Journal of Educational Psychology, 58,* 152–164.

deCharms, R. (1976). *Enhancing motivation: Change in the classroom.* New York: Irvington.

Deci, E., & Ryan, R. (1985). *Intrinsic motivation and self-determination in human behavior.* New York: Plenum.

Deci, E., Vallerand, R., Pelletier, L., & Ryan, R. (1991). Motivation and education: The self-determination perspective. *Educational Psychologist, 26,* 325–346.

Diener, D., & Dweck, C. (1978). An analysis of learned helplessness: Continuous changes in performance, strategy, and achievement cognitions following failure. *Journal of Personality and Social Psychology, 36,* 451–462.

Doyle, W. (1983). Academic work. *Review of Educational Research, 53,* 159–199.

Dweck, C. (1991). Self-theories and goals: Their role in motivation, personality, and development. In R. Dienstbier (Ed.), *Perspectives on motivation: Nebraska Symposium on Motivation 1990* (Vol. 38, pp. 199–235). Lincoln: University of Nebraska Press.

Dweck, C., & Elliott, E. (1983). Achievement motivation. In P. Mussen (Ed.), *Handbook of child psychology* (4th ed.), Vol. IV: *Socialization, personality, and social development.* New York: Wiley.

Eccles, J., & Wigfield, A. (1985). Teacher expectations and student motivation. In J. B. Dusek (Ed.), *Teacher expectancies.* Hillsdale, NJ: Erlbaum.

Elawar, M. C., & Corno, L. (1985). A factorial experiment in teachers' written feedback on student homework: Changing teacher behavior a little rather than a lot. *Journal of Educational Psychology, 77,* 162–173.

Feather, N. (Ed.). (1982). *Expectations and actions.* Hillsdale, NJ: Erlbaum.

Fowler, J. W., & Peterson, P. L. (1981). Increasing reading persistence and altering attributional style of learned helpless children. *Journal of Educational Psychology, 73,* 251–260.

Frieze, I., Francis, W., & Hanusa, B. (1983). Defining success in classroom settings. In J. Levine & M. Wang (Eds.), *Teacher and student perceptions: Implications for learning.* Hillsdale, NJ: Erlbaum.

Gardner, H. (1991). *The unschooled mind: How children think and how schools should teach.* New York: Basic Books.

Gottfried, A. (1985). Academic intrinsic motivation in elementary and junior high school students. *Journal of Educational Psychology, 77,* 631–645.

Grabe, M. (1985). Attributions in a mastery instructional system: Is an emphasis on effort harmful? *Comtemporary Educational Psychology, 10,* 113–126.

Heckhausen, H. (1991). *Motivation and action* (2nd ed.). New York: Springer-Verlag.

Hembree, R. (1988). Correlates, causes, effects, and treatment of test anxiety. *Review of Educational Research, 58,* 47–77.

Hill, K. T., & Wigfield, A. (1984). Test anxiety: A major educational problem and what can be done about it. *Elementary School Journal, 85,* 105–126.

Hughes, B., Sullivan, H., & Mosley, M. (1985). External evaluation, task difficulty, and continuing motivation. *Journal of Educational Research, 78,* 210–215.

Johnson, D., & Johnson, R. (1985). Motivational processes in cooperative, competitive, and individualistic learning situations. In C. Ames & R. Ames (Eds.), *Research on motivation in education.* Vol. 2: *The classroom milieu.* Orlando, FL: Academic Press.

Keller, J. (1983). Motivational design of instruction. In C. Reigeluth (Ed.), *Instructional-design theories and models: An overview of their current status.* Hillsdale, NJ: Erlbaum.

Kierwa, K. (1985). Investigating notetaking and review: A depth of processing alternative. *Educational Psychologist, 20,* 23–32.

Krampen, G. (1987). Differential effects of teacher comments. *Journal of Educational Psychology, 79,* 137–146.

Kruglanski, A. (1978). Endogenous attribution and intrinsic motivation. In M. Lepper & D. Greene (Eds.), *The hidden costs of reward: New perspectives on the psychology of human motivation.* Hillsdale, NJ: Erlbaum.

Ladas, H. (1980). Summarizing research: A case study. *Review of Educational Research, 50,* 597–624.

Lane, D., Newman, D., & Bull, K. (1988). The relationship of student interest and advance organizer effectiveness. *Contemporary Educational Psychology, 13,* 15–25.

Lepper, M. (1983). Extrinsic reward and intrinsic motivation: Implications for the classroom. In J. Levine & M. Wang (Eds.), *Teacher and student perspectives: Implications for learning.* Hillsdale, NJ: Erlbaum.

Lepper, M., & Greene, D. (Eds.). (1978) *The hidden costs of reward: New perspectives on the psychology of human motivation.* Hillsdale, NJ: Erlbaum.

Locke, E., & Latham, G. (1990). *A theory of goal setting and task performance.* Englewood Cliffs, NJ: Prentice-Hall.

Maehr, M., & Kleiber, D. (Eds.). (1987). *Advances in motivation and achievement.* Vol. 5. *Enhancing motivation.* Greenwich, CT: JAI Press.

Maehr, M., & Midgley, C. (1991). Enhancing student motivation: A schoolwide approach. *Educational Psychologist, 26,* 399–427.

Malone, T., & Lepper, M. (1987). Making learning fun: A taxonomy of intrinsic motivation for learning. In R. Snow & M. Farr (Eds.), *Aptitude, learning, and instruction: III. Conative and affective process analysis.* Hillsdale, NJ: Erlbaum.

Marshall, H. (1987). Motivational strategies of three fifth-grade teachers. *Elementary School Journal, 88,* 135–150.

Marshall, H. (1990). Beyond the workplace metaphor: The classroom as a learning setting. *Theory into Practice, 29,* 94–101.

Mayer, R. (1979). Can advance organizers influence meaningful learning? *Review of Educational Research, 49,* 371–383.

McCaslin, M. (1990). Motivated literacy. In J. Zutell & S. McCormick (Eds.), *Literacy theory and research: Analyses for multiple paradigms* (39th Yearbook, pp. 35–50). Rochester, NY: National Reading Conference, Inc.

McColskey, W., & Leary, M. R. (1985). Differential effects of norm-referenced and self-referenced feedback on performance expectancies, attributions, and motivation. *Contemporary Educational Psychology, 10,* 275–284.

McCombs, B. (1984). Processes and skills underlying continuing intrinsic motivation to learn: Toward a definition of motivational skills training and interventions. *Educational Psychologist, 19,* 199–218.

McGowan, T., Sutton, A., & Smith, P. (1990). Instructional elements influencing elementary student attitudes toward social studies. *Theory and Research in Social Education, 18,* 37–52.

Medway, F. M., & Venino, G. R. (1982). The effects of effort feedback and performance patterns on children's attribution and task persistence. *Contemporary Educational Psychology, 7,* 26–34.

Meece, J., Blumenfeld, P., & Hoyle, R. (1988). Students' goal orientations and cognitive engagement in classroom activities. *Journal of Educational Psychology, 80,* 514–523.

Midgley, C., Feldlaufer, H., & Eccles, J. (1989). Change in teacher efficacy and student self- and task-related beliefs in mathematics during the transition to junior high school. *Journal of Educational Psychology, 81,* 247–258.

Mitman, A., & Lash, A. (1988). Students' perceptions of their academic standing and classroom behavior. *Elementary School Journal, 89,* 55–68.

Morgan, M. (1985). Self-monitoring and attained subgoals in private study. *Journal of Educational Psychology, 77,* 623–630.

Naveh-Benjamin, M. (1991). A comparison of training programs intended for different types of test-anxious students: Further support for an information-processing model. *Journal of Educational Psychology, 83,* 134–139.

Newby, T. (1991). Classroom motivation: Strategies of first-year teachers. *Journal of Educational Psychology, 83,* 195–200.

Nolen, S., & Haladyna, T. (1990). Personal and environmental influences on students' beliefs about effective study strategies. *Contemporary Educational Psychology, 15,* 116–130.

Ogle, D. (1986). K-W-L: A teaching model that develops active reading of expository text. *Reading Teacher, 39,* 564–570.

Ortiz, R. (1983). Generating interest in reading. *Journal of Reading, 27,* 113–119.

Pintrich, P., & DeGroot, E. (1990). Motivational and self-regulated learning components of classroom academic performance. *Journal of Educational Psychology, 82,* 33–40.

Pressley, M. (Guest editor). (In press). Special issue on cognitive strategy instruction. *Elementary School Journal.*

Pressley, M., Johnson, C., Symons, S., McGoldrick, J., & Kurita, J. (1989). Strategies that improve children's memory and comprehension of text. *Elementary School Journal, 90,* 3–32.

Renninger, K., Hidi, S., & Krapp, A. (Eds.). (1992). *The role of interest in learning and development.* Hillsdale, NJ: Erlbaum.

Rohrkemper, M., & Corno, L. (1988). Success and failure on classroom tasks: Adaptive learning and classroom teaching. *Elementary School Journal, 88,* 297–312.

Schiefele, U. (1991). Interest, learning, and motivation. *Educational Psychologist, 26,* 299–323.

Schunk, D. (1991). Self-efficacy and academic motivation. *Educational Psychologist, 26,* 207–231.

Schunk, D. H., & Hanson, A. R. (1985). Peer models: Influence on children's self-efficacy and achievement. *Journal of Educational Psychology, 77,* 313–322.

Slavin, R. (1983). *Cooperative learning.* New York: Longman.

Stipek, D. (1988). *Motivation to learn: From theory to practice.* Englewood Cliffs, NJ: Prentice-Hall.

Stipek, D., & Daniels, D. (1988). Declining perceptions of competence: A consequence of changes in the child or in the educational environment? *Journal of Educational Psychology, 80,* 352–356.

Stipek, D., & Weisz, J. (1981). Perceived personal control and academic achievement. *Review of Educational Research, 51,* 101–137.

Thomas, J. W. (1980). Agency and achievement: Self-management and self-reward. *Review of Educational Research, 30,* 213–240.

Tollefson, N., Tracy, D., Johnsen, E., Farmer, W., & Buenning, M. (1984). Goal setting and personal responsibility for LD adolescents. *Psychology in the Schools, 21,* 224–233.

VanOverwalle, F., Segebarth, K., & Goldschstein, M. (1989). Improving performance of freshmen through attributional testimonies from fellow students. *British Journal of Educational Psychology, 59,* 79–85.

Weiner, B. (1984). Principles for a theory of student motivation and their application within an attributional framework. In R. Ames & C. Ames (Eds.), *Research on motivation in education.* Vol. 1. *Student motivation.* New York: Academic Press.

Weiner, B. (1992). *Human motivation: Metaphors, theories and research.* Newbury Park, CA: Sage.

Weinstein, C., & Mayer, R. (1986). The teaching of learning strategies. In M. C. Wittrock (Ed.), *Handbook of research on teaching* (3rd. ed.). New York: Macmillan.

Weisz, J., & Cameron, A. (1985). Individual differences in students' sense of control. In C. Ames & R. Ames (Eds.), *Research on motivation in education.* Vol. 2: *The classroom milieu.* Orlando, FL: Academic Press.

Wentzel, K. (1989). Adolescent classroom goals, standards for performance, and academic achievement: An interactionist perspective. *Journal of Educational Psychology, 81,* 131–142.

Whitley, B. E., & Frieze, I. H. (1985). Children's causal attributions for success and failure in achievement settings: A meta-analysis. *Journal of Educational Psychology, 77,* 608–616.

Wigfield, A., & Eccles, J. (1989). Test anxiety in elementary and secondary school students. *Educational Psychologist, 24,* 159–183.

Woolfolk, A., Rosoff, B., & Hoy, W. (1990). Teachers' sense of efficacy and their beliefs about managing students. *Teaching and Teacher Education, 6,* 137–148.

Zeidner, M., Klingman, A., & Papko, O. (1988). Enhancing students' test coping skills: Report of a psychological health education program. *Journal of Educational Psychology, 80,* 95–101.

Zimmerman, B. J., & Blotner, R. (1979). Effects of model persistence and success on children's problem solving. *Journal of Educational Psychology, 71,* 508–513.

Zimmerman, B., & Schunk, D. (Eds.). (1989). *Self-regulated learning and academic achievement: Theory, research, and practice.* New York: Springer-Verlag.

Zuckerman, G. (in press). A pilot study of a 10-day course in cooperative learning for beginning Russian first graders. *Elementary School Journal.*

FORM 6.1   Attributing Success to Causes

USE: Whenever teacher makes a comment to explain a student's success
PURPOSE: To see whether the teacher's statements support student
confidence and motivation to learn
For each codable instance, code each causal attribution category that
applies. How does the teacher explain good performance by students?

CAUSAL ATTRIBUTION CATEGORIES	CODES	
1. Effort or perseverance ("You worked hard, stuck to it")	1. ___	26. ___
	2. ___	27. ___
2. Accurate problem representation and solution ("You developed a good plan, followed the right process")	3. ___	28. ___
	4. ___	29. ___
3. Good progress in learning the domain ("You've really learned how to _____")	5. ___	30. ___
4. Native intelligence or ability ("You're smart")	6. ___	31. ___
5. Compliance ("You listened carefully, did as you were told")	7. ___	32. ___
	8. ___	33. ___
6. Irrelevant attributes ("You're a big boy")	9. ___	34. ___
7. Cheating ("You copied." "Did someone tell you the answer?")	10 ___	35. ___
8. Other (specify)	11. ___	36. ___
	12. ___	37. ___
NOTES:	13. ___	38. ___
	14. ___	39. ___
	15. ___	40. ___
	16. ___	41. ___
	17. ___	42. ___
	18. ___	43. ___
	19. ___	44. ___
	20. ___	45. ___
	21. ___	46. ___
	22. ___	47. ___
	23. ___	48. ___
	24. ___	49. ___
	25. ___	50. ___

FORM 6.2 General Motivational Strategies

USE: When the teacher has been observed frequently enough so that reliable information is available
PURPOSE: To assess the degree to which the teacher's general approach to instruction supports students' self-confidence and motivation to learn
How regularly does the teacher follow the motivational guidelines listed below? Rate according to the following scale:

5 = *always*
4 = *most of the time*
3 = *sometimes*
2 = *occasionally*
1 = *never*

A. ESSENTIAL PRECONDITIONS

_____ 1. Maintains a supportive learning environment (classroom atmosphere is businesslike but relaxed, teacher supports and encourages students' learning efforts)
_____ 2. Assigns tasks at an appropriate level of difficulty (students can achieve success with reasonable effort)
_____ 3. Assigns tasks with meaningful learning objectives (the tasks teach some knowledge or skill that is worth learning)
_____ 4. Demonstrates moderation and variation in use of motivational strategies (does not overuse particular strategies to the point that they become counterproductive)

B. MAINTAINING STUDENTS' SUCCESS EXPECTATIONS

_____ 1. Programs for success
_____ 2. Helps students to develop their skills for goal setting, performance appraisal, and self-reinforcement
_____ 3. Helps students to recognize effort-outcome linkages
_____ 4. Portrays effort as investment rather than risk
_____ 5. Portrays skill development as incremental and domain-specific (rather than as determined by fixed general abilities)
_____ 6. Focuses on mastery in monitoring performance and giving feedback (stresses student's continuous progress toward mastery rather than comparisons with other students)
_____ 7. If necessary, does remedial motivational work with discouraged students (to help them see that they have ability and can reach goals if they put forth reasonable effort)

C. STIMULATING STUDENTS' MOTIVATION TO LEARN

_____ 1. Models own motivation to learn (portrays learning as a self-actualizing activity that produces personal satisfaction and enriches one's life)
_____ 2. Communicates desirable expectations and attributions (implying that students see classroom activities as worthwhile and are eager to acquire knowledge and master skills)
_____ 3 Minimizes performance anxiety (treats mistakes as understandable and expected; minimizes the threat of tests)

NOTES:

FORM 6.3 Teacher's Response to Students' Questions

USE: When a student asks the teacher a reasonable question during a discussion or question–answer period
PURPOSE: To see if teacher models commitment to learning and concern for students' interests
Code each category that applies to the teacher's response to a reasonable student question. Do not code if student wasn't really asking a question or if he or she was baiting the teacher.

BEHAVIOR CATEGORIES	CODES	
1. Compliments the question ("Good question")	1. _4_	26. ___
2. Criticizes the question (unjustly) as irrelevant, dumb, out of place, etc.	2. _4_	27. ___
	3. _1,4_	28. ___
3. Ignores the question, or brushes it aside quickly without answering it	4. _4_	29. ___
	5. _4_	30. ___
4. Answers the question or redirects it to the class	6. _3_	31. ___
5. If no one can answer, teacher arranges to get the answer or assigns a student to do so	7. _4_	32. ___
	8. _4_	33. ___
6. If no one can answer, teacher leaves it unanswered and moves on	9. _7_	34. ___
	10. _4_	35. ___
7. Other (specify)	11. _4_	36. ___
	12. ___	37. ___
NOTES:	13. ___	38. ___
	14. ___	39. ___
#7 Explained that question would be covered in tomorrow's lesson.	15. ___	40. ___
	16. ___	41. ___
	17. ___	42. ___
	18. ___	43. ___
	19. ___	44. ___
	20. ___	45. ___
	21. ___	46. ___
	22. ___	47. ___
	23. ___	48. ___
	24. ___	49. ___
	25. ___	50. ___

Chapter
7

Students' Interactions with One Another

*I*n previous chapters, we have discussed the roles of teachers' expectations, classroom management, and motivational strategies in establishing productive learning environments. In subsequent chapters we will address teachers' instructional roles and strategies. Here, however, we shift focus from the teacher to the students, considering the makeup of the class and the ways in which students might interact with one another within productive learning environments.

Educators' thinking about issues of who should be in the regular classroom and how these students should interact with one another has evolved considerably in recent decades. At one time, there was heavy emphasis on excluding certain students from regular classrooms and on dividing the remaining students into more homogeneous groups through tracking at the school level and ability grouping at the classroom level. Definitions of effective teaching emphasized efficiency in moving students through progressive sequences of instructional objectives, and it was thought that this process would unfold with maximum efficiency if the students were as similar to one another as possible.

Educators' thinking has moved away from these notions in recent years, in several respects. Many educators object on philosophical grounds to policies of exclusion and homogeneous grouping, arguing that educational approaches should be assessed not only in terms of their efficiency but also in terms of equity. They argue for valuing diversity, policies of inclusion, and practices that meet the needs of all students rather than favoring some over others. These educators argue that heterogeneous classes are just as effective as homogeneous classes for accomplishing achievement and other cognitive outcomes, but in addition are more effective for accomplishing affective and social outcomes such as promoting cultural understandings and prosocial behaviors across racial and ethnic groups. To accomplish important social and affective goals, these educators argue, schools need to shift from homogeneous to heterogeneous grouping and from classroom discourse patterns that are mostly limited to teacher-student interaction to patterns that include a great deal of student-student interaction.

Recently developed social constructivist theories of teaching and learning (described in Chapter 10) reinforce these arguments by suggesting that increased emphasis on student-student interaction is important for achieving cognitive outcomes as well. In these views, learning should not be viewed as transmission of knowledge from a teacher to students who imitate or memorize it, but instead as social construction of new understandings accomplished primarily through sustained discussion. Besides learning through interacting with teachers, students learn by collaborating with peers in pairs and small groups and by interacting with them during class discussion. Assuming that everyone participates, diversity in students' backgrounds and points of view would be considered an asset, not a liability, so heterogeneous classes (and small groups) would be preferable to homogeneous ones.

In this chapter, we will discuss and consider the implications of theory and research on issues relating to the composition of the class and to students' interactions with one another. We begin with the goals of excellence and equity and their implications concerning student diversity and inclusion. Then we consider tracking and ability grouping. Finally, we address cooperative learning, peer tutoring, and other formats that allow students to learn by collaborating with one another.

EDUCATIONAL EXCELLENCE AND EQUITY

School quality (*educational excellence* as it has come to be called) is a continuing concern of the general public. By many criteria (including literacy rates and the percentage of the population who earn high school diplomas and college degrees) education in the United States has been quite successful both in absolute terms and in comparison with other countries. Historically, the general public has shown continuing commitment to the public schools and a perception that most of them are adequate, if not outstanding.

However, disenchantment sets in periodically, either in response to the writings of popular educational critics and would-be reformers or as a reaction to events perceived as indications of slippage in the nation's competitive position. The launching into orbit of *Sputnik* by the Soviet Union in the 1950s led to criticism of the schools' mathematics and science curricula. More recently, the economic successes achieved by the Japanese at the expense of American electronics and automobile manufacturers have produced a great deal of public debate about the schools and spurred a variety of reform movements.

When fueled by concern about educational excellence, reforms tend to concentrate on cognitive rather than affective or social objectives, and in particular on achievement test scores. Calls for upgrading schools commonly include recommitment to academic objectives and standards, mandated performance objectives and associated testing programs, increases in course requirements and reductions in course options, more rigorous grading, more challenging curricula, and more homework. Often there are calls for special programs to accommodate the perceived needs of "the best and the brightest": special tracks or courses for gifted elementary students and honors or advanced placement courses for qualifying secondary students.

In short, the "educational excellence" approach tends to identify school quality with success in maximizing achievement test scores. This is rejected as overly narrow by educators who wish to define school quality at least in part in terms of *educational equity*: fair and effective treatment of all students regardless of gender, race, ethnicity, socioeconomic status, or handicapping conditions. Equity concerns were the primary motives behind two of the most widespread changes introduced into the schools during the 1960s and 1970s: desegregation and mainstreaming.

Desegregation

Following the *Brown* v. *Board of Education* Supreme Court decision in 1954, separate schools for black students were abolished and district lines were redrawn so as to bring more black and white students together. Since then, attention has shifted from the legal and structural aspects of accomplishing desegregation to methods of addressing the equity issues it introduces: the need for multicultural awareness and fair treatment of different groups, the desire to elicit active participation of all students in classroom activities, and the attempt to get beyond mere tolerance by promoting positive, prosocial interactions among students of different backgrounds.

At the school level, this goal requires minimizing between-class achievement grouping. In most school populations, there are substantial correlations among race, socioeconomic status, and achievement, so that creating homogeneous classes in desegregated schools resegregates students and thus minimizes cross-racial contact.

At the classroom level, the degree to which the ultimate goals of desegregation are likely to be accomplished depends on the activities and organizational structures that the teacher introduces. Within-class grouping tends to resegregate students, and a heavy reliance on the traditional whole-class instruction/recitation/ seatwork approach to teaching minimizes students' opportunities to interact with their peers. Positive attitudes and frequent cross-race interaction are more likely in classrooms in which teachers frequently use small-group projects and other peer interaction formats (Nickerson & Prawat, 1981). The cooperative learning approaches that we describe later in the chapter have proven especially effective for improving cross-racial attitudes and behavior (Slavin, 1983).

Inclusion of Special Needs Students

In the past, schooling was treated as a privilege for students who fulfilled certain criteria rather than as a right guaranteed to all. Schools often denied enrollment to students whom they viewed as potential threats to smooth classroom functioning because of mental or physical handicaps, poor health, flagrant misbehavior, pregnancy, or even unconventional clothing or personal appearance. A series of court decisions in the 1960s and 1970s, however, established public education as a universal right rather than a privilege that schools could revoke capriciously. Also, resistance began to develop against the practice of placing students into special classes. There was concern about undesirable expectation and labeling effects on students diagnosed as handicapped and about special classes being dumping grounds for problems rather than improved educational settings that provide students with needed treatment.

Pressures for change culminated in Public Law 94-142, which became effective in 1977. This law directs public schools to search out and enroll all handicapped children and to educate them in the *least restrictive environment* in which they are able to function and still have their special needs met. The idea is to minimize the degree to which special students are labeled and treated as "different" and to maximize the degree to which they function as ordinary students participating in regular classes in usual ways. The following continuum of educational environments proceeds from most to least restrictive (Reynolds, 1978):

Full-time residential school

Full-time special day school

Full-time special class

Regular class plus part-time special class

Regular class plus resource room help

Regular class with assistance by itinerant specialists

Regular class with consultive assistance

Regular class only

The law calls for an individualized educational program (IEP) to be developed for each student who is recommended for special educational services. The IEP is developed by a committee that is likely to include the principal, teachers who instruct the student, a school psychologist or social worker who evaluates the student, and when feasible, a parent and the student. The IEP describes the student's present educational performance, identifies short-term and longer-term goals, and specifies a plan for achieving these goals through a combination of regular classroom teaching and whatever specialized instruction might be needed.

Research on regular versus special classroom placement suggests that the achievement progress of special education students depends not so much on what kind of classroom they are assigned to as on the amount and quality of the instruction they receive there. In general, the classroom management and instructional approaches that are effective with special students tend to be the same ones that are effective with other students (Crawford, 1983; Larrivee, 1985), although students with learning disabilities or handicaps may need individualized curricula and more one-to-one instruction (Leinhardt & Pallay, 1982; Madden & Slavin, 1983), and students with behavior disorders may need closer supervision (Thompson, White, & Morgan, 1982). Special students may be assigned to resource rooms where they receive instruction in basic skills from special education teachers who work with only 5 to 10 students at a time. These students spend the rest of their time in regular classrooms for instruction in other subjects.

"Mainstreamed" or "inclusion" students are likely to adjust well to regular classrooms if they receive acceptance and support from their teachers and peers. Teachers' attitudes and expectations are critical. It is important for teachers to think of these students as "their own" and as bonafide members of the class, not as visitors on loan from the special education teachers. These students should participate as fully and equally in classroom activities as possible and should be treated primarily in terms of what they can accomplish (or learn to accomplish with help) rather than with emphasis on what they cannot do because of their handicapping conditions. For detailed suggestions about teaching handicapped students, see Gearheart and Weishahn (1984), Good and Brophy (1990), Hewett and Watson (1979), or Reynolds and Birch (1988).

BETWEEN-CLASS GROUPING (TRACKING)

Between-class grouping involves assigning students to classes that are as homogeneous as possible. Two subtypes are grouping by ability or achievement and grouping by curriculum (Rosenbaum, 1980). *Grouping by ability or achievement* is more common in elementary and middle schools, where it is often called *homogeneous grouping*. To group 69 third graders homogeneously, for example, school staff would examine standardized achievement test scores and assign the highest 23 scorers to the top class, the next 23 to the middle class, and the last 23 to the bottom class. There might be some minor variations to the procedure, such as making the top class a little larger and the bottom class a little smaller. However, the result would be three classes, each much more homogeneous in achievement than if the students had been assigned randomly or in some other fashion that yielded heterogeneous grouping. Homogeneously grouped classes are usually taught essentially the same curriculum, but higher-ranking classes are taught in greater depth and breadth.

Grouping by curriculum is more frequently used in junior and especially senior high schools. It is commonly called *tracking*. Instead of merely introducing differences in the depth and breadth of instruction in the same curriculum, tracking creates separate curricula for students in the different tracks. College preparatory students take one curriculum, business-secretarial students another, vocational students another, and general education students another. Some ninth graders take algebra, some pre-algebra, some business math, and some general math.

American educators have always been ambivalent about between-class ability grouping (Rosenbaum, 1980). It is a sensible idea in theory because reducing heterogeneity should make it easier for teachers to meet more of their students' needs more consistently. In practice, however, it is less appealing. Its effects on achievement are weak and mixed rather than reliably positive, and it appears to have undesirable affective and social effects that conflict with the nation's egalitarian traditions. Consequently, opposition to tracking has been building and has culminated recently in policy statements by various blue ribbon panels and professional educational organizations calling for elimination or at least minimization of tracking (Oakes & Lipton, 1992).

Teachers' attitudes toward tracking tend to vary according to the subject they teach (Dar, 1985; Evans, 1985). Teachers who favor tracking tend to teach subjects such as mathematics or foreign languages in which the content is largely abstract and arranged hierarchically. In contrast, teachers of literature, history, and other humanities and social studies subjects see the least need for tracking, apparently because they can relate their subjects to everyday experience and develop them using commonsense explanations. Thus, it is easier for them to keep a heterogeneous class of students meaningfully focused on a common topic. Teachers whose subject matter lies in between these extremes of abstraction and hierarchical organization of content (science teachers, for example) tend to have mixed views of tracking.

Effects on Achievement

In theory, between-class ability grouping should improve achievement and be equally beneficial for both low and high achievers. In fact, however, reviews suggest only weak and mixed effects on achievement (Esposito, 1973; Gamoran, 1992; Kulik & Kulik, 1989; Oakes, 1992; Rowan & Miracle, 1983; Slavin, 1987, 1990a & b). We are not sure why tracking has not lived up to its theoretical potential, because most investigators have used a black box approach—looking only at outcomes without collecting information about curriculum and instruction in classrooms that might provide a basis for explaining conflicting results. If teachers provide essentially the same curriculum and instruction to both tracked and untracked classes, there is little reason to expect either benefits or detriments to student achievement. Such effects can be expected only when teachers differentiate their instruction to different classes (Gamoran, 1992; Good & Marshall, 1984). Thus, one reason tracking has not consistently had the expected positive effects on student achievement may be that teachers have not used it to focus instruction on fewer specific student needs. Another reason, however, is that any potential positive effects of tracking may be undercut by its negative effects.

Affective and Social Effects

Critics have identified four types of negative effects that tracking is likely to have on students (Gamoran, 1992; Oakes, 1992; Page, 1992; Page & Valli, 1990). First are the social labeling and teacher attitude and expectation effects we reviewed in Chapter 3. Investigators have found that teachers dislike teaching low-ability classes, spend less time preparing for them, and schedule less varied, interesting, and challenging activities in them (Evertson, 1982; Finley, 1984; Oakes, 1985). This is true even in elite schools where most students in low-track classes would be in higher tracks elsewhere (Page, 1992). Instead of being taught by means of curricula and methods suited to their needs, students in low-track classes may not be taught much at all. Often they are merely kept quiet with busywork rather than being challenged with effective instruction.

Even where the situation has not deteriorated to this extent, teachers tend to teach high- and low-track classes differently. Compared with their behavior in high-track classes, many teachers in low-track classes are less clear about objectives, introduce content less clearly or completely, make fewer attempts to relate content to students' interests or backgrounds, and are less receptive to student views. Instruction tends to be conceptually simplified and to proceed slowly in lower-track classes, with emphasis on rote memory, oral recitation, and use of low-level worksheets. In contrast, high-track classes study more interesting, complex material, taught at a faster pace and with more enthusiasm. Classroom discourse features discussion or debate rather than just recitation, and applications feature authentic activities calling for critical thinking and decision making, not just filling in blanks on worksheets. Much of what high-track students learn is likely to be applicable to their lives outside of school and to function as "cultural capital" that they can draw on in coping with modern society's complex demands.

The second problem with tracking is the undesirable peer structures it creates in low-track classes. In heterogeneously grouped classes, the brighter and better socially adjusted students tend to assume academic peer leadership, so that each class tends to function primarily as a learning environment and most time is spent engaged in academic activities. However, tracking systems place most of these academic peer leaders in upper-track classes, so that lower-track classes can become leaderless aggregations of discouraged and alienated students. These students may respond to their low status defensively by refusing to commit themselves seriously to academic achievement goals and by deriding classmates who do (Alexander, Cook, & McDill, 1978; Gamoran & Berends, 1987; Metz, 1978; Persell, 1979; Schwartz, 1981; Vanfossen, Jones, & Spade, 1987). Even if teachers approach these low-track classes with desirable attitudes and expectations, they may find it difficult to establish effective learning environments if they encounter defeatism, alienation, or flat-out resistance. Similarly, low-track students who want to accomplish as much as they can may have a difficult time doing so if classmates deride their efforts or if instructional continuity is often disrupted. Experimental data indicate that students assigned to higher groups achieve more than comparable students assigned to lower groups (Douglas, 1964; Mason et al., 1992; Tuckman & Bierman, 1971). Also, students in classes with primarily higher-achieving classmates tend to achieve more than students in classes with primarily lower-achieving classmates (Beckerman & Good, 1981; Veldman & Sanford, 1984; see also Leiter, 1983, for mixed results).

A third criticism of between-class ability grouping is that assignment to tracks tends to be permanent: There is little movement from one track to another once initial assignments have been made, and the movement that does occur tends to be downward. Thus, initial placement into a low track may categorize a student permanently and close off academic and career advancement options. For example, if students in low-track classes get general math instead of algebra, they will be prevented from enrolling in all future mathematics courses for which algebra is a prerequisite (and perhaps from enrolling in certain science and computer courses as well). Ultimately, even if they graduate from high school they will do so with a diploma but without many of the prerequisites demanded by high-quality college programs.

Thus, tracking decisions made even as early as first grade might affect students' academic progress from that point on, for good or ill. This might be of less concern if students were always grouped accurately, but there is reason to believe that many students are misclassified due to imperfection of tests as predictors of future performance. This problem is especially acute when test data are used to group young students or students with limited facility in the language in which the test is administered.

The lack of movement from lower to higher tracks is another indication that tracking typically does not lead to adaptive instruction of low achievers. If it did, many of these students would show improved achievement and move up to higher tracks.

The fourth problem with tracking is that it minimizes contact between students of differing achievement. As a result, it also minimizes contact between students who differ in social class, race, or ethnicity.

Taken together, the data on tracking suggest that it offers little or no advantage as a way to increase student achievement and has some important negative effects on affective and social outcomes. Consequently, we agree with the developing consensus that tracking should be minimized.

Where tracking is considered unavoidable, we recommend that it be delayed as long as possible and be confined to grouping by curriculum rather than grouping by ability or achievement. We do not see justification for grouping classes by ability or achievement when all students are going to be taught essentially the same curriculum.

Where conditions appear to compel homogeneous grouping, we recommend partial or compromise arrangements over arrangements that segregate different groups completely. One such compromise is the Joplin Plan and its many variations. In the original Joplin Plan, students were assigned to heterogeneous classes for most of the day but were regrouped for reading instruction across grades (teachers all taught reading at the same time to make such regrouping possible). For example, a fourth-grade, first-semester reading class might include high-achieving third graders. The class would be taught as a whole or perhaps divided into just two groups, but no more. Students would be assigned strictly according to reading achievement level (not IQ or some less direct measure) and would be reassigned when their performance warranted it.

The Joplin Plan requires coordinated scheduling and cooperation among teams of teachers, but it simplifies reading instruction by making it possible for each teacher to instruct the entire class as a group or to divide the class into only two subgroups instead of three or more. This simplifies management and increases the time that students receive instruction from the teacher rather than work independently on assignments. Slavin (1987) reported that the Joplin Plan showed significant positive effects on achievement compared with traditional homogeneous or heterogeneous grouping within grades, although Kulik and Kulik (1989) reported more modest effects.

Variations on the Joplin Plan call for grouping students for reading instruction within rather than across grades or for regrouping in subjects other than reading. Regrouping is more likely to be used for reading and mathematics than for science or social studies.

Three first-grade teachers we know devised a plan for regrouping students within grades for both reading and mathematics. Originally, students had been assigned randomly to each class. The teachers taught and carefully observed them for six weeks, then divided them into high, middle, and low groups for mathematics and reading instruction (the groups were not the same for each subject). The teacher who taught the low readers taught the high mathematic students, and vice versa, so that students did not come to view one classroom as the "dummy room" and another as the "brain trust room." Also, the teachers were careful to treat students as individuals even though they had been assigned together because of similar aptitudes.

The students remained with their regular teacher for all other activities (science, social studies, art, music, lunch, and recess), where they were taught in mixed-ability groups. They worked with two or even three teachers and yet spent most of the day with the same teacher (an arrangement we think facilitates young students' affective growth). When a student experienced academic difficulty, all three teachers frequently had pertinent knowledge to contribute to a group planning session to develop new strategies.

Another possibility is a plan developed in Baltimore that Findley and Bryan (1971) called *stratified heterogeneous grouping*. Under this plan, if 90 students were to be assigned to three classes, the students would be ranked according to test scores and then subdivided into nine groups of 10 each. Instead of assigning the top 30 students to Teacher A, the middle 30 to Teacher B, and the bottom 30 to Teacher C, class assignments would be as follows. (Group 1 contains the highest 10 ranked students, and Group 9 contains the lowest 10.)

Teacher A	Teacher B	Teacher C
Group 1 (1–10)	Group 2 (11–20)	Group 3 (21–30)
Group 4 (31–40)	Group 5 (41–50)	Group 6 (51–60)
Group 7 (61–70)	Group 8 (71–80)	Group 9 (81–90)

Note the several merits of this scheme. First, there is no top or bottom section; the sections overlap, so invidious comparisons between groups are minimized. Second, each class has a narrower range than a heterogeneous class would have. Teacher A can give special attention to the top 10 without worrying about "losing" the bottom 20 who are not in the class; Teacher C can concentrate on the bottom 10 without fear of holding up the top 20. Third, each class has academic peer leaders able to stimulate one another and their lower-achieving classmates. In Teacher

C's class, the top group is the third 10, students who probably have been playing second fiddle to those in the top 20. Finally, no teacher has to teach a clear-cut "low group" of leaderless and alienated students.

This method provides one way to develop a mix of students at different achievement levels in each room without forcing each teacher to prepare instruction for the full range of student learning needs. Even so, two important points should be considered.

1. The groups overlap, but they are still different. Class A is still the highest group and Class C the lowest. Although Class C has many capable students, in the minds of the teachers (and the students or parents) it may become the "difficult" group to teach. It is important that Class C not become a typical "low group."
2. If the primary motivation for grouping is to avoid working with large numbers of low achievers, this plan probably will not work. If teachers do not think that low-ability students can learn and are unwilling to engage in remedial activities with these students, no grouping pattern will be successful.

The Controversy Continues

Consensus is growing around the ideas that tracking should be minimized, should be delayed as long as possible, and when used, should be confined to grouping by curriculum rather than by ability or achievement. Controversy continues, however. Some reformers favor restructuring schools so as to eliminate tracking entirely and have begun to identify strategies for changing the culture of schools in ways that would make this possible (Oakes & Lipton, 1992; Wheelock, 1992). Other reformers have concentrated on methods of delaying the inception of tracking and modifying the forms that it takes (Braddock & McPartland, 1990). Suggestions include postponing tracking by deferring it as late in the grade span as possible; limiting it to basic academic subjects where differences in skills are clear detriments to whole-class instruction; using multiple placement criteria rather than a single test score to determine the track placement; experimenting with ideas such as offering students incentives for taking challenging courses; minimizing separate offerings for gifted and special needs students; rotating teachers among track levels; and encouraging students to move up to higher tracks and providing them with extra help if they need it.

Opposition to tracking is not unanimous, however. Proponents of tracking claim that many of the arguments against it are based more on ideology and theoretical commitments than on empirical findings demonstrating negative effects on students. In addition, advocates of acceleration programs and special courses for gifted students claim that the existing literature supports this particular form of tracking and that additional support would be forthcoming if a broader range of outcome criteria was used to judge its effectiveness (Allan, 1991). Opponents of tracking respond that the seeming advantages to tracking suggested by certain studies result from the enriched curriculum enjoyed by high-track students rather than from the homogeneity of their classes. They argue for an enriched curriculum for all students and maintain that there are no advantages but many disadvantages to grouping students homogeneously.

WITHIN-CLASS ABILITY GROUPING

Whether or not their schools employ tracking systems, teachers can arrange to instruct their students in homogeneous small groups rather than as whole classes. This system is used routinely for beginning reading instruction (Cazden, 1985; Hiebert, 1983) and often for elementary mathematics instruction as well (Hallinan & Sorensen, 1983).

Ability grouping within classes offers certain advantages over ability grouping between classes. First, only one teacher is involved, so that there is no need for cooperative planning and scheduling by teams of teachers. Within-class ability grouping is also more flexible in that it is easier for the teacher to vary the number and size of groups and to move students from one group to another. Whenever the teacher is instructing a small group, however, provisions must be made to keep the rest of the students profitably occupied. Consequently, instructional planning and classroom management are considerably more complicated than they are when the teacher uses whole-class methods. The result is that the potential advantages that within-class ability grouping offers to students (the opportunity to receive intensive small-group instruction in content and skills that are closely matched to current achievement) are offset by certain disadvantages (reduction in time taught directly by the teacher, increase in time spent in independent seatwork).

Even in districts that assign students with comparable achievement profiles to classrooms, some teachers regroup the students again to further reduce variations in achievement levels, at least in certain subjects. Mason and Good (1993) tested the effects of two models of active teaching on the mathematics learning of over 1700 fourth-, fifth-, and sixth-grade students drawn from 81 classrooms in a district that assigned students to classes on the basis of achievement (i.e., used regrouping in mathematics). Both models attempted to deal with student diversity by reducing the range of achievement levels that a teacher would deal with at a given time. One approach was a *structural approach* in which students' diversity was reduced before instruction. Students in these classrooms were divided into two groups on the basis of their previous year's performance, and teachers taught mathematics to these two groups separately. The second approach, the *situational approach*, involved changing student groups *after* instruction. That is, the teacher initially taught the class as a whole and then provided ad hoc instruction (review, enrichment, etc.) to a subset of students as needed. The situational approach is more consistent with the view that students' abilities are varied and that even within a subject, student learning may be more insightful in some topics than in others.

Mason and Good found that the situational model proved to be more effective than the structural model. In the situational model, teachers taught the whole class first and placed more emphasis on development (trying to explore and "connect" mathematical ideas) and on assessing student understanding (encouraging students to explain their thinking) than did teachers in the structural model. Importantly, the whole-class teachers also found more time to individualize instruction, in part because they spent less time on management issues associated with managing two groups.

More research is needed to consider the range of diversity that a teacher can handle at a given time; however, the situational model would appear to be a more adaptive model in many contexts. Thus, within-class ability grouping may be needed only when student populations are very diverse. This view is consistent with Kulik and Kulik's (1989) review reporting trivial-to-small positive effects of within-class grouping on student achievement.

Remarkably, in view of the near-universal use of reading groups, there are no clear research data comparing small-group versus whole-class instruction in beginning reading. However, within-class ability grouping for beginning reading is often criticized on logical grounds. First, ability grouping tends to exaggerate preexisting differences in achievement by accelerating the progress of students in the top groups but slowing the progress of students in the bottom groups (Rowan & Miracle, 1983; Weinstein, 1976). This effect is especially pronounced when the groups are notably different from one another and the teacher treats them very differently. Second, high groups seem to benefit not only from faster pacing but from better instruction from the teacher (Cazden, 1985; Hiebert, 1983), a more desirable work orientation, and greater attention to the lesson (Eder & Felmlee, 1984). Third, group membership tends to remain highly stable once groups are formed, so group assignments affect peer contact and friendship patterns in addition to achievement, more so as time goes on (Hallinan & Sorensen, 1985). In classrooms where race is correlated with achievement, ability grouping results in de facto resegregation of students, even though race as such may not be taken into account in making group assignments (Haller, 1985). Finally, ability grouping can result in the labeling effects, "low-group psychology" effects, and related undesirable expectation effects that we reviewed in Chapter 3.

Rist (1970) provided gripping examples of many of these potential problems with within-class ability grouping in a study of a class of students followed from kindergarten through second grade. Rist noted that after just a few days in the class, the kindergarten teacher began to call consistently on the same students to lead the class to the lavatory, to be in charge of the equipment, to take attendance, and so on. On the eighth day, the teacher made permanent seating arrangements.

At Table 1, located closest to her own desk, she placed the children who were generally the most verbal, who approached her without apprehension, who were free of body odor, and who came from relatively higher socioeconomic backgrounds. Interviews with the teacher suggested that these groupings were based on her expectations for students' success or failure. She spontaneously verbalized low expectations for the performance of children at Tables 2 and 3. Yet, these children, who were shy and had trouble communicating with her, were placed farthest from her, adding another barrier to overcoming these problems.

Rist followed 18 of these 30 children when they were assigned to the same first-grade classroom and noted that all of those who had been placed at Table 1 in kindergarten were placed at Table A (the highest group) in first grade. No student who had been placed at Table 2 or 3 in kindergarten was placed at Table A. Those who had been at Table 2 or 3 in kindergarten were placed at Table B, with the exception of one student placed at Table C. Most of the students at Table C were repeating the first grade.

Data from the second grade revealed the same pattern. There, the teacher termed the best group the Tigers, called the middle group the Cardinals, and unbelievably, labeled the low group the Clowns. No student who had not been at Table A in the first grade moved up to the Tigers. Students from Tables B and C formed the Cardinals, and students repeating second grade from the previous year were the Clowns. Rist saw the slow learners as locked into a self-defeating system at this point. No matter how well a child in the low group read, he or she was destined to remain in the low group. Other studies suggest the same conclusion: *Rigid* ability grouping does more harm than good, especially to low-group students (Eder, 1981).

Although Rist (1970) described an extreme case, enough problems with within-class ability grouping have been reported to cause educators to begin to question this practice and seek alternatives to it, even educators concerned with beginning reading instruction, where such grouping has been standard practice. The report *Becoming a Nation of Readers* (Anderson et al., 1985), for example, calls for reduced emphasis on oral reading in small homogeneous groups and suggests that teachers experiment with alternatives as settings for reading practice. Some programs have accomplished this through whole-class instruction followed by silent reading and comprehension assignments. As students work on their assignments, the teacher circulates to listen to individuals read orally. Other programs assign students to work in pairs, alternately taking the reader and the listener role.

It is too early to say whether such alternatives will prove more effective than teaching reading to homogeneous small groups. It is clear, however, that within-class ability grouping can have a great range of effects on students, depending on the decisions made when forming these groups and the nature of the instruction provided to the groups. We have several suggestions for those considering within-class ability grouping.

First, the number and composition of the groups should depend on the variation in achievement and instructional needs among students in the class. In other words, if you believe that within-class grouping is necessary to achieve homogeneity among students assigned to the same group, then make sure that such homogeneity is achieved—don't just arbitrarily divide the class into three equal-sized groups.

Second, grouping should lead to more effective meeting of instructional needs, not merely to differentiated pacing through the curriculum. Teaching will still have to be individualized within groups, and students who continue to have trouble will need additional instruction. This may mean simply repeating the material, but often it means reteaching a concept in a different way with new examples. Students who did not learn something the first time are unlikely to learn it the second time unless the teacher presents it in a new or more thorough way.

Third, group assignments should be flexible. Assignments should be reviewed regularly with an eye toward disbanding groups that have outlived their usefulness and forming new groups to respond to current needs.

Fourth, group scheduling and instructional practices should also be flexible. When there are good instructional reasons for it, a particular group might best meet for 40 minutes on one day and 20 minutes the next day, but this will not happen if the teacher rigidly adheres to a schedule calling for each group to meet daily for 30 minutes. Also, there is no need for the teacher to continue to work with the entire group throughout the time allotted. One way to meet the needs of individuals within the group is to release students who have mastered the day's objectives and let them get started on seatwork assignments while keeping the remaining students for more concentrated and individualized instruction.

Fifth, because of the potential dangers of labeling effects and because grouping affects peer contacts, teachers should limit the degree to which group membership determines students' other school experiences. Members of the same reading group should not be seated together or otherwise dealt with as a group outside of reading instruction, and if ability grouping is used for mathematics or other subjects, group assignments should be based on achievement in these subjects rather than in reading.

Finally, groups should be organized and taught in ways that provide low achievers with the extra instruction they need. For example, teachers can assign more students to high groups and fewer students to low groups, thus arranging for more intensive instruction of low achievers within the group setting (Dreeben, 1984). Or, teachers can spend more of their time providing direct instruction and supervision to low groups while high groups spend more time working cooperatively or independently (Anderson & Pigford, 1988).

Planned Heterogeneous Grouping

Small groups do not have to be formed based on student ability, especially if the object is merely to reduce the number of students to be taught together at one time and not necessarily to homogenize the group. For example, beginning reading instruction may be best conducted in small groups when it involves slow-paced oral reading, so even in classrooms composed of students of similar ability, teachers may want to use small groups for oral reading practice. If so, teachers do not necessarily have to group students by ability. Often, in fact, it may make more sense to group students randomly or on the basis of managerial considerations (e.g., separating students who tend to become disruptive when assigned to the same group).

Under some circumstances, you may want group assignments to achieve some kind of planned heterogeneity. For example, in activities designed to promote social awareness and acceptance, you might want to make sure that each group includes both genders and members of whatever racial or ethnic groups are represented in the class. We will consider such grouping in more detail in discussing cooperative group activities.

COOPERATIVE LEARNING

The traditional approach to schooling calls for whole-class lessons followed by independent seatwork. Cooperative learning approaches replace independent seatwork with small groups of students (typically four to six students) who work together on practice or application exercises. Thus, under cooperative learning arrangements students receive information and feedback from peers in addition to the teacher and the curriculum materials. Cooperative learning methods differ according to the task structures and incentive structures that are in effect (Slavin, 1983, 1990a & b).

Small-group learning has become popular because of its potential for engaging students in meaningful learning with authentic tasks in a social setting. Educators are increasingly calling for environments that allow students to construct knowledge actively (Chapter 10 provides details of this perspective), and, under appropriate conditions, small-group methods can support such social construction of knowledge (i.e., students learning from and with one another). However, small-group instruction varies widely in terms of tasks, group composition, and goals. Small groups can be used for drill, practice, learning facts and concepts, discussion, and problem solving. Even when the purpose of small-group instruction is inquiry or problem solving, those results are not automatic (Blumenfeld, 1992). Educators have much to learn about how to design small-group instruction in order to stimulate comprehension and higher-order thinking.

In the rest of this chapter we explore the possible uses and misuses of small groups. We want readers to consider both the potential payoff and inherent problems associated with small-group instruction. As we shall see, much more is known about the effects of small-group instruction than about how or why such effects occur, and more is known about its effects on skill and fact acquisition than about its effects on problem solving and conceptual understanding.

Task Structure

The term *task structure* refers to the nature of the task (its goal, the kinds of responses it requires, etc.) and the working conditions that accompany it. Task structures may be individual, cooperative, or competitive. *Individual task structures* require students to work on the task alone (except for help from the teacher if necessary). Traditional independent seatwork employs an individual task structure. *Cooperative task structures* require students to work cooperatively in order to meet task requirements. Assignments that call for students to assist one another in learning or to work together to produce a group product involve cooperative task structures. Finally, *competitive task structures*, such as contests, debates, and various competitive games, require students to compete (either as individuals or as teams) in order to fulfill task requirements.

Within groups, members may cooperate in working toward either group or individual goals. When pursuing *group goals*, the members work together to produce a single product that results from the pooled resources and shared labor of the group. For example, the group might paint a mural, assemble a collage, or

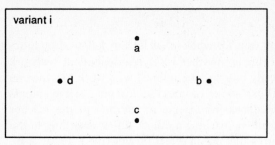

Figure 7.1 Children working individually on individual tasks for individual products.

Figure 7.2 Children working individually on identical tasks for individual products.

prepare a skit or report to be presented to the rest of the class. When working cooperatively to reach *individual goals,* group members assist one another by discussing how to respond to questions or assignments, checking work, or providing feedback or tutorial assistance. Cooperative work toward individual goals occurs when individual students are responsible for turning in assignments but are allowed to consult with one another as they work on those assignments.

Cooperative task structures also differ according to whether or not there is task specialization. When there is no task specialization, each member works on the same task. *Task specialization* is in effect when the larger task to be accomplished is divided into several subtasks on which different group members work. In preparing a report on a foreign country, for example, task specialization would be operative if one group member was assigned to do the introduction, another to cover geography and climate, another to cover natural resources and the economy, and so on.

Bennett and Dunne (1992) note that various organizational strategies facilitate different forms of work in small groups. Figures 7.1 through 7.5 illustrate five organizational models that vary in expectations for social and collaborative behavior. Variant i (Figure 7.1) illustrates four students (*) sitting together as a group but working on their own individual tasks (a, b, c, d) to achieve individual outcomes. This model might be used in a mathematics class where students work at different levels.

The second variant (see Figure 7.2) involves students (*) working on the same task (a) but to produce individual outcomes (e.g., each student writes his or her own story). Little academic discussion may occur in such settings because neither the setting nor the task encourages cooperative behavior. Indeed, given the socialization they have experienced, many students would interpret help from peers in variant ii as acceptable for procedural matters (clarifying the task, seeing if an expression is clear) but as cheating for exchanges about content (giving other students ideas to incorporate into their stories).

The third variant (in Figure 7.3) also involves students working individually on identical tasks to create individual products. Within this model, the teacher is encouraging cooperation—making clear that it is acceptable for students not only to talk but to contribute directly through sharing ideas, understandings, and so on.

Figure 7.3 Children working individually on "jig-saw" elements for a ioint outcome.

Figure 7.4 Children working jointly on one task for a joint outcome (or discussion).

Here, the task itself does not demand cooperation, but the teacher encourages it through directions to the students. From our perspective, variant iii would be a good place for students to begin to experience cooperative learning if they have not done so previously. This would allow students to break down the normative expectation that one cannot share ideas or give help in a classroom and it would help them to learn how to listen and interact constructively with peers.

Variant iv (in Figure 7.3) requires cooperation as part of the task structure itself. Here the task is divided so that each member must complete an activity if the group task is to be performed successfully. Both cooperation and individual accountability are built into the task structure in ways that encourage each student to do his or her share.

The fifth variant (Figure 7.4) is adapted from Johnson and Johnson (1975). In this model, students work together on one task to achieve a joint outcome. Collab-

Group evaluation	Always	Sometimes	Never
1 We checked to make sure everyone understood what we did	....	....	....
2 We answered any questions that were asked	....	....	....
3 We gave explanations wherever we could	....	....	....
4 We asked specific questions about what we didn't understand	....	....	....
5 Anyone who had difficulty got extra practice and help	....	....	....
6 We paraphrased what others said to be sure we understood	....	....	....

Group signatures

X .... X ....

X .... X ....

Figure 7.5 Evaluation of group processes.

orative exchange is built into the task because the group must jointly plan its approach and coordinate activities. Individual accountability, however, is low, because it is difficult to assess what each student has contributed during the problem-solving exchange. Teachers can supplement their knowledge of individual performance through follow-up activities, such as asking students to explain how their group arrived at the solution, but variant v is much more complex than variants iii and iv and individual accountability is more difficult to achieve.

Incentive Structure

Besides differing in task structure, group activities differ in incentive structure. *Incentive structure* (also called *reward structure* or *goal structure*) refers to methods used for motivating students to perform the task. These include the nature of incentives themselves (grades, concrete rewards, symbolic rewards) as well as rules specifying what must be done to earn rewards and how they will be delivered. Like task structures, incentive structures can be individual, cooperative, or competitive. Under *individual incentive structures*, any particular student's performance has no consequences for other students' chances of earning available rewards. That is, individuals are rewarded (or not) depending on whether they meet specified performance criteria, regardless of how the rest of the class performs. Under *cooperative incentive structures*, individuals' chances of earning rewards depend not only on their own efforts but on those of other members of their group. Thus, instead of or in addition to rewarding students as individuals, the teacher rewards groups of students according to the performance that results from their combined efforts. Finally, under *competitive incentive structures*, groups or individuals must compete for whatever rewards are available. The winners get the most desirable rewards, and the losers get less desirable rewards or no rewards at all. Classes in which grades are assigned according to preset curves explicitly involve competitive incentive structures, and any classes in which grades are assigned at least partly on the basis of comparative performance implicitly involve competitive incentive structures.

Cooperative and competitive incentive structures can also be differentiated according to whether they involve group or individual rewards. *Group rewards* are distributed equally to all members of the group. These may involve a single reward to be shared by the group (such as a prize or a treat) or assigning the same reward to each group member (if the group's product receives a grade of A, each group member receives a grade of A, regardless of that member's contribution to the group product). *Individual rewards* are assigned differentially to individual students depending on effort or performance. For example, students may be encouraged to cooperate with peers in discussing assignments and preparing for a test but be required to take the test individually and be graded according to their own performance.

Task and incentive structures are independent; cooperative task structure does not necessarily imply a cooperative incentive structure, and so on. In fact, any incentive structure could be imposed on any task structure, although some such arrangements would be highly artificial and unusual. For example, a teacher could require students to work on assignments alone (e.g., to use an individual task structure) but impose a competitive reward structure by dividing students into teams that never work together but are rewarded partly on the basis of how well team members do as a group on unit tests. Table 7.1 shows the combinations of task and reward structures that are typically used.

Well-Known Cooperative Learning Programs

We describe some of the best-known and widely researched cooperative learning programs here. For additional information about these programs and other cooperative learning programs, see Bohlmeyer and Burke (1987), *Educational Leadership* (1989–1990), Sharan et al. (1984), Slavin (1983, 1990a & b), or Slavin et al. (1985).

Learning Together

The Learning Together model of cooperative learning was developed by David and Roger Johnson (Johnson & Johnson, 1975; Johnson et al., 1984). Early versions called for students to work together in four- or five-member heterogeneous groups on assignment sheets. The major interest was in getting students who differed in achievement, gender, race, or ethnicity working together. The groups handed in a single sheet and were praised as a group for working well together and for their performance on the task.

Experimentation with this approach revealed that some variations worked better than others, and eventually the Johnsons identified four elements that should

Table 7.1　POSSIBLE COMBINATIONS OF TASK AND REWARD STRUCTURES
(all combinations are possible, but some are more typically used than others)

| | Incentive Structures | | | | |
| | I. Individual* | II. Cooperative† | | III. Competitive‡ | |
Task structures		A. Individual rewards	B. Group reward	A. Individual rewards	B. Group reward
I. *Individual.* Each student works alone.	Typical	Possible	Possible	Typical	Possible
II. *Cooperative.* Students work together or help one another.					
A. *Group goals.* Individuals cooperate to create a group product.					
1. *Undifferentiated roles.* Each student has the same task.	Possible	Possible	Typical	Possible	Typical
2. *Differentiated roles.* Different students perform different tasks.	Possible	Possible	Typical	Possible	Typical
B. *Individual goals.* Individuals help one another to fulfill their respective individual responsibilities.					
1. *Undifferentiated roles.* Each student has the same task.	Typical	Typical	Possible	Typical	Possible
2. *Differentiated roles.* Different students perform different tasks.	Typical	Typical	Possible	Typical	Possible
III. *Competitive.* The task requires students to compete.					
A. *Individual competition.*	Typical	Typical	Possible	Typical	Possible
B. *Team competition.*	Possible	Possible	Typical	Possible	Typical

*Reward depends strictly on one's own performance.

†Reward depends, at least in part, on group performance.

‡Reward depends, at least in part, on the outcome of a competition.

be included in any cooperative learning activity (Johnson & Johnson, 1985b; Johnson et al., 1984).

1. *Positive interdependence.* Students should recognize that they are interdependent with other members of their group in achieving a successful group product. Positive interdependence can be structured through mutual goals (goal interdependence); division of labor (task interdependence); dividing materials, resources, or information among group members (resource interdependence); assigning students unique roles (role interdependence); or giving group rewards (reward interdependence).

2. *Face-to-face interaction among students.* Tasks that call for significant interaction among group members are preferred over tasks that can be accomplished by having group members work on their own.
3. *Individual accountability.* Mechanisms are needed to ensure that each group member has clear objectives for which he or she will be held accountable and receives any needed assessment, feedback, or instructional assistance.
4. *Instructing students in appropriate interpersonal and small-group skills.* Students cannot merely be placed together and told to cooperate. They need instruction in skills such as asking and answering questions, ensuring that everyone participates actively and is treated with respect, and assigning tasks and organizing cooperative efforts (see Johnson & Johnson, 1982).

Group Investigation

Shlomo Sharan and his colleagues (Sharan & Sharan, 1976; Sharan et al., 1984) developed what they call Group Investigation models in Israel. Group Investigation students form their own two- to six-member groups to work together using cooperative inquiry, group discussion, and cooperative planning and projects. Each group chooses a subtopic from a unit studied by the whole class, breaks this subtopic into individual tasks, and carries out the activities necessary to prepare a group report. Eventually, the group makes a presentation or display to communicate its findings to the class and is evaluated based on the quality of this report.

Jigsaw

The Jigsaw approach (Aronson et al., 1978) ensures active individual participation and group cooperation by arranging tasks so that each group member possesses unique information and has a special role to play. The group product cannot be completed unless each member does his or her part, just as a jigsaw puzzle cannot be completed unless each piece is included. For example, information needed to compose a biography might be broken into early life, first accomplishments, major setbacks, later life, and world events occurring during the person's lifetime. One member of each group would be given the relevant information and assigned responsibility for one of the five sections of the biography, and other group members would be assigned to other sections. Members of different groups who were working on the same section would meet together in "expert groups" to discuss their sections. Then they would return to their regular groups and take turns teaching their groupmates about their sections. Since the only way that students can learn about sections other than their own is to listen carefully to their groupmates, they are motivated to support and show interest in one another's work. The students then prepare biographies or take quizzes on the material individually.

Several cooperative learning methods have been developed by Robert Slavin and others at Johns Hopkins University. Collectively, these methods are known as *Student Team Learning*. We will discuss four variations.

Teams-Games-Tournament (TGT)

The Teams-Games-Tournament approach (DeVries & Slavin, 1978; DeVries et al., 1980) calls for students to work together in four- to five-member heterogeneously grouped teams to help one another master content and prepare for competitions against other teams. After the teacher presents the material to be learned, team members work together, studying from worksheets. Typically they discuss the material, tutor one another, and quiz one another to assess mastery. Cooperative practice in this form continues throughout the week in preparation for tournaments held on Fridays.

For the tournaments, students are assigned to three-person tables composed of students from different teams who are similar in achievement. The three students compete at academic games covering the content taught that week and practiced during team meetings. Most of these games are simply numbered questions on a handout. A student picks a number card and attempts to answer the question corresponding to that number. Students can earn points by responding to questions correctly or by successfully challenging and correcting the answers of the other two students at the table. These points are later summed to determine each team's score, and the teacher prepares a newsletter that recognizes successful teams and unusually high scores attained by individuals. The newsletter may also contain cumulative team scores if tournaments last longer than a week. Prior to the next tournament, the teacher may reassign certain students to different tournament tables in order to keep the competition as even as possible at each table. This ensures that even though the teams are heterogeneous in composition and team membership remains the same, all students begin each tournament with an equal chance to earn points for their teams because they are competing against peers whose achievement is similar to theirs. This incentive structure motivates students not only to master the material on their own but also to help their teammates master the material.

Student Teams-Achievement Divisions (STAD)

Student Teams-Achievement Divisions is a simplification of TGT (Slavin, 1986). It follows the same heterogeneous grouping and cooperative learning procedures as TGT but replaces the games and tournaments with a quiz. Quiz scores are translated into team competition points based on how much students have improved their performance over past averages.

Both TGT and STAD combine cooperative learning task structures with team competition and group rewards for cumulative individual performance. However, STAD depersonalizes the competition. Rather than compete face-to-face against classmates at tournament tables, students in STAD classrooms try to do their best on quizzes they take individually. Over time, Slavin and his colleagues have emphasized STAD more and TGT less, because STAD is simpler to implement and reduces the salience of competition.

Jigsaw II

Jigsaw II is an adaptation of the original Jigsaw (Slavin, 1980b). In the new version, the teacher does not need to provide each student with unique materials. Instead, all students begin by reading a common narrative and then each group member is given a separate topic on which to become an expert. Next, as in the original Jigsaw, students who have the same topic assignments meet in expert groups to discuss topics and then return to their teams to teach what they have learned to their teammates. Then the students take the quiz and their individual scores are summed to compute team scores, and team accomplishments are recognized through a class newsletter.

Team-Assisted Individualization (TAI)

Team-assisted individualization (TAI) is an adaptation of individualized mathematics instruction that introduces cooperative learning methods and team competition with group reward, as in STAD (Slavin, 1985). TAI combines direct instruction (to small, homogeneously formed groups) by the teacher, follow-up practice using programmed curriculum materials, and a student-team learning approach to seatwork management (see Slavin, 1985 for details).

Controlled Conflict and Controversy in Small Groups

David and Roger Johnson and their colleagues developed an interesting variation on small-group cooperative learning methods in which controlled conflict or controversy is introduced into the group. We refer here to intellectual controversy involving conflict of opinion about academic issues, not physical aggression or other forms of personal conflict. In a review of these issues, Johnson and Johnson (1979) found that constructively managed controversy in the classroom promotes a healthy uncertainty about the correctness of one's views, curiosity for more information, and better achievement. Studies conducted since then have supported this interpretation.

Smith, Johnson, and Johnson (1981) studied the learning of sixth graders about controversial issues such as whether or not strip mining should be allowed. Students were presented with material offering pro and con views on the issues and directed to study the material either individually or in small groups. Controversy groups were subdivided to represent the two sides and encouraged to debate the issues, but concurrence-seeking groups were directed to study the material together and avoid arguing. The results indicated that the controversy group condition promoted higher achievement, more accurate understanding of both positions on each issue, interest in getting more information, and better attitudes toward classmates and the value of constructive controversy. Similarly positive results have been obtained in two subsequent studies (Johnson & Johnson, 1985a; Johnson, Brooker, Stutzman, Hultman, & Johnson, 1985). Teachers whose subjects lend themselves to controversy and debate (policy issues in social studies and science classes; interpretation issues in humanities and literature courses) should consider including controversy groups among their instructional activities. (For more information about how to deal with conflict constructively see Johnson and Johnson, 1992; Schmuck and Schmuck, 1988).

As we have seen, there is no single universal approach to cooperative learning, and the number of approaches continues to grow (Davidson & Worsham, 1992). Other approaches that may merit attention include Cohen's (1986) complex instruction approach, Kagan's (1990) structural approach, and the collaborative approach (Brubacher, Payne, & Rikett, 1990).

RESEARCH ON COOPERATIVE LEARNING METHODS

There has been a great deal of research on cooperative learning methods, and several summaries are available (Johnson, Johnson & Maruyama, 1983; Sharan, 1980; Slavin, 1980a, 1983, 1990a & b). The results are generally positive, although some studies are misleading because they begged the questions they were supposed to be studying by using learning tasks that are accomplished more effectively by groups than by individuals, or by allowing groups to work together on tests and then assigning a group's test score to each group member (many of whom would not have scored so highly if they had been required to take the test on their own). Even with such studies eliminated, however, the research indicates that cooperative learning methods are feasible in many classroom situations and that they are likely to have positive effects both on achievement and on other outcome variables.

Cooperative Versus Traditional Methods

The effects on *achievement* are positive, although they appear to be related to the use of specific group rewards based on members' individual performance rather than to the cooperative task structures used (Slavin, 1983). That is, the student team learning methods that include team rewards (TGT, STAD, Jigsaw II, TAI) tend to have consistently positive effects on student achievement, whereas the more purely cooperative methods (Learning Together, Group Investigation, and the original Jigsaw) are less likely to produce a significant achievement advantage over traditional techniques (Lew, Mesch, Johnson, & Johnson, 1986; Moskowitz, Malvin, Shaeffer, & Schaps, 1985; Okebukola, 1985; Slavin, 1983).

Also, methods ensuring the accountability of individual group members to their groupmates produce higher achievement than methods in which it is possible for one or two students to do the work while others take more passive roles. The most effective methods combine group goals with individual accountability (Slavin, 1988).

The findings on task specialization are mixed, probably because its appropriateness varies with subject matter and the instructional objectives pursued. Task specialization seems most useful in social studies and with assignments emphasizing higher-level cognitive skills (Graybeal & Stodolsky, 1985). It is difficult to use task specialization for mathematics or other linearly sequenced curricula.

There is no evidence that group competition offers advantages over other cooperative learning methods so long as arrangements are made to provide group rewards based on the cumulative performance of individual group members. Besides direct group competitions as in TGT and STAD, good results have been obtained by giving teams certificates for meeting preset standards independently of the performance of other teams and by using task specialization to motivate students to encourage their groupmates. Thus, although the effects of cooperative learning on achievement appear to be primarily motivational, the key is not motivation to win competitions against other teams but motivation to assist one's teammates to meet their individual goals and thus ensure that the team will do well.

Effects on outcomes other than achievement are even more impressive. Cooperative learning arrangements promote friendships and prosocial interaction among students who differ in achievement, sex, race, or ethnicity, and they promote the acceptance of mainstreamed handicapped students by their nonhandicapped classmates. Cooperative methods also frequently have positive effects, and rarely have negative effects, on affective outcomes such as self-esteem, academic self-confidence, liking for the class, liking and feeling liked by classmates, and various measures of empathy and social cooperation.

Group Composition and Processes

In addition to the research just summarized comparing cooperative with traditional learning methods, there have been studies of the effects on students' achievement of group composition and the nature of students' interaction during group meetings (Bennett & Cass, 1988; Peterson et al., 1984; Swing & Peterson, 1982; Webb, 1982, 1989; Webb & Cullian, 1983). These studies typically involved groups of four students whose interactions were tape-recorded for later analysis. Three main conclusions have emerged from this research.

First, whether students master the content to be learned depends not only on their entry-level achievement but on their experiences in the group. Giving explanations to other group members is positively correlated with achievement, even when entry-level ability is controlled. This confirms the findings from peer-tutoring studies and other research indicating that explaining material to others is an effective learning experience for the explainer as well as the person receiving the explanation. Receiving explanations usually also correlates positively with later achievement scores, indicating that students who know what to ask about and succeed in getting their questions answered are likely to master the material. In contrast, negative correlations with achievement have been noted for asking questions without getting a response or receiving only a direct answer to a question without an explanation of how to arrive at the answer.

A second, related finding is that quality of interaction in small groups can be enhanced through training. Compared with those in untrained control groups, students given training in how to interact during small-group activities have been shown to spend more time on-task (asking questions, giving feedback, checking answers) and to go beyond just giving answers by giving more detailed explanations designed to make sure that the listener understands the concept or process.

A third finding is that certain combinations of students seem to work better with one another than other combinations do. In mixed groups containing one high achiever, two average achievers, and one low achiever, most of the interaction involved tutoring of the low achiever by the high achiever, with the average achievers remaining relatively passive. Thus, heterogeneous small groups seemed to be relatively less effective with average achievers, at least when the students had not been trained in how to interact during small-group activities.

Homogeneous groupings produced mixed results. Groups of average students worked well together, helping one another and interacting actively. However, groups in which the students either were all high achievers or all low achievers did not work well together or interact much about the academic content. Members of homogeneous high-achieving groups apparently assumed that no one needed help, and members of homogeneous low-achieving groups often became frustrated because they were unable to explain material effectively to one another.

Bennett and Cass (1988) conducted a study in Britain to explore the effects of three types of groups on student performance. Groups studied included ability groups (high, average, low); mixed ability groups containing a high, an average, and a low student; and mixed groups that contained only high and low achievers. Two comparisons were built in. One group was composed of two high students and one low student (2HL), and the other included two low students and one high student (2LH).

The researchers found the 2LH performed much better than 2HL groups. When the low-achieving student worked with two high achievers, the low student was ignored or chose to withdraw from active participation. Lack of involvement led the low student to misunderstand the basis on which decisions were made and lowered performance. High achievers performed well in all group settings. These students provided more suggestions, had more suggestions accepted by group members, and provided both more explanations and more appropriate explanations. Thus, within the context of this study, high-achieving students' performance was not affected by working with low achievers.

LIMITATIONS OF FINDINGS ON SMALL-GROUP LEARNING

Although research illustrates that students can learn cooperatively under certain conditions, many issues about small-group instruction have not been resolved. Davidson (1985) notes that achievement comparisons have been made in reference to computational skills, simple concepts, and simple application problems. Thus, a relatively narrow range of dependent measures has been explored. Davidson argues that more information is needed about how higher-order skills are influenced by small-group mathematics learning, especially since educators increasingly advocate that instruction emphasize understanding rather than the learning of isolated skills.

Cooperative learning research has also been questioned on theoretical grounds. For example, many educators question the value of competition if cooperative learning is the goal. Research by Stipek (1986) and others who have explored intrinsic motivation concepts shows that teachers need to pay careful attention to what happens to students when cooperative behavior is maintained by the use of external incentives over an extended period.

Pepitone (1985) contends that the concept of group goals has largely been neglected in cooperative learning research, although distinctions between task goals and group goals have long been made. Some theorists contend that if a group is to work cooperatively, it must work on goals that are important to group members, not just on assigned work.

Yet another weakness of the research base on cooperative learning is that few observational data describe how students interact in groups and how achievement and affective gains actually occur. This deficiency is especially important for teachers and researchers who are interested in student development and not simply outcomes on an achievement test. Theorists such as Noddings (1989) would be interested in a broad range of outcomes (meaningful learning of subject matter, learning prosocial skills, developing alternative approaches to problem solving, exploring conjecturing, and growing in social intelligence).

Researchers have been encouraging more study of group processes in order to determine whether or not some of the putative goals of small-group instruction are being obtained (Bossert, 1988–1989; Good & Biddle, 1988; Good, Mulryan, & McCaslin, 1992). Bossert noted that researchers have often failed to verify whether students have even engaged in cooperative interactions, and that when they have observed instructional processes, their results have not always supported theories of cooperative learning.

As a case in point, Mulryan (1989) studied students' behavior during whole-class and small-group mathematics instruction. She found that students manifested more attending behavior in the cooperative mathematics small-group context than the whole-class context. However, not all students benefited in the same way from increased involvement during small-group work. High achievers exhibited significantly more quality attending behavior in cooperative small groups than did low achievers. Further, high achievers spent 5 percent of their time in cooperative small groups in off-task behavior, whereas low achievers were off-task 13 percent of the time.

Students did exchange information when working in small groups, but the frequency of question asking was relatively low. Low achievers asked more questions and high achievers did more information giving. Mulryan argued that the roles of helping that emerged in these small groups may not have been useful, especially when the same students played these roles consistently. Such circumstances create a "caste" system that discourages the active involvement of some students. During interviews some students indicated that they perceived low achievers as a burden to other members of cooperative groups.

Building on Good's (1981) passivity model, Mulryan identified six types of passive students: the discouraged student; the unrecognized student; the despondent student; the unmotivated student; the bored student; and the intellectual snob. The discouraged students were mainly low achievers who became passive because they perceived the group task as too difficult and thought it better to leave the work to peers who knew more content. The unrecognized students became passive because their initial efforts to participate were ignored or not recognized by other group members. Most unrecognized students were low achievers. Despondent students included both high and low achievers. They tended to be passive because they disliked or felt uncomfortable with one or more persons in their group. Some of their passivity appeared due to their perception of the cooperative learning task as unimportant or "only a game." Bored students also included both low and high achievers, although there were more high achievers than lows. They perceived the task as boring because it was too easy. Finally, intellectual snobs were passive in cooperative work because they thought their peers were less competent at math and they did not want to explain constantly to them.

Mulryan noted that some students were uninvolved in the official learning task but showed other active behaviors in their group. She identified social opportunists (students who wanted to talk with peers about social issues) and intentional loafers (students who allowed other students to do the work). Most social opportunists and intentional loafers were low achievers.

Other researchers have also observed problems of group interaction. King (1993) found that high-achieving students dominated group discussions and task initiation and generally played leadership roles. Even though low achievers were relatively passive during group work, they reported that they enjoyed working in small groups (especially the social aspects) and looked forward to more opportunities for group work.

As Good, McCaslin, and Reys (1992) have noted, students' affective reports of satisfaction on questionnaires or in interviews may mask important problems in group functioning. Thus, teachers who use small-group work as a method for engaging students in problem solving and higher-order thinking must be careful to monitor group processes in order to assess the quality of student interactions. Teachers need to develop strategies for monitoring group processes (occasionally tape-recording a group, sitting in on a group, etc.) in order to assess the quality of the discussions that take place.

POTENTIAL ADVANTAGES AND DISADVANTAGES OF COOPERATIVE GROUPS

Building on the research of Johnson and Johnson (1985a & b), Bossert (1988–1989) notes that four major explanations could account for the success of cooperative methods: (1) reasoning strategies—cooperative groups may stimulate more higher-order thinking; (2) constructive controversy—heterogeneous cooperative groups force the accommodation of the opinions of various members, and students must engage in problem solving and take another's perspective; (3) cognitive processing—cooperative methods increase opportunities for students to rehearse information orally and to integrate it; and (4) peer encouragement and involvement in learning. Positive interactions increase friendship, acceptance, and cognitive information processing.

There are at least eight additional reasons why cooperative groups may enhance students' achievement and social relations (Good, Mulryan, & McCaslin, 1992; McCaslin & Good, in press).

1. Subject-matter knowledge is increased. The knowledge of procedures and content that the group possesses is almost always greater than the knowledge of any individual student. Thus, with more knowledge, group problem-solving strategies can be more varied, fine-tuned, and powerful.

2. Students value shared academic work. It is likely that students will understand mathematics better in small groups because proportionately more group time is spent on conceptual understanding, in comparison to individual time, which tends to be spent on products. Thus, students may value shared academic work more because of the increased emphasis on understanding during small-group instruction.

3. Students can regulate their own resources. An individual's work pace can be more flexible in a group setting.

4. Students learn to manage others' resources. Students learn how to coordinate work with others, how to obtain information from peers, which peers to ask for what type of help, etc.

5. Students develop appropriate dispositions toward challenging work on shared tasks. Because academic work is done with others, challenging tasks are more malleable, approachable, or more do-able because of shared expertise.

6. School tasks are similar to those outside school. Tasks done in small work groups tend to be more like work done at home (and in many jobs), where everyone pitches in (or does his or her part) to get a job done.

7. Group members serve as models for one another. Students have the chance to learn important learning-to-learn skills from other students—for example, how to ask questions and how to self-regulate.

8. Students develop an expanded understanding of self and others. The opportunity to work with others helps students to identify and to appreciate individual differences in performance and motivation. Students learn that peers are not just "smart" or "dumb"; they develop a sense that everyone possesses both weaknesses and strengths. This awareness of variability in social and cognitive aptitude may allow students to be more creative, to view errors as acceptable, and to learn from failure.

Despite these ways in which small groups can provide useful learning experiences for students, problems that develop in some group situations may prevent or minimize constructive learning. Good, Mulryan, and McCaslin (1992) and McCaslin and Good (in press) identify several potential problems.

1. Students' misconceptions are reinforced. Students often have misconceptions about academic content and these may be reinforced during small-group interactions.

2. Students shift dependency from teacher to peers. The shift from whole-class to small-group instruction may be a superficial change (i.e., student as teacher) rather than an actual structural change (i.e., collaborative learning).

3. Students value the product more than the process. If group members focus too narrowly on the group product, speed may take precedence over

the problem-solving process, and groups may pay more attention to product rate than to the process of problem solution.

4. Students value group processes more than the academic product. In some classrooms, attention to group processes and "learning to learn with others" may take precedence over subject-matter learning so that much time is spent teaching students elaborate and potentially artificial procedures for dealing with controversy, and so forth.

5. Students receive differential attention and status. Some group situations may present little more than an opportunity for high-achieving students to perform for other students. In other groups, high achievers may feel excessive pressure to do the work for the group.

6. Some students believe they are not able to contribute. Some students will perceive themselves as having little to contribute to their peers during group learning. These students may become indebted to group members who consistently help them do most of the work.

7. Some students may learn that they do not need to contribute. Social comparison may exacerbate social loafing. Some students may consistently receive feedback suggesting that their skills are not valued as much as those of some of their peers. Both high- and low-ability students may recognize that their group makes progress whether or not they contribute actively. These students may learn to engage in social loafing—they do relatively little thinking or participating during group work either because they do not value the work or the group, or because they do not excel and, thus, are trying to protect their self-esteem.

8. Group accountability may mediate failure-avoiding and success-enhancing behavior. For example, students who have reputations as "know-it-alls" may withhold information so as not to enhance their (unwanted) reputations. Other students may withhold information in an attempt to be fair and to let other students contribute more. Such altruistic behavior may come at the expense of learning.

CONCLUSIONS FROM RESEARCH ON COOPERATIVE LEARNING

Cooperative learning methods have achieved impressive results. As Slavin (1983, p. 128) put it:

There are many important theoretical as well as practical issues yet to be resolved in research on cooperative learning. However, the research done up to the present has shown enough positive effects of cooperative learning, on a variety of outcomes, to force us to re-examine traditional instructional practices. We can no longer ignore the potential power of the peer group, perhaps the one remaining free resource for improving schools. We can no longer see the class as 30 or more individuals whose only instructionally useful interactions are with the teacher, where peer interactions are unstructured or off-task. On the other hand, at least for achievement, we now know that simply allowing students to work together is unlikely to capture the power of the peer group to motivate students to perform; structured methods with group rewards based on group members' demonstrated learning appear to be needed. For intergroup relations, acceptance of mainstreamed students, and general interaction among students, it is not yet clear whether structured groups and group rewards are absolutely necessary, but it is clear that these outcomes can be reliably produced at the same time as achievement and other outcomes are being improved for the entire class. This is a revolutionary development for attempts to improve intergroup and cross-handicap relationships, as programs designed only to improve relationships are seen as "frills" by many school districts, and are not supported if they take time away from instruction.

We share Slavin's enthusiasm and recommend cooperative learning methods to teachers, although with certain qualifications. First, it is important to view the cooperative learning approach not as a wholesale replacement of traditional whole-class instruction but as an adaptation of this approach in which active whole-class instruction by the teacher is retained but many follow-up practice and application activities are accomplished through small-group cooperation rather than through individual seatwork. Peers are not an acceptable substitute for active instruction by the teacher as the basic method for conveying content to students. Peers can deliver effective explanations about how to respond to specific questions or assignments, but they cannot be expected to have the subject matter and pedagogical knowledge needed to provide effective advance organization and structuring of content, systematic development of key concepts, or sophisticated remedial instruction. Nor can students be expected to tutor one another effectively on tasks that focus on higher-order objectives (Ross, 1988).

Second, cooperative learning approaches may be more feasible and valuable in certain classes than in others. So far, these methods have been used most frequently in (and most of the research supporting them comes from) classes in grades 4 through 9. They may be less relevant or more difficult to implement for teachers working with primary-grade students or upper secondary-school students. Also, methods that emphasize group rewards and individual accountability to other group members for one's own effort and performance (TGT, STAD, Jigsaw II, TAI) appear to be more appropriate for work in mathematics and other subjects that emphasize individual practice of sequenced skills. Methods that emphasize group discussion and investigation, structured controversy, differentiated roles and responsibilities, or cooperative development of a group product may be more appropriate for social studies and for assignments that focus on higher-level cognitive objectives (application, problem solving, analysis, synthesis, evaluation).

Third, it is not yet clear what the effects would be if cooperative learning methods were used in most courses year after year. Students who are social and those who receive considerable help from their peers would likely respond very positively, but other students might not. The latter include all students who enjoy working alone much of the time, as well as students who are academic leaders within teams and assume much of the responsibility for tutoring their teammates. Even students who enjoy learning cooperatively in moderation might tire of it if called upon to do so too often. Thus, there is probably some optimal level of use of cooperative learning methods, both within any course and across the school day or school year.

Fourth, although it may often be important to use methods that involve group rewards and individual accountability to the group for one's effort, we advise emphasizing cooperation but deemphasizing competition. Thus, STAD is preferable to TGT, for example. Competition is a form of extrinsic motivation that may distract students from basic learning goals unless it is handled carefully. Another problem is that competition creates losers as well as winners, and the bad feelings that result from losing competitions may undermine some of the potential contributions of small-group cooperative learning arrangements to improved personal and social outcomes (Ames & Felker, 1979).

Fifth, students need to be trained to work cooperatively, especially if they are not familiar with cooperative learning approaches. Some students may not know how to act in small-group situations or may even be hostile in responding to the contributions of their peers. Consequently, teachers may need to show students how to share, listen, integrate the ideas of others, and handle disagreements. In the early grades, most group assignments probably should be short, highly structured, enjoyable, and unlikely to produce conflict. Students can be moved gradually into longer and more demanding tasks as their skills develop. When structured effectively, cooperative small-group activities not only produce peer support and encouragement for learning but may result in the development of higher-quality strategies for understanding and responding to tasks than students develop when working alone (Johnson, Skon, & Johnson, 1980). In the process of discussing tasks and helping one another to learn, students discover a great deal about how to search efficiently and identify key information, recognize what is given and what is called for in a problem, and formulate problem-solving strategies that feature systematic hypothesis testing rather than random guessing and allow for checking of answers and identification of errors. This increases the likelihood that students will get the intended cognitive benefits, and not merely the right answers, from problem-solving exercises.

In discussing strategies for training students in group work skills, Bennett and Dunne (1992) suggest that cooperative skills need to be taught directly. Initially, if students have had limited experience in cooperative group work, they should receive a series of relatively simple tasks. This allows teachers to emphasize how to work cooperatively and to supervise students closely so that relevant feedback can be given about their cooperative and social skills. Students need to develop an awareness of what it means to work cooperatively in social settings and to learn the skills needed to do so. Some models, like variant v in Figure 7.4, may require considerable instructional time to help students develop needed social skills.

Although the teacher initially organizes such instruction, it is important that students gradually become more involved in their self-evaluation. According to Bennett and Dunne: "At the same time as the teacher encourages, develops and evaluates co-operation, there is a need for the children to be given tasks which enable them to monitor and evaluate their own behavior in groups and become responsible for their own group's performance. Thus both teacher and pupils need to participate in monitoring and evaluation, which will in turn have an impact on future co-operative activities" (p. 170).

What is critical in helping students learn to work cooperatively is to prepare them for both the social and cognitive demands of cooperation. Some models of cooperation require more ability to negotiate, compromise, and handle discontinuity and ambiguity. Teachers need to be aware of the need to help students understand both types of responsibilities more fully. One strategy that teachers have found useful to help students become more sensitive to required social and task dispositions is the use of T-charts.

Finally, teachers who wish to use cooperative learning effectively need to assign tasks and activities that are well suited to it. This often means adapting or substituting for traditional assignments meant for individuals. Good et al. (1989–1990), for example, found that small-group cooperative learning did not work well in many mathematics classes because most assigned tasks involved routine computation practice, an activity that students are accustomed to working on alone and that does not lend itself to cooperative interaction. If students are actually meant to cooperate rather than just compare answers, they need to be assigned to work on problems that admit to a range of formulation and solution strategies that can be discussed and debated, or else be assigned more complicated tasks that must be done in stages requiring cooperative planning and perhaps differentiation of roles for students in the group. Also, the activities assigned for cooperative learning must be continuous with the curriculum if cooperative learning is to be an integral part of subject-matter teaching rather than an isolated add-on. Thus, cooperative learning activities should engage students in exploring or applying the content currently being taught, with the scope of the task and the degree of autonomous cooperative work expected from students depending on their familiarity with both the academic content and the cooperative learning format.

IMPLEMENTATION GUIDELINES

Johnson et al. (1984) suggest the following steps for teachers interested in implementing small-group cooperative learning:

Objectives
1. Specify academic and collaborative skills objectives.

Decisions
2. Decide the size of the group (typically from two to six, depending on the nature of the task, the time available, and the experience of the teacher in using small-group methods).
3. Assign students to groups (preferably by ensuring heterogeneity rather than grouping by ability or allowing students to form their own groups).
4. Arrange the room so that the teacher has access to each group and group members can meet in a circle and sit close enough to each other to communicate effectively without disrupting other groups.

5. Plan instructional materials to promote interdependence (if necessary, give only one copy of the materials to each group or give each group member different materials so as to force task differentiation).

6. Assign roles to ensure interdependence (assign different members complementary and interconnected roles such as summarizer-checker, researcher-runner, recorder, encourager, and observer).

7. Explain the academic task.

8. Structure positive goal interdependence, peer encouragement, and support for learning (ask the group to produce a single product or use an assessment system in which individuals' rewards are based both on their own scores and on the average for the group as a whole).

9. Structure individual accountability (by using quizzes or randomly selecting group members to explain answers or present the group's conclusions).

10. Structure intergroup cooperation.

11. Explain success criteria.

12. Specify desired behaviors (define cooperative learning operationally by requesting that students take turns, use personal names, listen carefully to one another, encourage everyone to participate, etc.).

Monitoring and Intervening

13. Monitor student behavior (circulate to listen and observe groups in action; note problems in completing assignments or working cooperatively).

14. Provide task assistance.

15. Intervene to teach collaborative skills (where groups are experiencing major problems in collaborating successfully).

16. Provide closure to the lesson.

Evaluation and Processing

17. Evaluate quality and quantity of students' learning.

18. Assess how well the group functions (give feedback about how well the members worked with one another and accomplished assigned tasks and how they could improve).

USING EXTANT CURRICULUM AND TRAINING MATERIAL

A number of valuable sources provide ideas for helping students understand and respond to cooperative learning situations (e.g., Bennett & Dunne, 1992; Jenkin, 1989; Kagan, 1988). Such sources provide activities that teachers can adapt to their own classrooms. Teachers who are making decisions about group work must understand the long-term reasons why they are using cooperative learning and design activities that help students to work successfully under a specific model. Sometimes activities (even valuable activities) can become ends in themselves and lead to counterproductive behavior, beliefs, and norms.

Cohen (1986) provides a strategy that can be useful in getting students to monitor and to pay attention to group processes. The strategy, amended from Epstein

(1972), has been labeled the four-stage rocket. Students are divided into groups and presented with a short discussion task. The teacher observes various groups and notes appropriate and inappropriate discussion techniques. Then the teacher conducts a whole-class discussion of these observations. Students are told that they will have the opportunity to practice four skills that are necessary if the discussion is to "take off like a rocket." The four skills are conciseness, listening, reflecting, and everyone contributing. Students practice each skill.

Assuming that an appropriate discussion task has been selected, such an activity can provide an interesting orientation to small-group work. However, to reiterate, teachers must help students to see the broad purposes of small-group work. Conciseness of expression may be a virtue initially, but as they explore open-ended problems, students should be expected to deal with the ambiguities of going beyond the information given and explore problems. Further, an emphasis on time (only 15 seconds) may inadvertently suggest to students that *speed* is important. Hence, if teachers intend to develop a proactive and thoughtful approach to group problem solving, then they must establish these expectations with these students.

MEANINGFUL IMPLEMENTATION

The guidelines just presented appear deceptively simple. However, some of the steps may require much time to develop. Also, techniques that may be useful at certain stages (e.g., the assignment of roles) may become unnecessary or even counterproductive (role assignments may interfere with authentic communication when students work as a group—see variant v, Figure 7.4). For example, Good et al. (1989–1990) found that role assignment was often artificial and in some cases students spent more time discussing role boundaries than thinking about the task. Thus, it may make sense to use roles for a limited time for young students or when cooperative techniques are first being introduced and then to discard them and allow students to develop their own communication styles.

PROVIDING OPPORTUNITY FOR SELF-EVALUATION

Opportunities for self-evaluation are critical if students are to improve at monitoring and cooperative interactions. Clearly, students at different ages will need different kinds of evaluation activities, and students who have had more or less experience in cooperative settings will need different types of evaluation questions. For example, Figure 7.5 provides a straightforward method for helping young children reflect on group processes. One could have students fill out the sheet individually or in groups. In time, the teacher might allow individual students to explain why they disagree with other group members. However, again, it is important to stress the evolutionary nature of questions and activities that encourage students to become more sophisticated participants over time. For example, item 6 in Figure 7.5 might be appropriate when students are beginning to practice group skills, but in time, this question might be counterproductive (students spend time

1 What one word would you use to describe how the group was today?
   ....

2 What one word would describe the way you would like the group to be?
   ....

3 Is everyone participating?
   Yes, always .... Usually .... Occasionally ....
   Rarely .... No, never ....

4 Are you (everyone in group) trying to make each other feel good? If not, what are you doing?
   Yes, always .... Usually .... Occasionally ....
   Rarely .... No, never ....

5 Are you trying to help each other feel able to talk and say what you think?
   Yes, always .... Usually .... Occasionally ....
   Rarely .... No, never ....

6 Are you listening to each other?
   Yes, always .... Usually .... Occasionally ....
   Rarely .... No, never ....

7 Are you showing you are listening by nodding at each other?
   Yes, always .... Usually .... Occasionally ....
   Rarely .... No, never ....

8 Are you saying 'That's good' to each other when you like something?
   Yes, always .... Usually .... Occasionally ....
   Rarely .... No, never ....

9 Are you asking each other questions?
   Yes, always .... Usually .... Occasionally ....
   Rarely .... No, never ....

10 Are you listening and really trying to answer these questions?
   Yes, always .... Usually .... Occasionally ....
   Rarely .... No, never ....

11 Are you paying attention to each other?
   Yes, always .... Usually .... Occasionally ....
   Rarely .... No, never ....

12 Is any one person talking most of the time? Yes .... No ....

13 Is there a way to have a group where everyone talks about equally?

Figure 7.6 Evaluation of group processes.

clarifying when there is no point to the activity) and more mature issues should be addressed. Teachers must use student self-evaluation activities that are appropriate to the age and experience of students.

In evaluating the success of small-group work, it is useful to consider the needs of individual students as well as their responsibilities. For example, Samples (1992) argues that one fundamental obligation of teachers is to ensure that the cooperation and autonomy that they attempt to develop in the classroom are authentic. If there is authenticity in cooperation, some of the following characteristics should be present: students have a large voice in defining the task, real problem solving is required (outcomes are not known in advance); a primary source of satisfaction has to come from the experience itself; there are shifts of authority and responsibility within the group; students provide different types of leadership at different times and the teacher serves as resource and guide rather than as the dominant figure.

According to Samples, authenticity and autonomy are needed in an era that is encouraging cooperative education. Thus, teachers must be aware of the integrity of individual student autonomy while encouraging cooperation. He notes that consensus and fitting in can be overdetermined and that teachers must foster the integrity of both the solitary self and the social self in the process of cooperative learning. Some appropriate indicators for assessing authenticity and autonomy include: students are comfortable when they choose to be alone; students occasionally choose to withdraw from a group for temporary exploration; students respect what they know and what they do not know.

Another example of a self-evaluation or group evaluation form appears in Figure 7.6. This example is from Kagan (1988), who suggests that the first three questions should be addressed frequently and that the other questions on the scale would help students to focus on specific issues from time to time as appropriate.

A small-group format can take a variety of forms depending on whether more or less teacher direction and/or direct involvement is desired. Mason, Reys, and Good (1990) described three instructional models that could be used for small-group work. These models illustrate how small-group instruction might be organized. Although each model is teacher-directed to some extent, teacher direction and student group work vary (the role of teacher as director of learning decreases, and the role of students as directors or orchestrators of learning increases).

Model 1 (see Figure 7.7) is highly teacher directed; the lesson begins with a 30- to 40-minute teacher-led active teaching and learning component over a new concept. A single student work group session follows and varies from 5 to 10 minutes. Model 2 (see Figure 7.8) employs a recursive pattern in which teacher direction and facilitation components are alternated three or more times with student work in groups. Time allocated for work groups is increased to as much as 40 minutes (although this includes some time for teacher assessment, clarification, and new task assignment). In Model 3 (see Figure 7.9), the teacher's role changes from director to facilitator. Although the teacher fosters an appropriate environment for group work by creating interest and outlining pertinent questions, students in groups are the primary orchestrators of learning as they formulate and carry out the plan for addressing the question under study.

Model 1 is similar to traditional whole-class teaching except that students work together extending the ideas presented by the teacher rather than working individually on seatwork designed to reinforce the ideas. In Model 1 students see teacher demonstrations and explanations but also explore and discuss mathematical ideas and problem-solving strategies in both whole-class and small-group settings.

In Model 2, teachers engage students (through work groups) in a series of connected explorations, each building on the preceding one, and link those explorations with summarization of ideas and stimulation of new ideas. Teachers are asked not only to introduce students to each new task but to model strategies for solving the higher-level thinking problems.

Approximate Time	Activity	Locus of Control
30-40 min.		Teacher

Develop New Concepts and Skills with Stress on meaning
- Explanation
- Demonstration
- Illustration
- Discussion

Describe Work-Group Task
- Exploration
- Investigation
- Generalization
- Application

5-10 min.		Group

Work-Group Task
Inquiry, reinforcement, or extension of concepts using work-group task.
- Exploration
- Investigation
- Application

5-10 min.		Teacher

Review/Summarization of Task
- Brief review of Objectives
- Review of Work-Group Task
- Review of Findings
- Connections to Future/Past Study

Notes: *Time lines are suggested; particular lessons call for different time distributions, and lesson elements may vary substantially in length.

Review of seatwork, homework, and reteaching should be used as appropriate prior to beginning the active teaching and active learning component.

Establish routines to eliminate lengthy transitions, explanations, and directions.

Assure accountability on seat work and home work through direct method of monitoring.

Figure 7.7 A model of active teaching and active learning in mathematics using work groups as an extension of teacher development of a concept.

Approximate Time	Activity	Locus of Control
10 min.	**Introduce, Explore, Investigate Apply, or Reinforce Concept** • *Explore* New Concepts and skills with Stress on *Understanding* • Provide Problematic Situations and Modeling of Strategies • Guide Meaningful Discussion • Assign Task • Clarify Outcomes to be Attended	Teacher
5-10 min.	**Work Group: Task 1** Inquiry, reinforcement, or extension of concept using task • Exploration • Application • Investigation • Reinforcement	Group
5 min.	**Assess Progress/Process and Clarify** • Active Q/A Interactions • Discuss Problem Situation • Discuss Strategies/Process/Findings • Provide New Development • Provide New Tasks	Teacher
10-15 min.	**Work Group: Task 2**	Group
5 min.	**Assess Progress/Process and Clarify**	Teacher
10-15 min.	**Work Group: Task 3**	Group
5 min.	**Review/Summarization of Task** • Brief Review of Objectives • Review of Tasks • Review of Findings • Connections of Future/Past Study	Teacher

Notes: *Time lines are suggested; particular lessons call for different time distributions, and lesson elements may vary substantially in length.

Review of seatwork, homework, and reteaching should be used as appropriate prior to beginning the active teaching and active learning component.

Establish routines to eliminate lengthy transitions, explanations, and directions.

Assure accountability on seatwork and homework through direct method of monitoring

**During groups-of-four work, teacher monitors process and facilitates group-work in a nondirective manner.

Figure 7.8 A model of active teaching and active learning in mathematics using groups of four and teacher development in a recursive pattern.

Approximate Time   Locus of Control
10 min.   Teacher

Introduce Problematic Situation
- Guide Meaning Discussion
- Application/Transfer
- Solutions
- Brainstorming
- Teamwork/Cooperation
- Stress Sharing Strategies
- Assign Task
- Clarify Outcomes to be Attained

25-40 min.   Group

Work-Group Task
Problem formulation/clarification, solution strategy formulation, data collection, etc., depending on task.
- Exploration
- Investigation
- Application

5-10 min.   Teacher

Summarization of Group Progress
- Active Q/A Interactions
- Discussion of Problematic Situation and Findings
- Discussion of Strategies/Process
- Justification of Answers/Process
- Provision of New Alternatives
- Summary of Activity
- Direction for Continuing Exploration out of Class

----

60 min.

Notes: Time lines are suggested; particular lessons call for different time distributions, and lesson elements may vary substantially in length.

*Review of seatwork, homework, and reteaching should be used as appropriate prior to beginning the active teaching and active learning component.

Establish routines to eliminate lengthy transitions, explanations, and directions.

Assure accountability on seatwork and homework through direct method of monitoring.

**During groups-of-four work, teacher monitors process and facilitates group work in a nondirective manner.

Figure 7.9 A model of active teaching and active learning in mathematics using groups of four in a highly independent pattern.

In using Model 3, teachers simply introduce a problem by explaining to students that they have an opportunity to apply previously learned concepts or skills, seek multiple solutions, brainstorm with work-group teammates, and cooperate to develop strategies for solving the problem. Although teachers using Model 3 are asked not to model strategies for solving the problem, they should still review procedural rules as necessary and clarify the outcomes to be attained. -'

Each model encourages active student learning through teacher development and/or work-group activity. As appropriate, teachers are encouraged to organize activities involving exploration, discovery, problem solving, or application that enable students to construct or extend their understandings of mathematics with peers. For an illustration of how each model might be used with specific mathematics content, see Good, McCaslin, and Reys (1992).

Since research has not been conducted on these models, no sequence or value should be assumed (Good, McCaslin, & Reys, 1992; Mason et al., 1990). For example, some students may need considerable experience with Models 1 and 2 before they can function well in Model 3. However, extended participation in Models 1 and 2 could create misconceptions about Model 3 learning that would be difficult to correct.

Model 3 presents a way to provide students with more control and power over subject-matter knowledge and learning. The extent to which Models 1 and 2 are necessary instructional scaffolding is an interesting issue that will require considerable theory and research. Furthermore, we do not contend at this point that one model is better than the others. Experience in Model 2 with both frequent peer and teacher interaction may help students to develop mathematical power more effectively than will Model 3, which may place too much responsibility on students too soon. In contrast, Model 3 may be most productive for students who have the capacity for self-evaluation and autonomous mathematical reasoning. Model 1 may be optimal for other mathematical outcomes or types of students because it combines teacher modeling and whole-class discussion (with both teacher-student and student-student dialogue) with small-group exploratory work. Issues of authority and control (control of subject matter; control of discussion; control of evaluation) are important. The three models provide a theoretical basis on which to plan instructional sequences and research that will inform our understanding of these issues.

Small-group instruction has considerable potential for increasing student performance. There are data to suggest that small-group instruction can be used in ways to improve student motivation and performance on skills and facts. The method also can be used for increasing students' problem-solving abilities as well as encouraging students to work cooperatively in ways that build social skills. In this chapter we have provided information and strategies that can be of assistance as one implements small-group strategies.

However, as we noted earlier, there is a paucity of data describing successful group processes (how to establish and maintain them), especially processes that enable students to deal with significant problems and to solve them collaboratively. Thus, as teachers have students solve problems in cooperative groups, they must pay close attention to how groups function—to the norms groups are establishing and how those norms influence students' behavior and beliefs during small-group work.

ARRANGING TUTORIAL ASSISTANCE FOR STUDENTS

Individualized tutoring would be the optimal means of achieving most academic objectives, but classroom management responsibilities severely limit teachers' opportunities to provide such tutoring. We recommend that you tutor struggling students as often as you can, both by making time to help them individually during class and by arranging to tutor them outside class if possible (before or after school or between class periods). Even here, though, there are limits to what can be accomplished by even the most dedicated teacher.

One way to supplement instruction is to arrange for students to be tutored by someone other than the teacher. If teacher aides are available, this is one important function they could perform. The same is true of adult volunteers in the classroom and parents or older siblings at home. If you structure the tutoring by providing appropriate materials and exercises and by training the tutors in how to fulfill their roles effectively, you can significantly increase the amount of instruction that slower students receive, perhaps enough to make the difference between keeping up with the class or falling increasingly behind.

Students can also tutor one another, which we noted earlier as one benefit of student teams and other cooperative learning arrangements. Options include cross-age tutoring (older students work with younger students) and peer tutoring (students are tutored by classmates).

Cross-Age Tutoring

Cross-age tutoring is commonly used in elementary schools, where, for example, teachers may arrange for fifth- and sixth-grade students to tutor first- and second-grade students at designated times. Cross-age tutoring generally improves both the attitudes and achievement of students involved (Cohen, Kulik, & Kulik, 1982; Devin-Sheehan, Feldman, & Allen, 1976; Paolitto, 1976; Sharpley, Irvine, & Sharpley, 1983). Furthermore, these desirable outcomes are likely to occur not only for the tutees who receive instruction but also for the tutors who provide it. In part, this arrangement exemplifies the truism that we master material more thoroughly when we teach it to someone else than when we merely respond to it as learners.

The tutors' achievement gains may also be attributed to improved attitudes or self-concepts rather than to deeper exposure to academic content (because they are tutoring younger students on material several grades below their present status). Tutors often respond very positively to their responsibilities. The role involves serious concern about learning academic content, and it appears to stimulate many tutors to identify more closely with the teacher and to become more concerned about their own learning. The tutoring experience may cause underachievers to take their own work more seriously, or lead antisocial students to become more appreciative of their potential for prosocial interaction with others.

Thus, tutors should not be seen merely as performing a service for the teacher. If structured properly, cross-age tutoring presents opportunities for the tutors, and not just the tutees, to derive a variety of cognitive and affective benefits. Tutoring should not be overused, however, and students (especially high achievers) should not be asked to do so much of it that they lose opportunities to do challenging or interesting work at their own level. If anything, the potential benefits of assuming the tutor role are greatest for low achievers, who rarely get the opportunity to act as the competent expert giving instruction rather than receiving it. Yet, low achievers often can play this role effectively when tutoring younger students (Bar-Eli & Raviv, 1982).

The role of tutee also presents many potential benefits. Interactions with tutors are typically friendly and experienced as enjoyable and helpful (Fogarty & Wang, 1982), and they provide a change of pace from more typical learning situations. They also provide opportunities for tutees to take a more active role in structuring their learning experiences to meet their needs by asking questions or calling for particular forms of help. This may be especially important for discouraged or alienated students accustomed to feigning competency rather than seeking help, all the more so if the new behavior generalizes to their interactions with the teacher.

Under some circumstances, students may learn more readily from student tutors than from teachers. In the case of an unresolved personality clash or communication problem between a teacher and a student, for example, the student might not only be more comfortable but also learn more during individualized instruction from an older student. Also, student tutors may use language or examples that are more easily understood than those of the teacher, or may identify learning problems more accurately because they have experienced the same problems recently.

Thomas (1970) showed the value of student tutors in his study of the relative effectiveness of fifth and sixth graders versus college students as tutors of second graders in reading. He found that, in general, the elementary school tutors were just as effective as the college students (seniors enrolled in a reading methods course, who had almost completed undergraduate teacher education programs).

Although they lacked both the general intellectual development and the specialized knowledge about reading instruction that the college students had, the fifth and sixth graders were more comfortable and spontaneous in assuming the role of tutor. Thomas (1970) stated it this way:

> In analyzing the different groups of tutors, one is struck by the differences in their approach to the tutees. The college-aged tutors seemed to be attempting to coax the tutees into liking them, into enjoying the reading materials, and into practicing the reading skills. The elementary-aged tutors, for the most part, were more direct and businesslike. They seemed to accept the fact that the tutees had problems in their schoolwork, and seemed to feel that the tutoring sessions were for teaching those materials in front of them, not for going off in tangents and discussing matters outside the lesson.

Thomas's observations suggest that elementary-grade tutors can be as successful as adolescents or adults and that under some circumstances, they may even have certain advantages: (1) successful tutoring may demand direct instruction, and adults may tend to be too indirect; (2) the adults' vocabulary and examples may be too complex for young children to follow easily; and (3) tutors who are close in age to tutees may remember their own difficulties with materials and thus may be able to identify and respond to learning problems more effectively or maintain a patient, lesson-focused orientation longer than adults.

In general, though, adults are more effective tutors than children, especially in supplementing nonverbal demonstrations with verbal explanations of related concepts and in helping tutees learn the general principles that specific examples are designed to teach (Ellis & Rogoff, 1982). Thus, student tutoring is more likely to be successful when used to provide supervised practice and other follow-up to instruction originally presented by the teacher than when it is expected to stand on its own.

Peer Tutoring by Classmates

Teachers also can use peer-tutoring arrangements calling for one classmate to tutor another under specified conditions. Such peer tutoring must be handled carefully, however, because it "officially" identifies the tutee as needing help on the material being tutored. Some students may resist this role because they do not believe they need the help (Fogarty & Wang, 1982), because they are afraid of losing face before their peers, or because they believe they know more about the material than the students who are supposed to tutor them (Rosen et al., 1978). Problems of this sort are less likely to occur with cross-age tutoring or with tutoring that occurs within small-group cooperative learning arrangements, although they can occur even here if the same students are always tutored or if the teacher presents the tutoring as a remediation requirement rather than as an individualized learning opportunity.

LEARNING IN DYADS

Students can also learn new material together in pairs. Although one member of the pair may have a higher achievement profile, students of unequal ability can work together to explore new problems. For example, Kutnick and Thomas (1990) found that 11- to 12-year-old students did better on the cognitively based Science Reasoning Task than did students working individually. These results reflected improvement in both partners' individual performances, not just a simple sharing of abilities.

However, such gains are not automatic. Stacey (1992) explored mathematical problem solving by junior secondary students and found that in a written test of problem solving, randomly assigned students working alone did better than did students working as a group (mostly pairs with some triads). The test contained six items and required students to solve nonroutine mathematical problems. In exploring why group performance was not better than individual performance, Stacey found that during group discussions students consistently ignored right ideas in favor of simpler but incorrect ideas. The group was capable of generating many ideas; however, the choices they made between possible ideas were not considered carefully.

Thus, teachers who use peer tutoring or peer learning need to monitor the process of student exchange regularly to assure both the value of content and the sensitivity of communication. As in all aspects of classroom life, teachers need to make decisions about when and how to use peer tutoring and peer learning dyads. If teachers use dyads, they should consider the guidelines we presented earlier in the chapter. We give guidelines for peer tutoring (where one student explicitly helps another) in the section that follows. For more information on distinctions between peer tutoring, peer collaboration, and cooperative learning, see Damon and Phelps (1989).

We suggest the following guidelines for teachers considering peer tutoring (for additional suggestions see Goodlad & Hirst, 1989, or Jenkins & Jenkins, 1987).

Learning Outlook   Create the mental set that *we learn from one another.* This is more readily achieved when you consistently model and point out to students how you learn from them. Also, you can help reduce unnecessary competition by stressing that the goal is for all students to learn as much as they can and that the measure of success is how we compare with our own past performance rather than how we compare with others in the class.

Procedural Details   Decisions need to be made about the following procedural matters:

1. Definite times of the day should be set aside for tutoring, so that students quickly learn that only certain class times are for helping one another (to avoid continuous disruption of the class).
2. Specific assignments need to be outlined. The teacher should mimeograph the directions each tutor is to follow each week. For example, "Johnny, this week from 8:00 to 9:00 you will work with Jill and Terry. On Monday you will use flash cards to review the 7, 8, and 9 multiplication tables. Go through each table twice with them and then get individual responses from each. The last time, write down the mistakes that each makes and return the sheet to me. On Tuesday, play audiotape Number 16 for Jill and Terry and listen with them to the rhyming words. Then go to the word box and find the rhyming words and sheet. Read the material sentence by sentence and have Jill and Terry identify the rhyming words."
3. Allow a tutor to work with one or two tutees long enough (one or two weeks) so that you can make sequential assignments, and learning exercises are not constantly starting anew. However, switch tutoring assignments every couple of weeks to prevent attitudes such as "I'm your teacher" from developing.
4. Tutors should not be asked to administer real tests to tutees. One purpose of peer tutoring is to encourage cooperation between students. Asking tutors to quiz their tutees often defeats this purpose.
5. All students in the class should at times be tutors, and all should be tutees. In this way, students learn that they all can help and can benefit from one another. For example, if they are given the necessary answer

keys, slower students can help faster ones by listening to their spelling words or administering and scoring flash card drills in math.

6. Teachers need not adhere to the tutor model (one student flashes cards, the other responds) but can expand, when appropriate, to small work-team assignments (from two to eight students on a team). Shy students can be assigned to work with friendly extroverts. Students with artistic talents can be paired with bright but unartistic students in teams to gather facts and then represent them graphically. These combinations allow students to work together and gain interpersonal skills as well as to master content.

7. Both learning teams and peer tutoring take considerable teacher time to get off to a good start, especially if students have not participated in these activities before. Take your time at first and be sure that all students understand what to do. The first week you ask students to tutor, model the behaviors you want. For example, pass out instructions and have all students read them. Then tutor one or more students in accordance with the directions. Do not just describe what to do; actually do it, modeling the appropriate behaviors. After this demonstration, select another two students to model the next set of directions. Then break the group into pairs and go around listening and answering questions. After a couple of such practice sessions, most students are able to assist others effectively, at least in repetitious drill-like activities. The first week you implement a peer-tutoring program you may have a loud, somewhat disorganized room as students argue over where to go or what to do. Remember that learning does not necessarily require passive, quiet students and that any teacher trying new activities has minor adjustment problems as students learn new roles.

8. Pairing of best friends is often unwise, for several reasons: Friends tend to drift away from learning exercises; the number of classmates that a given student interacts with is reduced; and friends, in moments of anger, are more likely to become excessively critical or indulge in ridicule. Although many friends can work well together, many others cannot, and you should use caution in such groupings.

9. Communicate to parents that all students will both tutor and be tutored by classmates. This is especially important in high-socioeconomic-status areas where some parents may become upset on learning that their child is being tutored by a neighbor's child, fearing that the neighbors will see them as inadequate parents. Needless concern can be eliminated if you communicate to parents the purpose of the tutor program in a letter or visit and point out that tutoring occurs at particular times during the day. List these times and invite the parents to visit whenever they want to do so.

SUMMARY

As we have noted, educators' thinking has progressively moved away from policies of exclusion and homogeneous grouping toward an emphasis on the value of diversity, policies of inclusion, and practices that meet the needs of all students. More and more educators are arguing that heterogeneous classes are just as effective as homogeneous classes for obtaining achievement and other cognitive outcomes as well as affective and social goals such as cultural understanding and prosocial behavior across racial and ethnic groups.

In this chapter, following social constructivist theories of teaching and learning, we have argued for an increased emphasis on student-student interaction. We have noted that learning should not be viewed as transmission of knowledge from a teacher to students who imitate or memorize it, but instead as social construction of new understandings accomplished primarily through sustained discussion. Besides learning through interacting with teachers, students learn by collaborating with peers in pairs and small groups and by interacting with them during classroom discussion. Assuming that everyone participates, diversity in students' backgrounds and points of view should be considered an asset, not a liability.

Under certain conditions and for limited periods of time, it may be useful to accommodate student heterogeneity by grouping students on the basis of achievement profiles. Some educators advocate between-class ability grouping, and in theory such grouping should enable teachers to instruct all students more effectively. However, in practice, the effects of such grouping are weak and mixed. Further, critics have identified problems associated with between-class ability grouping including negative social labeling effects, removing academic peer leaders from low-ability classes, and countering progress toward desegregation and mainstreaming by minimizing contact between peers who differ in achievement. For these reasons, we recommend that between-class ability grouping be confined to grouping by curriculum in high school and that grouping by ability or achievement in earlier grades be avoided except in extreme circumstances.

A second strategy for coping with student heterogeneity is *within-class ability grouping*, especially for beginning reading instruction. We recommend that teachers minimize within-class ability grouping (using it only when necessary to achieve homogeneity, for example, and not merely to reduce the number of students to be taught at the same time). If within-class grouping is used, we recommend that it be used to meet particular needs rather than merely to pace students differentially through the same curriculum using the same instructional methods. Thus, we recommend that group assignments be flexible and reviewed frequently, and that teachers arrange to provide low-group students with extra and more individualized instruction.

Students should frequently be taught in heterogeneous groups in order to maximize the time for students to be active learners and to learn in a social context. Our focus is on valuing diversity and allowing students to respect differences in backgrounds and interests (more on this in Chapter 8). We think it important for different types of students to interact frequently for purposes of promoting both affective and cognitive gains.

Cooperative learning approaches involve assigning students to small groups for cooperative work on group tasks (group members cooperate to produce a single group product) or individual tasks (group members help one another complete individual assignments). Successful cooperative learning programs typically feature positive interdependence of group members, face-to-face interaction of group members, individual accountability for mastering assigned material, and instruction of students in how to interact effectively during small-group activities. Incentive structures involving group rewards appear to be responsible for the achievement benefits of cooperative learning (by motivating students within groups to help one another do as well as they can and thus ensure that the group does as well as it can). This feature is most characteristic of the Student Team Learning approaches (TGT, STAD, Jigsaw II, TAI) that have been used mostly with practice in mathematics and other basic skills.

The affective benefits of cooperative learning appear to occur either when there is an incentive structure featuring group rewards (even if students work on their own on individual tasks rather than on cooperative tasks) or when the task structure is cooperative and students work together to produce a common product (often under task differentiation conditions calling for each group member to take a unique role or fulfill a unique function). Such cooperative task structures are featured in the Learning Together, Group Investigation, and original Jigsaw methods commonly used in social studies classes or in activities designed to accomplish higher-level cognitive objectives.

In contrast to most other proposed adaptations of traditional classroom teaching, cooperative learning approaches have proven to be relatively easy to implement and likely to yield significant advantages (in both cognitive and affective outcomes). Consequently, we recommend that most teachers make at least some use of these methods as alternatives to traditional independent seatwork to provide students with opportunities to practice and apply what they are learning. However, most of our knowledge of small groups is based on research in which students worked on relatively simple content. Even when the purpose of small-group instruction is inquiry or problem solving, those results are not automatic (Blumenfeld, 1992). Educators have much to learn about how to design small-group instruction in order to stimulate higher-order thinking and comprehension.

Tutoring by teacher aides or other adult volunteers can be an important supplement to instruction from the teacher and a valuable means of providing extra assistance to slower students. So can cross-age tutoring, in which older students tutor younger students. Research has shown that cross-age tutoring benefits tutors as well as tutees. Peer-tutoring arrangements in which classmates work with one another can also be effective, but careful planning, training, and supervision are necessary so that the program is not more trouble than it is worth by upsetting parents or engendering resentment among students.

SUGGESTED ACTIVITIES AND QUESTIONS

1. Try to observe two small groups (three to five group members) working on the same topic. In what ways is group process the same and how does it differ? Is one group more cohesive than another? What accounts for the difference?

2. Try to interview the students you observed. What are their beliefs about the group process? Do those students who talked a lot feel differently from those who talked less? Do students who participated less see more talkative students as helpful or bossy?

3. If there is variation in the use of between-class ability grouping at the grade or subject you teach, arrange to observe in local schools that use heterogeneous grouping and others that use homogeneous grouping. What are the trade-offs involved, and what opportunities and constraints do they create for teachers? Which types of students (high or low achievers, phantom students versus social students) benefit more from homogeneously grouped classes? Why?

4. In which setting do you prefer to teach, and why? Given that you may not have this choice, what adjustments in your role as teacher will you have to make if you are assigned to a school that does not use the grouping arrangement you prefer?

5. If you plan to use within-class ability grouping, state the criteria you will use to assign students to groups initially. After these initial assignments, when and how will you schedule reassessments and arrange for regrouping?

6. What classes (in terms of grade, subject, and student composition) are most and least appropriate for within-class ability grouping? Why?

7. Why does placing students in a higher group than their achievement suggests tend to enhance their subsequent achievement?

8. In this chapter we have stressed the need for students occasionally to work in small heterogeneous groups; however, we have discussed both the advantages and disadvantages of small-group work. Given your intended (or present) teaching level and your goals, what reasons do you believe are most important for using small-group instruction?

9. What are the relative advantages and disadvantages of cross-age tutoring? Peer tutoring? Which types of students are most or least likely to benefit from peer tutoring (alienated, phantom, dependent)? Why?

10. How would you organize a cross-age student tutoring program at your school? What provisions could be made for evaluating and making adjustments in the program?

11. What can teachers do in advance to make peer-tutoring programs effective?

12. Given your preferred grade level and subject matter, are cooperative learning approaches likely to be worthwhile components of instruction? Why or why not?

13. Considering the differences among the cooperative learning methods described in the chapter, which would be the most appropriate for use in your preferred grade level or subject matter? Why?

14. If teachers group on the basis of one student characteristic (e.g., reading level), how might this affect other characteristics (dependency, sociability)? Does it make more sense to group on the basis of achievement than according to personal or social traits?

REFERENCES

Alexander, K. L., Cook, M., & McDill, E. L. (1978). Curriculum tracking and educational stratification: Some further evidence. *American Sociological Review, 43,* 47–66.

Allan, S. (1991). Ability-grouping research reviews: What do they say about grouping and the gifted? *Educational Leadership, 48*(6), 60–65.

Ames, C., & Felker, D. (1979). An examination of children's attributions and achievement-related evaluations in competitive, cooperative, and individualistic reward structures. *Journal of Educational Psychology, 71,* 413–420.

Anderson, L., & Pigford, A. (1988). Teaching within-classroom groups: Examining the role of the teacher. *Journal of Classroom Interaction, 23*(2), 8–13.

Anderson, R., Hiebert, E., Scott, J., & Wilkinson, I. (1985). *Becoming a nation of readers: The report of the commission on reading.* Washington, DC: National Institute of Education.

Aronson, E., Blaney, N., Stephan, C., Sikes, J., & Snapp, M. (1978). *The jigsaw classroom.* Beverly Hills, CA: Sage.

Bar-Eli, N., & Raviv, A. (1982). Underachievers as tutors. *Journal of Educational Research, 75,* 139–143.

Beckerman, T., & Good, T. (1981). The classroom ratio of high- and low-aptitude students and its effect on achievement. *American Educational Research Journal, 18,* 317–327.

Bennett, N., & Cass, A. (1988). The effects of group composition on group interactive processes and pupil understanding. *British Educational Research Journal, 15,* 19–32.

Bennett, N., & Dunne, E. (1992). *Managing small groups.* New York: Simon & Schuster.

Blumenfeld, P. (1992). The task and the teacher: Enhancing student thoughtfulness in science. In J. Brophy (Ed.), *Advances in research on teaching* (Vol. 3, pp. 81–114). Greenwich, CT: JAI Press.

Bohlmeyer, E., & Burke, J. (1987). Selecting cooperative learning techniques: A consultative strategy guide. *School Psychology Review, 16,* 36–49.

Bossert, S. (1988–1989). Cooperative activities in the classroom. In E. Rothkopf (Ed.), *Review of research in education* (Vol. 15, pp. 225–250). Washington, DC: American Educational Research Association.

Braddock, J., & McPartland, J. (1990). Alternatives to tracking. *Educational Leadership, 47*(7), 76–78.

Cazden, C. (1985). Ability grouping and differences in reading instruction. In J. Osborn, P. Wilson, & R. Anderson (Eds.), *Reading education: Foundations for a literate America.* Lexington, MA: Lexington Books.

Cohen, E. (1986). *Designing group work: Strategies for the heterogeneous classroom.* New York: Teachers College Press.

Cohen, P., Kulik, J., & Kulik, C. (1982). Educational outcomes of tutoring: A meta-analysis of findings. *American Educational Research Journal, 19,* 237–248.

Crawford, J. (1983). A study of instructional processes in Title I classes: 1981–82. *Journal of Research and Evaluation of the Oklahoma City Public Schools, 13*(1).

Dar, Y. (1985). Teachers' attitudes toward ability grouping: Educational considerations and social organizational influences. *Interchange, 16*(2), 17–38.

Davidson, N. (1985). Small-group learning and teaching in mathematics: A selective review of the literature. In R. Slavin, S. Sharan, S. Kagan, R. Lazarowitz, C. Webb, & R. Schmuck (Eds.), *Learning to cooperate, cooperating to learn* (pp. 211–230). New York: Plenum.

Devin-Sheehan, L., Feldman, R., & Allen, V. (1976). Research on children tutoring children: A critical review. *Review of Educational Research, 46,* 355–385.

DeVries, D. L., & Slavin, R. E. (1978). Teams-Games-Tournament (TGT): Review of ten classroom experiments. *Journal of Research and Development in Education, 12,* 28–38.

DeVries, D. L., Slavin, R. E., Fennessey, G. M., Edwards, K. J., & Lombardo, M. M. (1980). *Teams-Games-Tournament: The team learning approach.* Englewood Cliffs, NJ: Educational Technology Publications.

Douglas, J. (1964). *The home and the school: A study of ability and attainment in the primary school.* London: McGibbon and Kee.

Dreeben, R. (1984). First-grade reading groups: Their formation and change. In P. Peterson, L. Wilkinson, & J. Hallinan (Eds.), *The social context of instruction: Group organization and group processes.* Orlando, FL: Academic Press.

Eder, D. (1981). Ability grouping as a self-fulfilling prophecy: A microanalysis of teacher-student interaction. *Sociology of Education, 54,* 151–161.

Eder, D., & Felmlee, D. (1984). Development of attention norms in ability groups. In P. Peterson, L. Wilkinson, & M. Hallinan (Eds.), *The social context of instruction: Group organization and group processes.* Orlando, FL: Academic Press.

Educational Leadership. (1989–1990). The December 1989/January 1990 issue of this journal (Vol. 47, No. 4) focuses on cooperative learning.

Ellis, S., & Rogoff, B. (1982). The strategies and efficacy of child versus adult teachers. *Child Development, 53,* 730–735.

Epstein, C. (1972). *Affective subjects in the classroom: Exploring race, sex and drugs.* Scranton, PA: Intext Educational Publishers.

Esposito, D. (1973). Homogeneous and heterogeneous ability grouping: Principal findings and implications for evaluating and designing more effective educational environments. *Review of Educational Research, 43,* 63–179.

Evans, J. (1985). *Teaching in transition: The challenge of mixed ability grouping.* Philadelphia: Open University Press.

Evertson, C. (1982). Differences in instructional activities in higher- and lower-achieving junior high English and math classes. *Elementary School Journal, 82,* 329–350.

Findley, W. G., & Bryan, M. M. (1971). *Ability grouping, 1970 status: Impact and alternatives.* Athens: University of Georgia, Center for Educational Improvement.

Finley, M. (1984). Teachers and tracking in a comprehensive high school. *Sociology of Education, 57,* 233–243.

Fogarty, J., & Wang, M. (1982). An investigation of the cross-age peer tutoring process: Some implications for instructional design and motivation. *Elementary School Journal, 82,* 451–469.

Gamoran, A. (1992). Is ability grouping equitable? *Educational Leadership, 50*(2), 11–17.

Gamoran, A., & Berends, M. (1987). The effects of stratification in secondary schools: Synthesis of survey and ethnographic research. *Review of Educational Research, 57,* 415–435.

Gearheart, B., & Weishahn, M. (1984). *The exceptional student in the regular classroom* (3rd ed.). St. Louis: Mosby.

Good, T., & Biddle, B. (1988). Research and the improvement of mathematics instruction: The need for observational resources. In D. A. Grouws & T. J. Cooney (Eds.), *Perspectives on research on effective mathematics teaching* (Vol. 1, pp. 112–114). Hillsdale, NJ: Erlbaum.

Good, T., & Brophy, J. (1990). *Educational psychology: A realistic approach* (4th ed.). New York: Longman.

Good, T., & Marshall, S. (1984). Do students learn more in heterogeneous or homogeneous groups? In P. Peterson, L. Wilkinson, & M. Hallinan (Eds.), *The social context of instruction: Group organization and group processes.* New York: Academic Press.

Good, T., McCaslin, M., & Reys, B. (1992). Investigating work groups to promote problem solving in mathematics. In J. Brophy (Ed.), *Advances in research on teaching* (Vol. 3, pp. 115–160). Greenwich, CT: JAI Press.

Good, T., Mulryan, C., & McCaslin, M. (1992). Grouping for instruction in mathematics: A call for programmatic research on small-group processes. In D. Grouws (Ed.), *Handbook of research on mathematics teaching and learning* (pp. 165–196). New York: Macmillan.

Good, T., Reys, B., Grouws, D., & Mulryan C. (1989–1990). Using work groups in mathematics instruction. *Educational Leadership, 47*(4), 56–62.

Goodlad, S., & Hirst, B. (1989). *Peer tutoring: A guide to learning by teaching.* New York: Nichols.

Graybeal, S. S., & Stodolsky, S. S. (1985). Peer work groups in elementary schools. *American Journal of Education, 93,* 409–428.

Haller, E. J. (1985). Pupil race and elementary school ability grouping: Are teachers biased against black children? *American Educational Research Journal, 22,* 465–483.

Hallinan, M. T., & Sorensen, A. B. (1983). The formation and stability of instructional groups. *American Sociological Review, 48,* 838–851.

Hallinan, M. T., & Sorensen, A. B. (1985). Ability grouping and student friendships. *American Educational Research Journal, 22,* 485–499.

Hewett, F. M., & Watson, P. C. (1979). Classroom management and the exceptional learner. In D. L Duke (Ed.), *Classroom management (Seventy-Eighth Yearbook of the National Society for the Study of Education, Part II).* Chicago: University of Chicago Press.

Hiebert, E. (1983). An examination of ability grouping in reading instruction. *Reading Research Quarterly, 18,* 231–253.

Jenkins, J., & Jenkins, L. (1987). Making peer tutoring work. *Educational Leadership, 44*(6), 64–68.

Jenkins, L. (1989). *Making small groups work.* Oxford: Penguin Educational.

Johnson, D., & Johnson, R. (1975). *Learning together and alone.* Englewood Cliffs, NJ: Prentice-Hall.

Johnson, D., & Johnson, R. (1979). Conflict in the classroom: Controversy and learning. *Review of Educational Research, 49,* 51–70.

Johnson, D., & Johnson, R. (1982). *Joining together: Group therapy and group skills.* Englewood Cliffs, NJ: Prentice-Hall.

Johnson, D., & Johnson, R. (1985a). Classroom conflict: Controversy versus debate in learning groups. *American Educational Research Journal, 22,* 237–256.

Johnson, D., & Johnson, R. (1985b). Cooperative learning and adaptive education. In M. C. Wang & H. J. Walberg (Eds.), *Adapting instruction to individual differences.* Berkeley, CA: McCutchan.

Johnson, D., Johnson, R., Holubec, E. J., & Roy, P. (1984). *Circles of learning: Cooperation in the classroom.* Alexandria, VA: Association for Supervision and Curriculum Development.

Johnson, D., Johnson, R., & Maruyama, G. (1983). Interdependence and interpersonal attraction among heterogeneous and homogeneous individuals: A theoretical formulation and a meta-analysis of the research. *Review of Educational Research, 53,* 5–54.

Johnson, D., Skon, L., & Johnson, R. (1980). Effects of cooperative, competitive, and individualistic conditions on children's problem-solving performance. *American Educational Research Journal, 17,* 83–93.

Johnson, R., Brooker, C., Stutzman, J., Hultman, D., & Johnson, D. (1985). The effects of controversy, concurrence seeking, and individualistic learning on achievement and attitude change. *Journal of Research in Science Teaching, 22,* 141–152.

Kagan, S. (1988). *Cooperative learning: Resources for teachers.* Riverside: University of California.

King, L. (1993). High and low achievers' perceptions and cooperative learning in two small groups. *Elementary School Journal, 93,* 399–416.

Kulik, J., & Kulik, C. (1989). Meta-analysis in education. *International Journal of Educational Research, 13,* 221–340.

Larrivee, B. (1985). *Effective teaching for successful mainstreaming.* New York: Longman.

Leinhardt, G., & Pallay, A. (1982). Restrictive educational settings: Exile or haven? *Review of Educational Research, 52,* 557–578.

Leiter, J. (1983). Classroom composition and achievement gains. *Sociology of Education, 56,* 126–132.

Lew, M., Mesch, D., Johnson, D., & Johnson, R. (1986). Components of cooperative learning: Effects of collaborative skills and academic group contingencies on achievement and mainstreaming. *Contemporary Educational Psychology, 11,* 229–239.

Madden, N., & Slavin, R. (1983). Mainstreaming students with mild handicaps: Academic and social outcomes. *Review of Educational Research, 53,* 519–569.

Mason, D., & Good, T. (1993). Effects of two-group and whole-class teaching on regrouped elementary students' mathematics achievement. *American Educational Research Journal,* 328–360.

Mason, D., Reys, B., & Good, T. (1990). *Three models of active teaching and learning in mathematics using work groups* (Technical Report No. 492). Columbia: University of Missouri, Center for Research in Social Behavior.

Mason, D., Schroeter, D., Combs, R., & Washington, K. (1992). Assigning average-achieving eighth graders to advanced mathematics classes in an urban junior high. *Elementary School Journal, 92,* 587–599.

McCaslin, M., & Good, T. (in press). *Listening to students.* New York: HarperCollins.

Metz, M. (1978). *Classrooms and corridors.* Berkeley: University of California Press.

Moskowitz, J. M., Malvin, J. H., Shaeffer, G. A., & Schaps, E. (1985). Evaluation of Jigsaw, a cooperative learning technique. *Contemporary Educational Psychology, 10,* 104–112.

Mulryan, C. (1989). *A study of intermediate-grade students' involvement and participation in cooperative small groups in mathematics.* Unpublished doctoral dissertation, University of Missouri-Columbia.

Nickerson, J. R., & Prawat, R. S. (1981). Affective interaction in racially diverse classrooms: A case study. *Elementary School Journal, 81,* 291–303.

Noddings, N. (1989). Theoretical and practical concerns about small groups in mathematics. *Elementary School Journal, 89*(5), 607–624.

Oakes, J. (1985). *Keeping track: How schools structure inequality.* New Haven: Yale University Press.

Oakes, J. (1992). Can tracking research inform practice? Technical, normative, and political considerations. *Educational Researcher, 21*(4), 12–21.

Oakes, J., & Lipton, M. (1992). Detracking schools: Early lessons from the field. *Phi Delta Kappan, 73,* 448–454.

Okebukola, P. A. (1985). The relative effectiveness of cooperative and competitive interaction techniques in strengthening students' performance in science classes. *Science Education, 69,* 501–509.

Page, R. (1992). *Lower track classrooms: A curricular and cultural perspective.* New York: Teachers College Press.

Page, R., & Valli, L. (Eds.). (1990). *Curriculum differentiation: Interpretive studies in U.S. secondary schools.* Albany: State University of New York Press.

Paolitto, D. (1976). The effect of cross-age tutoring on adolescence: An inquiry into theoretical assumptions. *Review of Educational Research, 46,* 215–238.

Pepitone, E. (1985). Children in cooperation and competition: Antecedents and consequences of self-orientation. In R. Slavin, S. Sharan, S. Kagan, R. Lazarowitz, C. Webb, & R. Schmuck (Eds.), *Learning to cooperate, cooperating to learn* (pp. 17–67). New York: Plenum.

Persell, C. H. (1979). *Education and inequality.* New York: Free Press.

Peterson, P. L., Wilkinson, L. C., Spinelli, F., & Swing, S. R. (1984). Merging the process-product and the sociolinguistic paradigms: Research on small-group processes. In P. Peterson, L. Wilkinson, & M. Hallinan (Eds.), *Instructional groups in the classroom: Organization and processes.* New York: Academic Press.

Reynolds, M. (1978). Some final notes. In J. Grosenick & M. Reynolds (Eds.), *Teacher education: Renegotiating roles for mainstreaming.* Reston, VA: Council for Exceptional Children.

Reynolds, M., & Birch, J. (1988). *Adaptive mainstreaming: A primer for teachers and principals* (3rd ed.). White Plains, NJ: Longman.

Rist, R. (1970). Student social class and teacher expectations: The self-fulfilling prophecy in ghetto education. *Harvard Educational Review, 40,* 411–451.

Rosen, S., Powell, E., Schubot, D., & Rollins, P. (1978). Competence and tutorial role as status variables affecting peer-tutoring outcomes in public school settings. *Journal of Educational Psychology, 70,* 602–612.

Rosenbaum, J. E. (1980). Social implications of educational grouping. In D. C. Berliner (Ed.), *Review of research in education* (Vol. 8). Itasca, IL: Peacock.

Ross, J. (1988). Improving social-environment studies problem solving through cooperative learning. *American Educational Research Journal, 25,* 573–591.

Rowan, S., & Miracle, A. (1983). Systems of ability grouping and the stratification of achievement in elementary schools. *Sociology of Education, 56,* 133–144.

Schmuck, R., & Schmuck, P. (1988). *Group processes in the classroom* (5th ed.). Dubuque: William C. Brown.

Schwartz, F. (1981). Supporting or subverting learning: Peer group patterns in four tracked schools. *Anthropology and Education Quarterly, 12,* 99–121.

Sharan, S. (1980). Cooperative learning in small groups: Recent methods and effects on achievement, attitudes, and ethnic relations. *Review of Educational Research, 50,* 241–271.

Sharan, S., & Sharan, Y. (1976). *Small-group teaching.* Englewood Cliffs, NJ: Educational Technology Publications.

Sharan, S., et al. (1984). *Cooperative learning in the classroom: Research in desegregated schools*. Hillsdale, NJ: Erlbaum.

Sharpley, A. M., Irvine, J. W., & Sharpley, C. F. (1983). An examination of the effectiveness of a cross-age tutoring program in mathematics for elementary school children. *American Educational Research Journal, 20,* 103–111.

Slavin, R. (1986). *Using Student Team Learning* (3rd ed.). Baltimore: Johns Hopkins University, Center for Research on Elementary and Middle Schools.

Slavin, R. E. (1980a). Cooperative learning. *Review of Educational Research, 50,* 315–342.

Slavin, R. E. (1980b). *Using student team learning* (rev. ed.). Baltimore: Johns Hopkins University, Center for Social Organization of Schools.

Slavin, R. E. (1983). *Cooperative learning*. New York: Longman.

Slavin, R. E. (1985). Team-Assisted Individualization: A cooperative learning solution for adaptive instruction in mathematics. In M. C. Wang & H. J. Walberg (Eds.), *Adapting instruction to individual differences*. Berkeley, CA: McCutchan.

Slavin, R. E. (1987). Ability grouping and student achievement in elementary schools: Best evidence synthesis. *Review of Educational Research, 57,* 293–336.

Slavin, R. E. (1988). Cooperative learning and student achievement. *Educational Leadership, 46*(2), 31–33.

Slavin, R. E. (1990a). Ability grouping and student achievement in secondary schools. *Review of Educational Research, 60,* 417–499.

Slavin, R. E. (1990b). *Cooperative learning: Theory, research, and practice*. Englewood Cliffs, NJ: Prentice-Hall.

Slavin, R. E., Sharan, S., Kagan, S., Hertz-Lazarowitz, R., Webb, C., & Schmuck, R. (Eds.). (1985). *Learning to cooperate, cooperating to learn*. New York: Plenum.

Smith, K., Johnson, D., & Johnson, R. (1981). Can conflict be constructive? Controversy versus concurrence seeking in learning groups. *Journal of Educational Psychology, 73,* 651–663.

Stipek, D. (1986). Children's motivation to learn. In T. Tomlinson & H. Walberg (Eds.), *Academic work and educational excellence* (pp. 197–221). Berkeley, CA: McCutchan.

Swing, S. R., & Peterson, P. L. (1982). The relationship of student ability and small-group instruction to student achievement. *American Educational Research Journal, 19,* 259–274.

Thomas, J. (1970). *Tutoring strategies and effectiveness: A comparison of elementary age tutors and college tutors*. Unpublished doctoral dissertation. Austin: University of Texas.

Thompson, R. H., White, K. R., & Morgan, D. P. (1982). Teacher-student interaction patterns in classrooms with mainstreamed mildly handicapped students. *American Educational Research Journal, 19,* 220–236.

Tuckman, B., & Bierman, M. (1971). *Beyond Pygmalion: Galatea in the schools*. Paper presented at the annual meeting of the American Educational Research Association, New York.

Vanfossen, B., Jones, J., & Spade, J. (1987). Curriculum tracking and status maintenance. *Sociology of Education, 60,* 104–122.

Veldman, D. J., & Sanford, J. P. (1984). The influence of class ability level on student achievement and classroom behavior. *American Educational Research Journal, 21,* 629–644.

Webb, N. M. (1982). Student interaction and learning in small groups. *Review of Educational Research, 52,* 421–445.

Webb, N. M. (1989). Peer interaction and learning in small groups. *International Journal of Educational Research, 13,* 21–29.

Webb, N. M., & Cullian, L. K. (1983). Group interaction and achievement in small groups: Stability over time. *American Educational Research Journal, 20,* 411–423.

Weinstein, R. (1976). Reading group membership in first grade: Teacher behaviors and pupil experience over time. *Journal of Educational Psychology, 68,* 103–116.

Wheelock, A. (1992). *Crossing the tracks: How "untracking" can save schools.* New York: New Press.

FORM 7.1 Small-Group Interaction

USE: *Whenever a small group of students is working and the teacher is not a
    formal part of the group.*
PURPOSE: *To determine how the group spends its time*
    Make a code every 15 seconds to describe what the group is doing at
that moment.

Frequency		Type Contact
_____	1.	Reading (finding information, etc.)
_____	2.	Manipulating equipment
_____	3.	Task discussion: general participation
_____	4.	Task discussion: one or two person dominated
_____	5.	Procedural discussion
_____	6.	Observing
_____	7.	Nontask discussion
_____	8.	Procedural dispute
_____	9.	Substantive (task relevant) dispute
_____	10.	Silence or confusion

FORM 7.2 Individual Participation in Small-Group Work

USE: *When a small group is operating and the teacher is not part of the group*
PURPOSE: *To assess the involvement and participation of individual students
    during small-group work*
    Observe the target student for 15 seconds and make a code. Repeat the
cycle for the duration of the small-group activity. *

_____	1.	Reading (finding information)
_____	2.	Manipulating equipment (filmstrip, slide rule)
_____	3.	Participating in general discussion (telling and listening to others)
_____	4.	Listening to general discussion
_____	5.	Presents idea to group (others are listening to the target student)
_____	6.	Talking to individual (an aside: the conversation is not part of the group discussion)
_____	7.	Listening to individual (an aside: the conversation is not part of the group discussion)
_____	8.	Passive (can't tell if student is involved)
_____	9.	Misbehaving
_____	10.	Leaves group

*Note that it would be possible to use the form to code different individual
students in the group (code one student for a minute, then switch to another
student). Furthermore, the scale could be altered to provide information
about the group. For example, the percentage of the group that falls into
each category could be noted.

Teaching Heterogeneous Classes and Differentiating Instruction

SCHOOL-AGED POPULATION IS BECOMING MORE DIVERSE

The term *educationally disadvantaged* is defined differently by various educators. However, the number of disadvantaged students in U.S. schools seems certain to increase in the coming years. According to Natriello, McDill, and Pallas (1990, p. 13), "Some students will have suffered from a lack of appropriate formal educational experiences, others will have suffered from the lack of intellectual experiences in the family, and still others will have suffered from the lack of educational experiences in the community."

These authors report that the U.S. population under 18 will increase by about 4 percent between 1988 and 2020. The number of white students is expected to decline by about 27 percent (12.2 million students) during this period, whereas the number of Hispanic children will triple, from 6.8 million in 1988 to 18.6 million in 2020. The population of black youth under age 18 is predicted to increase 9 percent (from 9.6 million to 10.5 million), and the population of other groups is projected to double (increase by 2.3 million children).

Predicting population figures and related demographics is always difficult, because predictions are based on assumptions. The Census Bureau recently revised its projections from those released in the late 1980s. Birth rates were revised upward because of an increase in births among U.S. women and because of significant increases in immigration (both legal and illegal). According to Vobejda (1992), late in the 1980s, the bureau projected that the population would peak around 2038 and decline to about 300 million by 2050. However, the revised figures suggest an additional 80 million Americans and indicate that the population will not peak, but will continue to grow into the late twenty-first century. By the middle of the next century (2050), Hispanics are estimated to nearly quadruple—to one-fifth of the U.S. population, or 81 million people. However, Asians will remain the fastest-growing group, increasing from 9 million to 41 million by 2050. During the same period, the number of black Americans will nearly double, reaching 16 percent of the population, or 62 million people. As assumptions are altered, these figures will continue to change. Still, the trend clearly indicates an American population that is becoming much more diverse.

As Natriello et al. note, the projected change in composition of the school-age population suggests a substantial rise in the percentage of educationally disadvantaged students. Unfortunately, racial and ethnic group status are correlated with other indicators of educational disadvantage. Assuming a continuing relationship between race and poverty, as the proportion of black and Hispanic children increases, there will be more children living in poverty. Indeed, as can be seen in Figures 8.1 and 8.2, the projected number of U.S. children living with mothers who have not completed high school and having a primary language other than English will increase notably in the next decades.

Hopefully, new intervention programs (food programs, educational programs, etc.) may help reduce the relationship between socioeconomic status and educational progress. However, even with successful intervention programs, the number of educationally disadvantaged students will grow, and the total composition of students will become more diverse.

Hiebert (1991) notes that from some perspectives, diversity (differences among learners) has been conceptualized as a problem to be overcome, so that programs were designed to reduce or remove these differences. For example, students who knew fewer vocabulary words were taught separately. Many educators, however, are beginning to view diversity as a resource rather than a liability. According to

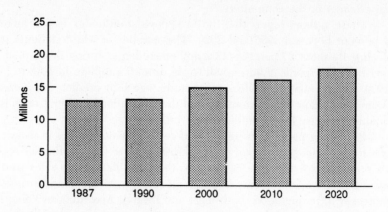

Figure 8.1 Projected number of U.S. children with mothers not completing high school, 1987–2020 (in millions).

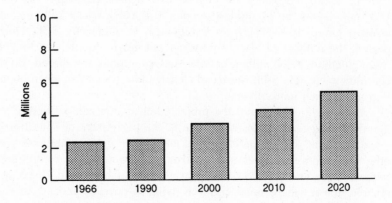

Figure 8.2 Projected number of U.S. children with a primary language other than English, 1986–2020 (in millions).

Hiebert, students with different backgrounds can interact with one another and learn how the same text material or concept can be interpreted differently by persons from different backgrounds. Thus, teachers can use unique pupil experiences to make classroom learning richer and more sensitive to differences among students.

We also view diversity as an opportunity to enrich classroom learning. Although widely diverse groups of learners can make teaching difficult, most instruction should occur in heterogeneous settings. In this chapter we note that dealing with diversity has become progressively more important as educational settings have become more inclusive at all levels. This chapter also discusses common strategies for responding to student diversity.

DEALING WITH DIVERSITY

At one time, only the children of the rich and powerful received formal education, typically in the form of private individualized tutoring. Such tutoring is the method of choice for most educational purposes, because both curriculum (what is taught) and instruction (how it is taught) can be individualized and because the teacher can provide the student with sustained personalized attention (Bloom, 1984). Unfortunately, private tutoring is too expensive for most families. Consequently, as systems for mass education developed, one constant feature was an arrangement whereby each teacher worked with many students (Kliebard, 1986).

Colonial times featured the one-room schoolhouse, into which students of all ages were crowded together for instruction in all subjects by a single teacher who had few if any commercially prepared texts or curriculum materials to work with (Grinder & Nelsen, 1985). Except for so-called primers for reading instruction (containing the alphabet and short sections such as proverbs, catechisms, or passages from the Bible), teachers made do with slates, chalkboards, and materials that they had purchased themselves or induced their students to bring from home (maps, books published for use by the general public). Recitations and rote memory exercises were relied on when texts or other curriculum materials were not available.

With the industrial revolution and the population shift to the cities, schools became larger and education became more standardized and formalized. Age grouping became the basis for assigning students to classes, curriculum guidelines and standards were established for each grade level, and teachers began using commercial textbooks and tests. Certain common practices for organizing and managing instruction in the public schools became well established and have continued as the traditional model of classroom teaching: the *lock-step curriculum* with its grade-level sequencing; division of the school day into periods for teaching different subjects, and division of instruction in each subject into units and lessons; *group pacing*, in which the whole class is moved through the same curriculum at roughly the same pace using largely the same materials and methods; and *whole-class instructional methods*, in which the teacher typically begins a lesson by reviewing prerequisite material, introduces and develops new concepts or skills, leads the group in a recitation or supervised practice or application activity, and then assigns seatwork or homework for students to do on their own. The teacher may occasionally teach small groups rather than the whole class (especially for beginning reading instruction) and may provide a degree of individualized instruction when "making the rounds" during seatwork times. However, despite these and other minor variations on the theme, the basic whole-class instruction/recitation/seatwork model has persisted as the dominant approach to public school teaching since it first became established, despite frequent criticism and calls for reform (Goodlad, Soder, & Sirotnik, 1990).

The fact that this traditional approach persists despite its many weaknesses suggests that it has certain enduring strengths. Indeed, the approach seems to work reasonably well for students whose rates of learning and responses to commonly used instructional materials and methods are similar to those of the mythical "average student" at a given grade. Furthermore, given that teachers must work with classes of 20 to 40 students, the traditional method, although clearly a compromise, may be the best approach available. Other things being equal, it may enable teachers to meet more of the needs of more of their students than they could meet using any other method that is feasible. The major constraints of the traditional approach are that the majority of students must work without close supervision whenever teachers work with small groups or individuals, and teachers cannot get around to each student often enough to provide effective individualized instruction.

The traditional approach has other important weaknesses, so that it periodically becomes the focus of criticism and calls for reform (e.g., Goodlad, 1984). Some critics describe the traditional system as unduly teacher dominant, rigidly structured, fostering passive and repetitive learning, or unimaginative and boring. Other critics acknowledge that the approach is adequate for average students but believe that brighter students should get more enrichment or accelerated pacing, that slower students should get extra instruction or more time to master material, and that students with special instructional needs should be taught using materials or methods different from those suitable for the majority. Critics commonly call for more variety in educational curricula and methods and for more attempts to adapt schooling to the needs and interests of students (Hiebert, 1991; Natriello et al., 1990). In particular, recent reform documents (e.g., *Mathematics for Everybody*, 1989) call for more active involvement of students (through discussion groups, project work, etc.) and more student responsibility for learning. We will discuss the implications of current theories of student learning more fully in Chapter 10. Here we discuss broad strategies that teachers can use to organize instruction for diverse learners in the same classroom.

MASTERY LEARNING

One fundamental, although modest, way to adjust traditional whole-class pacing is to allow slower students more time to master curriculum objectives. The traditional model of schooling allocates a fixed amount of learning time for each unit and accepts individual differences in mastery. An alternative to this is the Mastery Learning Model (Bloom, 1980), which calls for all learners to master a common set of curriculum objectives but allows for individual differences in learning time. The mastery approach assumes that the major difference between learners is the time it takes them to master curriculum objectives. Mastery approaches enable all students in a class to master all basic objectives by allowing slower learners more time (and usually additional tutoring or other assistance) to learn material that classmates have mastered more quickly. The original mastery approach emphasized individualized tutoring, but the approach has since been adapted for use in tandem with, rather than instead of, more traditional group-based instruction (Block & Anderson, 1975). Hence, principles of mastery learning have been integrated into diverse instructional methods (Gagné, Briggs, & Wager, 1992; Stallings & Stipek 1986).

At present, most mastery learning programs feature group-based rather than individualized instruction (Levine, 1985). These programs have certain common features. Anderson (1985) suggests that the following features are found in any true mastery learning program:

1. Clearly specified learning objectives
2. Short, highly valid assessment procedures
3. Preset mastery performance standards
4. A sequence of learning units, each composed of an integral set of facts, concepts, principles, and skills.
5. Provision of feedback about learning progress to students
6. Provision of additional time and help to correct specified errors and misunderstandings of students who are not achieving the present mastery learning standards

The heart of mastery learning is the cycle of teaching, testing, reteaching, and retesting. Students are informed of the objectives of a given unit and then receive instruction designed to enable them to master those objectives. Upon completion of instruction and related practice activities, students receive formative evaluation tests designed to assess their mastery. Those who achieve preset performance standards (usually, passing at least 80 percent of the items on the test) are certified as having mastered the unit and are not required to do further work on it. These students then move on to the next unit, or more typically, work on enrichment activities or activities of their own choosing until the entire class is ready to move on. Meanwhile, students who do not meet mastery criteria receive corrective instruction and additional practice before their mastery levels are assessed again. Theoretically, these cycles of assessment and reteaching could go on indefinitely until all students reach mastery, but in practice, attempts to bring students to mastery usually cease after the second test, and the class then moves to the next unit. Thus, in practice, group-based mastery learning programs are a compromise between traditional programs that allow little if any extra time for slow learners and ideal mastery programs that would allow all learners as much time as they needed.

Mastery approaches clearly can increase (often dramatically) the percentage of students who master basic objectives, and they benefit low achievers. They provide extra time and instruction to enable low achievers to master more content than they would master otherwise, and this additional mastery is likely to bring motivational benefits as well. In particular, mastery approaches are likely to convince chronic low achievers that the old academic "game" has been replaced by a new one that gives them a chance to "win" consistently if they have appropriate learning strategies and apply reasonable effort. Thus, at least some attempt to implement the mastery learning philosophy appears desirable.

It seems to us, however, that the emphasis should be on maximizing each student's achievement *progress*, even if this means maintaining or even increasing the range of student individual differences in achievement *levels* in a class. It appears that the mastery approach will not reduce the time that slow learners need to learn (relative to the time that fast learners need), so teachers can reduce individual differences in achievement progress only by deliberately holding back fast learners. This is not to say that teachers should continually push fast learners to master more of the curriculum instead of allowing them to engage in enrichment activities or alternative tasks. We do suggest, however, that the activities planned for fast learners should be selected for sound pedagogical reasons and not as mere time fillers designed to slow their progress through the curriculum in order to pursue the (inappropriate) goal of reducing individual differences in achievement levels within a class. A sensible compromise to this dilemma may be to identify learning objectives that seem most essential and see that all students master these objectives, while tolerating more variable performance on objectives considered less essential. Teachers can supplement the basic curriculum with enrichment opportunities that students work on individually or in groups during times when the teachers are busy teaching remedial or enrichment lessons to small groups of students. Furthermore, during some types of small-group assignments what is new content for some students is review material for others. Finally, although teachers' major task is to promote students' academic progress, teachers must also attend to other important outcomes like an ability to work constructively with others, fair play, and so on (McCaslin & Good, in press). Thus, while some activities meet students' academic needs, the same activities may meet other students' social or affective needs.

INDIVIDUALIZED INSTRUCTION

Mastery learning allows for student differences in time needed to learn, but it calls for using essentially the same methods and materials to move all students toward mastery of the same achievement goals. A more powerful form of accommodation is to retain the same achievement goals but introduce variation not only in time to learn but in the methods and materials used to accomplish this learning. Individualized instructional methods can allow more extreme forms of accommodation: They enable students to pursue different achievement goals and allow students a great deal of autonomy in deciding not only what to learn but how to learn it.

Some individualized approaches allow students to learn using different materials or methods but require them to show mastery in the same way. Still others allow demonstration of mastery in different ways (written report, written exam, oral exam, etc.). As Savage and Armstrong (1992) note, there are four major variables that can be altered to individualize instruction: rate of learning, content of learning, method of learning, and goals of learning. However, these variables can take many forms and can be combined in multiple ways. Thus, there is a range of individualized instructional concepts and programs. Teachers can create their own programs, for example, by adapting an individualized mathematics program to their classes but using whole-class methods to teach other subjects.

Wang and Lindvall (1984) list the following distinguishing features of *adaptive education* approaches:

1. Instruction is based on the assessed capabilities of each student
2. Materials and procedures permit each student to progress at a pace suited to his or her abilities and interests
3. Periodic evaluations inform the student concerning mastery
4. Students assume responsibility for identifying needs and abilities, planning learning activities, and evaluating mastery

5. Alternative activities and materials aid student acquisition of essential academic skills and content
6. Students exercise choice in selecting educational goals, outcomes, and activities
7. Students assist one another in pursuing individual goals and cooperate in achieving group goals

Few individualized instruction or adaptive education programs have all seven of these features, but most have several of them.

Reformers calling for individualization or adaptation of the traditional model of schooling have been active in every educational era, and at least some of their suggestions have been adopted by about one-third of the elementary teachers but less than one-fifth of secondary teachers at any given time (Cuban, 1984). Usually these innovations call for shifting responsibility for planning and accomplishing learning from the teacher to the student and for shifting responsibility for communicating content from the teacher to instructional materials, because it is not possible for one teacher to meet the needs of all students in a class simultaneously (Jackson, 1985). The innovations are popularized by committed advocates (usually without data to back up the claims made), thrive briefly, and then wane. Certain elements of the innovations sometimes are assimilated into traditional schooling, but the innovations are not retained as "total packages" that supplant traditional schooling. Typically, this is because reformers give too much emphasis to social and motivational aspects and not enough to curriculum and instruction, make unwarranted assumptions about students' capabilities for independent goal setting and learning, or produce materials that are focused too much on low-level isolated skills and involve too much testing or other managerial complexities (Grinder & Nelsen, 1985). Similar problems (low-level exercises) have been observed in computer software designed to assist in individualizing instruction (Beynon & MacKay, 1993).

Individualization has become easier in recent years with the development of materials and methods designed to allow teachers to differentiate instruction for different students. Many specialized materials are augmented with audiovisual components (filmstrips, audiotaped or videotaped instruction, computer software) and provide instruction and practice opportunities for students without involving the teacher. There is also advice about how to select appropriate media (see Gagné, Briggs, & Wager, 1992). Usually there is some initial assessment to determine where students should begin, and after that students work on their own. In heavily individualized programs, students receive more instruction from the curriculum materials than from the teacher, who acts more as a materials manager, tester, and progress monitor than as an instructor in the usual sense of the word. However, again we assert that teachers should be decision makers, and accordingly, teachers might adapt individualized programs and use them in some subjects (in part to develop students' skills for time management, etc.) but not others. Further, teachers need to critically assess the content of curriculum materials and supplement as necessary (e.g., higher-order questions and application exercises).

Most individualized instructional materials use principles of *programmed instruction* in which students are moved in small steps from "entry-level" performance toward ultimate objectives. Programs are divided into self-contained modules ready for independent use by individual students. Each module reviews prerequisite knowledge or skills and introduces new information and opportunities to practice by having students answer questions or carry out tasks. Students receive immediate feedback after they respond, and some programs have diagnostic and remediation features that allow students to skip segments they have mastered or to get extra instruction on material that they have not mastered by working through the regular program.

Research on Individualized Learning

Information about student achievement in individualized programs is often hard to evaluate because it is confined to scores on criterion-referenced tests that come with the programs. Such data usually show success in meeting the objectives of the program as formulated by its developers, at least in classes where the program is considered to be well implemented. However, such data do not allow conclusions about either the absolute effectiveness or the cost effectiveness of these programs in comparison with traditional approaches (Educational Products Information Exchange, 1974).

Comparisons of individualized programs with traditional instruction typically report no differences or minor differences, with more variation within than between the two types of programs (Bangert, Kulik, & Kulik, 1983; Horak, 1981). The best results appear to be associated with frequent assessment, student self-management and choice, and peer cooperation rather than with reliance on individualized progress through programmed materials.

Part of the problem in evaluating individualized programs is that their implementation differs from classroom to classroom and from year to year. Most models offer teachers flexibility in structuring the program. Thus, two teachers ostensibly using the same program may implement it very differently, and teachers using a presumably individualized program may do just as much group-based instruction and no more individualized instruction than teachers in traditional self-contained classrooms. Many evaluation attempts did not include classroom observation to verify whether a program was implemented as the designers intended, so it is not always clear what comparisons of "individualized" and "traditional" programs mean.

Slavin (1984) suggests that for any kind of instruction to be effective, four conditions must be satisfied: (1) The instruction must be high in quality, (2) the instruction must be appropriate to students' levels, (3) students must be motivated to work on tasks, and (4) students must have adequate time to learn. Slavin argues that individualized instructional programs have not lived up to expectations because they have concentrated on increasing the appropriateness of instruction but have not addressed the other three essential conditions. Quality of instruction was reduced because students were not taught directly by the teacher and were instead required to learn on their own. Students were not adequately motivated because individualized instruction was often boring and seldom offered incentives for moving through the curriculum rapidly. Finally, much classroom time was spent on procedural matters (passing out material, waiting for the teacher to check work, taking tests), to the point that time for learning was actually reduced in many cases.

Arlin (1982), Carlson (1982), Everhart (1983), and Jones et al. (1985) also provide discussion and examples of the difficulties teachers had implementing individualized instructional programs and how students' actual experience in the classroom fell far short of what the programs' developers had envisioned. Some of these problems are remediable: Developers can supply more and better materials to teachers, offer a more balanced and integrative curriculum rather than focus on low-level isolated skills, and supply multimedia components that reduce students' need to learn exclusively through reading. The basic problem, however, seems to be the student-teacher ratio. No individualized program is likely to work effectively if it depends on the teacher to provide individualized instruction simultaneously to all students in a class, especially if the teacher is expected to develop curriculum materials for the program as well. So, unless adaptive education programs are implemented in small classes, or unless significant help from aides or other adults is available, such programs have to rely on other strategies.

Computerized Instruction

Another approach to individualized instruction that might overcome the problems with learning systems is computerized instruction, especially now that personal computers (PCs) are widely available in classrooms. Assuming comparable instructional content, computerized instruction offers several advantages over conventional textbooks and programmed learning materials.

First, computer instruction brings novelty or at least variety to students' school experiences and thus is likely to be more enjoyable than conventional seatwork. Second, especially if combined with videodisc technology, computer instruction can incorporate animation, time-lapse photography, and other audiovisual techniques for communicating information and demonstrating processes in ways that are not possible through conventional print materials. Third, computers can allow students to respond more actively and in more varied ways than they can respond to conventional seatwork, and can provide students with immediate feedback following their responses. Fourth, computers can be programmed to keep track of students' responses to exercises and tests, thus accumulating records for teachers to use in monitoring progress and planning remedial instruction. Fifth, it is possible to build the capacity for identification and remediation of learning problems into the program itself so that students automatically skip parts that they do not need and work through appropriate remedial sequences (technologies for dynamic assessment have improved notably—see, for example, Lajoie & Lesgold, 1992). Sixth, programs can provide not only opportunities to practice and get feedback but also tutorial instruction and friendly encouragement similar to those students might receive from a tutor. Finally, computerized instruction can offer opportunities for higher-level problem solving and simulation activities that are seldom seen in conventional seatwork or programmed individualized instruction. For example, computer technology could allow students in Ann Arbor, Michigan; Tucson, Arizona; and Perth, Australia to work cooperatively to create networks of information in order to test hypotheses about environmental issues (Soloway, 1991). To the extent that these potential advantages of computerized instruction can be achieved at reasonable cost, transferring significant instructional functions from the teacher to the computer might be a feasible way of implementing individualized instruction or adaptive educational principles in typical classrooms (Lipson & Fisher, 1983; Taylor, 1980).

It remains to be seen whether computerized instruction's theoretical potential can become a practical reality. To date, reviewers interested in computer applications in ordinary classrooms have identified several important limitations on computers' usefulness (Amarel, 1983; Becker, 1982; Beynon & MacKay, 1992; Brophy & Hannon, 1985; Carver et al., 1992; Educational Products Information Exchange, 1985; Hancock, Caput, & Goldsmith, 1992; Lesgold, 1983; Sloan, 1985). One major problem is a paucity of appropriate software. Too many programs available even today are nothing more than electronic versions of traditional workbooks that provide drill and practice on low-level skills (Beynon & MacKay, 1993). Once the novelty of using the computer wears off, a steady diet of these programs is likely to be just as boring as repeated workbook exercises, and even less efficient (students with a grasp of the concepts and skills involved can move quickly through a workbook, but in working through a computerized version of the same exercise, they would have to type in each response and wait for confirmation before going on to the next item). Also, most programs are short modules (requiring only an hour or two at most to complete) designed to provide drill and practice on just one or a small set of related skills. They do not constitute systematically sequenced and integrated curricula designed to provide a full semester of instruction in conventionally taught elementary or secondary courses. Thus, teachers may have difficulty finding good software, and even when they do, they are likely to be unclear about when or how to use the program because it will not be integrated with official curriculum objectives and materials that underlie instruction. For this reason, most teachers use computerized instruction only for enrichment with faster students or remedial drill and practice with slower students, even when they are not hampered by the problems discussed here.

Limited access to computers creates additional problems. Cost considerations (including future projections) mean that school systems are unlikely to supply typical classrooms with more than one or two computers (except for classrooms equipped for instruction in computer programming). A great many more computers would be needed to implement programs that call for students to spend a significant amount of time at the computer. Survey data indicate that even in classrooms containing eight computers, students may spend as much as three-fourths of their time waiting for a turn at the computer (Center for Social Organization of Schools, 1984). This problem can be alleviated somewhat by having students work in small groups with a single computer (Clements & Nastasi, 1988), although almost all available software is designed for use by individuals, and adaptation to group use may be difficult. Further, it is clear that in many situations some students tend to dominate the computer while other students watch (Beynon & MacKay, 1993).

Although many exciting uses of computers are emerging (e.g., on-line searching of remote data bases, electronic newspapers, etc.), many teachers will continue to rely on drill and practice programs and educational games. Thus, computerized instruction is not yet a solution (e.g., limited software) to the practical problems involved in implementing individualized instruction in the typical classroom. Still, it offers worthwhile opportunities for teachers who have access to PCs. An evaluation of a computerized drill and practice curriculum tested in the Los Angeles schools (Ragosta, Holland, & Jamison, 1981) showed that even though students often complained of boredom, the program increased mathematical computation skills. Findings were mixed for mathematical concepts and were less positive in language and reading than in mathematics.

Some important advances in software are beginning to occur. For example, Stewart et al. (1992) describe simulation software (Genetics Construction Kit) that allows high school students to solve genetics problems. The investigators agree that the computer program allowed students to engage in many of the important activities of geneticists. Students were able to perform complex tests quickly, and the classroom approximated a professional scientific community. As more such programs are developed, the role of the computer in the classroom will expand.

Tucker (1983) provides advice about how schools can intelligently purchase and use computers. Lathrop (1982) offers guidelines (and a bibliography) for evaluating software. Finally, the Educational Products Information Exchange (1985) describes and critically reviews hundreds of software products sold for use in schools.

Need for Research

Sutton (1991) reviews research conducted during the 1980s on effects of race and ethnicity, social class, and gender on computer use in K through 12 classrooms. She documents that all three factors affect access to computers. Although gender differences in access appear to be small (several studies reported no significant differences), all analyses indicated that boys had more access. In no study were girls found to have greater access. Sutton reports that four national surveys conducted during the 1980s on computer access found that poor and minority children consistently had less access than other students to computers both at home and at school, although inequities in school-related access were lower in higher grades and decreased during the 1980s. Sutton concludes that the use of computers has maintained and exaggerated inequalities and that poor and minority students' access to computers in schools should be increased.

Computers: Advantages and Disadvantages

Lepper and Gurtner (1989) provide a balanced analysis of the potential uses and misuses of computers in the classroom. Concerning the former, they note:

> Imagine a 21st-century school in which each student is provided a portable computer comparable to current state-of-the-art machines in artificial intelligence. Imagine, as well, that these machines are linked to laser-disk devices, each capable of randomly accessing 56,000 "pages" of text on a single disk and are networked to one another. This entire system, moreover, is tied into a telecommunications network that permits classroom computers to communicate with students' homes, national data files, and other schools thousands of miles away. What opportunities for learning and motivation might such a truly technology-rich classroom provide? [p. 170]

Lepper and Gurtner point out that many have argued that the potential of the computer is immense. For example, the computer can be used as a personal tutor (making the learning of traditional school content more effective, providing detailed models of expertise in particular content areas, and providing students with precise analyses of their misconceptions), provide a context for experiential learning (e.g., simulations of scientific experiments that might be too complex or dangerous for students to undertake), or serve as a multipurpose tool (reduce the drudgery of editing one's work, help students organize their knowledge of a topic). Computer use also has motivational and social effects (e.g., to make learning fun, increase cooperation and collaboration among students, increase equality of opportunity).

Lepper and Gurtner note, however, that other educators have raised concerns about the use of the computer in the classroom. For example, some worry about regimentation and dehumanization of the classroom, and that computerization may bring homogenization rather than individualization of instruction. Computer use ultimately might increase inequality. For example, better software may be more expensive or harder to find. Hence, school districts with fewer resources are more likely to use drill and practice software. Others argue that computerization may inadvertently shape the curriculum in unintended ways. For example, subjects like mathematics and science may be more successfully adapted to computers than history, art, or literature, which involve a variety of thought processes. Students may focus primarily on rational problem solving rather than artistic or evaluative aspects of the last three subjects. Finally, some critics question the generalization of computer-based learning. For example, if student motivation depends on the use of features like color technology, will students be interested in material that does not contain such features?

The reader interested in more information about uses of the computer (e.g., as a personal tutor, for experiential learning, etc.) can consult Lepper and Gurtner. Although these authors are generally positive about the potential of computers, they indicate that there is little high-quality research in this area:

> Yet good research is sorely lacking. In part, this lack of research is a result of the unprecedented speed with which computers have moved into our lives, making it difficult for researchers to keep up with the latest advances in hardware and software and to distinguish transitory from lasting phenomena. At the same time, the dearth of empirical research is also the result of an attitude of disdain for systematic or evaluative research within some segments of the computer community. . . . Whatever the reasons underlying the paucity of good experimental research on educational computing, the result is clear: Seldom can one find unequivocal empirical answers to the debates we have just considered. [p. 175]

Conclusions About Individualized Instruction

It is difficult to generalize about programs for individualized instruction or adaptive education because of their variety and because, in practice, programs are often different from developers' views of implementation. Programs that use materials concentrating on repetitive drill of low-level isolated skills seem clearly inadequate. So do programs that actually reduce instructional time by requiring students to spend a great deal of time handling procedural matters or simply waiting for attention from the teacher.

Good and Stipek (1983) conclude that no dimension of individual differences has unambiguous implications for instruction. It seems more appropriate to develop high-quality instructional materials and methods intended for all students than to set out from the beginning to develop different materials and methods for various students. Still, some students need more instruction or learning time than others, students having difficulty learning may need to be retaught in a different way rather than using more of the same instruction, and teachers can include a degree of individualization within this general approach by drawing on their knowledge of students' individual needs, interests, and learning styles (see Corno & Snow, 1986 for a comprehensive discussion of student individual differences in educational settings).

Another criticism of individualized instruction is that although it is well suited to drill and practice in basic facts, concepts, and skills, it is not well suited to instruction in higher cognitive processes (problem solving, thinking, creativity) or to developing general dispositional states such as interests, attitudes, or values (Jackson, 1985). This criticism appears to be valid, and it is one reason why we recommend that individualized instruction requiring students to learn from curriculum materials be used in combination with, rather than instead of, whole-class or small-group instruction from the teacher.

Active instruction from the teacher has its own motivational and instructional advantages. It often saves both teachers and students a great deal of time, and teacher presentation underscores the importance of the content and provides the teacher with an opportunity to make it come alive for students. Also, research on factors associated with student achievement gain suggests that teachers who spend considerable time actively instructing students obtain better achievement than teachers who rely on curriculum materials to carry the content. Active instruction from the teacher is especially important for younger students, slower students, and students who come from less advantaged home backgrounds.

Even older, brighter students who seem to be progressing well through individualized learning programs can run into trouble if left on their own too long. Often, they do not even realize the problem. Erlwanger (1975) interviewed bright students who were consistently meeting mastery criteria on unit tests from their individualized mathematics curriculum. He found that many of them had misunderstood the material and developed mathematical conceptions that were at least partly incorrect, even though they were able to get the correct answers to application exercises and test items. The students had invented their own rules of thumb, which were useful for solving particular problems but would not work (and would leave the students badly confused) later on when they had to apply concepts to new situations. VanSledright and Brophy (1993) report similar problems in social studies education (i.e., to change students' naive concepts requires appropriate instruction).

Such findings illustrate a complaint that many teachers have voiced about individualized programs: Their students "can pass the tests but don't understand the concept." This is likely to happen if mastery criteria are set too low (70 to 80 percent instead of 90 to 100 percent) or if students continually retake the same test so that they actually memorize the answers. Even with stiffer mastery criteria and several forms of each test, however, student confusion can go undetected unless teachers monitor progress closely and require students to explain concepts in their own words or show their work in detail (not just supply answers to highly structured questions).

In conclusion, we do not recommend individualized instruction if it means that students spend most of their time working on their own trying to learn from curriculum materials. However, we do favor individualization when it accommodates individuals' needs within the group context and achieves an appropriate balance of instructional activities (whole-class instruction, small-group instruction, cooperative learning activities, individual work). Even within the traditional whole-class approach, teachers can individualize instruction to a degree by taking students' interests into account in presenting content and making assignments, by asking different kinds of questions or giving varied assignments to different students, by allowing student choice and autonomy when the objectives can be met in different ways, by providing enrichment for faster learners and extra instruction in basic skills for slower learners, and by using some of the specialized small-group and individualized learning approaches we discuss here and in Chapter 7.

SUPPLEMENTAL INSTRUCTION FOR AT-RISK STUDENTS

Before discussing individual work adjustments that teachers can make in the classroom without new equipment, materials, and so forth, we want to stress that most attempts to provide supplemental instruction for low achievers have failed. We believe this has occurred largely because educators have paid too much attention to deficits and too little attention to making instruction meaningful.

Shepard (1991) argues that most strategies for dealing with diversity have not improved the educational lives of students. In particular, tracking, special education through pull-out instruction, grade retention, kindergarten retention, and programs for at-risk kindergartners all have tended to individualize instruction by placing children in homogeneous groups where they could receive more "appropriate" instruction. Shepard and other researchers have concluded that, ironically, pupils in any of these arrangements are likely to receive poorer instruction than if they had remained in regular classrooms. Further compounding inequality is the more frequent assignment of students from culturally and linguistically disadvantaged backgrounds to these remediation programs.

Shepard articulates four principles that provide a theoretical perspective for planning appropriate instruction for diverse student populations. First, recognize that intelligence and reasoning are developed abilities. Students who have difficulty learning rote material and who are retained in first grade (and who receive similar instruction the following year) are unlikely to learn to read for meaning. Students need opportunities to plan and evaluate their own learning and to develop strategies for self-checking and problem solving, so a steady diet of work focused on structure and drill is ineffective.

Second, recognize that developed ability and learning-to-learn strategies are largely context specific, although some aptitudes for problem solving and strategies for integrating information may transfer across situations. For example, students who have a great deal of practical knowledge about mathematics (e.g., they frequently go to the store with parents, plan a budget, and so forth) will have developed the language and social interaction patterns necessary to appear capable during mathematics instruction. However, this does not necessarily mean that these students will be proficient at social studies or playing chess. Shepard contends: "The children who have developed the language and social interaction patterns appropriate in one context will look ignorant and deficient to teachers who are unaware of the arbitrary language and learning conventions they impose on the basis of their own cultural norms" (p. 294). Teachers need to be aware of and to use the learning strategies students have developed and need to show students how to use their knowledge in new ways.

Third, learning is a constructive process. Students do not learn effectively when they are presented with many discrete pieces of information, especially when these pieces seem unconnected. To learn successfully, students must be able to construct mental images of relationships among concepts, ideas, and facts. Students need the opportunity to think about material, not just to memorize and rehearse it.

Finally, *meaning is socially constructed.* How and what children learn are highly dependent on their histories as learners and the social arrangements that support their learning at home and school.

According to Shepard, these four principles provide a framework for considering appropriate instruction in diverse settings. She writes,

> It follows from these principles that effective instruction should engage children in meaningful, contextually situated tasks where the goal is to practice and develop strategic thinking about important subject matter. The progress of instruction should be designed to help students use what they already know to arrive at new understandings. Prior knowledge is defined not just as vocabulary and information mastery, but includes all of the images, language patterns, social relations, and personal experiences that a student relies on to make sense of something new. [p. 295]

Allington (1991) notes that although individualization is frequently mentioned as a strategy for dealing with students who have difficulty learning, there is actually little evidence that individualization occurs—that is, that the amount or type of instruction these children receive differs from what other students receive. Few reliable effects of individualized instruction can be documented in studies of schools (Leinhardt, Zigmund, & Cooley, 1981), primarily because students who receive individualized instruction typically do not receive adjustments in instruction that are appropriate or of high quality.

McGill-Franzen and Allington (1990) conducted an observational study to determine what individualized instruction actually meant for remedial and special education students. They found that at-risk learners usually worked alone on tasks involving low-level skills. Ironically, when learners were assigned to a remedial resource room, the "individualized" instruction was often identical for all students in the room, despite the fact that their "learning problems" often varied considerably. This finding is similar to the paradox that Fraatz (1987) found—that schools attempt to teach all children in a similar way in order to guarantee equity, although in order to provide appropriate individualization, it is necessary to teach each child differently.

Theoretically, individualized instruction can be effective. In practice, however, attempts to individualize instruction by removing students from the regular classroom or placing them in a separate program are usually fraught with difficulties. We agree with Allington (1991, p. 246):

> Little of what is done in the name of individualization in schools seems to address an individual child's instructional needs. When decisions abut individual needs lead to smaller amounts of instruction, to reduced curriculum coverage, to the neglect of comprehension development, and to perpetuation of low-achievement status for some children, one must question whether those children are well served.

RESEARCH ON DIFFERENTIAL CLASSROOM INSTRUCTION

There is some research on the topic of differential instruction. We discuss two research studies here that were conducted in secondary classes.

Instruction in Secondary English Classes

Some form of differentiated instruction to groups or individuals may be necessary when classroom composition is extremely heterogeneous. Research by Everston, Sanford, and Emmer (1981) illustrates methods teachers have used to cope with these difficult situations. The study focused on ways junior high English teachers adapted instruction in heterogeneous classrooms compared with the ways they taught more homogeneous classes. The heterogeneous classes had 8- to 10-year spreads in grade-level-equivalent units between low and high achievers.

Observations revealed that all of the heterogeneous classes got off to a bad start because the methods and materials used seemed poorly adapted to students' interests and abilities, and success rates in terms of completeness and correctness of assignments were low. This pattern then continued or deteriorated further in heterogeneous classes in which the teachers lacked the managerial skills to respond effectively to the problem. However, after about three weeks, the more effective teachers were able to overcome these problems to some extent by using the following strategies: (1) special attention and help for lower-ability students; (2) limited use of within-class grouping and differentiated materials or assignments; (3) limited differential grading based on individualized effort and continuous-progress criteria;

(4) limited use of peer tutoring; and (5) frequent monitoring and provision of academic feedback to all students, coupled with mechanisms to ensure student accountability for participating in lessons and completing assignments.

Because of these teachers' managerial and instructional skills, not to mention their sheer energy and determination, there was no difference in achievement gain between the heterogeneous and the homogeneous classes. Still, there were limits on what could be accomplished. The pressures of meeting the greater range of instructional needs in the heterogeneous classes left the teachers with little time for personalized interaction with students, especially interaction concerning non academic topics. In the poorly managed heterogeneous classes, there were also year-long problems of frequent student boredom or frustration due to inappropriate assignments. Probably because of these problems, ratings of student task engagement and cooperation remained lower in the heterogeneous classes throughout the year. Thus, this study illustrates that heterogeneous classes present difficulties, but that teachers can respond effectively to them by using appropriate techniques for managing the classroom and providing differentiated instruction. Teachers need to be sure that they use a variety of formats and consider both affective and cognitive goals when teaching heterogeneous groups. With careful planning, teachers can allow for new learning and appropriate practice and review for all students in the same lesson.

Response to Heterogeneity in a British School

Evans (1985) presented an interesting ethnographic study of what happened when a comprehensive secondary school (grades 7 through 9) in England switched from the traditional streamed (i.e., tracked) arrangement to mixed-ability grouping. Many teachers persisted with whole-class methods directed toward students with high or medium achievement within the class, just as they had done previously when students had been tracked. Typically teachers reduced teacher-led class instruction and increased individualized seatwork assignments, but essentially, these teachers taught the heterogeneous groups as whole classes.

Consequently, teachers were forced to slow the pace of instruction and concentrate even more than before on lower-level facts and skills rather than higher-level cognitive objectives. As a result, many of the brightest students were bored and many of the slowest students still had difficulty keeping up. Lacking the time to teach the latter students to the level of true mastery, teachers "piloted" these students through the curriculum. They often gave answers to students who did not supply them, responded to weak answers as if they indicated full understanding, and "summarized" answers in ways that actually elaborated on them considerably. Similarly, the teachers guided slower students through individualized seatwork assignments by simplifying directions and giving feedback in ways that converted cognitive tasks into mere procedural tasks. They often allowed students to copy answers from peers or to look them up in the back of the book without truly understanding how to arrive at these answers or why they were correct. Thus, teachers who persisted with whole-class methods in highly heterogeneous classes accepted the appearance of progress from slower students in the place of actual progress in mastering the curriculum. They also tended to leave high achievers underchallenged, or, in the case of foreign language classes, to use high achievers as the "steering group" to determine pacing of the whole class through the curriculum. Here, the high achievers appeared to be the only students who enjoyed the classes or understood the content as the year progressed.

Science teachers typically coped by emphasizing topic-centered, group-based instruction that allowed students to address common topics at a variety of levels of sophistication. All students worked on the same topic during a given unit, but the work was divided into a number of investigatory or practical activities on which the students worked in groups (predominantly from booklets). Activities were organized to include basic work that was required and optional enrichment work so that less able groups did only the former, but more able groups moved on to the latter. Because topics were not sequenced linearly, each new topic presented new opportunities for students to learn and achieve success, yet the variety of levels of sophistication at which each topic could be addressed provided opportunities for differentiated instruction. The brighter students tended to do much more writing, for example.

The advantages of this approach were counterbalanced by management problems. The teachers found it difficult to get around often enough to supervise the progress of each group and to establish workable classroom rules and routines that would encourage students to discuss content but at the same time discourage them from merely socializing during the group-work times. Pacing tended to be determined by the high achievers within groups, so that low achievers sometimes were ignored or ended up being directed by high achievers. Gender differences in student activities also were noticeable in these science classes: Boys tended to be more assertive in planning and conducting investigations and experiments, whereas girls were more likely merely to observe or record information. Not much truly cooperative learning occurred, in part because the materials and booklets were not written with that in mind, and also because teachers did not train students in cooperative learning principles. Mathematics teachers typically shifted from whole-class to individualized instruction based on programmed learning materials and encountered the problems we discussed earlier.

Most social studies teachers used a combination of whole-class instruction and individual seatwork. Seatwork assignments were not individualized as in math classes, but there usually was some differentiation of assignments according to student ability. Much of the seatwork was less effective than it could have been because of legibility problems and other physical deficiencies in the materials, and many assignments were at such low cognitive levels that they could be accomplished with little or no thinking or writing (beyond one word).

Extra materials and assignments (usually open-ended tasks) were provided to keep brighter students occupied until the class was ready to move on to new content. Teachers made rounds and dealt with individuals briefly as in the individualized math classes, but there usually was less need for help in social studies classes, so that teachers spent less time actually talking to students once whole-class instruction was finished. Thus, both the level and the amount of instruction in social studies were reduced for most of these students compared with what occurred previously during whole-class instruction in tracked classes.

English teachers could not be characterized in any simple way because they showed the most variability in curriculum (what they taught) and instruction (how they taught). In general, those who emphasized basic skills (spelling, grammar, etc.) stressed low-level seatwork assignments, whereas those who emphasized higher-level language arts objectives (critical reading of prose or poetry, written compositions, etc.) relied on whole-class instruction followed by differentiated assignments.

GENERAL PRINCIPLES FOR DIFFERENTIATING INSTRUCTION

The experiences just described and others involved with teaching heterogeneous classes suggest certain general principles. First, as the range of student ability increases, the role of whole-class teaching decreases, although students in mixed-ability classes can still benefit from exchanging ideas in a large-group setting (speaking before a group, etc.). Furthermore, managerial issues, unit introductions and reviews of use of equipment, demonstration of experiments, and certain other types of information exchange still lend themselves to whole-class presentations in mixed-ability classes. In general, though, the frequency and duration of whole-class teaching will be reduced, and teachers' use of individual assignments and small-group work will increase.

Matching Assignments to Student Ability

The following discussion focuses on ways to develop individual and small-group assignments that allow students of varying ability to work on similar projects. Some students can read well and do so enthusiastically; others have limited skills and interest in reading. If teachers are to allow students of mixed ability to work on similar projects, they must solve the reading problem. One strategy for doing this is to instruct students in independent reading and study skills. Another is to gather a wide assortment of materials written at varying levels of difficulty on a few core topics (it is unrealistic to try to acquire and store several books on every curriculum topic).

Although they read books that differ in detail or vocabulary, students can also read materials with a common focus on historical events (the Civil War) or famous persons (Booker T. Washington, Marie Curie, Babe Ruth). Furthermore, many stories of literary significance are written with a low vocabulary demand (e.g., *Tom Sawyer*). Students reading at different grade levels could benefit from reading these books, even though the teacher may eventually ask them to respond to the books in different ways.

Use of Multiple Reading Sources

Memory and Uhlhorn (1991) argue that despite the advantages of using textbooks and other sources that vary in readability, this instructional approach is less applicable than it appears. According to these authors, one reason teachers do not prepare a variety of reading materials in science is because previous research has provided little support for their doing so. However, Memory and Uhlhorn note that a more valid conclusion from extant research is "that weak readers do not benefit from materials originally written for more able readers and modified to present the same concepts in language that yields lower readability scores than the original language" (p. 66). Thus, less skilled readers are likely to learn less content from textbooks than are more capable readers, and curriculum materials to be used with students at different reading levels must be written with those students in mind from the start.

Memory and Uhlhorn note that there are many appropriate but easy-reading materials in science, and they offer suggestions for teachers who want to use text-books (or other materials) at different readability levels in their classes. First, as teachers select easier textbooks, they need to consider whether the books contain helpful comprehension questions at the end of brief chapters. Poor readers, at least initially, are unlikely to read for extended periods, and hence, selections should be relatively brief. Perhaps more important, the text should encourage students to consider content and to integrate it with their previous knowledge. Thus, appropriate comprehension questions must be raised—not simple, factual questions. In particular, Memory and Uhlhorn suggest that teachers should not use reading materials with the types of questions at the end of chapters that divert students' attention from key concepts by focusing on unimportant information.

A third consideration for using a variety of texts is to schedule comparable time for all students to work on reading assignments. Memory and Uhlhorn argue that even if students realize they are reading at different levels, there will be less social stigma if all students are expected to spend the same amount of time completing assignments (i.e., students with higher reading ability would read more words and pages and perhaps answer a few more questions).

In organizing and presenting a multilevel program in a way that students are likely to view as appropriate and equitable, teachers should outline the concepts that all students are to learn in each unit, regardless of the difficulty of texts students will use. Finally, Memory and Uhlhorn advocate the use of brief study guides presenting open-ended questions that alert students to significant content that all students are to master. Although teachers do not need to collect these written responses, they should emphasize that responding actively to material will help students prepare for class discussions and unit tests. Study guide questions should be prepared using the vocabulary of the text at the lowest reading difficulty. According to Memory and Uhlhorn, the potential benefits of using texts of varying difficulty are important enough to justify the extra planning and instructional difficulties they impose (e.g., explaining to parents, convincing administrators to purchase additional materials, etc.). Still, the authors note that little research supports the approach, and that teachers must adjust a reading program to meet the needs of their students. At least in science, however, textbooks written at different levels of difficulty exist, and teachers who are willing to develop multilevel programs should find them useful.

Ciborowski (1992) provides additional information about making textbooks suitable for work with low-achieving students. She argues that good readers and poor readers differ notably in how they think before, during, and after reading activities (these differences are presented in Table 8.1). For example, good readers are more likely than poor readers to think about what they already know about a subject when they begin reading. Hence, elementary and secondary teachers must help poor readers develop the skills and strategies that good readers already possess as well as make materials more accessible to poor readers. According to Ciborowski, many teachers need to teach students reading comprehension strategies so that students can understand what they read. The teacher cannot simply play the role of lecturer but rather must help low readers to take a more strategic, active role in reading. (For a review of research on strategy instruction see a special issue of the *Elementary School Journal* (November 1993) edited by Mike Pressely.) Teachers need to help readers to become more active, in having students predict what they think they will learn, what they would like to learn, and eventually summarize what they did learn and compare their conclusions with those of peers. Students need to contemplate the purpose of assigned work and to develop the skills for setting goals and self-evaluation. (See Figure 8.3. More of this in Chapter 10.)

Preparing Assignments

Even individualized assignments that do not demand a great deal of reading must be carefully prepared with low achievers in mind. If slow students are to comprehend written instructions and function independently, directions must be stated in clear and explicit terms. Otherwise, teachers spend too much time clarifying directions and responding to the managerial problems that occur when students do not know what to do. As students gain confidence in their independent learning skills, they can be challenged with progressively more complex tasks. Teachers must also be sensitive to the different backgrounds of students and ensure that students see the connection between tasks and their own experience.

Cooke (1976) suggests ways to develop individual seatwork cards for students of varying ability who are working on similar historical topics. Included in his suggestions are the following:

1. Develop a card for each topic and subtopic and require all students to complete these activities at their own pace.
2. Develop a number of option cards that provide guidelines for more intensive subject work, special activities, and so on, and allow students to choose from the option cards.
3. Do not try to develop option cards for each individual (both unnecessary and impractical) but do produce separate option (or even core) cards for *three or four ability levels.*

Figures 8.4, 8.5, and 8.6 illustrate work cards prepared for students at three ability levels. The figures show how the same historical topic could be pursued in different ways. Figure 8.4 shows the assignment for slow 12-year-olds. Notice that it focuses on concrete details (helping the student to search parts of a passage in order to find material to make comparatively simple judgments).

Figures 8.5 and 8.6 illustrate assignments for middle- and high-level students. Progressively, instructions are written in less specific terms, students are directed to search different books, page references are omitted in favor of references to

Table 8.1 A COMPARISON OF GOOD AND POOR READERS

Good Readers	Poor Readers
Before Reading	
Think about what they already know about a subject	Begin to read without thinking about the topic
Know the purpose for which they read	Do not know why they are reading
Are motivated or interested to begin reading	Lack interest and motivation to begin reading
Have a general sense of how the BIG ideas will fit together	Have little sense of how the BIG ideas will fit together
During Reading	
Pay simultaneous attention to words and meaning	Overattend to individual words; miss salience
Read fluently	Read slower and at the same rate of speed
Concentrate well while reading	Have difficulty concentrating, particularly during silent reading
Willing to "risk" encountering difficult words and able to grapple with text ambiguities	Unwilling to "risk;" easily defeated by difficult words and text
Constuct efficient strategies to monitor comprehension	Unable to construct efficient strategies to monitor comprehension
Stop to use a "fix-it" strategy when confused	Seldom use a "fix-it" strategy; plod on ahead, eager to finish
Reading skills improve	Reading progress is painfully slow
After Reading	
Understand how the pieces of information fit together	Do not understand how the pieces of information fit together
Able to identify what's salient	May focus on the extraneous, peripheral
Interested in reading more	See reading as distasteful

Adapted from the Orange County Public Schools, Department of Secondary Reading, Orlando Florida.

general sources or indexes, more deduction is demanded, and the use of supporting evidence for ideas is encouraged. For the most capable students, considerable initiative is required and more problem-solving questions are raised (dealing with conflicting accounts of history, etc.).

Students at all levels can benefit from problem-solving activities as well as from searching for facts and performing simple verification tasks. The work cards in Figures 8.4, 8.5, and 8.6 illustrate the relative emphasis that students of varying achievement levels need in seatwork assignments. To the extent that students who need "structure" receive and learn to handle appropriate learning assignments as depicted in Figure 8.4, they need more assignments like those in Figures 8.5 and 8.6.

Teachers have to decide when it is possible to keep students of mixed ability working on the same topic. Perhaps the best strategy in a subject like history is to

Chapter 6

**"Jamestown
The First
colony"**

What I think I'll learn

*where it
happened*

What I'd like to learn

*why it was
called Jamestown*

What I did learn
(to be completed in phase III)

*It was the 1st colony in 1608 and
it was a very hard colony to
happen because people got sick and
died but people worked hard and
prosperity came!*

Figure 8.3

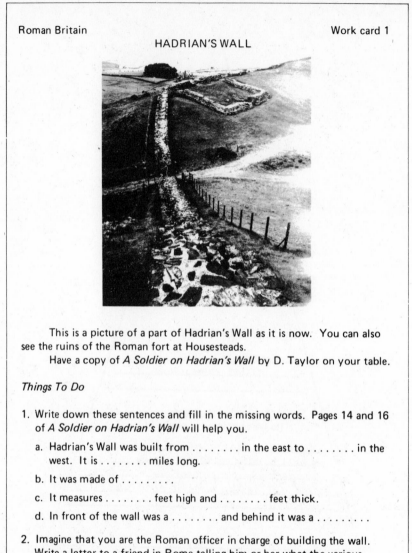

Roman Britain   Work card 1

HADRIAN'S WALL

This is a picture of a part of Hadrian's Wall as it is now. You can also see the ruins of the Roman fort at Housesteads.

Have a copy of *A Soldier on Hadrian's Wall* by D. Taylor on your table.

Things To Do

1. Write down these sentences and fill in the missing words. Pages 14 and 16 of *A Soldier on Hadrian's Wall* will help you.

 a. Hadrian's Wall was built from . . . . in the east to . . . . in the west. It is . . . . miles long.

 b. It was made of . . . .

 c. It measures . . . . feet high and . . . . feet thick.

 d. In front of the wall was a . . . . and behind it was a . . . .

2. Imagine that you are the Roman officer in charge of building the wall. Write a letter to a friend in Rome telling him or her what the various buildings on the wall are and what they are used for. You can find out about these buildings in your book, pp. 16-20.

3. Draw a diagram of one of the buildings in your letter. Label all the parts and sizes of it. If you prefer, make a model of it to scale.

4. Draw and color a picture showing a scene from Hadrian's Wall, perhaps an enemy attack or soldiers marching along it. From the picture on this card, imagine what it must have been like on the wall.

Figure 8.4 An example of a work card for low-achieving students.

Roman Britain

HADRIAN'S WALL

This is a picture of Hadrian's Wall today.

Read

> *A Soldier on Hadrian's Wall* by D. Taylor
>
> *Roman Britain* by R. Mitchell
>
> *Roman Britain* by J. Liversidge, pp. 16–33
>
> *The Romans in Scotland* by O. Thomson, Chapter 3

Things To Do

1. Answer these questions as fully as you can:

   a. Why did Hadrian build a wall across Britain?

   b. If you were an enemy of the Romans trying to break through the wall from the north, where do you think its weakest points would be? You will need to find information about the various forts and defenses along the wall.

   c. Another wall was built 20 years later by the Romans in Scotland. Which Emperor built it? Why was it built? How different was it from Hadrian's Wall?

2. Imagine that you are the Roman officer in charge of building Hadrian's Wall. Write a report to the Emperor telling him why you have decided to change the wall from turf to stone and to alter the size.

3. Draw a diagram of a cross-section of the wall, or of a fort, and label it carefully. If you prefer, make a scale model of it.

4. *Either,* as the Roman officer, write an entry for your diary describing an incident on the wall.
   Or, draw and color a picture of the incident.
   Do both of these if you wish.

Figure 8.5 An example of a work card for average students.

HADRIAN'S WALL

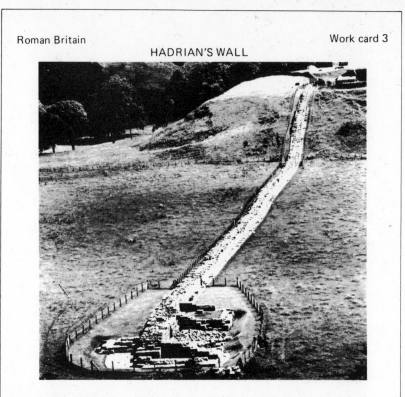

Consult the books in the class history library on Roman Britain, in particular *The Roman Frontiers of Britain* by D. R. Wilson; *The Roman Imperial Army of the First and Second Centuries* by G. Webster; *The Romans in Scotland* by O. Thomson; *Handbook to the Roman Wall* by I. A. Richmond.

1. Why did Hadrian build a wall across Britain between the Solway and the Tyne? Why were no other routes suitable?

2. Find a picture of a British hill fort (e.g., Maiden Castle or Hod Hill) and compare it with Housesteads as a fortification. Illustrate your answer.

3. If you were an enemy of the Romans trying to break through the wall from the north, where do you think its weakest points would be? Why?

4. The Emperor Antoninus Pius decided to build a wall in Scotland in about A.D. 142. Imagine and write a conversation between Antoninus and his senior advisor about building the wall in Scotland in which they discuss why Hadian's Wall is no longer suitable, and in what ways the new wall should be different.

5. *Either,* make a scale model *or* draw a picture of part of Hadrian's Wall. Do both if you wish.

Figure 8.6 An example of a work card for high-achieving students.

identify core topics that all students can learn and separate topics that more capable students can pursue at more complex and challenging levels. For example, all students might learn about the major causes of the Civil War, but only more capable students would be assigned to do research on the details of the leadership decisions that shaped them. For more about teaching mixed-ability students in a variety of subjects, see Evans (1985), Sands and Kerry (1982), or Wragg (1976).

Accommodating Students' Personal Characteristics

We have emphasized the need for building different assignments around common themes to allow students who differ in ability and achievement to address the same content at varying levels of sophistication. Students also differ, however, in personal and social traits such as energy, assertiveness, sociability, and patience. As teachers become more proficient at matching curriculum and instruction to students' achievement, they may wish to introduce additional individualization by accommodating differences in students' personalities, learning styles, or preferences.

The number of student factors that could be listed for consideration by teachers is endless, so there is no point in trying to construct an exhaustive list. However, we can present guidelines for differentiated instruction of a few common student types that teachers can expect to find in most classrooms. Good and Power (1976) identified the following five types of students:

1. Successful students are task oriented, academically successful, and cooperative. They typically participate actively in lessons, turn in complete and correct assignments, and create few if any discipline problems. They tend to like school and to be well liked by both teachers and peers.
2. Social students are more person oriented than task oriented. They have the ability to achieve but value socializing with friends more than working on assignments. They tend to have many friends and to be popular with peers but are usually not well liked by teachers because their frequent socializing creates management problems.
3. Dependent students frequently look to the teacher for support and encouragement and often ask for additional directions and help. Teachers generally are concerned about the academic progress of these students and do what they can to assist them. Peers may reject dependent students because they tend to be socially immature.
4. Alienated students are reluctant learners and potential dropouts. Extremely alienated students reject school and everything it stands for. Some are openly hostile and create disruptions through aggression and defiance. Others withdraw, sitting at the fringes of the classroom and refusing to participate. Teachers tend to reject students who express alienation openly and to be indifferent toward those who express it passively.
5. Phantom students seem to fade into the background because they are rarely noticed or heard from. Some are shy, nervous students; others are quiet, independent workers of average ability. They work steadily on assignments but rarely participate actively in group activities because they do not volunteer, and are rarely involved in managerial exchanges because

they do not create disruptions. Typically, neither teachers nor peers know these students very well or think about or interact with them very often. If asked to name all of their students from memory, teachers are likely to have the most difficulty remembering the names of phantom students.

After surveying the literature on these five types of students, Good and Power (1976) developed suggestions for ways that teachers might profitably introduce differentiated instruction to accommodate students' preferences and needs. We summarize some of their suggestions in Table 8.2.

Although based partly on research, the suggestions given in Table 8.2 are speculative rather than proven guidelines, for two reasons. First, accommodating students' preferences is not the same as meeting their needs. Several studies have shown that allowing students to choose their own learning methods or arranging to teach them in the ways that they prefer to be taught may produce *less* achievement than teaching them in some other way, even if it improves their attitudes toward learning (Clark, 1982; Schofield, 1981; Solomon & Kendall, 1979). Second, accommodating students' personal characteristics may reinforce these characteristics, including ones that the teacher would rather change if possible. For example, it would be easy to respond reciprocally to the behavior of phantom students and passive-withdrawn or alienated students by minimizing interaction with them— never calling on them unless they raise their hand or indicate a need for help. This behavior might even maximize the comfort of both the teacher and the students involved. However, it probably would not be in these students' best interests.

Even though such complexities must be kept in mind, Table 8.2 offers suggestions for introducing a degree of individualization into your instruction while primarily teaching the class as a group. Some of these suggestions can be incorporated easily (such as those that involve interacting more often or more affectively with certain students), whereas others would be more difficult or time consuming to implement (e.g., preparing different activities or assignments for different groups of students). It may not be possible to introduce such variation into the activities and assignments planned for each day, but these guidelines are useful for judging the appropriateness of longer-range plans. Each week or unit should provide enough balance to deliver something for everyone rather than involve activities and assignments that are well matched to the needs of only one or two subgroups but poorly matched to the needs of others.

A single teacher cannot provide optimal curriculum and instruction to all students in a class simultaneously, because different subgroups present conflicting needs and because classroom management considerations take first priority. For example, dependent students (at least until they are taught self-supervision skills and gain the confidence necessary for exercising these skills) need close supervision and frequent teacher feedback during independent seatwork. However, wise teachers reserve the first few minutes of seatwork to make sure that students in general and alienated students in particular get started on their assignments. Furthermore, teachers learn to keep their interactions with individuals brief so that they can continue to circulate around the room and be available to students who need immediate help. All students, even the most successful, need monitoring and feedback.

Despite these complexities, teachers who have developed a workable system for instructing the whole class can then use this system as a base from which to introduce differentiated instruction for various students. In this regard, it helps if a variety of work settings or assignment formats is available and if the number of students working individually at a given time is limited so that the teacher does not have to try to provide individualized feedback to the entire class. For example, an elementary-grade teacher might assign dependent, alienated, and social students to work on individualized seatwork during the early morning when these students are not involved in reading-group activities. These relatively brief times (typically two 20-minute periods) for individual work could be used profitably by these students (who may react less favorably to longer individual seatwork assignments), especially if the teacher supplies answer sheets or other self-checking devices that they can use to monitor their progress. Success students and phantom students might be engaged in brief small-group projects during these same periods. Then, after recess, the students might all be engaged in whole-class work in mathematics. In the afternoon, success students and phantom students could be assigned to spend large amounts of time in individual work while the teacher actively supervises the small-group work of other students.

However, there is only so much that can be accomplished even by experienced teachers who have developed sophisticated systems for organizing and managing instruction. Consequently, even the combination of methods we have discussed so far (ability grouping, differentiated curriculum materials and assignments, and differentiated teacher instruction) may not be enough to accommodate the diverse needs of students in heterogeneous classes. You may want to take the additional step of sharing instructional responsibilities with the students themselves by using cooperative learning approaches or by arranging for students to receive tutorial assistance (see Chapter 7). At least for certain purposes and for some types of student, such sharing may present a useful alternative or supplement to traditional methods.

INDEPENDENT WORK AND LEARNING CENTERS

Teachers can use well-chosen independent-work and learning center activities to enrich instruction and adapt it to individual differences. One way for teachers to create time for working with small groups and individuals is to structure time for students to engage in interesting, creative tasks of their own choosing. Some students, especially high achievers, finish their work quickly. Often these students are indirectly punished (given more of the same work to do, etc.) for their rapid work. Instead, teachers should allow them to engage in enrichment activities. However, other students work more slowly and take all available time to finish assigned seatwork; they are usually denied the opportunity to reflect on what they have done. For example, some students might finish writing their own ending to a story in 10 minutes, whereas other students may need all of the allotted 30 minutes. To give slower students time to reflect and improve, teachers might direct them to reread their work and reflect on it as an appropriate homework assignment.

Table 8.2 SUGGESTIONS FOR MEETING THE NEEDS OF FIVE DIFFERENT TYPES OF STUDENTS

	Success	Social	Dependent	Alienated	Phantom
1. Type of information needed from teacher					
a. Substantive explanation of content	Very high	Very high	High	High	High
b. Procedural directions	Low	Low	High	Moderate-high	Moderate-low
c. Socializing, emotional support, humor	Very low	Low-moderate	Moderate	Moderate (establish private rapport)	Low
2. Type of task needed					
a. Reading skills required	High	High	Low	Low	Moderate
b. Task difficulty level	Very high	High	Low-moderate	Low-moderate	Moderate
c. Abstractness level	High	Moderate	Low initially	Low initially	Moderate
d. Cognitive level	High	Moderate	Low-moderate	Low-moderate	Moderate
e. Degree of structure (specificity about what to do and how to do it)	Low	Moderate	High	High	Moderate
f. Opportunity to make active, overt responses	Not important	High	High	High	Moderate
g. Opportunity to make choices	Moderate (stress on enrichment)	Moderate (stress on choices to work with others)	Low	Moderate (stress on relevance)	Low

h. Interest value of task to student	Not important	Moderate	Low	High	Low
i. Length of task	Long	Short	Moderate	Moderate	Long
3. Type of response demanded					
a. Written	High	Low	High	Moderate	High
b. Oral	Low	High	Low	Low	Low
c. Physical	Low	Moderate	Moderate	High	Low
4. Individual versus group settings					
a. Individual	High	Low	High	High	High
b. Group	Low	Moderate	Low	Low-moderate	Low
5. Emphasis on competition	High	Moderate	Low initially	Low	Moderate
6. Type of feedback from teacher					
a. Personal praise	Low	Low	Moderate	Moderate (private)	Low
b. Personal criticism	Low	Low	Low	Very low	Low
c. Praise of good work	Low	Moderate	Moderate	Moderate (private)	Low-moderate
d. Criticism of poor work	Moderate	Moderate	Low	Low (but communicate demand)	Low-moderate

Source: Adapted from T. Good and C. Power, (1976). Designing successful classroom environments for different types of students. *Journal of Curriculum Studies, 8,* 45–60.

Older elementary students might develop an open-ended personal yearbook in which they write and illustrate stories or record their reaction after they finish assignments. What students put in these yearbooks is left completely up to them. Other possibilities include allowing students to read and review books on some curriculum topic (e.g., American Indians) or to act as resource specialists or tutors for other students. However, book reports, if overly structured, may do little to encourage reading for enjoyment and interest. Often it is useful for the teacher and the student to discuss the book, including not only the plot but also why the student liked or disliked it. Occasionally, teachers should carefully structure long periods of independent work for all students (not just those who finish quickly) and thereby create time for remediation, enrichment, and informal conversations with individuals.

The classroom can be arranged to facilitate independent study. Figure 8.7 shows how one teacher arranged her first-grade classroom. This diagram was made as the teacher instructed a reading group. Note how the room arrangement allows both group work and independent activities. Six students are in the reading group with the teacher, and two are reading at the independent-reading table. The reading center, separated by bookcases from the rest of the room, provides a place where students can read their favorite books in comfortable privacy when they finish their work. The teacher may, at times, use the reading center for an independent but structured learning activity. For example, students may be asked to write reports on chosen or assigned books.

Eight students are working at the listening center, which is a tape recorder with eight earphones that can be wheeled from table to table. One student has passed out pencils and accompanying exercise sheets; another is in charge of turning the tape recorder on and off. All students have been taught how to operate the recorder, and student helpers are assigned and rotated regularly. Similarly, four students are viewing filmstrips without teacher supervision. The student in charge today runs the machine and calls on students in turn to read the story that accompanies the pictures. When the students finish watching the filmstrip and complete written exercises, they move to another activity at their seats.

When the arrangement shown in Figure 8.7 was recorded, nine students were working independently at their seats and three were at the social studies center. Two of the latter were "buddy reading" stories about the social studies unit that had been printed by their fellow classmates, while the third was painting a picture. When the teacher terminated the reading group, all students rotated to a new activity.

Below we present one student's schedule for an entire day. Although a few other students would have the same schedule, there would be many different schedules within the room and the room would be divided to allow for various learning centers (see Figure 8.8). For example, another student might begin the day reading with the teacher in a reading group and end it at the listening post.

Johnny's schedule

8:30–9:15   Math corner
9:15–9:30   Math with his group
9:30–10:00   Reading with his group

Figure 8.7 Physical arrangement of a first-grade classroom.

Figure 8.8 A classroom divided into learning centers.

10:00–10:15	Morning recess
10:15–10:30	Social studies with entire class
10:30–11:15	Social studies in small-project group
11:15–11:45	Lunch
11:45–12:15	Story center (on alternative day or week the science center)
12:15–1:00	Free selection
1:00–1:30	Math instruction with entire class
1:30–2:00	Art center
2:00–2:15	Recess
2:15–2:30	Listening post (on alternative day or week at the writing center)
2:30–3:00	Reading instruction—independent work at the study area

Such scheduling allows students to work at different learning centers or in different project groups; the teacher then has free time for instruction of small groups or remedial work with individuals. Although many teachers may prefer not to use centers this heavily, such centers do provide excellent independent study areas and add flexibility by increasing the variety of assignments available.

Where there is room for only one or two centers at any one time, teachers can provide variety by setting up science and exploratory centers for a few weeks, then creative writing and mystery reading centers, and then art and historical centers. If such centers are more lesson oriented than project oriented they can be altered daily or weekly. The possibilities are limited only by a teacher's imagination.

Students need to learn how to use learning centers. As with all classroom assignments, tasks at learning centers need to be clearly specified if students are expected to work on their own with minimal teacher guidance. Rules for using equipment and handing in assignments must be established. Such rules, and the activities that take place in learning centers, vary with the ages and aptitudes of students.

Self-Regulation

It may be useful to have rules posted at each learning center to help the students function quasi-independently of the teacher. Teachers can use learning centers to expose students to a variety of interesting educational tasks. Young students, for example, might be asked to do independent work by listening to a story and then responding to questions about it. The questions can be simple, "How many bears were there in the story?" or complex, "Listen to the story and then write your own ending." Teachers are free to use their own imaginations and to create material when setting up learning centers. Although companies make filmstrips, tapes, and other materials that can be used for independent work, some of the best assignments come from spontaneous events that occur in the classroom.

For example, one day during a seventh-grade English class, the principal makes one of his frequent PA announcements. At the end of it, Joe Jordan says, loudly enough to be heard by half the class, including the teacher, "Wouldn't it be great if just one day he kept his mouth shut?" After the snickering dies down, the teacher, Mr. Thornton, appeals to logic: "But what would happen if he made no announcements?" The class concludes that nothing significant would be lost if the principal never spoke over the PA again, because teachers could make announcements. The teacher then gives the following assignment for independent work. "Assume there was no television, radio, or newspaper communication for two weeks. Write a theme on one of the following topics: (1) how your life would be affected; (2) how attendance at sports events would be affected; (3) how someone wanting to buy a house would be affected; (4) how supermarkets could advertise their specials; or (5) think of your own topic and have me approve it."

Let us look at a few other assignments that teachers can use.

Examples of Elementary Learning Center Assignments

The listening post is a popular learning place in first- and second-grade classrooms. It is a table equipped with a stack of answer sheets, a can of pencils, six to eight earphones, a tape recorder, and taped stories. The stories are taken from supplementary information in the teachers' editions of textbooks, Science Research Associates' commercially produced products, or the *Weekly Reader*, or are recorded by the teacher based on special interests or incidents that have emerged in the classroom.

To avoid confusion, one student is designated as leader. After the others sit down and put on the earphones, the leader starts the tape recorder, stops it at the signal given on the tape, passes out paper and pencils for the questions, starts the tape recorder again, stops it at the end, collects the paper and pencils, rewinds the tape, and sees that the table is ready for use by the next group. To make the learning activity more autonomous and to provide students with quicker feedback, teachers can put the correct answers at the end of the tape. After a few drills on procedure, even first graders are able to function independently at the listening post. Similarly, students can be taught necessary skills for using the computer, video players, and various other types of media.

In addition to tapes and filmstrips, learning centers can be equipped with a greater variety of photocopied learning sheets. The complexity of the tasks, of course, varies with the ages and aptitudes of the learners. For example, in the math corner on April Fool's Day, a second-grade teacher might give students the sheet in Figure 8.9 and ask them to circle all errors that appear in the calendar (or students could be asked to make their own calendars and see if their classmates can find the errors they included).

Many teachers have found special-feature learning centers to be useful. For example, the teacher may write an introduction to a mystery story (3 to 15 pages, the length varying with reader age and aptitude). Younger students are requested to tape-record their own endings to the story; older ones may be requested to write their own endings and compare them with those of others. Young children, if properly prepared, can prove helpful feedback about peers' writing (Beachy, 1992). At other times in the special-feature corner, the teacher may have students respond to interesting questions: "On one page respond to this question: How would you

Aqril, 19Γ2

S	M	T	W	T	ꟻ	S
				1	2	Ɛ
Ꮋ	5	6	8	7	9	10
11	21	1Ɛ	14	15	1ᘓ	17
18	19	20	12	22	23	2Ꮋ
26	27	28	2ꟼ	30	31	

Figure 8.9 An independent work sheet.

spend a million dollars? Think! Tell *why,* as well as *what* you would buy." "Relate in 200 words or fewer how you would feel if you (dropped, caught) the winning pass in a championship football game." "Assume that you woke up today in the year 2025. Describe what you will actually be doing in the year 2025. How old will you be then? What job do you expect to hold?" The ideas presented here are only a few of the many activities that teachers can use in learning centers. The really good activities will probably be exercises you prepare especially for a class or a smaller group based on special interests you have observed.

Teachers at the same grade level can share ideas for independent learning centers. In fact, one teacher could put together several weeks of math work while another makes multiple copies of listening tapes and assignment sheets and a third works on language arts units. Such cooperation enables teachers to produce high-quality units in less time, and once created, the units can be used year after year with only minor modifications (most changes involve the addition of new units based on the spontaneous interests of students).

Similarly, a good project for preservice teachers in a college course would be to form work teams (e.g., math, social studies, reading, or science), with each group preparing from five to ten projects. In this way, students could swap ideas and learn how to implement the learning-center concept by actually planning and writing sequential units. In addition, students could keep copies of all class materials and thus would be able to begin teaching with a number of units they could use in their own classrooms.

For more suggestions about learning centers in elementary classrooms, including the design of accountability and evaluation systems and the use of individualized contracting approaches in connection with learning centers, see McCarthy (1977), Gagné, Briggs, & Wager (1992), or Savage and Armstrong, (1992). Skilbeck (1992) provides a detailed account of how teachers, students, and parents work in a particular school to individualize instruction for students while maintaining a formal required curriculum.

Independent Work for Secondary Students

The learning center notion as discussed so far has more relevance for the elementary school teacher than for the secondary teacher who teaches one subject and sees students for only about one hour each day. However, certain subjects at the secondary level are well suited to independent study or independent group projects.

In addition to allowing students to learn from one another, independent group projects give secondary teachers time to meet with individual students or to pass from group to group, sharing ideas and talking informally. The guidelines here are similar to those suggested for younger students working in project teams, except that secondary students are able to work for longer periods without assistance. Students may be assigned to one- or two-week projects. Again, the assignments should involve interesting, enjoyable activities that encourage students to think about topics of interest and to discuss ideas or solve problems cooperatively.

Topics can be traditional assignments, such as having all groups first do basic research on four candidates seeking the presidential nomination (e.g., summarize their positions on selected issues), then having each group decide how one candidate would respond to a list of questions asked at press conferences in the South, North, East, and West, and then role-playing these press conferences.

The key points to note in such assignments are (1) students begin with a common reading assignment, so that they share a base of information and have knowledge that they can use to solve problems; (2) students are then required to summarize their information and apply it to a particular situation (typically, they are given a choice regarding which specialty group they want to work in); and (3) they share information with other groups by presenting the views of their candidate in a general classroom discussion; where (4) they receive evaluative feedback (correcting factual errors or contradictions in their position) from the teacher and fellow students.

Most students enjoy working independently to gather facts on a problem and using the information in simulated situations. Again, organization is the key. Teachers need to structure the learning task, identify pertinent resources, and let students know how they will be held accountable. Of course, teachers need not structure all assignments. After students have been through the process, the teacher can solicit and use students' ideas in creating new tasks. The important elements of group work are that the assignment has a clear focus (whether teacher defined or group defined), that each student is held accountable for at least part of the disucssion, and that group tasks are enjoyable and involve authentic learning tasks.

Topics need not always be traditional, content-centered assignments. Attitudes and awareness may be stimulated by combining factual knowledge with students' impressions and values. For example, the exercise just described involves mostly describing and reciting what journalists have written. Other assignments might begin with content and end with expression of feelings. For example, tenth graders in a world history class might be divided into four independent groups. Each group would be presented with summary descriptions of desirable physical and personality characteristics of women in four different countries in the 1850s. One group might then be asked to speculate about the cultural factors that led to these notions. Another might be asked to respond to such questions as "What were the roles of women in each of these countries and to what extent were women satisfied with these roles?"

Later, group discussion could center on the frustrations that led to women's rights movements in the United States and on why some countries allowed women to assume more responsibility than others. When and under what circumstances did women become activists? How did men respond to the emerging independence of women? What is male chauvinism? How has this definition changed across various periods—1920–1940; 1975–1995? Can a woman become president? What is women's role in contemporary American life?

Teachers who prefer not to devote much time to independent group work can still use brief assignments. Those who lecture daily or involve the entire class in daily discussion will be surprised at how effectively group assignments can enhance such a discussion. The basic procedure is as follows: (1) The previous night, the class is assigned certain pages to read; (2) at the beginning of the period, the class is broken into five small groups, each with two or three different questions to answer; (3) each group is allowed 10 to 15 minutes to discuss its answers, look up information, and so forth; (4) the class is brought back together, and the teacher calls on an individual to answer one of his or her group's questions. The teacher then encourages students from other groups to evaluate the answer and allows students who were in the original group to embellish the answer, defend it with logical argument, and so on.

Several good things can occur when teachers use small groups. First, students interact regularly with many of their peers, and, in discussing interesting questions about course material, have the chance to learn from one another. Students in small groups also have more chances to talk than they do in large groups, and shy students are likely to feel more comfortable expressing ideas in safer surroundings (when these students learn that they can express themselves and that others are interested in what they have to say, they will be more able to speak freely in front of the whole class). Students will be task oriented in these sessions when they know that any one of them may be called on to answer any one of the group's questions and that the teacher or a student in another group may ask for a clearer answer or more information. Perhaps most importantly, this procedure mobilizes students' attention, forces them to focus their thinking on relevant questions, and promotes learning. Finally, after listening and practicing their own responses, students will be interested in discussing their ideas and getting comments from others. If the teacher models interest in students' answers and responds to their comments constructively, students will learn that the teacher is genuinely interested in their learning, not just quizzing them about the reading assignment. Further, as we saw in Chapter 7, many students are passive during small-group instruction. Hence, teachers who use small groups may have to teach appropriate group work skills to students and regularly monitor discussions and be aware that some students do not automatically engage in group tasks (Mulryan 1992).

If teachers' goals include affective outcomes, then they may need to allow the same group of students to work together for fairly long periods (i.e., so students really have to learn how to get along). When groups are highly transitory, students may ignore real problems (e.g., why deal with the conflict if I'm in a different group tomorrow?).

CURRICULUM AND STUDENT DIVERSITY

As student groups become culturally more diverse, teachers will have to be aware that they need to consider all students' history, language, and culture. Balancing the curriculum to achieve both academic goals and fair representation of various groups is no easy task, especially if teachers are narrowing the content covered in order to deal more effectively with a smaller number of concepts in order to promote understanding and application.

Applebee (1991) considers the historical role of literature in the American curriculum and concludes that early educators selected literature that would reduce diversity and promote a core set of values and a common culture. Applebee reviews recent studies of what selections are used in secondary school literature programs. In schools with reputations for excellent English programs, literature was dominated by traditional British and American literature, with only token attention to world literature, contemporary literature, and works by women or minorities.

Applebee also reports on a representative national survey of secondary schools that he conducted earlier and that examined book-length works that students were required to read. Results from the survey (conducted in the spring of 1988) looked remarkably like those describing secondary schools at the turn of the century. Applebee notes, however, that other studies show that the secondary curriculum provides more diversity in areas such as short stories, poems, and nonfiction. Still, book-length works (epics, novels, and plays) receive the most attention and often are the core around which other selections are organized. According to Applebee, until this imbalance is changed, minority authors and women will continue to be placed at the margin of the culture, and in a dramatic way that is sanctioned by schools.

Consistent with the hypothesis that learning is socially situated and that students are more likely to be knowledgeable about topics that are more central to their own racial and ethnic groups, Applebee reports on recent national assessment data showing that students' knowledge of literature is linked to the diversity of their own backgrounds. Although African-American students did less well overall than white pupils, they did better than whites on questions dealing with literature by or about African-Americans. "To take a typical example, 53% of African-American students answered a question about Langston Hughes correctly compared with only 35% of white students and 27% of Hispanics" (p. 234).

Applebee argues that the issue is not one of simply guaranteeing that all students read works from their own heritage but rather of finding the proper balance among the many traditions, providing an appropriate mixture that represents the complex and changing fabric of American society, and striking a balance between a curriculum that is too standardized and one that is too particularized.

It is beyond the scope of this chapter to discuss in detail issues of multiculturalism. There are many excellent chapters and book-length manuscripts that focus exclusively on this topic (Agger, 1992; Appleton, 1983; Baker, 1983; Bullivant, 1981; Casanova, 1987; Grant, 1992; Lynch, Modgil, & Modgil, 1992; Sleeter, 1992). However, we do want to assert that teachers, especially if they have not had coursework in this area, need to explore the ethnic and cultural differences of their students. It is important to understand values and behaviors that make people similar as well as to appreciate differences that make them distinctive. Casanova (1987) notes that all students will react differently to instruction because of unique experiences each student brings to the classroom. Although many of these experiences do not interfere with learning, Casanova notes that some do, and that it is the teacher's responsibility to recognize such problems. Research findings illustrate that certain types of conflict can pose significant problems.

Heath (1983) illustrates how differences in communication patterns can lead erroneously to the perception of lack of ability. African-American children in Heath's study were much more adept at illustrating their comprehension of a story when they were invited to retell a story rather than to respond to isolated recall questions. Au and Mason (1981) have also demonstrated teachers' need to understand students' home learning context in order to provide students with appropriate school learning environments. Au and Mason found that allowing Hawaiian students to use conversational forms used in their homes (talking through a story) enabled them to achieve better in school.

Garcia (1991) discusses various issues associated with teaching in a pluralistic society. He recommends various strategies for helping students to become more sensitive to individual differences between cultures. Various strategies he suggests are presented in the box on pages 362–364. Other authors have discussed in-school opportunities for increasing multicultural contact (Bagley et al., 1992).

According to Casanova, it is difficult to write about cultural differences because the research base is very underdeveloped, and superficial discussions tend to solidify features of cultural groups in ways that lead to stereotyping. She argues that differences between cultural groups mask considerable individual differences within groups:

In our discussion, culture and ethnicity will be considered as part of everyone's personal being rather than special characteristics of people who differ from the dominant culture. At no time will the world *culture* be used to suggest artistic or intellectual

Strategies for Favorable Intergroup Relations

A study of family life patterns. This strategy requires that students study each other's families. The study, if handled maturely, should provide insight into the backgrounds and experiences of students from nontraditional families, extended families, and single-parent families. The study should include, but would not be limited to, an analysis of family roles, family livelihood, family problems and concerns, and family recreation patterns.

A study of minority and majority group communities. This strategy includes a study of minority and majority group communities. The study would include, but not be limited to, an analysis of organizing generalizations:

1. Communities have similarities and differences.

2. Communities require interlocking relationships, i.e., human interdependence.

3. Community conditions are results of current forces as well as the community's history.

A study of intergroup experiences. This strategy gets at the crux of the intergroup relations approach because all students are taught to analyze objectively the intergroup relations process. The strategy answers this question: What happens when a minority group and a majority group come into contact?

1. Students study in-group/out-group processes, stereotyping, ethnocentrism, elitism, racism, sexism, discrimination.

2. Students study attitudes, values, and beliefs of peers through surveys, personal interviews, and panel discussions.

3. Students study their own attitudes, values, and beliefs as well as their ancestral ties through genealogies, historical lifelines, and "roots" family study.

A study of sexism, gender-role stereotyping, and gender bias. This strategy emphasizes the idea that each person can develop a unique self concept and that gender-role attitudes are learned rather than innate characteristics.

1. Students study the sociocultural concepts of self-concept, social roles, gender roles, and gender-role stereotyping;

2. Students study how different societies teach their conception of gender roles through toys, games, and play activities;

3. Students study the autobiographies/biographies of men and women who have defied the gender-role stereotypes of their generation, e.g., Marie Curie, scientist, or Robert Frost, poet;

4. For more mature students, the study of existing biological differences between men and women and how they are interpreted differently in different societies. (This refers to the nurture/nature issue regarding sex differences; students would need to be able to read and evaluate studies conducted by adults for other adults.)

A study of social stratification in industrial and nonindustrial societies. This strategy emphasizes the universal nature of social stratification and the division of labor. By comparing stratification systems in industrial, hunting and gathering, and agricultural societies, students can gain insight into the economic and political reasons for social classes and social roles.

1. Students should study how families "make a living" in a hunting-gathering society, in an agricultural society, and in an industrial society;

2. Students should study the specific characteristics of the stratification systems of industrial societies;

3. Students should study how social classes are like ethnic groups which have distinct values, beliefs, behavioral patterns (customs, traditions, folkways), and dialects;

4. Students should study how social class membership is initially a matter of luck but that in dynamic societies some upward mobility is possible.

A study of handicapping conditions. This strategy requires accurate, timely information at the factual as well as the emotional levels regarding handicapping conditions. The strategy requires a candid examination of handicapping conditions and the social difficulties faced by handicapped individuals.

1. By reading and discussing biographies or autobiographies of handicapped individuals, e.g., Helen Keller or Louis Braille, students can learn about the social and personal impact of handicapping conditions;

2. By researching and group reporting, students can get accurate information about specific handicapping conditions, e.g., Down syndrome, dyslexia, hearing impaired;

3. By role playing and assuming a handicapping condition, students can gain an awareness of the condition's impact on the individual, e.g., ear plugs for hearing impaired or blindfold for visually impaired;

4. By practicing signing, students can learn how specific handicapping conditions require compensatory use of other senses to overcome the specific handicap.

A study of racism, prejudice, stereotyping in ethnically and racially homogeneous classrooms. This strategy is intended for classrooms where no visible ethnic or racial mixture of students exists.

1. Students experience in-group/out-group processes vicariously through open-ended stories, role playing, simulations.

2. Students visit and study ethnic minority community action agencies.

3. Students visit and study schools with high concentrations of ethnic minority students.

4. Resource speakers from ethnic minority groups are incorporated into courses of study.

A study of intergroup relations with emphasis on the nature of racism between in- and out-groups. Such a study requires a serious study of the following characteristics of racist and prejudiced thinking.

Emotional racism. This kind of racism ranges from slight distaste to extreme hate of ethnically and racially different out-groups.

Cognitive racism. This kind of racism focuses on perceptions of meanings and understandings of what out-group people are like. Whatever the facts may be about the out-group people, the racist person has his or her stereotypes as "facts" about out-group peoples.

Action racism. This kind of racism is observable; avoidance, discourtesy, exclusion, exploitation, and violence against out-group peoples are evident behaviors of this kind of racism. This is what is considered racial and ethnic discrimination.

Value racism. This kind of racism focuses on the values a racist person wishes to maintain or preserve. Preservation of racist values insures material gain; it becomes necessary to maintain racist values to insure material gain and economic security.

achievement, nor will it be used to refer to surface differences such as style of dress or music. Culture includes all the ways in which people think, feel, and act as they try to solve their particular problems. Because these things are not static, we view culture as dynamic. Part of our humanity is the ability to learn and grow. Some changes, like learning that one buys fruit at the store, come easy; some, like acquiring different rules of politeness, are more difficult; and some behaviors, like looking away from or looking directly at a person to whom one is speaking, are almost impossible to change because they are unconscious. [p. 373]

We echo the conclusions of Lynch, Modgil, and Modgil that teachers must be sensitive when they make judgments about students that come from cultural groups that differ substantially from their own. They argue that teachers " . . . need to be trained to be more circumspect in their judgments, more aware of the limits of reliability and validity of their assessment, not least in the use of so-called objective tests, and more able to recognize their own limitations to make judgments and to allocate life chances. Their judgments need, therefore, to be more easily reversible and the culture of teaching and learning needs to endorse that reversibility as a norm" (p. 451). Fortunately there is a growing body of knowledge that can help teachers be more sensitive to the issues of cultural diversity and more adequate to respond to these issues (Garcia, 1991, Grant, 1992; Harry, 1992; Jaspaert & Kroon, 1991).

To reiterate, a comprehensive discussion of issues like cultural influences on thought, culture, and communication, sociolinguistic differences, nonverbal communication, and school culture versus home culture is beyond the scope of this chapter. However, to teach heterogeneous classes, teachers need to value diversity and to encourage students to learn from one another and to appreciate different languages and traditions. For the most part, differences among students are to be respected and understood, not altered.

SUMMARY

In this chapter we argued that the United States and hence U.S. schools are becoming more racially and ethnically diverse. The school population will change dramatically in the next few decades. Many have seen diversity as a problem that must be overcome, and most strategies for dealing with diversity have not improved the educational lives of students. Programs like pull-out instruction, tracking, and grade retention (all designed to accommodate diversity by placing children in homogeneous groups where they can receive more "appropriate" instruction) have largely been unsuccessful. Indeed, most researchers have concluded that these arrangements are more likely to lead to poorer instruction for students than if they had remained in regular classrooms. Unfortunately, students from culturally and linguistically disadvantaged backgrounds are assigned to such remediation programs more frequently, further compounding educational inequality.

In this chapter we suggested that students with different backgrounds can interact with one another profitably and that teachers can use students' diverse, unique experiences to make classroom learning richer and more sensitive to differences among students. Although we view diversity as an opportunity for enriching classroom learning, dealing with widely diverse groups of learners can make teaching difficult.

We reviewed several ways teachers can respond to individual student differences (including individualized instruction, computer instruction, and supplemental instruction for low achievers). We discussed general principles for planning appropriate instruction for diverse student populations and presented many practical ideas for implementing these principles in elementary and secondary classrooms (e.g., learning stations, etc.).

We advocated more research on strategies for individualizing and making instruction more responsive to diverse student populations. Finally, we noted that if teachers are to teach heterogeneous classes successfully, they need to value diversity and to encourage students to respect differences in languages, traditions, and cultural beliefs.

SUGGESTED ACTIVITIES AND QUESTIONS

1. Observe or at least interview teachers who teach diverse learners. How do these settings compare with the classrooms in which you were instructed? How might your beliefs, norms, and preferences about teaching be influenced by diverse settings? What do teachers think is most rewarding and most difficult about teaching diverse classes? In what ways do their responses differ?

2. Visit a school that uses computers for activities other than drill and practice. Observe at least two students as they work on the computer and then interview them about their experiences. What were the students thinking about and attempting to accomplish while working? Many contend that students' thinking and intentions mediate instruction and thus affect instructional outcomes. To what extent do your interviews support or challenge this position?

3. Visit local schools or classes that purport to implement mastery learning. How do teachers' roles and responsibilities and students' opportunities in these settings compare with those in traditional classrooms? What is expected of students, and how do they respond to these expectations? Arrange a few interviews with students in both settings and ask them about their experiences. For example, do students in mastery learning classes think that speed is more important than do students in traditional classes? Do students in the two types of classes view mistakes differently (e.g., helpful, embarrassing)? What other questions should you ask students about their experiences in these two settings? Consider your own expectations as a college student. How much structure do you want, and how much freedom, in deciding what courses to take (given your goals)? Talk to others to get their views, and then design a system to manage college courses that will satisfy all students' needs. Is it possible to do so?

4. Often, pressure on schools to change comes from public sources (such as information in newspapers that achievement scores are declining) and from parents. Changes seldom take into account students' opinions. Should students, as consumers, be given more of a say about day-to-day school procedures and routines?

5. Outline a plan that allows students to spend parts of each day at learning centers. Specify the room arrangement required, the nature and location of learning centers, and typical schedules for groups or individual students.

6. In this chapter, we suggested that some teachers might want to organize courses around different textbooks that cover the same material but vary in amounts of material provided and reading difficulty. To what extent is it reasonable to match content to students' reading level? We also noted that materials of varying reading difficulty are available for secondary science instruction. Consider the subject you are going to teach and assess the extent to which reading materials could be adjusted for individual differences among students.

7. As a teacher, how much time would you want to spend in whole-class, individualized, and small-group instruction? Why? Would time allocations vary with particular units? What criteria would you use to make such decisions?

8. As a way to illustrate some of the differences in students, the chapter presents five types of students (successful, social, dependent, alienated, and phantom). Which types of students are most likely to benefit from computer instruction? The least? Why? Would your answers differ if you interpret "benefit" to mean learning versus interest?

REFERENCES

Agger, B. (1992). *Cultural studies as critical theory.* London: Falmer Press.

Allington, R. (1991). Children who find learning to read difficult: School responses to diversity. In E. Hiebert (Ed.), *Literacy for a diverse society: Perspectives, practices, and policies* (pp. 237–252). New York: Teachers College Press.

Amarel, M. (1983). Classrooms and computers as instructional settings. *Theory into Practice, 22,* 260–266.

Anderson, L. W. (1985). A retrospective and prospective view of Bloom's "Learning for mastery." In M. C. Wang & H. J. Walberg (Eds.), *Adapting instruction to individual differences*. Berkeley, CA: McCutchan.

Applebee, A. (1991). Literature: Whose heritage? In E. Hiebert (Ed.), *Literacy for a diverse society: Perspectives, practices, and policies* (pp. 237–252). New York: Teachers College Press.

Appleton, N. (1983). *Cultural pluralism in education: Theoretical foundation*. White Plains, NY: Longman.

Arlin, M. N. (1982). Teacher responses to student time differences in mastery learning. *American Journal of Education, 90*, 334–352.

Au, K., & Mason, J. (1981). Social organizational factors in learning to read: The balance of rights hypothesis. *Reading Research Quarterly, 17*, 115–152.

Baker, G. (1983). *Planning and organizing multicultural instruction*. Reading, MA: Addison-Wesley.

Bangert, R. L., Kulik, J. A., & Kulik, C. C. (1983). Individualized systems of instruction in secondary schools. *Review of Educational Research, 53*, 13–158.

Barth, J., Craycraft, K., Marker, P., Stitt, J., Willis, L., & Wineman, S. (1984). *Principles of social studies*. Lanham, MD: University Press of America.

Becker, H. (1982). Microcomputers: Dreams and realities. *Curriculum Review, 21*, 381–285.

Beynon, J., & MacKay, H. (Eds.). (1993). *Computers into classrooms: More questions than answers*. London: Falmer Press.

Biehler, R. (1971). *Psychology applied to teaching*. Boston: Houghton-Mifflin.

Block, J., & Anderson, L. (1975). *Mastery learning in classroom instruction*. NY: Macmillan.

Bloom, B. (1980). *All our children learning*. Hightstown, NJ: McGraw-Hill.

Bloom, B. (1984). The search for methods of group instruction as effective as one-to-one tutoring. *Educational Leadership, 41*(8), 4–17.

Brophy, J., & Hannon, P. (1985). The future of microcomputers in the classroom. *Journal of Mathematical Behavior, 4*, 47–67.

Bullivant, B. (1981). *Race, ethnicity, and curriculum*. Melbourne: Macmillan.

Carlson, D. (1982). "Updating" individualism and the work ethic: Corporate logic in the classroom. *Curriculum Inquiry, 12*, 125–160.

Carver, S., Lehrer, R., Connell, T., & Erickson, J. (1992). Learning by hypermedia design: Issues of assessment and implementation. *Educational Psychologist, 27*, 385–404.

Casanova, U. (1987). Ethnic and cultural differences. In V. Richardson-Koehler (Ed.), *Educators' handbook: A research perspective* (pp. 370–393). White Plains, NY: Longman.

Center for Social Organization of Schools. (1984, November). *School uses of microcomputers: Reports from a national survey* (Issue No. 6). Baltimore: Johns Hopkins University.

Ciborowski, J. (1992). *Textbooks and the students who can't read them*. Michael Pressley (Ed.). NY: Brookline Books.

Clark, R. (1982). Antagonism between achievement and enjoyment in ATI studies. *Educational Psychologist, 17*, 92–101.

Clements, D., & Nastasi, B. (1988). Social and cognitive interactions in educational computer environments. *American Educational Research Journal, 25*, 87–106.

Cooke, B. (1976). Teaching history in mixed-ability groups. In E. Wragg (Ed.), *Teaching in mixed-ability groups*. London: David and Charles Ltd.

Cuban, L. (1984). *How teachers taught: Constancy and change in American classrooms, 1890–1980*. New York: Longman.

Dollar, B. (1972). *Humanizing classroom discipline*. New York: Harper & Row.

Educational Products Information Exchange. (1974). *Evaluating instructional systems: PLAN, IGE, IPI* (Product Report No. 58). New York: EPIE Institute.

Educational Products Information Exchange. (EPIE Institute). (1985). *The educational software selector (TESS)*. New York: Teachers College Press.

Erlwanger, S. (1975). Case studies of children's conceptions of mathematics (Pt. I). *Journal of Children's Mathematical Behavior, 1,* 157–283.

Evans, J. (1985). *Teaching in transition: The challenge of mixed ability grouping*. Philadelphia: Open University Press.

Everhart, R. B. (1983). *Reading, writing, and resistance: Adolescence and labor in a junior high school*. Boston: Routledge and Kegan Paul.

Evertson, C., Sanford, J., & Emmer, E. (1981). Effects of class heterogeneity in junior high school. *American Educational Research Journal, 18,* 219–232.

Fraatz, J. (1987). *The politics of reading: Power, opportunity, and prospect for change in America's public schools*. New York: Teachers College Press.

Good, T., & Power, C. (1976). Designing successful classroom environments for different types of students. *Journal of Curriculum Studies, 8,* 1–16.

Good, T., & Stipek, D. (1983). Individual difference in the classroom: A psychological perspective. In G. Fenstermacher & J. Goodlad (Eds.), *Individual differences and the common curriculum* (82nd yearbook of the National Society for the Study of Education, Part I). Chicago: University of Chicago Press.

Goodlad, J. (1984). *A place called school*. New York: McGraw-Hill.

Goodlad, J., Soder, R., & Sirotnik, K. (Eds.). (1990). *Places where children are taught*. San Francisco: Jossey-Bass.

Grant, C. (1992). *Research in multicultural education: From the margins to the mainstream*. London: Falmer Press.

Grinder, R., & Nelsen, E. A. (1985). Individualized instruction in American pedagogy: The saga of an educational ideology and a practice in the making. In M. C. Wang & H. J. Walberg (Eds.), *Adapting instruction to individual differences*. Berkeley, CA: McCutchan.

Hancock, C., Caput, J., & Goldsmith, L. (1992). Authentic inquiry with data: Critical barriers to classroom implementation. *Educational Psychologist, 27,* 337–364.

Heath, S. (1983). *Ways with words*. New York: Cambridge University Press.

Hiebert, E. (1991). Introduction. In E. Hiebert (Ed.), *Literacy for a diverse society: Perspectives, practices, and policies* (pp. 1–6). New York: Teachers College Press.

Horak, B. (1981). A meta-analysis of research findings on individualized instruction in mathematics. *Journal of Educational Research, 74,* 249–253.

Jackson, P. W. (1985). Private lessons in public schools: Remarks on the limits of adaptive instruction. In M. C. Wang & H. J. Walberg (Eds.), *Adapting instruction to individual differences*. Berkeley, CA: McCutchan.

Jones, B. F., Friedman, L. B., Tinzmann, M., & Cox, B. E. (1985). Guidelines for instruction-enriched mastery learning to improve comprehension. In D. Levine (Ed.), *Improving student achievement through mastery learning programs*. San Francisco: Jossey-Bass.

Kliebard, H. (1986). *The struggle for the American curriculum, 1893–1958*. New York: Routledge.

Lajoie, S., & Lesgold, A. (1992). Dynamic assessment of proficiency for solving procedural knowledge tasks, 27, 365–384.

Lathrop, A. (1982). Courseware selection. In J. Lawlor (Ed.), *Computers in composition instruction*. Los Angeles: Southwest Regional Laboratory for Educational Research and Development.

Leinhardt, G., Zigmond, N., & Cooley, W. (1981). Reading instruction and its effects. *American Educational Research Journal, 18*, 343–361.

Lepper, M., & Gurtner, J. Luc. (1989). Children and computers: Approaching the twenty-first century. *American Psychologist, 44*, 170–178.

Lesgold, A. (1983). When can computers make a difference? *Theory into Practice, 22*, 247–252.

Levine, D. (1985). *Improving student achievement through mastery learning programs*. San Francisco: Jossey-Bass.

Lipson, J. (1974). IPI math—an example of what's right and wrong with individual modular programs. *Learning* (March), 60–61.

Lipson, J., & Fisher, K. (1983). Technology and the classroom: Promise or threat? *Theory into Practice, 22*, 253–259.

Lynch, J., Modgil, C., & Modgil, S. (Eds.). (1992). *Education for cultural diversity convergence and divergence* (vol. 1). London: Falmer Press.

McCarthy, M. (1977). The how and why of learning centers, *Elementary School Journal, 77*, 292–299.

McCaslin, M., & Good, T. (in press). *Listening to students*. New York: HarperCollins.

McGill-Franzen, A., & Allington, R. (1990). Comprehension and coherence: Neglected elements of literacy instruction in remedial and resource room services. *Journal of Reading, Writing, and Learning Disability, 6*, 149–180.

Memory, D., & Uhlhorn, K. (1991). Multiple textbooks at different readability levels in the science classroom. *School Science and Mathematics, 91*, 64–72.

National Research Council. (1989). *Everybody counts: A report to the nation on the future of mathematics education*. Washington, DC: National Academy Press.

Natriello, G., McDill, E., & Pallas, A. (1990). *Schooling disadvantaged children: Racing against catastrophe*. New York: Teachers College Press.

Ragosta, M., Holland, P., & Jamison, D. (1981). *Computer-assisted instruction and compensatory education: The EST/LAUSD study* (Final Report). Princeton, NJ: Educational Testing Service.

Sands, M., & Kerry, T. (Eds.). (1982). *Mixed ability teaching*. London: Croom Helm.

Schofield, H. (1981). Teacher effects on cognitive and affective pupil outcomes in elementary school mathematics. *Journal of Educational Psychology, 73*, 462–471.

Shepard. L. (1991). Negative policies for dealing with diversity: When does assessment and diagnosis turn into sorting and segregation? In E. Hiebert (Ed.), *Literacy for a diverse society: Perspectives, practices, and policies* (pp. 279–298). New York: Teachers College Press.

Slavin, R. E. (1984). Component building: A strategy for research-based instructional improvement. *Elementary School Journal, 84,* 255–269.

Sleeter, C. (1992). *Keepers of the American dream: A study of staff development and multicultural education.* London: Falmer Press.

Sloan, D. (Ed.). (1985). *The computer in education: A critical perspective.* New York: Teachers College Press.

Solomon, D., & Kendall, A. (1979). *Children in classrooms: An investigation of person-environment interaction.* New York: Praeger.

Soloway, E. (1991). *The promise of technology for promoting change.* Paper presented at the annual meeting of the American Educational Research Association.

Stewart, J., Hafner, R., Johnson, S., & Finkel, E. (1992). Science as model building: Computers and high-school genetics. *Educational Psychologist, 27,* 317–336.

Sutton, R. (1991). Equity and computers in the schools: a decade of research. *Review of Educational Research, 61,* 475–503.

Taylor, R. P. (Ed.). (1980). *The computer in the school: Tutor, tool, tutee.* New York: Teachers College Press.

Tucker, M. (1983). Computers in schools: A plan in time saves nine. *Theory into Practice, 22,* 313–320.

Vobeda, B. (1992). Births, immigration fuel population boom. *The Washington Post.*

Wang, M. C., & Lindvall, C. M. (1984). Individual differences in school learning environments: Theory, research, and design. In E. W. Gordon (Ed.), *Review of research in education* (Vol. 11). Washington, DC: American Educational Research Association.

Wragg, E. (Ed.). (1976). *Teaching in mixed ability groups.* London: David and Charles Limited.

FORM 8.1 Student Independence in Individual Work

*USE: When students interact with teacher during periods of individual work
assignment and/or in open settings.*
*PURPOSE: To see if individual students or students generally, over time, are
becoming more autonomous learners.*
*Below is a list of student behaviors that could occur during seatwork
assignments. Check each behavior as it happens.*

Frequency*   Type Contact

_____ 1. After beginning task, student seeks additional instructions
              about what to do.
_____ 2. Student seeks confirmation about being on the right track
              ("Is this okay?").
_____ 3. Student seeks substantive advice from teacher ("Is there
              another source that could be consulted?").
_____ 4. Student seeks evaluative feedback ("What do you think
              about this conclusion?").
_____ 5. Student tells teacher what was done and why (showing,
              justifying).
_____ 6. Student asks teacher what to do next after completing the
              initial assignment (seeks direction).

*In this particular example, the scale will yield information describing the
frequency of different types of contact that occur with the teacher during a
given amount of time. However, codes could be entered for individual students
or for types of students by assigning them a number (high achievers = 1, middle
achievers = 2, and so forth).

FORM 8.2   Learning Centers

USE: In classrooms containing one or more learning centers
PURPOSE: To describe the content and management of learning center
*   activities*
*   Enter a check mark (to indicate presence) or a 0 (to indicate absence)*
for each of the following questions.

CHECKLIST

_____   1. Has the center been created with clear curricular objectives in mind (that is, is it designed to ensure that the students learn something rather merely to entertain them)?

_____   2. Given the curricular goals, are the activities appropriate in difficulty level and otherwise likely to succeed in enabling the students to meet the objectives?

_____   3. Are the activities interesting or otherwise appealing to the students?

_____   4. Is there an appropriate amount and variety of materials and tasks (if necessary to accommodate a range of student ability levels)?

_____   5. Have the students been prepared (via demonstration and practice) in how to use the center?

_____   6. Has the center been equipped with appropriate furnishings and materials?

_____   7. Has the design and location of the center taken into account equipment storage and traffic patterns?

_____   8. Has the teacher posted a schedule or articulated clear guidelines to enable students to know when they can or should use the center?

_____   9. Are there clear management rules (concerning how many students may use the center at once, who should take charge of group activities, clean up and restoration of equipment, etc.)?

_____ 10. Do students know what to do when they get to the center (or can they consult clear guidelines posted at the center when they get there)?

_____ 11. Have provisions been made so that students can get feedback and check their work when they finish center activities?

_____ 12. Do the students know when and how to get help with center activities if they need it?

_____ 13. Is there a clear accountability system for center assignments (students know what they are supposed to do, know when and where to turn in completed work, and know that the work will be checked and followed up)?

_____ 14. Does the center emphasize hands-on activities that allow the students to explore or manipulate (rather than just provide more seatwork but in a different location)?

_____ 15. Have the activities been planned to allow students to work cooperatively or assist one another?

_____ 16. Does the teacher phase new activities into the center as the objectives of earlier activities are met?

COMMENTS:

Chapter
9

Active Teaching

*I*n previous chapters we addressed important factors involved in setting the stage for productive instruction: teacher expectations, classroom management, student motivation, and cooperative learning environments. We also noted that the task of teaching 20 or more students forces most teachers to rely on whole-class instructional methods as their basic approach, but that this approach can be modified in various ways to adapt to students' individual differences. We now turn to the core topic of instruction itself. Here in Chapter 9 we discuss research relating teacher behavior to student achievement and its implications about the role of the teacher in actively presenting information to students, involving them in discussions, and engaging them in learning activities and assignments. In chapter 10 we will discuss recent research and scholarship indicating that learning with understanding involves not only receiving information from a teacher or text but actively constructing understandings through social interaction. These ideas imply a need to modify traditional teaching methods so as to create more and better opportunities for students to construct understandings through productive interactions with the teacher and with their classmates. Once again we see that teacher decision making, guided by clear goals, is the key to effective instruction.

INSTRUCTIONAL METHODS AS MEANS TO ACCOMPLISH CURRICULAR GOALS

There are many different approaches to instruction. Some are mutually exclusive, but most are merely different. For example, Joyce and Weil (1986) described over 20 approaches to teaching, classified into four families or orientations—information processing, social interaction, focus on the individual person, and behavior modification. *Information-processing approaches* organize instruction to present material so that learners can process and retain it most easily. They also attempt to foster students' information-processing skills. *Social interaction approaches* stress the group-living aspects of schooling. Instruction is arranged so that students interact with and learn from one another as well as the teacher, who focuses on fostering group relations as well as on instruction. *Personal approaches* draw on humanistic psychology to promote intellectual and emotional development (self-actualization, mental health, creativity). Finally, *behavior modification approaches* sequence activities to promote efficient learning and shape behavior through reinforcement.

Specific teaching methods are useful for accomplishing certain purposes in certain situations. No one method is optimal for all purposes in all situations. Thus, one cannot teach effectively by using a single method all the time. Doing this would treat instructional method as an end in itself rather than as a means of accomplishing one's instructional goals.

An instructional method is most effective when used as part of a coherent instructional program that is *goals driven*—designed to accomplish clear goals that are phrased in terms of student outcomes or capabilities to be developed. A goals-driven program features *alignment* among the goals themselves and each of the program's components: the content selected for focus; the organization, sequencing, and representation of this content; its elaboration and application during lessons, activities, and assignments; and the methods selected for evaluating learning.

This notion of alignment among the elements in a goals-driven instructional plan implies the need for teacher decision making about goals and methods. Only certain methods are suited to particular goals, so that other methods will be irrelevant or even counterproductive. Given formulation of appropriate goals and identification of appropriate content, the primary planning task facing the teacher is to identify the combination of methods that is most likely to accomplish the goals. If several methods seem equally appropriate, the teacher might make the choice on the basis of secondary criteria such as personal familiarity or preference, student responsiveness, availability of materials, or cost in time and trouble.

It may seem obvious that curriculum planning should be goals driven and should feature alignment among its elements, but this ideal model is not often implemented in classrooms. Teachers typically plan by concentrating on the content they will teach and the activities their students will do, without giving much consideration to the goals that provide the rationale for the content and activities in the first place (Clark & Peterson, 1986). In effect, most teachers leave crucially important decisions about goals to the publishing companies who supply them with instructional materials. This would not be so bad if materials were clearly goals driven and featured alignment among their elements. However, analyses indicate that they tend to treat content coverage as an end in itself, so that too many topics are covered in not enough depth; that content exposition often lacks coherence and is cluttered with insertions and illustrations that have little to do with the key ideas that should be stressed; that skills are taught separately from knowledge content rather than integrated with it; and that, in general, there is little evidence of planning for development of key ideas and use of these ideas in ways that would help students to accomplish major instructional goals (Beck & McKeown, 1988; Brophy, 1992b; Dreher & Singer, 1989; Elliott & Woodward, 1990; Tyson-Bernstein, 1988).

Teachers cannot simply follow the suggestions that come with their textbooks and expect to achieve coherent programs of curriculum and instruction. They will have to be prepared to elaborate on or even substitute for much of the content in the texts and many of the activities suggested in the accompanying manuals. This implies that teachers will need not only sufficient content knowledge, but also familiarity with a variety of instructional methods and awareness of when and why these methods are used. Unfortunately, research findings have been slow to accumulate in this area and logical analyses are often framed in unproductive ways. For example, arguments about methods frequently are reduced to debates built around false dichotomies (phonics method versus whole-word method, didactic instruction versus discovery learning), as if there were only two choices available. Worse, such arguments often imply that there is one best way to teach, when we know that different situations and goals call for different methods, that a given method may have different effects on different students, and that the effectiveness of a method depends not just on its form but on how skillfully it is used. Once again, instructional methods are means to ends, not ends in themselves.

RESEARCH RELATING TEACHER BEHAVIOR TO STUDENT LEARNING

In addition to logical analysis, teachers' decisions about instructional methods need to be informed by research. So far, there exists only a limited and for the most part recently developed knowledge base to inform such decisions. Many important findings come from studies designed to assess the relationships between *processes* (what the teacher and students do in the classroom) and *outcomes* (changes in students' knowledge, skills, values, or dispositions). Two forms of *process-outcome research* are school effects research and teacher effects research. Each of these has emphasized identifying process variables that are associated with student gains on standardized achievement tests.

School Effects Research

School effects research has been done by creating process and outcome measures for entire schools and looking for correlations (Creemers & Scheerens, 1989; Cruickshank, 1990; Good & Brophy, 1986; Teddlie, Kirby, & Stringfield, 1989). The outcome measures are usually adjusted gain scores on standardized achievement tests. The process measures usually include school-level measures (administrative leadership, school climate) and classroom-level measures (teachers' attitudes and practices). The latter are averaged across teachers to produce a score for the school as a whole. Most school effects studies have focused on basic skills instruction, especially in schools serving socioeconomically disadvantaged populations. Because of research conceptualization and design problems, their findings are often subject to multiple interpretations. Thus, they do not have clear, straightforward implications for practice, even though many state- and district-level school improvement or accountability programs are based on them (Brophy, 1988).

Still, it is useful to know that school effects research has identified several characteristics that are observed consistently in schools that elicit good achievement gains: (1) strong academic leadership that produces consensus on goal priorities and commitment to excellence; (2) a safe, orderly school climate; (3) positive teacher attitudes toward students and expectations regarding their abilities to master the curriculum; (4) an emphasis on instruction (not just on filling time or on nonacademic activities) in using time and assigning tasks to students; (5) careful monitoring of progress toward goals through student testing and staff evaluation programs; (6) strong parent involvement programs; and (7) consistent emphasis on the importance of academic achievement, including praise and public recognition for students' accomplishments. We believe that these characteristics contribute to the effectiveness of any school, but especially schools serving primarily disadvantaged students. Some school improvement programs based on these findings have yielded significant gains in student achievement (Freiberg et al., 1990).

Teacher Effects Research

Process-outcome research at the classroom level (Brophy & Good, 1986; Cruickshank, 1990; Reynolds, 1992; Waxman & Walberg, 1991) has been done in more grades, in more subjects, and with a broader range of students than school effects studies, although it also has concentrated on basic skills instruction. The following are the most widely replicated findings concerning the characteristics of teachers who elicit strong achievement test score gains.

Teacher Expectation/Role Definition/Sense of Efficacy   These teachers accept responsibility for teaching their students. They believe that the students are capable of learning and that they (the teachers) are capable of teaching them successfully. If students do not learn something the first time, they teach it again, and if the regular curriculum materials do not do the job, they find or make other ones. In general, they display the qualities recommended in Chapter 3.

Student Opportunity to Learn   These teachers allocate most of their available time to instruction rather than to nonacademic activities or pastimes. Their students spend many more hours each year on academic tasks than do students of teachers who are less focused on instructional goals. Furthermore, the mix of academic tasks provided to their students allows them not just to memorize but to understand key ideas, appreciate their connections, and explore their applications (Blumenfeld, 1992).

Classroom Management and Organization   These teachers also organize their classrooms as effective learning environments and use group management approaches that maximize the time that students spend engaged in lessons and activities (see Chapters 4 and 5).

Curriculum Pacing   These teachers move through the curriculum rapidly but in small steps that minimize student frustration and allow continuous progress.

Active Teaching   These teachers actively instruct—demonstrating skills, explaining concepts and assignments, conducting participatory activities, and reviewing when necessary. They teach their students rather than expecting them to learn mostly from interacting with curriculum materials on their own. However, they do not stress just facts or skills; they also emphasize concepts and understanding.

Teaching to Mastery   Following active instruction on new content, these teachers provide opportunities for students to practice and apply it. They monitor each student's progress and provide feedback and remedial instruction as needed, making sure that the students achieve mastery.

A Supportive Learning Environment   Despite their strong academic focus, these teachers maintain pleasant, friendly classrooms and are perceived as enthusiastic, supportive instructors.

An Example

Table 9.1 shows a model for fourth-grade mathematics instruction developed by Good and Grouws (1979). The principles in the model were originally suggested by correlational studies and then tested through experimental studies. Results indicated that teachers trained to follow the model elicited greater achievement gains than control teachers who used whatever methods they had developed on their own. Good and Grouws's model is similar to traditional fourth-grade mathematics instruction in many ways, although it is more systematic. It includes time allocation guidelines to ensure that mathematics is taught for about 45 minutes each day and it calls for supplementing classroom instruction with homework assignments. There is a great deal of active instruction by the teacher. New concepts are presented in detail during the development portion of the lesson, the teacher makes sure that students know how to do an assignment before releasing them to work on it individually, and the assignment is reviewed the next day. The combination of active instruction, the opportunity to practice and receive feedback, and frequent testing helps ensure continuous progress (for more details, see Good, Grouws & Ebmeier, 1983).

Even for basic skills instruction in the elementary grades, *instructional models must be adapted to the subject matter, the students, and other contextual factors.* For example, Anderson, Evertson, and Brophy (1979, 1982) developed a model for small-group reading instruction in first grade, based on their teacher effects research. Their model is similar to the Good and Grouws model in its emphasis on active teaching, but it differs in many of its specifics because it is designed for different students and subject matter (it is a small-group rather than a whole-class model, its emphasis is on individual oral reading turns rather than on teacher-led problem solving, and it makes no mention of homework). These examples illustrate that although classroom research provides support for instructional principles of varying generality, it has not identified specific instructional behaviors that are ideal for all types of students and situations.

Table 9.1   SUMMARY OF KEY INSTRUCTIONAL BEHAVIORS

Daily review (first 8 minutes except Mondays)

1. Review the concepts and skills associated with the homework
2. Collect and deal with homework assignments
3. Ask several mental computation exercises

Development (about 20 minutes)

1. Briefly focus on prerequisite skills and concepts
2. Focus on meaning and promoting student understanding by using lively explanations, demonstrations, process explanations, illustrations, and so on
3. Assess student comprehension using
   a. Process/product questions (active interaction)
   b. Controlled practice
4. Repeat and elaborate on the meaning portion as necessary

Seatwork (about 15 minutes)

1. Provide uninterrupted successful practice
2. Momentum—keep the ball rolling—get everyone involved, then sustain involvement
3. Alerting—let students know their work will be checked at the end of the period
4. Accountability—check the students' work

Homework assignment

1. Assign on a regular basis at the end of each math class except Friday's
2. Should involve about 15 minutes of work to be done at home
3. Should include one or two review problems

Special reviews

1. Weekly review/maintenance
   a. Conduct during the first 20 minute each Monday
   b. Focus on skills and concepts covered during the previous week
2. Monthly review/maintenance
   a. Conduct every fourth Monday
   b. Focus on skills and concepts covered since last monthly review

Source: Good, T., & Grouws, D. (1979). The Missouri Mathematics Effectiveness Project: An experimental study in fourth-grade classrooms. *Journal of Educational Psychology, 71,* 821–829.

Different learning objectives (mastering well-defined knowledge or skills versus applying them to complex problem solving or using them creatively) require different instructional methods. Furthermore, other kinds of objectives (promoting the personal development of individuals or the social development of the class as a group) require still other methods. Research can inform teachers about the relationships between teacher behavior and student outcomes, but teachers must decide for themselves what outcomes they wish to promote and in what order of priority.

Throughout the rest of this chapter, we consider the principles involved in accomplishing three basic components of active teaching: presenting information, conducting recitations and discussions, and structuring activities and assignments. In the next chapter, we will consider methods of assisting students' efforts to construct meaning from these experiences.

PRESENTING INFORMATION TO STUDENTS

Presenting information to the whole class is an efficient way to expose students to content. It allows the teacher to control the material taught, is easily combined with other methods, and is adjustable to fit the available time, the physical setting, and other situational constraints. Presentation of information is part of the active teaching pattern that is associated with strong student achievement gains. These teacher presentations are typically short ones interspersed with questions or activities, however, not extended lectures. In this section, we offer guidelines about when and how to present information and we review research findings on clarity and enthusiasm.

When and How to Present Information

Despite its continuing popularity, educators have always been ambivalent about information presentation, especially when it is stereotyped as "the lecture method" (Henson, 1988; McLeish, 1976). The approach has been criticized as follows:

1. Lectures deny students the opportunity to practice social skills.
2. Lectures imply the usually incorrect assumption that all students need the same information.
3. Lectures often exceed students' attention spans, so that they begin to "tune out."
4. Lectures only convey information; they do not develop skills or dispositions.
5. Students can read facts on their own, so why not use class time for other activities?

These points are well taken. Most of us have known teachers whose lectures were ineffective because they were dull, vague, or simply too frequent and too long. However, most of these criticisms reflect overuse or inappropriate use of the lecture method, not problems inherent in the method itself. The lecture method also has much to recommend it, assuming that lectures are well organized, up to date, and presented appropriately. Ausubel (1963) pointed out that effective lectures provide students with information that would take hours for them to collect on their own. He and others would ask, "Why force students to search for information for hours when a lecture will allow them to get it quickly and then move on to application or problem solving?" Obviously, this point has merit. The important question is not "Should we lecture?" but "When should we lecture?"

Various authors (Davis & Alexander, 1977; Gage & Berliner, 1984; Henson, 1988; McMann, 1979) have suggested that *the lecture method is appropriate in the following situations:*

1. When the objective is to present information
2. When the information is not available in a readily accessible source
3. When the material must be organized in a particular way
4. When it is necessary to arouse interest in the subject
5. When it is necessary to introduce a topic before students read about it on their own or to provide instructions about a task
6. When the information is original or must be integrated from different sources
7. When the information needs to be summarized or synthesized (following discussion or inquiry)
8. When curriculum materials need updating or elaborating
9. When the teacher wants to present alternative points of view or to clarify issues in preparation for discussion
10. When the teacher wants to provide supplementary explanations of material that students may have difficulty learning on their own

These points also are well taken. Good lectures and presentations at these times do seem preferable to available alternatives. Also, many of the criticisms of the lecture approach can be met without abandoning the approach itself. For example, consider the criticism that lecturing does not allow students to learn actively or assist them to develop social skills. Teachers could adjust to this while retaining the advantage of lectures by giving short lectures (perhaps 15 minutes) to structure problems and provide students with necessary information, but then breaking the class into small problem-solving groups. Also, there is no need to view lectures merely as convenient devices for presenting information. When presented in interesting, enthusiastic ways, lectures can stimulate interest and raise questions that students will want to address in follow-up activities.

Lecturing is an *appropriate* method if used for the purposes outlined above. How *effective* it is will depend on the care and skill with which the lecture is prepared and delivered. Effective lectures (1) begin with advance organizers or previews that include general principles, outlines, or questions that establish a learning set; (2) briefly describe the objectives and alert students to new or key concepts; (3) present new information with reference to what students already know about the topic, proceeding in small steps sequenced in ways that are easy to follow; (4) elicit student responses regularly to stimulate active learning and ensure that each step is mastered before moving to the next; (5) finish with a review of main points, stressing general integrative concepts; and (6) follow up with questions or assignments that require students to encode the material in their own words and apply or extend it to new contexts (Chilcoat, 1989; Duffy et al., 1986).

Two key features of good lectures are the *clarity* of the information and the *enthusiasm* with which it is presented.

Clarity

Clarity is essential if students are to understand concepts and assignments. McCaleb and White (1980) identified five aspects of clarity that observers can attend to in classrooms:

1. *Understanding*. This is a prerequisite to clarity and involves matching the new information to the learners' present knowledge. Does the teacher
   a. Determine students' existing familiarity with the information presented?
   b. Use terms that are unambiguous and within the students' experience?

2. *Structuring*. This involves organizing the material to promote a clear presentation: stating the purpose, reviewing main ideas, and providing transitions between sections. Does the teacher
   a. Establish the purpose of the lesson?
   b. Preview the organization of the lesson?
   c. Include internal summaries of the lesson?

3. *Sequencing*. This involves arranging the information in an order conducive to learning, typically by gradually increasing its difficulty or complexity. Does the teacher order the lesson in a logical way, appropriate to the content and the learners?

4. *Explaining*. When explaining principles and relating them to facts through examples, illustrations, or analogies, does the teacher
   a. Define major concepts?
   b. Give examples to illustrate these concepts?
   c. Use examples that are accurate and concrete as well as abstract?

5. *Presenting*. This refers to volume, pacing, articulation, and other speech mechanics. Does the teacher
   a. Articulate words clearly and project speech loudly enough?
   b. Pace the sections of the presentation at rates conducive to understanding?
   c. Support the verbal content with appropriate nonverbal communication and visual aids?

Others have written more extensively about some of the aspects of clarity identified by McCaleb and White. Ausubel's (1963) concept of advance organizers is useful in thinking about how to structure presentations. Advance organizers tell students what they will be learning before the instruction begins. For example, before describing 20 penalties that can occur during hockey games, a physical education instructor could provide a way to organize the information: "Today we are going to discuss penalties that might be called during hockey games. We will discuss the differences between minor and major penalties and describe 15 minor penalties and 5 major penalties. At the end of the period, I will show you 20 slides and ask you to name the penalty illustrated and state whether it is major or minor."

Advance organizers give students a structure within which they can relate the specifics presented by a teacher or in a text. Without such a structure, the material may seem fragmented, much like a random list of unrelated sentences. A clear explanation of the nature of the content helps students to focus on the main ideas and order their thoughts effectively. Therefore, before lecturing, teachers should see that students know what they can expect to learn from the lecture and why it is important for them to know this information. After lectures, they should summarize the main points in a few simple sentences or ask questions to elicit a summary from students. Providing a clear introduction and a strong summary can make a big difference in the degree to which students remember essential facts and concepts (Luiten, Ames, & Ackerson, 1970; Schuck, 1981).

For extended presentations, periodic internal summaries of subparts may be needed in addition to a major summary at the end. Rosenshine (1968) discussed the value of these kinds of internal summaries and in particular the "rule-example-rule" approach, in which a summary statement is given both before and after a series of examples. He also stressed the importance of "explaining links"—words and phrases such as "because," "in order to," "If . . . then," "therefore," and "consequently" that make explicit the causal linkages between phrases or sentences. These linkages might not be clear without such language. For example, consider the following sentences:

1. Chicago became the major city in the Midwest and the hub of the nation's railroad system.
2. Because of its central location, Chicago became the hub of the nation's railroad system.

The first example presents the relevant facts but does not link them explicitly, as the second example does. If asked "Why did Chicago become the hub of the railroad system?" most students taught with the second example would respond, "Because of its central location," but many students taught with the first example would respond "Because it is a big city," or in some other way that would indicate failure to appreciate the linkage between a city's geographical location and the role it plays in a nation's transportation system.

In addition to these organization factors, presentations or questions can lack clarity because of vague or confusing language. Smith and Land (1981) reviewed studies indicating that the effectiveness of presentations is reduced by the presence of *vagueness terms* and *mazes*. They identified nine categories of vagueness terms:

1. Ambiguous designation (somehow, somewhere, conditions, other)
2. Negated intensifiers (not many, not very)
3. Approximation (about, almost, kind of, pretty much, sort of)
4. "Bluffing" and recovery (actually, and so forth, anyway, as you know, basically, in other words, to make a long story short, you know)
5. Error admission (excuse me, I'm sorry, I guess, I'm not sure)
6. Indeterminate quantification (a bunch, a couple, a few, a lot, a little, some, several)
7. Multiplicity (aspects, kinds of, sort of, type of)
8. Possibility (chances are, could be, maybe, perhaps)
9. Probability (frequently, generally, often, probably, sometimes, usually)

They gave the following as a brief example indicating how vagueness terms can distract from the intended message. The vagueness terms are italicized.

This mathematics lesson *might* enable you to understand *a little more* about *some things we usually call* number patterns. *Maybe* before we get to *probably* the main idea of the lesson, you should review *a few* prerequisite concepts. *Actually,* the first concept you need to review is positive integers. *As you know,* a positive integer is any whole number greater than zero.

Mazes refer to false starts or halting speech, redundantly spoken words, or tangles of words. The mazes are italicized in the following example:

This mathematics lesson will *enab* . . . will get you to understand *number, uh,* number patterns. Before we get to the *main idea of the,* main idea of the lesson, you need to review *four conc* . . . four prerequisite concepts. A positive *number* . . . integer is any whole *integer, uh,* number greater than zero.

In addition to looking for such problems in teachers' presentations, observers can study the effects of the presentations on students. The students' facial expressions, and especially their questions or responses to the teacher's questions, should indicate that they have received the message the teacher intended to communicate. Frequent evidence of student frustration, confusion, or misunderstanding suggests problems in teacher clarity (see Cruickshank, 1985 for related information about students' perceptions of teacher clarity; see Gliessman et al., 1989, for information about a training program for increasing teachers' clarity). Teachers who do not have access to observers but still desire to assess the clarity of their presentations can do so by collecting and studying students' notes or interviewing selected students to assess the depth and connectedness of their understandings (see McCaslin & Good, in press).

Enthusiasm

When teachers are enthusiastic about a subject, students are likely to develop enthusiasm of their own, and ultimately to achieve at higher levels (Rosenshine, 1970; Rosenshine & Furst, 1973). There is a bit of Tom Sawyer in all of us. In particular, young people develop interests through modeling others, including teachers. If teachers appear to enjoy knowledge in general and specific subject matter in particular, students are likely to develop similar interests. If the teacher shows no enthusiasm, students probably will not either (If the teacher does not like to paint fences, why should the students?).

Enthusiasm is a general teacher characteristic that includes at least two major aspects. The first is conveying sincere interest in the subject. This involves modeling, and even shy teachers should be able to demonstrate it. The second aspect is dynamic vigor. Enthusiastic teachers are alive in the room; they show surprise, suspense, joy, and other feelings in their voices and they make material more interesting to students by relating it to their experiences and showing that they themselves are interested in it.

Effective Demonstrations

When learning processes and skills, students need not only verbal explanations, but also physical demonstrations. It is important for teachers to learn to demonstrate effectively, because poor demonstrations can be more confusing than helpful. You may have discovered this for yourself if you have sought out a friend or relative for driving lessons or instructions about how to cook a complicated dish. Professional instructors teach these skills to beginners with ease and efficiency, but most other people do not, even if they are able to drive or cook very well.

What's the trick? Expert instructors tailor their demonstrations to learners' needs. They demystify the process by not only showing the physical movements involved but also verbalizing the thinking that guides these movements. As well, they emphasize the general principles involved rather than just the particular applications that apply to the example at hand. As a result, learners acquire strategies that they can use intelligently and adapt to varying situations, not just fixed routines learned by rote and applied without variation.

Expert instructors break processes down into step-by-step operations. They define each term they introduce and point to each part as they label it. They describe what they are going to do before each step and then talk through the step as they perform it. They have the learner master one step at a time rather than try to do the whole job at once. They give corrections in a patient tone so the learner can concentrate on the task and not worry about progressing quickly enough.

The same principles apply to teachers' demonstrations of new academic skills (e.g., word decoding, mathematical problem solving, research and report writing, use of laboratory equipment) and instructions for assignments. A good demonstration proceeds as follows:

1. Focus attention. Be sure that all students are attentive before beginning, and focus their attention by holding up an object or pointing to where you want them to look.
2. Give a general orientation or overview. Explain what you are going to do, so that students can get mentally set to observe the key steps.
3. If new objects or concepts are introduced, label them. If necessary, have the students repeat the labels. Students cannot follow an explanation if they do not know what some of the words mean.
4. Go through the process step by step. Begin each new step with an explanation of what you are going to do, and then describe your actions as you do them. Think out loud throughout the demonstration.
5. If necessary, perform each action slowly with exaggerated motions.
6. Have a student repeat the demonstration so you can observe and give corrective feedback. If the task is short, have the student do the whole thing and give feedback at the end. If it is longer, break it into parts and have students do one part at a time first.
7. In correcting mistakes, do *not* dwell on the mistake and the reasons for it, but instead redemonstrate the correct steps and have the students try again.

Thinking out loud at each step is crucial, especially when the task is primarily cognitive. While you demonstrate physical procedures such as pouring into a test tube, writing a number on the board, or making an incision, describe how you are filling the test tube exactly to the 20 ml. line, getting the sum by carrying two 10 units and adding them to the 10s column, or starting your incision at the breastbone and stopping short of the hipbones. Unless you verbalize the thinking processes that guide what you do and how you do it, some students may learn no more from watching your demonstration than they would from watching a magician perform a baffling trick.

If a demonstration is lengthy, help the students to follow it by summarizing its subparts and noting the transitions between them. If continuity is broken by student questions or discussion, reestablish the desired learning set by reminding the students of the overall structure of the presentation and of the place at which it is being resumed.

CONDUCTING RECITATIONS AND DISCUSSIONS

Teacher effects research has shown that teacher-led reviews, recitations, and discussions are important parts of the active teaching pattern that is associated with strong achievement gains. Furthermore, one common element in models for teaching school subjects for understanding is teacher-student discourse featuring thoughtful discussion or dialogue (Brophy, 1989). Thus, besides being able to make effective presentations, teachers need to know how to plan good sequences of questions that will help their students to develop understanding of the content and provide them with opportunities to apply it.

Teacher-student discourse relating to academic content occurs in a variety of formats. At one extreme is the *drill* or fast-paced *review* that is designed to test or reinforce students' knowledge of specifics. Here, the emphasis is on obtaining "right answers" and moving at a brisk pace. At the other extreme is *discussion* designed to stimulate students to respond diversely and at higher cognitive levels to what they have been learning. Here, the pace is slower and the emphasis is on developing understanding and pursuing implications. Higher-level questions that admit to a range of possible answers are used to engage students in critical thinking about the relative merits of proposed methods of solving problems or making decisions. In between reviews and discussions are *recitation* activities that vary in pace and cognitive level of question. They include the questioning and response segments that occur between teacher presentation segments, as well as most activities that teachers refer to as "going over the material" or "elaborating on the text."

Educational critics often speak warmly of discussion but criticize drill and most forms of recitation as boring, unnecessarily teacher dominant, restricted to low-level objectives, and tending to make students passive and oriented toward producing right answers rather than thinking. Clearly, recitation should not be used in ways that create such problems. Many of the problems result from inappropriate use of the recitation method, however, and thus can be minimized or avoided. Like the lecture method, recitation persists as a common approach to instruction because it has certain legitimate uses and is in some respects well suited to classroom teaching (Farrar, 1986). It allows the teacher to work with the whole class at one time, provides students with opportunities to learn from one another as well as from the teacher, is an efficient way to enable students to practice and receive immediate feedback on their learning of new content, is a convenient way for teachers to check on student understanding before moving on, and is much easier to manage than individualized instruction. Thus, as with lecturing, the operative question about recitation for most teachers is not whether to use it but when and how to use it effectively.

The more effective forms of recitation are blended with information presentation in lecture/recitation lessons that develop students' understanding of a topic's most important ideas. Questions are asked not just to monitor comprehension but also to stimulate students to think about the content, connect it to their prior knowledge, and begin to explore its applications.

Thus, unless recitation activities are explicitly intended as review or preparation for tests, they ordinarily should not take the form of rapidly paced drills or attempts to elicit "right answers" to miscellaneous collections of factual questions. Instead, such activities should be means for engaging students with the content they are learning. Questions should stimulate students to process that content actively and "make it their own" by rephrasing it in their own words and considering its meanings and implications. Furthermore, the questions should focus on the most important elements of the content and guide students' thinking in ways that move them systematically toward key understandings. The idea is to build an integrated network of knowledge anchored around powerful ideas, not to stimulate rote memorizing of miscellaneous information. Questions are devices for teaching, not just for testing.

We review advice about questioning techniques offered by various authors. Most of it is based not only on process-outcome research but on logical analyses of the characteristics of different types of questions and their appropriateness to different instructional goals (Carlsen, 1991; Dillon, 1988, 1990; Wilen, 1990).

Cognitive Levels of Questions

Teacher questioning has been a popular area of classroom research, partly because it is among the easiest of teacher behaviors to observe and code reliably. Many investigators have used hierarchies based on the Bloom taxonomy (Bloom et al., 1956) to classify questions according to the cognitive levels of the responses that they demand from students. Thus, *knowledge* questions would be considered low in cognitive demand; *comprehension* and *application* questions would be intermediate; and *analysis, synthesis,* and *evaluation* questions would be high. Other investigators have used simpler classifications such as fact versus thought questions or convergent versus divergent questions.

So far, research findings based on such classifications have been mixed and relatively uninformative about when and why different kinds of questions should be used (Good & Brophy, 1990). The research does at least underscore the complexities involved and cautions against attempts to substitute simple formulas for careful planning of question sequences. For example, higher-order questions do tend to elicit higher-order responses from students and the frequencies of higher-order questions often correlate positively with student achievement gains. However, students often respond at a lower cognitive level than the question called for, and the frequencies of lower-order questions often correlate positively with student achievement gains as well, even gains on higher-order objectives. Thus, it is not true that thought questions are always better than fact questions, that divergent questions are always better than convergent questions, or that higher-order or complex questions are always better than lower-order or simpler questions.

Even to phrase the issue this way is to impose a false dichotomy. Varying combinations of lower-order and higher-order questions will be needed, depending on the goals that a teacher is pursuing. Guidelines need to focus on *sequences* of questions designed to help students develop connected understandings, not just on the cognitive levels of individual questions considered in isolation from one another. Sequences that begin with a higher-level question and then proceed through several lower-level follow-up questions are appropriate for purposes such as asking students to suggest possible applications of an idea and then probing for details about how these applications might work. However, sequences featuring a series of lower-level questions followed by a higher-level question would be appropriate for purposes such as calling students' attention to relevant facts and then stimulating them to integrate these facts and draw a conclusion.

Issues surrounding cognitive level of questions should take care of themselves if sequences of questions are planned to accomplish worthwhile goals that are integral parts of well-designed units of instruction. However, plans will need to be revised if the questions appear to be random selections of test items or if the questions are all at the knowledge level when the activity is supposed to stimulate students to analyze or synthesize what they have been learning. Similarly, certain types of questions would be appropriate for arousing interest in a discussion topic, but other types would be needed to stimulate critical thinking about the topic or to see whether students have attained the intended understandings.

Questions to Avoid

Groisser (1964) identified questioning habits that often lead to underproductive responses. He described four types of questions that are particularly misused: (1) yes-no questions, (2) tugging questions, (3) guessing questions, and (4) leading questions.

Yes-No Yes-no questions typically are asked only as warm-ups for other questions. For example, the teachers asks, "Was Hannibal a clever soldier?" After a student answers, the teacher says, "Why?" or "Explain your reason." Groisser claimed that these initial yes-no questions confuse the lesson focus and waste time, so it is better to ask the real question in the first place.

We see two additional dangers in yes-no questions or other questions that involved a *simple choice between alternatives* ("Was it Hamilton or Jackson?"). First, such questions encourage guessing, because students will be right 50 percent of the time even when they have no idea of the correct answer. When a teacher asks too many of these questions, students are apt to try to "read" the teacher for clues about which answer is correct instead of concentrating on the question itself.

The other disadvantage of yes-no questions is that they have *low diagnostic power*. Because of the guesswork factor, responses to these questions do not reveal much about students' understandings. Choice questions sometimes are useful for low-achieving or shy students who have a difficult time responding, because they provide a warm-up that can help these students respond better to more substantive questions that follow. Ordinarily, however, these questions should be avoided.

Tugging Tugging questions or statements often follow a halting or incomplete response ("Well, come on." "Yes . . . ?"). Tugging questions essentially say "Tell me more." They provide no help to the student and may be perceived as nagging or bullying.

When students answer correctly but incompletely, teachers are more likely to elicit an improved response if they ask new, more specific questions than if they continue to ask: "What else?" "What's another reason?" and so forth. For example, a teacher might ask, "Why did the Pilgrims live in a fort?" A student might respond, "To protect themselves from the Indians and from animals." If the teacher wants to focus on the advantages of community living, the next question should cue the student to this aspect of Pilgrim life: "What advantages did the Pilgrims gain from living in a group?"

Guessing Guessing questions require students to guess or reason about a question, either because they do not have the facts ("How many business firms have offices on Wall Street?") or because the question has no correct answer ("If Columbus hadn't discovered America in 1492, what European explorer would have, and when?"). Guessing questions can be useful in capturing students' imagination and involving them in discussions. However, if such questions are overused or used inappropriately, they encourage students to guess thoughtlessly rather than to think carefully.

The value of guessing questions depends on how they are used. If the teacher just wants a guess, the question is probably pointless. However, if the teacher wants students to formulate hypotheses and make realistic estimates based on limited information, such questions can be valuable. *Guessing questions are useful if they are parts of larger strategies for helping students to think about what they are learning.*

Leading Leading questions ("Don't you agree?") and other rhetorical questions ("Johnny, you want to read about the Pilgrims, don't you?") should be avoided. *Questions should be asked only if the teacher really wants a response.* Students should develop the expectation that when the teacher asks a question, something important and interesting is about to happen.

Characteristics of Good Questions

Although the complete definition of a good question depends on context, certain guidelines can be applied. Groisser (1964) indicated that good questions are (1) clear, (2) purposeful, (3) brief, (4) natural and adapted to the level of the class, (5) sequenced, and (6) thought provoking.

Clear Questions should specify the points to which students are to respond. Vague questions can be responded to in many ways (too many), and their ambiguous nature confuses students. For example, Groisser wrote:

If a teacher of Spanish wished to call attention to the tense of a verb in a sentence on the board and asked, "What do you see here?" the student would not know exactly what was being called for. Better to ask, "What tense is used in this clause?"

Vague questions often result in wasted time as students ask the teacher to clarify or rephrase in order to identify the specific attack point. Questions can also be unclear if they are asked as part of an uninterrupted series. Groisser writes of a teacher who,

> in discussing the War of 1812 asks, in one continuous statement, "Why did we go to war? As a merchant, how would you feel? How was our trade hurt by the Napoleonic War?" The teacher is trying to clarify his first question and to focus thinking upon an economic cause of the war. In his attempt, he actually confuses.

This teacher should have asked a clear, straightforward question initially ("What was the cause of the War of 1812?"), waited for a response, and then probed for economic causes if the response failed to mention them.

Questions should clearly cue students to respond along specific lines. This does not mean that the teacher cues the answer; it means that the teacher communicates the specific question to which the student is asked to respond.

Purposeful Purposeful questions help achieve the lesson's intent. Advance planning is helpful here. Such planning should not be too rigid, because it may be worth pursuing an unanticipated teachable moment opened up by a student's question or comment. Still, it is worth remembering that teachers who improvise most of their questions ask many irrelevant and confusing questions that work against achievement of their own goals.

Brief Questions should be brief. Long questions are often unclear. The longer the question, the more difficult it is to understand.

Natural Questions should be phrased in natural, simple language (as opposed to pedantic, textbook language) and should be adapted to the level of the class. If students do not understand the question, they cannot begin to formulate responses and engage in the kind of thinking that the teacher intended to stimulate.

We do not mean that teachers should avoid unfamiliar words. Students benefit from learning new words and from exposure to modeling of sophisticated verbal communication. However, teachers must consider students' vocabularies. When teachers introduce new words, they should clarify their meanings and engage students in using the words within application contexts.

Sequenced If questions are intended as teaching devices and not merely as oral test items, they should be asked in carefully planned *sequences*, and the answers to each sequence should be integrated with previously discussed material before moving to new sequences. Initial questions might lead students to identify or review essential facts. Then the students might be asked to refine their understandings and apply them to real or hypothetical problems ("Now that we have identified the properties of these six types of wood, which would you use to build a canoe?").

Table 9.2   A REASONABLE QUESTIONING SEQUENCE

1. What was the Boston Tea Party?
2. What events preceded the Boston Tea Party?
3. What is a monopoly?
4. Under what conditions might a monopoly be justified?
5. Do we provide favorable circumstances for certain industries in this country that make it difficult for foreign countries to compete?
6. What did the Boston Tea Party mean to British citizens? To American citizens?
7. Who participated in the Boston Tea Party?
8. How much was the tea worth?

Table 9.3   AN UNREASONABLE SEQUENCE

1. What was the Boston Tea Party?
2. How many ships containing tea were in the harbor?
3. How did the colonists dress when they entered the ships to destroy the tea?
4. Define Townshend Duties.
5. Define Coercive Acts.
6. Who was Thomas Hutchenson?
7. On what date did the Boston Tea Party occur?

Alternatively, the teacher might initiate a problem-solving or decision-making discussion by first posing a question or issue to be addressed, then eliciting suggested resolutions, and then engaging students in critical thinking about the trade-offs that each of the suggested resolutions offers.

The sequence and the meaningfulness of information exchange are of critical importance, not the cognitive level of the question per se. For example, Table 9.2 shows how a sequence of relatively low-level factual questions can lead to a meaningful exchange of information and insights. In this sequence, the teacher helps students to understand the historical events that preceded the Boston Tea Party and to appreciate that events can be viewed from different perspectives. Here, key information is tied to the concept of monopoly and representative taxation, and the factual questions raised help students to *understand* the historical significance of events. For example, "What was the tea worth?"—a simple fact question—should help students to realize that in colonial times tea was quite valuable. The fact that the colonists were willing to dump the tea into the harbor rather than taking it home indicated how outraged they were. Similarly, the question, "Who participated in the Boston Tea Party?" is intended to develop appreciation of the wide range of citizens who participated in the demonstration.

In the unreasonable sequence shown in Table 9.3, the fact questions are often trivial and are not used to develop a thoughtful examination of what the Boston Tea Party represented. Questions about the number of ships in the harbor or how the colonists were dressed may allow the teacher to evaluate whether a student has read the book carefully, but they fail to develop important points. It is usually counterproductive to emphasize such trivial details. The questions evaluating knowledge of the Townshend Duties and Coercive Acts might have been productive if used to place the Boston Tea Party within the context of its antecedents and its subsequent effects, but in this sequence these questions merely test for knowledge of disconnected facts.

Distinctions among the cognitive levels of questions are useful in providing a basis for teachers to think about the cognitive demands that they place on students, but questions need to be planned in sequences designed to develop systematic discussion of a topic. A good set of questions is good not merely because it contains a significant percentage of higher-level questions but also because it helps students to think about the topic systematically and emerge from the discussion with connected understandings.

Thought Provoking   Good questions are thought provoking. Especially in discussions, questions should arouse strong, thoughtful responses from students, such as, "I never thought of that before," or "I want to find the answer to that question." Discussion should help students to clarify their ideas and to analyze or synthesize what they are learning. Fact questions often are needed to establish relevant information, but subsequent questions should stimulate students to use the information rather than just recite it and should motivate them to respond thoughtfully.

Groisser also suggested that questions should be followed by pauses that allow students time to think, balanced between fact and thought questions, distributed widely, asked conversationally, and sometimes asked to allow students to respond to classmates' answers.

Addressing questions to the class before calling on a student to respond involves first asking the question, then allowing students time to think, and then calling on someone. This makes everyone in the class responsible for the answer. If the teacher names a student to respond before asking the question or calls on a student immediately after doing so, only the student who is named is responsible for answering. Other students are less likely to try to answer it.

Groisser noted three special situations in which a teacher might want to call on a student before asking a question: (1) drawing an inattentive student back into the lesson, (2) asking a follow-up question of a student who has just responded, and (3) calling on a shy student who may be "shocked" if called on without warning.

Groisser's point that students need time to think seems self-evident but actually raises several complicated issues. First, optimal wait time varies with the question and the situation. A question calling for students to solve a complex problem or state a position on a difficult issue requires a much longer wait time than a question asking for a fact that a student either does or does not know.

Wait Time

Good questioning technique allows students sufficient time to think about and respond to questions. Rowe (1974a, 1974b) reported data that at the time seemed remarkable: After asking questions, the teachers she observed waited less than one second before calling on someone to respond. Furthermore, even after calling on a student, they waited only about a second for the student to give the answer before supplying it themselves, calling on someone else, or rephrasing the question or giving clues. These findings do not seem to make sense because they suggest that the teachers minimized the value of their questions by failing to give students time to think.

Rowe followed up these observations by training teachers, to see what would happen if they extended their wait times from less than one second to three to five seconds. Surprisingly, most of the teachers found this difficult to do, and some never did succeed. However, in the classrooms of teachers who extended their wait times to three to five seconds, the following desirable changes occurred:

1. Increase in the average length of student responses
2. Increase in unsolicited but appropriate student responses
3. Decrease in failures to respond
4. Increase in speculative responses
5. Increase in student-to-student comparisons of data
6. Increase in statements that involved drawing inferences from evidence
7. Increase in student-initiated questions
8. A greater variety of contributions by students

In short, Rowe found that longer wait times led to more active participation in lessons by a larger percentage of the students, coupled with an increase in the quality of this participation. Subsequent research replicated and extended these findings, verifying that increasing wait time leads to longer and higher-quality student responses and participation by a greater number of students (Rowe, 1986; Swift, Gooding, & Swift, 1988; Tobin, 1983a, 1983b; Tobin & Capie, 1982). These effects are most notable on the less able students in the class.

Subsequent research also verified Rowe's finding that many teachers experience difficulty in extending their wait times. DeTure (1979) found that even after training, no teacher attained an average wait time longer than 1.8 seconds. Why should this be? The answer lies in the pressures on teachers to maintain lesson pacing and student attention. Some teachers are reluctant to extend their wait times because they fear that they may lose student attention, or even control of the class, if they do. This illustrates one of the continuing dilemmas that require teacher decision making and adjustment to immediate situations. Longer wait times are generally preferable to shorter ones because they allow more thinking by more students, but the teacher may have to use shorter wait times when the class is restive or when time is running out and it is necessary to finish the lesson quickly.

Most teachers adjust wait times according to the type of question asked. They are likely to wait longer following higher-level questions (especially analysis and synthesis questions) than following lower-level questions (Arnold, Atwood, & Rogers, 1974). Furthermore, the causal linkages between question level and wait time seem to work in both directions. In addition to noting effects on students, some of the investigators who trained teachers to increase wait times noted that this change also led to interaction patterns in which the teachers asked fewer questions per time unit than before, but more questions at higher cognitive levels (Fagan, Hassler, & Szabo, 1981; Rice, 1977).

Thus, interactions featuring mostly lower-level questions tend to move at a quicker pace with shorter wait times than interactions featuring higher-level questions. *The appropriateness of these pacing and wait time factors depends on the objectives of the activity.* Although most studies in which teachers were trained to slow the pace and extend wait time have produced positive outcomes, these studies have focused on intermediate and upper grade levels and on instruction in abstract or difficult material. Anshutz (1975) reported no science achievement differences between short and long wait times for students in Grades 3 and 4, and Riley (1980) reported interaction effects on science achievement in Grades 1 through 5: A decrease in achievement occurred when wait time was extended from medium to long for low-level questions, whereas an increase in achievement was noted when wait time was extended for higher-level questions.

These studies show that pacing and wait time should be suited to the questions being asked and ultimately to the goals these questions are designed to accomplish. A fast pace and short wait times are appropriate for drill or review activities covering specific facts. However, if questions are intended to stimulate students to think about material and formulate original responses rather than merely to retrieve information from memory, it is important to allow time for these effects to occur. This is especially true for complex or involved questions. Students may need several seconds to merely process such questions before they can even begin to formulate responses to them. When a slow pace and thoughtful responding are desired, teachers should not only adjust their wait times but also make their goals clear to students. Unless cued, some students may not realize that they are supposed to formulate an original response rather than search their memories for something taught to them explicitly, and some may think that the teacher is looking for speed rather than quality of response.

Distributing Questions to a Range of Students

Teachers should distribute questions widely rather than allow a few students to answer most of them. Students learn more if they are actively involved in discussions than if they sit passively without participating. A few reticent students who rarely participate in discussions may still get excellent grades, but most students benefit from opportunities to practice oral communication skills, and distributing response opportunities helps keep them attentive and accountable. Also, teachers who restrict their questions primarily to a small group of active (and usually high-achieving) students are likely to communicate undesirable expectations (Good & Brophy, 1974) and generally to be less aware and less effective.

Feedback About Responses

Feedback is important both to motivate students and to produce learning. It lets students know how they are doing and how much progress has been made. This probably seems obvious, but teachers sometimes fail to give feedback, especially to low achievers (Brophy & Good, 1974).

Unless it is understood that no response indicates correctness, teachers should give some sort of acknowledgment every time students answer questions. Feedback need not be long or elaborate, although sometimes it has to be. Often a head nod or short comment like "Right" is all that is needed. Also, teachers do not always have to provide feedback personally. They can provide access to answer sheets that allow students to assess their own work or can arrange for students to provide feedback to one another.

Reasons for Questioning

Some types of questions suggest to students that the teacher is more interested in quizzing them than in sharing or discussing information (see Roby, 1988). Teachers who question students in harsh terms are likely to threaten them and make it difficult for them to share their thinking. In contrast, questions that present interesting challenges and invite friendly exchanges of views are likely to maximize motivation and yield productive responses.

That is what Groisser meant when he suggested that questions should be asked conversationally. He also suggested that allowing students to respond to one another is helpful:

> Many teachers seize upon the first answer given and react to it at once with a comment or with another question. . . . It is more desirable, where possible, to ask a question, accept two or three answers, and then proceed. This pattern tends to produce sustaining responses, variety, and enrichment. It encourages volunteering, contributes to group cooperation, and approaches a more realistic social situation.

Such techniques model teacher interest in the exchange of information about a topic (as opposed to pushing for the right answer) and indicate that there is not always a single correct answer. Students are likely to listen more carefully to one another if they are called on to respond to one another's answers occasionally. Wright and Nuthall (1970) found that teachers who redirected questions to other students during science lessons got better achievement than those who did not.

Inquiry Approaches

Although most approaches to teaching start with presentation of information to students and only then proceed to asking them questions, inquiry approaches *begin* with questions and rely on them heavily thereafter as ways to stimulate student exploration, discovery, and critical thinking about subject matter. Here questioning is the basic method of instruction.

Collins and Stevens (1983) described an inquiry approach built around ten instructional strategies: (1) select positive and negative examples, (2) vary case studies systematically, (3) select counterexamples, (4) generate hypothetical cases, (5) form hypotheses, (6) test hypotheses, (7) consider alternative predictions, (8) entrap students, (9) trace consequences to a contradiction, and (10) question authority. Examples are selected and sequenced to create dissonance or curiosity in students and set the stage for inquiry-oriented discussion. Students are challenged to form and evaluate hypotheses rather than given rules or principles, and are prodded to consider alternative predictions whenever they jump to conclusions without adequately considering alternatives. Hypothetical cases are used to challenge students' reasoning or force them to take into account factors that they are currently ignoring. Entrapment is used to reveal the inadequacies of erroneous preconceptions. It involves using the students' own thinking to show how it leads to incorrect predictions or conclusions. Tracing consequences to a contradiction is a similar strategy. Finally, questioning authority involves training students to think for themselves rather than to rely on the teacher or the book for correct answers.

In addition to discussing these instructional strategies, Collins and Stevens (1983) presented rules for structuring and sequencing dialogues designed to achieve particular objectives. We mention their work briefly here to underscore the point that thoughtful planning is just as important for inquiry approaches to instruction as it is for more didactic methods.

Conducting Discussions

Although drill and recitation occur frequently in classrooms, true group discussion is rare. Even activities that teachers call "discussion" tend to be recitations in which teachers ask questions and students respond by reciting what they already know or are now learning. Few such activities are actual discussions in which the teacher and students share opinions in order to clarify issues, relate new knowledge to their prior experience, or attempt to answer a questions or solve a problem (Alvermann, O'Brien, & Dillon, 1990; Tharp & Gallimore, 1988).

To conduct discussions, teachers must adopt a different role from the one they play in recitation activities, where they act as the primary source of information and the authority figure who determines whether answers are correct. Teachers lead discussions by establishing a focus, setting boundaries, and facilitating interaction, but in other respects, they assume a less dominant and less judgmental role. Even if a discussion begins in a question-and-answer format, it should evolve into an exchange of views in which students respond to one another as well as to the teacher and respond to statements as well as to questions.

If ideas are being collected, the teacher should record them (listing them on the board or on an overhead projector) but should not evaluate them. Once the discussion is established, the teacher may wish to participate in it periodically in order to point out connections between ideas, identify similarities or contrasts, request clarification or elaboration, invite students to respond to one another, summarize progress achieved so far, or suggest and test for possible consensus as it develops. However, the teacher does not push the group toward some previously determined conclusion (if the teacher were to do so, the activity would be a guided discovery lesson rather than a discussion).

The pace of discussions is notably slower than that of recitations, with longer periods of silence between speech. These periods provide participants with opportunities to consider what has been said and to formulate responses to it.

Dillon (1988, 1990) illustrated that teachers' statements can be just as effective as questions for producing lengthy and insightful responses during discussions. He also noted that questions may impede discussions at times, especially questions perceived as attempts to test students rather than to solicit their ideas. To avoid this problem, Dillon (1979) listed six *alternatives to questioning* that teachers can use to sustain discussions.

1. *Declarative statements*. In discussing the effects of war on the domestic economy, the teacher might respond to a student's statement by saying, "When the war broke out, unemployment dropped." The teacher could introduce this idea into the discussion by stating it directly rather than putting it into the form of a question such as "What happens to the unemployment rate in wartime?" or "What causes a drop in unemployment?" The statement provides information that the students have to accommodate and respond to; compared with a question, however, it invites longer and more varied responses.

2. *Declarative restatements*. Teachers can show that they have attended to and understood what students have said by occasionally summarizing. Such summarizing may be useful to the class as a whole, and reflecting students' statements to them may stimulate additional and deeper responding.

3. *Indirect questions*. When a direct question might sound challenging or rejecting, the teacher can make a statement such as, "I wonder what makes you think that" or "I was just thinking about whether that would make any difference." Such indirect questions might stimulate further thinking without generating anxiety.

4. *Imperatives*. Similarly, statements such as, "Tell us more about that" or "Perhaps you could give some examples" are less threatening than direct requests for the same information.

5. *Student questions*. Rather than asking all of the questions themselves, teachers can encourage students to ask questions in response to statements made by their classmates.

6. *Deliberate silence*. Sometimes the best response to a statement is to remain silent for several seconds to allow students to absorb the content and formulate follow-up questions or comments.

In general, if teachers expect an activity to involve genuine discussion and not merely recitation, they have to make this fact clear to students and alter their own behavior accordingly.

STRUCTURING ACTIVITIES AND ASSIGNMENTS

There are three main ways that teachers help their students to learn. First, they explain, demonstrate, model, or in other ways present information. Second, they lead the students in review, recitation, discussion, or other forms of discourse surrounding the content. Third, they involve students in activities or assignments that provide them with opportunities to practice or apply what they are learning (and in the process, provide them with coaching, task-simplification strategies, or other forms of scaffolding that may be needed to enable them to complete the activities successfully).

Only limited research is available on activities and assignments (Brophy, 1992a), even though most students spend half or more of their time in school working independently (Fisher et al., 1980). Similarly, although it is known that homework can provide a useful supplement to classroom instruction and may increase student achievement, at least in the secondary grades (Cooper, 1989; Epstein, 1988; Miller & Kelley, 1991; Rickards, 1982; Strother, 1984), little is known about how much or what kinds of homework to assign.

Process-outcome research suggests that *independent seatwork is probably overused and is not an adequate substitute either for active teacher instruction or for recitation and discussion opportunities.* This is especially the case when the seatwork emphasizes time-consuming but low-level tasks that reinforce memory for facts and mastery of subskills practiced in isolation but do not provide opportunities to think critically or creatively about what is being learned or apply it in problem-solving or decision-making situations.

So far, most research on activities has been conducted not by subject-matter specialists but by the researchers who developed principles for managing classrooms (Chapter 4) and motivating students (Chapter 6). This work suggests that activities and assignments should be varied and interesting enough to motivate student engagement, new or challenging enough to constitute meaningful learning experiences rather than pointless busywork, and yet easy enough to allow students to achieve high rates of success if they invest reasonable effort.

Student success rates, and the effectiveness of seatwork assignments generally, are enhanced when teachers *explain the work and go over practice examples with students before releasing them to work independently.* Furthermore, once students are released, the work goes more smoothly if teachers *circulate to monitor progress and provide help when needed.* If the work has been well chosen and explained, most of these "helping" interactions will be brief, and at any given time, most students will be progressing through an assignment rather than waiting for help.

Teachers should also monitor performance for completion and accuracy and provide students with timely and specific feedback. When performance is poor, teachers will need to provide not only feedback but reteaching and follow-up assignments designed to ensure that the material is understood.

Activities and assignments that provide students with opportunities to extend or deepen their knowledge and to apply what they are learning are important components of a well-rounded instructional program, but activities and assignments can also be pointless or even counterproductive. Critical analyses suggest that much of the seatwork assigned to students is just busywork or is defective in ways that make it unlikely to meet its intended objectives. This is just as true of the workbooks and other assignments provided with published curricula as it is of seatwork that teachers design themselves (Osborn, 1984). Frequently, these tasks are either too easy or too difficult for most students, poorly coordinated with what is being taught at the time, or more likely to confuse or mislead the students than to teach them target concepts. Osborn suggested the following guidelines for seatwork and workbook tasks.

1. A sufficient portion of these tasks should be related to current instruction in the rest of the unit.

2. Another portion should provide systematic and cumulative review.
3. Tasks should reflect the most important (and seatwork-appropriate) aspects of what is being taught.
4. Extra tasks should be available for students who need extra practice.
5. The vocabulary and conceptual levels of a task should relate to those used in the rest of the program used by the students.
6. The language used in a task should be consistent with that used in the rest of the lesson and in similar seatwork tasks.
7. Instructions should be clear and easy to follow; brevity is a virtue.
8. The layout of pages should combine attractiveness with utility.
9. Tasks should contain enough content to enable students to *learn* something, not just *be exposed* to something.
10. Tasks that require discriminations should be preceded by sufficient practice on the components of these discriminations.
11. The content should be accurate and precise; tasks should not present wrong information.
12. At least some tasks should be fun or have obvious benefits to students.
13. Most response modes called for should be consistent from task to task.
14. Response modes should be as close as possible to actual reading and writing (as opposed to circling, underlining, drawing arrows from one word to another, etc.).
15. The instructional design of individual tasks and of task sequences should be carefully planned.
16. There should be a finite number of task types and forms.
17. The artwork should be consistent with the prose of the task.
18. Cute, nonfunctional, space- and time-consuming tasks should be avoided.
19. Tasks should be accompanied by brief explanations of purpose.
20. English-major humor should be avoided.

Criteria to Consider in Selecting or Developing Activities

For teachers interested in selecting or developing their own activities and assignments, we suggest the following guidelines. First, *begin with a focus on the unit's major goals* and consider the kinds of activities that would promote progress toward those goals. With clear goals to provide guidance, teachers can make good decisions about whether to use activities suggested in the manual that accompanies a published curriculum and about what other activities may need to be included. Ideally, major goals will focus on students' understanding of the content and ability to apply it to their lives outside of school, and thus will guide teachers toward activities that are whole-application tasks that carry students through to the intended outcomes rather than just providing them with isolated practice of part skills.

Given the instructional goals, different activities might be considered: (1) essential; (2) directly relevant and useful, even if not essential; (3) directly relevant but less useful than other activities that serve the same functions more effectively; (4) tangentially relevant but not very useful because they do not promote progress toward major goals; or (5) irrelevant or inappropriate to the goals. For example, suppose than an American history course is designed to emphasize student understanding and appreciation of the development of American political values and policies. With these primary goals, a unit on the American Revolution and the founding of the new nation would emphasize the historical events and political philosophies that shaped the thinking of the writers of the Declaration of Independence and the Constitution. Essential activities for such a unit would be activities that call for research, debate, or various forms of critical thinking and decision making about the issues that developed between England and the colonies and about the ideals, principles, and compromises that went into the construction of the Constitution, especially the Bill of Rights. Less essential, but still relevant and perhaps useful activities might include studying more about the thinking of Jefferson and other key framers of the Constitution or about the various forms of oppression that different colonial groups had experienced. Activities that are similar in form but less useful in content would be studying the lives of Paul Revere or other revolutionary figures who are not known primarily for their contributions to American political values and policies, or studying the details of each of the economic restrictions that England imposed on the colonies. Irrelevant to the goals would be activities that focused on the details of particular Revolutionary War battles. To the extent that they were time consuming (e.g., construction of a diorama depicting the battle of Yorktown), such activities not only would fail to deliver goal-relevant benefits but would impose costs by reducing the scope and continuity of the goals-driven aspects of the program.

Activities that are not relevant to certain programs or courses might be highly relevant to others. For example, courses in military history would be developed with very different goals than those of the American history course described above. In teaching about the American Revolution, such courses would focus on its military aspects, so that activities that developed or applied knowledge of particular battles might be very useful or even essential to accomplishment of the course's goals. Thus, although generic concepts such as cognitive level of task demand are useful for examining activities, the potential pedagogical value of these activities ultimately must be assessed within the context of the major goals that a curriculum is designed to accomplish.

A second set of criteria concerns the *feasibility* and *cost-effectiveness* of a proposed activity. Is the activity feasible given its assumptions about students' prior knowledge and the time, space, and equipment that it will require? Do the benefits that the activity is expected to bring to the students justify its costs in time and trouble?

To be worthwhile in the first place, all activities considered for inclusion in an instructional program must meet these *primary criteria* of goal appropriateness, feasibility, and cost-effectiveness. Activities that do not meet these criteria should not even be considered.

In selecting from among activities that do meet these primary criteria, teachers might consider several *secondary criteria:*

1. Students are likely to find the activity interesting or enjoyable.
2. The activity provides opportunities for interaction and reflective discourse, not just solitary seatwork.

3. If the activity involves writing, students will compose prose, not just fill in blanks.
4. If the activity involves discourse, students will engage in critical or creative thinking, articulate and defend problem-solving or decision-making approaches, and so on, not just regurgitate facts and definitions.
5. The activity is targeted for students' zones of proximal development; it is not merely an occasion for exercising overlearned skills.
6. The activity focuses on application of important ideas, not incidental details or interesting but ultimately trivial information.
7. As a set, the activities offer variety and in other ways appeal to student motivation to the extent that this is consistent with curriculum goals.
8. As a set, the activities include many ties to current events or local and family examples or applications.

Structuring and Scaffolding Students' Learning

Besides being well chosen, activities need to be effectively presented, monitored, and followed up if they are to have their full impact. This means preparing the students for an activity in advance, providing guidance and feedback during the activity, and structuring postactivity reflection afterwards (Brophy & Alleman, 1991).

In introducing activities, teachers need to stress their purposes in ways that will help students to engage in them with clear ideas about the goals they are trying to accomplish. Such emphasis may need to be supplemented by statements or questions that call students' attention to relevant background knowledge, modeling of strategies for responding to the task, or scaffolding that will simplify the task for the students.

Teachers can scaffold by providing any needed information or help concerning how to go about completing task requirements. If reading is part of the task, for example, teachers might summarize the main ideas, remind students about strategies for developing and monitoring their comprehension as they read (paraphrasing, summarizing, taking notes, questioning themselves to check understanding), or provide them with advance organizers that will help them to approach the material in the intended ways. If necessary, teachers might provide additional scaffolding in the form of partial outlines or skeletal notes to fill in while listening to a presentation or reading an assignment (Kiewra, 1987), study guides that call attention to key ideas and structural elements, or task organizers that help students to keep track of the steps involved and the strategies they are using to complete these steps. For example, a teacher discussing careers in science in a seventh-grade life science class might distribute the outline presented in Table 9.4 as a way to help students to take notes effectively.

Once students begin working on activities and assignments, teachers should monitor their progress and provide assistance if necessary. Besides keeping these interventions short for the classroom management reasons described in Chapter 4, teachers should ordinarily confine themselves to minimal and indirect forms of help at these times. That is, assuming that students have a general understanding of what to do and how to do it, teachers should help them past rough spots by providing relatively general and indirect hints or cues. If their assistance is too

Table 9.4 OUTLINE FOR STUDENT NOTE-TAKING ON THE TOPIC OF CAREERS IN THE BIOLOGICAL SCIENCES

I. Major career fields in the biological sciences
   A. Botanists
   B. Zoologists
   C. Entomologists
   D. Microbiologists
   E. Anatomists
   F. Physiologists
   G. Geneticists
   H. Emerging areas of "synthesis"
II. Employment opportunities
   A. Universities and colleges
   B. Federal government
   C. Private industry
      1. Hospitals
      2. Clinics
      3. Laboratories
      4. Research foundations
III. Working conditions
   A. Qualifications—necessary training
   B. Prospects of employment
   C. Income/fringe benefits
   D. Degree of mobility
IV. References for additional information
   A. History of field
   B. Training programs
   C. Career opportunities

direct or extensive, teachers will end up doing tasks for students instead of providing them with scaffolding to enable them to do the tasks themselves.

Most tasks will not have their full effects unless they are followed by reflection or debriefing. Here, the teacher reviews the task with the students, provides general feedback about performance, and reinforces the main ideas as they relate to the overall goals. These debriefing and reflection activities should also include opportunities for students to ask follow-up questions, share task-related observations or experiences, compare opinions, or in other ways deepen their appreciation of what they have learned and how it relates to their lives outside school.

Homework

The same guidelines that apply to assignments done in the classroom apply as well to homework assignments, but with the additional constraint that the homework must be realistic in length and difficulty given the students' abilities to work independently. Thus, 5 to 10 minutes per subject might be appropriate for fourth graders, whereas 30 to 60 minutes might be appropriate for college-bound high school students.

Also, homework performance must be monitored and followed up. Voluntary homework may be of some use to those students who do it conscientiously, but if homework is to have instructional value for the class as a whole, it will be necessary to set up accountability systems to make sure that it is completed on time and to review it the next day. In addition, reteaching and follow-up assignments may be needed for certain students.

SUMMARY

In this chapter we began our consideration of instruction by reviewing research, relating teacher behavior to student achievement, and addressing three important components of active teaching: presenting information to students, involving them in recitations and discussions, and engaging them in learning activities and assignments. In the process, we noted that instructional methods are means, not ends. The appropriateness of such methods depends on the teacher's instructional goals, and their effectiveness depends on the quality of their implementation. Research can inform teachers about the trade-offs that different instructional methods offer, but it cannot tell teachers what their goal priorities should be.

School effects and teacher effects research have identified factors associated with gains on standardized achievement tests. School effects research points to the importance of strong academic leadership that produces consensus on goal priorities and commitment to instructional excellence, an orderly school climate, positive teacher attitudes and expectations, a focus on instructional use of the available time, careful monitoring of progress toward goals through student testing and staff evaluation programs, strong parent involvement programs, and consistent emphasis on the importance of academic achievement. Teacher effects research indicates the value of teacher role definitions that emphasize positive expectations and a sense of efficacy, time allocation policies that maximize student opportunities to learn, use of effective classroom management and organization approaches, curriculum pacing that moves students through the curriculum rapidly but in small steps that minimize frustration, active instruction by the teacher (as opposed to expecting students to learn mostly on their own from interacting with curriculum materials), making sure that students achieve mastery of basic objectives, and maintaining a supportive learning environment.

Lecture/presentation and drill/recitation activities are well suited to the classroom context in certain respects and have their place as parts of a comprehensive approach to instruction. However, teachers should avoid using these techniques too frequently or in ways that limit the curriculum to rote memorizing of miscellaneous items of information. These techniques are used most effectively in lecture/recitation segments of lessons in which teachers help their students to develop networks of knowledge that are built around connected sets of important ideas and are learned with their implications in mind so that they can be used in appropriate application situations.

Lectures and other forms of information presentation are useful for arousing students' interest in a topic, providing advance organizers and learning sets to help them appreciate the topic's significance and approach it with appropriate learning strategies, bringing together and efficiently communicating important ideas about the topic, and providing information that students will not get from their textbooks. Good presentations are delivered enthusiastically and in clear, well-organized language. Where the instruction focuses on processes or skills, students will need not only verbal explanations but physical demonstrations. Such demonstrations should focus on the general principles involved and demystify the processes by articulating the thinking that guides observable actions.

Most activities based on teacher questioning should be recitations or discussions designed to provide opportunities for students to actively think about, respond to, and apply the content being taught. The questions should address a variety of cognitive levels of response and should be clear, brief, natural, and thought provoking. Most of all, they should be selected and sequenced so as to accomplish significant instructional goals. Questions should be addressed to the class as a whole and should be followed by sufficient wait time to allow students to process what is being asked and to begin to formulate responses to it. Students' responses should receive immediate feedback or other appropriate follow-up.

Discussions do not occur as frequently as they should in most classrooms. They require teachers to switch from the role of information source and authority figure to that of discussion leader who establishes a focus for the discussion and facilitates interaction but does not dominate it unnecessarily. In addition to asking questions, teachers can stimulate contributions to the discussion by making declarative statements or restatements, offering opinions, encouraging students to ask questions or elaborate on their previous statements, or simply remaining silent and waiting for a student to take the initiative.

Learning activities and assignments also are important components of instruction, even though they can be overused (especially when they take the form of silent individual work on fill-in-the-blank worksheets and other low-level tasks). Learning activities and assignments are valuable to the extent that they promote progress toward important instructional goals and are feasible and cost-effective given the constraints that apply. The most valuable activities tend to provide opportunities for interaction and reflective discourse rather than just solitary seatwork, and to engage students in thinking critically and creatively about and applying what they are learning, not just regurgitating facts and definitions. In order to have their full impact, activities and assignments need to be structured sufficiently to enable students to engage in them with awareness of their goals, and student work needs to be monitored and scaffolded sufficiently to ensure that they accomplish those goals satisfactorily. The same principles apply to homework assignments, but with the additional constraint that the assignments must be realistic in length and difficulty given the students' abilities to work independently.

SUGGESTED ACTIVITIES AND QUESTIONS

1. Since research on teaching first began, the lecture-and-recitation approach has always been found to be used heavily, if not exclusively, in most classrooms, even though educational theorists have been critical of it. Why is this? Can you see ways to (a) avoid overuse of this approach in your own teaching and (b) make sure that you use the approach effectively when you do use it?

2. Give concrete examples of instances when lecturing might be desirable.

3. How can you make your information presentations and skill demonstrations easier for your students to follow and remember?

4. Role-play the process of introducing and ending lessons *enthusiastically* and with *clarity*. Describe the classroom situation (age of students, etc.) so that others may provide you with appropriate feedback.

5. We have stressed that questions should be asked not just to assess student learning but to promote it. What does this mean? How can questions help students to develop important understandings?

6. How should teachers' questioning and feedback strategies in recitations differ from those in discussions?

7. Plan a brief (15-minute) discussion. Write out the sequence of questions you will use to advance the discussion fruitfully, applying the criteria we suggested for effective oral questions. Role-play your discussion if possible.

8. The criteria for effective *oral* questions mostly apply to written questions as well, but there are some exceptions. Try to identify other criteria that are applicable only to written questions. In what important ways do written and oral questions differ?

9. Why should students be allowed to talk freely about opinions that differ from those of the teacher or the book?

10. What is the optimal difficulty level of an assignment?

11. Given your current or intended teaching context (grade level, subject matter, types of students), what kinds of learning activities and assignments will be most needed for enabling your students to meet your instructional goals?

12. Would regular homework assignments be appropriate for this teaching context? If so, what kinds of assignments and for what purposes?

13. Why does active teaching, in which the teacher presents content to students and structures their subsequent practice and application exercises, generally produce more learning than approaches in which students are encouraged to learn on their own?

14. Why is it impossible to give a precise definition of an *effective teacher?*

15. Interview some first- or second-year teachers and some veteran teachers (with at least eight years in service) concerning their beliefs about classroom discussions. Which group uses more discussion, and why? Are there differences in how they approach the discussion method or in the purposes for which they use it?

16. Think through your experiences with the discussion method as a student, and discuss them with peers. Can you agree on the trade-offs that the method offers students? In what ways is it a desirable learning method? In what ways is it frustrating or otherwise problematic? What does this imply about when, why, and how to use discussion in your teaching?

REFERENCES

Alvermann, D., O'Brien, D., & Dillon, D. (1990). What teachers do when they say they're having discussions of content area reading assignments: A qualitative analysis. *Reading Research Quarterly, 25,* 296–322.

Anderson, L., Evertson, C., & Brophy, J. (1979). An experimental study of effective teaching in first-grade reading groups. *Elementary School Journal, 79,* 193–223.

Anderson, L., Evertson, C., & Brophy, J. (1982). *Principles of small-group instruction in elementary reading.* Occasional Paper No. 58. East Lansing: Michigan State University, Institute for Research on Teaching.

Anshutz, R. (1975). An investigation of wait-time and questioning techniques as an instructional variable for science methods students microteaching elementary school children. (Doctoral dissertation, University of Kansas, 1973). *Dissertation Abstracts International, 35,* 5978A.

Arnold, D., Atwood, R., & Rogers, V. (1974). Question and response levels and lapse time intervals. *Journal of Experimental Education, 43,* 11–15.

Ausubel, D. (1963). *The psychology of meaningful verbal learning: An introduction to school learning.* New York: Grune & Stratton.

Beck, I., & McKeown, M. (1988). Toward meaningful accounts in history texts for young learners. *Educational Researcher, 17*(6), 31–39.

Blumenfeld, P. (1992). The task and the teacher: Enhancing student thoughtfulness in science. In J. Brophy (Ed.), *Advances in research on teaching.* Vol 3. *Planning and managing learning tasks and activities* (pp. 81–114). Greenwich, CT: JAI.

Bloom, B., Englehart, M., Furst, E., Hill, W., & Krathwohl, D. (1956). *Taxonomy of educational objectives: The classification of educational goals.* Handbook I: *Cognitive domain.* New York: Longmans Green.

Brophy, J. (1988). Research on teacher effects: Uses and abuses. *Elementary School Journal, 89,* 3–21.

Brophy, J. (Ed.). (1989). *Advances in research on teaching.* Vol. I: *Teaching for meaningful understanding and self-regulated learning.* Greenwich, CT: JAI.

Brophy, J. (Ed.). (1992a). *Advances in research on teaching.* Volume 3. *Planning and managing learning tasks and activities.* Greenwich, CT : JAI Press.

Brophy, J. (1992b) The *de facto* national curriculum in U.S. elementary social studies: Critique of a representative example. *Journal of Curriculum Studies, 24,* 401–447.

Brophy, J., & Alleman, J. (1991). Activities as instructional tools: A framework for analysis and evaluation. *Educational Researcher, 20*(4), 9–23.

Brophy, J., & Good, T. (1974). *Teacher-student relationships: Causes and consequences.* New York: Holt.

Brophy, J., & Good, T. (1986). Teacher behavior and student achievement. In M. C. Wittrock (Ed.), *Handbook of research on teaching* (3rd ed.). New York: Macmillan.

Carlsen, W. (1991). Questioning in classrooms: A sociolinguistic perspective. *Review of Educational Research, 61,* 157–178.

Chilcoat, G. (1989). Instructional behaviors for clearer presentations in the classroom. *Instructional Science, 18,* 289–314.

Clark, C., & Peterson, P. (1986). Teachers' thought processes. In M. C. Wittrock (Ed.), *Handbook of research on teaching* (3rd ed.). New York: Macmillan.

Collins. A., & Stevens, A. (1983). A cognitive theory of inquiry teaching. In C. Reigeluth (Ed.), *Instructional-design theories and models: An overview of their current status.* Hillsdale, NJ: Erlbaum.

Cooper, H. (1989). *Homework.* New York: Longman.

Creemers, B., & Scheerens, J. (Guest editors). (1989). Developments in school effectiveness research. *International Journal of Educational Research, 13,* 685–825.

Cruickshank, D. (1985). Applying research on teacher clarity. *Journal of Teacher Education, 36,* 44–48.

Cruickshank, D. (1990). *Research that informs teachers and teacher educators.* Bloomington, IN: Phi Delta Kappa Educational Foundation.

Davis, R., & Alexander, L. (1977). *The lecture method.* East Lansing: Instructional Media Center, Michigan State University.

DeTure, L. (1979). Relative effects of modeling on the acquisition of wait-time by preservice elementary teachers and concomitant changes in dialogue patterns. *Journal of Research in Science Teaching, 16,* 553–562.

Dillon, J. (1979). Alternatives to questioning. *High School Journal, 62,* 217–222.

Dillon, J. (Ed.). (1988). *Questioning and teaching: A manual of practice.* London: Croom Helm.

Dillon, J. (Ed.). (1990). *The practice of questioning.* New York: Routledge.

Dreher, M., & Singer, H. (1989). Friendly texts and text-friendly teachers. *Theory into Practice, 28,* 98–104.

Duffy, G., Roehler, L., Meloth, M., & Vavrus, L. (1986). Conceptualizing instructional explanation. *Teaching and Teacher Education, 2,* 197–214.

Elliott, D., & Woodward, A. (Eds.). (1990). *Textbooks and schooling in the United States, Eighty-ninth yearbook of the National Society for the Study of Education, Part I.* Chicago: University of Chicago Press.

Epstein, J. (1988). *Homework practices, achievements, and behaviors of elementary school students* (Report No. 26). Baltimore: Center for Research on Elementary and Middle Schools, the Johns Hopkins University.

Fagan, E., Hassler, D., & Szabo, M. (1981). Evaluation of questioning strategies in language arts instruction. *Research in the Teaching of English, 15,* 267–273.

Farrar, M. (1986). Teacher questions: The complexity of the cognitively simple. *Instructional Science, 15,* 89–107.

Fisher, C., Berliner, D., Filby, N., Marliave, R., Cahen, L., & Dishaw, M. (1980). Teaching behaviors, academic learning time, student achievement: An overview. In C. Denham & A. Lieberman (Eds.), *Time to learn.* Washington, DC: National Institute of Education.

Freiberg, H., Prokosch, N., Treister, E., & Stein, T. (1990). Turning around five at-risk elementary schools. *School Effectiveness and School Improvement, 1,* 5–25.

Gage, N., & Berliner, D. (1984). *Educational psychology* (3rd. ed.). Boston: Houghton Mifflin.

Gliessman, D., Pugh, R., Brown, L., Archer, A., & Snyder, S. (1989). Applying a research-based model to teacher skill training. *Journal of Educational Research, 83,* 69–81.

Good, T., & Brophy, J. (1974). Changing teacher and student behavior: An empirical investigation. *Journal of Educational Psychology, 66,* 390–405.

Good., T., & Brophy, J. (1986). School effects. In M. C. Wittrock (Ed.), *Handbook of research on teaching* (3rd. ed.). New York: Macmillan.

Good, T., & Brophy, J. (1990). *Educational psychology: A realistic approach* (4th ed.). New York: Longman.

Good, T., & Grouws, D. (1979). The Missouri Mathematics Effectiveness Project: An experimental study in fourth-grade classrooms. *Journal of Educational Psychology, 71,* 355–362.

Good, T., Grouws, D., & Ebmeier, H. (1983). *Active mathematics teaching.* New York: Longman.

Groisser, P. (1964). *How to use the fine art of questioning.* New York: Teachers' Practical Press.

Henson, K. (1988). *Methods and strategies for teaching in secondary and middle schools.* New York: Longman.

Joyce, B., & Weil, M. (1986). *Models of teaching* (3rd ed.). Englewood Cliffs, NJ: Prentice-Hall.

Kiewra, K. (1987). Notetaking and review: The research and its implications. *Instructional Science, 16,* 233–249.

Luiten, J., Ames, W., & Ackerson, G. (1970). A meta-analysis of the effects of advance organizers on learning and retention. *American Educational Research Journal, 17,* 211–218.

McCaleb, J., & White, J. (1980). Critical dimensions in evaluating teacher clarity. *Journal of Classroom Interaction, 15,* 27–30.

McCaslin, M., & Good, T. (in press). *Listening to students.* New York: HarperCollins.

McLeish, J. (1976). Lecture method. In N. Gage (Ed.), *The psychology of teaching methods* (Part I). *(75th Yearbook of the National Society for the Study of Education).* Chicago: University of Chicago Press.

McMann, R. (1979). In defense of lecture. *Social Studies, 70,* 270–274.

Miller, D., & Kelley, M. (1991). Interventions for improving homework performance: A critical review. *School Psychology Quarterly, 6,* 174–185.

Osborn, J. (1984). Workbooks that accompany basal reading programs. In G. Duffy, L. Roehler, & J. Mason (Eds.), *Comprehension instruction: Perspectives and suggestions.* New York: Longman.

Reynolds, A. (1992). What is competent beginning teaching? A review of the literature. *Review of Educational Research, 62,* 1–35.

Rice, D. (1977). The effect of question-asking instruction on preservice elementary science teachers. *Journal of Research in Science Teaching, 14,* 353–359.

Rickards, J. (1982). Homework. In H. Mitzel (Ed.), *Encyclopedia of educational research* (5th ed.). New York: Free Press.

Riley, J. (1980). *The effects of teachers' wait-time and cognitive questioning level on pupil science achievement.* Paper presented at the annual meeting of the National Association for Research in Science Teaching, Boston.

Roby, T. (1988). Models of discussion, In J. Dillon (Ed.), *Questioning and discussion: A multidisciplinary study* (pp. 163–191). Norwood, NJ: Ablex.

Rosenshine, B. (1968). To explain: A review of research. *Educational Leadership, 26,* 275–280.

Rosenshine, B. (1970). Enthusiastic teaching: A research review. *School Review 78,* 499–514.

Rosenshine, B., & Furst, N. (1973). The use of direct observation to study teaching. In R. Travers (Ed.), *Second handbook of research on teaching.* Chicago: Rand McNally.

Rowe, M. (1974a). Science, silence, and sanctions. *Science and Children, 6,* 11–13.

Rowe, M. (1974b). Wait time and rewards as instructional variables, their influence on language, logic, and fate control: Part I—Wait time. *Journal of Research in Science Teaching, 11,* 81–94.

Rowe, M. (1986). Wait time: Slowing down may be a way of speeding up! *Journal of Teacher Education 37,* 43–50.

Schuck, R., (1981). The impact of set induction on student achievement and retention. *Journal of Educational Research, 74,* 227–232.

Smith, L., & Land, M. (1981). Low-inference verbal behaviors related to teacher clarity. *Journal of Classroom Interaction, 17,* 37–42.

Strother, D. (1984). Homework: Too much, just right, or not enough? *Phi Delta Kappan, 65,* 423–426.

Swift, J., Gooding, C., & Swift, P. (1988). Questions and wait time. In J. Dillon (Ed.), *Questioning and discussion: A multidisciplinary study* (pp. 192–212). Norwood NJ: Ablex.

Teddlie, C., Kirby, P., & Stringfield, S. (1989). Effective versus ineffective schools: Observable differences in the classroom. *American Journal of Education, 97,* 221–236.

Tobin, K. (1983a). The influence of wait-time on classroom learning. *European Journal of Science Education 5*(1), 35–48.

Tobin, K. (1983b). Management of time in classrooms. In B. Fraser (Ed.), *Classroom management.* Bentley, Australia: Western Australia Institute of Technology.

Tobin, K., & Capie, W. (1982). Relationships between classroom process variables and middle-school science achievement. *Journal of Educational Psychology, 74,* 441–454.

Tyson-Bernstein, H. (1988). *A conspiracy of good intentions: America's textbook fiasco.* Washington, DC: Council for Basic Education.

Waxman, H., & Walberg, H. (Eds.). (1991). *Effective teaching: Current research.* Berkeley, CA: McCutchan.

Wright, C., & Nuthall, G. (1970). The relationships between teacher behaviors and pupil achievement in three experimental elementary science lessons. *American Educational Research Journal, 7,* 477–492.

FORM 9.1   Teacher Lectures, Presentations, and Demonstrations

USE: *When the teacher lectures, presents information, or demonstrates skills to the class*
PURPOSE: *To assess the effectiveness of the presentation*
Enter a checkmark for each of the following features that was included effectively in the presentation, and a 0 for each feature that was omitted or handled ineffectively. Add your comments below, emphasizing constructive suggestions for improvement.

CHECKLIST

INTRODUCTION

_____ 1. States purpose or objectives
_____ 2. Gives overview or advance organizer
_____ 3. Distributes a study guide or instructs the students concerning how they are expected to respond (what notes to take, etc.)

BODY OF PRESENTATION

_____ 4. Is well prepared; speaks fluently without hesitation or confusion
_____ 5. Projects enthusiasm for the material
_____ 6. Maintains eye contact with the students
_____ 7. Speaks at an appropriate pace (neither too fast nor too slow)
_____ 8. Speaks with appropriate voice modulation (rather than a monotone)
_____ 9. Uses appropriate expressions, movements, and gestures (rather than speaking woodenly)
_____ 10. Content is well structured and sequenced
_____ 11. New terms are clearly defined
_____ 12. Key concepts or terms are emphasized (preferably not only verbally but by holding up or pointing to examples, writing or underlining on the board or overhead projector, etc.)
_____ 13. Includes appropriate analogies or examples that are effective in enabling students to relate the new to the familiar and the abstract to the concrete
_____ 14. Where appropriate, facts are distinguished from opinions
_____ 15. Where appropriate, lengthy presentations are divided into recognizable segments, with clear transitions between segments and minisummaries concluding each segment
_____ 16. Where necessary, questions the students following each major segment of a lengthy presentation (rather than waiting until the end)
_____ 17. Monitors student response; is encouraging and responsive regarding student questions and comments on the material

CONCLUSION

_____ 18. Concludes with summary or integration of the presentation
_____ 19. Invites student questions or comments
_____ 20. Follows up on the presentation by making a transition into a recitation activity, a follow-up assignment, or some other activity that will allow the students an opportunity to practice or apply the material

COMMENTS:

FORM 9.2 Questioning Techniques

USE: When teacher is asking class or group questions
PURPOSE: To see if teacher is following principles for good questioning practices
For each question, code the following categories:

BEHAVIOR CATEGORIES

CODES

A. TYPE OF QUESTION ASKED
1. Academic: Factual. Seeks specific correct response
2. Academic: Opinion. Seeks opinion on a complex issue where there is no clear-cut response
3. Nonacademic: Question deals with personal, procedural, or disciplinary matters rather than curriculum

B. TYPE OF RESPONSE REQUIRED
1. Thought question. Student must reason through to a conclusion or explain something at length
2. Fact question. Student must provide fact(s) from memory
3. Choice question. Requires only a yes-no or either-or response

C. SELECTION OF RESPONDENT
1. Names child before asking question
2. Calls on volunteer (after asking question)
3. Calls on nonvolunteer (after asking question)

D. PAUSE (AFTER ASKING QUESTION)
1. Paused a few seconds before calling on student
2. Failed to pause before calling on student
3. Not applicable; teacher named student before asking question

E. TONE AND MANNER IN PRESENTING QUESTION
1. Question presented as challenge or stimulation
2. Question presented matter-of-factly
3. Question presented as threat or test

	A	B	C	D	E
1.	1	2	2	1	2
2.	1	2	2	1	2
3.	1	3	2	1	2
4.	1	2	2	1	2
5.	1	2	2	1	2
6.	1	3	2	1	2
7.	1	2	2	1	2
8.	2	1	2	1	1
9.	1	2	2	1	2
10.	1	2	2	1	2
11.	1	2	2	1	2
12.	1	2	2	1	2
13.	—	—	—	—	—
14.	—	—	—	—	—
15.	—	—	—	—	—
16.	—	—	—	—	—
17.	—	—	—	—	—
18.	—	—	—	—	—
19.	—	—	—	—	—
20.	—	—	—	—	—
21.	—	—	—	—	—
22.	—	—	—	—	—
23.	—	—	—	—	—
24.	—	—	—	—	—
25.	—	—	—	—	—
26.	—	—	—	—	—
27.	—	—	—	—	—
28.	—	—	—	—	—
29.	—	—	—	—	—
30.	—	—	—	—	—
31.	—	—	—	—	—
32.	—	—	—	—	—
33.	—	—	—	—	—
34.	—	—	—	—	—
35.	—	—	—	—	—
36.	—	—	—	—	—
37.	—	—	—	—	—
38.	—	—	—	—	—
39.	—	—	—	—	—
40.	—	—	—	—	—

Record any information relevant to the following:
Multiple Questions. Tally the number of times the teacher:
1. Repeats or rephrases question before calling on anyone *II*
2. Asks two or more questions at the same time *0*

Sequence. Were questions integrated into an orderly sequence, or did they seem to be random or unrelated?
Teacher seemed to be following sequence given in manual (led up to next history unit).
Did students themselves pose questions? *No*

Was there student-student interaction? How much? *None*

When appropriate, did the teacher redirect questions to several students, or ask students to evaluate their own or others' responses? *No*

Chapter 10

Helping Students to Construct Usable Knowledge

*T*he following is an abbreviated version of part of the transcript of a fifth-grade literature lesson recorded by Quirk and Cianciolo (1993). The teacher is asking her students to consider the importance of the setting in the book under discussion (*The Lion, the Witch, and the Wardrobe*), and in fanciful fiction in general. Note her reliance on questioning rather than didactic explanation. How would you assess her method as a way to develop her students' understanding and appreciation of the concept of setting as an element of literature? Would you do anything differently? How might you follow up this segment after Martha makes her concluding comment?

During a discussion about *The Lion, the Witch, and the Wardrobe*, Ms. Williams asked her students to consider the importance of the setting in this book and in fanciful fiction in general. An abbreviated version of the transcript of the lesson follows:

TEACHER: How important is the setting to this story?

SUSIE: Very, very.

TEACHER: Why?

SUSIE: Because if the setting was in a different place, they wouldn't have got [sic] the wardrobe. And then they wouldn't have gone to Narnia.

TEACHER: Okay. Jessica.

JESSICA: I think they could have changed the setting a little. They had to make it into a different world, but they didn't have to make it all snow. They could have made it spring and the children always wanted it to be winter.

TEACHER: Okay. So they could have changed the seasons very easily. But you said something about it had to be Narnia.

JESSICA: It didn't have to be Narnia, but it had to be a different world.

TEACHER: A different world. Why? That's a very good point, Jessica. Why would it have to be a different world? Darrin?

DARRIN: Because it makes you like, interested because you could go through a wardrobe and walk and walk, and then you enter into a new world.

TEACHER: Okay, and what do you think Steve?

STEVEN: I think it [the setting) is very important, because if you put them [the characters] in a setting like [our town] it wouldn't be exciting. I mean, like in Narnia you have all these monsters and the witch.

TEACHER: What does it do to our imagination when we have, as Jessica suggested, another world, or another time, or another place? Barbara?

BARBARA: If it's exciting, we want to read more. You can make it the world you want it to be.

TEACHER: Absolutely, very good. Jason?

JASON: When it's another world it makes your mind wander and makes you want to get out of everything. But it also makes you think that you're actually in that world. It's kinda boring if it was just in the professor's house or something. But it's more exciting when it's in another world.

TEACHER: Why is it okay to have this other world situation in Narnia, but in *The Tales of a Fourth Grade Nothing*, it is a familiar situation. Judy Blume books are set in familiar places we can identify like [our town], or whatever. Why is it okay for those books, but I'm hearing some of you say Narnia has to be way out some place. Barbara?

BARBARA: Because Judy Blume's telling what could really happen, but here in C. S. Lewis' books it's imagination and imagination has to lead you the way or else you aren't gonna get anywhere.

TEACHER: Okay. One last comment. Martha?

MARTHA: I think that it can be different because of the titles. There wouldn't be a lion, a witch, and a wardrobe in [our town]. It has to be somewhere, where anything can happen.

In Chapter 9 we reviewed research that documented the connections between active teaching (presenting information, structuring discourse, monitoring work on assignments) and student gains on achievement tests. These widely replicated research findings are gratifying for several reasons. First, they reaffirm the fact that teachers make a difference, by showing that some teachers elicit more achievement gains than others do and by pointing to the classroom management and instructional behaviors associated with these achievement gains. Also, such findings move the field beyond unsupported claims about effective practices toward scientific statements based on credible data. Finally, the findings are gratifying to most teachers because they validate principles that teachers have developed through experience.

TEACHING FOR UNDERSTANDING, APPRECIATION, AND APPLICATION OF KNOWLEDGE

Even as the contributions of research on school effects and teacher effects were being consolidated and applied in teacher education, research on teaching was moving on to new phases. One reason for this was increasing recognition of certain limitations in process-outcome research. First, this research focused on important but very basic aspects of teaching. Its findings differentiated the least effective teachers from other teachers, but they did not address the subtler fine points that distinguish the most outstanding teachers. Second, most of this research relied on standardized tests as the measures of learning. Consequently, its assessment focused on mastery of relatively isolated knowledge items and skill components without including the degree to which students had developed understanding of networks of connected content or could use this content in realistic application situations.

These concerns led to new forms of research on subject-matter teaching. The new studies focused on teaching for *understanding*, which implies that students learn not only the individual elements in a network of related content but also the connections among them, so that they can explain the content in their own words and can access and use it in appropriate application situations in and out of school (Bereiter & Scardamalia, 1987; Brophy, 1989; Glaser, 1984; Prawat, 1989; Resnick, 1987). Students who learn content with understanding not only learn the content itself but appreciate the reasons for learning it and retain it in a form that makes it usable when needed. Recent research on subject-matter teaching has involved exemplary teachers who know their subjects thoroughly and emphasize developing understanding when planning their instruction. The research focuses intensively on particular curriculum units or lessons, taking into account the teacher's instructional goals and assessing students' learning accordingly. The researchers find out what the teacher is trying to accomplish, record detailed information about classroom processes, and then assess learning using evaluation measures keyed to the instructional goals. Often the evaluation methods include detailed interviews or collection of portfolios of student work in addition to or instead of more conventional short-answer tests.

While deepening our understanding of the role of the teacher in stimulating student learning, recent research has also emphasized the role of the student. This reflects the influence of developmental and cognitive psychologists who hold *constructivist* views of learning and teaching (Davis, Maher, & Noddings, 1990; Resnick & Klopfer, 1989; Steffe, Cobb, & von Glasersfeld, 1988). Constructivists believe that students learn through a process of active construction that involves making connections between new information and existing networks of prior knowledge. Constructivists emphasize the importance of relating new content to the knowledge that students already possess, as well as providing opportunities for students to process and apply the new learning. They believe that before knowledge becomes truly *generative*—usable for interpreting new situations, solving problems, thinking and reasoning, and learning generally—students must elaborate and question what they are told, examine the new content in relation to more familiar content, and build new knowledge structures (Resnick & Klopfer, 1989). Otherwise, the knowledge may remain *inert*—recallable when cued by questions or test items very similar to those that were used in practice exercises, but not applicable when it might be useful in everyday living.

Although the term *constructivist* is relatively new, many constructivist ideas can be traced to John Dewey and Jean Piaget and some go back at least as far as Socrates. Many are embodied in historically significant educational movements such as open education, inquiry learning, and discovery learning, as well as in contemporary movements such as whole-language teaching and portfolio assessment. Current constructivist approaches to teaching for understanding include a variety of theoretical rationales and suggested teaching methods, but they all involve some subset of the following key ideas drawn from recent scholarship on cognitive development and learning.

Knowledge as Constructed

Common to all approaches to teaching for understanding, appreciation, and application of knowledge is the core idea of constructivism: *Students develop new knowledge through a process of active construction*. They do not merely passively receive or copy input from teachers or textbooks. Instead, they actively mediate it by trying to make sense of it and relate it to what they already know (or think they know) about the topic. This is precisely what we want them to do, because unless students build representations of the new learning, "making it their own" by paraphrasing it in their own words and considering its meanings and implications, the learning will be retained only as relatively meaningless and inert rote memories. However, each student builds his or her own unique representation of what was communicated, and this may or may not include a complete and accurate reconstruction of what the teacher or textbook author intended to convey. Sometimes the learning is incomplete or distorted.

Even when the basic message is reconstructed as intended, it gets connected to each learner's unique set of prior understandings. As a result, each learner constructs a unique set of meanings and implications of "the same" set of ideas, and "files" it in memory accordingly. For example, on reading a fictional or nonfictional narrative about mountain climbers who overcame potential disasters to achieve their goals successfully, one reader might remember and think about the text primarily as a story about achievement motivation, another as a story about the value of teamwork, another as a story about how shared adventure seals the bonds of friendship, and yet another as an illustration of the challenges and specialized techniques involved in mountain climbing. The students were exposed to the same narrative as constructed by its author and their reconstructions of it all include the same basic storyline, but they emphasize different meanings and potential implications.

Constructivists differ in their ideas about the nature of knowledge. Empirically oriented constructivists believe that knowledge is anchored in the external environment and exists independently of the learner's cognitive activities, so they tend to speak about helping learners to construct accurate conceptions (Case, 1982; Ginsburg & Opper, 1979; Rumelhart & Norman, 1981). In contrast, radical constructivists believe that knowledge resides only in the constructions of learners. Consequently, one cannot teach precise representations of "truth," but can only negotiate shared meanings with students and provide them with opportunities to construct useful understandings by overcoming obstacles or contradictions that arise as they engage in purposeful activity (Cobb, 1986; Cobb, Yackel, & Wood, 1992; von Glasersfeld, 1984). Whatever their underlying philosophical views, however, all constructivists emphasize that teachers need to go beyond information transmission models (teachers or texts tell, students memorize) and move toward knowledge construction models of teaching and learning. These involve structuring reflective discussions of the meanings and implications of content and providing opportunities for students to use the content as they engage in inquiry, problem solving, or decision making (Brooks, 1990).

Knowledge construction models of teaching and learning have been emphasized in the curriculum and instruction guidelines released in recent years by the American Association for the Advancement of Science, the National Council of Teachers of Mathematics, the National Council for the Social Studies, the National Council of Teachers of English, and other professional organizations concerned with K–12 education in general or with the teaching of particular school subjects. In addition, organizations concerned with the education of young children have emphasized knowledge construction models of teaching and learning in documents dealing with the concept of developmentally appropriate practice in preschool and primary classrooms (Bredekamp, 1987; National Association of State Boards of Education, 1988).

Knowledge Networks Structured Around Powerful Ideas

As educators, we want students not just to retain information but to develop deep understandings and reflect thoughtfully about what they are learning. We want them to become scientific inquirers, critical thinkers, systematic problem solvers, and value-based decision makers. If these lofty goals are to be accomplished, we need to teach with emphasis on higher order thinking about and applications of what is learned. However, misuse of hierarchical schemes such as the Bloom taxonomy of cognitive objectives (Bloom et al., 1956) to guide curriculum development has implanted the notions that instructional strands are hierarchies of knowledge and that one must proceed through them in sequence, moving linearly from lower levels to higher levels. Thus, one introduces a topic by beginning at the knowledge level and staying there until a complete base of information has been developed, then moves to the comprehension level by helping students begin to translate the information into different terms and probe its connections, then moves to the application level, and so on. Movement to higher levels (analysis, synthesis, and evaluation) occurs only after mastery of lower levels has been accomplished.

Recent theory and research suggest that there is no need to impose such a rigid, linear hierarchy on teaching and learning (Brophy, 1989; Marzano et al., 1988). The argument is that, instead of viewing knowledge as composed of linear hierarchies, we should view it as composed of networks structured around key ideas. These networks include facts, concepts, and generalizations, along with related values, dispositions, procedural knowledge (implementation skills), and conditional knowledge (of when and why to access and apply parts of the network). An important implication of this conception of knowledge is that one can enter and begin to learn about a network almost anywhere, not just at the low end of a linear hierarchy. Learning can be couched within an applications context and students can be engaged in higher-order thinking about a topic right from the beginning of instruction. For example, a teacher might begin teaching about a mathematical operation by posing a problem that requires the operation for efficient solution. Or, the teacher might begin a lesson on climate and weather by asking students to speculate about why there often is wet weather on one side of a mountain range but dry weather on the other side.

Shifting from a linear to a network conception of knowledge structuring fits well with ideas about teaching subjects for understanding, appreciation, and application. Because comprehension (i.e., understanding) is near the bottom of the Bloom taxonomy, teaching for understanding is sometimes viewed as a low-level cognitive objective. However, scholars have pointed out that, in order to achieve a reasonably complete understanding of a network of knowledge, students will have to engage in application, analysis, synthesis, and evaluation activities, not just in activities designed to build knowledge and comprehension. Consequently, the notion of separating cognitive levels of learning and addressing them in sequential order breaks down when one is confronted with the kinds of integrated instruction involved in teaching for meaningful understanding.

The preceding paragraphs assume that the content has been selected and organized as means to move students toward important educational goals. That is, they assume that the content is *worth* understanding, appreciating, and applying in the first place. If so, it will be structured as a series of networks of connected knowledge, not as a disconnected parade of facts and isolated skills. Furthermore, it will be taught with emphasis on the powerful ideas that anchor the networks and provide a basis for potential applications.

Many more things are worth teaching than we have time to teach in school, so breadth of topic coverage must be balanced against depth of development of each topic. This is an enduring dilemma that can only be managed in sensible ways, not a problem that can be solved once and for all. However, recent research suggests that we have drifted in the direction of addressing far too many topics and including too many trite or pointless details. Curriculum analyses in all of the subject areas suggest the need for teacher decision making about how to reduce breadth of coverage, structure the content around powerful ideas, and develop these ideas in depth.

The Role of Prior Knowledge

Construction of knowledge goes more smoothly when learners can address new content in the context of relating it to their existing background knowledge. New content is not first understood in some abstract way and only later related to existing knowledge; instead, it is interpreted from the beginning within contexts supplied by that existing knowledge. Collections of prior knowledge that provide contexts for meaningful interpretation of new content are usually called *schemas* (Anderson, 1984; diSibio, 1982). If new content can be related to existing schemas, activation of these schemas can help learners to develop expectations about the nature of the content, identify and pay special attention to its most important elements, and fill in gaps where information is implied rather than stated explicitly. Consider the following paragraph:

> When Mary arrived, the woman at the door greeted her and checked her name. A few minutes later, she was escorted to her chair and shown the day's menu. The attendant was helpful but brusque, almost to the point of being rude. Later, she paid the woman at the door and left.

You probably were able to interpret this rather sketchy narrative because you recognized that the events took place in a restaurant, that Mary had made reservations, and that she was seated by a hostess at a table (not merely in a chair), that the "attendant" was a waiter, and that the "woman at the door" was a cashier. You could infer all of this information, even though none of it was explicit in the text, because you possess a "restaurant" schema that includes such slots as "being seated," "ordering," and "paying the check" (Schank & Abelson, 1977).

Activation of relevant background knowledge can make learning of new content easier and more efficient, at least if the activated schemas are suited to the instructional goals (Adams, 1990; Anderson, 1984; Gagne & Dick, 1983). Teachers can prepare students for story reading by telling them what the story is about and asking them questions to activate schemas that they will find useful in comprehending it. Teachers also can help students to activate relevant prior knowledge by drawing analogies or suggesting examples that link the new content to familiar ideas or experiences, by taking an inventory of what students know (or think they know) about the topic before beginning instruction, or by asking questions that require students to make predictions about the content or to suggest solutions to problems based on it. The K-W-L technique described in Chapter 6 is another way to stimulate relevant prior knowledge when introducing new content.

Knowledge Restructuring and Conceptual Change

Learning is a constructive process that involves "seeking after meaning," so students routinely draw on prior knowledge as they attempt to make sense of what they are learning. Whether schemas are activated through the students' own initiative or in response to comments or questions from the teacher, activation of relevant schemas will facilitate learning if the schemas are accurate and support accomplishment of the instructional goals. When schemas are not accurate or not well suited to the goals, however, their activation will interfere with learning

(Alvermann, Smith, & Readence, 1985). If the new content is filtered through schemas that are oversimplified, distorted, or otherwise invalid, students may develop misconceptions instead of the target conceptions that the teacher is trying to teach. For example, many students believe that the sun orbits the earth, because they have "seen" it do so. Sometimes this prior knowledge is so well entrenched that it causes certain students to miss what the teacher or textbook is saying when discussing cycles of day and night. Such students may emerge from a lesson having learned that particular parts of the earth experience daylight at times when they are exposed to the sun, yet still believing that cycles of day and night are due to orbiting of the sun around the earth instead of vice versa.

Besides adding new elements to an existing cognitive structure, active construction of knowledge may involve changing the structure through processes of *restructuring* and *conceptual change*. Sometimes the needed restructuring is relatively minor and easily accomplished, but sometimes students need to undergo more radical restructuring that involves simultaneous change in large networks of connected knowledge (Carey, 1985; Chinn & Brewer, 1993; Vosniadou & Brewer, 1987). Radical restructuring can be time consuming and difficult to accomplish.

Mere exposure to correct conceptions will not necessarily stimulate the needed restructuring because learners may activate long-standing and firmly believed misconceptions that cause them to ignore, distort, or miss the implications of aspects of the new learning that contradict their powerful misconceptions. It may be necessary to help students first to see the contradictions between what they currently believe and what the teacher is trying to teach, and then to appreciate that the target concepts are more valid, more powerful, more useful, or in some other way preferable to their existing concepts.

Knowledge as Socially Constructed

Some constructivist accounts of learning, especially those that have been influenced heavily by the developmental psychology of Jean Piaget, depict learning as primarily a solitary activity. The focus is on the individual child who develops knowledge through exploration, discovery, and reflection on everyday life experiences. However, most constructivist accounts are variants of *social constructivism*. In addition to emphasizing that learning is a process of active construction of meaning, social constructivists emphasize that the process works best in social settings in which two or more individuals engage in sustained discourse about a topic. Participation in such discussions helps participants to advance their learning in several ways. Exposure to new input from others makes them aware of things that they did no know and leads to expansion of their cognitive structures. Exposure to ideas that contradict their own beliefs may cause them to examine those beliefs and perhaps restructure them. The need to communicate their ideas to others forces them to articulate those ideas more clearly, which sharpens their conceptions and often leads to recognition of new connections. As a result, cognitive structures become better developed (both better differentiated and better organized). Social constructivist ideas have been influenced heavily by the writings of the Russian developmental psychologist Lev Vygotsky (1962, 1978). Vygotsky believed that children's thought (cognition) and language (speech) begin as separate functions but become intimately connected during the preschool years as children learn to use language as a mechanism for thinking. Gradually, more and more of their learning is mediated through language, especially learning of cultural knowledge that is difficult if not impossible to develop through direct experience with the physical environment. Children initially acquire much of their cultural knowledge through overt speech (conversations with others, especially parents and teachers). Then they elaborate on this knowledge and connect it to other knowledge through inner speech (thinking mediated through language, or self-talk).

Literacy, numeracy, and knowledge in the subjects taught at school are prominent examples of the kinds of cultural knowledge that Vygotsky viewed as socially constructed. He suggested that this learning proceeds most efficiently when children are consistently exposed to *teaching in the zone of proximal development*. The zone of proximal development refers to the range of knowledge and skills that students are not yet ready to learn on their own but could learn with help from teachers. The children already know things that are "below" the zone, or can learn them easily on their own without help. They cannot learn things that are "above" the zone, even with help.

Ideas about teaching within the zone of proximal development, sometimes summarized in the term *zone theory*, resemble in some ways the ideas connected with the notion of *readiness* for learning. However, readiness is passive in its implications, suggesting that teachers can do little but wait until children become ready to learn something (presumably due to maturation of needed cognitive structures) before trying to teach it to them. Zone theory assumes that children's readiness for learning something depends much more on their accumulated prior knowledge about the topic than on maturation of cognitive structures, and that advances in knowledge will be stimulated primarily through the social construction that occurs during sustained discourse, most rapidly through teaching in the zone of proximal development (Moll, 1990; Newman, Griffin, & Cole, 1989; Rogoff & Wertsch, 1984; Tharp & Gallimore, 1988; Wertsch, 1985, 1991; Wertsch & Tulviste, 1992).

Social constructivists emphasize teaching that features sustained dialogue or discussion in which participants pursue a topic in depth, exchanging views and negotiating meanings and implications as they explore its ramifications. Along with teacher-structured whole-class discussions, this includes cooperative learning that is constructed as students work in pairs or small groups. Key features of social constructivist approaches to teaching and learning are summarized in Table 10.1.

Situated Learning and Authentic Tasks

Many social constructivists, especially those interested in teaching procedural and conditional knowledge (knowing how and when to use skills and other procedures, as opposed to knowing facts, concepts, and other propositional knowledge) believe that instruction in schools should be modeled as much as possible on the instruction that occurs in natural settings. Schooling brings people together and thus makes possible the social construction of knowledge, but it is an artificial environ-

Table 10.1   TEACHING AND LEARNING AS TRANSMISSION OF INFORMATION VERSUS AS SOCIAL CONSTRUCTION OF KNOWLEDGE

Transmission view	Social construction view
Knowledge as fixed body of information transmitted from teacher or text to students	Knowledge as developing interpretations coconstructed through discussion
Texts, teacher as authoritative sources of expert knowledge to which students defer	Authority for constructed knowledge resides in the arguments and evidence cited in its support by students as well as by texts or teacher; everyone has expertise to contribute
Teacher is responsible for managing students' learning by providing information and leading students through activities and assignments	Teacher and students share responsibility for initiating and guiding learning efforts
Teacher explains, checks for understanding, and judges correctness of students' responses	Teacher acts as discussion leader who poses questions, seeks clarifications, promotes dialogue, helps group recognize areas of consensus and of continuing disagreement
Students memorize or replicate what has been explained or modeled	Students strive to make sense of new input by relating it to their prior knowledge and by collaborating in dialogue with others to conconstruct shared understandings
Discourse emphasizes drill and recitation in response to convergent questions; focus is on eliciting correct answers	Discourse emphasizes reflective discussion of networks of connected knowledge; questions are more divergent but designed to develop understanding of the powerful ideas that anchor these networks; focus is on eliciting students' thinking
Activities emphasize replication of models or applications that require following step-by-step algorithms	Activities emphasize applications to authentic issues and problems that require higher-order thinking
Students work mostly alone, practicing what has been transmitted to them in order to prepare themselves to compete for rewards by reproducing it on demand	Students collaborate by acting as a learning community that constructs shared understandings through sustained dialogue

ment in many respects and tends to teach generic knowledge and skills that have been abstracted and removed from the application settings that gave birth to them. Too often, the generic knowledge and skills are forgotten or remain inert—not easily accessible when needed in out-of-school settings.

Scholars who have studied learning in home and job settings believe that it is a mistake to separate knowing from doing, or what is learned from how it is learned and used (Brown, Collins, & Duguid, 1989; Lave & Wenger, 1991; Rogoff, 1990). They believe that *cognition is situated;* that is, that knowledge is adapted to the settings, purposes, and tasks to which it is applied (and for which it was constructed in the first place). Consequently, they argue, if we want students to learn and retain knowledge in a form that makes it usable for application, we need to make it possible for them to develop the knowledge in the natural setting, using methods and tasks suited to that setting. In this view, the ideal model for schooling is the on-the-job training that occurs as experienced mentors work with novices or apprentices.

Whatever the merits of this notion, there are obvious limits to the degree to which it is feasible to consider shifting significant portions of the school's curriculum from in-school to out-of-school settings. However, the notion of situated cognition has implications for the design of in-school instruction as well. In particular, it implies that we ought to be more conscious of potential applications when we select and plan our teaching of curriculum content, and we should emphasize those applications in presenting the content to the students.

Also, as much as possible, we should allow students to learn through engagement in authentic tasks. *Authentic tasks* require using what is being learned for accomplishing the very sorts of life applications that justify the inclusion of this learning in the curriculum in the first place. If it is not possible to engage students in the actual life applications that the curriculum is supposed to prepare them for, then one can at least engage them in realistic simulations of these applications. Examples of authentic activities are listed in Table 10.2.

The notion of situated cognition implies that students will need to learn such things as inquiry, critical thinking, and problem solving by engaging in them under realistic conditions. Teachers will have to work within the constraints imposed by students' current readiness and by access to settings and equipment, but they still can engage their students in inquiry into worthwhile and meaningful questions, critical thinking about significant policy issues, and discussion of potential methods of solving real problems.

Scaffolding and Transfer of Responsibility for Managing Learning from Teacher to Learner

Ideas about situated learning and about teaching in the zone of proximal development tend to cluster around the notions of scaffolding and gradual transfer of responsibility for managing learning from the teacher to the student. Instructional *scaffolding* is a general term for the task assistance or simplification strategies that teachers might use to bridge the gap between what students are capable of doing on their own and what they are capable of doing with help. Scaffolds are forms of support provided by the teacher (or another student) to help students progress from their current abilities to the intended goal (Rosenshine & Meister, 1992). Like the scaffolds used by house painters, the support provided through scaffolding is temporary, adjustable, and removed when it is no longer needed. Examples of scaffolding include cognitive modeling (in which the teacher demonstrates task performance while articulating the thinking that guides it), prompts or cues that help students move on to the next step when they are temporarily stuck, and questions that help them to diagnose the reasons for errors and develop repair strategies.

Following Wood, Bruner, and Ross (1976), Rogoff (1990) suggested that appropriately scaffolded instruction includes the following six components:

1. Developing student interest in accomplishing the intended goal of the task
2. Demonstrating an idealized version of the act to be performed

Table 10.2 AUTHENTIC ACTIVITIES

K–3

Math: Apply basic four functions to problems in saving/budgeting money, sharing/dividing treats

Science: Observe and take notes on plant growth and decomposition, events occurring in the class aquarium

Social Studies: Recreate the school day in a nineteenth-century one-room schoolhouse, implement Mini-Society or other economics simulations calling for students to produce, buy, and sell goods and services

Reading: Listen to and discuss story read by teacher, read good children's literature

Writing: Correspond with pen pals, write thank-you notes to classroom visitors

4–6

Math: Develop specifications for a garden or construction project

Science: Monitor air pollution on each of the four sides of the school building, collect and analyze life forms and residues found in a nearby pond

Social Studies: Plan an extended vacation trip, with maps and itinerary; debate whether the American Revolution was justified

Reading: Read genre fiction, discuss and write reactions; learn and apply content-area reading and study skills

Writing: Poems and short essays for self-expression; journals for recording observations and insights

7–12

Math: Apply probabilities to making predictions about the relative effectiveness of alternative strategies for addressing a problem or issue, use algebra for solving compound interest problems to inform decisions about loans and investments

Science: Apply scientific principles to household engineering problems (spot removal, appliance troubleshooting), develop projects for science fairs and displays

Social Studies: Debate current policy issues, simulate legislative budget debates (e.g., acting as state legislators representing districts with different agendas)

Reading: Read and discuss youth theme novels, compare and contrast different authors who work in the same genre or different works by the same author

Writing: Compose short stories, term papers, and other research reports

3. Simplifying the task by reducing the number of steps required to solve a problem, so that the student can manage certain components and recognize when these are being accomplished successfully

4. Controlling frustration and risk in problem solving

5. Providing feedback that identifies the critical features of discrepancies between what the student has produced and what is required for an ideal solution to a problem

6. Motivating and directing the student's activity sufficiently to maintain continuous pursuit of the goal

Closely associated with the notion of scaffolding is the notion of *gradual transfer of responsibility for managing learning*. Early in the process, the teacher assumes most of the responsibility for structuring and managing learning activities and provides students with a great deal of information, explanation, modeling, or other input. As students develop expertise, however, they can begin to assume responsibility for regulating their own learning by asking questions and by working on increasingly complex applications with increasing degrees of autonomy. The teacher still provides coaching or other scaffolding needed to assist with challenges that students are not yet ready to handle on their own, but this assistance is reduced little by little in response to gradual increases in student readiness to engage in independent and self-regulated learning.

Tharp and Gallimore (1988) described a model of *assisted performance* that involves teaching in the zone of proximal development, scaffolding learning through responsive assistance, and transferring responsibility to the child as expertise develops. Teacher assistance is contingent on and responsive to the learner's level of performance. The emphasis is on patience and on allowing learners to handle as much as they can on their own and to learn through their mistakes, except where mistakes might be costly or dangerous and thus must be minimized through more direct and controlling forms of instruction.

Tharp and Gallimore identified six means of providing responsive assistance:

1. Modeling, especially cognitive modeling that includes overt verbalization of strategies
2. Contingency management, especially praise of good performance
3. Providing feedback about the correctness of responses
4. Instructing—telling the student specifically what to do; to be used sparingly
5. Questioning, to stimulate the student to think and communicate about the task, especially if this will produce mental operations that might not be produced otherwise
6. Cognitive structuring—stating principles or generalizations that pull things together and make for better organized representation of the learning

Cognitive structuring may focus on the content being learned or on the learners' cognitive activities. When focused on the content, cognitive structuring provides explanations (e.g., that the expansion of gases that occurs as they are heated during chemistry experiments occurs because molecular activity increases with temperature, or that the next story in the reader is about the dangers and challenges faced by a group of mountain climbers as they work their way up a mountain). When cognitive structuring focuses on the learners' cognitive activity, it provides explanation or reminders of the strategies that students are expected to use as they work on academic tasks (e.g., "So, whenever you come to a new word that you are not sure about, you first look for clues, then put the clues together with what you already know about the word to decide on a meaning, and then check to see if that meaning fits with the rest of the sentence").

Similarly, Collins, Brown, and Newman (1989; see also Collins, Brown, & Holum, 1991) have drawn on ideas about situated cognition and about learning through apprenticeship in the work place in order to develop the *cognitive apprenticeship* model of schooling. The model includes four important aspects of traditional apprenticeship: modeling, scaffolding, fading, and coaching. The master models task performance for the apprentice, provides coaching and other forms of scaffolding as the apprentice practices portions of the task, and then fades these forms of assitance as the apprentice becomes proficient enough to accomplish tasks independently. Cognitive apprenticeship in the classroom includes these same elements, along with additional ones that are needed because of the more abstract content taught there. The modeling includes thinking out loud in order to make the teacher's cognition perceptible to students, and the teacher asks many questions designed to make student cognition perceptible to the teacher as well. Also, by emphasizing authentic tasks and contexts for learning that make sense to students, teachers attempt to build in some of the task meaningfulness and motivation that are ordinarily built into learning that is situated in the work place. Finally, because the teacher must teach for transfer, cognitive apprenticeship exposes students to a range of tasks and encourages them to note their common elements and consider the implications for application to life outside of school.

The emphasis placed here on students becoming more active learners is consistent with the view of classroom management expressed in Chapters 4 and 5. There is a growing consensus that education must include problem solving, integration, and elaboration of meaning (Good, McCaslin, & Reys, 1992; McCaslin & Good, 1992). If students are to become active learners, teachers must align management and instructional goals so that students are consistently expected to engage in appropriate problem-solving behavior.

SUMMARY AND IMPLICATIONS

Recent research on teaching school subjects for understanding, appreciation, and application has begun to move beyond the basics implied in the term *active teaching* in order to identify the subtleties involved in the best teaching. Along with ideas drawn from educators' writings about curriculum and instruction, these studies have been informed by the writings of psychologists and cognitive scientists on thought and language, cognitive development, situated cognition, and the social construction of knowledge. Different authors emphasize different theoretical rationales and instructional methods, but for the most part, their ideas are compatible with one another and with notions about active teaching developed from earlier research. Compatibilities are especially evident when instructional goals are taken into account and it is recognized that different goals call for somewhat different approaches to curriculum and instruction.

The notion of teaching for understanding implies helping students construct connected networks of knowledge by relating new content to existing knowledge in ways that allow them to appreciate the connections and to access the knowledge for use in appropriate application situations. Students develop new knowledge through a process of active construction in which they develop and integrate a network of associations linking the new content to preexisting knowledge and beliefs anchored in concrete experience. Thus, teaching involves inducing conceptual change, not infusing knowledge into a vacuum. To the extent that students' preexisting beliefs about a topic are accurate, they facilitate learning and provide a natural starting place for teaching. To the extent that students harbor misconceptions, however, these misconceptions will need to be corrected so that they do not persist and distort the new learning.

When the new learning is complex, the construction of meaning required to develop clear understanding of it takes and is facilitated by the interactive discourse that occurs during lessons and activities. Clear explanations and modeling from the teacher are important, but so are opportunities to answer questions about the content, discuss or debate its meanings and implications, and apply it in problem-solving or decision-making contexts. These activities allow students to process the content actively and "make it their own" by paraphrasing it in their own words, exploring its relationships to other knowledge and to past experience, appreciating the insights it provides, and identifying its implications for personal decision making or action. The teacher provides whatever structuring and scaffolding the students need in order to accomplish the goals of learning activities successfully, but this assistance is faded as student expertise develops. Ultimately, students engage in independent and self-regulated learning.

RESEARCH ON TEACHING FOR UNDERSTANDING

Research on teaching school subjects for understanding and higher-order applications is still in its infancy, but it already has produced successful experimental programs in most subjects. Even more encouraging, analyses of these programs have identified a set of principles and practices that are common to most if not all of them (Anderson, 1989; Brophy, 1989; Prawat, 1989). These common elements, which might be considered components in a model or theory describing good subject-matter teaching, include the following:

1. The curriculum is designed to equip students with knowledge, skills, values, and dispositions that they will find useful both inside and outside of school.
2. Instructional goals emphasize developing student expertise within an application context and with emphasis on conceptual understanding of knowledge and self-regulated application of skills.
3. The curriculum balances breadth with depth by addressing limited content but developing this content sufficiently to foster conceptual understanding.
4. The content is organized around a limited set of powerful ideas (basic understandings and principles).
5. The teacher's role is not just to present information but also to scaffold and respond to students' learning efforts.
6. The students' role is not just to absorb or copy input but also to actively make sense and construct meaning.
7. Students' prior knowledge about the topic is elicited and used as a starting place for instruction, which builds on accurate prior knowledge and stimulates conceptual change if necessary.

8. Activities and assignments feature tasks that call for problem solving or critical thinking, not just memory or reproduction.
9. Higher-order thinking skills are not taught as a separate skills curriculum. Instead, they are developed in the process of teaching subject-matter knowledge within application contexts that call for students to relate what they are learning to their lives outside of school by thinking critically or creatively about it or by using it to solve problems or make decisions.
10. The teacher creates a social environment in the classroom that could be described as a learning community featuring discourse or dialogue designed to promote understanding.

Teaching for understanding requires "complete" lessons that are carried through to include higher-order applications of content, which means that the breadth of content addressed must be limited in order to allow for more in-depth teaching of the content that is included. Unfortunately, both state and district curriculum guidelines (which often feature long lists of knowledge items and subskills to be "covered") and typical curriculum packages supplied by educational publishers (which respond to these state and district guidelines by emphasizing breadth over depth of coverage) discourage in-depth teaching of *limited* content. Teachers who teach for understanding and higher-order applications of subject-matter content both (1) limit what they try to teach by focusing on what they see as most important and omitting or skimming over the rest, and (2) structure what they do teach around important ideas and elaborate it considerably beyond what is in the text.

Besides presenting information and modeling skill applications, such teachers structure a great deal of discourse surrounding the content, in which they use questions to stimulate students to process and reflect on the content, recognize relationships among and implications of its key ideas, think critically about it, and use it in problem solving, decision making, or other higher-order applications. Such discourse is not mere factual review or recitation featuring rapid-fire questioning and short answers, but instead is sustained and thoughtful examination of a small number of related topics, in which students are invited to develop explanations, make predictions, debate alternative approaches to problems, or otherwise consider the implications or applications of the content. Some of the questions admit to a range of possible correct answers, and some invite discussion or debate (e.g., concerning the relative merits of alternative suggestions for solving problems). In addition to asking questions and providing feedback, the teacher encourages students to explain or elaborate on their answers or to comment on classmates' answers, and also capitalizes on "teachable moment" opportunities offered by students' comments or questions (by elaborating on the original instruction, correcting misconceptions, calling attention to implications that have not been appreciated yet, and so on).

Skills are taught holistically within the context of applying the knowledge content, rather than being practiced in isolation. Thus, most practice of reading skills is embedded within lessons involving reading and interpreting extended text, most practice of writing skills is embedded within activities calling for authentic writing, and most practice of mathematics skills is embedded within problem-solving applications. Also, skills are taught as strategies adapted to particular purposes and situations, with emphasis on modeling the cognitive and metacognitive components involved and explaining the necessary conditional knowledge (of when and why the skills would be used). Thus, students receive instruction in when and how to apply skills, not just get opportunities to use them.

Activities, assignments, and evaluation methods incorporate a much greater range of tasks than the familiar workbooks and curriculum-embedded tests that focus on recognition and recall of facts, definitions, and fragmented skills. Curriculum strands or units are planned to accomplish gradual transfer of responsibility for managing learning activities from the teacher to the students in response to growing student expertise on the topic. Plans for lessons and activities are guided by the overall curriculum goals (phrased in terms of student capabilities to be developed), and evaluation efforts concentrate on assessing the progress that has been made toward accomplishing these goals.

SUBJECT-SPECIFIC EXAMPLES

In discussing what is involved in teaching school subjects for understanding, appreciation, and application, we have so far concentrated on generic aspects that cut across the various school subjects. In the following sections, we provide examples showing how these principles have been embodied in programs developed to foster such teaching in particular subjects.

Reading

We recommend the report *Becoming a Nation of Readers* (Anderson et al., 1985) for its integration of research-based principles for teaching reading for understanding and application. The report calls for teaching reading as a sense-making process of extracting meaning from texts that are read for information or enjoyment (not just to get reading practice). Thus, the emphasis is on reading and interpreting text rather than on practicing fragmented skills. Important skills such as decoding, blending, and noting main ideas are taught and practiced, but primarily within the context of application (reading for meaning). There is considerable explicit instruction and modeling of skills currently being phased in, but such skills instruction is phased out as students develop expertise. Phonics and blending, for example, receive a great deal of emphasis in the first grade but are phased out by the end of the second grade.

Activities and assignments feature more reading of extended text and less time spent with skills worksheets. Students often work cooperatively in pairs or small groups, reading to one another or discussing the meanings or implications of the text. Rather than being restricted to the somewhat artificial stories found in basal reading series, students often read genuine literature written to provide information or pleasure to the reader (children's literature, poetry, biography, nonfictional material about the physical or social world).

Most current innovations in reading instruction feature attempts to incorporate these principles. The California State Department of Education (1987), for example, has revised its reading and language arts guidelines to call for more holistic instruction with emphasis on reading genuine literature. The principles apply at least as much to instruction of disadvantaged students or to remedial instruction of students having difficulty learning to read as they do instruction of other students (Knapp & Shields, 1991). They are featured prominently in the KEEP program that was developed to meet the needs of native Hawaiian children who previously had difficulty learning to read (Au et al., 1985; Tharp & Gallimore, 1988), as well as in the Reading Recovery program that is being used successfully with first graders who have failed to learn to read when taught by traditional methods (Anderson & Armbruster, 1990; Pinnell, DeFord, & Lyons, 1988). The principles are also embedded in several theoretically derived and empirically validated experimental programs.

Paris, Cross, and Lipson (1984) developed Informed Strategies for Learning (ISL), a program designed to increase awareness and use of effective reading strategies. The program contains 14 weekly modules that show students what is involved in using each strategy, when to use it, and what benefits can be expected from using it. Students first observe models using the strategies and then practice the strategies themselves with guidance and feedback from the teacher. The strategies are explained and illustrated using metaphors familiar to the students. For example, a lesson on preassessment to discover clues to the topic, length, and difficulty of a passage uses the metaphor "Be a reading detective." Similarly, comprehension-monitoring strategies are taught using analogies to traffic signs such as a "Stop—say the meaning in your own words," or "Dead end—go back and reread the parts you don't understand." ISL has been used successfully in third- and fifth-grade classes (Cross & Paris, 1988).

Hansen and Pearson (1983) improved fourth graders' reading comprehension using a program that featured strategy training and practice in answering questions. Strategy training was conducted through story introductions in which students were asked to relate their prior knowledge about situations like those depicted in the upcoming story, then predict what the protagonist would do. They wrote down their prior knowledge answers on one sheet of paper and their predictions on another, then combined the two to demonstrate that reading involves combining what one knows with what is in a text. Following these preparations, students read the story and compared their predictions with what actually occurred.

The other part of the treatment involved changing the nature of the questions asked following story reading. Typically, students are asked about 80 percent factual questions and only 20 percent inferential questions. For this study, the students were asked only inferential questions concerning such issues as the characters' motives or the larger moral or meaning that the story was meant to communicate. Evaluation data showed that this combination of strategy training and inferential questions improved the experimental students' reading comprehension over that of control students taught in traditional ways. The treatment was especially effective with poor readers.

Duffy, Roehler, and their colleagues (Duffy, 1993; Duffy & Roehler, 1987, 1989; Duffy, Roehler, & Herrmann, 1988; Duffy et al., 1987) have shown that poor readers in the intermediate grades learn to read with better comprehension and increased awareness of their strategies when they are provided with *explicit instruction* in these comprehension strategies. The strategies are the same ones taught typically, such as identifying the main idea in a paragraph or using the dictionary, but they are taught much more explicitly and thoroughly than usual. Teachers learn to explain the nature of each strategy in detail, tell when and why it is used, model by verbalizing the mental processes that occur when using it, point out sequential aspects and salient features of these processes, and then provide students with opportunities to use the strategy and see its effectiveness for themselves.

During the practice and application phases, teachers provide *responsive elaboration* on their original instruction. That is, they tailor their feedback to the specific misunderstandings that emerge during the reading and discussion of text (for example, failure to use a strategy when it was applicable suggests the need to clarify when and why the strategy is useful, whereas failure to use a strategy correctly suggests the need for additional modeling). Instruction continues until students not only can use the strategy effectively to make sense of what they read but also can explain when and why the strategy should be used.

Palincsar and Brown (1984) developed a *reciprocal teaching* method for teaching four comprehension-fostering and comprehension-monitoring strategies to poor readers: summarizing, questioning, clarifying, and predicting. In the reciprocal teaching method, the teacher does most of the initial modeling and explaining but gradually turns over these responsibilities to the students. Eventually, students take turns acting as the teacher and leading small-group discussions of texts.

To begin, the teacher notes the title and asks for predictions about the content of the passage. Then the group reads the first segment silently and the student "teacher" asks a question about it, summarizes it, and then offers a prediction or asks for clarification if appropriate. If necessary, the adult teacher provides guidance by prompting, "What questions do you think a teacher might ask here?"; instructing, "Remember, a summary is a shortened version; it doesn't include detail"; or modifying the activity, "If you are having a hard time thinking of a question, why don't you summarize first?" The adult teacher also provides feedback about the quality and specificity of questions, the logic involved in making predictions, and so on.

The following dialogue (from Palincsar & Brown, 1989) illustrates reciprocal teaching as implemented in a first-grade classroom.

TEACHER: The pipefish change their color and movements to
(*reading from text*) blend with their surroundings. For example, pipefish that live among green plants change their color to a shade of green to match the plants.

CLAIRE: One question that I had about this paragraph is: "What
(*the child leading* is special about the way that the pipefish looks?"
the discussion)

KEITH (*clarifying*): Do you mean the way that it is green?

ANDY (*elaborating*): It's not just that it's green; it's that it's the same color as the plants around it, all around it.

CLAIRE (*resuming*): Yes. That's it. My summary is this part tells how the pipefish looks and that it looks like what is around it. My prediction is that this is about its enemies and how it protects itself and who its enemies are.

MONTY: They also talked about how the pipefish moves . . .

KEITH: It sways back and forth.

ANDY: Along with the other plants.

TEACHER: What do we call it when something looks like and acts like something else? The way that the walkingstick was yesterday? We clarified this word when we talked about the walkingstick.

ANGEL: Mimic.

TEACHER: That's right. We said, we would say, that the pipefish mimics the . . .

SEVERAL STUDENTS: Plants.

TEACHER: OK! Let's see if Claire's predictions come true.

Over time, as students become more familiar with reciprocal teaching activities, the dialogue becomes less routinized and the strategies are used in more flexible ways. The teacher turns over more responsibility for leading and sustaining the dialogue to the students, gradually engaging less in modeling and instruction but more in coaching students' participation in the discussion.

The reciprocal teaching method has produced sizable gains on tests of reading comprehension in several studies (Palincsar & Brown, 1989). It combines key elements of teaching for understanding and self-regulated learning (modeling of strategic application of skills, scaffolded instruction that gradually releases increasing responsibility to the students themselves) with provision of opportunity for students to learn cooperatively in small groups.

Strategy training in reading is not just for elementary students. It can be helpful to secondary students too if it is focused on strategies needed for accomplishing tasks encountered at their grade levels. Dimino et al. (1990) illustrated this in a study comparing two methods of improving low-achieving ninth graders' comprehension of short stories. Compared to a group taught using traditional basal instruction, students taught to analyze stories using strategies based on story grammar did significantly better on several outcome measures. These students learned to analyze stories by identifying the primary problem or conflict, the main character, the character's attempts to solve the problem or conflict, the resolution of these efforts, twists in the plot, information about the character's reactions to the depicted events, and the overall theme suggested. Andre and Anderson (1978–1979) trained high school students to generate questions about the main points of a text as they studied it. These students learned more than a group who simply read and reread the text and also a group who were directed to ask themselves questions but were not trained in strategies for doing so.

Cook and Mayer (1988) showed that training in strategies for content-area reading and text study can significantly improve learning even in college students. The students they studied initially had difficulty in sorting passages from chemistry texts into categories on the basis of their organizational structures (e.g., generalizations supported by examples or elaboration, enumeration of lists, linear sequences, classification systems, comparison and contrast passages). After training in strategies for recognizing these text structures and using this information to aid study, trained students showed considerably improved recall of highly conceptual information and ability to use what they had learned when responding to application questions.

Michael Pressley and his colleagues have analyzed and synthesized a great many studies of training students in strategies for improving reading comprehension. Pressley et al. (1989) concluded that research support is particularly strong for the following strategies: summarizing the gist of a paragraph or set of paragraphs, emphasizing the main ideas; constructing images to represent visually what the text is describing verbally; using mnemonic devices to help remember the meanings of new words; generating story grammar analyses or constructing story maps for narrative passages; generating questions to ask oneself about the meanings and implications of the text; attempting to answer any questions that have been included in the text as aids to checking for understanding; and activating relevant prior knowledge by making predictions about the text and by comparing depicted events with one's own experiences.

Pressley and his colleagues developed what they called transactional methods to teach students to become "good strategy users" through classroom discourse and provision of support and guidance as students engage in content-area reading and study (Pressley et al., 1992). They also illustrated ways in which good strategy instruction incorporates many of the methods advocated by social constructivists, even though these approaches are often viewed as quite different or even contradictory (Pressley, Harris & Marks, 1992). They argued that good strategy instruction differs from social constructivist recommendations in its emphasis on explicit statement, modeling, and explanation of strategies, but that otherwise it emphasizes classroom discourse, scaffolded and responsive assistance to students, and related constructivist notions.

Many students appear to develop efficient reading and study strategies on their own and do not need much explicit instruction or practice, but many need help with this. Low-achieving students in particular stand to benefit considerably from instruction and guidance in self-regulated reading and study strategies. For more information, see Dole et al. (1990) and Paris, Wasik, and Turner (1991).

Writing

When writing is taught for understanding and application, the instructional goals focus on teaching students to use writing for organizing and communicating their thinking to particular audiences for particular purposes, and skills are taught as strategies for accomplishing these goals. There is explicit instruction concerning when, why, and how to use the skills, and this is elaborated later during responsive feedback to students' composition efforts. Key basic skills such as printing and cursive writing are taught explicitly and practiced to mastery, but a great deal of this practice is embedded within writing activities that call for composition and communication of meaningful content. Composition activities emphasize "authentic" writing intended to be read for meaning and response, not mere copying or exercises focused on displaying skills for the teacher (Applebee, 1986; Bereiter & Scardamalia, 1987; Calkins, 1986; Florio-Ruane & Lensmire, 1989; Graves, 1983; Rosaen, 1989).

Thus, composition is taught, not as an impersonal exercise in writing a draft to conform to the formal requirements of a genre, but as communication and personal craftsmanship calling for developing and revising an outline, developing and revising successive drafts for meaning, and then polishing into final form. The emphasis is on the cognitive and metacognitive aspects of developing compositions, not just on writing mechanics and editing.

In helping students plan and work through successive drafts, teachers concentrate first on purpose, audience, and content and organization of the ideas to be communicated, and only later on the fine points of grammar and spelling. Writing is done for a variety of purposes and audiences, so that students learn to consider not just what they want to say but how their message will need to be phrased if it is to have the intended effects on the intended audience. Also, writing is used as a method of learning school subjects, through assignments calling for students to analyze, synthesize, evaluate, or in other ways use higher-order thinking to respond to what they have been learning in science, social studies, literature, or other subjects.

One experimental program that embodies many of these principles is the Cognitive Strategies in Writing program developed by Englert and Raphael (1989). In addition to providing initial explicit explanation and modeling and follow-up responsive elaboration concerning writing goals and strategies, this program offers scaffolded assistance to students' composition efforts. Students are provided with sets of questions to guide their planning, outline forms, and suggestions for recording and organizing ideas on "think sheets."

For example, a think sheet to assist students in planning their compositions asks them to respond to the following questions: Who am I writing for? Why am I writing this? What do I already know about my topic? and How do I group my ideas? To further assist planning, the think sheet contains numbered lines under the "What do I already know about my topic?" question (so that students can enter separate ideas on separate lines), as well as boxes with lines underneath them under the "How do I group my ideas?" question (so that students can enter group labels in the boxes and then list examples on the lines under the boxes). Similarly, a think sheet for organizing information for comparison and contrast writing contains boxes for identifying the dimensions on which comparisons will be made and then separately listing the ways in which the things to be compared are alike and different.

Mathematics

The National Council of Teachers of Mathematics (1989) has released guidelines for mathematics instruction that emphasize teaching for understanding and higher-order applications. Goals focus on developing students' mathematical *power*, a term that refers to their abilities to explore, conjecture, and reason logically, as well as to use a variety of mathematical models effectively to solve nonroutine problems. The notion of developing mathematical power is based on the recognition that mathematics is more than a collection of concepts and skills to be mastered; it includes methods of investigating and reasoning, means of communication, and notions of context.

An ideal program would emphasize teaching of mathematical concepts, not just mathematical operations. Both the concepts and the operations would be embedded in networks of knowledge structured around key ideas and taught within an application context right from the beginning. Compared with what is typically done now, students would spend less time working individually on computation skills sheets and more time participating in teacher-led discourse concerning the meanings and implications of mathematical concepts and their application to problem solving. Teachers would explain and model the mathematical reasoning used to address classes of problems, then stimulate students to engage in such reasoning themselves. In addition to well-structured exercises that merely require them to recognize problem types and then apply familiar formulas, students would often be exposed to the kinds of ill-structured problems that occur in real life and require us to discover and invent ways of framing and solving the problem. Often such applications can be approached in many different ways, thus providing opportunities for students to examine potential solution strategies. Teacher-led discourse surrounding such applications would involve sustained, thoughtful examination of a small number of related questions rather than fast-paced recitation of number facts. It would feature a great deal of higher-order mathematical reasoning in generating and debating ideas about how the problems might be approached.

One experimental approach that embodies many of these principles is Cognitively Guided Instruction (CGI), a program developed by Fennema, Carpenter, and Peterson (1989) for increasing primary grade teachers' effectiveness in introducing young children to mathematics. CGI places more emphasis on word problems than on computational practice. The problems emphasize applications to students' current lives, and teachers elicit and foster discussion of students' own invented strategies for solving such problems. Teachers learn that problems that can be solved through addition and subtraction fall into eight basic types and that children possess intuitive knowledge about and strategies for solving each problem type that can be used as a starting point for instruction. Problems are taken up in the order in which children naturally develop interest in them, and the students are encouraged to discover knowledge and invent strategies in addition to learning from teacher explanation and modeling. Evaluation data have revealed that students in CGI classrooms showed significant advantages in problem solving and mathematical confidence compared to students in control classrooms, with no loss in computation skills (Carpenter et al., 1989).

Two other approaches to introducing mathematics in the primary grades feature similar philosophies and have achieved similar results to those described for CGI. Hiebert and Wearne (1992) provided first graders with "conceptually based" instruction on place value and on addition and subtraction, using methods reflecting the guidelines published by the National Council of Teachers of Mathematics

(1989). Compared with students who were taught the same content using more traditional methods, the experimental students showed more understanding of key concepts and ability to apply the strategies they had learned. Cobb and his colleagues (Cobb et al., 1991; Wood, Cobb, & Yackel, 1990) drew on the same principles and on social constructivist ideas to develop a method of teaching mathematics to second graders that emphasized teacher-led discussion of alternative suggestions about solving problems. Compared to students taught more conventionally, the experimental students developed higher levels of conceptual understanding in mathematics as well as a preference for collaborating with others to achieve understanding rather than competing with them for rewards.

As with the CGI program, students taught using the Hiebert and Wearne program and the Cobb et al. program not only outperformed comparison students on measures of conceptual understanding and higher-order applications, but also equaled or exceeded their performance on arithmetic computations, even though the experimental programs placed much more emphasis on problem solving than on computation practice. Soled (1990) achieved similar results with seventh-grade science students and ninth-grade mathematics students. Thus, within limits at least, the gains in understanding, appreciation, and strategic application of skills that can be achieved through instruction that emphasizes authentic applications over isolated skills practice apparently can be accomplished without a corresponding reduction in skills development.

Lampert (1989) has emphasized teaching for understanding and developing mathematical power in the intermediate grades. She teaches not just skills but a language to use in describing mathematical phenomena, connects mathematical operations and relations to more familiar and concrete operations and relationships, and guides students' construction of meaning concerning mathematical symbols and operations so that it centers on key ideas drawn from the discipline. Lampert instructs actively, but with stress on processes, relationships, multiple methods, and chances for students to evaluate and discuss proposed solutions to problems. Group inquiry featuring dialogue or argument is emphasized over teacher presentations, and discussion focuses on the relative merits of alternative suggestions for approaching problems rather than on finding a "right answer."

Lampert identified five keys to her approach: (1) involving learners with phenomena that feel problematic to them, so that finding solutions *matters* to them; (2) using multiple representations of concepts to ensure that students understand their meanings; (3) emphasizing dialogue (including argument, not just discourse) as the vehicle for joint establishment of meaning; (4) diagnosing students' levels of understanding and needs for corrective explanation as the dialogue progresses, and providing the needed instruction; and (5) teaching the students to become willing and able to collaborate in solving problems and constructing new knowledge.

These approaches to mathematics teaching that have been developed recently in the United States have much in common with methods emphasized in Japan and China (Stigler & Stevenson, 1991). Mathematics classes in these countries consist of coherent lessons that are presented in a thoughtful, relaxed, and nonauthoritarian manner. They are oriented toward problem solving rather than rote mastery of facts and procedures. Teachers use many different types of representational materials and often rely on students as sources of information. They lead the class in discussions of problems, acting as knowledgeable guides who seek to stimulate students to produce, explain, and evaluate potential solutions rather than as prime dispensers of information and arbiters of what is correct.

Science

Anderson and Roth (1989) have developed an approach to teaching science that emphasizes depth over breadth and focuses on the teaching of powerful ideas in ways that encourage students not only to learn them with understanding but to recognize their value for describing, explaining, making predictions about, or gaining control over real-world systems or events. Through real-life examples and involvement of students in discussion of applications, their approach aims to make science content more meaningful to students by connecting it with their experience-based knowledge and beliefs. The focus is on producing *conceptual change*, building on accurate current knowledge and correcting misconceptions.

Students often find science harder to learn than other subjects. In part, this is because science courses typically require them to learn a great many new concepts very quickly (the average science course introduces more new vocabulary than the average foreign language course!). An additional problem, however, is that students typically enter these courses with misconceptions about the content they will be studying. For example, most middle-school science textbooks contain units on plants that emphasize their roles as food producers via the photosynthesis process. Students typically enter these courses knowing little about photosynthesis, but a great deal about food, especially food for people. They know that (1) food is something that you consume or eat, and it is taken in from the outside environment; (2) there are many different kinds of food.

These beliefs may produce distorted understandings if they lead students to assume that, like people, plants must take in food from their environment in many different forms. However, plants make their own food. Neither soil nor water nor fertilizers (despite their sometimes being called "plant food") are taken in as food or consumed for energy. Nor do plants take in any other other form of food. Their only source of food is that which they manufacture themselves through the photosynthesis process. They transform light energy from the sun into chemical potential energy stored in food and available for use both by the plant and by animals. The matter that they take in during this process (carbon dioxide, water, and soil minerals) is not food because it is not a source of energy. Students must go through a process of conceptual change if they are to attain understanding of photosynthesis and the food production function of plants. They must abandon their assumptions about the metabolic similarities between plants and humans and restructure their thinking about the nature of food (focusing on the scientific definition of food as potential energy for metabolism).

Unless misconceptions are corrected, they are likely to persist and distort new learning. Unfortunately, neither curriculum writers nor teachers typically are very aware of common misconceptions that students are likely to harbor about scientific content, so that the instruction they provide not only fails to confront these misconceptions directly but often is presented in such general or imprecise terms that students can interpret the new input as consistent with their existing misconceptions (Anderson & Smith, 1987).

For example, Smith and Anderson (1984) found that less than a quarter of students had dropped misconceptions about plants as producers of food and acquired the correct scientific conceptions following a unit of instruction on photosynthesis. Analyses of the instruction documented ways in which students' misconceptions affected their interpretations of what they were learning.

One crucial experiment involved growing plants in the light and in the dark. To set the stage for an explanation of photosynthesis, students were to observe that the plants in the dark would begin to grow at first but then wilt. The scientific explanation for this is that the plants in the dark die because they cannot engage in photosynthesis without light, and photosynthesis is their only source of food once food stored in their seeds is used up. However, the students' misconceptions caused them to interpret the experiment differently. Because they assumed that plants take in water, minerals, and other "food" from the soil, they saw no connection between the experimental findings and the question of where plants get their food. They interpreted the results as showing that plants need light in order to stay green and healthy (for reasons that they were not very clear about), but they missed the point that the plants were dying of starvation because they could no longer produce food through the photosynthesis process (which requires sunlight).

None of the 14 teachers was very successful in getting students to abandon their misconceptions in favor of scientific conceptions. *Activity-driven teachers* focused on the activities to be carried out (textbook assignments, demonstrations, experiments, etc.). These teachers seemed to think that students would learn automatically if they engaged in these activities. However, the teachers often unknowingly modified or deleted crucial aspects of the program in ways that made it difficult if not impossible for the students to discover the intended concepts.

Didactic teachers presented information directly to the students and regarded the text as a repository of knowledge to be taught. They did not seem to be aware of student misconceptions and thus did not see a need to be certain that the students had interpreted the information as intended. Also, because these teachers did not question students in ways that would allow them to express their own thinking, the teachers denied themselves the opportunity to become aware of students' misconceptions.

Discovery-oriented teachers tried to avoid telling answers to their students and instead encouraged them to develop their own ideas about the results of the plant-growing experiment. These teachers did not realize that the program they were using, although described as a discovery program, calls for direct instruction concerning certain concepts, including photosynthesis. Also, rather than question students in ways that would challenge their misconceptions and lead them to consider specific theoretical issues, the teachers merely invited students to interpret their own observations in their own ways. Unfortunately, most students used their *misconceptions* as the basis for interpreting the experiments.

The teachers failed to develop understanding because they failed to surface and correct students' misconceptions. Posner et al. (1982) have suggested that four conditions must be satisfied if students are to be induced to change their understandings of key concepts: (1) Dissatisfaction with existing concepts must be induced, (2) the new concepts must be intelligible, (3) the new concepts must be initially plausible, and (4) the new concepts must appear fruitful.

Anderson and Roth (1989) have developed a conceptual change teaching approach designed to accomplish these goals. Two general features of the approach are (1) a curricular commitment to teaching limited content for understanding rather than to covering a wide range of content superficially, and (2) recognition that teaching for conceptual change requires an array of teaching strategies used flexibly in response to students' needs. These strategies all share an important characteristic, however: They engage students in conceptual change sense-making by involving them in actively struggling with ideas rather than just witnessing the teacher's performance.

The process begins by adjusting the curriculum. In contrast to typical textbook treatments, Anderson and Roth's treatments omit much of the technical vocabulary and detail—all that can be omitted without sacrificing much explanatory power. Their materials on photosynthesis, for example, do not present the scientific formula for photosynthesis or discuss the role of chlorophyll, because these are not seen as crucial elements for developing understanding of the process. Instead, the materials are developed around the central problem of "food" for plants: What is "food" for plants and how is it similar to and different from food for people and animals? The unit begins by asking students to define food and food for plants and to respond to a problem. This provides the teacher with information about students' conceptions and makes the students more aware of these conceptions.

Next, students are given explanations about different ways of defining food, including the scientific definition of food as energy-containing matter. Then the students are asked to address questions that give them a chance to use this new definition of food to explain everyday phenomena (Is water food? Juice? Vitamin pills? Can you live on vitamin pills alone? Why or why not?).

Throughout the unit, students use this definition of food to analyze experimental observations of plants, think about similarities and differences between plants and animals, distinguish materials taken into plants from materials made by the plants during photosynthesis, and distinguish between energy-containing and non-energy-containing materials that people consume. These activities encourage students to make connections between their own ideas and scientific concepts, as well as to use their newly structured conceptions to make predictions and to develop more satisfying explanations of familiar everyday phenomena.

Anderson and Roth speak of creating learning communities in which teacher and students work together to develop and use scientific knowledge. When operating most successfully, these learning communities feature three kinds of activities.

First, the teacher establishes problems that engage students in scientific thinking. Instruction begins with questions that elicit students' reasoning about the topics they will be studying. This activates prior knowledge and helps make the students aware of its limitations, provides diagnostic information to the teacher, and engages the teacher and students in dialogue about commonly understood issues. In the photosynthesis unit, for example, students are asked at the outset to (1) write down their ideas about how plants get food, (2) write down their ideas about what kind of food plants use, and (3) draw pictures on a diagram of a plant to show how they think food moves inside the plant. At the end of the unit, the students reread what they had written and describe how their ideas have changed.

A second feature is modeling and coaching through scaffolded tasks and dialogue. The teacher models by showing how scientific knowledge can be used to solve problems, then provides problem-solving opportunities. The students' initial attempts are scaffolded through simplification or clarification of tasks and through classroom dialogues in which teacher and students listen carefully and respond to one another, sometimes critically but in ways that reflect respectful attention to the speaker's ideas. In the photosynthesis unit, for example, students are asked at several points to answer sets of questions that require them to make predictions and explanations about plants. Scaffolding is provided via reminders of key ideas that need to be kept in mind or provision of chart outlines to help students make key comparisons (e.g., between food for plants and food for people).

The third feature is student work that leads to independent use of scientific knowledge and integration with scientific ideas developed in other contexts. As students develop expertise, they are encouraged to work more independently to describe, explain, make predictions about, or exert control over scientific phenomena in everyday life.

The work of Anderson and Roth (1989) is representative of recent trends in science education that place greater emphasis on eliciting students' prior knowledge (including misconceptions) when introducing topics and then developing the topics through social constructivist teaching. A great deal has been learned in recent years about the kinds of misconceptions that students develop in various areas of science (Glynn, Yeany, & Britton, 1991; Novak, 1987) and about addressing these through conceptual change teaching (Roth, 1990). For information about programs and techniques that have been used at various elementary and secondary grade levels, see Driver (1987), Hand and Treagust (1991), Minstrell (1989), Neale, Smith, and Johnson (1990), and White (1992).

Social Studies

Newmann (1990, 1992) has conducted research on social studies teaching that is built around his conception of higher-order thinking. He defines higher-order thinking as challenging students to interpret, analyze, or manipulate information in response to a question or problem that cannot be resolved through routine application of previously learned knowledge. In order to meet such higher-order thinking challenges successfully, students need a combination of (1) in-depth knowledge of content, (2) skills in processing information, and (3) attitudes or dispositions of reflectiveness.

Instruction is organized to offer depth on a few related topics rather than breadth in covering a great many topics, and activities encourage students to go beyond gathering information in order to participate in disciplined inquiry by scrutinizing arguments for logical consistency, distinguishing between relevant and irrelevant information and between factual claims and value judgments, using metaphor and analogy to represent problems and solutions, developing and defending positions by referring to relevant information, and making reasoned decisions. These activities both develop and reflect a set of student dispositions that together constitute *thoughtfulness:* a persistent desire that claims be supported by reasons (and that the reasons themselves be scrutinized), a tendency to be reflective by taking time to think problems through rather than acting impulsively or automatically accepting the views of others, a curiosity to explore new questions, and a flexibility to entertain alternative and original solutions to problems.

Newmann identified six key indicators of thoughtfulness observed in high school social studies classes:

1. Classroom interaction focuses on sustained examination of a few topics rather than superficial coverage of many.
2. Interactions are characterized by substantive coherence and continuity.
3. Students are given sufficient time to think before being required to answer questions.
4. The teacher presses students to clarify or justify their assertions, rather than accepting and reinforcing them indiscriminately.
5. The teacher models the characteristics of a thoughtful person (showing interest in students' ideas and their suggestions for solving problems, modeling problem-solving processes rather than just giving answers, acknowledging the difficulties involved in gaining a clear understanding of problematic topics).
6. Students generate original and unconventional ideas in the course of the interaction.

Thoughtfulness scores based on these scales distinguished classrooms that featured sustained and thoughtful teacher-student discourse not only from classrooms that featured lecture, recitation, and seatwork, but also from classrooms in which teachers emphasized discussion but did not foster much thoughtfulness (because they skipped from topic to topic too quickly or accepted students' contributions uncritically). Other noteworthy findings were that

1. Teachers with high thoughtfulness scores tended to make writing assignments that required students to draw inferences, give reasons, integrate information from a number of sources, develop an idea or theme, or generate original responses.
2. Thoughtfulness scores were unrelated to entry levels of achievement, indicating that teachers can structure thoughtful discourse with students at all ability levels.
3. High-scoring teachers were more likely to mention critical thinking and problem solving as important goals.
4. In talking about the satisfactions of teaching, high-scoring teachers tended to mention evidence of good student thinking about the content, whereas low-scoring teachers tended to talk about student interest or positive response to lessons (but without emphasizing good thinking).

5. In talking about their goals for students, high-scoring teachers were more likely to mention longer-range and farther-reaching dispositional goals in addition to more immediate knowledge and skill goals.
6. High-scoring teachers were more confident that they could influence the performance of below-average students.
7. All teachers mentioned that students are likely to resist higher-order thinking tasks, but the high-scoring teachers nevertheless emphasized these tasks.
8. All teachers felt pressure to cover more content, but high-scoring teachers experienced this primarily as external pressure and tended to resist it by favoring depth of topic development over breadth of coverage, whereas low-scoring teachers experienced it primarily as internal pressure and thus emphasized breadth.
9. Students identified high-scoring teachers' classes as more difficult and challenging, but also as more engaging and interesting.

Newmann's findings provide cause for optimism because they suggest that thoughtful, in-depth treatment that fosters higher-order thinking about social studies topics is feasible in most classrooms (not just those dominated by high achievers) and that teachers with the knowledge and determination to do so can overcome students' resistance to higher-order thinking activities and even bring the students to the point where they see such activities as more engaging and interesting than lower-order recitation and seatwork. Only limited research relevant to Newmann's work has been done at the elementary level, but Thornton and Wenger (1990) reported observing lessons that exhibited many of the characteristics of thoughtfulness described by Newmann, and Stodolsky (1988) reported that the quality of students' task engagement was higher during more cognitively complex activities than during lower-level activities.

CONCLUSIONS

Teaching well is difficult, especially if one aims high by teaching for understanding, appreciation, and application. It requires a good working knowledge of the subject (including its purposes and goals, its most powerful ideas, and the ways in which these ideas are connected and applied), of students (their likely prior knowledge about the subject, including misconceptions; what important knowledge and skills are within their current zones of proximal development), and pedagogy (how to represent these aspects of the subject to the students and assist them in constructing new understandings). Development of this kind of expertise takes time, although researchers are beginning to learn more about it (Brophy, 1991) and about how to develop it through preservice and inservice teacher education (see Chapter 11).

The best teaching is adapted to the situation, including the instructional purposes and goals, the students, and the subject matter. For example, the techniques associated with the terms *active teaching, strategy instruction,* and *situated learn-*

ing are most relevant when the situation calls for presenting new information, modeling skills, or coaching students as they attempt to implement skills or procedures. In contrast, the techniques associated with terms such as *social constructivism* or *teaching for thoughtfulness* are most relevant when one wishes to develop understanding and appreciation of networks of knowledge through shared construction and negotiation of meanings and implications. A principle such as transferring responsibility for managing learning from the teacher to the students applies to all teaching situations, but figuring out exactly how to apply it (how much modeling, explanation, coaching, and other scaffolding to provide and how quickly to fade this support) takes experience with the content and the students. Even then, some trial and error may be required. What worked well with last year's class might not work well with this year's class.

Research findings sometimes reflect these complexities. Swing, Stoiber, and Peterson (1988) compared the effects of two contrasting interventions on fourth-grade students' mathematics achievement. In the thinking skills intervention, teachers learned how to teach the cognitive strategies of defining and describing, thinking of reasons, comparing, and summarizing. In the learning time intervention, teachers learned how to increase students' engagement and academic learning time. The researchers expected that the thinking skills intervention would produce better results than the learning time intervention, but the effects differed according to student achievement level. Higher-achieving classes did better with the thinking skills intervention, but lower-achieving classes did better with the learning time intervention. Within the classes that received the thinking skills intervention, however, lower achievers benefited more than the higher achievers. Thus, the same treatment can have different effects on different types of students.

Also, an approach that is well adapted to one situation might not work well in another. We noted earlier that the reciprocal teaching method developed by Palincsar and Brown has shown impressive results as a method of improving students' reading comprehension. However, two attempts to teach mathematical problem solving using the same basic strategies that are used in reciprocal teaching produced unsatisfactory results (Brown & Campione, 1990; Resnick, 1989). The reasons are not yet clear, but it is obvious that the reciprocal teaching method is well adapted to teaching reading comprehension but not to teaching mathematical problem solving. Similarly, the Kamehameha Early Education Project (KEEP) that had been developed for teaching native Hawaiian children had to be adjusted when it was implemented with Navajo children. Native Hawaiian children are accustomed to learning collaboratively through lively discussions and cooperative work on tasks, so the KEEP program built on these strengths by incorporating a great deal of conversational discussion of reading selections during group lessons and cooperative learning in independent activity centers. However, Navajo children tend to be less verbally interactive in groups and more independent in their patterns of task engagement, so the KEEP program elements that had been specifically incorporated for and worked well with native Hawaiian children did not work well at all with Navajo children (Tharp & Gallimore, 1988).

Rather than viewing these complexities in research findings simply as frustrations or even as failures, researchers and teachers need to appreciate them as indications of the complexities involved in adapting instruction to students and situations. Researchers are making progress in learning about these complexities and their potential implications for instruction, and they will continue to build on this knowledge base. Still, research-based information can only inform teachers about the trade-offs involved in decision alternatives; it cannot make those decisions for them. It is teachers who must decide what goals to pursue with their students and what combinations of content representations, instructional methods, and learning activities will be most helpful in assisting their students to accomplish the goals.

To cope with these complexities and keep their curriculum and instruction well matched to each successive class of students, teachers need to be reflective about their practice and prepared to engage in diagnosis and experimentation when goals are not being met. Teacher colleagues can help one another here by meeting regularly to share insights, identify and generate possible solutions to common problems, and coordinate efforts to expand students' opportunities to assume responsibility for self-regulated learning. In-service professional development programs that promote such collegial collaboration are discussed in Chapter 11.

Eventually, research might point to one or more highly specific methods for accomplishing each of a great many highly specific objectives. So far, research has focused on the more general goals of teaching school subjects for understanding, appreciation, and application, and it indicates the value of the principles and techniques we have reviewed in Chapters 9 and 10. The work of Blumenfeld (1992) and of Fraenkel (1992) provides two recent examples.

Blumenfeld (1992) drew on case studies of fifth- and sixth-grade science teaching to identify practices that promote student thoughtfulness in learning science. She listed the following as characteristics of the more successful teachers:

Opportunities: Topic coverage focuses on a few key ideas developed in depth; learning activities relate to these main ideas, focus on application rather than mere verification, and involve engagement in meaningful problems relating to children's experience or to real events; the products produced through these activities also relate to the main ideas and require processing at higher cognitive levels.

Instruction: Clear presentations highlight main points and critical information, take into account students' prior knowledge, and use examples, analogies, and metaphors; these presentations build connections by linking with prior knowledge, making relationships among new ideas evident, focusing on similarities and differences among ideas, and showing their application; they include scaffolding in the form of modeling of learning and of metacognitive and problem solving strategies.

Press (use of questions and feedback): Questions focus attention on main ideas; teacher checks understanding by asking comprehension questions, asking for summarization, asking for application, focusing on content rather than procedures, adding higher-level questions to worksheets, and asking for alternative representations of content; teacher draws out student reasoning by probing, asking for justification or clarification, and elaborating on student responses; teacher uses errors to diagnose and clear up misunderstandings; teacher encourages making of connections by asking about relationships of key ideas to prior knowledge, relationships among new ideas, how an activity's procedures relate to its content, and how the results of the activity illustrate main ideas; teacher ensures widespread responding by calling on many students, using debate, and using voting or asking who agrees or disagrees with a statement.

Support: Teacher helps students to accomplish tasks by breaking down problems, simplifying procedures, modeling procedures, or providing models and examples; teacher promotes independence, self-regulation, and cooperation by encouraging students to work together, providing time for planning, asking about students' individual contributions to group work, and asking students whether they agree or disagree with their group's conclusions.

Evaluation: Teacher holds students accountable for understanding by adding questions to worksheets that focus on the meanings of key ideas; evaluation focuses on learning rather than performance, features recognition of individual contributions and improvement, and deemphasizes grades and correct answers.

Similarly, Fraenkel (1992) drew on case studies of instruction in high school social studies classes, looking for factors associated with differences in effectiveness. Like Newmann (1990, 1992), Fraenkel found that the major factor determining the success of a class was the teacher, not student achievement levels, the subject matter, or other aspects. Impressive teachers were found in non-elite as well as in elite schools, and many of the teachers in the elite schools were not impressive.

The less effective teachers tended to present ideas ready-made rather than to ask students to develop ideas for themselves. They tended to talk *to* students rather than *with* them. They often did not seem to have a clear sense of where they were heading. They tended to engage students in busywork and to stress memorization and regurgitation of facts rather than understanding of ideas. These teachers often did not seem to like what they were doing, to like their students, or to be having much fun. Unsurprisingly, their students rarely were active learners and often were discipline problems.

In contrast, the more effective teachers often engaged students in discussions. When they did lecture, they combined lectures with use of the overhead or showing pictures, maps, or other visuals. Their questions tended to elicit discussion rather than mere recitation and they often asked students to respond to one another's comments. Students often worked in pairs or small groups while the teacher circulated and interacted with them. They were often required to function as active learners by role-playing or giving presentations in class. The teachers made a point of engaging students in activities to help them understand and require them to use the ideas they were learning.

In the process, these teachers appeared to like what they were doing, like their students, and like their subjects. They had high expectations for their students, emphasized depth rather than breadth of coverage, were able to explain things clearly using examples that related to the students' lives, had good wait times and were good listeners when students talked, demonstrated patience when students did not initially understand, varied their instructional approaches and types of activities, and displayed considerable command of their subject and ability to relate it to a variety of daily-life examples.

They were highly attuned to their students. They encouraged them to take public risks by contributing their opinions to discussions and publicly discussing their mistakes or confusions. Yet they were quick to notice indicators of confusion or anxiety and to react by providing additional explanations, alternative assignments, or other scaffolding. They emphasized bringing to light students' thought processes for public examination and discussion. They established personal contacts with their students and arranged for frequent interaction among students through cooperative small-group activities.

For some time we have known that teachers who emphasize conceptual development in their instructional techniques are much more likely to promote student understanding than teachers who emphasize procedures and seatwork (e.g., Good, Grouws, & Ebmeier, 1983). However, what is becoming clear is that designing academic tasks that encourage problem solving and pressing students for responses during dialogue that reflect their understanding are also important components of the process (Blumenfeld, 1992; Brophy, 1992).

Keep the Goals in Sight

In order to make good decisions about what to teach and how to teach it, teachers need to establish worthwhile goals and keep these goals in sight as they develop and implement their plans. This can be difficult, because as curriculum guidelines get translated into separate strands and then become segmented by grade level and by units within grades and lessons within units, the goals that are supposed to guide the entire process sometimes fade into the background, along with many of the originally recognized connections and intended life applications (Brophy & Alleman, 1993). For example, consider the following goals drawn from social studies:

District-wide goal: Prepare young people to become humane, rational, participating citizens in an increasingly interdependent world.

Program-area goal for social studies, K–12: Enable students to appreciate that people living in different cultures are likely to hold both common values and also different values that are rooted in experience and are legitimate in terms of their own cultures.

Grade-level goal for social studies, Grade 1: To understand and appreciate that the roles and values of family members may differ according to the structure of the family, its circumstances, and its cultural setting.

Unit-level goal for social studies, Grade 1: To understand that families differ in size and composition.

The last (unit-level) goal is phrased in purely descriptive, knowledge-level language, and it is trite for a unit goal even at the first-grade level. It makes no reference to the concepts concerning cultures and roles that are referred to in the higher-level goals, nor to the related values and dispositions (multicultural appreciation and citizen participation). Unless the teacher has a coherent view of the purposes and nature of social education, or unless the manual does an unusually good job of keeping the teacher aware of how particular lessons fit within the big picture, the result is likely to be a version of social studies that is long on isolated practice of facts and skills but short on integration and application of social learning.

Unfortunately, typical manuals do little or nothing to help teachers put these lower-level goals into perspective as pieces of a larger plan to move students toward major goals. Often, in fact, the curriculum materials were developed not to systematically accomplish major goals, but instead only to cover long lists of disconnected knowledge topics and isolated skills. In this case, students might learn a few obvious generalities about families (they differ in size and composition, they grow and change, and their members work and play together), but not much about variations in family roles across time and culture, the reasons for these variations, or the life-style trade-offs that they offer. This will not do much to advance students' knowledge of the human condition, help them put the familiar into broader perspective, or even stimulate their thinking about family as a concept.

To avoid such problems, teachers need to think through their goals, identifying the capabilities and dispositions that they want to develop in their students throughout the year as a whole and in each of their curriculum units. Then they can examine curriculum materials in the light of these goals. Taking the viewpoint of the students, they can first read the student text (i.e., not the teacher's manual, which contains more guidance and information) to see what information is included and emphasized and what information is not, noting places where additional structuring or input will be necessary to focus students' learning on important ideas. Then teachers can study the manual, assessing its suggested questions, activities, and evaluation devices to determine the degree to which they will be useful as tools for helping students accomplish their primary goals. To help their students focus on important aspects of the content, teachers may need to augment the text with additional input (or replace it with something else if necessary), skip pointless questions and activities, and substitute other questions and activities that support progress toward major goals.

Through such planning, teachers can overcome some of the limitations in materials that feature trite goals, parade-of-facts content, and parade-of-skills-exercises activities. Ideally, they can begin to teach for understanding, appreciation, and application to life outside of school by developing a limited number of important ideas in depth; organizing the content into networks structured around these important ideas; teaching the ideas with an emphasis on their connections; asking questions and making comments that produce reflective discourse that focuses on these key ideas; engaging students in activities that provide opportunities for authentic applications of what they are learning; and evaluating the learning using measures that feature authentic tasks and assess accomplishment of major goals.

SUGGESTED ACTIVITIES AND QUESTIONS

1. Teaching for understanding requires reducing breadth of content coverage so as to be able to develop the most important content in greater depth. This creates dilemmas for teachers, who are caught between their desire to focus on important topics in depth and their felt responsibilities to cover a broader range of content. Focusing on grades at which you teach or intend to teach, interview several teachers about how they respond to this dilemma.

2. Focusing on particular grades and school subjects, interview teachers to determine what they consider to be authentic activities for their students. To what extent do they use similar criteria and identify similar activities? Do they actually use these authentic activities in their teaching, or do they rely more on worksheets and other less authentic assignments? If the latter, why?

3. We discussed several aspects of teaching in this chapter; however, we did not provide a summary synthesizing this information. Show your mastery of the important aspects of the chapter by writing your own summary in a couple of typewritten pages. Compare your summary with those made by classmates and fellow teachers.

4. What are some of the advantages and disadvantages involved when students are asked to summarize material on their own?

5. Much of the research reviewed in this chapter was conducted by scholars who believe that standardized achievement tests are incomplete or even inappropriate as measures of student learning. To find out what you think about this, obtain samples of standardized achievement tests to study and discuss with peers. What do you see as their strengths and weaknesses as measures of learning outcomes? What does this imply about the strengths and weaknesses of the research reviewed in Chapter 9?

6. Some educators think that there are important differences between active teaching as described in Chapter 9 and helping students to construct usable knowledge as described in Chapter 10. Others believe that the former is subsumed within the latter and that the differences are more in underlying philosophy than in what would actually be done in the classroom. Discuss this with peers and see whether you come to agreement on implications for classroom teaching.

7. Examine samples of K–12 textbooks that you use now or likely will use in the future. Do they present networks of connected knowledge structured around powerful ideas, or just parades of disconnected facts? What does this suggest about your use of such texts with students?

8. Learning with understanding is usually described as a process of relating new content to one's existing prior knowledge. But what if students are so unfamiliar with certain content that they possess no readily available schemas within which to assimilate it and very little useful prior knowledge to bring to bear? Is it possible to develop their understanding of such content? If so, can it be done through social constructivist methods or will it

be necessary to begin by providing information through texts, teacher explanations, or other input sources? Using a realistic example from your current or future teaching, plan how you would introduce and develop a topic for which students had little or no prior knowledge.

9. How might you determine your students' zones of proximal development with respect to a particular curriculum unit or topic? What does this imply about forms of preinstructional assessment of student knowledge and thinking that you might incorporate into your teaching?

10. For each subject that you teach or plan to teach, establish a file of authentic activities and assignments that will allow your students to use what they are learning in the process of conducting inquiry, solving problems, or making decisions. Be prepared to use these activities and assignments in place of those supplied with or suggested in the manuals that accompany your curriculum materials, whenever the latter activities or assignments are not worth using.

11. How does ideal scaffolding of students' learning efforts differ from forms of teacher assistance that are less desirable?

12. Define *conceptual change teaching* in your own words. Why is more time for instruction not always effective?

13. What is the difference between teaching "main idea" as a concept and teaching about how identifying and focusing on main ideas can be a useful strategy for guiding one's efforts to learn with understanding? What does this imply about your teaching about main idea (regardless of whether you teach reading to your students)?

14. What is meant by the phrase *writing to learn*? What does this imply about the kinds of writing assignments that you should include in your teaching?

15. We suggested that there might be limits on the degree to which one could emphasize authentic applications over skills practice without experiencing reductions in skills development. What might these limits be? In the subjects that you teach, are there certain things that simply must be memorized or practiced repeatedly? If so, why?

16. The discovery-oriented teachers studied by Smith and Anderson (1984) used methods similar in many ways to those advocated by social constructivists. However, they did not get positive results. What were some crucial differences between these teachers and teachers who use social constructivist methods to teach for understanding?

17. Can you relate the goals and objectives of each of your lessons and activities to larger purposes and goals? Can you see how each lesson or activity contributes to the long-run development of knowledge, skills, values, and dispositions that school subjects are ostensibly designed to develop? Test yourself by selecting a few lessons and activities at random and seeing whether you can explain to others' satisfaction why they are needed in the curriculum. If you have trouble doing this, you may need to think through larger purposes and goals and keep them in mind as you develop your teaching plans.

18. Review and revise (as necessary) the statements you made after reading Chapter 1, when you attempted to identify teaching behaviors and characteristics that are signs of effective teaching. How much has your view of effective teaching changed?

19. You have now completed reading the substantive chapters of this book that describe effective teaching. What important aspects of teacher and student behavior have we neglected? Why do you believe these behaviors are important? What information do you need as a teacher that we have not addressed? Compare your list with others.

REFERENCES

Adams, M. (1990). *Beginning to read.* Cambridge, MA: MIT Press.

Alvermann, D., Smith, L., & Readence, J. (1985). Prior knowledge activation and the comprehension of compatible and incompatible text. *Reading Research Quarterly, 20,* 420–435.

Anderson, C., & Roth, K. (1989). Teaching for meaningful and self-regulated learning of science. In J. Brophy (Ed.), *Advances in research on teaching.* Vol. 1: *Teaching for meaningful understanding and self-regulated learning.* Greenwich, CT: JAI.

Anderson, C., & Smith, E. (1987). Teaching science. In V. Richardson-Koehler (Ed.), *Educators' handbook.* New York: Longman.

Anderson, L. (1989). Implementing instructional programs to promote meaningful, self-regulated learning. In J. Brophy (Ed.), *Advances in research on teaching.* Vol. 1: *Teaching for meaningful understanding and self-regulated learning.* Greenwich, CT: JAI.

Anderson, R. (1984). Role of the reader's schema in comprehension, learning, and memory. In R. Anderson, J. Osborn, R. Tierney (Eds.), *Learning to read in American schools: Basal readers and content texts.* Hillsdale, NJ: Erlbaum.

Anderson, R., & Armbruster, B. (1990). Some maxims for learning and instruction. *Teachers College Record, 91,* 396–408.

Anderson, R., Heibert, E., Scott, J., & Wilkinson, I. (1985). *Becoming a nation of readers: A report of the Commission on Reading.* Washington, DC: National Institute of Education.

Andre, M., & Anderson, T. (1978–1979). The development and evaluation of a self-questioning study technique. *Reading Research Quarterly, 14,* 605–623.

Applebee, A. (1986). Problems in process approaches: Toward a reconceptualization of process instruction. In A. Petrosky & D. Bartholomae (Eds.), *The teaching of writing* (85th Yearbook of the National Society for the Study of Education). Chicago: University of Chicago Press.

Au, R., Tharp, R., Crowell, D., Jordan, C., Speidel, G., & Calkins, R. (1985). The role of research in the development of a successful reading program. In J. Osborn, P. Wilson, & R. Anderson (Eds.), *Reading education: Foundations for a literate America.* Lexington, MA: Lexington Books.

Bereiter, C., & Scardamalia, M. (1987). An attainable version of high literacy: Approaches to teaching higher-order skills in reading and writing. *Curriculum Inquiry, 17*(1), 9–30.

Bloom, B., Englehart, M., Furst, E., Hill, W., & Krathwohl, D. (1956). *Taxonomy of educational objectives: The classification of educational goals.* Handbook I: *Cognitive domain.* New York: Longmans Green.

Blumenfeld, P. (1992). The task and the teacher: Enhancing student thoughtfulness in science. In J. Brophy (Ed.), *Advances in research on teaching.* Vol. 3: *Planning and managing learning tasks and activities* (pp. 81–114). Greenwich, CT: JAI.

Bredekamp, S. (Ed.). (1987). *Developmentally appropriate practice in early childhood programs serving children from birth through age 8.* Washington, DC: National Association for the Education of Young Children.

Brooks, J. (1990). Teachers and students: Constructivists forging new connections. *Educational Leadership 47*(5), 68–71.

Brophy, J. (Ed.). (1989). *Advances in research on teaching.* Vol. 1. Greenwich, CT: JAI.

Brophy, J. (Ed.). (1991). *Advances in research on teaching.* Vol. 2. Greenwich, CT: JAI.

Brophy, J. (1992). Probing the subtleties of subject-matter teaching. *Educational Leadership,* *49*(7), 4–8.

Brophy, J., & Alleman, J. (1993). Elementary social studies should be driven by major social education goals. *Social Education, 57,* 27–32.

Brown, A., & Campione, J. (1990). Interactive learning environments and the teaching of science and mathematics. In M. Gardner, J. Greeno, F. Reif, A. Schoenfeld, A. diSessa, & E. Stage (Eds.), *Toward a scientific practice of science education* (pp. 111–139). Hillsdale, NJ: Erlbaum.

Brown, J., Collins, A., & Duguid, P. (1989). Situated cognition and the culture of learning. *Educational Researcher, 18*(1), 32–42.

California State Department of Education. (1987). *Handbook for planning an effective literature program, kindergarten through grade 12.* Sacramento: Author.

Calkins, L. (1986). *The art of teaching writing.* Exeter, NH: Heinemann.

Carey, S. (1985). *Conceptual change in childhood.* Cambridge, MA: MIT Press.

Carpenter, T., Fennema, E., Peterson, P., Chiang, C., & Loef, M. (1989). Using knowledge of children's mathematical thinking in classroom teaching: An experimental study. *American Educational Research Journal, 26,* 499–532.

Case, R. (1982). Learning, maturation, and the development of computation strategies in elementary arithmetic. In T. Carpenter, J. Moser, & T. Romberg (Eds.), *Addition and subtraction: A cognitive perspective* (pp. 156–170). Hillsdale, NJ: Erlbaum.

Chinn, C., & Brewer, W. (1993). The role of anomolous data in knowledge acquisition: A theoretical framework and implications for science instruction. *Review of Educational Research, 63,* 1–49.

Cobb, P. (1986). Making mathematics: Children's learning and the constructivist tradition. *Harvard Educational Review, 56,* 301–306.

Cobb, P., Wood, T., Yackel, E., Nicholls, J., Wheatley, G., Trigatti, B., & Perlwitz, M. (1991). Assessment of a problem-centered second-grade mathematics project. *Journal for Research in Mathematics Education, 22,* 3–29.

Cobb, P., Yackel, E., & Wood, T. (1992). A constructivist alternative to the representational view of mind in mathematics education. *Journal for Research in Mathematics Education, 23,* 2–33.

Collins, A., Brown, J., & Holum, A. (1991). Cognitive apprenticeship: Making thinking visible. *American Educator, 15*(3), 6–11, 38–46.

Collins, A., Brown, J., & Newman, S. (1989). Cognitive apprenticeship: Teaching the craft of reading, writing, and mathematics. In L. Resnick (Ed.), *Knowing, learning, and instruction: Essays in honor of Robert Glaser.* Hillsdale, NJ: Erlbaum.

Cook, L., & Mayer, R. (1988). Teaching readers about the structure of scientific text. *Journal of Educational Psychology, 80,* 448–456.

Cross, D., & Paris, S. (1988). Developmental and instructional analyses of children's metacognition and reading comprehension. *Journal of Educational Psychology, 80,* 131–142.

Davis, R., Maher, C., & Noddings, N. (Eds.). (1990). *Constructivist views on the teaching and learning of mathematics. Journal of Research in Mathematics Education Monograph No. 4.* Reston, VA: National Council of Teachers of Mathematics.

Dimino, J., Gersten, R., Carnine, D., & Blake, G. (1990). Story grammar: An approach for promoting at-risk secondary students' comprehension of literature. *Elementary School Journal, 91,* 19–32.

diSibio, M. (1982). Memory for connected discourse: A constructivist view. *Review of Educational Research, 52,* 149–174.

Dole, J., Duffy, G., Roehler, L., & Pearson, P. (1990). Moving from the old to the new: Research on reading comprehension instruction. *Review of Educational Research, 61,* 239–264.

Driver, R. (1987). Promoting conceptual change in classroom settings: The experience of the Children's Learning in Science Project. In J. Novak (Ed.), *Proceedings of the second international seminar on misconceptions and educational strategies in science and mathematics* (Vol. 2) (pp. 97–107). Ithaca, NY: Cornell University.

Duffy, G. (1993). Rethinking strategy instruction: Four teachers' development and their low-achievers' understandings. *Elementary School Journal, 93,* 231–247.

Duffy, G., & Roehler, L. (1987). Improving classroom reading instruction through the use of responsive elaboration. *Reading Teacher, 40,* 514–521.

Duffy, G., & Roehler, L. (1989). The tension between information-giving and mediation: Perspectives on instructional explanation and teacher change. In J. Brophy (Ed.), *Advances in research on teaching.* Vol. 1: *Teaching for meaningful understanding and self-regulated learning.* Greenwich, CT: JAI.

Duffy, G., Roehler, L., & Herrmann, B. (1988). Modeling mental processes helps poor readers become strategic readers. *Reading Teacher, 41,* 762–767.

Duffy, G., Roehler, L., Sivan, E., Rackliffe, G., Book, C., Meloth, M., Vavrus, L., Wesselman, R., Putnam, J., & Bassiri, D. (1987). Effects of explaining reasoning associated with using reading strategies. *Reading Research Quarterly, 22,* 347–368.

Englert, C., & Raphael, T. (1989). Developing successful writers through cognitive strategy instruction. In J. Brophy (Ed.) *Advances in research on teaching.* Vol. 1: *Teaching for meaningful understanding and self-regulated learning.* Greenwich, CT: JAI.

Fennema, E., Carpenter, T., & Peterson, P. (1989). Learning mathematics with understanding. In J. Brophy (Ed.), *Advances in research on teaching,* Vol. 1: *Teaching for meaningful understanding and self-regulated learning.* Greenwich, CT: JAI.

Florio-Ruane, S., & Lensmire, T. (1989). The role of instruction in learning to write. In J. Brophy (Ed.), *Advances in research on teaching.* Vol. 1: *Teaching for meaningful understanding and self-regulated learning.* Greenwich, CT: JAI.

Fraenkel, J. (1992, November). *A comparison of elite and non-elite social studies classrooms.* Paper presented at the annual meeting of the National Council for the Social Studies, Detroit.

Gagne, E., & Dick, W. (1983). Instructional psychology. In M. Rosenzweig & L. Porter (Eds.), *Annual review of psychology.* Palo Alto, CA: Annual Reviews.

Ginsburg, H., & Opper, S. (1979). *Piagetian theory of intellectual development* (2nd ed.). Englewood Cliffs, NJ: Prentice-Hall.

Glaser, R. (1984). Education and thinking: The role of knowledge. *American Psychologist, 39,* 93–104.

Glynn, S., Yeany, R., & Britton, B. (Eds.). (1991). *The psychology of learning science.* Hillsdale, NJ: Erlbaum.

Good, T., Grouws, D., & Ebmeier, H. (1983). *Active mathematics teaching*. New York: Longman.

Good, T., McCaslin, M., & Reys, B. (1992). Investigating work groups to promote problem solving in mathematics. In J. Brophy (Ed.), *Advances in research on teaching*. Vol. 3. *Planning and managing learning tasks and activities* (pp. 115–160). Greenwich, CT: JAI.

Graves, T. (1983). *Writing: Teachers and children at work*. Exeter, NJ: Heinemann.

Hand, B., & Treagust, D. (1991). Student achievement and science curriculum development using a constructive framework. *School Science and Mathematics, 91,* 172–176.

Hansen, J., & Pearson, P. (1983). An instructional study: Improving the inferential comprehension of fourth-grade good and poor readers. *Journal of Educational Psychology, 75,* 821–829.

Hiebert, J., & Wearne, D. (1992). Links between teaching and learning place value with understanding in first grade. *Journal for Research in Mathematics Education, 23,* 98–122.

Knapp, M., & Shields, P. (Eds.). (1991). *Better schooling for the children of poverty: Alternatives to conventional wisdom*. Berkeley, CA: McCutchan.

Lampert, M. (1989). Choosing and using mathematical tools in classroom discourse. In J. Brophy (Ed.), *Advances in research on teaching*. Vol. 1: *Teaching for meaningful understanding and self-regulated learning*. Greenwich, CT: JAI.

Lampert, M. (1990). When the problem is not the question and the solution is not the answer: Mathematical knowing and teaching. *American Educational Research Journal, 27,* 29–63.

Lave, J., & Wenger, E. (1991). *Situated learning: Legitimate peripheral participation*. Cambridge: Cambridge University Press.

Marzano, R., Brandt, R., Hughes, C., Jones, B., Presseisen, B., Rankin, S., & Suhor, C. (1988). *Dimensions of thinking: A framework for curriculum and instruction*. Alexandria, VA: Association for Supervision and Curriculum Development.

McCaslin, M., & Good, T. (1992). Compliant cognition: The misalliance of management and instruction goals in current school reform. *Educational Researcher, 21,* 4–17.

Minstrell, J. (1989). Teaching science for understanding. In L. Resnick & L. Klopfer (Eds.), *Toward the thinking curriculum: Current cognitive research: 1989 Yearbook of the Association for Supervision and Curriculum Development*. Alexandria, VA: Association for Supervision and Curriculum Development.

Moll, L. (Ed.). (1990). *Vygotsky and education: Instructional implications and applications of socio-historical psychology*. Cambridge: Cambridge University Press.

National Association of State Boards of Education. (1988). *Right from the start: The report of the NASBE task force on early childhood education*. Alexandria, VA: Author.

National Council of Teachers of Mathematics. (1989). *Curriculum and evaluation standards for school mathematics*. Reston, VA: Author.

Neale, D., Smith, D., & Johnson, V. (1990). Implementing conceptual change teaching in primary science. *Elementary School Journal, 91,* 109–131.

Newman, D., Griffin, P., & Cole, M. (1989). *The construction zone: Working for cognitive change in school*. Cambridge: Cambridge University Press.

Newmann, F. (1990). Qualities of thoughtful social studies classes: An empirical profile. *Journal of Curriculum Studies, 22,* 253–275.

Newmann, F. (Ed.). (1992). *Student engagement and achievement in American secondary schools.* New York: Teachers College Press.

Novak, J. (Ed.). (1987). *Proceedings of the second international seminar on misconceptions and educational strategies in science and mathematics* (Vol. 2). Ithaca, NY: Cornell University.

Palincsar, A., & Brown, A. (1984). Reciprocal teaching of comprehension-fostering and comprehension-monitoring activities. *Cognition and Instruction, 1,* 117–175.

Palincsar, A., & Brown, A. (1989). Classroom dialogues to promote self-regulated comprehension. In J. Brophy (Ed.), *Advances in research on teaching.* Vol. 1: *Teaching for meaningful understanding and self-regulated learning.* Greenwich, CT: JAI.

Paris, S., Cross, D., & Lipson, M. (1984). Informed Strategies for Learning: A program to improve children's reading awareness and comprehension. *Journal of Educational Psychology, 76,* 1239–1252.

Paris, S., Wasik, B., & Turner, J. (1991). The development of strategic readers. In R. Barr, M. Kamil, P. Mosenthal, & P. Pearson (Eds.), *Handbook of reading research* (Vol. 2) (pp. 609–640). New York: Longman.

Pinnell, G., DeFord, D., & Lyons, C. (1988). *Reading recovery: Early intervention for at-risk first graders.* Arlington, VA: Educational Research Service.

Posner, G., Strike, K., Hewson, K., & Gertzog, W. (1982). Accommodation of a scientific conception: Toward a theory of conceptual change. *Science Education, 66,* 211–228.

Prawat, R. (1989). Promoting access to knowledge, strategy, and disposition in students: A research synthesis. *Review of Educational Research, 59,* 1–41.

Pressley, M., El-Dinary, P., Gaskins, I., Schuder, T., Bergman, J., Almasi, J., & Brown, R. (1992). Beyond direct explanation: Transactional instruction of reading comprehension strategies. *Elementary School Journal, 92,* 513–555.

Pressley, M., Harris, K., & Marks, M. (1992). But good strategy instructors are constructivists! *Educational Psychology Review, 4,* 3–31.

Pressley, M., Johnson, C., Symons, S., McGoldrick, J., & Kurita, J. (1989). Strategies that improve children's memory and comprehension of text. *Elementary School Journal, 90,* 3–32.

Quirk, B., & Cianciolo, P. (1993). *The study of literature in a fifth-grade classroom: One teacher's perspective* (Elementary Subjects Center Report No. 83). East Lansing: Michigan State University, Institute for Research on Teaching, Center for the Learning and Teaching of Elementary Subjects.

Resnick, L. (1987). *Education and learning to think.* Washington, DC: National Academy Press.

Resnick, L. (1989). Treating mathematics as an ill-structured discipline. In R. Charles & E. Silver (Eds.), *The teaching and assessing of mathematical problem solving.* Hillsdale, NJ: Erlbaum.

Resnick, L., & Klopfer, L. (Eds.). (1989). *Toward the thinking curriculum: Current cognitive research: 1989 Yearbook of the Association for Supervision and Curriculum Development.* Alexandria, VA: Association for Supervision and Curriculum Development.

Rogoff, B. (1990). *Apprenticeship in thinking: Cognitive development in social context.* New York: Oxford University Press.

Rogoff, B., & Wertsch, J. (Eds.). (1984). *Children's learning in the "zone of proximal development."* San Francisco: Jossey-Bass.

Rosaen, C. (1989). Writing in the content areas: Reaching its potential in the learning process. In J. Brophy (Ed.), *Advances in research on teaching.* Vol. 1: *Teaching for meaningful understanding and self-regulated learning.* Greenwich, CT: JAI.

Rosenshine, B., & Meister, C. (1992). The use of scaffolds for teaching higher-level cognitive strategies. *Educational Leadership, 49*(7), 26–33.

Roth, K. (1990). Developing meaningful conceptual understanding in science. In B. Jones & L. Idol (Eds.), *Dimensions of thinking and cognitive instruction* (pp. 139–175). Hillsdale, NJ: Erlbaum.

Rumelhart, D., & Norman, D. (1981). Analogical processes in learning. In J. Anderson (Ed.), *Cognitive skills and their acquisition* (pp. 335–359). Hillsdale, NJ: Erlbaum.

Schank, R., & Abelson, R. (1977). *Scripts, plans, goals, and understanding.* Hillsdale, NJ: Erlbaum.

Smith, E., & Anderson, L. (1984). *The Planning and Teaching Intermediate Science study: Final report.* East Lansing: Institute for Research on Teaching, Michigan State University.

Soled, S. (1990). Teaching processes to improve both higher and lower mental process achievement. *Teaching and Teacher Education, 6,* 255–265.

Steffe, L., Cobb, P., & von Glasersfeld, E. (1988). *Construction of arithmetical meanings and strategies.* New York: Springer-Verlag.

Stigler, J., & Stevenson, H. (1991). How Asian teachers polish each lesson to perfection. *American Educator, 15*(1), 12–20, 43–47.

Stodolsky, S. (1988). *The subject matters: Classroom activity in math and social studies.* Chicago: University of Chicago Press.

Swing, S., Stoiber, K., & Peterson, P. (1988). Thinking skills versus learning time: Effects of alternative classroom-based interventions on students' mathematics problem solving. *Cognition and Instruction, 5,* 123–191.

Tharp, R., & Gallimore, R. (1988). *Rousing minds to life: Teaching, learning, and schooling in social context.* Cambridge: Cambridge University Press.

Thornton, S., & Wenger, R. (1990). Geography curriculum and instruction in three fourth-grade classrooms. *Elementary School Journal, 90,* 515–531.

von Glasersfeld, E. (1984). An introduction to radical constructivism. In P. Watzlawick (Ed.), *The invented reality* (pp. 17–40). New York: Norton.

Vosniadou, S., & Brewer, W. (1987). Theories of knowledge restructuring in development. *Review of Educational Research, 57,* 51–67.

Vygotsky, L. (1962). *Thought and language.* Cambridge, MA: MIT Press.

Vygotsky, L. (1978). *Mind in society: The development of higher psychological processes* (edited by M. Cole, V. John-Steiner, S. Scribner, & E. Souberman). Cambridge: Harvard University Press.

Wertsch, J. (1985). *Vygotsky and the social formation of mind.* Cambridge: Harvard University Press.

Wertsch, J. (1991). *Voices of the mind: A sociocultural approach to mediated action.* Cambridge: Harvard University Press.

Wertsch, J., & Tulviste, P. (1992). L. S. Vygotsky and contemporary developmental psychology. *Developmental Psychology, 28,* 548–557.

White, R. (1992). Implications of recent research on learning for curriculum and assessment. *Journal of Curriculum Studies, 24,* 153–164.

Wood, D., Bruner, J., & Ross, G. (1976). The role of tutoring in problem solving. *Journal of Child Psychology and Psychiatry, 17,* 89–100.

Wood, T., Cobb, P., & Yackel, E. (1990). The contextual nature of teaching: Mathematics and reading instruction in one second-grade classroom. *Elementary School Journal, 90,* 497–513.

FORM 10.1 Teaching Content for Understanding and Application

PURPOSE: To assess the degree to which the teacher teaches content not just for memory but for understanding and application.
USE: When you have detailed information about the curriculum, instruction, and evaluation enacted during a content unit or strand.

    Enter a checkmark for each of the following features that was included effectively in the content unit or strand, and a zero for each feature that was omitted or handled ineffectively. Then add detailed comments on a separate sheet, emphasizing constructive suggestions for improvement.

Checklist

_____   1. *Goals* were expressed in terms of long-term student outcomes (acquisition of knowledge, skills, values, or dispositions to be applied to life outside of school), not just in terms of short-term content mastery.

_____   2. Limited content was taught in sufficient *depth* to allow for development of understanding.

_____   3. The *knowledge* content was represented as *networks* of related information structured around powerful key ideas.

_____   4. In presenting and leading discussions of the content, the teacher helped students to recognize the centrality of key ideas and to use them as bases around which to structure larger content networks.

_____   5. In addition to providing explicit explanations, the teacher asked questions and engaged students in activities that required them to process the information actively, test and if necessary repair their understanding of it, and communicate about it.

_____   6. *Skills* (procedural knowledge) were taught and used in the process of applying information (propositional knowledge) content rather than being taught as a separate curriculum.

_____   7. Most skills practice was embedded within inquiry, problem solving, decision making, or other whole-task application contexts rather than being limited to isolated practice of part skills.

_____   8. If skills needed to be taught, they were taught with emphasis on modeling their strategic use for accomplishing particular purposes, as well as explaining when and why the skills would be used.

_____   9. Content-based *discourse* emphasized sustained and thoughtful discussion featuring critical or creative thinking about key ideas, not just fast-moving recitation over specifics.

_____   10. *Activities and assignments* called for students to integrate or apply key ideas and engage in critical and creative thinking, problem solving, inquiry, decision making, or other higher-order applications, not just to demonstrate recall of facts and definitions.

_____   11. In *assessing* student learning, the teacher focused on understanding and application goals, not just low-level factual memory or skills mastery goals.

FORM 10.2 SOCIAL CONSTRUCTION OF KNOWLEDGE

USE: When a teacher engages students in reflective discussion designed to stimulate construction of knowledge.

PURPOSE: To assess the degree to which the discussion includes features that support social construction of knowledge.

Check each feature that was included in the discussion:

A. Poses a well-chosen problem

___ 1. Problem is appropriate in familiarity, difficulty: Students have enough prior knowledge to allow them to discuss it intelligibly, but they also must engage in reasoning and higher-order thinking

___ 2. Problem is authentic, significant to the students

___ 3. Teacher requires them to predict, explain, develop justified problem-solving or decision-making strategies that call for applying the powerful ideas being developed

B. Elicits suggestions and related justifications

___ 1. Students act as learning community, teacher facilitates

___ 2. Poses problem, calls for ideas about how to approach it

___ 3. Lists suggestions on board or overhead

___ 4. Doesn't judge but calls for clarification, elaboration, justification

C. Elicits assessments and discussion

___ 1. Invites students to critique by offering justified arguments for or against contributed ideas

___ 2. Invites contributors to revise their thinking if they wish

___ 3. Encourages student-student interaction and debate

___ 4. If necessary, scaffolds by breaking question into separate issues or substeps, asking about a neglected aspect, listing what is given or has been agreed upon separately from what still is at issue

D. As issues get clarified, moves students toward resolution (s)

___ 1. Tests for consensus when it appears to have developed; if disagreement still exists, asks about unresolved issue(s)

___ 2. If necessary, asks questions to focus attention on unwarranted assumptions, misconceptions, or complications that have not yet been recognized

___ 3. If necessary, temporarily interrupts discussion to allow students time to get more information or interact more intensively in subgroups

___ 4. When consensus is finally achieved, asks questions to help students reformulate what they have discovered about this particular case into more general principles

E. Constructs summary of main ideas and their connections

___ 1. Invites students to summarize what has been learned

___ 2. If necessary, asks clarification and elaboration questions to make sure that the summary includes all main points and connections between them that need to be emphasized

___ 3. Follows up by having students work individually or in small groups to reconstruct the new knowledge (by writing in journals or composing reports, etc.) and perhaps to apply it to new cases

NOTES:

Chapter
11

Improving Classroom Teaching

INTRODUCTION

We have described a variety of instructional behaviors and learning opportunities that should appear in the classroom and outlined ways of measuring their quality. In this chapter we present guidelines for in-service training and self-improvement. Although the ideas we provide are practical and useful, they are not intended as prescriptions for how to teach. As we stress throughout the book, teachers have different needs and interests; hence, in-service programs must be tailored to participants, and teachers must adapt program content to meet their own needs.

You need to integrate the theory, research, and concepts we have presented with your own personality and teaching style and apply them to your teaching context. This view is similar to Biddle and Anderson's (1986) perspective on the role of theories in research on teaching: "They provide a synthesis and explanation for findings to date, they suggest predictions that we might make for teaching contexts we have not yet examined, they make explicit the assumptions with which we think about events, and they provide tools we can use to think about and comprehend the confusing phenomena of teaching" (p. 246).

You must go beyond theory and research by reflecting on your own earlier experience as a student, your beliefs about what appropriate teaching is, and your actual teaching experience as well as by learning to use other teachers to gain insight into their teaching (Ball & Goodson, 1985; Carter, in press; Gitlin et al., 1992). Exciting developments are occurring in teaching today—a growing citizen awareness of the importance and complexity of teaching and the willingness of some administrators to share with teachers power and responsibility for staff development and evaluation (Maeroff, 1988). We discuss ways to design in-service programs to facilitate your personal growth. We begin with sections about individual programs of self-growth and informal study groups of volunteer teachers. Then we discuss staff development that occurs as part of a school system's official in-service program.

Teachers, like everyone else, are sometimes unwilling to engage in self-evaluation. Is this because teachers are not committed to their profession or are unwilling to do the extra work necessary to improve? We doubt it. Teachers seek opportunities to evaluate and improve their teaching if acceptable and useful methods are available (Good & Mulryan, 1990). However, certain obstacles minimize self-improvement in some teachers, and these must be removed if continual development is to take place. The following vignettes illustrate how colleagues can assist or hinder self-evaluation.

A Junior High Example

Janice Taylor is an ambitious social studies education major who is student-teaching at Oak Junior High. Oak students come from the same kinds of middle-class homes that Janice comes from. Still, she is sometimes apprehensive about teaching. She has not been in a junior high for several years, and although she has gained useful information in her college classes, she has never taught. Will students obey her? Can she make them enjoy schoolwork? These doubts increase as the time for her to begin teaching nears. She has been observing Ms. Woodward's class for two weeks. In another week she is to become the teacher.

Janice watches Ms. Woodward intently because she wants to learn how to get students to respond and obey. She believes Ms. Woodward is a good teacher who treats students fairly and is respected by them. However, Janice is a shy and soft-spoken person who frequently becomes nervous when she is around loud, assertive people. Consequently, she is often upset by the forceful way in which Ms. Woodward runs the class. She speaks in a booming voice and does not hesitate to give misbehaving students a tongue-lashing or send them out of the room. Her favorite tactic when students are disruptive is to yell, "I'm telling you once and for the last time, listen to your classmates when they talk!" Students typically stop after Ms. Woodward yells at them.

One week later, when Janice is teaching the class, she loudly addresses some misbehaving students in the same way, "I'm telling you once and for the last time, listen to your classmates!" Think about these two questions:

1. Why did Janice imitate Mrs. Woodward's teaching style?
2. How might Janice have taught if she had had a different cooperating teacher?

A High School Example

Ralph Tyler has taught chemistry for 15 years at Riverside High School, an affluent high school in a western state. He is respected as a teacher by both colleagues and students. Today he is meeting with Sharon Jenkins, a first-year history teacher. Mr. Tyler believes that peer teacher observation and feedback are useful. Although math teachers typically work with math teachers, and so forth, the principal encourages teachers to cross subject-matter lines on occasion to help colleagues better understand instructional issues that are not subject-specific (clarity, etc.). Today, Ralph observed Ms. Jenkins's third-period class. Now, during fifth period they are meeting to discuss the observation. Mr. Tyler begins the conversation immediately. "Sharon, it was a pleasure to observe in your class. I enjoyed it a lot. It was a good lesson. There are only a few mistakes that I'd like to talk about."

What do you think about peer observation? Should teachers observe other teachers? Would you like for classmates to observe you? What should happen during a feedback conversation? What do you think of the way Mr. Tyler began the conversation?

Obstacles to Teacher Self-Improvement

One obstacle to teacher self-improvement results from the way we were socialized. Most of us have seldom taken part in self-evaluation designed not just to uncover weaknesses but to eliminate those weaknesses. We may occasionally engage in destructive self-criticism, but we rarely link such behavior with constructive plans for improvement.

We act this way in part because our socialization (especially our experience in schools) has not helped us to develop the needed skills. For example, has a teacher ever returned an "A" paper to you with instructions to reflect on the paper and to improve it? Certainly, most of us have had to rewrite papers, but seldom "A" papers, and rarely have we been asked to rethink and incorporate new ideas of our own into such work.

Indeed, school seldom allowed most of us time to *think* about what we were doing. We were too busy finishing assignments to reflect on them. Remember the feeling of relief when major tasks or final exams were completed? No matter how well or poorly we think we have performed, we feel liberated when we are finished. We no longer have control over the paper, and we do not think about it anymore.

Socialization in schools tends to emphasize this idea: Do not look back, keep moving forward. Yet we must examine our past and present performances so that we can monitor progress and determine whether we are moving forward or merely traveling in circles.

A second obstacle to self-improvement is that our school experience has often emphasized analytical thinking, not synthesis. The following tenth-grade social studies dialogue represents analytical thinking:

> TEACHER: John, what's wrong with electing members of Congress every two years?
>
> JOHN: (*Hesitantly and in a soft tone*) Well, ah, I think that they spend too much time trying to be reelected. (*The teacher is beaming and nodding, so John begins to speak more confidently and loudly.*) Since they face reelection every two years, they always need money for reelection. They build their campaign chest primarily with funds from the people who financed their original candidacy, so they owe these people a double debt. It's hard for them to be their own person.
>
> TEACHER: Good answer, John. Carol, what did John imply when he said, "be their own person"?
>
> CAROL: Well, that the candidates' debts and their continual dependency on special interests who have given money make them cater to these groups. But even if members of Congress are strong, the two-year election procedure is bad because they continue to run, make speeches, raise money, and have little time to do their real job.

Although such discussions are important, they seldom go beyond an analysis stage that defines the problem. However, the teacher might point out the desirability of controlling campaign spending and making the sources of contributions public knowledge and then challenge students to go beyond these common solutions that *others* have suggested. For example, the teacher might "playfully" suggest that senators, even though they are elected for six-year terms, spend much time running for reelection and make most of their decisions accordingly. The teacher could also have students suggest ways in which elected representatives could be held accountable: Should they keep daily logs of how their time is spent, hold regular office hours for the public, or spend a designated number of days in the district or state they represent? Students could be encouraged to speculate on the effects of term limits that have been approved in some states.

Demands are seldom made on students for original, practical suggestions because most teachers were socialized in schools that demanded and rewarded analytical thinking. This emphasis gave most of us plenty of practice in pinpointing weaknesses but comparatively little experience in solving problems by generating constructive alternatives.

Also, most of the evaluation we experienced in schools was external and nonconstructive. The way it was handled told us where we stood, but not how we could improve. Thus, we tended to avoid evaluation. Since evaluation was so strongly associated with negative consequences, it often evoked the fear that "I'm going to be exposed" rather than the anticipation "I'm going to receive useful feedback." Consequently, evaluation may make us anxious, even when it is just self-evaluation.

Another factor that has limited teachers' ability to grow as professionals is that teacher education programs have not assisted students in developing skills in collegiality and in learning about themselves through feedback from others. Teachers need to study models of collegial relationships and to practice giving and receiving feedback.

Smylie (1992), in studying teachers' reports of their interactions with teacher leaders, concludes that teachers and teacher leaders often conceptualize the role of the teacher leader differently. Hence, often teachers perceive their needs differently from teacher leaders. Further, it is clear that teacher leaders in Smylie's sample wanted to provide more classroom support for teachers (observe, teach, offer resources), but the organizational structure in which they worked often made it impossible for them to work with teachers during the instructional day. Thus, if peer leadership programs are to work, there must be both careful goal conceptualization and appropriate structural supports (i.e., time).

EXPERIMENTING AND IMPROVING

As a teacher you are an individual with a unique pattern of strengths and weaknesses. You have to develop a style that allows you to express yourself and teach students in your own way. To do so, you may have to experiment with different methods before you find an approach that is right for you (i.e., you feel comfortable using it and your students learn and respond positively to it). If you try an approach systematically for a reasonable time and it does not work, *then discard it and develop techniques that do work for you.* There is no need to teach the way your cooperating teacher did without regard to your own feelings or to the response of your students.

Even after identifying a satisfying style, successful teachers continue to experiment with new methods and to find new ways to stimulate student learning. They also constantly reflect on their teaching and stay abreast of new research and developments. Given the demands of preparing for class and grading papers, finding time for professional reading is often difficult. But continued reading is essential if teachers are to grow professionally and to become knowledgeable colleagues.

Teaching Is Difficult

Few teachers are excellent in all aspects of teaching. Too often, teachers enter the classroom with unrealistically high expectations ("I will capture the interest of every student at every moment, and every lesson I teach will be completely successful."), so that when outcomes do not match expectations, they may become depressed, blame students, or begin to justify and rationalize their behavior rather than to search for new styles of teaching. This occurs in part because they do not realize that other teachers also have difficulties. All teachers occasionally teach lessons that fail, say the wrong thing to students, and so forth. Although teaching is difficult, one can succeed at it by continuing to strive for improvement.

Like everyone else, teachers tend to talk about successes, not failures. Thus, some teachers, especially new ones, may become anxious and discouraged when they have trouble because they hear nothing but the good or interesting things that other teachers are doing. They experience feelings of disappointment and ineptness when they do not achieve easy success, yet are reluctant to ask veteran teachers for help because they believe they would be admitting failure (Rosenholtz, 1989).

If you have thoughts like these, dismiss them. Teaching is challenging and exciting work, but it takes time to develop and refine teaching skills. Most experienced teachers are sympathetic to the problems of beginning teachers and are glad to help them. However, few of us like to be approached by someone who says, "Tell me what to do." It is better to approach other teachers by telling them you have a teaching problem and would like to exchange ideas with them and benefit from their experience. Experienced teachers can also learn from beginning teachers.

Identifying Good Teaching

You must decide what is good practice by observing the effects of your behavior on students. (Do tests reveal appropriate learning? Do lectures lead students to raise their own questions? Do students enjoy and understand assignments?) There is no single formula specifying good teaching because no one set of teaching behaviors is clearly related to student achievement in all situations (Brophy, 1992; Brophy & Good, 1986; Leinhardt, 1992) and, in any case, achievement is only one of many student outcomes that must be considered. Our advice is based on research, but we have often gone beyond the data in order to provide suggestions. The statements in this chapter are not intended to tell you how to teach but rather to provide you with a way of looking at and analyzing classroom life.

Many resources are available to help teachers analyze and improve instruction. Important practical research findings and concepts are summarized in fundamental references such as the *Handbook of Research on Teaching* (Wittrock, 1986). This handbook discusses a wide range of subjects comprehensively and critically, such as the cultures of teaching, teaching functions, and teachers' thought processes. It also contains several chapters on adapting teaching to learners (e.g., teaching creative and gifted learners) as well as on teaching each of the major school subjects. Research results are especially useful for teachers who want to engage in self-study programs but who realize that although empirical data provide direction, teachers have to evaluate their own classroom behavior (Good & Weinstein, 1986).

Another excellent source is the *Educators' Handbook*, edited by Virginia Richardson-Koehler (1987). It provides research-based information about a variety of educational topics, including peer teaching, professional collaboration, and classroom management. It is an especially good source of information about the teaching of various subjects, including mathematics, reading, science, social studies, and computers and higher-order thinking skills.

Millman and Darling-Hammond (1990) have edited a comprehensive book, *Teacher Evaluation*, providing an authoritative review of factors (political, social, organizational) that influence the evaluation of elementary and secondary teachers. The text also deals with self-evaluation. Professional societies have prepared a growing number of handbooks (for example, the volume on mathematics teaching that Grouws, 1992, edited for the National Council of Teachers of Mathematics).

Teachers should seek recent research publications from their professional societies (e.g., National Council of Teachers of English, etc.).

A number of sources encourage teachers to reflect on their personal experiences (as a child, as a student, as a student teacher, etc.) in order to understand their current beliefs about instruction. Reflecting on experiences (one's own or reading stories of other teachers) can stimulate self-insight and new goals or approaches to teaching (Ball & Goodson, 1985; Carter, 1993; and Gitlin et al., 1992). Finally, numerous valuable sources discuss self-evaluation (e.g., Barber, 1990) and how self-improvement and staff development can hinder or facilitate teachers' personal and professional growth depending on program goals and quality of feedback (Gitlin & Smyth, 1989).

Starting Self-Evaluation

The first step in improving teaching is to evaluate your current strengths and weaknesses. Go back through this text and list your behaviors on three pages entitled (1) *Perform Capably*, (2) *Needs Work*, and (3) *Not Sure*. Take the first list, which represents progress you have made as a teacher, and store it in your desk so you can examine it from time to time and add to it.

You may note that you already ask a variety of factual and higher-order questions and that you ask questions before calling on students. On your list for *Needs Work*, you may note a tendency not to follow through on warnings and an inconsistency as a classroom manager. After a few hours of thinking about strengths and weaknesses, you will have an outline of your ability as a teacher and will be ready to begin work on the list of needed improvements.

If you have trouble deciding where to start, you might have a teacher or supervisor whom you respect observe your class and make suggestions. Alternatively, you could listen to a tape-recorded session of your class. It is difficult to evaluate what occurs in classrooms because so much happens so quickly, so it may take some time to identify strengths and weaknesses.

Making Explicit Plans

To improve your teaching, you must decide what you want to do and how to determine whether your plans are working. Too often, our half-hearted New Year's resolutions are never acted on because they are vague. Goals such as "I want to teach in diverse ways" are seldom accomplished simply because they are not concrete goals that can guide planning. Resolutions are more likely to be fulfilled when they specify the desired change: "I want to increase the time I spend in small-group and project-based work by 25 percent."

Self-evaluation is relatively simple in many teaching situations, although certain teacher behaviors are more difficult to evaluate than others. Teachers frequently set goals for students as well as for themselves. A teacher may say, "I want all of my ninth-grade students to participate actively during small-group lab projects." This resolution calls for evaluating the behaviors of both the teacher and the students.

The message is simple. If you do not know where you are going, you are unlikely to get there. By understanding the problem you are addressing, it is easier to clarify the beliefs, norms, and behaviors you are trying to improve. However, we recognize that problem identification is not always easy and that change can be complex at times. For example, teachers who want to implement small-group cooperative learning may find that they must do considerable reading and visit other classrooms in order to decide what role small-group teaching will play in their classrooms.

Action

After developing appropriate goals (or needs for knowledge from which to form goals), the next step is to choose two or three behaviors or beliefs to change or new ones to try. Do not try to change too many things at once, lest you become overwhelmed and discouraged. Consider a few issues at a time and carefully monitor your progress. For example, if you try to call on students randomly, you may have to write their names on flash cards and shuffle the stack periodically. Always calling on students who have their hands up is a difficult habit to break. You may improve classroom communication by explaining why you ask questions, thus helping students to understand their roles.

As you implement a change, assess its effectiveness. After you introduce lessons by telling students why the lessons are important, try to assess whether more students follow the directions or seem interested. Similarly, if you call on students to react to other students' responses, note whether students pay greater attention to the discussion (and whether student essays reflect more awareness of diverse opinion, etc.).

Individual Self-Study

Some questions that might be useful for self-study include the following:

> What aspects of teaching do I most enjoy and what does this imply about my beliefs about good teaching?

> How do my instructional goals match those of my peers? (As an algebra teacher, how much time do I spend on particular topics? As a social studies teacher, do I emphasize history as much as other teachers do?)

> Do my low and high achievers indicate that I have equal interest in them?

> Do low- and high-achieving students have different beliefs about the value of subject matter?

> Do my questions emphasize understanding or only quick, correct answers?

> How long do I wait for students to respond? Is this figure different for high and low achievers?

> When students work in small groups, do some students do most of the work?

Which students want to work in small groups the most? The least? Why?

What percentage of my day is spent in actual instruction?

When I teach my subject specialty (biology, honors English, French), how do I teach the content I am most knowledgeable about and interested in versus content I am least knowledgeable about?

What percentage of a student's day is spent learning new material versus reviewing?

Do some students who need help rarely seek me out to get it? Which students initiate contact with me and which ones don't? Why?

How much time do I spend with individual students in a given day?

How much time do I spend in math, social studies, language arts? Do students' achievement gains reflect time spent?

Are undesirable gender roles or inappropriate cultural expectations being communicated?

How often do I get requests from students to tailor an assignment to their interests? Do I handle such requests appropriately?

How much time do my students spend on their homework? Do I need to work to get some students to take homework more seriously?

How do students study for exams (in groups, individually, in pairs)? Does it seem to make any difference?

How interesting do students rate various lessons or assignments? Does this interest vary as a function of gender or achievement?

Responding to such questions would provide you with information about aspects of your classroom that you might want to change. That is, the results could lead you to ask questions such as: Can I raise the average amount of time I spend with individual low achievers during mathematics from two minutes to five minutes a day? If so, what effect will this have on their attitudes, achievement, and attention spans (when they work independently)? When I implement learning centers and peer-tutoring activities, do I have more time to work with individual students? Can I change certain routines to make the classroom more interesting for me and my students?

Classroom Example

Let us consider an example to see how a teacher could use information to improve instruction. Assume that sixth-grade teacher Joe Bean's students do less well in math than in all other subjects. Joe is puzzled by this. He enjoys teaching math and feels well qualified to do so. Students' attitudes measured earlier in the year were generally positive toward him and the instructional program. However, math drew the most criticism when students commented on specific subjects.

Joe decides to obtain anonymous information from students about the problems they encounter in math and about how the program might be improved. Upon doing so, he is discouraged to find that much of the information is contradictory (what some students prefer is disliked by others) or does not lead to suggestions for action (students do not believe that the math period is too long). However, one theme is evident in the comments of several students: "I often don't know what I'm supposed to do for my assignment"; "When we start a new unit, I'm always lost"; "I don't understand my work until you explain it the next day."

Subsequently, Joe notices that students engage in more neutral or aimless activity when working on math assignments than at any other time during the day. He decides that he does not spend enough time explaining how the work relates to preceding work, modeling how to do problems, and allowing students to generate and discuss examples before he has students begin work on assignments. In particular, he wants students to discuss more of their background knowledge and to think about the bridge between what they already know and the current instruction.

If students had expressed low interest, Joe might have considered peer tutoring or devising a mathematics learning center to add novelty and provide more time for him to work with individuals. However, students' self-reports ("Often I'm confused, but after a while I catch on.") match his own observations that the problem is not low motivation (boredom) but lack of understanding. Joe's plan is to increase his ratio of explanation, modeling, and student verbalization of thinking to practice work, especially at the beginning of a unit, and to see whether this strategy improves students' attitudes and achievement.

Note that Joe's plan is based on only a hypothesis, a hunch about how to proceed. It must be judged by its effects on students' performance. Plans must not become "answers" adopted without consideration of their effects on students. Joe might find that some other factor (assignments too long, feedback inadequate) is related more directly to student achievement. By evaluating the effects of his changes in classroom processes on student outcomes (achievement, attitude), eventually he will find procedures that work for him in the class.

The preceding example focused on changes in instruction. However, self-improvement plans might also focus on changing knowledge. Teachers could evaluate and then enhance their knowledge of particular subjects (geometry) or concepts. Similarly, teachers might improve curriculum units (How can I promote more higher-order thinking about social studies topics? How can I teach fewer topics but make them more integrated and meaningful?). And, of course, teachers might focus on collegial relations (How can I find more time to discuss important issues with peers? How can we arrange to do guest lectures to extend our own knowledge?). We continue to focus our discussion on changing instruction, but you should note that the general process of change is similar across different types of outcomes.

You Are Not Alone

You may wish to begin your evaluation and operate for a while without feedback from others. Nevertheless, all teachers will eventually benefit from discussing classroom teaching with other teachers.

If you have access to videotape equipment, arrange to have one or two of your typical lessons videotaped. Do not attempt to construct special units or to review old material. Teach your regularly scheduled lessons in your normal fashion. After a couple of weeks, tape some similar lessons so you can watch for signs of progress in your classroom behavior, your decision making, and in the responses of students. If your school does not have video equipment, check with your principal to see if you can get it from the central office. Central school officials are usually delighted to loan video equipment. If it is impossible to secure video equipment, cassette audio recorders are readily available and can be used to collect useful information.

You can obtain feedback from other sources too. Many people teach in teams or other situations where it is easy to arrange for another teacher to observe them. You can also request release time to work with peers or make arrangements to trade weekly visits with other teachers during free periods. Finally, you can use student teachers, student observers, or parents on occasion.

It usually is best to specify what an observer is to look for, because there is so much to see that he or she may not notice the things you would like to receive feedback about. The observer, of course, can always volunteer additional information.

Curriculum supervisors also can provide you with relevant feedback. Most supervisors are delighted when teachers make explicit observation requests. However, supervisory visits are often frustrating for the supervisor as well as for the teacher (McDaniel, 1981). Since supervisors may not know the goals of a lesson or how it fits into a unit, it is difficult for them to provide helpful feedback. Armed with a specific request, though, they can provide relevant comments about areas of interest to teachers.

Students are another source of information. Informal conversations and anonymously administered questionnaires provide useful information (McCaslin & Good, in press; Rohrkemper, 1981; Weinstein, 1983; Wittrock, 1986). Teachers who have never solicited student evaluations may be dismayed at first when they see the variety of comments. Students have unique perspectives, and different students may label the same behavior as a weakness or a strength. However, feedback usually includes some comments on which most students agree.

We have found that student feedback is most useful if it is given anonymously. Also, rather than requesting global comments or ratings, it is usually better to ask for specific reactions. One method is to request three or more statements about strengths and three or more about weaknesses, which forces students to be specific and to provide a more balanced critique than do global, free-response methods.

Various standardized instruments are available for obtaining student feedback. One especially good source (Anderson, 1983) provides extensive coverage of affective assessment, including examples of self-report measures, procedures for developing new measures, and strategies for interpreting affective data.

Richards (1987) describes questions she used in attempting to motivate secondary students who did not want to learn. She provides an intriguing discussion of how she was able to increase students' motivation by increasing her understanding of the students' perspectives. Teachers who collect anonymous information should demonstrate to students the usefulness of this information; that is, they should call students' attention to program changes made in response to their feedback.

Self-Study Groups

You can often use regularly scheduled in-service time for work in self-improvement groups. This procedure is especially useful when the time is devoted to small-group work with teachers who have common problems (e.g., elementary teachers working at the same grade, secondary teachers who teach the same subject). Self-study groups can also be formed on the basis of interest (e.g., beginning teachers who want to form a support group). Small groups provide an excellent place for teachers to receive feedback and suggestions from peers.

Different goals call for different groupings. For example, to improve curriculum continuity, teachers in contiguous grades should work together. However, if the goal is to allow elementary and secondary teachers to realize that some of their assumptions about what occurs at the other level do not apply, then it is important to mix teachers from the two levels. To promote the exchange of information about teaching style or classroom climate, teachers who teach different subjects and at various grade levels are needed. Beginning teachers should sometimes meet together (where they feel free to express problems); at other times, experienced teachers should meet with beginning teachers (i.e., to offer the benefit of experience in responding to problems).

Self-improvement teams may wish to view and provide feedback about tapes of one another's teaching, especially feedback about aspects that are of special interest to the teacher taped. This procedure contrasts markedly with the typical in-service program, which provides teachers with information on issues that the consultant wishes to discuss. Many staff development programs are designed by persons outside schools to "fix" teachers' deficiencies as these persons perceive them. Too often teachers view in-service activities as unrelated to their teaching needs (Spencer, 1984).

Some self-study group programs are created to encourage teachers to teach in one and only one way. We believe, however, that the role of self-study groups is to help teachers to develop their own styles, not to impose a style on them. The goal is self-development through professional reflection, not standardization of teaching practice (see Gitlin & Smyth, 1989).

Participation in self-study groups usually should be voluntary. Nothing hurts a program that involves discussing and evaluating teaching more than someone who takes part solely because it is required. Consideration should be given, however, to teachers who want to assess their instructional programs and develop their own goals before joining a group. Such teachers should have a chance to join self-study groups when they are ready to do so.

Three rules should be kept in mind when in-service groups begin to function. First, group structure and feedback exist to provide teachers with information that augments their self-development. The group provides the unique perspectives of its members as well as resources that enable it to give a teacher feedback regarding specific instructional plans. Thus, teachers function as decision makers, setting their own developmental goals. The group functions as a barometer, telling how it views the teacher and suggesting alternative ways to reach the goals the teacher has set. Teachers in the group will have their own viewpoints, of course, and each will react in terms of his or her own perspective.

Each teacher lists current goals and outlines what behaviors and techniques the group should examine when they view videotapes or observe the classroom. So as not to do too much at once, the teacher initially focuses on improving a few areas, and the group restricts its comments to these. After the group has functioned for a few weeks, the "video teacher of the week" may be ready to ask the group to focus on all dimensions of teaching that were exhibited.

The second rule to follow, then, especially in the group's formative weeks, is not to overwhelm a teacher with information. Restricting discussion to a few areas will help, and it may be useful to limit the number of comments each group member makes. We can profit from only so much information at one time, particularly negative feedback.

In-service groups may benefit from a rule such as this: Each participant provides a written discussion of two or three strengths and two or three weaknesses of the presentation. This guideline limits the amount of information a teacher receives and focuses attention on a small, manageable list of "points to consider." The rule also allows the teacher to have in writing (for future review) the reactions of each participant to the lesson.

Useful feedback focuses on specific ways to improve teaching. Ensuing discussions should include alternative procedures that the teacher might use to produce more desirable student responses. Thus, the teacher should receive both realistic reactions (positive and negative) to his or her performance (on goals that are of personal value) and information about alternative behaviors to consider.

A third rule is to be honest. Self-study groups lose their effectiveness when individuals engage in either of two participatory styles: Pollyanna and Get-the-Guest. Too many teachers are unwilling to say what they feel about another teacher's behavior, perhaps because they are afraid that frankness will lead other teachers to respond in kind when they are being evaluated, or because they believe that the teacher will be hurt by an honest reaction. Yet teachers can improve only if they receive honest, objective feedback. Criticism followed by new ideas or approaches that may improve teaching is the best way the group can assist a teacher in self-development. To be sure, teachers should communicate the good things that a teacher does. We all like to know when we have done well, and it is especially important to receive acknowledgment and encouragement for improvement.

The other undesirable participant role is that of the carping critic who criticizes excessively and thoughtlessly. Perhaps such behavior is motivated by the need for self-protection ("If everybody looks bad, I'll be okay"). Perhaps such teachers are just insensitive to the needs of others. At any rate, their behavior rarely does any good, and they need to be helped to deliver criticism tactfully and to link it with positive suggestions. Those who are not willing to temper excessive criticism should not continue in the group.

Opportunities to Observe and Obtain Feedback

Supervisory Feedback   Research has established that teachers often profit from feedback about their instruction when it is supplied by knowledgeable, sensitive classroom observers. Eash and Rasher (1977) reported that classroom observation was an important component of an in-service program to help teachers cope with the greater student diversity due to desegregation, and thus to improve students' achievement. The supervisory personnel who observed classrooms needed additional training for this role, however, because observation does not automatically improve instruction. It is useful only when conducted by competent persons who have a framework for observation.

Feedback from Researchers   In interviews with teachers, Good and Brophy (1974) found that teachers were unaware of much of their differential behavior toward high and low achievers, such as the percentage of time that they "stayed with" or "gave up" on students who did not immediately give a correct response. When teachers were presented with information about their behavior that both intrigued and bothered them, they wanted to change. Subsequent observation showed that they succeeded in doing so, and there were signs that students altered their behavior as a result of changed teacher behavior.

Feedback from Peers   Martin and Kerman's Equal Opportunity in the Classroom project (see Martin, 1973) attempted to help teachers become aware of self-defeating treatment of low-achieving students and learn new ways to interact with these students. First, teachers were presented with detailed information about teacher behavior that might be occurring in their own classrooms. They were then trained to treat low achievers in specific ways and also to observe and be observed by fellow teachers.

Teachers' reports about the project were enthusiastic. In particular, they benefited from feedback from other teachers and from observing other teachers themselves. Watching other teachers provides a valuable way to see new techniques. Observational data illustrated that project teachers began to treat low achievers much differently, whereas control teachers did not. In addition, the attitudes of low-achieving students in project classrooms were better than those in control classes.

Researchers continue to provide evidence that feedback can improve instruction. Sparks (1986) studied 19 junior high teachers who were given workshop training on how to increase low achievers' time on task and to improve interactive teaching. The teachers were placed into one of three groups. The first group participated only in the workshops. They were trained to use a coding system (SSOI; see Stallings, 1986), examined their own teaching profiles as exhibited by the SSOI, and discussed recent research findings. The second group participated in the workshops and also received the results of two classroom observations by a peer following the workshop training. The third group of teachers participated in the workshops and received two in-classroom coaching sessions from the trainer. Results showed that teachers who received workshops plus peer observations made the most change.

Sparks listed several possible reasons why the peer observational treatment was most effective. She noted that secondary teachers rarely observe other secondary teachers instruct and that observing another teacher can generate new ideas about teaching. A second advantage of peer observation is that the teachers were also collecting and coding data as they observed. This may have helped them to analyze both their peers' and their own teaching behavior more reflectively.

Feedback from Students   Feedback from students also can be useful in changing teacher behavior, although teachers do not change their behavior simply because they receive information (Kepler, 1977). To be useful, the information must relate to goals that are important to teachers. When evaluation forms do not reflect teachers' goals or needs, teachers are likely to reject the feedback as meaningless.

When teachers are given specific and accurate information, and especially when their collection of student feedback is voluntary, they can use it to improve instruction. Pambookian (1976) reported that when a group of college teachers was informed of significant discrepancies between their own perceptions and their students' perceptions of their teaching, they changed their teaching behavior. Instructors with student ratings lower than their own ratings improved their teaching the most. If student feedback is to have optimal value, teachers must be involved in the construction of the evaluation instruments to see that questions of personal importance are included, and instruments need to be changed occasionally to present teachers with information about different behaviors.

Quality of Feedback   Quality of feedback is critically important, irrespective of its source (supervisor, researcher, peer, student). Unfortunately, little research has focused on this topic. Pajak and Glickman (1989) examined the extent to which teachers and supervisors could discriminate among three types of supervisory communication: information only, information with suggestions, and information with directives. They showed each experimental group videotapes simulating supervisory conferences that differed in the use of informational versus controlling language. The information-only treatment ended with the following message: "The only thing I notice for future improvement is that three students were not following the assignment. I went over to them and noticed that they were unclear as to what they were supposed to do. They had hardly begun the assignment by the end of the class" (p. 96). The information-with-suggestions treatment ended in the following way: "What you might do is meet with those three students before next class and ask them about the directions. During seatwork time, you could move around the classroom and look over their shoulders to see how they are doing. You can check their work while they are still doing it. You may want to make these changes" (p. 96). The information-with-directives treatment ended in the following way: "What you must do is meet with those three students before next class and ask them about the directions. During seatwork time you should move around the classroom and look over their shoulders to see how they are doing. You have to check their work while they are still doing it. I want you to make these changes" (p. 97).

Teachers in each of the three treatment conditions were asked to rate the videotaped conference in terms of supportiveness, authenticity, loyalty, trust, and productivity. Teachers gave their highest ratings to the conference in which the supervisor communicated with suggestions, followed by the conference in which the supervisor communicated information only and then by the conference in which the supervisor communicated information with directives.

Teachers saw information with directives, which implies little choice for teachers, as undesirable. This finding is consistent with Deci and Ryan's (1985) theory of information and control, which suggests that the more choice individuals are given over their activities, the more productive and satisfied they are. If the degree of choice alone was what determined the favorable perceptions, teachers would prefer information only over information with suggestions, because this procedure would allow them more choice about their subsequent behavior. In the context of professional supervision, however, teachers expect supervisors to give them suggestions for improvement. Information alone fails to provide teachers with a basis for improving their instruction, whereas information with suggestions provides teachers with a guide for reflecting on supervisors' advice (i.e., a basis for accepting, revising, or rejecting the suggestions).

These results indicate that the way information is provided—in this case, the degree of control communicated—may determine whether teachers listen to the information. Efforts to help teachers to be specific about the types of information they want from observers may help the latter to be informative without being perceived as "controlling."

Individualizing Feedback   There is growing interest in making teaching assessment and feedback (whether for development or evaluation) more sensitive to individual teachers' needs and interests. In their book, *Marching to Different Drummers*, Guild and Garger (1985) raise issues associated with teaching styles and discuss the value of such information for teacher supervision and staff development. For example, drawing on the work of Witkin et al. (1977), Guild and Garger illustrate how administrators' understanding of individual teachers' field dependence and field independence can be useful in designing supervisory conferences (see Tables 11.1 and 11.2).

Table 11.1   WHAT TEACHERS EXPECT FROM AN ADMINISTRATOR

Field dependence	Field independence
To give warmth, personal interest, support	To focus on tasks
To provide guidance, to model	To allow independence and flexibility
To seek their opinions in making decisions	To make decisions based on analysis of the problem
To like them	To be knowledgeable about curriculum and instruction
To have an open door	To maintain professional distance
To "practice what they preach"	To be professionally experienced in appropriate content areas
To use tones and body language to support words	To give messages directly and articulately

Source: Guild, P., & Garger, S. (1985). *Marching to different drummers.* Alexandria, VA: Association for Supervision and Curriculum Development.

Table 11.2 HOW TEACHERS WANT TO BE EVALUATED

Field dependence	Field independence
With an emphasis on class "climate," interpersonal relationships, and quality of student-teacher interaction	With an emphasis on accuracy of content, adherence to learning objectives, and assessment of learning
With a narrative report and personal discussion	With a specific list of criteria
With consideration of student and parent comments	With consideration of academic achievement and test scores
With credit for "effort" and for trying	With evidence and facts to support comments

Source: Guild, P., & Garger, S. (1985). *Marching to different drummers.* Alexandria, VA: Association for Supervision and Curriculum Development.

We include these suggestions as a way to stimulate thinking about differential needs. Individuals are not dichotomous (most teachers will demonstrate both field orientations). Hence, principals or teachers should interpret these tables as heuristical models—suggesting that teachers have different needs. In order to establish communication with an individual teacher, the emphasis should be placed on open communication, understanding of goals, and frequent feedback, not a static definition of teacher style.

IMPROVING WORK PLACE CONDITIONS FOR TEACHING

Lanier (1986) reviews research indicating that collaboration among teachers is often undermined by the actual conditions of work. She notes that sometimes teachers are taught various collaborative strategies in in-service programs but then do not get the opportunity to use what they have been taught. For example, teachers are encouraged to plan cooperatively but are not given time during the school day to do so. According to Lanier, if in-service programs are to be effective, certain important (and expensive but necessary) changes must occur in work conditions. For example, induction programs for new teachers would require administrators and veteran teachers to give more attention to the potential and competence of beginning teachers. According to Lanier, "More extensive and coherent staff development programs would require giving up the notion that experience by itself is an adequate teacher of teachers. Finally, the lack of progression in the teaching career would have to be confronted and challenged, as indeed it is being challenged in many states today" (p. 563). We agree, and in the sections that follow, we discuss the importance of having teachers play a more central role in regulating their growth.

Increasing Professional Opportunities for Teachers

Maeroff (1988) argues that raising teachers' status by increasing their competence in some aspect of teaching or inviting them to play a role in decision making leads to enhanced commitment and better teaching. Maeroff's optimistic conclusions come from conversations with teachers who were participating in a program intended to raise teachers' morale, deepen their intellectual background, allow them to make decisions, and increase their confidence and ability. The program also was designed to help teachers develop increased knowledge in various areas (including teaching critical thinking), improve their writing, build interdisciplinary units with other teachers, and explore new content.

Maeroff acknowledges that such large-scale programs require outside money and leverage (to get release time for teachers, etc.) and that sometimes there were problems in obtaining administrators' permission for teachers to participate in programming decisions or in securing space and time to plan, implement, and institutionalize the changes. It was also difficult to get teachers to view themselves as change agents who demand the opportunity to shape instructional philosophy and content rather than simply carrying out what is dictated to them by others. Teachers' willingness to act to reform their school environments is a key variable, especially in districts that do not have outside funding to support change or to legitimate the importance of restructuring schools and increasing teachers' professional opportunities (Smylie, 1992).

Types of Professional Collaboration

There has been an increasing recognition of the need to involve teachers as colleagues in a variety of educational programs. Teachers are collaborating more often with professors in conducting classroom research (e.g., Lieberman, 1986), and the need for teacher education programs to develop skills for collegial interaction is evident (e.g., Rosenholtz, 1989). Teachers find such professional opportunities stimulating and rewarding (e.g., Bradford, 1986). Glatthorn (1987) notes at least five ways in which teacher teams can work together: professional discussion, curriculum development, peer supervision, peer coaching, and action research.

Professional Discussion Professional dialogue facilitates reflection about teaching. In groups, teachers can discuss issues of common interest—issues specific to a particular subject (e.g., the teaching of controversy in social science, available software for teaching a particular subject) or applicable to all subjects (student motivation, ability grouping, critical thinking). Thus, discussion groups do not have to focus on changing teacher behavior; they also can emphasize general professional issues.

There are no systematic data concerning the effects of professional dialogue, but participants' reports about such opportunities are generally positive. Although there are many ways to design discussion groups, Glatthorn suggests one model based on his experience.

The model includes guidelines that increase the likelihood of focus and productive exchange of ideas. The first stage emphasizes external knowledge, or what can be found in the literature about a particular problem (e.g., Do experts agree on the issue—or on strategies for how to respond to such problems?). In the first stage, participants should not attempt to dispute external knowledge but rather should explore and try to understand it. In the second stage, discussion centers on personal knowledge (What does my experience with the problem suggest? How does our collective sense of the problem compare with what others say about it in the literature?). Glatthorn suggests that by active listening, sharing, and reflection, teachers learn from a healthy tension between personal and external knowledge and from attempting to integrate the two types of knowledge. The third stage explores future actions (How does the discussion inform future teaching plans? What actions might be taken as a result of increased awareness of the problem and reflection about possible actions?). Depending on the interests of the group, this stage could focus on the needs of individual teachers or on implications for the entire school.

This model is a reasonable one for exploring topics like the pros and cons of ability grouping; however, discussion groups might have to explore and adopt new models that support their inquiry, especially topics that deal with personal values. For example, if teachers are sharing insights about why they decided to become (or remain) a teacher, they might want to examine their own feelings in depth before reading literature reviews (Brookhart & Freeman, 1992) or before exploring the personal examples of how other teachers' decisions have evolved (Bullough, Knowles, & Crow, 1992; Carter, 1990a, 1990b).

Another of the many possible topics for discussion group exchange is the study of teachers' beliefs. As we noted in Chapter 3, teachers' beliefs about student potential can have important consequences for how teachers plan and enact curriculum. However, teachers hold many beliefs, and systematic exploration could be most stimulating and helpful. For example, Pajares (1992) synthesized research about teachers' beliefs and their potential effects on teachers' thinking and action. He emphasizes that his synthesis yielded only assumptions based on extant data and that some of these assumptions will be clarified or transformed as more research occurs. Pajares argues that

1. Beliefs are formed early and tend to self-perpetuate, persevering even against contradictions caused by experience.
2. Individuals develop a belief system that contains all beliefs acquired through the process of cultural transmission.
3. The belief system has an adaptive function in helping individuals define and understand themselves and society.
4. Knowledge and beliefs are inextricably intertwined, but the potent affective, evaluative, and episodic nature of beliefs makes them a filter through which new phenomena are interpreted.
5. Thought processes may well be precursors to and creators of belief, but the filtering effect of belief structures ultimately screens or reshapes subsequent thinking.
6. Epistemological beliefs play a key role in knowledge interpretation and cognitive monitoring.
7. Individuals rank their beliefs according to their connections or relationships to other beliefs or other cognitive and affective structures. Apparent inconsistencies may be understood by exploring the functional connections and centrality of the beliefs.

8. Belief substructures, such as educational beliefs, must be understood in terms of their connections not only to each other but also to other, perhaps more central, beliefs in the system.

9. By their very nature and origin, some beliefs are more incontrovertible than others.

10. The earlier a belief is incorporated into the belief structure, typically, the more difficult it is to alter.

11. Belief change during adulthood rarely occurs. Individuals tend to hold onto beliefs based on incorrect or incomplete knowledge, even after scientifically correct explanations are presented to them.

12. Beliefs are instrumental in defining tasks and selecting the cognitive tools with which to interpret, plan, and make decisions regarding tasks; hence, beliefs play a critical role in defining behavior and organizing knowledge and information.

13. Beliefs strongly influence perception, but they can be an unreliable guide to the nature of reality.

14. Individuals' beliefs strongly affect their behavior.

15. Beliefs must be inferred, and this inference must take into account the congruence among individuals' belief statements, the intention to behave in a predisposed manner, and the behavior related to the belief in question.

16. Beliefs about teaching are well established by the time a student gets to college.

Reading Pajares's review and related research could be a logical starting point for a discussion group. However, other teachers might want to start with an examination of their own personal experience and beliefs and then integrate the views of other teachers (Ball & Goodson, 1985) or researchers.

Yet another possibility for such groups would be a general discussion organized around understanding the dynamics of and improving teacher-parent communication. At one level, teachers might want to consider their own role in minimizing contact with families. As Weinstein and Mignano (1993) indicate, there are various reasons why teachers are reluctant to involve families in school activities—or even to maintain contact with parents. For example, simply calling each parent in a class of 30 and spending only 10 minutes on the phone would require that teachers spend a minimum of 5 hours on the telephone, assuming teachers do not have to call parents back repeatedly in order to reach them. Calling parents would be an additional demand on a workload that often does not leave teachers time to grade papers adequately, let alone design and undertake new activities. Teachers are aware of their time commitments and are sometimes reluctant to seek parental involvement because they recognize that parents also have pressing responsibilities.

A third reason Weinstein and Mignano cite to explain why teachers do not involve families in schooling (e.g., homework, etc.) is that teachers have sometimes encountered angry or apathetic parents. Teachers have concluded that parents are not interested in developing relationships with schools and that parents see the school as a free babysitting service. Finally, some teachers are reluctant to involve parents in schooling because the teachers want to enjoy their authority and freedom to make decisions. Parents who become more involved in schooling may seek a broader role in classroom activities and curriculum, and perhaps challenge the teachers' professional competence.

Teachers' reluctance to work closely with families is also due partly to the perception (often accurate) that many parents are reluctant to become involved in schooling. In addition to being busy, some parents feel that schooling should be left to teachers and principals (the experts) or that parents support teachers best by not bothering them. Other parents remember school as a place where they were uncomfortable and hence do not want to come into contact with the institution again. Further, some parents are embarrassed because they believe that their children's difficulties (whether academic or behavior) are their fault. Finally, as we have noted earlier in the text, sometimes students' problems are directly caused by parents (e.g., child abuse).

Teachers interested in exploring such topics could begin with an examination of some of the extant literature (Hoffman, 1991; Hoover-Dempsey, Bassler, & Brissie, 1987; Kauffman et al., 1993; Lightfoot, 1978; and Weinstein & Mignano, 1993). However, other teachers might want to begin their professional discussion with an examination of their own personal beliefs and experience before conducting research reviews.

Curriculum Development   According to Glatthorn (1987), curriculum development involves cooperative activity in which teachers enhance the district's curriculum guides (e.g., English teachers might create a unit on local or regional dialects). Others have suggested additional ways for teachers to work on curriculum issues. Mitman et al. (1984) concluded that too little attention is given to the processes of science (conducting experiments, making and testing inferences) and too much time is spent on low-level memorization. Their work suggests that it is valuable to study curriculum materials to determine the extent to which the curriculum encourages thinking versus memorization. Teachers might profitably exchange ideas about textbooks, assignments, learning stations, learning kits, computer labs, problem sets, quizzes, tests, unit reports, and so on.

In addition to analyzing materials, teachers can also help one another by developing and sharing materials. For example, teachers might design clever ways to begin selected science units with experiments or assignments that have practical value to students. Developing such units takes time, and if teachers worked together they could have more time to develop a few themes in greater depth. In most schools, teachers working in isolation are so busy getting ready for the next day or unit that they do not have sufficient time for curriculum development.

Peer Observation   Peer observation, or peer supervision, as Glatthorn (1987) refers to it, is a process in which classroom observation is used to improve teaching (as we have discussed earlier in the chapter). The observation is data based and focuses on the teacher's own goals. Under the right conditions—teachers know what information they want, and peers are sensitive—peer feedback encourages teachers to improve their performance (see Roper & Hoffman, 1986). Moreover, the teachers who observe may gain as much as those who are observed (Sparks, 1986).

Peer Coaching According to Glatthorn, peer coaching is similar to peer observation but involves some key differences. Peer observation suggests more choice for individual teachers with regard to what will be observed. In contrast, peer coaching is usually based on a staff development theme (often selected by district staff or administrators). That is, teachers would be given theoretical orientation to a model or set of skills, would observe the model or skills being implemented, and then would try to implement the model or skills while receiving frequent feedback.

Showers (1984) has written a training manual that emphasizes several major aspects of peer coaching: companionship (reduces teacher isolation), technical feedback (match between observed behavior and model), objective rather than evaluative feedback, assistance from peer coaches to teachers in adjusting the model to a class, and support and encouragement provided by the coach. Peer coaching can be helpful in changing teacher behavior and in improving student performance (see Showers, 1984), although gains are not automatic.

Structure and follow-up appear to be vital to successful staff development efforts. Joyce (1981) argued that all of the following elements should be included in good staff development programs:

1. Presentation of theory or description of teaching skills or strategies
2. Modeling or demonstration of teaching skills or strategies
3. Practice in simulated and real classrooms
4. Structured and open-ended feedback about performance
5. Coaching for application—in-classroom, hands-on assistance in transferring new knowledge and skills to the classroom

Joyce (1981) estimates that fewer than 20 percent of the trainees master the skills of a training program if they do not receive feedback about their performance and if they are not coached in how to apply new skills. These conditions are often missing in staff development programs.

Action Research Lieberman (1986) notes that action research can be used as a means for pursuing various goals, including increasing teacher reflection, collegial teacher interaction, and teacher status and efficacy; reducing the gap between doing research and implementing its results; and legitimating the professional value of practical classroom concerns.

According to McKernan (1987), action research is self-reflective problem solving that enables practitioners to better understand and solve problems in social settings. He suggests that the critical aspect of action research is that it allows practitioners to improve their performance by the direct study of their work. He notes that action research is defined differently by various persons and that some individuals define it narrowly.

We agree with McKernan that narrow definitions of how to conduct action research are self-defeating. Engaging in self-reflective inquiry independently or with peers is productive. Whether teachers collect data, compare and contrast curriculum units, or develop new tests is less important than the quality of action research—the opportunity to apply scholarship to a practical problem.

Our endorsement of the concept of action research suggests a view of teachers not only as recipients of knowledge but also as professionals who can produce knowledge for themselves and for others. Teachers are not necessarily expert researchers but are inquirers who see knowledge about curriculum and instruction as open to question. In its best form, action research is a basis for not only curriculum reform but also professional development.

If action research is to be successful, teachers must have the time and resources to collect and organize data and to discuss implications of their findings. Although good teaching involves considerable art (e.g., timing, using an example that appeals to students' affective and aesthetic needs as well as cognitive ones), it also has a scientific basis (a gradually increasing set of findings from studies of classroom practice). As Billups and Rauth (1987) persuasively argue, if the public views teaching only as an art, with no scientific basis, it is unlikely to accept teaching as a profession.

What is crucial about action research is the opportunity it provides for teachers to discuss ideas, reflect on teaching, and extend their knowledge of alternative practices. However, teachers need time if they are to engage in reflective scholarship (time to observe, make tapes, keep journals about their teaching, and discuss these ideas with colleagues).

SCHOOLS AS SOCIAL SYSTEMS

So far we have discussed the effects of professional collaboration and staff development on teachers' development. But there is also evidence that school settings influence teachers' expectations and performance.

Rosenholtz (1989) showed that the social structure of the work place varies remarkably from school to school and that the social organization in which teaching takes place significantly affects teachers' commitment, leadership, cooperation, and the quality of both teachers' and students' school lives. She analyzed questionnaire data provided by over 1200 teachers from 78 elementary schools concerning social organizational variables within schools (e.g., teacher goal setting, teacher collaboration, etc.). Results indicated that perceptions about work place conditions were generally similar among teachers within each school and that in schools where teachers perceived high goal consensus, they also reported high commitment, and so forth.

To understand the teacher perspective better, Rosenholtz interviewed randomly selected teachers in schools that represented particular types of social organization. These interviews revealed that individual teachers' reports were heavily influenced by the social environments in which they taught. For example, in high-consensus schools, only 8 percent of the teachers felt that "there is no time to talk," whereas in moderate- and low-consensus schools 11 and 20 percent of the teachers, respectively, felt this way. These data describing little time for teachers to talk in school are similar to findings presented in the 1989 report, *What Works:*

Research About Teaching and Learning. In some studies as many as 45 percent of the teachers reported *no* contact with one another during a school day, and another 32 percent reported infrequent contact with colleagues.

In comparing what high- and low-consensus teachers discussed (when they had the opportunity to talk), Rosenholtz found that only 4 percent of the high-consensus teachers mentioned that they complained about student behavioral problems when they talked with other teachers, but 54 percent reported discussing issues related to curriculum and instruction. In contrast, 28 percent of the teachers in low-consensus schools reported talking about student problems, whereas only 19 percent said they discussed curriculum and instruction.

In terms of leadership, teacher leaders in schools that had collaborative orientations were seen as helping other teachers to solve problems, but no teacher leader in schools that had isolated climates was seen as willing to help other teachers to solve problems. Among teachers who sought help, those whose comments focused on students' problems were largely relegated to dealing with problems reactively, whereas, those who focused on curriculum and instruction were able to use the skills and resources of other teachers proactively.

When asked, "Where do your new teaching ideas come from?" teachers in "learning-enriched" schools reported learning from a variety of sources. Ninety percent reported learning from other teachers, 45 percent from professional conferences, and 72 percent from their own problem solving and creativity. In the "learning-improved" schools only 32 percent of the teachers reported learning from other teachers, none from professional conferences, and only 4 percent from their own problem solving and creativity.

A key concept in Rosenholtz's theoretical position is uncertainty about how teaching can best be conducted to help students learn. She notes that a technical culture is uncertain if outcomes of work are unpredictable. According to Rosenholtz, work in schools reflects an uncertain technical culture because there are few codified means for helping individual students achieve specific goals (e.g., learn problem solving or engage in complex, abstract synthesis). Thus, work in schools is seen as nonroutine, and the role of teaching at a given moment is often fraught with uncertainty.

Rosenholtz notes that organizational uncertainty has consequences for individual teachers, just as uncertainty affects behavior and beliefs in any social situation. When we are unable to control situations or to make positive things happen, we may question our ability or develop self-protective strategies (refuse to participate, not try) in order to avoid embarrassment. Rosenholtz argues that in schools where principals' or teachers' views of their job competence are sufficiently threatened, they too engage in self-defensive tactics to protect their own sense of self-worth.

Rosenholtz notes that uncertainty is endemic to teaching but that the reaction of schools to uncertainty—the social culture in which teaching takes place—is central to whether the uncertainty becomes a disability (e.g., teachers develop routine, predictable ways to deal with situations that are not routine, deny problems, etc.) or a creative tension (teachers learn to discuss ideas and to collaborate to solve problems and to improve teaching). According to Rosenholtz, uncertainty is reduced by two conditions. First, teachers have the opportunity to obtain positive feedback about their abilities from peers and principals in a variety of ways. Second, teachers are provided with occasions to increase their technical knowledge (i.e., knowledge of teaching) and hence to gain more expertise in dealing with more situations. Rosenholtz argues that teachers' commitment to schools and to continued learning is heavily influenced by three work place conditions: (1) task autonomy—teachers' sense that they can adapt instruction to their own contexts; (2) continuous opportunities for learning that provide them with greater mastery and control of the environment; and (3) "psychic" rewards that ensure their continuous contributions to schools (their opinions are requested, they have the opportunity to interact with peers, they receive needed information when appropriate, etc.).

THE GROWING IMPORTANCE OF STAFF DEVELOPMENT

The ideas we presented earlier are organized and written as informal suggestions that a group of teachers at a given school might implement. However, self-improvement programs can also be an important part of the official school district in-service program. Fenstermacher and Berliner (1985) note that staff development today is not the same as the in-service education of earlier decades, when teachers were thought to have primary responsibility for their professional development and self-renewal. There is, however, growing interest in broadening the concept of staff development and including teachers more in the decision-making process. Today's teachers function in a complex environment of policy, law, regulation, special programs, and professional associations. Modern staff development usually involves groups of teachers working together with specialists, supervisors, administrators, parents, and university personnel. In some districts a large percentage of the budget is spent on staff development.

Despite the perceived importance of staff development, planning for it in some districts is not as systematic as it should be. In-service programs are frequently one-time events (a speaker is brought in, but little, if any, follow-up occurs), and there is too little attention to assessing program effects.

Improving the Entire School

A staff development program should first help teachers to address their individual needs. Once these needs are met, teachers can address broader school concerns through cooperative in-service programs. Ultimately, staff development should lead to the improvement of a school's entire teaching staff. Working collectively to improve is a potent determinant of the value of a staff development program. Little (1981) writes,

> First, the school as a workplace proves extraordinarily powerful. Without denying differences in individuals' skills, interests, commitment, curiosity, or persistence, the prevailing pattern of interactions and interpretations in each building demonstrably creates certain possibilities and sets certain limits. . . . we are led from a focus on

professional improvement as an individual enterprise to improvement as particularly an organizational phenomenon. Some schools sustained shared expectations (norms) both for extensive collegial work and for analysis and evaluation of and experimentation with their practices; continuous improvement is a shared undertaking at schools, and these schools are the most adaptable and successful of the schools we have studied. [pp. 9, 10]

Rosenholtz (1989) reached similar conclusions.

Along these same lines, McDonnell (1985) argues that staff development programs should include a strong affective component. That is, they should boost morale and raise (or maintain) positive expectations. She notes that these qualities are critical to creating an effective school; therefore, staff development programs need to help principals and teachers not only develop new skills but also feel good about using those skills.

Staff Development in Effective Schools

The way in which resources in schools are used and the manner in which teachers are encouraged to interact with one another help to predict the overall effectiveness of a school (Good & Brophy, 1986; Little, 1981; Rosenholtz, 1989). Hence, it is important to consider how best to develop the talents of the teaching staff. School and classroom processes must be considered at the same time in an attempt to identify processes and interrelationships that facilitate or hinder goals at each level. How can schools focus on high-quality instruction at the same time that individual teachers are helping students to develop their talents as effectively as possible? How can opportunities for practice, display, and reward of learning accomplishments be improved? How best can activities such as school newspapers, journals, and assemblies be used to supplement the efforts of teachers in individual classrooms (Good & Weinstein, 1986)? Although much research remains to be conducted in this area, some practical, innovative ideas have already emerged (Deal, 1985).

Teacher-Teacher Communication

Teachers must work jointly to build a favorable school environment. However, the most basic contribution that an individual teacher can make to a school is to develop an effective classroom. Only then can the teacher help other teachers understand what they are doing in their classrooms. There is no need for teachers in the same school or district to use similar styles and practices; there are many different ways to instruct effectively. Through working with peers, however, teachers can exchange ideas and improve instruction. If schools are to affect student outcomes significantly, teachers must be cognizant of how other teachers in the same school teach.

It is not uncommon to visit schools in which assignments for fifth graders are less demanding than those for third graders. Students in lower grades often have more choices of books to read, more freedom to work with other students, and more opportunities to plan work on assignments than students in higher grades. In some secondary schools, seventh graders write original essays, but ninth graders only answer questions about various works of history and English. Such discrepan-

Table 11.3   STAGES OF INTERACTION CONTEXT

1. Nonteaching duties
   a. Clerical routines (attendance, forms)
   b. Simple management routines (lineup, etc.)
   c. Playground supervision
   d. Lunchroom supervision
2. Materials
   a. Seatwork assignments
   b. Homework assignments
   c. Laboratory assignments
   d. Daily quizzes
   e. Unit tests
3. School-level meetings
   a. Committee meetings
   b. Before- and after-school duties
   c. Extracurricular activities
   d. Ceremonies, special events
4. Preactive teaching
   a. Lesson plans
   b. Evaluation plans
5. Adult relationships
   a. Principals
   b. Other teachers
   c. Parents
   d. Secretaries
   e. Other building staff members
   f. Outside administrators
   g. Board members
   h. Representatives of teacher organizations

6. Classroom management
   a. Getting/maintaining attention
   b. Responding to student misbehavior
   c. Task management—time allocation during seatwork
   d. Interruptions
   e. Student record keeping
7. Teacher behavior
   a. Lesson introduction
   b. Quality of teacher explanations
   c. Quality of questions asked
   d. Pace of lesson
   e. Appropriateness of assigned task
8. Student learning
   a. Student-initiated questions
   b. Student explanations
   c. Student responses
   d. Student understanding
   e. Student interest
9. Explanatory mechanisms
   a. Motivation theory
   b. Development theory
   c. Learning theory
   d. Instructional theory
   e. Classroom management/organization theory
   f. Research on teaching

cies not only fail to challenge students to become progressively more independent and self-reliant but may lower older students' interest in schoolwork. Unfortunately, many teachers do not provide appropriately challenging assignments because they are unaware of what other teachers in the same school are doing.

What we are advocating here is broader than teachers simply sharing information, although the exchange of information is vital. We are also referring to a sense of community among teachers who try to develop appropriate, positive expectations for all students and to challenge students by designing tasks based on information obtained in carefully planned and coordinated discussions with other teachers, in-service training, and so on.

Teachers should have regular time built into their schedules to exchange ideas with other teachers. Table 11.3 summarizes some of the topics that teachers might discuss. Rosenholtz's (1989) work makes it clear that, in schools where little effective instruction takes place, teachers tend to communicate infrequently and to complain rather than to solve instructional problems when they do talk. In effective schools, teachers want to discuss professional concerns, including curriculum and instruction.

The Principal as Facilitator

One clear mandate from the effective schools literature is that principals need to be active leaders and to support the instructional efforts of teachers. It is nevertheless important to have realistic expectations for principals because they are busy simply running their schools, and a typical day is filled with conflicts and interruptions. If teachers are interested in additional assistance and if administrators are able and willing to play a facilitative rather than merely an evaluative role, then principals and teachers can work together to improve instruction.

Principals can arrange for teachers to observe and provide feedback to one another. They can allow teachers to use in-service time for discussion, self-study groups, or action research—not just listening to lectures. Principals can facilitate self-study efforts by soliciting funds to buy appropriate video equipment and by scheduling videotaping so that optimum use can be made of it.

Building on Teachers' Interests

When teachers find in-service training programs boring and a waste of time, it is usually because the programs are unrelated to their needs. Much time and effort are currently spent developing curricula that are more interesting to students and allow them more opportunity to pursue topics collaboratively. Perhaps corresponding emphasis should be placed on identifying ways for teachers to become more active in the development of in-service training programs that meet their needs and interests rather than subject them to a passive role. Allowing teachers to use in-service time to engage in independent self-improvement activities, either as individuals or in groups, would be valuable.

After teachers begin to work on self-improvement, they are in a position to advise the principal about the type of university consultant who would facilitate their program. Teachers who plan their own in-service training typically take the task seriously and work earnestly to develop useful programs. As a resource specialist and facilitator, the principal can aid immeasurably by supplying teachers with copies of recent books and journals that focus on classroom practice, research, and theory.

The Principal's Role

Observing Classrooms Many principals have been trained primarily as managers rather than as instructional leaders; hence, some of them do not have the skills necessary to observe teachers and to provide them with information about their classroom behavior. Most teachers welcome ideas from principals about how to improve their work, but they rarely receive them. The average teacher is visited by a supervisor only once a year and then receives only general and vague feedback. In contrast, principals who are good supervisors frequently visit classrooms and help teachers to improve by giving feedback that is of interest and value to teachers. Such principals encourage teachers to come to them for help without branding these teachers as "weak." Principals need to develop skills for this role by reading recent books on teaching, curriculum, and supervision. Even principals who are adequate observers will gain by allowing teachers to assume more responsibility for self-evaluation and improvement of teaching.

Feedback to Individual Teachers   An interesting question for future research is how principals influence instructional behavior of teachers. It is not enough simply to observe in classrooms—principals must provide teachers with appropriate and useful information in a sensitive fashion. Many interesting issues merit exploration. How do principals communicate expectations and establish instructional priorities? If principals encourage teachers to determine their own instructional goals, how do principals become aware of each teacher's goals and how do they monitor and provide feedback about progress? Dwyer et al. (1982) provide a helpful profile that characterizes effective principals as *active*. Considering that effective principals are more visible to teachers and students in their schools, it is important to know whether or not their decisions and actions are related to student progress. For example, when and how often do principals visit particular classrooms? Do successful principals spend more time with teachers they believe to be average, or do they observe less capable teachers more closely? How specific is the feedback they provide to teachers? On what topics do conferences focus? Do effective principals discuss curriculum and instruction, or do they talk only about general issues of classroom management, resources, and human relations?

We believe that what is critical is not the frequency of teacher-principal interaction but the nature of the interaction and whether it leads to more thoughtful instruction. Table 11.4 illustrates that principals can communicate their expectations to teachers in various ways.

Stimulating Teachers' Growth   Although principals must build a school climate and an instructional program, they cannot lose sight of the need for teachers to have flexibility and to function as decision makers. Principals can help classrooms function more productively by making teaching more satisfying and stimulating—a profession rather than an occupation that requires the performance of a limited number of classroom skills.

Furthermore, it is important that principals involve teachers in discussing and planning school as well as classroom change. Schools where teachers engage in considerable job-related discussion and share in decisions about instructional programs and staff development are more effective than schools where decisions are made by rule-bound bureaucratic procedures (Schlechty & Vance, 1983). Thus, one challenge confronting principals is how to provide teachers with the time to reflect and grow.

Bruce Joyce (Brandt, 1987) points out that teachers need more than one period to prepare for five or six teaching periods and that time for planning must increase if teachers' roles expand. Joyce argues that to provide more time for teacher reflection, students must spend considerably more time working independently. However, he adds that if teachers are to have time to develop more complex lessons that stimulate student thinking, students must be prepared to accept the extra responsibility for their own learning.

Table 11.4 PRINCIPALS' COMMUNICATION OF COMPETENCY EXPECTATIONS TO INDIVIDUAL TEACHERS

1. Classroom visitation
   a. Frequency of classroom visitation
   b. Frequency of feedback conferences
   c. Types of exchanges—social versus instructional
   d. Content of focus (to the extent that interactions focus on instruction, what is the content of these interactions?)
2. Opportunity to have contact with other teachers
   a. Be visited by other teachers
   b. Visit other teachers
   c. Visit teachers in other schools
   d. Planning time with other teachers
3. Resource allocation
   a. Equipment budget
   b. Materials budget
   c. Free time/extra assignments
   d. Availability of substitutes so teachers can participate in in-service workshops
   e. Active voice in how in-service funds will be used
4. Leadership roles
   a. Principal selects teachers to represent school at district or state meeting
   b. Teacher serves as chair of committee (e.g., textbook selection)
   c. Principal solicits teachers' opinions privately and publicly
5. Curriculum teaching assignment
   a. Principal assigns teachers advanced section
   b. Principal assigns honor students to these teachers
   c. Teacher has free period at advantageous time

Obviously, teaching students to assume more responsibility for independent study and self-evaluation also takes instructional time (Rohrkemper & Corno, 1988). Thus, the best uses of independent study or other instructional approaches (computerized instruction, parent volunteers, more classroom teachers, etc.) to increase release time for teachers are not clear. However, principals who can find some extra time for teachers to plan and communicate with peers will be providing the necessary conditions for expanding teachers' roles—and eventually improving student learning.

TEACHER EVALUATION

It is beyond our purpose here to discuss in detail the principal's role as evaluator. However, we do want to discuss evaluation problems briefly. Part of the difficulty in evaluating teachers is that we have too little information about teacher behaviors that consistently relate to desired student outcomes in predictable ways. In some areas (e.g., student achievement in basic subjects), extensive empirical findings exist. Such information could, if properly used, help to identify teachers who need assistance. However, there is a paucity of information about how classroom processes relate to most affective goals and to many important cognitive goals (e.g., problem solving). We have reviewed topics here (expectations, modeling, management, motivation, instruction) that should be of considerable value to principals who must evaluate teachers. Still, teachers and principals must discuss this information so that they agree on how it can be applied appropriately in the classroom (see Brophy, 1988; Good & Mulryan, 1990; Zumwalt, 1986).

There are many indices of teaching effectiveness, and behavioral indicators can sometimes be misleading. Students who appear to be on task may not really be thinking about assigned work. Some teachers may take more time than others to introduce a concept or to establish classroom rules and hence may appear to be ineffective. However, these teachers may be able subsequently to cover content more quickly and with fewer interruptions because they have thoroughly prepared students. Doyle (1983) reports that it is possible to identify teachers who are poor managers (using criteria from recent classroom management research) but who nevertheless obtain high student achievement. Although it is unlikely that many such teachers exist, it is noteworthy that some teachers can compensate for poor management skills so that they still promote student achievement.

Wise et al. (1985) contend that quality control achieved through the enforcement of a professional standard of practice differs from quality control that is obtained through prescribed curricula and standardized testing. Explicit recommendations for how teachers ought to teach make teaching less attractive, which then lowers the quality of the teaching force. This, in turn, causes school districts to become even more prescriptive in their attempts to monitor teachers' behavior. In contrast, the professional approach depends on teachers' judgments and places more importance on the development of teacher-responsive practices than on the definition of standardized practice. In time, such a system eliminates teachers who are unable or unwilling to develop competence.

Professional control and broad standards are preferable to narrow lists of behaviors because virtually all the concepts generated by classroom research have to be interpreted and applied to particular classrooms. Teachers can wait too long for students to respond as well as not long enough, and there can be too much alerting and accountability as well as too little. Again, we argue that concepts (e.g., wait time, action zone, teaching for understanding) enable teachers, supervisors, and principals to examine more aspects of teaching and to assess more extensively why a particular classroom is or is not effective. Nevertheless, to be used well, concepts must be related to instructional goals and learners' needs (Zumwalt, 1986).

We agree with Dillon-Peterson (1986) that administrators need to trust teachers to know what is good for them and to allow teachers more opportunity for planning and evaluating in-service programs. Teachers can assume more responsibility for self-growth and self-evaluation when given appropriate training, support, and time. Although administrators have considerable responsibility for teacher evaluation, effective administrators involve teachers in this process and use their professional knowledge to good advantage.

RECENT DEVELOPMENTS IN TEACHING

Two recent developments have enriched teachers' opportunities for professional growth: (1) the attempt to differentiate teachers' career roles (master teacher programs), and (2) the growing involvement of teachers in beginning teacher induction programs.

The Master Teacher

There is currently a great deal of interest in differentiating the work of teaching and in designating some teachers as master teachers. In part this effort is intended to attract and retain good teachers by rewarding teacher effectiveness. According to Griffin (1985), there are two dominant ways to describe and identify a master teacher. The first is based on a "better than" assumption: One teacher engages in essentially the same activities as another but is judged to be better at accomplishing those activities. This approach raises questions about the specification of criteria for evaluating performance, as well as about the objectivity, validity, and reliability of human judgments in a complex social situation.

Doyle (1985) notes that the "better than" definition tends to create a narrow set of criteria for differentiating effective teachers. That is, under pressure to identify teachers who are better than other teachers, there is a tendency to reify and to overapply classroom research.

A second conception of the master teacher that Griffin describes is based on a "more than" perspective. In this view, the master teacher, who may or may not engage in traditional teaching, performs specialized functions in schools and classrooms (National Education Association, 1983). For example, the master teacher may plan curriculum for a group of other teachers, monitor student progress, formulate and administer evaluation schemes, or serve as a mentor by helping beginning teachers with special instructional or curricular needs.

Griffin believes that master teacher plans may increase the professional status of teachers, but only if these plans move away from narrow definitions of good teaching and provide greater freedom for teachers to make curriculum decisions. In this view, proposals that differentiate teachers on the basis of varied role expectations have more promise than ones that assume a few teachers can perform presumably key teaching tasks better than others.

Doyle (1985) defines master teachers as those who are consistently able to design tasks that convey the curriculum to students in appropriate ways and to orchestrate these tasks successfully in a complex classroom environment. Effective teaching, from Doyle's point of view, is more than modeling a master teacher. It consists of the constructive adaptation of instruction to specific contexts. This conception of effectiveness holds that mastery is supported by knowledge and skills that are accessible to all practitioners rather than residing in the magic qualities of a few extraordinary teachers.

Henson and Hall (1992) illustrate that plans to provide teachers with more professional status and rewards do not always translate into successful academic programs. In their study of career ladder plans, they found that plans created considerable conflict between teachers, instructional leaders, and principals.

Beginning Teachers

The transition from preservice to in-service teaching can be traumatic as teachers move from the idealistic world of the college classroom to the reality of everyday teaching. For a variety of reasons, teachers may experience role-adjustment problems. They may be poorly trained in teacher preparation programs and develop unrealistic expectations, so that they do not perceive that teaching is a demanding and difficult but do-able and rewarding job. We have emphasized (beginning in Chapter 1) that classrooms are complex settings that demand decision making and the application of general principles to particular situations.

New teachers may experience some problems because they have had only general training and are thus not ready for a specific job. For example, one may student-teach in an inner-city first-grade classroom but then be assigned to teach full time in a sixth-grade class in a suburban school district. For this reason, we recommend that teachers-in-training spend time in various types of schools. After learning about their first assignments, new teachers should talk with other teachers who teach at the same grade level.

There are other reasons why teachers may have difficulties when they start to teach, and there are some problems that teachers cannot prepare for in advance. First-year teachers are not only becoming teachers and learning to deal with students, parents, and other adults; they are also assuming new responsibilities (making new friends, paying off loans, etc.). Thus, anxiety and role conflict are expected at this time.

Goodson (1991) argues that one of the problems for beginning teachers is that they are typically asked to implement a curriculum that has been developed by others. In addition to learning to negotiate the school, a new role, and new students, now teachers must simultaneously implement an unfamiliar curriculum and also develop a teaching style that fits their particular context. Bullaugh (1992) expresses the potential dilemma this way: "At times the two demands are contradictory: the adopted curriculum prohibits establishing a satisfying role; and the desired role makes it difficult to implement the established curriculum" (p. 239).

Becoming a teacher affects individuals in different ways. Some teachers alter their behavior after their initial teaching experiences. Bergmann et al. (1976) found that 57 percent of beginning teachers reported that they changed their initial student-focused teaching to a more traditional instructional model. A more student-centered style can be effective, but many new teachers do not have the necessary management and curriculum skills to maintain such an approach. Moskowitz and Hayman (1974) reported that many beginning teachers ignore too much misbehavior (seemingly in the hope that, if not acknowledged, it will disappear).

Reported Problems   Veenman (1984) reviewed the problems beginning teachers reported in 83 studies. The most serious problem reported was *classroom discipline*. The next most salient problem was *motivating students*. Other frequently reported problems were dealing with individual differences among students, assessing students, and communicating with parents.

Despite the fact that many teachers report problems, most teachers enter teaching successfully. Several studies (Broeders, 1980; deVoss & Dibella, 1981; Edmonds & Bessai, 1979; Tisher, Fyfield, & Taylor, 1979) showed that over 80 percent of beginning teachers were satisfied with their schools and jobs.

Different Needs   Beginning teachers with different skills and needs react to teaching in different ways. Glassberg (1980) found that more mature beginning teachers emphasized the need to understand individual students and to be flexible, whereas less mature novices held a more restricted view of teaching. Thus, new teachers may need different types of in-service training.

There are several models for analyzing the development level of teachers (e.g., Hunt & Joyce, 1981; Sprinthall & Thies-Sprinthall, 1983). The first explicit theory describing teacher development was proposed by Fuller (1969) and elaborated by Fuller and Bown (1975). The first stage of teaching is concern with *survival.* (Will I be liked? Can I control students? Will others think I am a good teacher?) The second stage is concern with the *teaching situation* (methods, materials, etc.), and the third stage reflects concern with *students* (their learning and needs). The early, self-centered concerns are considered less mature than later, more student-centered concerns. However, until teachers deal with early concerns (Will I survive? Can I refine my teaching skills?), they will have less ability to respond to individual students' needs.

Realistic resources, relevant experience, content knowledge, and good supervision (i.e., during student teaching) can help many new teachers at least to be past the survival stage when they enter the classroom. Teachers need to work through a variety of personal (Will anybody listen to me?) and procedural teaching concerns (how to use the computer, how to structure small-group instruction) before they can devote most of their attention to the effects of teaching (i.e., student learning).

The advice and strategies for self-growth we have provided are useful for all teachers, even those who have taught successfully for several years. However, the recommendations are especially important for beginning teachers. Unfortunately, too many teachers who experience difficulty deny their problems (at least to others) and fail to avail themselves of the experience of other teachers and supervisors. New teachers need to use discretion in deciding which teachers to approach for information; some teachers are better sources of information and are more empathic than others, and obviously student teachers and beginning teachers need to exercise tact when they ask for assistance. However, a broader, more pervasive problem is failing to obtain help.

Huling-Austin (1986) argues that induction programs can help in five areas:

1. Improve the teaching performance of beginning teachers
2. Increase the retention rate of promising beginning teachers during the induction year
3. Screen out the least promising teachers

4. promote personal and professional well-being by fostering each teacher's professional self-esteem
5. Satisfy mandated requirements related to induction and certification

She notes, however, that it is *unreasonable* to expect induction programs to (1) overcome major problems that exist in schools, such as misplacement of teachers (teaching in an area that they have not been trained for), overcrowded classrooms, or too many classroom preparations; (2) develop into successful teachers those who enter the classroom without the necessary ability and personal characteristics to be competent professionals; and (3) substantially improve the long-range retention of teachers if changes are not made in the broader educational system as well (improved status in the eyes of society, better salaries and working conditions).

Mentor Teachers' Roles   In many districts, experienced and successful teachers are appointed to help beginning teachers adjust to their role in the school. Mentor teachers need to realize that beginning teachers' needs may be different from their own (for more information about mentor-beginning teacher relationships, see Galvez-Hjornevik, 1986; Huffman & Leak, 1986; Wildman et al., 1989). Beginning teachers have more concerns about self and classroom management, whereas other teachers have more concerns about student learning (i.e., beginning teachers' views of teaching may be different from those of other teachers until they develop a better understanding of curriculum content and classroom procedures).

New teachers must recognize that their questions naturally differ from those of successful, experienced teachers. Some beginning teachers believe that they should "think" like veteran teachers and hence are hesitant to ask questions. However, all teachers—experienced as well as inexperienced—should obtain knowledge about any topic of concern. Beginning teachers ask many questions about management, planning, and motivation (experienced teachers also discuss motivation and management), but in time, beginners' concerns move from general class issues to adapting instructional and motivational models to the needs of specific students.

Mentors will be most helpful if they heed the advice presented earlier in this chapter: allowing beginning teachers to structure their own self-improvement plans and helping by providing appropriate feedback. Mentors must also realize that many different teaching styles can be effective.

Zeichner and Tabachnick (1985) note some advantages to loose supervision of first-year teachers. For example, some first-year teachers they observed maintained their own styles and perspectives despite a differing school philosophy (Tabachnick & Zeichner, 1984). Mentors, supervisors, and principals should offer teachers assistance, but beginning teachers (and student teachers, for that matter) should not be guided so rigidly that their independent role in adapting content and designing classroom environments is eroded.

TEACHER PLANNING

In the following discussion we illustrate the value of planning for classroom teaching and highlight potential differences between beginning and more experienced teachers. We use the example of planning, but beginning and more experienced teachers are apt to show differences concerning many other aspects of teaching.

Models of Planning

Considering that teachers develop and use different types of plans, what models describe how teachers do, in fact, plan? For many years, those writing on the topic of planning cited Ralph Tyler's (1950) work as a good example of appropriate planning for classroom instruction. Tyler's linear model consists of four steps: (1) specify objectives, (2) select learning activities, (3) organize learning activities, and (4) specify evaluation procedures. Tyler's model was accepted at face value for about 20 years before researchers examined directly the planning process that teachers used and compared what teachers actually did with their plans.

Borko and Niles (1987) discuss the implications of classroom research on planning for teachers in training (e.g., preservice teachers). They argue that preservice teachers can learn from research that planning typically focuses on subject matter and the selection of corresponding activities, and that teachers pay relatively little attention to objectives or evaluation. However, they note that if teachers are to use this information appropriately, they must understand *why* experienced teachers plan this way and why their plans include certain elements and exclude others. According to Borko and Niles, experienced teachers do not specify objectives because these are implied in the materials and curriculum guides. However, preservice teachers have not had as many opportunities as experienced teachers to work with these objectives and most likely will need to focus more on them. Teachers should realize that it is natural for experienced teachers to use indirect means to determine which students have reached objectives for a particular lesson. Experienced teachers have a broader range of exerience and a variety of procedures for receiving and interpreting information from students (e.g., the way they ask questions, examination of seatwork, etc.). Borko and Niles conclude that Tyler's model, which includes objectives and evaluation, may have more relevance for preservice and beginning teachers than for experienced teachers. Hence, it may be important for less experienced teachers to begin with a formal model for planning and later to adapt that model to their own classes. Mentor teachers need to expect and to accept the fact that beginning teachers may use different models from the ones other teachers use.

Avoiding Rigid Planning

The concept of excessive planning is an important one for *preservice* teachers. Experienced teachers told Borko and Niles that student teachers should learn to *plan thoroughly.* By thorough planning, experienced teachers mean developing more than enough activities for a given time period; they do not imply the specification of a detailed, *rigid* script (I will ask this question and, if given this student answer, will follow it with this question, etc.). In fact, experienced teachers discouraged their protégés from using detailed scripts. Recent planning research supports this advice. Plans are valuable to the extent that they provide organization and direction for the teacher and students in the class; however, they can cause teachers to react rigidly to students and may impede creative responding. Simply put, plans need to be thorough but not rigid.

Practical Ideas About Planning

As we have seen, teachers need to plan proactively if they are to be successful in the classroom. You can use a variety of planning strategies, but it is best to start with a few simple, straightforward ideas about what you want to accomplish and then later develop more elaborate plans about what to do at different stages in the lesson. In Table 11.5 Posner (1985) presents a preliminary planning sheet that provides a framework for organizing the initial questions you might want to ask as you plan a unit. Subsequently, a more detailed plan could be developed that answers more questions and integrates the learning unit more fully. The initial plan helps you to understand your unit goals. When you examine that plan, you undoubtedly will discover that some issues merit more attention than others. Ultimately, then, you need to develop a plan that will allow you to respond to these issues. Clearly, any plan must be adapted to a particular situation on a given day, but a plan should provide you with confidence and a good base for teaching a unit. As we have stressed before, mentor teachers can be of considerable benefit to beginning teachers by sharing their planning outlines and discussing how they *think* about preparing for teaching.

DO LOOK BACK

Our intent here is to encourage you to look at your classroom behavior and to plan ways to make the classroom a more meaningful and exciting place. We have stressed that objective, improvement-oriented self-evaluation is difficult for many of us to engage in because we have not been trained to do it. Any significant new experience is always a challenge, and self-evaluation is no exception. Your first efforts to examine your instructional decisions will be difficult and perhaps frustrating. However, such analysis, if it is attempted one step at a time and linked to systematic strategies for improving behavior, will lead to better teaching and the satisfaction that accompanies it.

We have included observation forms and materials to help you assess your behavior and plan new instructional strategies, but ultimately you and only you can evaluate the effects of your teaching. Do not avoid your responsibility by uncritically accepting someone else's advice or teaching philosophy.

Remember, a teaching strategy is good when two basic conditions are satisfied: (1) students understand and can apply key subject matter concepts, and (2) students find the learning process so interesting and rewarding that they initiate efforts on their own and can progressively assume more responsibility for planning and evaluating their work.

It is up to you to identify instructional plans and decisions that meet these criteria and develop a teaching style with which you feel so comfortable that you

Table 11.5   PRELIMINARY PLANNING SHEET

Planning element	Planning question	Preliminary answers (plans)
I. Direction		
1. Activity	What activity do you plan to initiate or lead?	
2. Objectives	What are the students supposed to learn from the activity?	
3. Entry characteristics	What prior skills and understandings do you expect the learners to bring to the lesson?	
II. Specifics (use separate sheet for specifics as necessary)		
4. Content	What specific content will you cover?	
5. Procedures	What specifically will you and the learners do during the activity?	
6. Results	What results do you expect?	
III. Provisions		
7. Resources	What facilities and materials will you and the learners need in order to carry out the activity?	
8. Feedback	How will you and the learners be provided with feedback regarding their progress?	
9. Time	How long will the activity take?	
10. Follow-up	What activities will you assign as a means of extending or reinforcing the lesson?	

Source: Posner, G. (1985). *Field experience: A guide to reflective teaching.* New York: Longman.

look forward to your work. You are the teacher, and *you* must assume responsibility for establishing a learning atmosphere that is stimulating and exciting for you as well as for students. If you do not enjoy class, your students will not either!

SUMMARY

We have urged you to assess your strengths and weaknesses as a teacher by collecting objective information on your classroom decisions, behavior, task selection, and their effects on students. A good way to begin is to consider the concepts and guidelines presented throughout this book, listing those that you are using effectively, those that you need to work on or have not tried, and those for which you are uncertain about your performance. The question marks can be reduced by arranging to obtain feedback. You can collect information about some behaviors by keeping records, consulting your students, or arranging to be audiotaped or videotaped. For many behaviors, however, it will be necessary for you to arrange to be observed by someone who agrees to visit your classroom and conduct focused observation designed to obtain objective information about the behaviors of interest to you. Your choices of content and what to examine briefly or in depth can be compared in dialogue groups with those of peers.

Observational feedback is also important in providing you with information about the effects of new curriculum plans or teaching techniques that you are trying for the first time. We have offered suggestions for enlisting the help of peer teachers and principals in self-improvement efforts and, in particular, for working with other teachers in cooperative self-help groups. The group approach is likely to be especially valuable, provided that each teacher sets individual priorities and goals, focuses on a few issues at a time, and receives balanced and honest feedback. Self-help programs that follow these guidelines have been popular with teachers and have helped them to increase their awareness of and control over their classroom behavior. We have also argued that at least a part of a school district's in-service program should be organized around the needs of individual teachers and designed to promote professional satisfaction and growth.

Finally, we have discussed two current trends that contribute to the professionalization of teaching: master teacher programs and beginning teacher induction programs.

SUGGESTED ACTIVITIES AND QUESTIONS

1. Read some of the literature on teachers' personal stories about their involvement in changing their educational practice (see, for example, Gitlin et al., 1992). How do teachers' personal stories or action research differ from the use of other types of research information? In general, how would you compare and contrast the systemization of a given teacher's knowledge based on her or his experience, the integration of experience across several teachers (perhaps four or five teachers relating their common and differing experiences), and formal research? In this chapter, we have taken the position that all of these sources of knowledge are data. Do you agree or disagree?

2. Try to interview briefly three or so teachers who are relatively inexperienced (first- or second-year teachers) and a few teachers who have several years of experience (eight or more years). Compare and contrast their attitudes about in-service activities. Would one group want more responsibility for in-service activities than another? How much time are they willing to devote? What topics and strategies would the teachers like to be involved in? To what extent is experience a relevant factor in planning in-service programs?

3. The authors in this chapter argue that teachers should take progressively more responsibility for their own in-service education. How realistic is this? What percent of teachers would want to actively participate in in-service activity if it were voluntary? Would participation vary according to type of organizational setting (elementary, middle school, high school, rural, suburban, etc.)?

4. Make a list of all the books and ideas you want to explore. Do not limit your selection to materials listed in this text. Rank the three things you most want to learn, which will serve as your in-service map. Compare your notes with other teachers', and if you have

similar needs and interests, share material and collectively urge the principal to design in-service programs that will satisfy these needs.

5. Make a list of the two concepts or topics you believe are the most difficult for you to teach. Arrange to see other teachers present these topics, or discuss with other teachers how they teach these concepts.

6. Make a list of your teaching strengths and weaknesses. Make specific plans to improve your two weakest areas.

7. What are the possible advantages and disadvantages of using parents or retired, capable adults as observers who supply teachers with feedback about their behavior?

8. Why is it difficult for most of us to engage in self-evaluation?

9. How can teachers initiate self-improvement programs?

10. Should new teachers seek advice from veterans? If so, under what circumstances and in what manner?

11. As a teacher, how can you help your students to develop skills and attitudes for evaluating their own work nondefensively?

12. What are some of the dangers involved in having teachers evaluate other teachers? What are the advantages of peer evaluation?

13. What are your views about master teachers? What criteria are most important for teachers to satisfy if they are to become master teachers? What percentage of teachers should be able to become master teachers—only a few, or most? Why do you feel this way?

14. Reread the narratives at the end of Chapter 1. If these teachers were members of your self-study team, what advice would you offer? Be specific.

15. What is the role of research in defining effective teaching? Can teachers be effective in one school district and not in another? How likely is it that teachers might vary in effectiveness because districts use different criteria for judging effectiveness?

16. We have stressed the need for you to seek evaluative comments and to analyze your behavior if you are to grow and to improve. In that spirit, we seek your comments about this book. We would like to know how useful it is to you and about any deficiencies that can be remedied in future editions. We encourage you to write us (Tom Good, College of Education, University of Arizona, Tucson, AZ 85721; Jere Brophy, College of Education, Michigan State University, East Lansing, MI 48824) with your comments (What was your general reaction to the book? Is it relevant to teachers and future teachers? What topics are omitted that you believe should be included in future editions? What advice or suggestions do you disagree with, and why? Did we communicate negative expectations or provide contradictory advice, and if so, where and how? Were some sections of the book especially helpful, and why?). We will be delighted to receive your suggestions and criticisms and will give your comments serious consideration for the next edition.

REFERENCES

Anderson, C. (1983). The causal structure of stituations: The generation of plausible causal attributions as a function of the type of event situation. *Journal of Experimental Social Psychology, 19,* 185–203.

Ball, S., & Goodson, I. (Eds.). (1985). *Teachers' lives and careers.* London: Falmer Press.

Barber, L. (1990). Self-assessment. In J. Millman & L. Darling-Hammond (Eds.), *The new handbook of teacher evaluation: Assessing elementary and secondary school teachers* (pp. 216–228). Newbury Park, CA: Sage.

Bergmann, C., Bernath, L., Holmann, I., Krieger, R., Mendel, G., & Theobald, G. (1976). *Schwierigkeiten junger Lehrer in der Berufspraxis.* Giessem: Zentrum fur Lehrerausbildung der Justus Liegig-Universitat.

Biddle, B., & Anderson, D. (1986). Theory, methods, knowledge, and research on teaching. In M. C. Wittrock (Ed.), *Handbook of research on teaching* (3rd ed., pp. 230–254). New York: Macmillan.

Billups, L., & Rauth, M. (1987). Teachers and research. In V. Richardson-Koehler (Ed.), *Educators' handbook: A research perspective* (pp. 624–640). New York: Longman.

Borko, H., & Niles, J. (1987). Descriptions of teacher planning. In V. Richardson-Koehler (Ed.), *Educators' handbook: A research perspective* (pp. 167–187). White Plains, NY: Longman.

Bradford, D. (1986). The Metropolitan Teaching Effectiveness Cadre. *Educational Leadership, 43,* 53–55.

Brandt, R. (1987). On teachers coaching teachers: A conversation with Bruce Joyce. *Educational Leadership, 44,* 12–17.

Broeders, A. (1980). *Beginnende leerkrachten: Werksituate en arbeidssatisfactive.* Doctoraal scripte, Instituut voor Onderwijskunde, K. U. Nijmegen.

Brookhart, S., & Freeman, D. (1992). Characteristics of entering teacher candidates. *Review of Educational Research, 62,* 37–60.

Brophy, J. (1988). Research on teacher effects: Uses and abuses. *Elementary School Journal, 89*(1), 3–22.

Brophy, J. (1992). Probing the subtleties of subject-matter teaching. *Educational Leadership, 49,* 4–8.

Brophy, J., & Good, T. (1986). Teacher effects. In M. C. Wittrock (Ed.), *Handbook of research on teaching* (3rd ed., pp. 328–375). New York: Macmillan.

Bullaugh, R., Jr. (1992). Beginning teacher curriculum decision making, personal teaching metaphors, and teacher education. *Teaching and Teacher Education, 8,* 239–252.

Carter, K. (1990a). Meaning and metaphor: Case knowledge in teaching. *Theory into Practice, 39,* 128–132.

Carter, K. (1990b). Teachers' knowledge and learning to teach. In W. Houston (Ed.), *Handbook of research on teacher education* (pp. 291–310). New York: Macmillan.

Carter, K. (1993). The place of story in the study of teaching and teacher education. *Educational Researcher, 22,* 5–12.

Deal, T. (1985). The symbolism of effective schools. *Elementary School Journal, 85,* 601–620.

Deci, E., & Ryan, R. (1985). *Intrinsic motivation and self-determination in human behavior.* New York: Plenum.

deVoss, G., & Dibella, R. (1981). *Follow-up of 1979–80 graduates at the Ohio State University's College of Education Teacher Certification Programs.* Columbus: Ohio State University, College of Education.

Dillon-Peterson, B. (1986). Trusting teachers to know what is good for them. In K. Zumwalt (Ed.), *Improving teaching.* Alexandria, VA: Association for Supervision and Curriculum Development.

Doyle, W. (1983). *How order is achieved in classrooms.* Paper presented at the annual meeting of the American Educational Research Association, Montreal, Canada.

Doyle, W. (1985). Effective teaching and the concept of master teacher. *Elementary School Journal, 86,* 27–34.

Dwyer, D., Lee, G., Rowan, B., & Bossert, S. (1982). *The principal's role in instructional management: Five participant observation studies of principals in action.* San Francisco: Far West Laboratory for Educational Research and Development.

Eash, M., & Rasher, S. (1977). Mandated desegregation and improved achievement: Longitudinal study. *Phi Delta Kappan, 58,* 394–397.

Edmonds, E., & Bessai, F. (1979). *First class: A survey of Canadian teachers in their first year of service.* Charlottetown: University of Prince Edward Island.

Fenstermacher, G., & Berliner, D. (1985). Determining the value of staff development. *Elementary School Journal, 85,* 281–314.

Fuller, F. (1969). Concerns of teachers: A developmental conceptualization. *American Educational Research Journal, 6,* 207–226.

Fuller, F., & Bown, O. (1975). Becoming a teacher. In K. Ryan (Ed.), *Teacher education* (74th yearbook of the National Society for the Study of Education). Chicago: University of Chicago Press.

Galvez-Hjornevik, C. (1986). Mentoring among teachers: A review of the literature. *Journal of Teacher Education, 37,* 6–11.

Gitlin, A., Bringhurst, K., Burns, M., Cooley, V., Myers, B., Price, K., Russell, R., & Tiess, P. (1992). *Teachers' voices for school change: An introduction to education research.* New York: Teachers College Press.

Gitlin, A., & Smyth, J. (1989). *Teacher evaluation: Educative alternatives.* New York: Falmer.

Glassberg, S. (1980). *A view of the beginning teacher from a developmental perspective.* Paper presented at the annual meeting of the American Educational Research Association, Boston.

Glatthorn, A. (1987). Cooperative professional development: Peer-centered options for teacher growth. *Educational Leadership, 44,* 31–35.

Good, T., & Brophy, J. (1974). Changing teacher and student behavior: An empirical investigation. *Journal of Educational Psychology, 66,* 390–405.

Good, T., & Brophy, J. (1986). School effects. In M. C. Wittrock (Ed.), *Handbook of research on teaching* (3rd ed., pp. 570–604). New York: Macmillan.

Good, T., & Mulryan, C. (1990). Teacher ratings: A call for teacher control and self-evaluation. In J. Millman & L. Darling-Hammond (Eds.), *Handbook of teacher evaluation* (2nd ed.). Beverly Hills, CA: Sage.

Good, T., & Weinstein, R. (1986). Teacher expectations: A framework for exploring classrooms. In K. Zumwalt (Ed.), *Improving teaching* (pp. 63–86). Alexandria, VA: Association for Supervision and Curriculum Development.

Griffin, G. (1985). The school as a workplace and the master teacher concept. *Elementary School Journal, 86,* 1–16.

Grouws, D. (Ed.). (1992). *Handbook of research on mathematics teaching and learning.* New York: Macmillan.

Guild, P., & Garger, S. (1985). *Marching to different drummers.* Alexandria, VA: Association for Supervision and Curriculum Development.

Henson, B., & Hall, P. (1992). Linking performance evaluation and career ladder programs: Reactions of teachers and principals in one district. *Elementary School Journal, 93*(4), 323–353.

Hoffman, S. (Ed.). (1991). Special issue of the *Elementary School Journal*. Educational partnerships: Home-school community.

Hoover-Dempsey, K., Bassler, O., & Brissie, J. (1987). Parent involvement contributions of teacher efficacy, school socio-economic status, and other school characteristics. *American Educational Research Journal, 24,* 417–435.

Huffman, G., & Leak, F. (1986). Beginning teachers' perceptions of mentors. *Journal of Teacher Education, 37,* 22–25.

Huling-Austin, L. (1986). What can and cannot reasonably be expected from teacher induction programs. *Journal of Teacher Education, 37,* 2–5.

Hunt, D., & Joyce, B. (1981). Teacher trainee personality and initial teaching style. In B. Joyce, C. Brown, & L. Peck (Eds.), *Flexibility in teaching*. New York: Longman.

Joyce, B. (1981). A memorandum for the future. In B. Dillon-Peterson (Ed.), *Staff development/organization development*. Alexandria, VA: Association for Supervision and Curriculum Development.

Kauffman, J., Hallahan, D., Mostert, M., Trent, S., & Nuttycombe, D. (1993). *Managing classroom behavior: A reflective case-based approach*. Boston: Allyn & Bacon.

Kepler, K. (1977). *Descriptive feedback: Increasing teacher awareness, adopting research techniques*. Paper presented at the annual meeting of the American Educational Research Association, New York.

Lanier, J. (1986). Research on teacher education (with J. Little). In M. C. Wittrock (Ed.), *Handbook of research on teaching* (3rd ed., pp. 527–569.). New York: Macmillan.

Leinhardt, G. (1992). What research on learning tells us about teaching. *Educational Leadership, 49,* 20–25.

Lieberman, A. (1986). Collaborative research: Working with, not working on . . . *Educational Leadership, 43,* 28–33.

Lightfoot, S. (1978). *Worlds apart: Relationships between families and schools*. New York: Basic Books.

Little, J. (1981). *School success and staff development in urban desegregated schools: A summary of recently completed research*. Paper presented at the annual meeting of the American Educational Research Association, Los Angeles.

Maeroff, G. (1988). *The empowerment of teachers*. New York: Teachers College Press.

Martin, M. (1973). *Equal opportunity in the classroom* (ESEA, Title III: Session A Report). Los Angeles: County Superintendent of Schools, Division of Compensatory and Intergroup Programs.

McCaslin, M., & Good, T. (in press). *Listening to students*. New York: HarperCollins.

McDaniel, T. (1981). The supervisor's lot: Dilemmas by the dozen. *Educational Leadership, 38,* 518–520.

McDonnell, L. (1985). Implementing low-cost school improvement strategies. *Elementary School Journal, 85,* 423–438.

McKernan, J. (1987). Action research and curriculum development. *Peabody Journal of Education, 64,* 6–19. [Special issue: Potential and Practice of Action Research, Part I. Editors: D. Kyle & R. Hovda.]

Millman, J., & Darling-Hammond, L. (Eds.). (1990). *The new handbook of teacher evaluation: Assessing elementary and secondary school teachers.* Newbury Park, CA: Sage.

Mitman, A., Mergendoller, J., Packer, M., & Marchman, V. (1984). *Scientific literacy in seventh-grade life science: A study of perceptions and learning outcomes* (final report). San Francisco: Far West Laboratory for Educational Research and Development.

Moskowitz, G., & Hayman, J. (1974). Interaction patterns of first-year, typical, and "best" teachers in inner-city schools. *Journal of Educational Research, 67,* 224–230.

National Education Association. (1983). *Statement by the National Education Association on excellence in education.* Paper presented to the House Budget Committee Task Force on Education and Employment, Washington, DC.

Pajak, E., & Glickman, C. (1989). Informational and controlling language in simulated supervising conferences. *American Educational Research Journal, 26,* 93–106.

Pajares, M. (1992). Teachers' beliefs and educational research: Cleaning up a messy construct. *Review of Educational Research, 62,* 307–332.

Pambookian, H. (1976). Discrepancy between instructor and student evaluation of instruction: Effect on instruction. *Instructional Science, 5,* 63–75.

Posner, G. (1985). *Field experience: A guide to reflective teaching.* New York: Longman.

Richards, M. (1987). A teacher's action research study: The "bums" or "8H". *Peabody Journal of Education, 64,* 65–79. [Special Issue: Potential and Practice of Action Research, Part I. Editors: D. Kyle & R. Hovda.]

Richardson-Koehler, V. (Ed.). (1987). *Educator's handbook: A research perspective.* White Plains, NY: Longman.

Rohrkemper, M. (1981). *Classroom perspective study: An investigation of differential perceptions of classroom events.* Unpublished doctoral dissertation, Michigan State University, East Lansing.

Rohrkemper, M., & Corno, L. (1988). Success and failure on classroom tasks: Adaptive learning and classroom teaching. *Elementary School Journal, 88,* 299–312.

Roper, S., & Hoffman, D. (1986). *Collegial support for professional improvement: The Stanford collegial evaluation program.* Eugene: University of Oregon, School Study Council.

Rosenholtz, S. (1989). *Teachers' workplace: The social organization of schools.* New York: Longman.

Schlechty, P., & Vance, V. (1983). Recruitment, selection, and retention: The shape of the teaching force. *Elementary School Journal, 83,* 469–487.

Showers, B. (1984). *Peer coaching: A strategy for facilitating transfer of training.* Eugene: University of Oregon, Center for Educational Policy and Management.

Smylie, M. (1992). Teachers' reports of their interactions with teacher leaders concerning classroom instruction. *Elementary School Journal, 93,* 85–98.

Sparks, G. (1986). The effectiveness of alternative training routines in changing teacher practices. *American Educational Research Journal, 23,* 217–225.

Spencer, D. (1984). The home and school lives of women teachers: Implications for staff development. *Elementary School Journal, 84,* 299–314.

Sprinthall, N., & Thies-Sprinthall, L. (1983). The teacher as an adult learner: A cognitive-developmental view. In G. A. Griffin (Ed.), *Staff development* (82nd yearbook of the National Society for the Study of Education). Chicago: University of Chicago Press.

Stallings, J. (1986). Using time effectively: A self-analytic approach. In K. Zumwalt (Ed.), *Improving teaching*. Alexandria, VA: Association for Supervision and Curriculum Development.

Tabachnick, R., & Zeichner, K. (1984). The impact of the student teaching experience on the development of teacher perspectives. *Journal of Teacher Education, 35*, 28–36.

Tisher, R., Fyfield, J., & Taylor, S. (1979). *Beginning to teach: The induction of beginning teachers in Australia* (Vols. 1, 2). Canberra: Australian Government Publishing Service.

Tyler, R. (1950). *Basic principles of curriculum and instruction*. Chicago: University of Chicago Press.

Veenman, S. (1984). Perceived problems of beginning teachers. *Review of Educational Research, 54*(2), 143–178.

Weinstein, C. & Mignano, A., Jr. (1993). *Elementary classroom management: Lessons from research and practice*.

Weinstein, R. (1983). Student perceptions of schooling. *Elementary School Journal, 83*, 287–312.

Wildman, T., Niles, J., Magliaro, S., & McLaughlin, R. (1989). Teaching and learning to teach: The two roles of beginning teachers. *Elementary School Journal, 89*(4), 471–494.

Wise, A., Darling-Hammond, L., McLaughlin, M., & Bernstein, H. (1985). Teacher evaluation: A study of effective practices. *Elementary School Journal, 86*, 61–119.

Witkin, H., Moore, C., Goodenough, D., & Cox, P. (1977). Field-dependent and field-independent cognitive styles and their educational implications. *Review of Educational Research, 47*, 1–64.

Wittrock, M. (1986). Students' thought processes. In M. C. Wittrock (Ed.), *Handbook of research on teaching* (3rd ed., pp. 297–314). New York: Macmillan.

Zeichner, K., & Tabachnick, R. (1985). The development of teacher perspectives: Social strategies and institutional control in the socialization of beginning teachers. *Journal of Education for Teachers, 7*, 1–25.

Zumwalt, K. (Ed.). (1986). *Improving teaching*. Alexandria, VA: Association for Supervision and Curriculum Development.

Name Index

Abelson, R., 417
Ackerson, G., 382
Adams, M., 417
Adams, R., 54
Agger, B., 360
Alexander, K., 269
Alexander, L., 244, 379
Alhajri, A., 54
Alkin, M., 1
Allan, S., 272
Alleman, J., 34, 400, 444
Alleman-Brooks, J., 153
Allen, V., 304
Allington, J., 29, 30
Allington, R., 31, 35, 103, 336
Almasi, J., 431
Alton-Lee, A., 243
Alvermann, D., 395
Amarel, M., 330
Ames, C., 212, 215, 221, 223, 227, 247, 294
Ames, R., 212
Ames, W., 382
Anderson, C., 181, 417, 435, 436, 437, 467
Anderson, D., 457
Anderson, L., 29, 114, 141, 153, 275, 276, 324, 325, 377, 425, 427
Anderson, R., 154, 417, 428
Anderson, S., 173
Anderson, T., 430
Andre, M., 430
Anshutz, R., 393
Anttonen, R., 86
Applebee, A., 359, 432
Appleton, N., 360
Archer, A., 383
Archer, J., 215

Arlin, M., 329
Armbruster, B., 428
Arnold, D., 392
Aronson, E., 283
Ashton, P., 104
Atwood, R., 392
Au, K., 361, 428
Aussiker, A., 129, 174, 195, 200
Ausubel, D., 244, 379, 381

Babad, E., 102
Baker, G., 360
Ball, S., 458, 463, 476
Ballard, K., 199
Bandura, A., 176, 216, 217, 218
Bangert, R., 328
Barber, L., 463
Bar-Eli, N., 305
Bash, M., 199
Bassler, O., 477
Basta, S., 173
Beady, C., 105, 106
Beck, I., 374
Becker, H., 330
Beckerman, T., 269
Beez, W., 86, 95
Benevento, A., 107
Bennett, N., 140, 278, 287, 294, 296
Bereiter, C., 413, 432
Berends, M., 105, 269
Bergman, J., 431
Bergmann, C., 489
Berliner, D., 32, 138, 379, 481
Bernath, L., 489
Berndt, T., 214

Subject Index

Ability
concepts of, 217
intellectual, types of, 111–112
Ability grouping, 104, 475
between-class, 267–276
within-class, 265
Abstract information, 242–243
Abusive verbal attacks, 178
Academic tasks. *See* Tasks, academic
Accountability, student, 280, 283
maintaining, 151–152
Achievement
between-class ability grouping effects, 268
cooperative learning effects, 286
factors that influence, 32–34
gender and, 13
motivation, 216
teacher expectation effects on, 106–107
and teacher-student interaction,
30–32, 104
tests, standardized, 33
Action research, 478–479
Action-system knowledge, 2–3
Action zones, classroom, 54, 487
Active instruction, 333
Active listening, 37, 173
Active responses, 229, 251
Active teaching, 373–404
conducting discussions, 395–396
example, 377–379
Activities. *See* Tasks, academic
Activity-driven teachers, 436
Adaptive education, 326
Adjustment problems, serious, 182–191
Advance organizers, 244, 381–382

Aggression
against peers, 186–188
substitute methods of expressing, 188
Alienated students, 347, 349
Allocated time, 32–33, 299, 376
Analyses, classroom, 7–8, 14–15
Anecdotal records, 63
and running records compared, 64
Answers, writing, on worksheets, 78
Anxiety, 189, 190
performance, 228, 238
student, 228
teacher, 42
test, 223
Appreciation
task, 240
teaching for, 413–424
Argumentative essays, 226
Assertive discipline, 195–196
Assignments. *See also* Homework; Seatwork
criteria in selecting, 398–400
failure to complete, 190–191
follow-up, 397
learning center, 356–358
matching student ability to, 339
preparing, 341
structuring, 396–402
worthwhile, criteria for, 153–155
Assisted performance model, 423
At-risk students, 334–336
Attainment value, 214
Attention, student, 37, 141
getting/holding, 150–153
level of, 72–73
minor inattention, 168–170